Retail Marketing Management

David Gilbert

FINANCIAL TIMES
Prentice Hall

An imprint of **Pearson Education**

Harlow, England · London · New York · Reading, Massachusetts · San Francisco · Toronto · Don Mills, Ontario · Sydney
Tokyo · Singapore · Hong Kong · Seoul · Taipei · Cape Town · Madrid · Mexico City · Amsterdam · Munich · Paris · Milan

Pearson Education Limited

Edinburgh Gate
Harlow
Essex CM20 2JE
England

and Associated Companies throughout the world

Visit us on the World Wide Web at:
www.pearsoneduc.com

First published 1999
Second edition 2003

ISBN 0273 655116

British Library Cataloguing-in-Publication Data
A catalogue record for this book is available from the British Library

10   9   8   7   6   5   4   3   2   1
06   05   04   03   02

Typeset in 10/12.5pt Sabon by 35
Printed and bound by Bell & Bain Limited, Glasgow

The publisher's policy is to use paper manufactured from sustainable forests.

Retail Marketing Management

We work with leading authors to develop the
strongest educational materials in marketing,
bringing cutting-edge thinking and best
learning practice to a global market.

Under a range of well-known imprints, including
Financial Times Prentice Hall, we craft high quality print and
electronic publications which help readers to understand
and apply their content, whether studying or at work.

To find out more about the complete range of our
publishing, please visit us on the World Wide Web at:
www.pearsoneduc.com

Contents

About the contributors

David Gilbert, BA, MA, DipM, PhD, is Professor of Marketing in the School of European Studies at the University of Surrey. Prior to working in academia he was employed as a marketing manager for Rank Leisure. He also has experience of working with Littlewoods on various aspects of their strategic planning and was retained as a Research Director of major studies into image, promotion awareness and change of corporate identity. He has extensive consultancy experience, having worked on an assignment for M&S in the restructuring of their marketing, has carried out location studies, and acted as lead consultant in the improvement of retail outlets in museums, zoos and other leisure attractions. Dr Gilbert has published extensively in applied marketing journals and is very involved in the fields of tourism marketing, consumer behaviour and relationship marketing.

Joshua Bamfield, MA, MPhil, MBCS, is Director of the Centre for Retail Research based in Nottingham and Professor of Management. He runs his own consultancy and has carried out work over the last twenty years for a range of large and medium-sized retailers, mainly dealing with EPOS and IT as well as strategic innovation. He has also conducted a number of studies into the costs of crime and the use of technology to combat theft.

James Bell, BA, CertEd, MBA, is a Senior Lecturer in Retail Management in the School of Management Studies for the Service Sector at the University of Surrey. Before starting an academic career, he worked for a number of years in food retail operations. Current research interests include the management of retail service quality and of consumer co-operatives.

Hayley Myers, BA, PhD, is currently Director of European Retail Research with Retail Intelligence, Mintel International Group and Visiting Fellow at the University of Surrey. Previously she spent three years as a Lecturer in Retail Management in the School of Management Studies at the University of Surrey, where her teaching and research interests included the international activity of retailers. Prior to this she completed a PhD, which focused upon the internationalization of European food retailers.

Preface

Retailing occupies a pre-eminent position in the economies of all modern societies. However, retailing is by no means static. In the twenty-first century we are witnessing an ever-increasing series of changes in retailing including the decline of once powerful icons, such as Marks & Spencer, as well as a turbulent introduction of applications of the Internet to retailing. Market stability is a thing of the past as technology advances and retailers have to seek out ways to add value to their services.

In order to address contemporary change the second edition of this book has been revised and updated, based upon new knowledge related to retail marketing as well as feedback from a number of anonymous reviewers. As part of the incorporation of the latest developments the book has been restructured with the marketing mix expanded and extended into separate chapters to incorporate sections such as retail formats and category management. More emphasis has been placed on electronic aspects of retailing and all chapters have been extended and revised.

The main philosophical underpinnings of the book remain. In short, it is based upon the belief that in order to gain success retail management has to be carried out within the context of a marketing approach. As such the need for a retailer to look at the business from the customer's point of view is essential. Each of the chapters emphasizes a consumer-led approach so as to reflect the key marketing issues facing today's retail marketplace. The aim of this edition is to provide the theory, concepts and practice of retailing so that the needs of undergraduate and/or postgraduate students, managers and practitioners are met. The continuation in the blurring of areas of retail with the inclusion of financial services, catering outlets and electronic retailing has made it even more important to have specific chapters on service and quality, IT, consumerism and retail brand management. In addition retailing is becoming much more international and there is a need to understand the complexity of the process of deciding on international expansion given the number of pitfalls that can occur. The book has a number of topical minicase studies that help the reader to relate more easily to the theories because of the practical nature of the content.

The latest book could not have been produced without the help of others, prime among whom are James Bell, Hayley Myers and Joshua Bamfield. I am also indebted to advice from Chris Dutton and Harvey Ells at Brighton University, Bonny Yu, and Charles Stancomb at SRI Consulting Business Intelligence. My thanks are also due to those staff at Surrey University who have helped in my quest to find material for this book or improve different sections, including Karen Choi, Gavin Eccles, Ailsa Kolsaker, Jenny Long, Haiyan Song, Harmen Oppewal and Jan Powell-Perry. I need especially to thank Jean Gilbert, who made many comments regarding the draft manuscripts, and Paul Gamble who was supportive of my efforts throughout the second edition's production.

David Gilbert

Acknowledgements

We are grateful to the following for permission to use copyright material:

Figure 13.3 from 'Strategy and the Internet' by Porter, M.E., in *Harvard Business Review*, March, pp. 63–78, reprinted by permission © 2001 by the Harvard Business School Publishing Corporation; all rights reserved.

Minicase 2.1 from 'Does M&S have a future?' in *The Economist* © The Economist Newspaper Limited, London, October 31, 2000; Minicase 3.1 from 'Youth, Inc' in *The Economist* © The Economist Newspaper Limited, London, December 23, 2000; Minicase 3.2 from 'Think Ethnic, Act Ethnic', reproduced from *Marketing* magazine with the permission of the copyright owner, Haymarket Business Publications, July 5, 2001; Minicase 4.2 from 'The Personal Touch' in *The Economist* © The Economist Newspaper Limited, London, November 11, 2000; Minicase 6.1 from 'M&S' perfect solution?', reproduced from *Marketing* magazine with the permission of the copyright owner, Haymarket Business Publications, September 13, 2001; Minicase 8.1 from 'Get the most out of window space', reproduced from *Marketing* magazine with the permission of the copyright owner, Haymarket Business Publications, August 2, 2001; Minicase 8.4 from 'Point of Purchase: POP designers add creative ingenuity', reproduced from *Marketing* magazine with the permission of the copyright owner, Haymarket Business Publications, May 24, 2001; Minicase 10.1 from 'Has the Body Shop lost its direction for good?', reproduced from *Marketing* magazine with the permission of the copyright owner, Haymarket Business Publications, May 10, 2001; Minicase 11.2 from 'Market Forces' in *The Economist* © The Economist Newspaper Limited, London, October 7, 2000; Minicase 12.1 from 'The right to grey goods?', reproduced from *Marketing* magazine with the permission of the copyright owner, Haymarket Business Publications, July 19, 2001; Minicase 12.2 from 'How should Monsoon go about expansion?', reproduced from *Marketing* magazine with the permission of the copyright owner, Haymarket Business Publications, August 2, 2001; Minicase 13.1 from 'Opinion: Online shopping – the next five years', FT.com, *The Financial Times Limited*, October 26, 2000 © Richard Hyman, Chairman Verdict Research Limited; Minicase 16.2 from 'How can KFC catch the UK's fast food retailers?', reproduced from *Marketing* magazine with the permission of the copyright owner, Haymarket Business Publications, August 16, 2001.

We are grateful to the Financial Times Limited for permission to reprint the following material:

Minicase 1.2 from 'Rewriting the rules', © *Financial Times*, August 17, 2001 © John Hunt; Minicase 5.3 from 'M&S hopes tills will revive with the sound of music' © *Financial Times*, July 26, 2001; Minicase 8.2 from 'Persuading viewers to pay for services could be tough' © *Financial Times*, September 5, 2001; Minicase 10.2 from '7 from Eleven wants to cut it the UK way' © *Financial Times*, July 25, 2001; Minicase 12.3 from 'Back to cheap and cheerful – Own Label' © *Financial Times*, June 19, 2001; Minicase 13.2 from 'How the fittest survived the dotcom meltdown: Online Retailing' © *Financial Times*, August 27, 2001; Minicase 14.2 from 'Brussels drops compact disc price-fixing probe' © *Financial Times*, August 18, 2001; Minicase 15.1 from 'Creating a warm fuzzy feeling' © *Financial Times*, August 31, 2001; Minicase 15.2 from 'Kingfisher's new chief executive wants a run of good fortune' © *Financial Times*, August 2, 2001; Minicase 15.3 from 'UK plc: overspent, overstretched, over there' from www.FT.com/retail (2001 News Analysis) © *Financial Times*, June 19, 2001.

In some instances we have been unable to trace the owners of copyright material, and we would appreciate any information that would enable us to do so.

1 An introduction to retailing as an activity

This chapter should enable you to understand and to explain:

- the importance of the retail industry;
- what retailing is;
- the major theories of change which underpin the study of retail management;
- the structure of retailing in the UK.

THE RETAIL ENVIRONMENT

It is often stated that the only constant in retailing is change and it is certainly true that the pace of development within retailing is accelerating. More than at any other period before we are witnessing the emergence of new forms of retailing, in part as a response to demand from increasingly sophisticated consumers. The market is becoming more segmented with retail formats focusing on the needs of particular consumer groups. The result of this is the development of a more complex retail environment.

Where once it was manufacturers' brands that were all important, the 2000s are witnessing the power of retailers' brands challenging the position of suppliers. The traditional forms of independently owned small businesses and co-operatives have lost significant market share and, in developed economies, the retail sector is now characterized by large-scale multiple chains run by powerful and sophisticated organizations.

The increasing size of retailers and intensifying rates of competition in the markets in which they are operating has led retailers to search for new ways in which to grow their businesses. More recently we have observed the trend in retailers moving away from their core businesses into such areas as financial services – exemplified by leading grocers Tesco and J. Sainsbury linking up with the Royal Bank of Scotland and the Bank of Scotland respectively.

The other main avenue of growth has been to move retail operations into new markets. Many follow a border-hopping strategy moving into nearby markets, while others have focused on markets they perceive to be culturally close – for example, US retailers such as Gap entering the UK. Certainly retail internationalization has boomed in recent years, resulting in the same familiar logos, liveries, store fascias and retail formulas being found throughout the world. All this illustrates that retailing is a truly dynamic industry.

More recently the impact of e-retailing has received considerable attention – however, after the initial hype, the success model for most retail sectors now seems established as one of multi-channel retailing. Many pure-play Internet retailers are having a tough time attempting to make profits, even if they are able to increase sales (for example the e-tailer Amazon). The Internet is also used as a complementary channel by established bricks and mortar retailers moving to a multi-channel 'bricks and clicks' approach, as exemplified by UK grocer Tesco, among others, with its Tesco.com online grocery offer.

THE GROWING IMPORTANCE OF THE RETAIL INDUSTRY

Retailing is not only an integral part of our economic structure but also shapes, and is shaped by, our way of life. While the trading of goods has always been a part of traditional societies, in recent times the buying and selling of products has become a much more formalized and brand-dominated activity. Even as recently as the 1960s, retailing was predominately seen as having a smaller and significantly less important role than other industries such as manufacturing. However, the retail sector is increasingly being viewed as an important activity in the economy and its impact on society in general is readily acknowledged. This acceptance is a reflection of a number of factors; for example, retailing accounts for a significant proportion of the economy, it employs a large proportion of the workforce, and retailers today are among the largest and most sophisticated of organizations.

The power of individual retail organizations is growing; they are now comparable with, and even bigger than, many manufacturers, which is an indication of the growing dominance of retailers within the supply chain. Certainly the annual turnovers achieved by retailers are comparable with the largest companies in other service industries. If the retail sector is compared with organizations within the hospitality sector, and indeed with major corporations outside the service sector, the relatively powerful position of retailers is clear (Table 1.1).

The increasing importance of the retail sector is reflected in its contribution to GDP. In 1999, the UK retail sector accounted for about 10 per cent of GDP, thus a very significant proportion of the economy is linked to retailing. While public policy tends to recognize its importance as a driving force of the economy and aims to promote its sustained growth, other regulations, such as planning restrictions on large new stores and limits on store opening hours, act in favour of some consumer groups and small independent retailers – and balance the power of the multiple retailers.

A significant historical reason underlying the perceived increasing importance of retailing is that its contribution to the economy is much more visible in the modern era than it was in the past. In less developed economies retail structures are less developed and are dominated by informal retailing, such as markets. In such environments bartering

Table 1.1 Annual turnovers for a variety of companies, 2000

Company	Sector	Turnover 2000 (£m)
Tesco UK	Food retailing	16 958
Unilever	fmcg	28 963
Unilever UK	fmcg	2 299
Marks & Spencer	Variety retailing	6 483
Glaxo SmithKline	Pharmaceuticals	8 300
Whitbread Group	Hospitality	3 095

Sources: Company annual reports; Retail Intelligence, 2001a

may be an important way of trading, making it very difficult to estimate transactions. Even when currency is used, informal retailing methods are much less likely to include the recording of transactions in a systematic way, in part due to the sellers not being faced with the same regulations as formal retailers. As a retail structure becomes increasingly developed, characterized by large multiple chains rather than small-scale independent retailers, the retailers' businesses become more sophisticated and successful and hence turnover and profit are more visible. The formalization and growing importance of distribution channels has resulted in the retail sector's contribution to economic vitality becoming more obvious – as a matter of public record.

Another indication of the important role retailers play in today's society is their status as employers. It is estimated that the retail industry employs one in nine of the UK workforce. Retailers employ a significant proportion of the overall workforce, and they are particularly important employers of some groups. Notably, the retail sector has higher levels of female employees than many other sectors; indeed, it is estimated that more than two-thirds of the retail labour force are female. Also more than half of retailing employees are employed on a part-time basis (Labour Market Trends, 1998), in part due to the need to maintain a highly flexible workforce capable of adapting to the differing labour demands. In the past the retail sector has had a reputation for not supporting its employees and for having lower pay and longer hours than other sectors. However, increasingly there are examples of retailers implementing innovative and supportive working conditions. For example, the DIY retailer B&Q has marketed itself to both its workforce and consumers as an organization supportive of part-time and older employees.

Retailers are becoming increasingly important in their role as gatekeepers within the channel of distribution. In the past, when suppliers were dominant, retailers supplied the merchandise that was on offer and consumers selected from this. However, as retailers have become significantly more powerful they are more able to exert their power over suppliers and stock only the brands they wish to sell, depending on their overall retail strategy and supplier relationships. The effect of this is that consumers are able to purchase only what is selected and offered to them by the retailers, as opposed to manufacturers, and so retailers may be considered to be shaping consumer demand (see Minicase 1.1 which highlights this debate).

MINICASE 1.1

Britain: Supermarket profits boom while food poverty increases

At the outbreak of the foot and mouth crisis, Prime Minister Tony Blair accused Britain's supermarkets of having farmers in an 'arm-lock' to produce cheap food. Ever careful not to bite the hands that feed New Labour – Blair's cabinet contains Lord Sainsbury, head of one of Britain's top five supermarket chains and a major financial backer of the party – this populist jibe at the food retailing giants was soon dropped.

This is an issue that Labour cannot wish away, however. The so-called 'cheap-food' policy of the supermarkets is the opposite of how it is portrayed by Labour. It is a policy of maximising profits at the expense of both their suppliers and, more importantly, their customers. The arm-lock employed by Britain's supermarkets is first of all placed on farmers, in order to drive down the price that the major food retailers pay for agricultural produce. But the supermarkets do not pass this saving on to the millions of working people who use their facilities. Instead shoppers are being forced to pay over the odds for the food they eat.

This situation was exemplified by last week's announcement by the Tesco supermarket chain of record profits of over £1 billion – the equivalent of £2.7 million a day. Britain's food retailing is the most concentrated in Europe, with the top five supermarket chains – Asda, Morrison, Safeway, Sainsbury and Tesco – controlling 70 percent of all food purchased. This trade was valued at £76.78 billion in 2000, an increase of 4.5 percent over the previous year.

Developing international operations are increasingly necessary as the UK food retailing market is so heavily saturated. In reporting Tesco's record profits, business weekly *The Economist* writes that the company's 'growth prospects now depend upon expanding overseas'. The magazine pointed out that Tesco has already opened 68 foreign hypermarkets, with overall foreign sales growing by 43 percent to £2.9 billion, and increasing by a massive 85 percent in Asia. The purchasing power of these supermarket chains is such that it 'has forced margins down at many food suppliers. Price discounting by the large supermarkets has been passed on to suppliers, and a number of suppliers have lost contracts as supermarkets have rationalised their supply arrangements.'

The expansion of large supermarket outlets, often in out-of-town locations that are poorly served by public transport, has been at the expense of locally based shops, able to serve those without cars. Industry figures record that between 1975 and 1995, the number of produce outlets fell from 30,000 to just 8,000. The powerful position of Britain's supermarket chains has created an oligopoly, with a very few players controlling virtually all outlets for food and fresh produce, and able to dictate terms to the primary producers. A 1996 report in the *Australian Agribusiness Review* pointed out that 'the UK leads the world in food retailer supply chain linkages for meat and produce'. These are horizontal retail alliances, where individual retail chains are powerful buyers in their own right. 'In Europe, the chains combine in buying groups to further enhance their buying power. These groups account for one third of the total European food market', the report notes.

The final report produced by the Competition Commission last year found that UK food prices were on average 12–16 percent higher than in France, Germany and Holland and that this could only partially be accounted for by the relative strength of the pound against European currencies. The investigation concentrated on two main areas of complaint. Firstly, pricing practices, where the Commission concluded that three of the current practices 'distorted competition and gave rise to a complex monopoly situation'. These areas were identified as: persistent below-cost pricing, 'price flexing' – varying prices in different geographical locations – and the adoption of pricing structures that concentrated competition on a very small number of lines across the majority of the outlets from ostensibly competing chains. However, the Commission gave the supermarkets a free hand to continue their operations unchecked. The Commission recommended 'no remedy for identified adverse effects', arguing that imposing regulations would cost too much.

Secondly, concerning the relationship between the supermarket chains and their suppliers, the Commission found that two common practices in this area 'also operated against the public interest'. Evidence of coercive practices is clear from the report, which states, 'Most suppliers were unwilling to be named, or to name the main party that was the subject of the allegation. There appeared to us to be a climate of apprehension among many suppliers in their relationship with the main parties'. Here, the Commission merely recommended the establishment of a Code of Practice, which would be drawn up by the retailers and suppliers themselves, but 'approved by the Director General of Fair Trading'.

Source: Richard Tyler: www.wswg.org, 23 April 2001

For example, if organic produce is difficult to obtain or is sold at a relatively high price, sales are likely to be limited – the retailer thus shaping consumer purchasing behaviour. Furthermore, as retailer own-brand lines take an increasingly large proportion of the market, retailers are also influencing the development of new products. Many retailers use new product development as a competitive tool – for example, Marks & Spencer led the way with added value 'ready meal' products and continues to develop innovative products such as their range of 'Steam Cuisine' meals.

The issue of retailers as gatekeepers brings into question the concept of social responsibility. It has been suggested that the only responsibility of businesses is to make profits

(Friedman, 1970), although the late Lord Sainsbury had put it more succinctly and fairly by leaving room for ethical concern, seeing profit as 'a first motive for a commercial business'. However, such is the current lack of trust of the public in large business that the degree of social responsibility taken by retailers is being questioned more and more. In some cases regulations are brought in to try and make the retail environment a fairer one. However, retailers are increasingly using the idea of self-regulation and social responsibility as a marketing tool (*see* Chapter 14).

No existing business can relax in the competitive nature of the retail marketplace. Large retail multiple chains are constantly looking for new opportunities or new areas in which to grow their business. This is especially the case in markets with highly developed retail structures, such as the UK and France, where competition is fierce and regulation often restricts the development of further stores. One strategy of expansion has been for retailers to move away from their core business and into broader retail activities: for example, moving from the food sector to the DIY or clothing sector, or diversifying into financial services. It is in part a reflection of the high esteem in which retailers are held that many of the personal banking services are proving to be a success. Customers are displaying increasing loyalty to the retailer fascia or brand rather than manufacturer brands. It appears that consumers are willing to trust the likes of J. Sainsbury or Marks & Spencer with their financial needs in part because they trust their retail offer and organizational culture. In fact many companies are moving from a self-concept of being a trader to one of being committed to the development and marketing of a brand. This market-led approach requires the development of a sophisticated set of marketing programmes, as exemplified in some later chapters of this book. By strong brand positioning and image creation a retailer can improve trade rather than trading itself being the main business focus. The rise in competitive pressure in the industry has led to an endless search for competitive advantage – currently based on the precept that it is much cheaper to retain an existing customer than to acquire a new one. This has led to the development of loyalty card schemes that provide for targeted marketing while providing the benefit of valuable market data for the retailer.

Factors illustrating the growing importance of the retail sector

- large and increasing contribution to GDP
- economic importance more visible
- major employer
- retailers as gatekeepers
- retailers diversifying their activities
- organizations growing on an international scale
- size of operations allowing for supply chain control
- blurring of areas of retail to include wider area of business activity

---

Increasingly retailers are also expanding their businesses internationally. Although there have long been examples of international retailers, they often focused on the luxury goods markets. Despite earlier examples, it was not until the late 1980s that the process of retail internationalization occurred on any significant scale. Furthermore, it is a process that is increasing at an accelerating rate: not only are more retailers operating internationally, but they are moving into an increasing number of markets and expanding into more geographically and culturally distant markets. Thus, whereas in the past retailers were essentially domestic operations, but often dealing with multinational suppliers, by the 2000s many are operating as multinational companies, thus strengthening their negotiating position (*see* Chapter 15 for a full discussion of retail internationalization).

THE STUDY OF RETAILING

Interest in the study of retailing has to some extent mirrored the growth and increasing prominence of the retail industry. Retailing has emerged from a number of interrelated disciplines: geography, economics, planning and, more recently, management and marketing. In the past it has not been acknowledged as a subject area in its own right, indeed Potter (1982, p. 2) described the academic study of retailing as 'the Cinderella of the Social Sciences'.

Increasingly retailing is being focused upon as an accepted area of academic debate, in part a reflection of the industry's growing importance and visibility as a contributor to national economic development. Brown (1992) has suggested that the development of the study of retailing may be considered as following the wheel of retailing (*see* discussion below of cyclical theories of retail change). Changes in academia have also resulted in the development of the subject area. University research centres focused on retailing have become established and professorial appointments in retailing have been made. One outcome of the recognition of the study of retailing is the fact that academic journals focusing on retailing are being published as well as specific retail industry consultancy reports.

As marketing and management disciplines have become more established, degree courses specializing in retailing have been developed in North America, the UK and elsewhere within Europe – in part in response to calls from industry for significant increases in graduate recruitment in the retail sector. Although retailers may have been considered to be behind other industries in terms of recruitment processes, they are becoming more sophisticated as organizations and they are realizing the importance of appropriate recruitment and retention. As a result, they are beginning to use similar procedures and offer employment packages that compete favourably with those of established blue chip organizations in the market for graduates.

RETAIL DEFINITION

There are many approaches to understanding and defining retailing; most emphasize retailing as the business activity of selling goods or services to the final consumer. We have defined retail as:

> **any business that directs its marketing efforts towards satisfying the final consumer based upon the organization of selling goods and services as a means of distribution.**

The concepts assumed within this definition are quite important. The final consumer within the distribution chain is a key concept here as retailers are at the end of the chain and are involved in a direct interface with the customer. However, the emphasis on final consumer is intentionally different from that on customer: a consumer is the final user of a purchase whereas a customer may have bought for his or her own use, as a present or as part of an own business activity. Purchases for business or industrial use are normally not retail transactions. Additionally, retailing includes more than the sale of tangible products, as it involves services such as financial services, hair cutting or dry cleaning.

Retailers are often referred to as 'middlemen' or 'intermediaries'. This suggests they occupy a middle position, receiving and passing on products from producers and whole-salers to customers. This is accomplished by the addition of service and the provision of the store in a convenient location to provide a successful channel of distribution. The key objective for any successful channel is to ensure availability of the right product, in the right quantity, at the right time via the right channel. All marketing channel decisions need to be related to ensuring the customer is a focal point for the selection and display of stock so as to make the sales operation as effective as possible.

In demand-led Western economies we usually consider retailing as providing a neces-sary service and a positive contribution to the economy. This is due to the effectiveness of the retailer in supporting manufacturing by buying in bulk (either directly from the manufacturer or through a wholesaler) on the basis of knowing what the consumer requires. However, in supply-led economies such as the former centrally planned economies (CPEs) of Eastern and Central Europe, retailing has traditionally been viewed as an unnecessary and unproductive link in the channel of distribution (Myers and Alexander, 1997). Jack (2001) highlights this as:

> The norm throughout most of the developed world is modern shop design, products you can pick up to examine, and reasonably helpful shop assistants. Such things are a rarity in Russia, where you are more likely to be screamed at, ordered to produce the exact change and charged for a plastic bag to carry away what you have bought. During the Soviet era, which was plagued by shortages, the shop assistant was king. In pharmacies, the inferiority of the customer was institutionalised by health regula-tions. Clients were meant to bend down to speak through a tiny window – supposedly for the sake of hygiene – through which they received orders on which drugs to buy.

The actual term 'retailing' is thought to be derived from the old French word *'retailler'* which means 'a piece of' or 'to cut up' (Brown, 1992). This implies the breaking-of-bulk function of the retailer – that is, the acquiring of large amounts of the products they sell and dividing them up into smaller amounts to be sold to individual consumers.

Thus a retailer carries out a specific service and this should not be confused with the wholesaler. Retailers and wholesalers are different in nature and perform distinct func-tions. Some specific differences that characterize a retailer are listed below:

1 The retailer's interface with the customer is predominately service based, often with social interaction and interpersonal sales techniques masking the sophistication of computer-based ordering, stocking and transaction systems.

2 Retailers sell small quantities of items on a frequent basis unlike wholesalers who sell in bulk but on a less frequent basis.

3 Retailers attempt to provide convenience in terms of location, payment and credit facilities, range of merchandise, after-sales service, etc.

4 Retailers offer selection – an assortment of merchandise related to the target market in order to provide choice.

5 Retailers set up in business to trade with the general public whereas wholesalers may restrict the general public from purchasing from their warehouses.

6 Retailers normally charge higher unit prices than would a wholesaler.

7 A retailer's pricing policy tends to be simpler than that of the wholesaler, with less use of a discounting structure.

8 The retailer bears a different kind of risk to the manufacturer and wholesaler.

THE DYNAMIC NATURE OF RETAIL CHANGE

Retailing, however judged, is dynamic. One of the areas of retailing that has been addressed by authors is the way in which the retail environment changes. Brown (1987) has reviewed the research in this area and suggests that theories of retail institutional change may be classified into three groups: environmental, cyclical and conflict theories. Environmental theories seek to explain developments in the retail industry as resulting from changes in the wider environment such as variations in lifestyle patterns. Cyclical theories, allied to the business cycle, suggest there are patterns of development which may predict changes in the retail industry, just as cycles can be seen in general economic conditions. Conflict theories propose that institutional retail change is an outcome of the relationships between, and competitive behaviour of, retailers.

MINICASE 1.2

Rewriting the rules (factors of change)

Destruction is essential for creativity: Dyson attacked Hoover; Diesel attacks Levi's. What did Schumpeter tell us about successful challengers? First, emergent industry leaders change the rules of the game. For example, current marketeers do not see themselves as selling a product but as creating an experience. So Starbucks challenged the might of Nestlé and others in the coffee business by offering a coffee bar experience.

Other challengers that radically changed the rules of the game include easyJet, Nokia and Southwest Airlines. New World wine producers, car importers, non-finance intruders in pensions and mortgages and online retailing have all dramatically changed the rules of their industries. All have offered an experience, not simply a product.

Several decades ago, would you have invested your money in a plan to build huge, poorly serviced, isolated warehouses full of inexpensive Swedish flat-packed furniture? Changing the rules means breaking with the past. This requires energy. Schumpeter observed that new industry leaders are motivated by an entrepreneurial drive. Someone with power sees an opportunity and grabs it to restructure the company and, eventually, the industry.

Selecting the 'right' new experience appears complex, especially when academics try to explain it. Yet from my experience, those who successfully predict the future do so with disarming, even naive simplicity. Schumpeter is often quoted by critics for his concept of destruction rather than creativity. But he was not suggesting doom and gloom for leaders. Many retain their thrones for years. If they react swiftly, the threat passes. In Schumpeter's terms, equilibrium is restored to the market.

In a recent paper,* four US academics tested Schumpeter's theory, to establish how challengers increase the probability of dethroning the industry leader. They offered four conclusions and one challenge for success: be aggressive; use a complex repertoire of actions; be unpredictable; and delay the leader's reaction time.

Their challenge was to keep the company fit. The first conclusion – be aggressive – refers to the ferocity of a sustained attack by the challenger. Between 1987 and 1990, Microsoft launched 43 more new actions (new products, ideas and promotions) into the market per year than any competitor. Between 1991 and 1993 it launched 131 more actions than the number two in the business. This raised Microsoft from fourth to first, bypassing Lotus, Word Perfect and Computer Associates.

The second conclusion was to strike with a complex repertoire of actions – that is, several different attacks on the same product. So change product, pricing, production, people, distribution, promotion. In short, make it impossible for any competitor to replicate. Nokia did this to the mobile phone market, Wal-Mart to K Mart and Sears and Tesco to Sainsbury.

Third, maximise unpredictability. Effective challengers plan unpredictable actions. They use misinformation and gossip to increase uncertainty. They circulate stories of products, of market penetration, of customer surveys and of appointments in order to raise anxiety.

Last, delay the leader's reaction. The longer the leader takes to react, the greater the probability that it will lose market share. The researchers add one last but important suggestion: keep fit. Some models of strategic management suggest it is possible for a competitor to avoid the effects of competition. This paper rejects that view: the challenger must engage the industry leader, not avoid it. This is a refreshing conclusion. In an age of hyper-competition there is no haven.

Source: FT.com site; 17 August 2001

* Smith, K., Ferrier, W. and Grimm, C. (2001) 'King of the hill: Dethroning the industry leader', *Academy of Management Executive*, 15, 2.

Environmental theory

A whole array of factors shape the nature of retail environments: factors of an economic, social, political, regulatory, cultural and demographic nature all impinge upon the environment in which retailers operate. It is easy to see direct links between some environmental conditions and retail change: for example, a relaxation in regulations governing store opening hours changes the retail offer available. Other changes in the wider environment may be less direct but still play a fundamental part in shaping the nature of retail development; for example, increasing acceptance of female waged labour influencing lifestyle and consumer purchasing patterns (Myers, 1996). Changes in government planning guidelines may provide further examples of significant environmental factors.

There are specific examples illustrating how environmental factors have directly influenced the development of particular types of retail format. For example, Appel (1972) suggested that the success of the import of the self-service format from the USA to Europe in the 1940s was due – in part – to environmental conditions. The format was based on price competitiveness which made it particularly appropriate in a time of economic downturn. Some consumer groups were characterized by increasing rates of car and refrigerator ownership, which meant there was a growing demand for less frequent buying. More recently superstores have transformed the grocery retailing marketplace in the UK and now account for the majority of retail expenditure each week by UK consumers. The development of superstores is a means by which the leading grocery retailers have increased their market shares. Customers have switched to this relatively new form of grocery retailing, moving away from smaller local stores. Superstores (sales areas greater than 25 000 square feet) have grown to what could be a saturation point for the market as there are now over 1100 such outlets. Figure 1.1 indicates the growth patterns of these stores in the UK. It is interesting to note that the top four grocery retailers account for just under 90 per cent of all superstores. Environmental theories have taken a 'Darwinian' approach and suggest that only retailers with the most appropriate organizational structure and formats will survive (Gist, 1968; Davidson *et al.*, 1983; Brown, 1987). This implies that if retailers expand into new markets where there are different environmental conditions in terms of, for example, economy and culture, they may need to adapt in order to succeed. It also suggests that if retailers are to survive over

	1965	1970	1980	1993/4	1995/6	1997/8	2000/01
Tesco	–	–	–	229	247	286	319
Sainsbury's & Savacentrre	–	–	–	203	239	268	293
Asda	–	–	–	192	196	205	232
Safeway	–	–	–	109	143	173	185
Somerfield	–	–	–	N/A	N/A	27	13
Morrisons	–	–	–	54	72	78	99
Waitrose	–	–	–	3	5	7	10
TOTAL	4*	19*	239*	790	902	1045	1151

Fig. 1.1 Indicative growth in number of grocery superstores by leading players

Source: Institute of Grocery Distribution, 1997* (totals only), 2001

time they must respond appropriately to the evolution of market conditions or otherwise face the possibility of extinction.

The major environmental factors

1 Changes related to the consumer:
   - demographic changes – increases or decreases in population numbers, age groups, racial groups, socio-economic groups, etc.;
   - attitudes and preferences to purchasing, brands and products;
   - changes in lifestyle, whereby time is more important and therefore fast food, telephone banking, credit card payments and suchlike are becoming important;
   - economic influences based upon real incomes, confidence, numbers of women working, etc.

2 Changes in technology:
   - microwave cookers, food freezers, motor cars, the Internet, computer applications to business, just-in-time delivery systems, and so on.

3 Changes in competition:
   - the competitive strength or otherwise of actual or alternative channels of distribution, depending upon the nature and type of the retail organization. The impact of the Internet is a fundamental example of new types of competition that can appear.

Cyclical theories

The wheel of retailing

One of the original theories addressing the issue of retail institutional change is the wheel of retailing (McNair, 1931, 1958). This concept proposes 'a more or less definite cycle', as follows. When retailers enter a market they compete by offering goods at the lowest possible price or 'the bold new concept, the innovation', in order to attract customers. As retailers develop their experience and gain capital, they tend to increase their level of service and quality – and therefore their price. This success allows mature retailers to move steadily into an upmarket position. However, retailers in this position may become vulnerable due to high costs, declining efficiency and, perhaps, stagnating management strategies which culminate in a downturn in sales. If this is the case the retailer may plunge into decline and even be forced to withdraw from the market. The consequence of this move around the wheel of retailing is that a gap is left at the bottom end of the market – an opportunity for a new retailer to enter.

An example of this process is provided by changes within the UK food retail sector. In the 1970s the main players were very much price oriented, illustrated by Tesco's sales cry of 'pile it high, sell it cheap'. However, throughout the 1980s the main grocery retailers moved to a higher quality and service orientation, operating larger stores from more accessible sites. This trend has resulted in further consolidation of the market during the 1990s and a considerable gap being left at the lower end of the market. This opportunity has been seized by the Continental hard discounters who have moved into the UK market. For example, German retailers Aldi and Lidl have followed an aggressive expansion strategy, rolling out smaller-scale stores and offering heavily discounted limited lines relying on high volumes and an efficient operation to make their money.

In the classic phases of the wheel of retailing there are three stages: entry; trading up; and vulnerability. At the entry stage a retailer enters the market as a low-price, low-status competitor with operating expenses reduced to a minimum. This is reflected in restricted services, low rent location, modest shopping atmosphere and limited product mix. As the retailer becomes successful, and accepted, others emulate the original business. The retailer then tradesup through success to improved facilities, and offers enhanced services and improved or additional product lines. With maturity, the retailer becomes more vulnerable due to an inability to adapt, producing a decline in the rate of return from the business. The entry of new lower-price innovators signals decline for the mature business.

In practice the wheel of retailing can explain some of the changes in the UK retail marketplace. The changes from corner store to supermarket as price vulnerability occurred fits the model. However, the factors in modern retailing such as size of operation of leading retailers, the importance placed on branding and loyalty schemes, and a continual drive for efficiency by all personnel create highly competitive operations. The basic difficulty in utilizing the wheel of retailing approach is the timescale. It can vary extensively, depending on the speed of economic, social and technological change.

The retail accordion theory

The retail accordion theory suggests that retailers initially enter a market as a general retailer; with experience they focus down on particular product sectors and/or consumer groups. Over time they begin to diversify their offer in order to grow, but again will revert to specialization. The premise of the retail accordion is that the changes in retail operations are related to strategies that alter the width (selection) of the merchandise mix. An example of this type of pattern is the establishment of small-scale specialist food retailers such as grocers or bakers followed, over time, by the takeover of the food retail sector by large-scale superstores with diverse product ranges. We are now witnessing the next stage in this pattern: the re-emergence of the small store in the guise of convenience formats such as Tesco's Metro and Sainsbury's Local and Central with limited ranges for a different market but trading under the same name, brand and reputation.

We can see this specialization occurring due to:

- store sizes in some locations being unable to accommodate greater variety in order to compete and therefore specialization occurs;
- greater disposable income and large urban populations allowing for profitable segmentation;
- the importance of the specialist shopping experience and convenience stores;
- established retailing brands wanting to obtain more specialist coverage of the market.

Potted history of the UK retail marketplace

1950s
Rationing ends and austerity and shortage still prevalent; Population is careful about expenditure and debt; Launch of the self-service supermarket format in the UK; Very few national retail chains; TV advertising helps to boost sales of the leading branded products; Manufacturers set the retail price of their products, e.g. through price-marked packs.

1960s
Increased wealth and UK population increase fuels demand; Repeal of the Price Maintenance Act – allows retailers greater freedom to compete on price; First motorways built – making it more economical to distribute goods over longer distances; There is a change in social attitudes developing growth of a consumer society – especially with the young; Retailers become large enough to deal with manufacturers directly, rather than buying through wholesalers; The fashion and leisure industry develops.

1970s
Youth market continues to develop and retailers develop segmentation strategies; UK joins the European Community; Scanning technology first introduced to stores, replacing traditional price tickets; Supermarkets begin to extend beyond their traditional range of packaged products to sell more fresh foods: meat, fish, dairy, fruit and vegetables, etc.; Marks & Spencer develops new chilled products, e.g. desserts and ready meals.

1980s
Co-op relinquishes its long-held position as the UK's leading grocer; Major decline in specialist local stores (butchers, bakers, greengrocers, etc.) as the public accepts the benefits of the one-stop shopping approach of out-of-town and large formats; Superstores (over 25 000 sq. ft) replace smaller supermarkets as the leading retail format triggering a race between retailers to find the best sites; Retailers centralize their purchasing (buying through head office) and distribution (suppliers deliver to regional warehouses); Growth of the fast-food sector: pizzas, burgers, kebabs, etc.; Steep rise in the proportion of own-branded products.

1990s
Large chains (such as Sainsbury's, Tesco and ASDA) achieve national coverage and the high street fascias are similar in all main centres; Continental retailers (Aldi, Netto, Lidl) enter the UK

marketplace; Sunday opening legalized; Broadening base of retail offers – supermarkets become leading petrol retailers and branch out to other forms of retailing including financial services; Longer opening times – 24-hour opening in some stores; Large-category retailers enter the market; Internationalization of retailers with UK retailer chains expanding overseas and others entering the UK, e.g. America's Wal-Mart, the world's biggest retailer acquires ASDA; Rapid uptake of the Internet prompts the launch of e-commerce shopping services.

2000s
Smart cards and new ways of paying are adopted; E-commerce becomes more sophisticated; The traditional retailers hit back at the new 'clicks and mortar' e-tailers by developing their own Internet sites; More emphasis on value for money and brand values as C&A disappears and M&S suffers; Need for more convenience as time is at a premium.

The trend to become more general is due to:

- expansion of complementary lines as part of the retail offer;
- a skimming policy – that is, carrying more of the profitable lines and creaming these off from those of the competition;
- a move to increase the density of shoppers in-store by providing a complete range offering (one-stop shopping);
- the growth of large shopping centres with outlets which allow for expansion of lines and ranges.

The retail life-cycle theory

The retail life-cycle theory suggests that retail developments pass through stages. At birth (termed the embryonic stage in the context of industry life cycles), there are slow rates of growth due to limited resources and experience. This is followed by a time of rapid growth as efficiency and experience increase. Eventually growth will level off into the mature stage due to increased costs and competition and reduced efficiencies. In a mature market the competition remains intense, growth slows and profits begin to fall. A continued decrease in market share and profitability will eventually cause the development to decline and, if the situation worsens, ultimately to withdraw from the market. The less competitive companies, which have previously entered the market, will be forced out early as the market goes through a shake-out period. An example of a company which has had problems in relation to the life cycle is Woolworths. In an attempt to remain competitive its range was expanded to a point where the offer was undefined and it became a store of last resort. The group realized it was not adequately providing for the needs of the contemporary consumer and survived only because it recognized the value of adopting a focused strategy. Figure 1.2 illustrates the way a retail business may grow from the embryonic stage into a period of maturity and, perhaps, to final decline.

Conflict theory

Competition between retailers causes changes in the nature of the retail environment. However, it is not so much the day-to-day competition between companies that causes

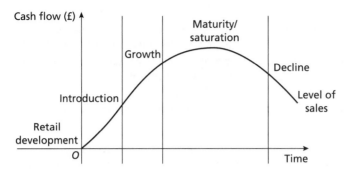

Fig. 1.2 The retail life cycle

institutional change, but rather the imbalance caused by innovations. Brown (1987) states that a response to innovation follows a process of four stages. Initially, retailers are in shock at the innovation; secondly, they deny the threat by means of defensive retreat; thirdly, they then move into a stage of acknowledgement and assessment; finally, they develop a strategy of adaptation.

Types of retailer response to innovation

● shock

● defensive retreat

● acknowledgement and assessment

● adaptation

The question is the timescale and strategy requirements which may occur as a result of the call for adaptation. There is a need to understand the type of change needed, the cost of any adaptation and the resultant profitability of a change.

An example of retail innovation as a catalyst for change is the introduction of self-service supermarkets. As the supermarket developed and increasingly took market share from the traditional specialist retailers a direct reaction by the independents was necessary; in order to remain competitive, they formed themselves into voluntary groups and buying alliances. As part of their strategy companies such as Spar copied the trend by offering self-service. The buying alliances also helped the independents to remain in touch with the prices offered by the developing supermarket chains. A more recent example is multi-channel retailers. Traditional bricks and mortar players felt threatened by this new channel of distribution and by the new pure-play e-tailers. They seized the opportunity to develop a competing offer, and one that would complement their existing offer, hence the bricks and clicks approach. Due to the heavy losses incurred by e-retailing specialists it is now the multi-channel operators that, on the whole, are more successful.

> **Theories of retail institutional change – a summary**
>
> 1 environmental
> 2 cyclical:
>   - the wheel of retailing
>   - the retail accordion
>   - the retail life cycle
> 3 conflict

THE STRUCTURE OF RETAILING IN THE UK AND EUROPE

A number of structural changes in the retail environment have become evident during the post-war era. These developments have occurred throughout Europe, although they are apparent to differing extents in different markets. Three fundamental and inter-related transitions have occurred in the European retail environment: first, the balance of power has shifted along the distribution channel from the manufacturers to the retailers; secondly, traditional independent retailers and co-operatives have lost market share to multiple chain organizations; and thirdly, markets have become increasingly consolidated and concentrated. The second point above is reinforced by Hollinger (1998), who identified that the Co-op had fifty mutual retail societies, of which the fifteen largest accounted for more than 90 per cent of the movement's trade. In fact in 1985 the Co-operative movement as a whole could boast that it was the UK's leading grocery retailer, as well as a banker, insurance provider, funeral services group and agricultural operator. The Co-op business allowed its competitors such as Tesco, J. Sainsbury, ASDA and Safeway to invest heavily in store development, delivering a consistent product range to customers while the Co-op's individual societies were left to languish.

Table 1.2 indicates the sales of some of the major UK retailers with foreign operations.

These structural trends are intrinsically linked. Retailers have been able to use their power against suppliers, in part, due to the growth of multiple organizations. Multiples

Table 1.2 Major UK retailers with foreign operations, 2000

Retailer	Sector	Sales 2000 (£m, excl VAT)	Countries operated in
Dixons Group	Electricals	3 618	UK, Scandinavia, Ireland, Spain, Portugal
Kingfisher	Multi-sector	10 885	UK, France, Germany, Belgium, Netherlands, Italy, Luxembourg, China, Singapore, Taiwan, Czech Republic, Slovak Republic, Turkey, Canada, Brazil
J. Sainsbury	Grocery	16 135	UK, USA
Tesco	Grocery	18 796	UK, Ireland, Hungary, Czech Republic, Poland, Slovak Republic, France, Thailand, South Korea, Taiwan

Source: Retail Intelligence, 2001b

have grown dominant by being more competitive and achieving economies and efficiencies of scale, in turn owing to their enhanced negotiating position because of their power over suppliers.

The extent of the domination of the market by multiples varies throughout Europe. The highest levels of concentration and multiple dominance are in the structurally advanced markets of the UK and Germany, where the top three to five players account for almost half the market share in the grocery sector. This trend decreases slightly in the structured markets of France and the Netherlands, while in intermediary and traditional markets such as Spain, Italy, Portugal and Greece small-scale independent retailers still maintain a strong market presence. However, even in these markets the trend is towards market dominance by multiples. Just as we can follow these structural trends since the 1960s and 1970s, so we can trace geographical trends.

Independent and co-operative retailers have fought to maintain their market share. To varying degrees throughout Europe public policy has favoured them, for example by restricting the development of new stores or controlling acquisitions of large companies. They have also attempted to fight back strategically by joining together in voluntary groups and alliances and by providing a complementary retail offer to the multiples. For example, small grocery stores may be unable to compete with the range of merchandise of a superstore but they can increase their competitiveness by locating in neighbourhoods rather than out-of-town sites and offering longer opening hours for local consumer convenience.

Retailers are constantly having to assess the changing environment in which they operate and adapt accordingly. One outcome of this has been the way in which retailers have altered their store format, size and location. Outcomes of environmental changes are the dichotomous trends in store size, the development of dominant formats in national markets, and locational issues such as the move of stores to out-of-town sites.

Structural trends in European retailing

- increasing dominance of retailers over suppliers
- increasing market share held by multiples and associated loss by independents and co-operatives
- increasing rates of market concentration
- technical superiority of the big players providing cost-effectiveness

All of the trends occur to differing extents throughout Europe. The most advanced markets have the most power held by retailers, highest proportion of multiple chains and the highest levels of market concentration.

CONCLUSION

Retail organizations have grown in size dramatically, particularly in the food sector. This has mirrored a growth in store size, for example, the emergence of the superstore in the UK and the hypermarket in France. At the same time as food retailers have been increasing the size of new stores, they have also been selling off the smaller stores in their portfolio. These older, smaller stores are typically located on the high street and in town centres, while the new very large stores tend to be on out-of-town sites. Thus the upgrading of store size has altered the locational strategy of food retailers from within towns to their outskirts. The major players have consolidated their positions with the use of improved branding, relationship marketing schemes, own-brands and improved retail environments.

Store size may be considered in terms of the polarization model. While on the one hand large-scale formats are becoming increasingly large in order to benefit from economies and efficiencies of scale, they have left a gap at the other end of the market for small-scale stores. While we are seeing fewer specialist retail outlets, small-scale convenience formats and stores are very much in evidence. Not only are these operated by independent retailers and voluntary chains, but even the multiple retailers have recognized an opportunity for small-scale stores that complement their large-scale operations – as exemplified by Tesco's Metro and Sainsbury's Local and Central fascias.

Similarly, though the hard discounters have entered the UK market to fill a gap at the lower end of the pricing structure, their entry may also be viewed in terms of polarization of store size and location. Whereas the superstores are increasing their size and moving to out-of-town locations, the discount supermarkets and convenience stores are of a significantly smaller scale and tend to be located in town centres – in part because they are able to find sites of adequate size, unlike the superstores which need very large sites, and in part because they are focused on consumer demand within retail centres, not the need for 'one-stop' shops.

Leading retailers have tended to move towards large-scale retailing, in terms of multiple chains and store size, in order to gain from efficiencies and economics of scale. However, small-scale operators do have certain advantages. First, they often benefit from supportive public policy, for example, legislation limiting the development of large out-of-town stores. Second, they attempt to gain their own economics by developing voluntary groups and buying alliances. Third, small-scale retailers may benefit from clustering in town centres and thus creating a critical retail mass to attract and more easily satisfy consumers.

It is interesting to note that in terms of large-scale food retailing different formats are apparent in various markets. For example, the UK food sector is dominated by the quality and service oriented superstore; in contrast the French market is characterized by the large-scale, out-of-town hypermarket that is price oriented and has a high ratio of non-food ranges. Germany has a mix of hypermarkets and discount supermarkets, while in the Benelux countries the high street supermarket format is dominant. This begs the question: is the development of these dominant formats in markets a reaction by retailers to national consumer demand or have retailers imposed particular retail conditions upon consumers?

EXERCISES

The exercises that follow help to place the information in this chapter in a practical context. We suggest they are worked through before you move on to Chapter 2.

1 What is a retailer and what is their function? Which retailers would fall into the categories outlined in the grid below? Add your responses in the spaces in the grid.

Retailer that has developed through cyclical theory change	**Who:**	**How:**
Retailer that has developed through accordion theory change	**Who:**	**How:**
Retailer that has developed through conflict theory change	**Who:**	**How:**

Of the theoretical approaches you have considered, which one offers the clearest understanding of change and why?

2 Think about the trends that have occurred in your local high street. Read Minicase 1.1 about the increasing power of the supermarkets. What are the main changes in high street retailing which may affect the consumer due to the power of the large players? Is this inevitable given the change theories you have read in this chapter and if so what theories apply more than others?

3 Consult the statistics on the performance of different types of retail businesses (e.g. Internet, DIY stores, superstores, corner shop grocers, department stores, bespoke tailors, mail order). You then need to provide a breakdown by company of at least three areas from this list with at least three years' figures. Now comment on what are some of the important statistics you have found and the changes which may occur in the next decade. Also comment on the ways change theories help us understand these trends.

4 Read Minicase 1.2 and then identify those retailers who are changing the rules of the game by developing new formats and retail experiences. What do you predict will happen as an outcome of these changes?

REFERENCES AND FURTHER READING

Appel, D. (1972) 'The supermarket: early development of an institutional innovation', *Journal of Retailing*, 48, 39–53.

Brown, S. (1987) 'Institutional change in retailing: a review and synthesis', *European Journal of Marketing*, 21 (6), 5–36.

Brown, S. (1992) *Retail Location: a micro-scale perspective.* Aldershot: Avebury.

Davidson, W.R., Sweeney, P.J. and Stampfl, R.W. (1983) *Retailing Management.* 5th edn. New York: John Wiley.

Financial Times (2001) 'Rewriting the rules', FT.com site: 17 August.

Friedman, M. (1970) 'The social responsibility of business is to increase profits', *New York Times Magazine*, September, 13.

Gist, R.R. (1968) *Retailing: Concepts and decision.* New York: Wiley and Sons.

Hollinger, P. (1998) 'Survey – future of mutuality: the Co-op: Members urged to co-operate', *Financial Times*, 10 March.

Jack, A. (2001) 'Healthy break with the past: Russian retailing', *Financial Times*, 6 August.

Institute of Grocery Distribution (1997) *Grocery Retailing 1997: The market review.* Watford: IGD Business Publications.

Institute of Grocery Distribution (2001) www.igd.com fact sheets.

Keh, H.T. and Park, S.Y. (1997) 'To market, to market: The changing face of grocery retailing', *Long Range Planning*, 30 (6), 836–46.

Labour Market Trends (1998) 'Employee jobs', *Labour Market Trends*, June, S. 21.

McNair, M.P. (1931) 'Trends in large scale retailing', *Harvard Business Review*, 10, 30–9.

McNair, M.P. (1958) 'Significant trends and developments in the post-war period', in Smith, A.B. (ed.) *Competitive Distribution in a Free High-Level Economy and its Implications*. Pittsburgh, PA: University of Pittsburgh.

Myers, H.A. (1996) 'Internationalisation: The impact of the European Union. A study of the food retail sector'. Unpublished PhD thesis. School of Management Studies, University of Surrey.

Myers, H.A. and Alexander, N. (1997) 'Food retailing opportunities in Eastern Europe', *European Business Review*, 97 (3), 124–33.

National Accounts (1998) *Annual Abstract of Statistics 1997*. London: The Stationery Office.

ONS, Department of Manpower Services, Annual abstract of Statistics (2000).

Potter, R.I.B. (1982) *The Urban Retailing System: Location, cognition, behaviour*. Aldershot: Gower.

Ratchford, B.T. (1998) 'Introduction to the special section: Economic perspectives on retailing', *Journal of Retailing*, 74 (1), 11–14.

Retail Intelligence (1998) *The European Retail Handbook – 1998 edition*. London: Retail Intelligence Research Publications.

Retail Intelligence (2001a) *The UK Retail Rankings*, London: Retail Intelligence Research Publications.

Retail Intelligence (2001b) *The World's Top 100 Retailers*. London: Retail Intelligence Research Publications.

Tyler, R. (2001) 'Britain: Supermarket profits boom while food poverty increases', www.wswg.org, 23 April.

2 An introduction to retail marketing

This chapter should enable you to explain:

- the origins of marketing;
- business philosophies and the differences between the production, sales and marketing eras;
- definitions, concepts and functions associated with marketing;
- the differences between marketing and sales and what constitutes a marketing orientation.

RETAILING AND MARKETING

Retailing was introduced in Chapter 1 in terms of its function and structure and why it is so visible in our everyday lives. However, not everyone may be clear that retailing involves the activity of shopping, purchasing by means of the Internet, dealing with financial services or even visiting a local fast-food outlet or hairdresser. This daily involvement is interpreted in different ways and underlies the complexity of retail marketing operations. This complexity has to be understood in relation to the revolution occurring in the whole of the retail area that is transforming the way goods and services are being offered to the market. For a fuller understanding we require a framework of concepts to ensure that we have a basic knowledge of what may constitute retail marketing.

Retailing in its various guises can be traced back for centuries but because the elements of retailing and conditions of the marketplace have changed substantially there has been a requirement for a corresponding change in both techniques and approaches. Reid (1995) has described retailing as a once-Cinderella business which has now evolved as a leader in business innovation and the management of complexity. Retailing comprises all the activities involved in the marketing and distribution of goods and services. Therefore, marketing is a core area for any retail operation as the success or failure of retailers is based upon how well they understand and serve the needs of their customers.

Change in consumer behaviour is constantly occurring. For example, there has been increasing pressure on people's time given the growth in the number of families with both partners working; more children arrive home to organize their own cooking or purchases; and extra time is being spent on leisure activities, including shopping as a leisure pursuit. This has led to a number of segments which have higher disposable income but little discretionary time for more routine purchasing. Such changes produce intense competition among retailers. These changes are so dramatic, we are witnessing major shifts in the way that consumers interact with some of the more traditional areas of the retail sector – prime among these are the financial service providers. Changes in consumer lifestyles have required elements of the banking relationship to be handled in a more convenient manner and more economically. This has led to the development of banking services using automated teller machines (ATMs), the post, telephone or by electronic means. Non-branch banking is an important development which reflects the needs of the modern consumer.

This trend, known as *disintermediation*, is even more pronounced in the insurance sector. The traditional use of an insurance broker to organize car, house or personal insurance has given way to a major growth in direct marketing. Companies such as Direct Line in insurance and Citibank in banking have pioneered the changes. The use of telephone sales, the Internet and other methods of marketing has transformed both the distribution and the cost structure of the industry. This has been made possible not only by rapid and focused technological development but also by consumers' acceptance of the new services and their price advantage. However, at the same time as we are witnessing these changes, such as e-banking, there is growing pressure from some consumers to retain local banks in order to counteract concerns about the exclusion of certain sections of society from financial services provision.

NEED FOR A STRATEGIC APPROACH

Any change that occurs has to be underpinned by an appropriate marketing strategy if it is to be successful. As part of the development of retail marketing there is a need to ensure that both the positioning of any offer, and the image of that offer, are sound and logically linked. *Positioning* as a marketing concept is based upon a market position of image, price and quality rather than geographical position. It is where a retailer will decide on the 'placing' of their business in a market position where it will be able to compete favourably with other similar retail outlets. This position should be perceived clearly by the consumer so that the retailer gains some advantage, either through being different from others in the mind of the consumer or more clearly identified as offering a particular type of retail offer by the choice of that position. This type of approach can provide a positive image of the retailer. For example, one success story in positioning is Toys "Я" Us, which has positioned itself in a 'category'. Category retailers dominate through specializing in very large-scale, high volume formats with value-for-money pricing and strong branding. However, the cut-price operations and the operating costs of Toys "Я" Us has caused a number of financial problems and the closures of some of its European outlets. Notwithstanding the setback for Toys "Я" Us, the success of such positioning has led to the coining of the term 'category killers', so called because the concept destroys or snuffs out various parts of a traditional chain and dominates an entire category of merchandise. This recent retail marketing approach has led to the early domination of some areas of the market for toys, sports goods, electrical goods and DIY needs.

The approach of many retailers is to aim for growth and domination of their chosen position in order to create leadership. Leadership in the marketplace cannot be gained overnight. Even Wal-Mart, now the world's largest retailer, had only fifty stores and sales of $50 million in the 1970s. We should, however, be aware that there is a reverse to these successes; a high number of ventures end in failure. In the USA in 1993, Sears announced that – after 107 years – the company would no longer offer its mail order catalogue. This was because of increasing competition through the penetration of retailers such as Wal-Mart stores into rural areas, changes in the use of the car, and changing consumer purchasing patterns. However, many other catalogues were doing far better than that of Sears. The problems of companies such as Sears may be related to their inability to squeeze sales from mature markets and the need to improve their retail marketing approach. However, Sears is still a large retailer with consolidated operations. The company has its main international operations in America, Puerto Rico and Canada. In 1999 they had what they term full-line stores (858) with exclusive bands such as Canyon River Blues, Fieldmaster, Crossroads, Kenmore and Craftsman, as well as their speciality stores (2100).

The maturation of the retail marketplace has led to the development of schemes which allow improved relationship building with the customer. There is a recognition that relationship marketing schemes will reduce the long-term costs of attracting customers owing to the retention benefits they provide. Therefore, recent developments in retail marketing have been associated with building customer loyalty (*see* Chapter 8 for definitions and a full discussion of retail loyalty schemes).

Dick and Basu's (1994) framework of customer loyalty conceptualizes loyalty as the relationship between relative attitude towards an entity (product/service/brand/store) and patronage behaviour. This means that cognitive, affective, and behavioural components of attitude will all contribute to levels of loyalty. These attitudes will be based upon the function of pre- and post-appraisal. The following are possible loyalty states:

- *No loyalty*: Low relative attitude and low repeat patronage signal an absence of loyalty (Dick and Basu, 1994). This may occur when there has been a recent introduction of a new store brand and/or inability to communicate the distinct advantages or differences of a new store brand.

- *Spurious loyalty*: Describes a low relative attitude and high repeat patronage and is characterized by non-attitudinal influences on behaviour. It is similar to inertia when consumers perceive little brand differentiation as in a low involvement purchase situation and it may involve repeat purchases based upon situational cues, such as familiarity.

- *Latent loyalty*: A high relative attitude and a low repeat patronage is a sign of latent loyalty. Consumers may display high relative attitudes toward a particular outlet, but patronize other stores that offer superior promotions.

- *Loyalty*: Clearly the favoured situation for any retailer. Loyalty is based upon a favourable correspondence of both relative attitude and relative patronage. A store-loyal customer prefers and visits the same store to purchase certain merchandise. Thus, the retailer's objective is to increase customers' store loyalty.

The ability of a retailer to enhance and build customer loyalty is highly dependent on identifying and understanding the target market, and offering the right type of reward or scheme to ensure the retention of the bulk of their custom over the long term. It also requires superior service, few stockout problems and convenience of operation. This is not just for the larger retailer. There are small businesses based upon local owner-managed retailers, mobile shops or door-to-door trading. Each of these relies on building relationships and delivering some form of added value in order to be successful. Just as

Transaction marketing	Relationship marketing
• short-term orientation • 'me' oriented • focus on result of a sale as the sale is the end of the process • enphasis on persuasion to buy • need to win, manipulation • stress on conflict inherent in achieving a transaction	• long-term orientation • 'we' oriented • focus on retention and repeat sales • stress on creating positive relationships • providing trust and service • partnership and co-operation to minimize defection and provide longer-term relationships (with customers or strategic alliances, joint ventures, vendor partnering, etc.)

Fig. 2.1 Transaction and relationship marketing – a comparison
Source: Gilbert, 1996

customers may be unique in their demands, there is a need for different types of loyalty building. Sopanen (1996) carried out research for the SOK group and found there are six different kinds of loyalty:

1 *monopoly loyalty* – where no choice is available;

2 *inertia loyalty* – where customers do not seek alternatives;

3 *convenience loyalty* – attributed solely to the location of a retail outlet;

4 *price loyalty* – where customers believe in seeking out low prices, but will shift if lower prices are identified elsewhere;

5 *incentivized loyalty* – based upon loyalty reward schemes for accumulating benefits;

6 *emotional loyalty* – found in brand loyalty: this is the most elusive to create.

Each of these is important and requires attention by marketing people to establish the future direction with regard to providing competitive prices, offering the appropriate loyalty schemes and developing stronger branding. The current use of relationship marketing can be seen to be in direct contrast to transaction marketing approaches which have been the traditional approach to markets; Fig. 2.1 provides a clear comparison of their differences in approach. As can be seen, relationship marketing has a longer-term perspective, emphasizing the retention of the customer.

Gengler *et al.* (1997) carried out research into relationship marketing and found that, because of the importance of repeat business and measuring attitudes, it is a vital tool for retail businesses. Loyalty schemes have recently been extended to include improved targeted groupings such as OAPs, students, families with children, etc. The schemes now offer rewards such as air miles or extra loyalty points linked to seasonal promotions and financial services. The benefit of these schemes to a retailer is that by utilizing personal data collected for the scheme along with the transaction data the retailer can carry out data mining of the information collected in order to provide improved promotional and targeting benefits. Once customers utilize their store credit card it is possible to monitor them in terms of what, when, and where they purchase so that a retail database can be provided.

An important business need of modern retailing is to do things better than the competition, in the case of loyalty schemes to offer better types of incentives or relationship clubs. This fits with the need to develop sustained competitive advantage, with each aspect of the business being improved to a level which gives a superior position to that of the competition. This will be related to decisions over retail location and design, service provision or merchandise selection, technology, financial cost control, and communication plans.

Communication programmes are especially important for retailers. It will not have been long since you last saw a promotion for either a fashion product, brand of food or discounted good. We are continually bombarded with advertising and sales material. Each day the post brings yet another letter containing one type of retail offer or another. There are numerous advertisements placed in the media each day and all shops have a myriad of promotional messages. We are surrounded by invasive messages and communication paid for out of marketing budgets. However, as we shall see later in this chapter, marketing is far more than the promotion of a retail product – this constitutes only one aspect of marketing. Promotion is often used to build brand image and we witnessed a great deal more activity or investment in stronger branding at the end of the 1990s. This may be in relation to the retailer's name or the own-brand products which cover a wide spectrum of price and quality positioning. Improvement of brand image creates more added psychological value to the retail operation.

The need to offer value in the retail clothing marketplace

The table below highlights the relative under-performance of the traditional mass market leaders. In the case of Marks & Spencer, the (non-food) figures are a serious downturn. The company had ignored marketing, allowed quality standards to slip and failed to offer value for money, just as consumers were becoming more demanding and used to improvements from other retailers. The M&S share of the UK clothing market suffered major decline and there was the need for a marketing turnaround.

Clothing retailers: Estimated UK trading area and sales growth, 1996/97–2000/01

Retailer	Trading area growth (%)	Sales growth (%)
Matalan	+145	+216
New Look	+99[a]	+127[a]
Peacocks	+116	+153
The Officers Club	+500[b]	+392[b]
TJ Hughes	+130	+149
Marks & Spencer (non food)	+19.1[a]	−6.5
Arcadia	+36.8[a]	+92.0[a]
Next (retail)	+51.3	+76.3

Source: Retail Intelligence, 2001
Note: [a] 1995/96–1999/2000, [b] 1996/97–1999/2000

The background to these changes is a continuous rise in the potency of retail companies. Over a relatively short period of time the retail industry has developed enormous power and is now exercising considerable control over manufacturers. This change has occurred alongside a continuing concentration of the retail business into fewer large international companies. This is especially the case in food retailing; in the UK, for example, five chains account for the major share of the market. Many of the recent changes in the size of organizations have led to the creation of a widening gulf between managers of the business and consumers. A consequence of the distance which has been created is the lack of first-hand knowledge of the consumer's wants and needs. Where marketing thinking has been adopted, the emphasis is on developing a full understanding of the dynamics of consumer behaviour. We should be aware that organizations which use marketing are influenced by historical changes such as the change of power from the manufacturer to the retailer, and the change in perception of consumers and their resultant behaviour.

Gabor (1977) in McGoldrick (1990) lists three major indicative trends in the transfer of power to the retailer in the UK:

1 The abolition of resale price maintenance (RPM) in 1964 in the UK, in most product sectors. This represented a significant landmark in the shift of power, although pressures for change existed well before the legislation. This process has been ongoing. In 1997 the Monopolies and Mergers Commission decided to support a ban on recommended retail prices (RRPs) across a wide range of electrical goods. This means large electrical manufacturing companies cannot refuse to supply discount retailers.

2 The spread of own-brands, which accounted for nearly 22 per cent of retail sales and 25 per cent of food sales by 1986. By 2000 own-brand sales represented over 50 per cent of grocery sales (ACNielsen, 2001).

3 Increased retail concentration – which is both an effect and a cause of further retail power. By 1986, large multiple chains (ten or more outlets) held almost 60 per cent of retail trade in Britain. This concentration has increased as the leading grocers increase their retail offers with financial services, new store developments, and a broadening of the product range.

Retail concentration in grocery retailing is clearly illustrated in Figs 2.2 and 2.3.

The changes represented in Fig. 2.3 need to be placed in the context of the 1960s, when business in the UK had become increasingly uncompetitive by world standards. This was identified to be a failure of management and new courses were set up introducing the concepts and applications of marketing to a new breed of managers. However, changes have often been slow to materialize. Within the marketplace the companies that have adapted most successfully to contemporary changes are those which have directed management resources to supporting research into market and consumer trends, and to improving channels of distribution and communication campaigns. The stress is shifting to brand building and involves the development of own-labels. This dates from as late as the 1980s due to the retail industry being one where custom and tradition have been particularly strong, based upon an emphasis on trading or buying. According to Wileman and Jary (1997), in most retail companies a marketing function does not exist; even if it does, they point out, it is likely to be subordinate to the trading function. McGoldrick (1990) indicated the marketing concept was late in its application to the retailing industry and that even though there had been a use of marketing it did not mean the concept had been properly or fully applied. The interpersonal sales, trading service aspects of the industry have created styles of interaction with customers which only began to alter in the late 1990s. As with many other industries in the service sector this sales mentality has

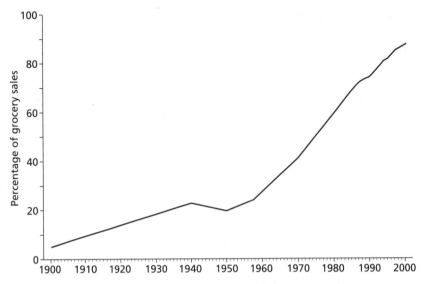

Fig. 2.2 Percentage of grocery sales through multiples, 1900–2000

Sources: ACNielsen, 2001; Board of Trade

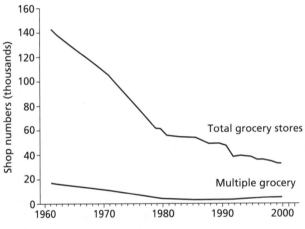

Fig. 2.3 Number of grocery outlets, 1960–2000

Source: ACNielsen, 2001

preserved the customary, long-established ways of doing business. The need for change has been forced upon the industry by the changes which have occurred in relation to the consumer and market forces. Modern retail marketing has emerged as a business reaction to changes in the social and economic environment, with the most successful companies having demonstrated a keen sense of providing the right organization structure and complete package offer for the retail consumer. This emergence relies as much on an approach or attitude to business or the market as it does to specific management expertise. Marketing is, therefore, a philosophy which initially relies on the art and science of different management approaches.

THE DEVELOPMENT OF MARKETING

We have discussed some of the important retail changes which may be associated with marketing. If we state that we live in an era of marketing, what does this mean? One method for perhaps understanding the development of marketing is to treat it as the development of ideas and trace what has been written about them. Unfortunately, while historical accounts show that trade has always existed, the term marketing was only used as a noun in the first part of the twentieth century. The use of the word marketing in the early stages of the twentieth century was associated with a number of factors which were loosely related to the activity of achieving a sale. Therefore, marketing as it is known at the beginning of the twenty-first century must be considered to be a recent development.

One way of attempting to answer a question about the meaning of marketing is to look at the definition which is presented later in this chapter. It is very easy to describe, using a definition, what is meant by marketing; but it is far more difficult to describe the practice of marketing. This is because central to marketing is the body of underlying concepts which forms the general guide for organizational and managerial thinking, planning and action. Therefore, to achieve a comprehensive understanding of marketing, it is necessary to master the underlying concepts.

Marketing has evolved against a background of economic and business pressures which have required an increased focus on adopting a series of managerial measures based upon satisfying consumer needs. Key to the importance of marketing within retail has been the level of economic growth throughout the twentieth century – growth which has led to improvements in living standards, enlargement of the population, a dramatic improvement in educational standards and increases in the discretionary time of consumers. Such changes enabled the Disney management to launch the Disneyland theme park concept and McDonald's to open their first fast-food restaurant, in the USA in 1955. Not all retail management was well conceived. Early retailing followed a passive supply-led approach; markets were assumed to exist and the retailer only had to provide an acceptable outlet, or means, for the consumer to make a purchase (channel management). At the early stage of retailing there was only minimal branding and competitive advantage was gained through creating efficiencies in operational costs.

The development of marketing is fashioned as the outcome of social and business pressures. The most widely accepted account of the development of marketing is that proposed by Keith (1996) outlining the 'production to sales, to marketing' evolvement of the Pillsbury company in the USA. In 1960 Keith argued that the growing recognition of consumer orientation would 'have far-reaching implications for business, achieving a virtual revolution in economic thinking'. He inferred that, at the time of writing, consumer orientation was only just beginning to be accepted as a business concept. A survey of the literature reveals an account of the history of marketing and modern business practice as having developed in three distinct stages: the production era, the sales era, and the marketing era.

1 *The production era.* During this stage there was a belief that if products were priced cheaply enough they would be bought. Therefore, it was important to plan supply to the marketplace, with the emphasis on consistently reducing costs. The focus of management was on increasing the efficiency of production, which involved an inward,

product-oriented emphasis to reduce unit costs rather than an outward, market-oriented emphasis. The overriding objective for management was standardization of the production of the offer, in order that it could be sold at the lowest price to the market.

2 *The sales era.* This is an evolvement phase where companies attempted to sell the products they believed in. If the consumer did not agree with the company's assessments – and so did not buy – there had to be a search for more effective means of selling. As competition increased, companies realized they could not survive without knowing more about different markets and improving their sales techniques. Therefore, the attempts of companies to influence demand and tailor it to meet their supply – in terms of retail product and outlet – characterized a sales era.

3 *The marketing era.* This is the phase that characterizes the end of the twentieth century and start of the twenty-first, and is dominated by a reversal of the preceding philosophy. Companies started to provide the products or merchandise they could sell – the goods people wanted – rather than trying to sell what they had. They adopted a consumer-led approach and concentrated on improving the marketing mix. It was recognized that customer needs and satisfaction were the most effective basis for planning and that a company has to be outward looking to be successful. With this approach, customer needs are key: the starting point for retail business processes. More recently the emphasis has subtly shifted to include the building of lasting relationships with customers. This approach focuses on an increase in profitability by concentrating on the achievement of higher lifetime value from the customer through cost-effective retention strategies.

There are continuing arguments as to the dates encompassed by the above eras, or even whether they can be treated as discrete periods. For our purposes, in the majority of texts the marketing era is identified as having been established from the 1950s onwards. For a full discussion, *see* Gilbert and Bailey (1990). The important factors, which have ushered in the marketing era during the late twentieth century, are discussed in some detail in the following paragraphs.

First, the increases in demand were occurring at a lower rate than the rises in productivity. This culminated in an oversupply of retail outlets serving similar markets and too many companies in the marketplace. The increase in competition, coupled with the risks associated with the retail marketplace, has led to greater reliance on the use of marketing. Selling strategies can only dominate when there is a lack of competition. As competition increases, the weaker competitors are squeezed or bought out of the marketplace. Concentration, contraction and mergers produce a 'battlefield' for retailers and provide the incentive to adopt marketing as a superior business philosophy. With the growth in market concentration, the larger companies are able to benefit from increased negotiating and buying strength.

The retail business system may be viewed as an organism that is concerned solely with survival and a wish for proliferation. Following this argument, when a business system is threatened it will take functional steps to improve the situation. The reaction by competitors, such as Sainsbury and Safeway, to Tesco's launch of their loyalty card is an example of the way change occurs through competition and the need to develop marketing to suit new environments. This response did not stop Tesco creating a competitive advantage from the launch of its Clubcard in 1995 or Clubcard Plus in 1996, nor did it halt Tesco's rise to the position of the UK's most successful grocery retailer. Marketing may provide for tactical change and modification of the system in times of risk, over-supply or market saturation. When the marketplace is competitive, marketing assumes a much more important role.

Second, the consumer was becoming more affluent and, therefore, it was possible to develop retail products which could be sold using a range of non-price attributes. This has required the development of methods of creating, and changing, consumer attitudes and beliefs; it is noticeable that promotion and image, managing quality and services, and improving store/retail atmosphere have all become significantly more important.

Third, the distance between the retailer and consumer had been continuously increasing. This led to a need for marketing research in relation to the gathering of information on market trends, evaluating levels of satisfaction, and understanding consumer behaviour. This has been compounded by the centralization of retail decision-making away from individual unit or store managers and into head office. This development was fuelled by the need for retailers to take advantage of the economies of scale of central buying. However, retail technology has provided much more detailed information about customers and their buying habits along with increased operational efficiency in such areas as checkout processes, and shelf and inventory replenishment. Larger retailers were in a position to regain relationships with their customers and the ability to do this through available resources and technical development has allowed this.

Fourth, as society developed, the mass market splintered into a number of sub-markets while at the same time methods of reaching the mass market became increasingly difficult. This was due to the increase in specialist media and the potential for a whole range of new retail products. The changes required improved expertise in the segmentation of markets and the formulation of different marketing mix strategies which would maximize demand for individual segments. Segmentation in retailing can take a number of different approaches. These are often based upon customer groups, product groups and shopping/usage occasions.

MINICASE 2.1

Does M&S have a future?

Marks & Spencer's big store in London's Kensington High Street has just had a re-fit. Instead of the usual drab M&S interior, it is now Californian shopping mall meets modernist chrome and creamy marble floors. Roomy walkways and designer displays have replaced dreary row after row of clothes racks. By the end of the year M&S will have 26 such stores around Britain – the first visible sign that the company is making a serious effort to pull out of the nose-dive it has been in for the past two years.

Things have become so bad that M&S, until recently a national icon, is in danger of becoming a national joke. It does not help that its advertisements featuring plump naked women on mountains – the

first-ever TV ads the company has produced – have met with an embarrassed titter; nor that, last week, the BBC's *Watchdog* programme savaged M&S for overcharging and poor quality in its range of garments for the fuller figure. As the attacks grow in intensity, so do the doubts about M&S's ability to protect its core value: a reputation for better quality that justified a slight price premium – at least in basic items, such as underwear. It is a long time since any self-respecting teenager went willingly into an M&S store to buy clothes. Now even parents have learned to say no. Shoppers in their thirties and forties used to dress like their parents. Now many of them want to dress like their kids. M&S's makeover comes not a moment too soon. Compared with the jazzy store layouts of rivals such as Gap or Hennes & Mauritz, M&S shops look like a hangover from a bygone era. The makeover aims to bring it into the present. The 26 stores being overhauled account for around a fifth of M&S's turnover. According to one former director, the retailer makes most of its profit from around 40 stores. So it makes sense to play to the company's strengths. But M&S will still be left with a long tail of some 270 relatively dowdy stores. Before the company rolls out its new look nationwide, it will have to work out how many of the stores are even worth hanging on to. M&S has always had difficulties with such issues. When its profits were growing strongly, it was inclined to add floor space, such as the 19 stores it took over from Littlewoods three years ago – just before profits peaked. It rarely closed down any of its high-street shops. Worse, the company had no satisfactory system for evaluating which of its stores, most of which it owns outright, were making money: M&S did not, until recently, charge notional rents to its stores. M&S does not disclose the performance of individual stores. But, judging by recent changes in retailing, its future lies increasingly with the most prominent. According to Verdict, a retail consultancy, the 100 top shopping locations in Britain (ranging from the biggest high streets, such as Oxford Street, to shopping centres, such as Lakeside in Essex) now account for around 60% of retailers' total high-street takings, but only around 40% of their space. No wonder M&S's chairman, Luc Vandevelde, is thinking of closing more than 20 mostly small stores. The details will be announced next month, when M&S is expected to reveal yet another set of appalling results, and yet another reorganisation.

The rot began appearing two years ago, when M&S announced a 23% fall in half-year results and warned of further bad news. In the event, pre-tax profits halved from £1.2 billion to £546m, then fell again to £418m for the year to March 2000. The biggest problems were in M&S's core British retailing, but foreign operations in North America and continental Europe were also going sour.

Behind this decline lie two basic faults. The first is the rigid, top-down, 'head office knows best' culture built on M&S's proud record of success. This was fine so long as customers kept coming and the competition lagged behind, but it also made it difficult to question the M&S way of doing things. M&S is only now scrapping outmoded rules that meant staff spent too much time on rituals such as checking stock or counting cash in the tills, just because somebody at Michael House, its head office in London's Baker Street, had decreed years ago that such tasks were essential.

Add to this in-bred top management. People tended to join M&S straight from college and work their way slowly up the ranks. Few senior appointments were made from outside the company. This meant that the company rested on its laurels, harking back to 'innovations' such as machine-washable pullovers and chilled food. Worse, M&S missed out on the retailing revolution that began in the mid-1980s, when the likes of Gap and Next shook up the industry with attractive displays and marketing gimmicks. Their supply chains were overhauled to provide what customers were actually buying – a surprisingly radical idea at the time. M&S, by contrast, continued with an outdated business model. It clung to its 'Buy British' policy and it based its buying decisions too rigidly on its own buyers' guesses about what ranges of clothes would sell, rather than reacting quickly to results from the tills. Meanwhile, its competitors were putting together global purchasing networks that were not only more responsive, but were not locked into high costs linked to the strength of sterling. In clothing, moreover, M&S faces problems that cannot be solved simply by improving its fashion judgments. Verdict points out that overall demand for clothing has at best stabilised and may be set to decline. This is because changing demographics mean that an ever-higher share of consumer spending is being done by the affluent over-45s. They are less inclined than youngsters to spend a high proportion of their disposable income on clothes.

The results of M&S's rigid management approach were not confined to clothes. The company got an enormous boost 30 years ago when it spotted a gap in the food market, and started selling fancy convenience foods. Its success in this area capitalised on the fact that, compared with clothes, food generates high revenues per square metre of floor space. While food takes up 15% of the floor space in M&S's stores, it accounts for around 40% of sales. But the company gradually lost its advantage as mainstream food chains copied its formula. M&S's share of the British grocery market is under 3% and falling, compared with around 18% for its biggest supermarket rival, Tesco. M&S has been unable to respond to this competitive challenge. In fact, rather than leading the way, it has been copying rivals' features by introducing in-house bakeries, delicatessens and meat counters.

Perhaps the most egregious example of the company's insularity was the way it held out for more than 20 years against the use of credit cards, launching its own store card instead. This was the cornerstone of a new financial-services division, also selling personal loans, insurance and unit-trust investments. When, in April this year, M&S eventually bowed to the inevitable and began accepting credit cards, it stumbled yet again. It had to give away around 3% of its revenues from card transactions to the card companies, but failed to generate a big enough increase in sales to offset this. Worse, it had to slash the interest rate on its own card, undermining the core of its own finance business. And this at a time when the credit-card business was already becoming more competitive, with new entrants offering rates as low as 5%.

How has M&S managed to escape a hostile takeover bid, despite its increasing woes? The break-up merchants had a crucial calculation to make. How much would they have to pay in relation to M&S's underlying assets (i.e., the stores, the retail business and financial services)? For the numbers to work for any bidder, especially one looking to break up M&S, the market value of its properties needs to be significantly higher than the value shown in its books. This is because the costs of breaking up M&S, which has around 75,000 employees, would be huge. Although some experts think the properties are worth more than enough to cover closure costs, others are not so sure. It is all very well, they say, to look at how easily the 100 C&A stores were disposed of (when the Dutch retailer started closing down its British operations earlier this year), but this misses the point. The problem is: if you do not use a prime M&S site on a high street for mainstream retailing, what can it be used for? Any break-up merchant could well face a complex task of selling property in smaller lots. This means that anyone seeking to take over M&S would have to be prepared to run at least the core, profitable part of the business, while managing the closure and disposal of the long tail of lacklustre shops. This is precisely the strategy with which the present management is grappling. Despite the firm's advantage of scale in a saturated clothing market, it is increasingly hard to avoid the conclusion that M&S's future is a slow and inevitable decline – with the only question being who is going to manage that process. If shrunk to its profitable core, M&S may become an attractive target for another big retailer. At the moment, however, while its food division may be attractive to the likes of Tesco, the clothing side represents a daunting challenge. Why take the risk now, when the brand may be damaged beyond repair?

Source: © *The Economist* Newspaper Ltd, London, 28 October, 2000

The four factors discussed on pages 28–9 have combined to force retailers and suppliers (manufacturers or providers) to work even more closely with one another in an effort to provide for the precise needs of the customer. Both retailers and suppliers are combining their talents in areas such as product design and research and development to ensure systems, services and goods will continue to satisfy current and future customers.

DEFINITIONS AND CONCEPTS OF MARKETING

Any conceptual definition of a business discipline is, by nature of its condensed form, a limited abstraction of values, techniques and practices which are the focus of its activity. Therefore, no single definition can be comprehensive enough to describe the true essence or complexity of marketing. Various definitions of marketing have been offered based upon the values prevalent at the time. Early definitions, reflecting the business philosophy and environment of the time, stressed the importance of selling. A popular definition utilized for many years stressed marketing being a managerial process of providing the right product, in the right place, at the right time and at the right price. This definition is mechanistic and stresses the provision of the product offer without due regard to those involved in the process.

No modern definition of marketing can ever disregard the importance of Philip Kotler, who has established himself as the most widely referenced proponent of general marketing theory. Kotler *et al.* (1999) define marketing as:

a social and managerial process by which individuals and groups obtain what they need and want *through creating and exchanging products and value with others*.

Kotler *et al.* argue that the definition is built on the main concepts of wants, needs, demands and satisfaction through exchange, transactions and relationships because these aspects are central concepts to the study of marketing. In 1984 the British Chartered Institute of Marketing defined marketing as:

the management process responsible for identifying, anticipating and satisfying customers' requirements profitably.

A comparison of both definitions reveals that there are significant core similarities. On examination it is found that both stress marketing as a management process. In addition, the British Chartered Institute clarifies the management responsibility as being one of assessment of consumer demand through the identification and anticipation of customer requirements. This denotes the importance of research and analysis as part of the overall process. One important difference is that Kotler's definition is more appropriate to not-for-profit organizations where there is free entrance or a subsidization towards the cost of a service. However, the most important implication which should be at the heart of any definition is the emphasis which is placed on the consumer's needs as the origin of all of the company's effort. The marketing concept has been expressed in many succinct ways, from Burger King's 'Have it your way' to the 'You're the boss' of United Airlines. This is the basis of the modern marketing concept which holds that the principal means of success is based upon not only identifying different consumer needs but also in delivering a retail product, the experiences of which provide sets of satisfactions which are preferable to those of the competitors. In addition, these satisfactions have to be delivered with attention to their cost-effectiveness as marketing has to be evaluated on the basis of its expenditure.

The concept of value within retailing

It should be noted that delivering value is an important aspect of the marketing approach. Companies have to find ways to ensure they optimize the delivery of value. This requires a way of uncovering the value sought by the customer, the development of that within the company and then the delivery of optimum value to the end customer (*see* Fig. 2.4).

The value of a retail product includes a number of different aspects, among them the perception of price, quality, and image as well as the economic and social aspects of the consumer. Consumers of today have far more information with which to make comparisons between alternative offers. As we are dealing with perceptions these will differ as they are based upon the available time individuals have to carry out comparison shopping. Also, some individuals have a wide network of acquaintances and may consult alternative information sources in making a decision about what offer delivers more value than another. A retailer or channel does not project a single image. It is likely to generate various images which differ according to a specific group, such as customers,

Approaches	Uncovering value needs	Developing value	Delivering value
Gathering	Data/feedback	Operations	Logistics
Analytical	EDI, surveys, etc.	Customer interfaces/purchasing	In-store, online services
Organizational	Interpretation	Training/retail strategies	Improved attitudes and behaviour

Fig. 2.4 A system for delivering value

employees, and shareholders, each of whom has a different type of experience with the company. This means perceptions of value will fluctuate within the population. The information box lists the components of retail product perceived value.

Retail product perceived value

This is based upon:

- actual price asked and the relativity to prices for same or similar product offered elsewhere
- perceived quality of the brand / product
- retailer or channel image, and its congruence with the image of the customer
- consumer characteristics by disposable income and level of difficulty in assessing the benefits / relative price of the product
- experience associated with the purchase or consumption process

---

However, it will be seen from the last point in the box that the focus on the cognitive – or functional – aspects of value for money should include intrinsic aspects, so that either the purchase or a shopping experience can be treated as of value for its own sake. For example, an experiential perspective may include the symbolic, hedonic and aesthetic aspects of the consumption process. This means that consumer judgement through utilitarian criteria has to include hedonic criteria, based on an appreciation of the good or service for its own sake. Value can be based upon the thinking and feeling dimensions of purchase and consumption behaviour. Consumption by value criteria is based upon a multiplicity of inputs which contribute in varying ways to consumer judgement in different choice situations.

Value is an essential aspect of the creation of retail success. If we consider the success of McDonald's, the value is not simply the hamburger or fries: it is the way the service, cleanliness, and speed of food production has provided an added value to the food. McDonald's customers are made up of a whole series of segments who value a fast, light and reasonably priced meal. This is all achieved by means of a great deal of planning and understanding. The company sets itself a series of high standards to achieve, known internally as QSCV, which is Quality, Service, Cleanliness and Value. These provide a defined target of value delivery for its operations. This is only one aspect that is important in the running of the company. The marketplace is dynamic and therefore

McDonald's has had to renew itself on a constant basis by introducing new menu items which fit with the values of health and nutrition in order to react to the changing market environment.

Understanding the retail experience from a marketing perspective is extremely important. However, the marketing concept – where the consumer is the driving force for all business activities – must not be confused with a sales approach. The next section ensures that the difference is understood and then we will introduce you to the notion of marketing orientation.

THE DIFFERENCES BETWEEN MARKETING AND SELLING

By now it should be obvious to the reader that marketing and selling are not synonymous. Levitt (1960) described the difference as follows:

> Selling focuses on the need of the seller; marketing on the needs of the buyer. Selling is preoccupied with the seller's need to convert his product into cash; marketing with the idea of satisfying the needs of the customer by means of the product and the whole cluster of things associated with creating, delivering and finally consuming it.

Current changes in the retail marketplace, from Internet e-commerce to telephone banking, have placed greater emphasis on the use of marketing rather than selling.

Retailing is much more than a sales transaction. Marketing has led us to focus on the full experience of the customer. Even though shopping may take place in a number of different types of retail setting, each offers a unique set of diverse experiences. Whether a shopper goes to the convenience store as opposed to an upmarket boutique in a shopping mall, or a fast-food outlet rather than a sandwich bar, there is a *total retail experience* of the occasion. This includes everything about the purchase, from the journey and parking until the checkout or payment and leaving. The total retail experience involves all elements of the retail offering which provide satisfactions or dissatisfactions to that retail episode. This will include the number and type of salespeople, and their level of service and demeanour; the displays on the floor and in the window; the merchandise – by brands, depth and width; and the atmosphere of the retail outlet in terms of music or other factors which will affect the senses. Marketing has to consider these and many other variables in order to ensure that each and every experience by the consumer is as satisfactory as possible. In fact, the marketing management team have to exceed customer expectations if they are to provide a 'wow' factor to the whole experience. All this is very important because satisfied consumers return and will tell others; they act as advocates of the retailer if their experience is consistently good.

The contrast between the sales and the marketing approaches highlights the importance of marketing planning and analysis related to customers and the marketplace (*see* Fig. 2.5 for a summary comparison of the two concepts). The sales concept focuses on the merchandise or goods being offered, and uses selling and promotion to achieve profits through sales volume. The underlying weakness is that the sales concept does not necessarily satisfy the consumer and may only culminate in short-term, rather than long-term company success. If the customer does not value the product, more resources and effort will have to be provided at the sales stage in order to achieve the sale. The marketing concept, on the other hand, has as its focus customer needs and it stresses the requirement for an integrated marketing effort throughout the company to achieve

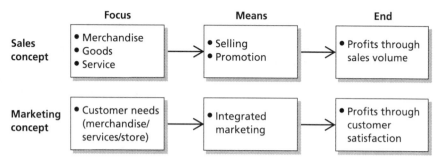

Fig. 2.5 The sales and marketing concepts compared

profits through customer satisfaction. Thus we begin to see the importance of the pervasive influence of marketing for the whole of the company.

Example: IKEA

Adherence to the marketing concept has rewarded IKEA with a major return on its investments. IKEA, the Swedish home furnishings retailer, started in 1958 with one store and now operates in 29 countries with over 140 stores and plans for further expansion. The company has a range of products that are based upon the benefits of design, quality and affordability. Its international marketing success is the envy of other retailers. The brand is a recognized concept based upon customer needs, including: ease of parking, stock availability and self-assembly take-away packs, modern designs, good value, children's play areas, and the offer of a leisure day out experience. In addition, products are constantly updated to match changing consumer lifestyles. The target group matches the product as it is young, new homeowners and middle-income families. Emphasis is placed upon in-store service and staff training programmes. Given the description of IKEA's retail operation, the adoption of the marketing concept (as outlined above) can be identified as central to the company's success. The success of IKEA can be gauged by sales per foot being over 2.5 times the industry average.

MARKETING MANAGEMENT TASKS

A marketing orientation relies on a series of management responsibilities. To clarify the situation, marketing can be seen to provide for a business to customer interface with responsibility for specific management tasks. These tasks are more clearly explained in Chapter 5 which provides a discussion of the marketing mix. It should be made quite clear here, however, that retail companies without a proper commitment to a marketing orientation have little likelihood of effectively executing the marketing function. Moreover, they will have an even lower expectation of success if their competitors adopt and commit themselves to a marketing orientation.

The full retail marketing function requires a combination of many activities. Whether they are those involving staff, producers or customers, they are all focused on facilitating and expediting transaction exchanges. The tasks listed in Fig. 2.6 ensure that potential buyers and sellers will be able to offer value to each other, will be informed and will communicate with each other. Surrounding this set of tasks is the requirement for all activity to be focused on creating customer satisfaction.

The marketing function may, therefore, be treated as a system which is designed to be an interface with the customer. This marketing system is illustrated in Fig. 2.7.

Task	Retail Marketing Function
1 identifying customers' needs and buying patterns for a store's retail offer	marketing research and EPOS data mining
2 analysing marketing opportunities	analysis and selection of target markets (segmentation) and understanding buyer/supplier relationships
3 translating needs into products (assortments and store layouts)	retail product planning and formulation as well as merchandise and stock management
4 determining the retail product's value to the customer at different seasonal periods	pricing policy – management to provide value
5 making the product available	establish distribution outlets, inventory systems, location analysis
6 informing and motivating the customer	promotion (selling and advertising, relationship marketing schemes), signage and in-store display

Fig. 2.6 The business to customer interface of marketing functions

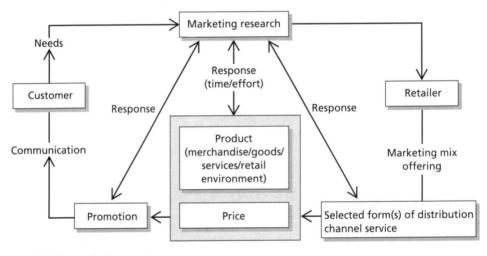

Fig. 2.7 The marketing system

THE ADOPTION OF MARKETING

There are numerous examples within retail of a change to a marketing orientation resulting in success. The retail industry, owing to its high service-based content, has been characterized by a history of custom and tradition rooted in trading practice. Until recently there has been a lack of vision in the industry which has resulted in the demise of many of the traditional companies during the final 25 years of the twentieth century. During this period we have seen a growing concentration and power shift towards retailers. However, there are weaknesses in historical trends which are still pertinent now. For example, O'Reilly's (1984) comments are apposite and still relevant; they are based on some areas of concern:

1 surplus floorspace capacity arising from rapid geographical expansion may cause space productivity to fall;

2 the intensification of competition as retailers' strategies converge in terms of locations, retail formats, assortments and private brands;

3 a possible serious decline in high street property values, especially as new technology reduces the financial institutions' reliance on large networks of branches;

4 the sheer scale of retailers' investment in stores, distribution systems, information systems, etc. could make them less flexible and more vulnerable to those offering new formats, improved economies and superior systems to the market.

As the marketplace becomes ever more complex, there is a need to ensure that the marketing function is attuned to current customer requirements. It would seem a simple change to listen to customers and provide what they say they want. If we examine the service marketing mentality of a very important piece of leisure equipment – a television – we can see that it began to change as late as the 1980s and 1990s. If you want to rent a TV, or have one repaired, there is a history of intractability and inflexibility of suppliers, who work to their own delivery and work schedules. This leads to consumers having to wait in after taking days off work, or cancelling social arrangements, or reorganizing the children's travel to or from school. By 1989, Radio Rentals had finally recognized the advantage of offering to install or repair televisions and a range of other equipment at a time when it was convenient to the consumer. This was further improved – albeit almost a decade later – with the use of larger vans to carry spares, mobile telephones, and flexible hours to suit the client including various times at weekends and/or in the evenings. As installations take only minutes and because repairs more often than not involve the replacement of a complete circuit board or parts, the time costs to the company are not excessive. At the same time, the company is able to build customer loyalty and stabilize the number of accounts it holds.

THE MARKETING ENVIRONMENT OF THE COMPANY

In 1995 Argyll (ASDA) tried to reinvent itself to counteract the way it had been caught in the increasingly competitive environment of grocery retailing. As such the Safeway supermarket group announced 124 store closures and 4800 job losses (Cope, 1995) as part of a major restructuring intended to allow the company to become more competitive with the market leaders Sainsbury and Tesco. At the time, the chairman Sir Alistair Grant said, 'I want Safeway to be a leader rather than a follower so that we are in a better position to come up with new initiatives.' The environmental forces of competition and change can be seen to have caused major problems for the retail sector. In order to compete more effectively, ASDA became part of Wal-Mart in July 1999, and by 2001 had 240 stores and 19 depots across the UK. The company is more able to compete on price and mix – fresh food, grocery, clothing, home, leisure and entertainment goods. Given the strength of Wal-Mart, ASDA is able to plan for investing over £1 billion and to open a number of new stores. The Wal-Mart brand was utilized on a UK store for the first time in 2000 in Bristol and other supercentre stores are planned.

These environmental forces affect each individual retail enterprise as well as the total retail market structure. This environment is made up of different levels of influence

Table 2.1 Four levels of marketing environment affecting the company

Level 1: The company	Level 2: Company markets	Level 3: Company stakeholders	Level 4: The wider environment
Marketing sub-functions need to be well organized and integrated with other company functions. Marketing has to communicate the needs of the market environment as described in levels 2, 3 and 4; and marketing thinking needs to dominate any strategy formulation.	The existing distribution systems and trends in specific forms of retail selling or outlet will affect the retail marketplace. The degree of rivalry, extent of consumer sophistication and the intensity of competitive activity will affect market activity choice.	Interest groups will affect the context of decision-making, e.g. shareholders, competitors, customers, employees, unions, government, suppliers, debtors, local community, banks, etc. – all of whom may have conflicting values but all of whom have a stake in the company.	Analysis is required of various forces: • political • economic • social • technological. Interrelationships of these different forces and changes in them are powerful market environment determinants.

which will affect the opportunities and marketing decisions that need to be made as a consequence of their actual or forecast pressures. Historical conditions affecting competition and rivalry in company markets; the values of stakeholder groups; and the political, economic, social and technological changes of the wider environment – these all affect the likely performance of the company and its brands. These influences are discussed in greater detail in Chapter 10, which deals with marketing planning.

The company marketing environment can be considered to be related to four levels (*see* Table 2.1):

- Retail marketing operates as a demand management function within an organizational context (*level 1*) and as such it needs to be adequately resourced and managed in order to be effective.

- A small retailer may have grown (*level 2*) through supplying to a local consumer market and using superior service and knowledge of customer needs over the competitors. However, later growth may require a more sophisticated development of new markets and a fuller understanding of the range of customer requirements. Retail is predominantly an intermediary service which, like any other market type, will be affected by the market environment in which the company operates. Therefore, competitors are as important as the customers served. As a result of the price-led strategies of companies new to the UK, such as Aldi (Germany) and Netto (Denmark), considerable growth was achieved in a relatively short time period. In fact the price-led discounters' marketplace changed rapidly and by 1996 it accounted for 8 per cent of the grocery sector (*Retail Week*, 1996). The most significant casualty at that time, due to the environmental changes, was J. Sainsbury. For the first time in 20 years Sainsbury's announced a fall in profits from £809 million in 1994 to £765 million in 1995. In 2000 Sainsbury's sold its Homebase DIY business to Schroder Ventures for £750 million. At the time Sir Peter Davis, group chief executive of Sainsbury's, said: 'Our priority now is to focus on food retailing and to devote our management and financial resources to the profit recovery in our UK supermarket business and in becoming first choice for food shopping.'

- The stakeholder system (*level 3*) involves all those participants in the company's value chain – a system within which different relationships have to be carefully fostered and reinforced. The power of stakeholder influence can be harnessed in a positive way to ensure a greater likelihood of competitive advantage in brand management, company reputation, product and service acceptability, etc.

- The wider macro-environment (*level 4*) places pressures on a company which are beyond the control of management. The broad categories of Political, Economic, Social and Technological (mnemonic: PEST) involve a series of different levels of aggregation – regional, national and international – related to business constraints and opportunities. (See page 245 for further discussion.)

All retailers need to take account of the environment and its likely effects on business. Those companies following a market-led business philosophy will take the influences and pressures of the different levels into account. The following section helps to clarify further what a company marketing approach is, describing the market-led company in terms of a business philosophy.

ALTERNATIVE BUSINESS PHILOSOPHIES

Marketing is a business philosophy which places consumers and their needs at the forefront of all activities. For example, at Men's Wearhouse in the USA customers are not given less service because it is a discount outlet with prices up to 30 per cent below those of department stores; they are offered added services: free pressing and alteration of any suit bought in the outlet. In addition, after 15 days a telephone call is made to ensure the suit fits properly. Shoppers need to feel they are getting added value for a purchase even though it may be discounted. A valuable knowledge of the process related to the purchase of men's suits only occurs when someone bothers to identify the key needs of the shopper.

While it is important to recognize the importance of structuring any organization so that the focus is the customer, there are a number of alternative philosophies which can be recognized. Each of these philosophies acts as a guiding orientation and a system of approaching the market. Figure 2.8 illustrates an important set of approaches, especially for those retail companies creating their own-brand products. In order to follow these philosophies it is important to understand the initial starting point within each chain system. This is because the first stage in the sequence of events demonstrates most clearly the locus of the company's approach to effecting exchange transaction relationships.

The product-oriented company (*see* Fig. 2.8(a)) may be ineffective due to problems encountered in having the wrong retail product or store layout for the market, and therefore having to waste extra resources on promotion and selling in order to achieve a sale. With this business type it is normal to find that companies believe their products to be acceptable and all that is required for sales to occur is the identification of prime markets and methods of selling. Such an approach to the marketplace by retailers who make, as well as buy in, products is associated with a lack of understanding of the true needs of

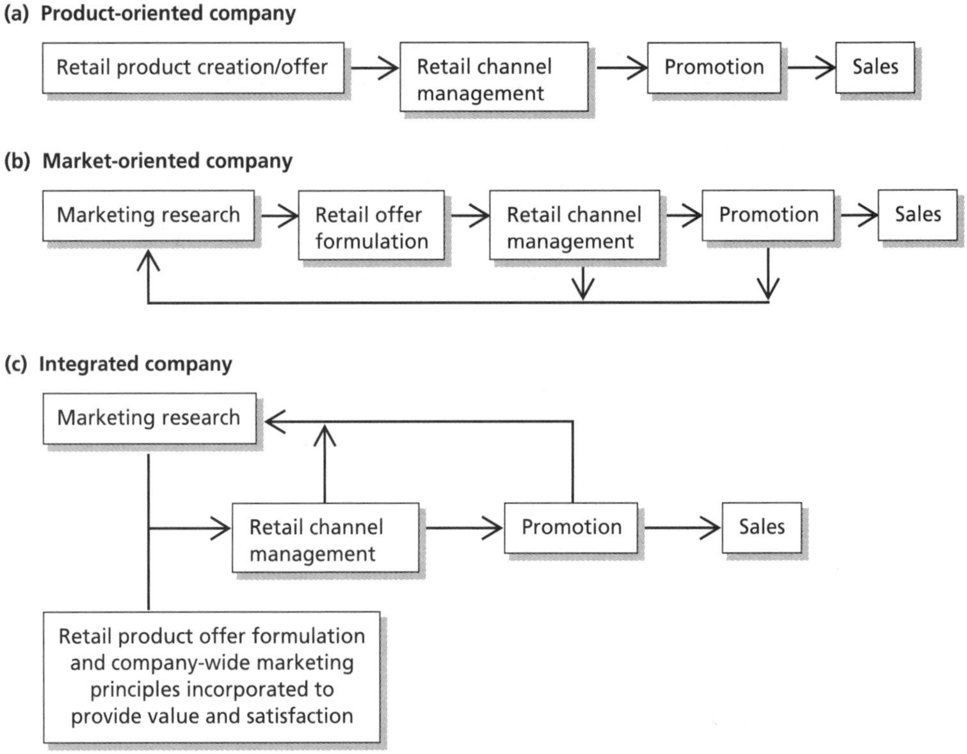

(a) Product-oriented company

Retail product creation/offer $\rightarrow$ Retail channel management $\rightarrow$ Promotion $\rightarrow$ Sales

(b) Market-oriented company

Marketing research $\rightarrow$ Retail offer formulation $\rightarrow$ Retail channel management $\rightarrow$ Promotion $\rightarrow$ Sales

(c) Integrated company

Marketing research

Retail channel management $\rightarrow$ Promotion $\rightarrow$ Sales

Retail product offer formulation and company-wide marketing principles incorporated to provide value and satisfaction

Fig. 2.8 Three possible business philosophies

the customer. A focus and emphasis on the merchandise as product, rather than an understanding of the benefits the consumer is seeking, is still the basis of a great deal of current marketing. Being product focused is misguided because the retailer should offer *benefits* such as:

- the promise of attractive looks, not simply a stress on clothes;
- good-looking feet and pleasure from walking, not simply a stress on the offer of shoes;
- hours of pleasure and the benefit of knowledge, not simply a stress on books or magazines;
- the 'snob' effect of certain brands – where richer groups purchase expensive merchandise in order to manipulate the management of their impression on others.

In short, the retailer is not selling simply 'things'; the sale has to incorporate aspirations, benefits, pleasure and new emotions.

Retail managers should take heed of success stories such as that of Wal-Mart; the late Sam Walton argued he had one abiding principle: to give customers what they wanted. In addition the strategy was to discount, concentrate on small town locations and aim for excellent employee relations. A product-focused philosophy is acceptable when there is a shortage or during boom times which are characterized by little competition. However, this approach usually indicates inward-looking management which concentrates on improvement within the company rather than outward-looking management, concentrating on the consumer and emerging retail needs.

The examples in Fig. 2.8(b) and (c) offer the ideal approach to organizing business in the modern retail marketplace. They are driven by research which creates an understanding of the consumer, the business and the marketplace. Research will be both secondary and primary. Information has to be collected from within and outside the company in order to establish a clear picture of the marketing environment. The integrated approach provides for a sequence of events that commences with an understanding of the consumer, the competitors, and the types of product that the company is capable of providing. It also requires a system that sensitizes the whole company to a marketing orientation. The integrated system helps to ensure that methods of improving the satisfaction levels of the consumer are incorporated into each department's objectives. Within these two examples of company philosophy, it can be seen that the feedback process allows the marketing department to develop products – as well as different forms of promotion – which are right for the consumer. This establishes a more effective means of ensuring that products are successful and that marketing budgets are used more efficiently. Marketing starts with the consumer and the market; the sovereignty of the consumer is clear. This has to be the correct strategy as it is the consumer alone who can dictate what they may want from tomorrow's retail marketplace. The retail industry is spending vast sums of money on developing new promotions, improving products, building or refurbishing new outlets and investing in technology. The only way for the risk level to be kept to a minimum is through the adoption of a marketing philosophy which provides products related to the needs of consumers.

MARKETING ORIENTATION

Markets are ever-changing and characterized by risk and threat; retail marketing, therefore, requires an appreciation of the types of decision needed in relation to the complexity of situations faced by the company. The factors creating complexity are:

- the need to consider a vast number of changing situations related to the scale of the modern retail market and its competitive forces (for example, there is a need to consider the multi-channel nature of retailing rather than focus on a bricks and mortar mentality – as such Internet, mobile phones, kiosks, digital TV all need to be considered);
- the uncontrollable nature of the above forces, and the unstable and unpredictable character of markets;
- the scarcity of reliable and comprehensive information;
- the continual improvement in marketing by competitors;
- the changing nature of consumers.

In order to deal with markets in a systematic way marketing has introduced a number of key approaches. These have been developed to capitalize on the many different sales and marketing opportunities in the retail industry. The industry has thrown off many of the traditional attitudes it had towards the customer, largely due to a realization of the importance of a marketing orientation. Five main areas can be identified which offer a truly marketing-based approach and these are discussed below.

1 It is a management orientation or philosophy

When a company is truly marketing oriented, the focus of company effort is placed on the consumer and this then leads to an integrated structure and customer focus within the company. There is the recognition that the conduct of the organization's business must revolve around the long-term interests of the customers it serves. It adopts an outward-looking orientation which requires responsive action in relation to external events. The overriding philosophy is to maximize customer satisfaction. This is achieved through offering merchandise or ways of purchasing which provide benefits of satisfaction through the buying process, as well as through use and possession of different items. The utilities delivered can be both perceived and real, as store image, sales techniques and branding can all affect the overall satisfaction level of the consumer. The focus of retailers in the 1980s and early 1990s was on new ways to satisfy consumers. This is characterized by Currys, large DIY retailers and the superstores which pioneered out-of-town developments. The late 1990s witnessed a focus on new product development, loyalty schemes, a concern with branding, and the broadening of retail channels. This has culminated in grocery retailers moving into petrol forecourts, own-brand developments and smaller, city-centre formats, and Dixons setting up Freeserve. In addition, the Internet is in the process of rapid development for appropriate types of product and where more direct methods of selling are the norm.

2 It encourages exchange transactions

This involves affecting the attitudes and decisions of consumers in relation to their willingness to make purchases. Marketers have to develop innovative methods to encourage exchange to take place. They also need to ensure the service offers value for money which may have to be linked to building intrinsic value into the retail offer. This can be related to the retailer's decisions over the intrinsic qualities of design, workmanship, materials used and features of the merchandise they offer. The customer will be looking for quality, suitability, value and acceptability. Marketers are required to ensure that they understand what the consumer values in order to create high levels of exchange transaction. Relationship marketing is a more refined aspect of this, with marketers attempting to retain the customer over longer periods of time through club or loyalty programmes.

3 Long- and short-term planning

This concerns strategic planning and tactical activity. There is a need for the efficient use of resources and assets for the long-term success of a company, while tactical action will be required to keep plans on course. All retail planning needs to create some match between the differences in consumers' purchasing and usage needs on the one hand, and the retailer's buying and selling requirements on the other. This may involve merchandise planning, trading area and store planning, market targeting, merchandising techniques, own-product development, as well as sales and tactical promotions (*see* Chapter 10 for a marketing planning approach to business). Such planning is used to create innovative formats or to target niche markets. The retailing success stories of the late 1990s were those of:

- B&Q Warehouse – a DIY 'category killer' (in 1998 B&Q merged with France's leading DIY retailer, Castorama, to become the largest DIY retailer in Europe. The group's DIY brands include Brico-Depot and Dubois Materiaux in France and Reno-Depot in Canada. In 1999 B&Q opened its first store in mainland China);
- Crazy George's – in 2001 there were 86 Crazy George's which were part of Thorn Financial Services Ltd prior to being aquired by the Principal Finance Group of Nomura in 1998. Thorn's format offers household goods to low income groups;
- Daisy and Tom – children's superstores;
- Disney Store – character merchandising and toy retailer;
- Internet Bookshop – WH Smith was the first UK bookseller to utilize cyberspace;
- MVC – music retailer offering discounted CDs, magazines and videos to its members.

4 Efficient cost-effective methods

Marketing's principal concern for any company has to be the delivery of maximum satisfaction and value to the customer at acceptable or minimum cost to the company, in order to ensure long-term profit. A large marketing budget may achieve a great deal but this may not constitute an acceptable cost to the retailer. Retailers have to be able to judge the operational and financial performance of their business in relation to the level of marketing expenditure. The productive use of any marketing budget relies on the knowledge and expertise of those employed in the marketing department and varies according to the type of trade involved, for example fashion, food or DIY.

5 The development of an integrated company environment

The company's efforts and structure must be matched with the needs of the targeted customers. Everybody working for the company must participate as much as they can in a holistic, total corporate marketing environment, with each retail department maximizing the satisfaction level of consumers. Integration is not just a smile or politeness; the emphasis has to be on creating assured quality and the highest standards of service (*see* Chapter 4 for a full discussion of this important area). Any company barrier to satisfying the customer or improving service must be removed. The onus is on the company to provide organizational structures which are responsive and are flexible enough to undergo change to suit changing customer needs.

CONCLUSION

From the discussion in this chapter it should be abundantly clear that retail marketing involves a number of special characteristics, as outlined below:

1 Marketing is a philosophy with the overriding value that the decision-making process of any company has to be led by the consumer's needs, the marketplace, and the company's assets and resources.

2 Successful marketing requires a specific type of organization structure which supports the belief in integrating the principles of consumer orientation throughout the company.

3 It requires innovative methods of thinking and planning so that new ideas are generated to take advantage of opportunities or to improve existing methods of marketing. As such, retailers need to create clear propositions of their retail offer. The clear differentiation of a Sainsbury's position from an Aldi or that of a 7–Eleven from a Marks & Spencer are examples of the clarity of retail marketing thinking and planning.

4 The retailer has to create the right environment, additional advantages and value, or loyalty schemes in order to ensure the customer is offered a complete package of benefits.

Retail marketing has evolved due to the different business and social changes which have occurred throughout the twentieth century and the beginning of the twenty-first. This chapter emphasizes that marketing has developed as a reaction to the different conditions which impinge on business operations. While we can identify different business philosophies, clarify the marketing concept and describe the benefits of a marketing orientation, the heart of marketing lies in the way marketing management functions in an attempt to create consumer satisfactions.

EXERCISES

The exercises that follow help to place the information given in this chapter in a practical context. We suggest they are worked through before you move on to Chapter 3.

1 Discuss the way you believe marketing is being used by the retailer types listed in the top left-hand box of the grid below. You need to identify the ways in which aspects of marketing may be changing. You need to think about this with regard to the marketing mix. For example, do supermarkets now offer more clothing or electrical products?

Major grocery chains – ASDA/Tesco Banks and building societies Petrol stations Chemists Others (provide types)	**What is the marketing emphasis?**
Can you identify any trends or emphases by type of retailer?	**What are they and do they seem successful?**

Now share your ideas with other students and come to some agreement as to what are the five most important trends occurring in today's retailing arena. You need to agree a system of voting or ranking to obtain this list.

2 Ask some of your colleagues or friends what they believe retail marketing to be. Also ask them what marketing people are responsible for. Now explain the philosophy and concepts of retail marketing, highlighting the differences between the theory you have read in textbooks and the ideas of those to whom you have spoken.

3 Think about the contemporary pressures from the wider environment and list all those that you believe will have an impact on a retail company's business. Are companies addressing these? If not, what action should be taken for retail companies to react to the most important changes you have identified? What, if any, are the wider and more general implications of the environmental changes you have identified?

REFERENCES AND FURTHER READING

ACNielsen (2001) *The Retail Pocketbook*. Oxford: NTC Publications.

British Chartered Institute of Marketing (1984) The Institute of Marketing, Cookham, Maidenhead.

Business Week (1993) 'History collides with the bottom line', *Business Week*, 8 February, 34.

Cook, D. and Walters, D. (1991) *Retail Marketing: Theory and practice*. Hemel Hempstead: Prentice Hall.

Cope, N. (1995) 'Kwik Save starts price war', *Independent*, 3 May, 34.

Dibb, S. and Meadows, M. (2001) 'The application of a relationship marketing perspective in retail banking', *Service Industries Journal*, 21 (1), 169–94.

Dick, A.F. and Basu, K. (1994) 'Customer *Loyalty*: Towards an Integrated Conceptual Framework', *Journal of the Academy of Marketing Sciences*, 22 (2), 99–113.

Drucker, P. (1974) *Management Tasks, Responsibilities, Practices*. London: Heinemann.

The Economist (2000) 'Does M&S have a future?', *The Economist*, 28 October.

Egan, J. (2000) 'Drivers to relational strategies in retailing', *International Journal of Retail and Distribution Management*, 28 (8), 379–86.

Gabor, A. (1977) *Pricing, Principles and Practices*. London: Heinemann.

Garbarino, E. and Johnson, M.S. (1999) 'The different roles of satisfaction, trust and commitment in customer relationships', *Journal of Marketing*, 63 (2), 70–87.

Gengler, C.E., Leszczyc, P. and Popkowski, T.L. (1997) 'Using customer satisfaction research for relationship marketing: a direct marketing approach', *Journal of Direct Marketing*, 11 (1), 23–9.

Gilbert, D.C. (1996) 'Relationship marketing and airline loyalty schemes', *Tourism Management*, 17 (8), 575–82.

Gilbert, D.C. and Bailey, N. (1990) 'The development of marketing – a compendium of historical approaches', *Quarterly Review of Marketing*, 15 (2), 6–13.

Keith, R.J. (1960) 'The marketing revolution', *Journal of Marketing*, January, 35–8.

Keith, R.J. (1996) 'The marketing revolution', in Enis, B.M. and Cox, K.K. (eds) *Marketing Classics*. 8th edn. London: Allyn & Bacon.

Kotler, P., Armstrong, G., Saunders, J. and Wong, V. (1999) *Principles of Marketing*. 2nd European edn. Englewood Cliffs, NJ: Prentice Hall.

Levitt, T. (1960) 'Marketing myopia', *Harvard Business Review*, July/August, 45–56.

Lusch, R.F., Dunne, P. and Gebhart, R. (1993) *Retail Marketing*. Ohio: South-Western Publishing Co.

McGoldrick, P.J. (1990) *Retail Marketing*. Maidenhead: McGraw-Hill.

Moss, S. (2000) 'The Gospel according to IKEA', *Guardian*, 26 June, 2.

O'Reilly, A. (1984) 'Manufacturers versus retailers: The long-term winners?', *Retail and Distribution Management*, 8 (2), 55–8.

Reid, M. (1995) 'Survey of retailing (1): Change at the check-out – economies of scale and information technology have given top retailers awesome power. But can they keep it?', *The Economist*, 4 March, 334.

Retail Intelligence (2001) 'UK retail report', May, 120.

Retail Week (1996) *Retail Week*, November, 18–20.

Sivakumar, K. and Weigand, R.E. (1997) 'Model of retail price match guarantees', *Journal of Business Research*, 39 (3), 241–55.

Sopanen, B. (1996) 'Enhancing customer loyalty', *Retail Week*, December, 21–4.

Sweeney, J.C. and Soutar, G.N. (2001) 'Consumer perceived value: The development of a multiple item scale', *Journal of Retailing*, 77 (2), 203–20.

Wileman, A. and Jary, M. (1997) *Retail Power Plays*. London: Macmillan.

3 Consumer behaviour and retail operations

This chapter should enable you to understand and explain:

- the benefits of studying consumer behaviour;
- the decision-making process as part of buying behaviour theory;
- motivation theory and Maslow's hierarchy of needs;
- the content of simple as well as complex consumer behaviour models;
- the influence of demographics and family roles on retail purchase behaviour.

CONSUMER BEHAVIOUR IN THE RETAIL CONTEXT

It is important to realize that management cannot be effective unless it has some understanding of the way in which retail consumers make decisions and act in relation to the consumption of retail products. There is, therefore, a need to understand the different ways in which consumers choose and evaluate alternative retail services. While the term 'consumer' would seem to indicate a singular concept of demand, the reality is that there is a wide diversity of consumer behaviour – with decisions being made for a range of reasons. We need to study consumer behaviour to be aware of:

- the needs as well as the purchase motives of individuals;
- how demographic change may affect retail purchasing;
- the different effects of various promotional tactics;
- the complexity and process of purchase decisions;
- the perception of risk for retail purchases;
- the different market segments based upon purchase behaviour;
- how retail managers may improve their chance of business success based upon understanding what is required as part of the retail experience, and how customers react to that experience process based upon all the retail marketing approaches utilized.

Many variables will influence the way consumption patterns differ. These will change based upon the different types of retailers in the marketplace and the way individuals have learnt to approach purchase opportunities. The variations are countless and this makes it more practical to deal with general behavioural principles which are often discussed within a framework that includes the disciplines of psychology, sociology and economics.

Table 3.1 Needs, wants and demand functions for the purchase of clothes

Motivation	Characteristics
Needs	Basic human requirements that pre-exist for warmth, covering, social status
Wants	Potential to purchase occurs as the individual feels a drive to satisfy those needs – retail marketing attempts to direct needs to a specific want for the retailer's own channel or service and merchandise
Demands	Those wants for which the customer is able to pay

The principles that apply will help explain retail purchases – whether they are from a store, a catalogue, or some other form of retail offer. A market-based system assumes that individuals enter the marketplace with money to spend. Consumer spending is directly related to an individual or household's income, the first call upon which will be for necessities such as food, rent, insurances, energy and home costs. The amount of money someone has left after paying for necessities and their taxes is known as *discretionary income*. From this discretionary income individuals may purchase luxury items. However, discretionary income is not an easy concept to pin down because some individuals and households treat particular purchases as necessities while others treat them as luxuries.

First, we should all be aware that there is a process of purchasing which takes into account the needs, wants and demands for products; Table 3.1 describes this process for the purchase of clothes.

The simplest of models of buying generated from the states of motivation outlined – needs, wants and demands – is illustrated in Fig. 3.1. This process is based upon the response to a stimulus. The decision to buy the clothes may be linked to feeling a need to impress friends at a party, that something is wearing out, that there is a need for more fashionable clothes and knowing where to go to purchase the favoured brand. The retailer engenders wants which lead to demand by affecting consumer behaviour through the image of the store, its layout and the ways the customer is brought into visual and sensory contact with the merchandise.

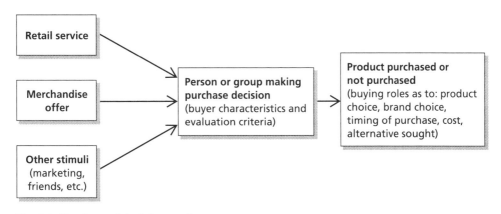

Fig. 3.1 Simple model of the purchase process

Buyer characteristics (*see* Table 3.1 and Fig. 3.1) will influence the type of purchases made. For example, the culture, social class, age, occupation, personality and beliefs of the individual will affect the types of product they purchase. Hollinger (1998) has indicated that in the UK the mail order market has historically served lower income groups owing to the attraction of financial credit which may have been difficult to obtain elsewhere. This is argued to be a UK phenomenon whereby mail order is not attractive to the middle classes. However, it does not have the same image within other parts of Europe. This is because the buyer will be attempting to establish his or her self-worth by buying products as part of impression management. The purchase process has been influenced by marketers to ensure that products and brands are chosen to create a social comparison between the purchaser and others. This is based upon the symbolic meaning that brands have built up over a period of time. Nevertheless, the final choices made by consumers are by no means simple.

Time taken to shop

There are differences in the type of shopping behaviour embarked upon. For example, sometimes a shopping trip is merely a functional or complex activity whereas at other times it will be a leisure activity. Shopping expeditions can combine different behavioural influences whereby some individuals want a predictable set of events as part of complex or functional shopping whereas in contrast others want some novelty and interest. In complex shopping the customer will probably contemplate the purchase of a technical product. This will lead to prior research of information or the need to take advice from retail staff as there is normally a higher risk associated with the intended purchase. This takes more time than in functional shopping but is required to reduce the level of perceived risk associated with a purchase (see later section on perceived risk). The leisure shopper is different, as he or she will not be concerned with the time taken to shop but is more interested in browsing and discovering wants rather than simply satisfying needs. The continuum for this is shown in Fig. 3.2.

A simple account of differences between the functional and leisure shopping occasion needs to be further enlarged by understanding how the leisure shopper is developing their demand patterns for certain styles and fashion. The next section uncovers the process by which fashion trends may develop.

Example of process – retail fashion buying

Snyder and Fromkin (1980) explained the dichotomy of individuality and conformity in fashion adoption. According to this theory, humans strive towards individuality (uniqueness) and conformity in appearance. Through a social comparison process individuals evaluate their level of uniqueness in relation to others, resulting in both emotional and behavioural reactions. It would appear that individuals have the most positive reactions

Functional (time efficient)	**Complex** (time required)	**Leisure** (time-rich activity)
Focused predetermined routine habitual action	- - - - Pre-planned/researched - - - - higher risk	Emphasis on browsing and serendipity

Fig. 3.2 Simple model of time-related shopping expeditions

when they perceive their appearance to be moderately similar to others. The most negative reactions occur when individuals perceive themselves as either dissimilar or very similar to the comparison individual or group. Consequently change occurs towards similarity when perceived similarity is low, and towards dissimilarity (uniqueness) when perceived similarity is high. Accordingly, fashion merchandising and sensible stock levels at perceived realistic prices can satisfy the need both for individuality as well as for conformity.

There are three theoretical approaches that may explain the way by which adoption processes for fashion occur in retailing:

1 *Trickle-down theory* is based upon the premise that new innovative fashions and styles originate in the wealthier classes owing to ability to purchase designer clothing and are passed down through the middle classes to the lower socio-economic groups.

2 *Trickle-up theory*, as a hypothesis, is based upon a process of fashion and style creation by the lower socio-economic groups which is followed by the upper classes prior to being adopted by the middle classes.

3 *Trickle-across theory* is based upon the notion that fashion and style can originate in any one of the social classes. If the opinion leaders within one or more of the classes take up the fashion development then that fashion and style is more likely to be adopted. This is because the opinion leaders will be instrumental in endorsing the acceptability of the fashion change. In this process the fashion will extend horizontally through the population and may affect all classes in its turn.

The purchase of fashion items and accessories can also be seen to follow Veblen's notion of *conspicuous consumption*: the theory that consumption often takes place as a means of displaying one's wealth. Conspicuous consumption is the acquisition and displaying of products that are purchased to gain recognition and respect from others. It could be argued that some forms of conspicuous consumption are declining as those individuals with the wealth to purchase extravagantly deliberately adopt more frugal lifestyle purchases. However, when dressing in styles associated with the working classes or urban groups, as has occurred with jeans, there is still the opportunity to achieve the 'snob effect' of purchasing designer or expensive brand labels. The wealthier groups, or those who have been willing to pay higher amounts for clothing, have remained important as it is the *trickle-down* effect of reference group influence which may account for the adoption of different products by less wealthy individuals. Sometimes the fashion product is created in large numbers to bring down unit price and thus enable trickle down; at other times products, such as mobile phones or electronic diaries, are accepted at the height of their pricing.

Retail buying roles

Choices over purchase are subject to a vast number of forces acting collectively. As part of the way the whole process is influenced we also need to realize that there are different roles – initiator, influencer, decider, buyer, user – which individuals may play in the buying process (*see* Table 3.2). Within these roles the potential consumer exhibits varying types of purchase behaviour. These will be based upon the nature and importance of the decision to be made and who needs to be consulted prior to purchase. Buying a wedding

Table 3.2 Buyer roles

Buyer role	Characteristics
Initiator	First individual who suggests product/service should be evaluated/purchased
Influencer	Provides views and advice which are valued by others and can subsequently influence the final decision
Decider	The individual who will take the decision in the buying process as to what, how, when and where to buy (store choice), etc.
Buyer	The individual who actually makes the purchase
User	The individual who consumes or uses the service/product

present for a best friend will probably involve all the above buying role types and may involve a number of people.

Decision over store choice

The decider in Table 3.2 has decision power over where the purchase will be made (store choice). Consumer motives in store selection have been researched for many years and little development has been made over the work of Kelly and Stephenson (1967) who identified eight basic dimensions in store choice:

1 general store characteristics (reputation, number of stores);
2 physical characteristics of the store (decor, cleanliness, checkout services);
3 convenience of reaching the store from the customer's location (time, parking, etc.);
4 products offered (variety, dependability, quality);
5 prices charged by the store (value, special sales);
6 store personnel (courteous, friendly, helpful);
7 advertising by the store (informative, believable, appealing); and,
8 friends' perception of the store (well known, liked, recommended).

The next question that needs to be asked is: how free are individuals to make choices or purchase decisions? Some would argue that behaviour is conditioned and that it is possible through effective marketing to persuade individuals to adopt specific purchase behaviour. The question remains as to how rational human beings are in the purchase process. The assumptions of how consumers may approach retail purchases are well summed up by Ajzen and Fishbein (1980):

> Generally speaking, human beings are usually quite rational and make systematic use of the information available to them. We do not subscribe to the view that human social behaviour is controlled by unconscious motives or overpowering desires, rather people consider the implications of their actions before they decide to engage or not engage in a given behaviour.

However, it is still debated whether consumers act in a rational way by consideration of the alternatives or whether they are more compulsive in action. The difficulty we have in

Table 3.3 Behaviourist and cognitivist perspectives

Behaviourist	Cognitivist
• Observed behaviour is all important • Behaviour is predictable • People are information transmitters • People are all alike • Behaviour is rational • Human characteristics can be studied independently • Emphasis is on what a person is and does • Behaviour can be understood	• What goes on in a person's mind is the key to comprehension • Behaviour is not predictable • People are information generators • Each person is unique • Behaviour is irrational • People must be studied as a whole • Emphasis is on what a person can be • Behaviour can never be completely understood

understanding this is that individuals have expressed conscious rationalizations as well as having unexpressed attitudes to purchase. The analysis of the different patterns that take place – and why – is therefore complex.

COMPARISON OF BEHAVIOURIST AND COGNITIVIST APPROACHES

The study of consumer behaviour as a whole can be found to lie either within or between two major approaches: the behaviourist approach and the cognitivist approach. It is not always clear from the literature the approach that any one author is taking. To enable you to have a clearer idea of the difference in perspective between the two approaches, simplified key points are listed in Table 3.3.

As with most polar opposites, reality probably occurs somewhere between the two extremes of these views. Behaviour is predictable to a certain extent, yet can never be completely understood. Decisions are made that have both rational and irrational elements. The importance of identifying both extremes is that it sets a framework within which to work and helps us to understand the more extreme stances taken by some theorists. What we do know is that socio-economic, demographic, social and psychological buying decision variables will affect the purchase patterns of consumers. These influences are examined later in the chapter; first, there is an explanation of some of the main theories of consumer behaviour.

THE MAIN THEORIES OF CONSUMER BEHAVIOUR

Perhaps the most fruitful approach to an understanding of retail demand is to identify and evaluate the broader theories of consumer behaviour linked to purchase behaviour. This is far from simplistic as we are faced with a proliferation of research within a discipline which has displayed significant growth and diversity. The discipline of consumer behaviour has borrowed a range of concepts from the quantitative and behavioural sciences in order to generate integrated models of action. Because of the difficulties which are involved in proving that one model is superior to another, we are confronted by a range of models which rely on a correspondence of belief rather than any logical proof that they are right or wrong. Theories can only be assessed on the contribution they make to our understanding of the purchase process. Complex models may never be proven or validated beyond any doubt; they can offer only intuitive criteria based upon existing knowledge to predict the likely process of decision-making. However, behaviour is not totally random or beyond our comprehension due to the patterns of consumer behaviour which may be predicted.

Models of behaviour are a useful means of organizing disparate bodies of knowledge regarding social action into a somewhat arbitrary yet plausible process of intervening psychological, social, economic and behavioural variables. The early major theories were those of Engel *et al.* (1968); Engel *et al.* (1986); Howard and Sheth (1969); and Nicosia (1966). These models can be found to share several commonalities:

1 they all exhibit consumer behaviour as a decision process. This is integral to the model;

2 they provide a comprehensive model focusing mainly on the behaviour of the individual consumer;

3 they share the belief that behaviour is rational and hence can, in principle, be explained;

4 they view buying behaviour as purposive, with the consumer as an active information seeker – both of information stored internally and of information available in the external environment. Thus the search and evaluation of information is a key component of the decision process;

5 they believe that consumers limit the amount of information taken in, and move over time from general notions to more specific criteria and preference for alternatives;

6 they all include a notion of feedback – that is, outcomes from purchases will affect future purchases.

A brief overview of some models will provide a better understanding of the decision-making process.

The Engel–Kollat–Blackwell (EKB) model

The Engel–Kollat–Blackwell (EKB) model has been widely referenced and is acknowledged as one of the most comprehensive explanations of consumer behaviour. The original model has undergone three major revisions since 1968 and the current model, while retaining some of the fundamentals, has become more sophisticated in definitional and explanatory aspects and therefore varies from the original version. This reflects the progress made in knowledge which required some adaptation to the original model for its continued survival.

The EKB model (*see* Fig. 3.3) takes a broad view, incorporating inputs such as perception and learning which are discussed in great detail. A key feature of the EKB model is its incorporation of the differences between *high* and *low involvement* as part of the buying process.

High involvement is normally present in the decision-making process when the perceived risk in the purchase is high. This element of risk is higher when the consumer is unsure about the outcome of his or her purchase decision. This arises when:

● information is limited;

● the buyer has low confidence;

● the price relative to income is high.

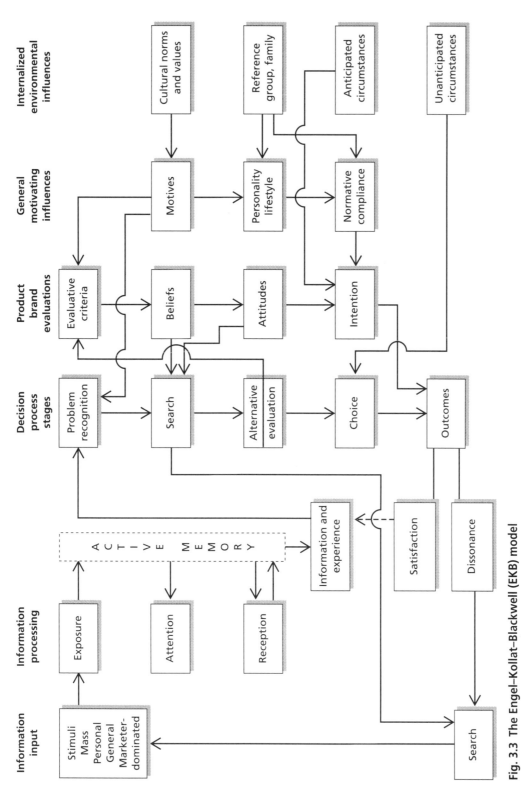

Fig. 3.3 The Engel–Kollat–Blackwell (EKB) model

Source: Engel, Kollat and Blackwell, 1968

This has obvious connections to demand. Engel, Blackwell and Miniard (EBM) in 1986 stated that limited problem-solving (LPS) activity takes place when there is little perceived risk that a wrong decision will be made. As they also point out, most consumer decisions are of the LPS type. However, when present, extended problem-solving (EPS) affects the amount of effort put into the search to reduce the perceived risk. This will involve a great deal more external searching.

The EKB model has the decision process as pathways of convergence passing through various stages of processing prior to any choice being made. The central process can be seen to incorporate five stages:

1 problem recognition/arousal;

2 internal search – alternative evaluation;

3 external search – alternative evaluation;

4 choice/purchase;

5 outcomes as dissonance or satisfaction.

The environmental factors, such as cultural norms and values, motives, etc., which influence these stages are important. The model incorporates influence which moves from the general to the specific, which is from the macro level (reference group, social class, norms) to the micro level (belief, intention, attitude).

Minicase 3.1 illustrates the importance of changes in age profile and its resultant impact on culture, beliefs and behaviour in relation to consumers' shopping behaviour.

MINICASE 3.1

The importance of the Teenager – Youth, Inc

Sure, the young are going to change the world. But first they are going to buy a huge amount of stuff. The economic influence of the young has never been greater. Just in America alone, the 31m kids between 12 and 19 control $155 billion-worth of consumer spending, according to Teenage Research Unlimited, a market-research firm. Their numbers are slightly smaller than those of the boomers at the same age, but their spending power, adjusted for inflation, is five or six times as large. No wonder the young consumer has gone from afterthought to perhaps the most important retail sector today. If society seems obsessed with youth, it is at least partly because companies are. Like it or not, the young increasingly pick the styles and brands that trickle up to the rest of the population.

Now that dual-income families have become the norm, parents spend money on their children to compensate for their absence. Divorce and remarriage compound this effect. Young people's money tends to flow in concentrated streams that can make or break companies. This year, for example, Pokémon, a series of fighting cartoon characters, generated more than $3 billion in revenue for its owner, Nintendo, in America alone. When urban teens got bored with Tommy Hilfiger's clothes in mid-1999, the firm's share price plummeted by 85% in a matter of months. Push scooters were a 1950s anachronism; now, thanks to an overnight youth craze there is an updated model called the Razor.

A thriving industry has emerged to try to understand young consumers and predict what they will like. Companies have entire research arms dedicated to youth trends. Microsoft set up a youth house to watch teenagers work and play. Market-research firms send out pint-sized spies into the malls to report back on the latest spontaneous fashions and brand loyalties.

So who are they? A lot of things. They are the 'echo boomers', offspring of the baby boomers, that huge wave of children of the post-war reconstruction. They are also the 'net generation', the first to grow up never knowing a time before computers, and not much time before the Internet. They were bathed in bits, immersed in a revolutionary technology that the rest of the world is still struggling to understand. And they are the 'millennials', with the clean slate and new day that implies: born in the 1980s, the richest generation in history, the best educated, healthiest, the first to grow up knowing nothing of war, famine, disease and poverty.

The gradual departure of the boomers from the workforce over the next 25 years will leave a huge vacuum for the millennials to fill, and the likely failure of Social Security will force them into the role of saviour, helping the state to support their parents. Unimaginatively, they are better-known as Generation Y, a reference to their once-troubled predecessors, 'Generation X'.

Source: © The Economist, London, 23 December 2000

Sheth's family model of behaviour

Quite often the purchase decision process is investigated in terms of the individual; for example, some models have stressed the individual as the single focus of attention. It is clear that for the purchase of high price items the decision process involves a high level of risk that the decision may be a poor one. It also often involves the preference resolution of more than one individual. This creates a complex situation whereby, more often than not, the purchase has to satisfy the divergent needs of the group. Obviously a family decision involves multiple influences from its members. Within the theory of family buying behaviour there is the concept of role structure, that is, individual members of the family take on roles such as collecting information, deciding on the available budget, etc. Whatever way a family makes its final decisions we have to realize we are not dealing with a homogeneous unit but with a collection of individuals with different goals, needs, motives and interests.

The Sheth model of the family decision process (Fig. 3.4) provides one of the few examples of an attempt to replicate the behaviour of group decision-making. The problem with the schema of Sheth is that aspects of search, motives, beliefs and predispositions occur in tandem with each member of the group prior to there being a resolution of the group to a final decision, whereby joint or autonomous outcomes occur. While we have to applaud Sheth for breaking away from an overreliance by theorists on individual decision models, we may need to question the reality of his model as to how groups bargain and trade off parts of the larger decision, especially in relation to products shared by members of the family.

THE BUYING DECISION PROCESS AND THE IMPLICATIONS FOR RETAIL MANAGEMENT

Retail has developed rapidly over the past few decades, led by a marketing thrust which has created diversity of supply, focused on important consumer segments and stimulated high levels of demand. Within this development, marketing has often concentrated more on improving the product than understanding the consumer and the complexity of their decision processes. Whatever approach is taken it is normally agreed that the act of buying retail products is characterized as a process of different stages. As part of this approach, the buying decision is the involvement of some or all of the stages outlined in Fig. 3.5 and listed on pages 57–60.

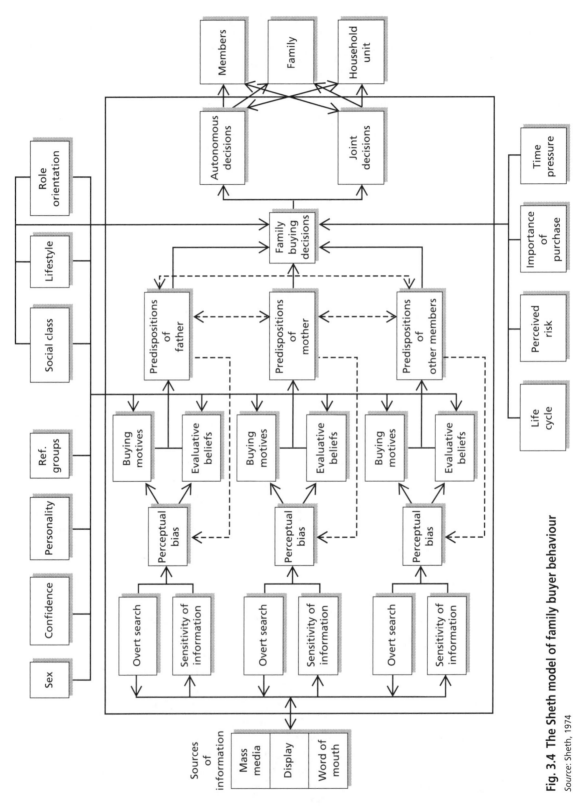

Fig. 3.4 The Sheth model of family buyer behaviour

Source: Sheth, 1974

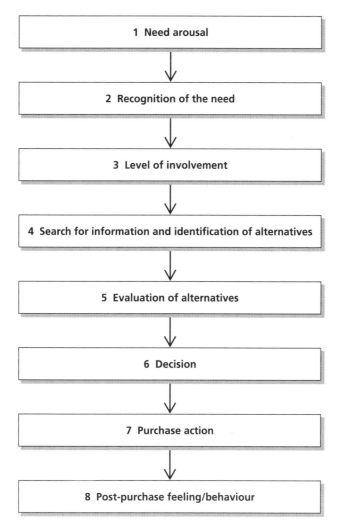

Fig. 3.5 Eight-stage model of the retail buying process

The retail buying process outlined

The starting point is where a need is recognized and the individual is energized into becoming a potential customer.

1 Need arousal

The buying process is triggered by the emergence of an unsatisfied need. The stimulus for this is a *cue* (social or commercial) or a *drive* (physical, when the senses are stimulated) which motivates or arouses the individual to act.

2 Recognition of the need

This is the prerequisite stage based upon the recognition of the need to perhaps replenish the stock of food or a need for new clothes because of a forthcoming function or holiday.

Retailers can affect this stage using good window displays, advertising and promotion, and stimulating in-store merchandise displays. The stimulation of demand is important given that many shopping trips are simply to browse.

The recognition may be that other secondary needs emerge. For example, the desire for a holiday may require new luggage and leisurewear. A new suit may also be part of a complex need that includes buying a shirt, tie and shoes as well. Good retailers recognize the opportunity to group complementary products or to provide cues as to what else the customer may require. The marketing-oriented retailer will present a total merchandise package to the consumer but also will train their staff to prompt the customer to think about his or her accessory requirements.

3 Level of involvement

This is the amount of time and effort invested in the decision process, for example the depth of search for information. Involvement will differ based upon the complexity of the product, the individual customer perceptions and the buying situation in which the purchase is to be made. This is discussed further below in the context of simple or complex decision-making.

4 Search for information and identification of alternatives

Brands which initially come to mind when considering a purchase are referred to as the *evoked set*. However, friends, shop assistants, merchandise, leaflets, magazine adverts, etc. may provide a consideration set. The search for information occurs on an internal and external basis (Fig. 3.6 illustrates this). Individuals will draw upon actively and passively acquired memory as to which products and/or stores will satisfy their needs best. Clearly any brands or stores which come to mind – evoked sets – are going to achieve a distinct advantage over competitors. The promotional campaigns of brands or new products, as well as peer group influence, will also have a major impact on what is to be considered for purchase. This will be via the external search process.

Some customers who enjoy shopping will search more than those who do not enjoy shopping. The individual who enjoys shopping is more likely to spend time in shops assessing the alternatives and gathering information from different sales staff. It is important to realize that if this type of buyer does not obtain the required information from one retailer they will visit another for more appropriate information. There are those customers who are more self-confident and as such will be found to search less. In addition, there are the routinized shoppers who know in advance what they want to spend and where to find the products they want. The situational factors which affect search phases are the number of competing brands and stores available, and the time pressure within which the purchase has to be made. Typically, the potential customer will continue to collect information until the point when he or she is satisfied that the risk of their intended purchase is acceptable.

5 Evaluation of alternatives

Comparisons are made of the salient attributes based upon the criteria of the potential purchaser. These could be criteria such as cost, reputation or performance expectation. This is a complex stage based upon comparing attributes within the context of brand

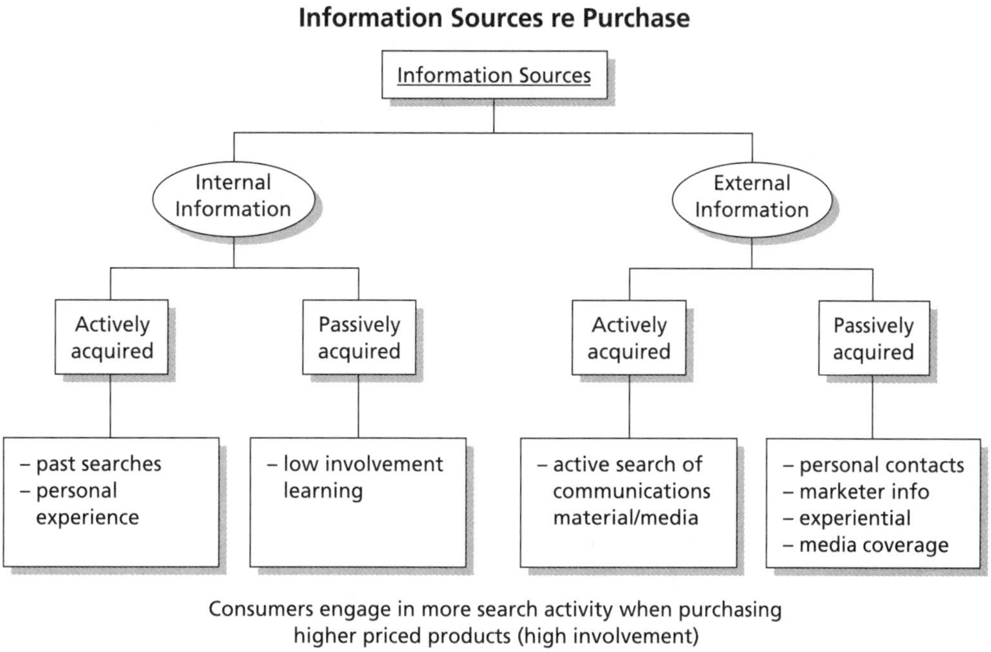

Information Sources re Purchase

Consumers engage in more search activity when purchasing
higher priced products (high involvement)

Fig. 3.6 Information source consideration prior to purchase

beliefs and attitudes. As they come to their final choice customers will form some ranking of preference among the alternatives. Also, the customer may be trying to satisfy both functional needs related to the performance of the product as well as psychological needs associated with the gratification shoppers obtain in terms of self-image. For example, a designer label shirt may not be functionally as good as another shirt but may be chosen because it will say something about the wearer. Usually the customer will form a purchase intention at this stage but they could also seek additional information or delay the purchase if they remain unsure of the outcome.

The attitudes of consumers are dynamic and as channel management improves so the expectations of the retail customer will change. Table 3.4 indicates some changes that are occurring.

6 Decision

Choice is made as part of a problem-solving exercise to select on the basis of the overall balance of evaluation, with the most favoured offer, brand and method of purchase being selected.

7 Purchase action

This may be affected by the available merchandise: for example, colours or size. The type of transaction, based upon credit facilities or payment methods, may also affect a purchase event.

Table 3.4 Attitude change

20th-century attitudes to retail	21st-century attitudes to retail
• I need to seek out an offer • When are your opening hours? • When can you deliver? • I have to make a shopping trip • I am an unknown customer • I will not worry if quality is low • I am looking for the right product, in the right place, at the right time . . .	• You should make the offer to me • I want the convenience of 24-hour 7-day opening • Delivery time should be short and suit me • I want an experience and discovery event • You should build a relationship with me • I expect quality problems to be resolved • I expect choice of channels (Internet, WAP, high street etc.) with anywhere–anytime–anything service.

8 Post-purchase feeling/behaviour

This is the feeling the individual experiences after the purchase. Quite often with important purchases the purchaser will doubt the wisdom of their choice or have some dissatisfaction; they may have a need for reassurance to reduce what is known as *cognitive dissonance* or disequilibrium. This state is when tension results from holding two conflicting ideas or beliefs at the same time. If the doubt over purchase is high, it may affect use of the product or result in a decision not to repurchase. This psychological state of anxiety is reduced by the means of guarantees, telephone helplines to deal with queries, or 'no-quibble' return policies such as those operated by Marks & Spencer. It is also reduced through advertising which reinforces the wisdom of having made the purchase. The post-purchase process is related to how well the customer has been satisfied on the basis of their expectations of the product and store.

The buying decision process can be simple or complex

In the case of high risk purchases such as expensive items, medicinal cures or presents for those we care about, the purchase is often of a complex nature where an individual will be likely to go through each of the eight stages outlined. This type of purchase routeing is sometimes termed a *complex* or '*high involvement*' purchase. We have already touched upon this with the EKB model of consumer behaviour. As part of the high involvement process, customers will spend more time and effort to seek out information and evaluate alternative products. Customers who are trying to satisfy important needs may require, or be reassured by, in-store merchandise displays which reduce uncertainty and risk. For example, a purchase of a bed to help with a bad back may require a cutaway mattress to show how the springs will provide support. The provision of in-store videos, brochures and leaflets to explain the merchandise and describe its specifications – in terms that the customer understands – will assist in the sale of merchandise.

For routine, habitual or normal day-to-day purchase items, however, the process is more elementary and often termed *simplistic* or '*low involvement*'. The phases at 3, 4 and 5 above are often ignored or skipped through. For example, the purchase of regular items such as salt, sugar and matches will be low involvement. As a general rule goods

Table 3.5 Product categories and level of purchase involvement

Product category	Characteristics of purchase
Convenience	There is frequent purchase with little effort exerted to compare or judge alternatives – the typical process is low involvement
Shopping	Price, quality and value comparisons are made – the typical process is medium involvement
Speciality	Due to the specialist aspects of the purchase, the perception of quality and value are relevant. Given ignorance often exists regarding the product, the risk is higher. The typical process is therefore high involvement
Fashion	Fashion products are highly susceptible to peer and reference group influences. However, some fashion products have slower rises to popularity than others with gradual declines – the typical process is medium to high involvement

that are purchased more frequently, are less expensive and perform functional roles are related to a simplified process of purchase. With low involvement the customer relies more on personal knowledge due to successful prior experiences; even if the purchase is expensive, through prior satisfaction the process may be simplistic. The consumer may be brand or store loyal because they have been highly satisfied with previous purchases and, therefore, may adopt a low involvement route of purchase.

Store loyalty exists when consumers habitually visit the same store because they are satisfied with the shopping experience and products on offer. Store loyalty may be enhanced by selecting the right location, offering breadth and depth of merchandise selection, creating the right sales ambience or atmosphere, promoting goods intelligently, providing optimum service standards and rewarding frequent customers through loyalty schemes.

We can examine the product categories of retail to understand the links to different characteristics of the purchase (*see* Table 3.5).

The different aspects of perceived risk

The retail service encounter can be characterized as a moment of self-realization: that is, the customer assesses the quality of the service encounter as well as his or her own personal feelings about the possible purchase. Retail purchases are associated with:

- some risk of the decision-making leading to a negative physical or tangible consequence;
- the uncertainty of the decision with regard to subjective consequences.

Uncertainty is often associated with personal reservations and risk. Therefore, there is a requirement placed on retailers to understand its complexity. For example, the purchase of some product categories involve a sense of more risk than others. The purchase of baby food is perceived as more risky than groceries. For some customers own-brand products may not be favourably evaluated against national brands whereas for others they will be. Therefore, perceived risk is based upon personal factors and the magnitude of an expected adverse consequence of a purchase. This means that in the decision-making process it is the *likelihood* of a problem occurring which will heighten the risk factor associated with a purchase.

Retail products may involve complex decision-making because the purchase is often personal and thus often of relatively high risk. Quite often the perceived risk is related to the problem of making a mistake. This is promulgated on the basis of worries about the *economic*, *physical*, *psychological* and *performance* aspects of the purchase.

Economic risk

The risk can be *economic*, involving the purchaser in the problem of deciding whether or not the product offer is of good value or not. Consumers face economic or financial risk when they purchase retail products that they cannot be sure will deliver the desired benefits. Retail sometimes involves the purchase of an expensive product which cannot be easily assessed prior to purchase and being taken home. This type of risk is heightened for those with low levels of disposable income for whom the purchase represents a major expenditure.

Physical risk

Some products may be perceived to be dangerous such as children's toys or electrical goods which have unknown brand names. It may be the case that some people have a fear of electrical goods or medicines, irrespective of what brand they purchase.

Psychological risk

Status can be lost through patronizing the wrong stores or using companies which have a poor image. The fear is that the peer group of the consumer may ask, 'Where on earth did you buy this?' This risk occurs when the potential customer feels the purchase may not reflect the self-image they wish to portray.

Performance risk

This risk is experienced where the effectiveness of different brands cannot be assessed in advance. This type of risk is associated with feelings that the product may not deliver the desired benefits. For those who made a bad purchase such as a poor holiday or an uncomfortable new bed, there is unlikely to be an opportunity to make up for it by attempting to have another, better holiday or to replace the bed in the same year. Most consumers do not have the additional money or holiday entitlement to make good the purchase if it goes wrong.

From a marketing point of view these risks have to be minimized through product and promotion strategies. Creating and delivering communication campaigns helps to convince the potential customer of the reliability of the company and will lessen the feeling of risk. By acquiring information the consumer builds up mental pictures and attitudes which create the expectation of positive benefits from the retail or consumption experience.

Consistency of offering will allow the consumer to learn to worry less about risk. It is therefore important for retailers to have an understanding of how expectations will affect the service experience. The development of brand or store loyalty is far easier if the consistency of service is managed properly. If this is successful, the resulting reputation will lead to risk-reduction perceptions.

Influences on the consumption process

The consumer decision processes can be found to fall within a simplified framework of influence. Many different authors have researched these influences. It can be found that investigation has centred on the following four areas.

1 *Energizers of demand.* These are the forces of motivation that lead a potential consumer to decide upon a shopping visit or to seek out a product.

2 *Filterers of demand.* Even though motivation may exist, demand is constrained or channelled due to: economic factors (social class and disposable income), sociological factors (reference groups, cultural values), and psychological factors (perception of risk, personality, attitudes). In addition, evaluative criteria will filter the different retailers' offers with regard to location, assortment, value for money, store personnel, and services.

3 *Effecters.* The consumer will have developed ideas of a product or brand from its promotion, development of image, and information which is generally available (learning, attitudes, associations). These effecters will heighten or dampen the various energizers which lead to consumer action. In addition, an effecter could be the position, display and type of merchandise which creates an impulse purchase. For example, grocery items which are located at end-of-aisle displays, and placed at eye level, often exhibit increased demand.

4 *Roles.* The important role is that of family member who is normally involved in the different tasks of the purchase process and the final resolving of decisions about when, where and how the group will consume the retail product (family influence, cultural influence).

Energizers or motivational forces – the need and involvement stage

The classic dictionary definition of motivation is derived from the word 'motivate' which is to cause (a person) to act in a certain way due to compelling forces; or to stimulate interest. There is also reference to the word 'motive' which is concerned with initiating movement or inducing a person to act. As would be expected, the concept of motivation offers insight as one of the major determinants of consumer behaviour.

Tauber (1972) suggested shoppers utilize six categories of personal motivation:

1 *role playing* – shopping may be a learned and expected behaviour pattern which, for some, becomes an integral part of their role;

2 *diversion* – shopping may provide an escape from the daily routine, a form of recreation; it can provide a diversionary pastime for individuals or free entertainment for the family;

3 *self-gratification* – the shopping trip may represent a remedy for loneliness or boredom, with the act of purchasing being an attempt to alleviate depression;

4 *learning about new trends* – includes a desire for continuation of personal education. Many people enjoy shopping as an opportunity to see new things and get new ideas;

5 *physical activity* – the exercise provided by shopping is an attraction to some, especially those whose work and travel modes provide little opportunity for exercise;

6 *sensory stimulation* – the shopping environment may provide for many forms of stimulation, through light, colours, sounds, scents and through handling the products.

In addition to the above, shopping activity is also characterized by the following five social motives.

1 *Social experiences outside the home.* In a similar way to the social setting of the traditional market, the shopping area can provide the occasion for social interaction – meeting friends or simply 'people watching'.

2 *Communication with others having a similar interest.* Hobby, sports and even DIY shops allow the opportunity to associate with staff and shoppers with similar interests.

3 *Peer group attraction.* Using a particular store may reflect a desire to be associated with the group to which one chooses or aspires to belong. This may be particularly significant in patronizing a store which is seen to be associated with a high status or a 'trend' image.

4 *Status and authority.* In the stores that seek to serve the customer – especially when they are contemplating high-cost, comparison purchases – some shoppers enjoy being 'waited on' while in the store.

5 *Pleasure of bargaining.* Some derive satisfaction from the process of haggling or from shopping around to obtain the best bargains.

As with most of the authors dealing with motivation the research is qualitative; therefore, the proportion of shopping which would exhibit one type of motivation rather than another is difficult to judge. What we do know is that the patronage of a retail outlet will be based upon certain common motives. These are:

- its *convenience* in terms of the time required to reach the outlet, perhaps park, walk around to find the product and then pay;
- the *reputation* of the retailer as judged by self, friends and other retailers;
- *retail environment characteristics* such as ambience, decoration, displays, lighting, heating or air conditioning. Many customers seek to browse and explore the retail outlet offerings;
- *service encounter expectations* of the friendliness of the staff, their knowledge, return policy arrangements, the efficiency and courteousness of the transaction, the after-sales service; the expectation of queues and other shopper numbers;
- *expectations of the merchandise* – that the variety, value for money, quality and brands will fulfil the needs of the visit;
- *expectations of value* – value for money through fair pricing, loyalty rewards, guarantees.

If the retail outlet image, or service delivery policy, corresponds to the customer's need priority then improved loyalty is a likely result. If the priority is convenience, then a customer will be willing to patronize an outlet which is close but perhaps more expensive. We should be aware that convenience in terms of the ease of shopping and paying is becoming more important. This is because, owing to social pressures, the time that an individual is willing to allocate to shopping has been declining – explaining the popularity of convenience stores. Alternatively some customers may value the shopping experience and want better levels of service. This is why some retailers play music in stores to encourage longer browsing times and the higher probability of a sale. Once a consumer has found a retail experience which suits him or her, repeat visits and store loyalty are more likely.

There are different types of shopping trip. A number of studies have identified that households have a routine of supermarket shopping which includes one weekly main trip and other secondary purchases. The main trip is planned to cover most of a household's grocery needs. In the USA nearly all supermarket trips are by car whereas in the UK about 80 per cent are by car. Larger outlets are able to draw in customers from longer distances as consumers are willing to spend more time travelling to utilize these stores because of the wider range of merchandise on offer and ancillary services such as an integral snack and coffee bar.

UNDERSTANDING MOTIVATION – MASLOW'S HIERARCHY MODEL

It could be argued that, due to its simplicity, Maslow's need hierarchy is probably the best-known theory of motivation. It is used in industrial, organization and social science texts on a regular basis. The theory of motivation proposed by Abraham Maslow (1943) is in the form of a ranking, or hierarchy, of individuals' needs. Maslow considered the factors which led to an ultimate goal of achieving self-actualization or fulfilment. He argued that if some of the higher needs in the hierarchy were not satisfied, then the lower needs – the physiological ones – would dominate behaviour. If a lower need, or needs were satisfied, however, they would no longer motivate and the individual would be motivated by the next level in the hierarchy. He initially proposed that the individual would endeavour to satisfy the needs of each level on a sequential basis but later accepted that individuals would attempt to satisfy needs at more than one level simultaneously.

The model shape given to Maslow's series of motivations is normally triangular which seemingly indicates a narrowing towards a higher level set of motivations. Alternatively it is illustrated by way of five steps. There seems little empirical evidence to suggest why any of these shapes – as opposed to, say, overlapping Venn diagrams which blur the changes in motivation – are more accurate as a representation. Therefore, the following hierarchy list, rather than a model, is offered.

High	5	**Self-actualization** – self-fulfilment and realization, enriching experiences
	4	**Esteem** – ego needs, success, status, recognition, accomplishments
	3	**Belongingness** – acceptance, affection, giving and receiving love
	2	**Safety** – security, shelter, freedom from fear and anxiety
Low	1	**Physiological** – hunger, thirst, sex, rest, sleep, activity

Maslow (1968) identified that there are two motivational types of sequence mechanism in motivation. These can be greatly simplified as:

- deficiency or tension reducing motives;
- inductive or arousal seeking motives.

Maslow maintained that his theory of motivation is holistic and dynamic and can be applied to both work and non-work spheres of life. Despite his claims, Maslow's hierarchy of needs has received no clear support from research.

Maslow treats his need levels as universal and innate. However, he accepts that they have inherent weaknesses due to instinctual reasons; they can be modified, accelerated or inhibited by the environment. He also states that while all the needs are innate, only those behaviours that satisfy physiological needs are unlearned. While a great deal of demand theory has been built upon Maslow's approach, it is not clear from his work why he selected five basic needs; why they are ranked as they are; how he could justify his model when he never carried out applied observation or experiment; and why he never tried to expand the original set of motives. His theory was developed out of a study of neurotic people and he argued that he was not convinced that the selective use of its application elsewhere (in organizational theory) was legitimate (1965).

The early humanistic values of Maslow seem to have led him to create a model where self-actualization is valued as the level 'man' should aspire to. It is not as if Maslow has been extended or distorted by behaviour theorists but simply that he has provided a convenient set of containers which can be relatively easily labelled. The notion that a comprehensive coverage of human needs can be organized into an understandable hierarchical framework is of obvious benefit for authors. If individuals are satisfying basic needs and seeking self-fulfilment, then retailers have to understand the need to offer products which allow consumers the opportunity to fulfil their higher needs of self-improvement, the attainment of individuality, provide status and give some deeper meaning in life. Some exclusive brands achieve this but many other brand strategies set out to create these associations.

Within Maslow's model human action is connected to predetermined, understandable and predictable aspects of action. This is very much in the behaviourist tradition of psychology as opposed to the cognitivist approach, which stresses the concepts of irrationality and unpredictability of behaviour. However, Maslow's theory does allow for people to transcend the mere embodiment of biological needs, an ability which sets them apart from other species.

To some extent the popularity of Maslow's theory can be understood in moral terms. It suggests that, given the right circumstances, people will grow out of their concern for the materialistic aspects of life and become more interested in 'higher' things. In examining the needs that Maslow has isolated, we should question some of those that may be absent. For example, individuals often strive for dominance or abasement, for intrinsic as well as extrinsic reward, and they often sublimate one need for another.

One trend which may be loosely linked to Maslow's need for improvement in self-esteem is the *compulsive shopper*. In recent years there has been the identification of the deviant pattern of compulsive shopping. This type of shopper has been identified in Europe and in other countries. In the USA about 6 per cent of shoppers are thought to exhibit some form of this trait. The characteristic is associated with the purchase of a range of clothes, shoes and goods that are not required and may never be used. This type of behaviour is at the extreme end of a continuum as other individuals also have strong urges to buy which they find difficult to hold in check. The compulsive shopper situation is different as it can be based upon a psychological difficulty which leads to a financial problem and thereby causes great distress. The behaviour often occurs among individuals who are unhappy and are suffering emotional difficulties. Compulsive buyers obtain emotional release or improved mood states when they purchase. The urge to purchase is stronger than their decision not to purchase. It is found that women who have low self-esteem mainly carry out compulsive buying. It is also associated with emotional disturbances such as unsatisfactory relationships with partners. Sufferers are usually trying to reward themselves through conspicuous consumption and in order to gain recognition will often talk about their purchases.

There are other shoppers who have been identified as definite behavioural types. There is the *economic consumer* who is oriented to be as careful as possible in the use of their finances and time. This consumer is focused on the value of purchases. The *befriending consumer*, sometimes referred to as 'personalizing', likes to develop strong personal attachments with store employees as a substitute for social contact. This type of shopper seeks out more intimate store types. The *ethical consumer* is happiest shopping in a small business and wants to help out local store merchants, particularly the 'little guy'. The *apathetic consumer* does not like to shop. Convenience is paramount to minimize the time and trouble of shopping. The *habitual shopper* goes 'grazing' in the field of shops on a very regular basis. He or she cannot think of anything else to do with their time and derives a comfort feeling in making regular purchases.

Motivations are an important clue to the purpose and type of shopping individuals will undertake. This helps retailers position their store to appeal to the different preferences based upon merchandise, price and quality. This leads to decisions in terms of which type or types of shoppers to attract and how many of them can be targeted.

DEMOGRAPHIC FACTORS

Demographic factors which influence demand are based upon the aggregate of individual social patterns within society. These factors may not be subject to dramatic change but account for powerful effects on the volume and nature of demand for different products. Demographic factors form the bedrock of the way individuals adopt different forms of lifestyle in their own social worlds.

As shown in Fig. 3.7, the changes over the past decades are creating both problems and opportunities for marketers. Most countries are experiencing changes now and facing predicted and projected ones.

Demographic changes – problems and opportunities

Slowing birth rate

Predictions in some countries are indicating the total population will decline. However, with smaller families the first born still requires the baby-related goods of furniture, clothes and additional items which are normally passed on to other siblings. Age is an important demographic variable as many purchases, such as those for babies and children, are age dependent. The trends are linked to important changes in relation to the baby, youth and mature markets. Retailers are keen to influence children under 12 years of age rather than treat them as passive in the consumer behaviour process. This is

ASPECTS		AFFECTS
Population size, growth rate and projections	Age structure profile, distribution by gender, birth/death rates, life expectancy	Types of shopping trip, given age and mobility of shopper
Geographic density of population	Location by different demographic variables, migration patterns	Geographic shifts and transit patterns by region and city. Ethnic groups, location and trends
Household size Family size	Patterns of child rearing: single parents, childminding, extended family, etc.	Trends of marriage/divorce/ cohabitation and family life cycle (FLC) needs
Income and wealth distribution	Population who are working or unemployed, pensions, unearned income	Levels of disposable income and ability to purchase at different price levels
Socio-economic groups	Social groups, occupational groups, retirement patterns, reference groups, peer groups	Patterns of educational attainment and changing values and culture

Fig. 3.7 Demographic factors which influence patterns of demand

because children influence their parents' consumption patterns, constitute a very large annual purchasing market, are tomorrow's adult consumer and learn to know how to buy for themselves and their future dependants.

Average life expectancy

Average life expectancy for both males and females is continuing to increase. This, in combination with lower birth rates, is creating an ageing population – the so-called grey market. According to the government actuary's department in the UK, male life expectancy rates rose from 48 years in 1901 to 74.9 years in 1998–9 and for females from 52 years to 79.7 years in the same period. By 1998 about 20 per cent of the UK population were over 60 years of age and this will rise to 30 per cent by 2038. Such trends will have an impact on those companies with products targeted on specific age groups. Many of the older generation, for a number of reasons, did not pay into pension schemes and consequently their pensions and benefits barely keep up with inflation. These groups and the unemployed are likely to adapt their lifestyle to basic activities linked to the home and family. However, the mature market of the 45-years-plus groups offers significant profit potential due to its spending power now and better future pension entitlements.

The actual and projected UK population by age (1971–2031) is provided in Table 3.6. The predicted percentage change in the UK population by age (1995–2031) is illustrated graphically in Fig. 3.8.

The social structure

The UK's social structure may develop into a polarized society based upon the rich becoming richer while the poor become poorer. There are other divisions such as the healthy or unhealthy, the technologically literate or technologically illiterate, those who

Table 3.6 Actual and projected UK population by age, as a percentage of the total population, 1971–2031

	1971	1981	1991	1995	2001	2011	2021	2031
Under 16	25	22	20	21	20	18	18	17
16–34	26	29	29	27	25	24	23	22
35–54	24	23	25	26	29	29	26	25
55–64	12	11	10	10	10	12	14	13
65–74	9	9	9	9	8	9	11	13
75+	5	6	7	7	7	7	8	11
Total (millions)	55.9	56.4	57.8	58.6	59.5	60.5	61.1	60.7

Source: Office for National Statistics, 1997

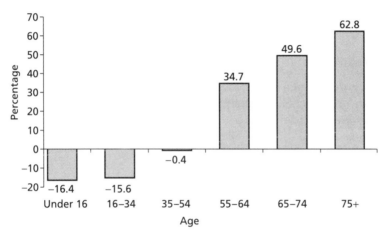

Fig. 3.8 Projected percentage changes in UK population by age, 1995–2031
Source: Office for National Statistics, 1997

are mobile or immobile, and those who are time-rich or time-poor. The implications are that those who are time-rich but money-poor will have to be careful with their budgets and will need to shop around for the lowest prices. This social category may well include the retired as well as disadvantaged groups. However, lack of mobility and the high cost and/or unavailability of public transport may restrict the money-poor to shop nearer home. Fear of technology or lack of expertise in utilizing technology will not liberate these groups. If the majority of the middle and older aged groups are technologically illiterate then penetration of the Internet and their use of other means of IT-based home shopping will be limited.

The target group for retailers will be the money-rich and time-poor group, as this segment will demand quality products for which they will be prepared to pay a premium. This group are also more likely to embrace IT as a solution to the problems of time constraints and the offer of greater convenience of shopping. The average household expenditure on food – per person per week – increased by 5.4 per cent to £15.63 in 1995. While this increase may be in part linked to inflation according to the Institute of Grocery Distribution (1997) it is also attributable to changing consumption patterns. It is argued that this is based upon convenience purchases and higher priced premium products. The report also indicates that lifestyle trends – such as vegetarianism, eating out, snack foods, healthier eating and preferences for foreign or ethnic foods – have created purchase behaviour changes. In the UK, Sunday opening and late night shopping are retail strategies which alleviate the constraints of dual-worker families especially if they have children.

Delay of marriage

Couples are continuing to wait until they are older than previous generations before they marry. They also wait longer to have their children. This will mean a trend towards more compact housing units, smaller packaged food items, etc. It also means there are higher levels of disposable income prior to child rearing. This allows for the sale of more luxury items and a higher preponderance to consume leisure products. The term often used for these households is 'dinky' (dual income, no kids yet) and relates to a group with higher than average consumption patterns due to their joint incomes and freedom from the time and money constraints of supporting children.

Value of education

There is a desire among young people to obtain a good education and a greater number than ever before are entering higher and further education. This means individuals are entering the workforce later and are often in debt, with sizeable student loans to pay off. Occupation trends are for more white collar jobs which places an emphasis on the purchase of formal styles of clothing.

Number of households

The number of households is increasing due to single occupancy and parents living separately from their children. As consumption units become smaller there is more purchase for personal rather than group use (*see* Table 3.8 on page 77 for an indication of household size).

Working women

More women are working outside the home and they are predominately entering the service sector or becoming the sole breadwinner. The rise in the number of females in the workforce has to be assessed in conjunction with their traditional roles of wife/partner and mother. This means they are more likely to spend higher amounts of money on labour-saving devices in the home, be more independent in their purchases, and have higher levels of disposable income for leisure activities. Working women are apt to seek individualism and personal identity through their consumption patterns and therefore the sale of a cars, clothing or appliances has to be attuned to female requirements. However, time constraints will be important and retailers may have to extend their hours of operation and their product range to ensure that they serve the needs of the working woman.

Population mobility is increasing

The younger groups under 35 years of age are the most mobile. In addition, companies relocate or expand on an international basis. The implication for retailers is that well-known chains or franchises will be more successful, especially if they take the opportunity to expand by way of franchising or licensing. There is also the implication that advertising or PR, which gains a wider recognition for the retailer, will help to create and maintain a stronger presence and image for the company.

Ethnic groups

The interests of ethnic groups are becoming more important because of their increasing percentage share of the population. According to Curtis (2001), a survey of 93 organizations by Race for Opportunity (RFO) – a forum of public and private sector organizations promoting race and diversity issues in business including Lloyds TSB, Sainsbury's, Marks & Spencer, BT, Boots and British Airways – indicates how ineffective companies are in marketing to ethnic minorities. The conclusion was that only a fifth successfully reach out to ethnic minority consumers. An amazing 29 per cent admitted to not making any effort to target ethnic communities at all and only 19 per cent sought the opinion of minority consumers in focus groups and research. In 1996 the estimated ethnic minority share of the British population was 6 per cent or around 3.3 million people (Institute of Grocery Distribution, 1997). Because in Britain the ethnic minorities' group is generally younger than the rest of the population, the difference in birth rates and family composition lead to different retail and product demands. All this means that there is potential profit for those companies which can target their promotions to this growing segment. In the USA Sears, McDonald's and K Mart have attempted to appeal more to the ethnic market by the use of African-American models in a variety of their promotions, or by the introduction of special merchandise. In the UK WH Smith have stocked ethnic greetings cards and BT advertise in Hindi to promote long-distance phone calls. In addition, many food manufacturers and multiple retailers have responded to demand in areas with large ethnic communities by stocking and promoting ethnic foods.

SOCIO-ECONOMIC CATEGORIES

A main division of consumer groups is that of socio-economic or class division. The groups listed below are based upon type of employment of the head of household. The middle-class groups are categorized as those in the groups A, B and C1.

A	Upper middle class	– higher managerial/administrative or professional, e.g. doctor, director
B	Middle class	– intermediate manager/administrative or professional *ABs are 22.8 per cent of the population
C1	Lower middle class	– supervisory/clerical/junior managerial/administrative *C1s are 27.2 per cent of the population
C2	Skilled working class	– skilled manual worker *C2s are 22.0 per cent of the population
D	Working class	– semi-skilled or unskilled worker *Ds are 17.6 per cent of the population
E	Lowest level of subsistence	– pensioners, casual worker, widows and others *Es are 10.5 per cent of the population

(*taken from NRS, 1999/2000 for adults over the age of 15)

THINK ETHNIC ACT ETHNIC: Marketers are missing out by failing to target the UK's specific minority niches

While marketing to ethnic minorities is an accepted and profitable practice in the US, British business remains reluctant to play the race card. Ethnicity is not routinely ignored by UK marketers, but considering the size and spending power of different ethnic segments, remarkably little effort is made to target each culture discretely.

Research conducted by Race for Opportunity – a division of Business in the Community (BITC) – showed that just one-fifth of British companies think they target ethnic communities effectively. And 29% admit to not attempting to reach them at all. The study, which includes the views of 90 BITC-member companies, such as HSBC, Boots and Lloyds TSB, also discovered that 25% do not seek feedback from ethnic minorities in focus group research. And only 19% thought they were effective in their efforts to test marketing strategies against ethnic-minority consumers. The 2001 Census will provide a more complete picture of the UK's ethnic mix, but the last survey, taken in 1991, revealed that 5.5% of the UK's 55 million population comes from ethnic minority groups. In London, that figure rises to 40%. The 850,000-strong Indian community is the biggest of the ethnic groups, with black Caribbeans second on the list, numbering 500,000. And the ethnic population is growing rapidly. As the number of whites in the UK remains almost static, minorities are growing by 2% to 3% a year, driven by higher fertility rates and immigration. The Commission for Racial Equality (CRE) estimates that by 2020, ethnic communities will account for 10% of the UK populace. In some areas of the country, minorities are rapidly becoming the majority population. Leicester, for example, is 38% non-white and there, as well as in some inner-city areas of London and Birmingham, the ethnic population is expected to be in the majority by the end of the decade.

This growth is highly significant for marketers. One major factor is youth. According to the CRE, 70% of Asians in the UK are under 35 and, by 2010, it expects that 40% of under-25s in London and Birmingham will be black or Asian. A second factor is disposable income. The spending power of ethnic groups is now estimated to be £15bn (two-thirds of ethnic people have a disposable income of more than £30,000 a year).

So, armed with databanks full of customer information, why are UK marketers not embracing ethnic diversity? Michael Williams, director of marketing and communications at Focus Consultancy, says: 'British businesses are scared of approaching ethnic groups directly. They tend to tip-toe around, afraid of what to say and what not to say, whereas in the US it's all about money. Marketers are missing a great opportunity because brands are extremely important to ethnic-minority consumers. When you live in a society that questions your value, brands are a way of demonstrating your worth through what you buy.'

If brands are nervous about targeting ethnic groups, the fault is not all their own. Although there is a wealth of specialist ethnic media – particularly for Asian communities – audiences are relatively small and some media owners struggle to provide reliable data. There is also little conventional industry research covering ethnic-minority consumers, which makes it hard for advertisers to plan campaigns with confidence. As a result, many advertisers settle for using mainstream media, even though it may result in a high degree of wastage. As a survey in *New Nation*, the newspaper for the black community, revealed, two-thirds of black people in the UK think mainstream media has no relevance to them. Specialist ethnic media is growing rapidly in the UK, with more than 180 press titles and an increasing number of digital TV channels. The Asian market is particularly well-served, with 15 digital TV channels. The big four – Zee, Sony, B4U (Bollywood for You) and the recently launched Star TV – have access to between 250,000 and 300,000 Asian households in the UK. Then there are specialist channels, such as the highly regarded Prime TV, which serves the Pakistani community (40,000 homes), and Reminiscent TV, which offers a range of channels catering for Punjabi, Gujarati, Tamil, Bengali, Urdu and Hindu communities. It claims to have 15,000 subscribers. There are also five principal Asian radio stations. The biggest, Sunrise Radio in London, has about 300,000 listeners, while Birmingham's XL and Manchester's ASR both claim audiences of 250,000.

Source: James Curtis, Marketing, 5 July 2001

While social class is often used to describe the readership or viewing patterns of various media it is probably not as relevant as an understanding of lifestyle, demographics and cultural values for segmenting markets or positioning products. There are interesting trends towards more home-based working; more women working, especially in managerial roles; more occupations being classified as middle class, etc. A number of changes make it difficult to adhere to traditional methods of designating class.

1 While class position may have provided fairly clear demarcations of buying power prior to the 1960s, increases in disposable and discretionary income by occupational group type has blurred the class groups.

2 Class is treated as being relatively permanent whereas people's careers and jobs may change – which affects the basis of the measure of current or past status.

3 Class groups are treated as if they are homogeneous and individuals are expected to behave like each other. If a broader set of measures are used incongruence may arise, with an individual registering high on one measure and low on another.

4 The number of women working and the type of work they do will affect the definition and measurement of the 'head of the household's' occupation. An indication of trends is the forecast that in the UK and USA women will soon represent almost 50 per cent of the workforce. The impact of more women working and the consequent lack of family shopping time is likely to result in:

- increased sales of labour-saving appliances and equipment;
- women having more independence over purchase decisions, with the seeking of identity from purchases;
- leisure time taking on increased importance with the resultant need for leisurewear and related products;
- shopping being skewed more to evening and extended opening hours or perhaps being increasingly based upon direct purchasing. Once attracted to the store, consumers will require the retailer to ensure there is good, clear signage and labelling in order to facilitate quicker shopping. Limited time may lead to more opportunities for telesales or Internet sales functions;
- limited time leading to greater opportunity for pre-prepared and convenience foods or quick service restaurants or takeaway outlets. Retailers may have to examine the need for more self-service and pre-packaging of various products. There may also be a greater demand for reductions in payment and checkout time functions;
- service companies (repairs etc.) having to ensure that services are offered outside normal work hours or at weekends;
- the purchase of more luxury items due to an increase in affluence among some families;
- advertisers promoting more heavily to the employed female, as a segment, and this may be based on evening television commercials and the daily press.

As indicated above, the attitudes of the general public to health and leisure are changing. These values are reflected in the type of clothing and fashions which are based upon leisure-related activity. However, as Harverson (1998) pointed out, the numbers of 20–34 year olds in the UK are on the decline, which means the group responsible for the

Table 3.7 Ownership of consumer durables, Great Britain, 1972–98

Households with	1972 %	1979 %	1985 %	1987 %	1991 %	1994 %	1998 %
Home computer	–	–	13	18	21	24	34
Colour TV	–	66	86	90	95	97	98
Satellite TV	–	–	–	–	–	–	29
Video recorder	–	–	31	46	68	77	85
CD player	–	–	–	–	27	47	68
Washing machine	66	74	81	83	87	89	92
Dishwasher	–	3	6	8	14	19	24
Microwave	–	–	–	30	55	67	79
Telephone	42	67	81	83	88	91	96
Car or van	52	57	62	64	67	69	72

Source: General Household Survey, 1998

bulk of demand in the sports group market is shrinking rapidly, but the retailers remain confident they can counteract any negative effects of this demographic trend by selling more goods and clothing to existing customers.

The changes occurring in society are dynamic and will lead to further changes in men's and women's roles. Men will often do the shopping and it may be the female who is the main 'breadwinner'. Such changes may produce different patterns of retail use, shopping habits and responsibilities. The opening up of higher education in the UK and the increased level of foreign travel will influence further changes. Consumers are more knowledgeable and sophisticated in their tastes. The degree of education of younger people is leading them to be less conforming, less open to pressure to follow different fashion trends and to be more confident over purchases. However, they are also aware of their rights and, therefore, will expect more attention to be given to quality control. In addition, their early schooling will have implanted in them the values of protecting the environment and seeing the resources of the earth as in need of being sustained. Issues of developing new retail sites, purchasing products which do not misuse the earth's resources, or the questioning of the exploitation of workers in Third World countries may become more important. Some retailers are accepting this trend and changes to methods of doing business have already been championed by The Body Shop.

The changing values of households and the ability to purchase create a pattern for ownership of a range of consumer durables. Increasing affluence and the importance of technology, linked to purchases based upon leisure activity and help with household chores, can be gauged from the household purchasing patterns outlined in Table 3.7. Many of these trends are linked; for example, the microwave may supplement or replace the cooker but it also ensures the future of the freezer.

ROLE AND FAMILY INFLUENCE

As the fundamental social unit of group formation in society, the influence of a family on retail demand is extremely important. A family acts as the purchasing unit which may be supplying the needs of perhaps two or more generations. In addition, it socializes children to adopt particular forms of purchasing and acts as a wider reference group. Given the importance of family behaviour in the purchase of products we may want to question the preponderance of literature that treats consumer behaviour as a model of individual action.

The concept of family life cycle (FLC) helps us to understand how situation-specific life stage conditions exert a great influence on buying behaviour. The FLC is not just a progression by phase or age but represents likely fluctuations in disposable income and changes in social responsibilities. For example, the bachelor stage represents an individual living away from home with few responsibilities but with the need for affiliation with others and the likelihood of purchases of leisure and entertainment, personal care items and clothes. As we grow older our preferences for products and activities change in relation to the different demands placed on income and time. In addition, as we grow older we will have accumulated durable goods, such as furniture, which we do not replace unless necessary. Wells and Gubar (1966) have conceptualized the life cycle of families in the USA, from the bachelor to solitary survivor stage, as follows:

1 **Bachelor stage:** young single people not living at home (low earnings, few financial responsibilities, purchase clothing, leisure and electronics).

2 **Newly married couples:** young, no children (double income, therefore ability to obtain credit for mortgage or different household goods, leisure, entertainment).

3 **The full nest I:** young married couples with dependent children (one or two earners if child care arranged, more careful spending and logical purchase related to house purchase or appliances).

4 **The full nest II:** married couples with dependent children over six (less likely to be influenced by advertising, concentrate on future needs, the children, family activities and vacations).

5 **The full nest III:** married couples with dependent children (higher income level providing ability to purchase higher quality items and enjoy more expensive leisure pursuits).

6 **The empty nest I:** older married couples with no children living with them. Head of household in the labour force (travel and recreation important, ability to spend money by choice on grandchildren or self).

7 **The empty nest II:** as above, but head retired (careful and prudent over consumption).

8 **The solitary survivor I:** older single people in labour force (may sell home, purchase inexpensive leisure and travel).

9 **The solitary survivor II:** as above, but retired (poor income, security conscious and likely to join local social groups).

Many of these different stages represent attractive market segments for those who market and retail products and services such as insurance, banking, children's wear, etc. However, the trends in divorce, delayed-child marriages and single-parent family households indicate that a large number of individuals do not easily fit into the above life-cycle pattern. In order to take account of social trends and ensure the above model remains applicable, the definition of 'married' needs to be relaxed to include any couple living together who are in a long-term relationship.

Each member of a family fulfils a special role within the group. They may act as husband/father, wife/mother, son/brother or daughter/sister. Family decision-making assigns roles to specific members of the family. Decision-making may be shared or decisions may be made by one person. One member of the family may be the facilitator, while another may gather information. The family acts as a composite buying unit with the different role patterns leading to particular forms of retail product purchase.

We should not expect family decisions to be taken easily. Olsen and McCubbin (1983) suggest that it should be assumed there is disagreement and a lack of congruence among family members rather than assume the family is an integrated and highly congruent group of individuals. Indeed, while much research has been conducted in order to determine the differentiation and distribution of roles within the family in relation to purchasing behaviour, there has been little theoretical endeavour to determine the effects of lack of consensus on family decision-making. Olsen claims that family decision-making moves away from egalitarian preferences towards a more centralized structure as families move along the stages of the life cycle.

In addition to particular commodities that are linked with joint decision-making, Sheth (1974) defined certain situations where joint decisions are made. He identified that where the level of perceived risk in buying is high then joint decisions are more likely in order to reduce individual risk; similarly, where the purchasing decision is important to the family as a whole or where there is high involvement in the purchase, joint decisions are also probable. Finally, where there are few time pressures, consensus decision-making may be seen as more appropriate (a shortage of time will usually encourage one member to make a quick decision). Certain demographic groups are identified as more syncretic, e.g. middle-income groups, families in the early stages of the life cycle, childless families, and families where only one parent is employed.

There are other classifications of consumers by life cycle, with each system taking a slightly different approach in its emphasis. This is because the concept of a family or household is dissimilar within different countries. For example, the age at which we define a child or adult as having reached adulthood varies widely throughout the world – even within the EU.

Table 3.8 indicates the number of single person households and the resultant opportunity to develop smaller packs and single servings to reduce the price to the consumer and wastage. In particular, elderly women and males aged between 25 and 34 are increasingly likely to live alone.

UK households with one person have changed from 22 per cent of all households in 1981 to 28 per cent in 1996. Four or more people in a household has declined in the same period from 29 per cent to 22 per cent of all households.

The company CACI (CAC Inc. International) has provided a national breakdown, placing each UK household into a classification group. It was found that a database system of splitting the different residential neighbourhoods into segments could have predictive power for the market targeting of different products. This system known as ACORN (a classification of residential neighbourhoods) identified 40 variables from census data in order to describe the different types of people living in each enumeration district. This was further refined to take into consideration postcode matches to address and housing type. This information is used in different ways based upon lifestyle groups to provide profiles of consumption patterns for food, drink, car ownership, central heating, kitchen equipment, etc. There are several levels of abstraction of the data with the

Table 3.8 Percentage of people in UK households by sex, age and family type, 1996

Age/sex	One person	Couple, no children	Couple, with children	Lone parent, with dependent children	Lone parent, with non-dependent children only
Males					
under 16	0	–	78	22	–
16–24	15	7	64	8	7
25–34	21	22	51	1	5
35–44	14	12	69	2	3
45–54	12	27	57	1	3
55–64	16	57	25	–	2
65–74	21	68	9	–	2
75 and over	34	59	4	–	3
Females					
under 16	0	–	78	22	–
16–24	14	11	55	14	5
25–34	12	20	51	15	2
35–44	7	11	67	13	2
45–54	11	32	47	4	5
55–64	21	58	15	1	5
65–74	40	50	5	–	4
75 and over	68	25	1	–	5

Source: Office for National Statistics, 1997

simplest illustrated in Table 3.9. Table 3.9 is based upon small group classification of no more than 150 homes and then aggregated to form the different ACORN types. The assumption is that neighbours, due to the similarity in housing type, will purchase similar products. In 2000 ACORN was further improved to take into account lifestyle aspects of those living in specific housing types. The importance of ACORN is that it offers the opportunity to carry out micro-marketing by currently classifying the population of Great Britain into one of 17 groups and then of 54 types. This can help in aspects such as selecting a profitable location for a retailer, deciding on the merchandise range and targeting different areas with sales promotion campaigns.

Psychographics

Psychographics is sometimes termed lifestyle as both are used as a description or analysis of the consumer's activities, interests and opinions. This approach allows the grouping of individuals into a profile of the way they may spend their time; their beliefs related to different issues about the home, work or politics or themselves. Clearly the way that an individual may view themselves and act will affect a whole range of product needs. For example, an individual who is interested in environmental issues and has beliefs about the protection of natural resources is likely to seek out those brands that are ethically and environmentally acceptable.

Table 3.9 CACI ACORN profile of Great Britain, 1997

ACORN category	Category percentage of population (16+)		ACORN group	Description	Group percentage of population (16+)	
	1991	*1997*			*1991*	*1997*
A Thriving	20.17	20.37	1	Wealthy achievers, suburbia	15.18	15.35
			2	Affluent greys, rural communities	2.35	2.37
			3	Prosperous pensioners, retirement areas	2.64	2.65
B Expanding	10.85	10.89	4	Affluent executives, family areas	3.46	3.47
			5	Well-off workers, family areas	7.39	7.42
C Rising	8.41	8.31	6	Affluent urbanites, town and city areas	2.41	2.39
			7	Prosperous professionals, metropolitan areas	2.25	2.24
			8	Better-off executives, inner city areas	3.75	3.68
D Settling	24.49	24.5	9	Comfortable middle-agers, mature home-owning areas	13.78	13.85
			10	Skilled workers, home-owning areas	10.71	10.65
E Aspiring	13.93	13.88	11	New home owners, mature communities	9.91	9.88
			12	White collar workers, better-off multi-ethnic areas	4.02	4.00
F Striving	21.53	21.37	13	Older people, less-prosperous areas	3.87	3.85
			14	Council estate residents, better-off homes	10.74	10.66
			15	Council estate residents, high unemployment	2.82	2.79
			16	Council estate residents, greatest hardship	2.27	2.24
			17	People in multi-ethnic, low-income areas	1.83	1.83

Source: CACI, 1998

SRI Consulting Business Intelligence has developed a value and lifestyle analysis of consumer markets (VALS analysis) by placing individuals into one of eight groups (*see* Fig. 3.9). The VALS segmentation approach has three premises: a general segmentation is more effective than a product-specific segmentation; demographics alone are an insufficient basis for modelling segmentation; psychographics are more powerful as they reveal the key attitudes driving behaviour.

The VALS model is based upon a continuum measuring three fields of self-orientation. These three are made up of groups that are **principle oriented** (grounded in the field of ideas, knowledge and ideals), **status oriented** (motivated to achieve a clear social position) or **action oriented** (based upon direct experience). On the other axis an individual's resources are considered (income, education, health, self-confidence, energy level) as either abundant or minimal. Different levels of resource enhance or constrain an individual's ability and motivation to act, given his or her own self-orientation. The components of the VALS approach are those identified as *principle oriented* – fulfilleds or believers; *status oriented* – achievers or strivers; *action oriented* – experiencers or

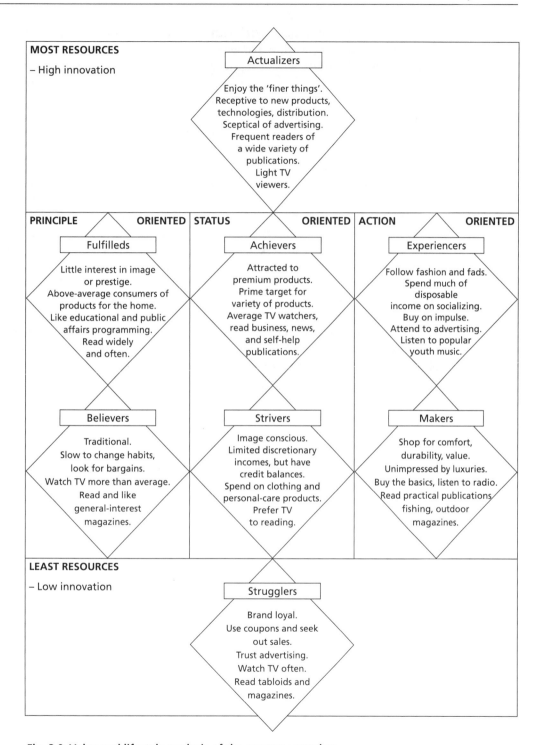

Fig. 3.9 Value and lifestyle analysis of the consumer market

Source: Reproduced with permission of SRI Consulting Business Intelligence

makers. Actualizers or strugglers fall either side of the central area of *status oriented* as the actualizers are very wealthy while the strugglers are quite poor. One difference here is that the actualizers are wealthy enough to be able to choose any of the three orientations on the horizontal access whereas the strugglers are constrained and find it more difficult to exhibit any particular orientation.

In the *principle-oriented* group those who are the fulfilleds are described as mature, satisfied, well educated, responsible and professional people. They are flexible and reflective thinkers, accepting of change, home-centred and aware of the events of the world. They are high income and practical, value-seeking consumers. Believers as the second principle-oriented group are less wealthy, conservative, traditional, more rigid in thinking and likely to purchase the established brands. In the second part of the model the status-oriented consumer is more likely to take notice of the opinions of others and be guided by them. Achievers are successful work-oriented people whose satisfaction is based upon succeeding in a work and family environment. They are in favour of stability and the status quo and purchase products that are well established and can provide a clue of their success to their peers. Strivers are almost identical to achievers yet they lack the same level of resource and therefore style is more important as a means to emulate others. In addition, strivers are sensitive to the tastes and opinions of others as they exhibit low esteem and want to obtain a lifestyle beyond their means. As identified, those groups either side of the achiever and striver area are based upon high or low resource. They include the actualizers – who are successful and wealthy and therefore can have choice over consumption which reflects their taste, character and independence – and the strugglers – who have the lowest incomes, have restricted choice, yet will remain more brand loyal. Finally there is the *action-oriented* group. These individuals are judged to be driven by a desire for social or physical activity, variety and risk taking. The experiencers with a median age of 25 and mainly single are found to be the youngest of all the VALS groups and as such have high energy and like physical and social activities. This group is still developing its norms and will be ambivalent, enthusiastic at one stage and then less eager at the next. They spend heavily on clothing, technology, eating out, music and youth culture. The other group, the makers, are those who are more self-sufficient and as such will place more emphasis on what is familiar. They are less likely to focus any interest on the broader world and will place their energy into family, work and physical activity. They carry out do-it-yourself activities and are consumers who will not value the pursuit of material possessions or status goods that have no practical or functional purpose.

The use of VALS or lifestyle analysis allows the retailer to understand the customer better as well as the target market because it does not take simplistic demographic data as the basis for the approach. It allows a current analysis of how people live and the way they may consider others as well as themselves as part of their choice over spending and consumption.

The role of children in the consumer behaviour process

The influence of children in the family decision-making process has not received the attention from researchers that it deserves. While the parents are responsible initially for a child's consumer behaviour, as the child learns about purchasing and consumption primarily from his or her parents, the child eventually becomes a dominant force in certain purchasing decisions. Families where both parents are working are increasing which means less time is spent with children. In America in the early 1990s 70 per cent of mothers worked full- or part-time (Gubar and Berry, 1993) compared to 30 per cent in 1980. Parents may overcome their guilt of not providing enough attention to their children by spending more money on them or giving them extra pocket money. Moreover, children between the ages of 6 and 14 are expected to do more around the house than in the past, with many having to cook for themselves on weekdays. This means that children are taking on different roles and becoming more self-reliant.

Companies target children at an early age so as to build brand loyalty. There are promotions utilizing long-term collector schemes, direct contact forms of promotion or membership of clubs. The long-term collector schemes rely on the child saving tokens from packaging to obtain a reward. This may be a reward for a school project – for example, to collect tokens in order to obtain books as in the case of a Walkers Crisps promotion involving thousands of schools – or it can be for a personal reward. Many children want instant gratification of their needs and, therefore, scratch card promotions by companies such as Golden Wonder have been used to provide an instant reward for a minority of purchasers. The most successful brand building schemes are probably the clubs which banks and building societies have deployed in order to capture the early saver. Clubs such as the 'saver's gang' may provide free gifts, organized outings to zoos and museums, and free personal insurance. Some supermarkets and fast-food chains in the USA and Europe have formed clubs which provide children with comic books, coupons for purchasing certain foods, and information packages on environmental and educational issues. Burger King has used to good effect a passport which gives the child certain entitlements to free gifts, magazines and other incentives. Banks realize that it is important to capture the younger saver as they are likely to stay loyal. This has led to a number of schemes including offering incentives to school leavers to open an account. Each of the schemes described has the ability to influence the child at an early age and bias their brand loyalties and prejudices when they become an adult consumer.

In order to use direct marketing techniques, marketers are faced with several issues. The main issue is to deal with any negative reaction the parents would have. Parents may perceive direct marketing as a means of increasing children's desires, and thus increasing the 'pester' factor in their own homes. In order to eliminate these problems, marketers need to orient their messages to both parents and children. This can be quite a challenge, as the message has to reach and influence two separate target groups. The parents will want to have sufficient information on the promotion whereas the child will want to see some fun in the offer, such as humour, visual attraction, excitement and reward. Another possible solution is for the marketer to contact the parents first in order to gain their consent for a further mailing to the child. This sort of approach is often used by the financial service sector.

After discussing various aspects of family decision-making, it is interesting here to conclude with a brief overview of the relative influences of family members. Figure 3.10 provides an account of the individual (adult partners) as opposed to joint decision-making which may take place in families. This model is of an average of all findings and it should be noted that it will be affected by the number of years of marriage (or relationship), socio-economic background of partners, time available for both parties, etc.

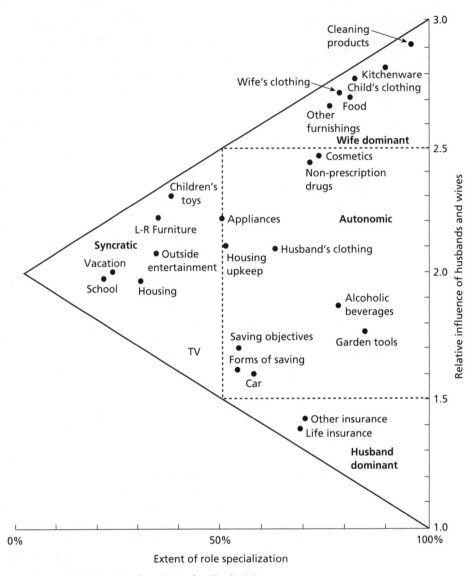

Fig. 3.10 Husband and wife roles in family decisions
Source: Davis and Rigaux, 1974

SOCIAL INFLUENCE

The family may introduce political ideas and consumer attitudes to purchasing to the children. However, the reference group of the individual is just as important. Purchases take place on the basis of thinking about the way the purchase may help provide status within the group, how the purchaser may need to consider other members and what messages the purchase communicates to those from whom an individual wants recognition and acceptance.

There are four types of reference groups:

- primary reference groups;
- secondary reference groups;
- aspirational groups;
- disassociative groups.

Primary reference groups include the family as well as groups of close friends, co-workers and so on. Secondary reference groups are those where there is formal contact but it is less continuous. This will be based upon membership of clubs, professional associations, religious organizations or a result of the contacts from the area someone lives in, or the occupation they have. There are also aspirational groups to which the purchaser has positive feelings; they would like to be considered a member. Personalities are often used to endorse products as part of the marketing of expensive aspirational products. Finally there are disassociative groups, with which the individual does not want to be associated. For example, if yuppie group association is not valued then the type of products a member of a yuppie group may purchase, such as a palmtop, may be avoided.

Approaches to decisions

According to Carmouche and Kelly (1995), when an individual considers the choice between the alternative fast-food outlets of Burger King and McDonald's they will pass through a number of phases. To understand the process we need to:

1 **identify the relevant decision-maker**
In this case it would be the individual involved but if a family, or group of friends, were dining out the complexity of parents' and children's wishes would need to be considered.

2 **identify the courses of action available**
In this case there are only two alternative outlets, but in more complex situations the evoked brands and those considered are important.

3 **identify the relevant uncertainties in the purchase situation**
Possibly the time available, food preferences, choice of menu, etc. If it is time, the three possibilities envisaged could be:

- there will be no queues and food will be served immediately;
- there will be long queues and consequently considerable delay in being served;
- the outlet will be closed.

4 **create a matrix that includes the relevant information**
This will be based on a set of values related to the above scenarios in relation to the two outlets. This provides for six possible utility values which can then be summed based on the two outlets in order to provide for the subjective utility of each individual. The likelihood of choice can be assessed based upon the calculation which indicates the highest expected value of outcome of utilizing either one of the outlets. Of course in reality this iteration is carried out in seconds.

CONCLUSION

In order to satisfy customer needs the retailer must have a thorough understanding of how customers make store choice and purchase decisions. Consumer behaviour provides some valuable insights into the process and, therefore, is useful for retail management decision-making. It is important to realize that the purchase of products involves motivational, social, psychological and economic factors. In addition, there are important stages involved in the purchase process and the type of purchase – as well as the risks of the purchase – that will affect the buying behaviour.

Retail consumers need to be understood on a variety of levels.

- They are problem-solvers, deciding on what offer satisfies their needs. All retail activities and promotions should therefore aid the consumer to make a decision.
- Consumers seek to reduce the risk of their purchase. Retailers need to provide information, guarantees, and after-sales services to reduce the perception of risk.
- Consumers will go shopping for a variety of reasons. The complexity of the shopping trip *per se* should be clear to retail staff.
- There are a number of demographic and other changes which are having an impact on the patterns of purchasing and consumption.

EXERCISES

The exercises that follow relate to the contents of this chapter. It is suggested that you work through them before you move on to Chapter 4.

1 Think about the last time you bought an expensive item. Write down why you think you recognized the need to buy the item, what information you looked at, who you talked to about the purchase and why you bought the brand you did. Did you then worry that you may have made a poor purchase decision?

What links are there between the theory of consumer behaviour discussed in this chapter and your purchase? Are there any other influences you can identify?

2 List the key demographic changes which are occurring throughout Europe. Assess what implications these and the following will have for different types of retailers. Use the grid below as a guide.

Change to birth rates and long-term prediction of fewer younger people	Implications for grocery retailers, DIY retailers, etc.
Smaller families and households	Implications for grocery retailers, DIY retailers, etc.
Other key trends identified	Implications

3 Produce a decision-making flow diagram based upon a choice between going to the cinema or hiring a video for the evening. The choice process should include your best friend. Ensure you

include all the key aspects of the process through to post-decision phase as well as the other influences which you would consider could affect the perception of risk in this decision.

4 Using Maslow, list the type of products and brands, or retail stores that utilize a Maslow approach which will appeal to individual self-esteem rather than those which will satisfy more basic needs. What can a retailer learn from this? Relate this to changes in consumer lifestyle which may be affecting the current retail marketplace.

REFERENCES AND FURTHER READING

Ajzen, I. and Fishbein, M. (1980) *Understanding Attitudes and Predicting Social Behaviour*. Englewood Cliffs, NJ: Prentice Hall.

Assael, H. (1987) *Consumer Behaviour and Marketing Action*. Boston, MA: Kent.

CACI (1998) *Geodemographic Pocketbook*. Henley: NTC Publications.

Carmouche, R. and Kelly, N. (1995) *Behavioural Studies in Hospitality Management*. London: Chapman and Hall.

Chisnall, P.M. (1994) *Consumer Behaviour*. Maidenhead: McGraw-Hill.

Curtis, J. (2001) 'THINK ETHNIC ACT ETHNIC: Marketers are missing out by failing to target the UK's specific minority niches', *Marketing*, 5 July.

Davis, H. and Rigaux, B. (1974) 'Perception of marital roles in decision processes', *Journal of Consumer Research*, 1, June, 51–60.

Dellaert, B.G., Arentze, T.A., Bierlaire, M., Borgers, A.W. and Timmermans, H.J.P. (1998) 'Investigating consumers' tendency to combine multiple shopping purposes and destinations', *Journal of Marketing Research*, 35 (2), 177–88.

The Economist (2000) 'Youth Inc', *The Economist*, 23 December.

Engel, J.F., Blackwell, R.D. and Miniard, P. (1986) *Consumer Behavior*. New York: The Dryden Press.

Engel, J.F., Kollat, D.J. and Blackwell, R.D. (1968) *Consumer Behavior*. New York: Holt, Rinehart and Winston.

Fant, D. (1998) 'Understanding customers: The key to retail success', *Marketing News*, 32 (4), 7.

General Household Survey (1998) Office for National Statistics, Social Survey division, 1998–1999, Colchester.

Gubar, S. and Berry, J. (1993) *Marketing To and Through Kids*. Maidenhead: McGraw-Hill.

Harverson, P. (1998) 'Sports retailing: relegating less active sectors', *Financial Times*, 17 March.

Hollinger, P. (1998) 'Home shopping: homing in on niche markets', *Financial Times*, 17 March.

Howard, J.A. and Sheth, J.N. (1969) *The Theory of Buyer Behavior*. New York: J Wiley and Sons.

Hurley, R.F. (1998) 'Customer service behavior in retail settings: A study of the effect of service provider personality', *Journal of the Academy of Marketing Science*, 26 (2), 115–27.

Institute of Grocery Distribution (1997) *Grocery Retailing 1997: The Market Review*. Watford: IGD Business Publications.

Kelly, R.F. and Stephenson, R. (1967) 'The semantic differential: An information source for designing retail patronage appeals', *Journal of Marketing?*, 31, October, 43–7.

Living in Britain – Results from the 1994 General Household Survey. London: The Stationery Office.

Maslow, A.H. (1943) 'A theory of human motivation', *Psychological Review*, 50, 370–96.

Maslow, A.H. (1954) *Motivation and Personality*. New York: Harper and Row.

Maslow, A.H. (1965) *Eupsychian Management*. Homewood, IL: Irwin.

Maslow, A.H. (1968) *Toward a Psychology of Being*. 2nd edn. New York: Van Nostrand, Reinhold.

Maslow, A.H. (1970) *Motivation and Personality*. 2nd edn. New York: Harper and Row.

National Readership Survey, July 1999–June 2000, NRS Ltd.

Nicosia, F.M. (1966) *Consumer Decision Processes: Marketing and advertising implications*. Englewood Cliffs, NJ: Prentice Hall.

Office for National Statistics (1997) *1994-based National Population Projections Report*. London: The Stationery Office.

Olsen, D. and McCubbin, H. (1983) *Families, What Makes Them Work?* Beverley Hills, CA: Sage Publications.

Qualls, W. (1987) 'Household decision behaviour: The impact of husbands and wives sex role orientation', *Journal of Consumer Research*, 14 (2), 264–78.

Riche, M. Farnesworth (1989) 'Psychographics for the 1990s', *American Demographics*, July, 25–31.

Severin, V., Louviere, J.L. and Finn, A. (2001) 'The stability of retail shopping choices over time and across countries', *Journal of Retailing*, 77 (2), 185–202.

Sheth, J. (1974) 'A theory of family buying decisions' in Sheth, J.N. (ed.) *Models of Buyer Behavior*. New York: Harper and Row.

Snyder, C. and Fromkin, H. (1980) *Uniqueness: the human pursuit of difference*. New York: Plenum Press.

Solomon, M., Bamossy, G. and Askegaard, S. (1999) *Consumer Behaviour – A European Perspective*. Upper Saddle River, NJ: Prentice Hall Europe.

Tauber, E.M. (1972) 'Why do people shop?', *Journal of Marketing*, 36 (4), 46–59.

Tuck, M. (1976) *How Do We Choose?* London: Methuen.

Wells, W. and Gubar, G. (1966) 'Life cycle concepts in marketing research', *Journal of Marketing Research*, November, 355–63.

Williams, T.G. (1982) *Consumer Behaviour, Fundamentals and Strategies*. St Paul, MN: West Publishing Co.

4 The management of service and quality in retailing

This chapter should enable you to understand and explain:

- the characteristics of the retail and service product;
- the basics of the service encounter;
- some of the ways in which service and quality are managed, monitored and controlled;
- quality both as a concept and within the context of a model.

A great deal of retail management involves taking decisions based upon judgement, information and experience. All areas of retail management should, therefore, be fully informed of the ways in which the quality of the service and product offer are a key to the processes used by customers to judge competing retail services. On 21 December 1999 customers who had ordered Christmas presents through Toys "Я" Us were informed that the fulfilment of their order may not be achieved prior to Christmas. In 2000 shoppers were obviously affected by the previous year's bad publicity, or experience, as the majority purchased earlier with sales slowing after 10 December. Service standards are therefore directly related to the way service activities create store or channel selection, loyalty and fulfilment. The changing expectation of the consumer is driving the need to ensure that services are planned to be acceptable. The fastest-growing area is e-commerce; where in previous times Amazon.com could have been successful with delivery services of a week or even more, today no e-tailer could survive without a service function that delivered within a few days. There have to be returns management schemes which are easy and have no additional cost to the customer, and remedial schemes which are proactive and trusted.

Changes are constantly occurring which leads to a variety of options for the delivery of services. If the trend in delivering lower contact services is examined its growth is often due to the benefit of a company achieving lower costs. However, less contact is not necessarily a service weakness, as it is perceived to be beneficial for certain customers. In banking, for example, there are a number of service alternatives:

- make a personal visit to interact with staff and make transactions or queries;
- conduct the queries and transactions by telephone with a customer service representative;
- use an automated teller machine (ATM);

- use a postal service to send payments or account deposits;
- carry out transactions utilizing the touch keys of a telephone to respond to automated voice commands;
- conduct home banking operations through a personal computer and special software; and
- carry out personal banking operations by means of a password and personal link via the Internet.

Research by the Midland Bank (now part of HSBC) prior to First Direct being set up found that 51 per cent of account holders wanted to visit their bank as little as possible and 38 per cent reported banking hours were inconvenient. Therefore, the operational and service level provision of traditional banking is not necessarily the most preferred form of service interaction.

Quality is another important area for retail marketing management. In order for retail managers to be better at managing quality they need to start with knowledge of the specific characteristics of retailing, based upon its tangible and intangible nature. When the retail experience is more tangible it is easier to assess the quality because physical aspects of the store and merchandise can be subjected to examination. However, retail transactions include a service element that is difficult to assess until the sale has taken place. This is especially the case with direct services such as insurance, banking and travel, all of which indicated growth throughout the final decades of the twentieth century. Therefore, when marketing any one of the retail operations we find in the marketplace, there are a number of tasks and attributes we need to be aware of. The first major factor modern retail managers have to understand is the growing expectation by consumers that they will receive a quality product and service. The management of quality is associated with the need to understand these customer expectations – and to attempt to respond to them – by monitoring and control methods. However, for retailers to be successful at quality management it is necessary that they should also understand the special services marketing characteristics related to retailing.

WHAT CONSTITUTES RETAILING?

We can begin with the separation of the retail offer into two broad areas:

1 Tangible features

Retailing is an amalgamation of goods and services. It is a channel service but may also involve a mix of the physical surroundings, signage, uniforms, changing rooms, displays and other tangible features such as the merchandise. Retailing provides, most of all, the beneficial utility of a place for purchase. It also includes the characteristics of the service component, such as the 'intangible' interaction with sales staff and other retail departments. Other characteristics take into consideration the type and timing of the service delivery, other customers and the nature of a retail sales transaction. These are based upon the ability of retail staff to add extra value to the retail environment through advice on the use of the product, any need for maintenance and care, or, if it is a garment, the type of alterations that can be made to improve its fit and so on.

2 Intangible services

Retailing is also largely intangible and at the extreme matches the main characteristics of pure services with operations such as banking, insurance and investment services.

These broad categories are further explained by comparing 'transaction with' merchandise with 'transaction without' merchandise (*see* relevant sections below).

To understand the nature of retailing from a store environment perspective we need to understand it in relation to its special features. With retailing we are dealing with an amalgam – a mixture – of a good and a service that has specific characteristics. These characteristics set retail marketing apart from some other principles of marketing and the marketplace. As discussed, retailing can be pure services such as insurance and banking or an amalgam between services and goods based upon their relationship to different types of shops and merchandise offers.

The blurring of the boundaries between the areas comprising retail is clear when it is considered how many different services could easily be included within retailing: dry cleaners and laundries, photographic studios, hairdressers, shoe repairers, undertakers, health clubs and centres, reprographic shops, public houses, garage services, car hire, cinemas, catering outlets, travel agents, banking, insurance, investment. With many of these service-dominant retail businesses there is little or no movement of physical goods through a distribution channel.

THE SERVICE–PRODUCT CONCEPT

An understanding of the complexity of the service–product concept is an essential pre-requisite for successful retail marketing. Some important factors and basic differences are identified below.

Transaction with merchandise

In retailing there are three types of services with goods: owned-goods service, rental-goods service, and service with bought goods.

1 **Owned-goods service** would be the traditional outright purchase and ownership of a good from a retailer. The retailer would have performed the service of channel management.
2 **Rental-goods service** would deliver a tangible good, such as a car, for the personal use of the customer. No ownership exists and the good has to be returned.
3 **Service with bought goods** indicates that the retailer performs/supplies extra services. These could include delivery, wrapping, providing credit, etc.

Transaction without merchandise

In retailing there is also service without goods: pure services without goods. **Pure services** are provided by a wide range of retailers who are involved in arranging or organizing travel, financial transactions and services, or providing personal services such as dry cleaning, a haircut or shoe repairs.

The onus is increasingly being placed on the marketer to develop a deeper understanding of the links which correspond to consumer benefits sought, through to the nature of the service delivery system. A starting point is an examination of the traditional dimensions of the various concepts of service.

THE INTANGIBLE–TANGIBLE PRODUCT CONTINUUM

All products fall on a continuum between pure services and goods, with most products being a combination of the two. A pure service would be consultancy or financial advice, whereas a pure good would be more tangible, such as a can of beans or a bottle of lemonade. Very few products are purely intangible or entirely tangible; services such as retailing, however, tend to be more intangible than manufactured goods. Some products will have more of a service content than others and if they are assessed as being placed to the left of the centre of the continuum they may be termed service products (*see* Fig. 4.1). Retailing falls to the service end of this continuum, despite being associated with the sale of goods. This is due to the nature of transactions involving the interpersonal skills of service providers. The added service element is a core part of the transaction.

Services, such as retailing, can be characterized as having the following attributes (discussed in more detail below):

- intangibility;
- perishability;
- inseparability.

Intangibility

This means that some products cannot be easily stored, evaluated or demonstrated in advance of their purchase. For example, a travel agent cannot allow for the testing or sampling of the tourism product; a bank cannot easily demonstrate its service. On the other hand, a car or a computer game can be tested prior to purchase and clothing may be tried on – but this occurs in a retail environment and not in the home. Mail order sales or similar methods of selling have to utilize printed literature to communicate the benefits of the product. In addition, mail order sales offer only limited visual clues as to the benefits of the product. Prior to the arrival of the goods the potential customer has to make use of intangible clues. However, the clearest example of retailing related to intangibility is telephone banking, where transactions can be carried out by voicemail and no personal or tangible interface exists. Moreover, the experience of retail purchases is not something that can easily be explained or demonstrated away from the branch, store or mall.

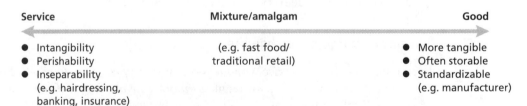

Fig. 4.1 Service–good/product continuum

Greater difficulty is faced by the marketers of the more intangible services which make up retailing. Because of fixed time and space constraints, they cannot easily demonstrate the benefits of the retail offer or any merchandise they may be selling. The challenge for the retail service marketer is to overcome intangibility through the use of selling techniques, the physical layout of the store or a depiction – by graphical, video or display means – of the product in use. In addition, the creation of a positive image surrounding the service will enable the consumer to envision the retail experience benefits.

MINICASE 4.1

Improving service for the consumer

Granada's television rental arm completed the roll-out across the UK of a revamped service that is expected to generate significant cost savings. Roger Mavity, group managing director of the media and leisure group's TV rental business, said the new system of operation had increased the rate of first-time fixes from 75 to 91 per cent after initial trials. The group has torn up the old image of its TV repairman, now equipped with mobile phones. The initial spur was puzzlement that 3 million service calls a year were being made when statistics showed that modern televisions do not often go wrong. A survey threw up a tale of missed appointments, repeat visits and reluctance by staff to concede defeat on repairs in the home. Astra estate cars have been swapped for large Mercedes trucks so that a big stock of televisions can be carried. The working week has been changed from 9a.m.–5p.m. Monday to Friday to 9a.m.–8p.m. Monday to Saturday. The repairmen, who use their mobile phones to check on appointments, have also been trained as salesmen. If a problem cannot be solved in minutes, the customer is either given a replacement set or offered a deal on a better model. The latest action follows the 1997 decision to close 100 shops. Mr Mavity said the cost of revamping the repair service would be almost nothing as the phones and vehicles were leased.

Source: David Blackwell, *Financial Times*, 9 March 1998

Perishability

This means that, unlike goods, the service product cannot be stored for sale on a future occasion. For example, if customers do not enter the store when it is fully staffed sales may not occur, for which the revenue can never be recouped. This perishability factor leads to the high risk nature of the retail industry. Marketers in the retail industry have to devise complex pricing and promotion policies in an attempt to create demand in 'off season' periods and create greater synchronization of staffing levels and supply with demand patterns. Weak demand is not the only problem; the industry is also characterized by seasonal demand, such as during the Christmas period, when shoppers are more selective where they shop due to overcrowding and related problems that occur. Stores have a fixed capacity with a maximum upper level demanding constraint. In peak periods retailers often have difficulty in coping with demand; therefore, they offer only full prices or have to resort to queuing systems. In the low periods of demand, however, there is a need for greater marketing activity.

The challenge for marketers arising from perishability problems is to try to smooth out demand curves by careful use of the marketing mix. To achieve this the forecast of demand must be relatively accurate to ensure a productive use of staff.

Inseparability

This means retailing delivers a service which is utilized and produced simultaneously for each customer. Because there is less opportunity to pre-check each sales activity, it may vary in the standard of its service delivery. This is sometimes characterized by theorists as *heterogeneity*. Variance occurs due to the inseparable nature of the retailing product's delivery where the customer is part of the sales process. The simultaneous process of production and consumption may lead to situations where it is difficult to assure the overall satisfaction of consumers. For example, peak loads of demand cannot always be forecast and may create dissatisfaction and secondary problems. There is also a constant threat of problems being caused by one set of customers who may upset another. This provides for the potential for conflict on various levels. Whether it is the young out enjoying themselves, perhaps congregating by the tapes and CDs or in the electrical department by the computer games and annoying older customers, or restaurant users involved in a clash of social values, sets of unacceptable behaviour may be exhibited by various groups. Manufactured goods, on the other hand, are produced in advance of being sent to the warehouse and there is little or no contact with the end consumer.

The service aspects of retail are inseparable – service is intrinsic to retailing. Staff may have personal problems or be feeling ill or tired and this type of problem may affect their level of commitment to giving good service or resolving problems. Because the nature of the retail service product is one of interpersonal relationships, where the performance levels of staff are directly related to the satisfaction experience of the consumer, there is a need for quality assurance mechanisms. Staff are emotional and changeable and if a high content of the sales experience is based upon interpersonal relationships between 'strangers' – as client and a service provider – it is important to ensure standardized service levels are understood and adhered to by everyone. In order to reduce the problems associated with inseparability there is a need to invest in company training programmes.

The problems discussed above make it clear that there is a need to ensure that quality is managed as a basis of planning to achieve competitive advantage. The following section on service and quality classifications will provide insight into the process of service delivery.

A CLASSIFICATION OF SERVICE AND QUALITY

We can classify the different approaches to quality management into two categories: first, the product-attribute approach; second, the consumer-oriented approach (Gilbert and Joshi, 1992). The product-attribute approach is based upon trying to match the product's conformance to standardized requirements which have been set by reference to what company managers think the failure point to be. Product-attribute approaches rely on trying to control the company's output by using an internal standard-setting perspective. This relies on an inward-looking and trading-led management style, rather than a marketing-led approach.

It would seem more appropriate to adopt a consumer-oriented approach which recognizes that the holistic process of service delivery has to be controlled by taking into consideration the expectations and attitudes of retail customers. If the starting point for management is the understanding of how quality is judged by customers then the

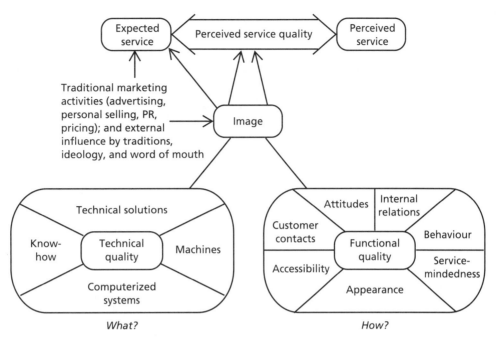

Fig. 4.2 Managing the perceived service quality

Source: Gronroos, 1982

perception processes of this judgement, as to whether a service is good or bad, can be managed. Gronroos is a leading author who has defined this concept.

The Gronroos model of perceived quality management

Gronroos (1982) developed a model, which is a form of gap analysis, to explain what he calls the 'missing service quality concept'. The model (*see* Fig. 4.2) focuses mainly on the construct of an image which represents the point at which a gap may occur between expected service and perceived service. Gronroos allows us to be aware of the ways in which image is created from the aggregation of different aspects of technical and functional variables. By following his model of different inputs we are alerted to the fact that we should not reduce quality to a simplistic description of itself but that we should try to understand the full range of inputs. This is because to speak simply of quality gives the manager no indication of what aspects of the whole retail experience should be controlled. Gronroos argues that the function and range of resources and activities includes what customers are looking for, what they are evaluating, how service quality is perceived, and in what way service quality is influenced. Gronroos defines 'perceived quality' of the service as dependent on two variables: *experienced service* and *perceived service*, which collectively provide the outcome of the evaluation.

Gronroos distinguishes between *technical quality* and *functional quality* as the components of the service image delivery:

1 *technical quality* – refers to what the customer is actually receiving from the service. This is capable of objective measurement, as with tangible goods

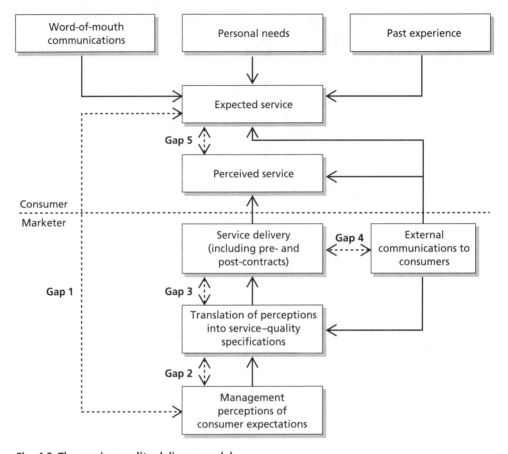

Fig. 4.3 The service quality delivery model

Source: Reprinted with permission from the American Marketing Association from Parasuraman *et al.*, 1985

2 *functional quality* – refers to how the technical elements of the service are transferred or perceived. We know that a customer in a restaurant will not only evaluate the quality of the food consumed but also the way in which it was delivered (the style, manner and appearance of the staff or the ambience of the place itself). Figure 4.2 shows that the attitudes, behaviour and general service-mindedness of personnel can be influenced by management.

The Parasuraman, Zeithaml and Berry model

Parasuraman *et al.* (1985) have also developed a model of service quality, which claims that the consumer evaluates the quality of a service experience as the outcome of the difference (gap) between expected and perceived service (*see* Fig. 4.3). The model highlights the main requirements for a service provider delivering the expected service quality. From the model five gaps may be identified that could lead to unsuccessful service delivery. By understanding this model, it is possible to provide greater management control over retail customer service relationships. This should lead to an improved realization of the key points at which the marketer can influence the satisfactions of the consumer. The marketer is then in a better position to be able to reduce or close the gaps.

Gap 1: Ignorance of the customer's expectations

This is the gap between consumer expectation and management perception. The gap may result from a lack of understanding of what consumers expect from a service. The literature confirms this disparity by revealing that what providers perceive as being important to consumers is often different from what consumers themselves actually expect. The gap may relate to a lack of communication or feedback from customers or an unpreparedness to address important changes that are required.

In the early 1990s, Sears failed to realize that customer buying habits had changed and the company retained its traditional catalogue when the customers had embarked upon different modes of shopping. In the modern marketplace there is a need for responsive and adaptive adjustment to the service provision, based upon feedback from staff at all levels in the company. In addition, good relationship marketing programmes should also help in the reduction of customer and company problems arising from different expectations of what constitutes an 'appropriate' service.

Gap 2: Requirement for service design standards

This is the gap between management perception and service quality specifications. It results when there is a discrepancy between what management perceives to be consumer expectations and the actual service quality specifications established. Management may not set quality standards; the ones they set may not be very clear; or the quality standards set may be clear but unrealistic. Alternatively, although the standards are clear and realistic, management may quite simply not be committed to enforcing them. The need here is to provide service design standards which are supported by everyone and form the yardstick against which all service standards are judged. These standards will then provide the guidelines against which the overall service and retail staff may be evaluated.

Gap 3: Not delivering to service standards

This is the gap between service quality specifications and service delivery. Even where guidelines exist for performing a service well, service delivery may not be of the appropriate quality owing to poor employee performance. The employee plays a pivotal role in determining the quality of a service. This is because retail staff and their actions are visible to the customer, and can be assessed and judged on a constant basis. Companies may have service standards but not facilitate the service with adequate technology, the appropriate human resource policies or a positive company culture.

Gap 4: Inconsistency between performance and promises

This is the gap between service delivery and external communications. Consumer expectations are affected by the promises made by the service provider's promotional message. Marketers must pay close attention to ensure consistency between the quality image portrayed in promotional activity and the actual quality offered. The problem is any discrepancy between those who describe and promote the service and those who are delivering the service. If a marketing promotion promises a certain offer or service, it has to be available when customers demand it. Marketing has a key role in ensuring that all promotions are co-ordinated effectively and monitored closely.

Gap 5: The service shortfalls

This is the gap between perceived service and delivered service. This gap results when one or more of the other gaps described occurs. If these shortfalls arise, company staff have to ensure they reduce or close the gaps where problems have appeared.

The focus on perceptions and expectations provides a guideline for quality management intervention strategies. To this end, the model proposed by Parasuraman *et al.* has the following two main strengths:

1 The model presents an entirely dyadic view to the marketing task of delivering service quality. The model alerts the marketer to consider the perceptions of both parties (marketers and consumers) in the exchange process.

2 Addressing the gaps in the model can serve as a logical basis for formulating strategies and tactics to ensure a consistent marketing approach to the creation of experiences and expectations.

Zone of tolerance

Within the delivery of services the consumer will have different levels of tolerance as to what may be judged adequate or expected service. This is known as the *zone of tolerance*: customers are willing to accept different levels of service which fall within a zone between the desired and adequate levels of performance. The area of the zone of tolerance can increase or decrease for individual customers depending on other variables such as alternatives provided by the competition, how much was paid and whether it represented value for money, or other differences in the retailer's service. It is important to realize that there are differences between individual customer's perceptions; similarly each customer may have different expectations of one brand in comparison with another. For example, if Marks & Spencer delivered more consistent service over time than Bhs then the expectations for the M&S brand are higher. If Marks & Spencer service were to decline to the level consistently offered by Bhs, the customer might be more disappointed by the service received from Marks & Spencer – even though the service standards are similar.

Further factors in service quality delivery

Providing promotional methods which lead staff to achieve high levels of customer care and service quality is becoming increasingly important. One poster targeted on staff read, 'Good enough is not good enough' which set the standards and aims of the company personnel above the average. This type of inward marketing is used as a means to change the general attitudes of staff towards quality.

A well-positioned service enables the company to:

- differentiate its position so as to distinguish itself from competitors;
- deliver superior service to that accepted as the norm (sometimes described as creating customer delight or 'wow' factors).

This allows the company to plan and build competitive advantage by establishing leadership principles of service standards and delivery. Once the standards are established there should be a policy to communicate and reinforce the service provision philosophy at every possible opportunity: meetings, training and internal marketing programmes,

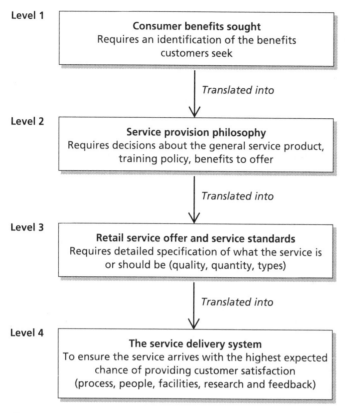

Fig. 4.4 An approach to deconstructing service delivery

induction programmes and appraisal systems. The human resource function needs to be aware of marketing so as to ensure that the different levels in the service delivery process (*see* Fig. 4.4) are always clearly understood and reinforced throughout the company – in its culture and in its reward systems. Without good internal company procedures and relationships it is unlikely that even the most well conceived of quality programmes will be successful.

IMPLEMENTATION OF SERVICE MANAGEMENT

For the model in Fig. 4.4 to be successful there is a need for the implementation process to consider the following areas vital to success:

1 Leadership and commitment by senior management, with clear goals and a policy on quality being set and communicated to others. There is also the need to release the appropriate resources to create changes and achieve the required results. Sam Walton, founder of Wal-Mart, adopted the following philosophy to direct his retail staff and gain pre-eminence in the retail marketplace:

   ● realize that customer service is key;

   ● design for comfort and convenience;

   ● provide one-stop shopping;

- customize;
- invert the organizational chart so that the customer is on top and company management is on the bottom;
- empower the sales staff;
- provide servant leadership – Wal-Mart's managers are servants to the needs of their employees and customers;
- recognize that the customer is always right.

2 The focus of all changes and objectives should be defined by the customer. All the definitions of quality delivery and standards have to be delineated in all of the dimensions of the service delivery with reference to customers' needs. These should be incorporated into the training policy and induction programmes.

3 The orientation of the organization needs to adopt a process and systems approach to match or exceed customer expectations. This relies on a workable quality audit system which applies measurement and inspection to ensure defects are corrected and the system delivers optimum quality results.

4 Human resource management is required to motivate, reward, train and educate staff to understand and deliver the concepts of quality. Teamwork values with champions of quality product delivery are a prerequisite for competitive advantage.

5 Assessment needs to be made of the added value and benefit of any change rather than there being an emphasis on costs and profit implications. That is, the long-term benefits of any change need to be the focus of decision-making.

6 A need for quality audits and control to ensure the service meets or exceeds customer expectations must be recognized.

An organization has to create a quality management culture and not just attempt to be the clone of a system learnt elsewhere. This requires honest two-way communication between management and staff which will build confidence in the implementation process. It also means that staff have to be allowed to own up to weaknesses and problems of poor quality in a supportive atmosphere where the company attempts to learn from weaknesses rather than punish them. Such an atmosphere will foster teamwork, confidence and commitment. However, there is also the need for competence to deliver the changes. This may require further training and seminars for staff and follow-up sessions. The recognition that other members of staff should be treated as internal customers will assist the transition to a total quality management (TQM) system. It is obvious that organizations have customers from within as well as from outside them. If employees visualize the relationships between each other based upon supplier and customer links as a quality chain, then the question is always: am I meeting the full requirements of my role? For example, the secretary is a supplier to the boss and needs to provide timely, error-free work in order to assist the boss work as supplier to his or her internal customer, who may be a director. A company, therefore, is a web of internal suppliers and customers. Such chains are easily weakened or broken by faulty equipment or people. The important issue is that an internal quality chain failure will ultimately have some effect on the outside customer.

Minicase 4.2, in discussing a high level service approach, indicates how this can be applied to the retail industry.

The personal touch

How do you persuade people not to buy a car-insurance policy purely on price? Progressive, an insurance company based in Ohio, has an answer. If a policyholder has an accident, a claims officer goes straight to the scene, gives him a cellphone and a cup of coffee, pulls out a laptop and, in 95% of cases, hands him a claim cheque on the spot. Some customers say: 'I wasn't a member until I was hit by one.' The service, not the price, sells the product. 'It creates a "wow" experience.'

For the technology companies that have pioneered many business applications, customer support is one of the first opportunities for change the Internet provides. 'Some customers simply want to talk to someone,' admits John Fiore, the chief information officer. But the scarcer support staff become, and the longer telephone inquirers have to hold on, the easier it is to encourage customers to look up the answer to their problem online. And there are huge gains to be made from applying the usual 80/20 rule, says Ward Hanson of Stanford Graduate School of Business: if the staff answer only the complicated 20% of questions, their work is far more interesting and productive. 'The grey area,' he adds, 'is trying to hide the help-desk telephone number from the remaining 80%.' More savings are to be had if the customer can be trained to place orders online. Savings in online selling do not come only from lower transaction costs. Dell's Mr Marengi argues that the best thing about moving to online ordering has been to dispose of endless arguments over whether the customer ordered this keyboard or that keyboard. 'If the customer puts in the order,' he says cheerfully, 'that conflict is eliminated.'

Source: © *The Economist*, 11 November, 2000

The findings of research into hotels by Cadotte and Turgeon (1988) led to a simple typology of what may lead to complaints or compliments. This acts as a framework which may inform retail managers of what is required for a desirable service. The research showed that weak performance of the technical service (parking availability, prices, speed of service, credit availability, checkout times) will seriously detract from the customer's evaluation, whereas high performance did not enhance the hotel's image. However, the compliments of helpful attitudes and service knowledge of employees, neatness and spaciousness of the building and convenience of location can all lead to high satisfaction if present, while few complain if they are absent or the performance is only indifferent.

The potential for compliments and complaints can be illustrated diagrammatically (*see* Fig. 4.5) in terms of four categories: dissatisfiers, satisfiers, criticals and neutrals. These may be described as follows:

1 *Dissatisfiers.* Low performance or an absence of the desired feature is more likely to produce a complaint. Exceeding the threshold performance standard will not, however, generate a compliment. For example, if a customer arrives at an out-of-town retail

		Potential for compliments	
		Low	*High*
Potential for complaints	*High*	**Dissatisfiers**	**Criticals**
	Low	**Neutrals**	**Satisfiers**

Fig. 4.5 Factors with potential for prompting complaints and compliments
Source: Cadotte and Turgeon, 1988

store and cannot find a place to park they may complain; whereas if a parking space is found, this is what a customer expects and so it will not prompt a compliment.

2 *Satisfiers*. Unusual performance beyond expectation will elicit compliments but average performance or even absence of such an aspect of service will not cause dissatisfaction or prompt a complaint. For example, providing large portions in a restaurant.

3 *Criticals*. These are capable of eliciting both negative and positive feelings. The quality of service is important as it ranks high in both compliments and complaints along with employee knowledge of the service.

4 *Neutrals*. There are performance ratings which receive few compliments or complaints and, therefore, are not important to the judgements made by customers regarding standards of service provision.

WHY THERE IS GROWING EMPHASIS ON CONTROL OF QUALITY

Quality has emerged as a major competitive component of company strategies. There are four main reasons that may account for the increasing relevance of quality management.

1 Companies need to find new ways of creating differential advantage by providing better service levels than their competitors. Retail competition has increased because services and goods are available from a wide range of channels and manufacturers are creating technically satisfactory goods that require little after-sales service.

2 The increased levels of consumerism and the greater media attention on quality have meant that companies have to be more responsive to quality issues. Consumers are far more aware of their rights and are less likely to suffer quietly from the results of poor quality.

3 There has been a growing sophistication of consumer markets, with the non-price factors of image, retail offer positioning and service delivery processes becoming more important.

4 Technology is one of the new applications to quality enhancement. It can aid service by providing higher levels of convenience: for example, automatic vending or ticketing machines, bar code checkout systems to improve accuracy and speed of transaction, or smart card developments – all of which provide memory of purchases.

It is important for the quality of retailing to be controlled, especially in relation to the process of service delivery. This is because relative quality between service providers or retailers has linkages to market share and profitability. Quality is, therefore, one of the key components that leads to a successful strategy. This is why quality has emerged as a major competitive component of service company strategies. However, when we examine the use of the term 'quality' there appears to be almost a superabundance of its use in relation to the way management operates. Overall, there is a crusade for quality management and improvement within industry worldwide. The campaign for improved quality can be traced to its roots in the manufacturing industries prior to its expansion into the service industry. However, many individuals in industry are still unaware of the theoretical grounding of quality management. Knights and McCabe (1997) have carried out research which illustrates that management often does not understand either the weaknesses or the underlying philosophy of TQM. They argue that management continues to adopt 'inconsistent' approaches, such as concentrating on the control of costs and employees while advocating the importance of the customer and the need for a trust-based culture.

WHAT ARE THE KEY TERMS FOR QUALITY?

Kay (1995) reminds us that the quality of MFI's flatpack furniture was the butt of jokes in the 1980s. However, the senior management at MFI recognize that it still has an image problem even though the days of ill-fitting flatpack furniture are long gone. It is reported that although the jokes are slowly dying, many people remember MFI the way it was and have not been back since. This indicates the importance of a quality image and shows that a poor image is not easily improved. To understand the complexity of quality management there are several key concepts which have to be mastered, and these are discussed below.

Quality is the totality of relationships between service providers (functional aspects) and the features of retailing (technical aspects) which are related to the delivery of satisfaction. It is, therefore, important to create systems of *quality control*, which are checks, and also monitoring processes to ensure that measurement of service delivery is taking place. To this end *total quality management* (TQM) is a holistic organizational approach which systematically attempts to improve customer satisfaction by focusing on continuous quality improvements without incurring unacceptable cost increases. These improvements are part of an unending quest for excellence in all aspects of quality service delivery. Therefore, TQM has to influence the values and form the mindset of all employees, leading to the creation of an integrated corporate culture because quality is required to be the concern of all employees. The culture should not be based upon a departmental or technical understanding of quality but on a holistic view of quality as a systematic process extending throughout the organization. From a retail perspective, the focus of any change in quality must be based upon external customer expectations and not on internal company ideas.

TQM is managed by *quality assurance* arrangements; that is, a system is instituted to allocate responsibility for planned and systematic activities which will ensure that the product will provide the right levels of satisfaction for all concerned. Hart (1988) has postulated that a service guarantee system allows for more quality control and data capture in the organization. This information on what goes wrong allows for improved service. A good service guarantee is identified as unconditional, easy to understand and communicate, meaningful, and easy to invoke and obtain recompense. It is also recognized that there is a need not to:

- promise something your customers already expect;
- shroud a guarantee in so many conditions that it is meaningless;
- offer guarantees so mild that they are never invoked.

A guarantee can set clear standards and allow company personnel to be clear about what the company stands for. If customers can make complaints without difficulty, the company has the benefit of being able to collect data on common problems which need to be addressed and eradicated. This is because a guarantee system trains the spotlight on why the failure occurred and what needs to be done about it to improve service quality.

Moreover, a guarantee adds credibility and weight to the marketing effort of the company. It allows for the emphasis of the guarantee which also provides for a reduction in the perception of risk associated with purchase and may lead to higher levels of customer loyalty.

In order to measure whether the quality delivery complies with the planned delivery of the service a *quality audit* needs to take place to judge the effectiveness of the total service delivery arrangements. For a system to be audited correctly a method of creating unbiased feedback must be found. While a range of aspects of quality can be assessed, a number of categories exist. These may include the following, which are based upon various research studies which have attempted to establish categories of service quality determinants.

CHARACTERISTICS OF QUALITY

There are two sets of quality characteristics which are important to a retailer. These are the characteristics related to either merchandise or service categories.

Merchandise (products)

Merchandise categories include the following elements:

- performance based upon inherent operating characteristics, such as the sound and clarity of a hi-fi system;
- features which add to the basic function of the product;
- reliability of the product not to break down in normal use;
- conformance to standards of safety or operating performance needs;
- durability based upon the length of time a product will last;
- serviceability – relating to the after-sales service and ability to be repaired;
- aesthetics of the look, feel, design, sound and smell of the product;
- image of the brand association, reputation and personality of the product.

Services

Service categories include the following elements.

1 *Tangibles*: what can be experienced from personnel, company literature and signs, and the physical environment of the retail encounters. These include aspects of the store or material the customer can see, touch, use, etc., such as:
   - physical facilities;
   - appearance of personnel;
   - tools or equipment used to provide the service;
   - physical representation of the service, e.g. store credit card, fascia design;
   - other customers in the service facility.

2 *Reliability* of staff to deliver the expected or promised service dependably and accurately. This involves consistency of performance and dependability. It means the

company should perform the service right the first time, and honour its promises. This factor also demands that the company is able to trust employees with the responsibility to deliver service which, consistently and accurately, meets policy standards, including:

- accuracy in charging;
- keeping the correct records;
- performing the service at the designated time – for example, accurate to opening hour promise.

3 *Responsiveness* of staff to help customers and provide timely service. This concerns the willingness or readiness of employees to provide service – to help customers and give timely service, such as:

- mailing a transaction slip immediately;
- calling a customer back quickly after a query;
- giving prompt service (e.g. arranging an appointment).

4 *Competence*: an assurance of employees' ability to convey trust and confidence through company and product knowledge, as well as by the courtesy of their interpersonal skills:

- knowledge and skill of the contact personnel;
- listening to customer needs and explaining the desired product or service;
- reinforcing the company's reputation;
- personal characteristics of the contact personnel;
- ability to respect confidentiality, and display financial and personal security.

5 *Empathy*: having an understanding of what customers as individual humans require in relation to psychological as well as physical needs. This is not a universal occurrence. A cashier when asked why she had not provided a 'thank you' for a payment was heard to say that her receipt had 'thank you' written on it. Empathy concerns individualized attention to customers – a caring, individual concern and attention for others and their emotions:

- recognizing regular customers;
- learning the customer-specific requirements and anticipating their needs;
- being attentive and providing individualized (customized) service;
- ensuring that if there is a problem it is acknowledged, responsibility is taken, and some action is carried out to ensure the service fault is compensated for.

The above points allow a retailer to focus on a systems perspective which identifies the linkage between consumers' needs and service delivery. This highlights the management principles associated with service products. It may also be utilized in the establishment of benchmark points against which the service can be positioned. In retail, *waiting time*, whether in a store, when contacting a call centre or utilizing the Internet, is an important concept. It should be remembered that unoccupied time is perceived to be longer than occupied time; relaxation and lack of anxiety makes a wait seem shorter; uncertain waits are more stressful than expected waits; and unexplained waits seem longer than ones where the time and reason are explained.

The elements which could be assessed in the course of establishing the position of a service could also include: availability of items the customer demands; after-sales service and contact (e.g. Amazon.com has an e-mail system to let customers know when a book has been despatched); the way the telephone orders and queries are handled; the reliability and safety of the items being sold; availability of sales literature and brochures; the number and type of items which can be demonstrated; technical knowledge of staff; the way an employee deals with a complaint, etc.

MINICASE 4.3

Service can include the customer

IKEA of Sweden has managed to be highly successful because of the service role it has developed with its customers. IKEA recognized that customers are happy to be part of the business system by taking on responsibility for the services normally carried out by paid service staff. When customers enter the store they are given a catalogue, tape measure, pen and notepaper. This means they are able to perform the function normally carried out by the salesperson. The new role of some of the staff is to look after customers' children in a supervised child centre, allowing a less stressful decision-making process for the parents. After choice and payment customers can then take the purchase to their car on a cart. If necessary they can hire, or buy, a roof rack for the transport of larger items. Once home the customer assembles the new furnishings with the aid of carefully written instructions. Complete service is not always necessary as sometimes less service is better service. This is especially the case if the customer enjoys more involvement in the manufacture and retail process in order to achieve lower prices. The new role for the customer developed at IKEA provides added personal value and contributes to the overall satisfaction experience.

Source: Based on company information

The following section indicates some of the ways that quality may be assessed. It is important to realize, however, that whatever system is used to audit quality, at the end of the day, that which is not measured cannot be controlled.

QUALITY AUDITING SYSTEMS

There are various methods that may be used to measure and monitor quality. Figure 4.6 lists some methods of internal inspection and of auditing.

Buttle (1994) indicated that following research of loyal Jaeger customers a list of 180 service variables was reduced to 26 key attributes against which mystery shoppers could assess a store's service performance. It is important to note that the final list was based upon *customer preferences* and did not correlate with what Jaeger's own employees had identified as being important. The key items identified by customers were:

● external appearance of the branch;
● merchandise pricing in window display;
● greeting upon entry;
● staff approachability;
● staff availability to help;

Internal inspection	Auditing
• statistical process – control based upon quality failure information and objective measures • visual inspections to check against standards and consistency • management by walking about • quality control group feedback • inspection of competitors' offer and assessment of own company offer	• internal auditors of quality • external bodies • consultants, regular users, non-user surveys and feedback • cross-department audits • mystery shoppers • content analysis of complaint and praise letter and documented problem • free phone line feedback

Fig. 4.6 Summary of some methods of internal inspection and auditing

- manager availability;
- whether the manager is recognizable;
- the number of customers served simultaneously by one staff member;
- efficiency/promptness of enquiry handling;
- branch stock levels;
- staff awareness of fashion trends;
- speed of stock location;
- staff awareness of advertised lines;
- helpfulness of staff advice;
- honesty of staff advice;
- standard of fitting rooms;
- availability of advertised stock;
- colour/size availability;
- selection within size;
- availability of alterations advice;
- availability of garment reservation;
- eye-catching quality of window displays;
- eye-catching quality of interior displays;
- speed of till transaction;
- comparability of service in other Jaeger branches.

Benchmarking

A method now widely used for assessment of the service standards of a company is to compare them with those which are deemed to be the best available – the benchmark. Benchmarking is a continuous process of selecting the best practices and services against which to judge. It is based upon the Japanese concept *dantotsu*, meaning 'the best of the best', the underlying philosophy which emphasizes that if you seek out and match best practice there is the possibility of the attainment of superiority. By identifying a guideline, benchmarking will allow a company to know what operating standards to apply.

Four types of benchmarking exist:

- *internal*, where the best internal company examples are utilized;
- *competitive*, based upon external directly competing retailers and their merchandise;
- *functional*, which measures against the best external market leaders or functional operations;
- *generic*, which is to take measures of the best practices regardless of what sector or industry is represented.

Companies such as American Express may be benchmarked for service standards, Marks & Spencer for specification of product, TGI Friday for service training, etc. For example, American Express has a service tracking report which systematically assesses customer satisfaction and employee performance on a worldwide basis. The report is generated each month based on measurement against 100 service quality factors grouped into the three major service dimensions of responsiveness, timeliness and accuracy. Within the first three years of the adoption of this system American Express improved service delivery by 78 per cent and reduced costs of the average transaction by 21 per cent. Therefore, a retail operation could try to learn from American Express by benchmarking its service tracking system as this makes marketing sense.

IS QUALITY A COST OR A LONG-TERM BENEFIT?

It is found that smaller firms embarking upon service quality programmes (SQP) perceive them as costly, needing a lot of management time, difficult to measure the intangible benefits, and finally not easy to implement. Given the nature of retailing (people-based with employee performance and interaction being of paramount importance), it is clear that errors are inevitable. In addition to this element of human error is the nature of human response to it. It is estimated that there is a ratio of 4 : 1 where individuals will speak of poor service to good service and therefore pass on more negative than positive aspects of service delivery. The moment of truth – the impact on the bottom line of any organization – is the judgement of customers on the quality of its service.

Figure 4.7 is based upon the model of Heskett *et al.* (1990) who argue that the linkages of service encounters create a self-reinforcing mechanism. Figure 4.7 indicates the relationship between the customer on the left with the service provider on the right. This overcomes the notion that improvement in quality is associated with increased costs. The model indicates that, in the long term, true quality improvement leads to an improved trading position.

This proposition, that a continuous improvement in service is not a cost but an investment in a customer who will return more profit in the long term, is becoming more widely supported. The premise is based upon research which indicates that the cost of acquiring a new customer is much higher than that of retaining an existing customer through providing quality service. Such an argument is based upon non-traditional accounting practices which stress that satisfied customers will be willing to pay higher prices due to the service quality they have experienced and liked; there is a free advertising

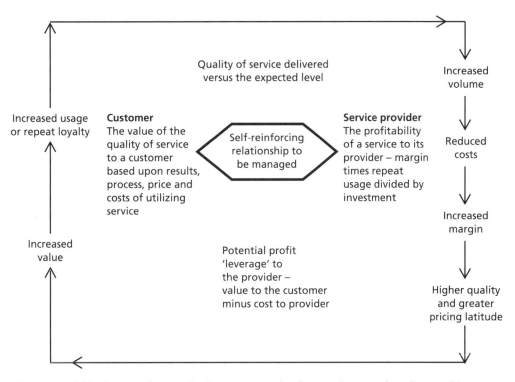

Fig. 4.7 Model indicating that quality improvement leads to an improved trading position
Source: Based on Heskett *et al.*, 1990

benefit due to the positive word of mouth recommendation; and there is a different cost in acquiring new customers as opposed to retaining existing customers over longer time periods. In general, following the ideas of relationship marketing, it is suggested that to keep a customer over the long term provides important savings. On a cost–benefit basis, good service quality is thought to increase revenue and reduce long-run costs.

Service recovery

Service recovery is a broad term that relates to the planned systems and effort that a firm provides to correct a problem following a service failure with the specific objective of retaining a customer's goodwill. Given that the estimated cost of finding a new customer is five times that of retaining an existing one, there is growing emphasis on customer retention and relationship marketing. When a dissatisfied customer defects, the lifetime value of that individual and anyone else who switches due to negative comments is affected. Long-term revenue can be enhanced by *service recovery* strategies. Good service recovery procedures allow a customer to refocus on the satisfactions received from the service delivery process rather than to question why corrective action was not taken. A problem tests the system and if a customer complaint is dealt with appropriately the customer is likely to become more loyal.

Effective recovery requires: *acting fast* to resolve the problem on the spot or within short time periods; being open and *admitting mistakes* if the retailer is in the wrong rather than being defensive; providing *empathy* by attempting to understand the problem through the perceptions of the customer so as to acknowledge their feelings; providing a *relationship* whereby there is a partnership of looking at the problem to see how both parties may best resolve it as part of a mutually acceptable solution; *informing and clarifying* the steps which will be taken to resolve the situation, ensuring the customer understands these and any *remedial action* to be taken to ensure a repeat of the problem does not arise.

Individual service recovery strategies may include some of the factors discussed below.

Watching for sign language

Consideration needs to be given to enabling those customers who are reticent or mute when it comes to complaints to break their silence. Companies need the opportunity to prove their commitment to the customer through service quality measures. However, the silent customer who is not satisfied will escape company notice but may tell many of their acquaintances of the problem. Some companies have Freephone numbers for complainants to make a call to complain, or adopt employee training to enable staff to test for weak signals of a customer's dissatisfaction. Many companies empower staff to provide immediate remedial action if they suspect poor service. A long wait to be seated in a restaurant, for example, may be acknowledged by a reduction in the bill or free coffee. Others place emphasis on mystery customers or research feedback.

Preplanning

There is a need to analyse the service delivery process so as to anticipate those aspects of service which may exceed the tolerance level of customers. Times of peak demand, or low levels of staffing may affect the judgement of the customer in relation to the overall level of service quality delivery.

Training

As service is an interpersonal performance activity, the provision of communication and customer relation skills training will enhance the ability of staff to deal with the most difficult of situations. Perhaps more important, training will allow staff to feel confident in the service encounter transaction and allow them to deal professionally with all situations. Training has to be allied to labour retention strategies; overall service recovery may suffer if there is too high a proportion of untrained staff or seasonal employees.

Empowerment

A great deal of staff service delivery goes unsupervised. Front-line retail staff, therefore, need to react quickly to service problem situations without the input of supervisors. Empowerment is where a retail staff member is motivated to service a customer problem and has the skills, resources and authority to do so. A staff member who provides some extra means of satisfying a customer may stave off a more difficult or serious situation. Empowerment conveys responsibility, too – an obligation to act; front-line staff are trusted to act, not simply to focus on who is to blame for a poor service encounter. The benefits of empowerment are that decisions are taken more quickly and service recovery occurs on the spot, allowing employees to feel more responsible and in control of the situation. This is likely to motivate the staff more and may affect the whole service encounter due to staff feeling better about themselves as well as the customers. This is because empowerment often leads to increased job satisfaction, reduced role stress and less ambiguity of responsibility and action. Widening the scope for employee empowerment requires acceptance of the need for training schemes and the need for trust in any employee's decision. However, it should be recognized that the extent to which empowerment can take place is reliant upon the competency of the member of staff, the complexity of the task and the nature of the service or retail operation.

A summary of the key components of a quality-led approach

1 An unending quest for excellence in all things.

2 A system which offers continuous improvement and reduces failure repetition. A feeling that there is no such thing as an insignificant improvement in quality or service. However, this has to be cost-effective.

3 An orientation which focuses on the customer and stakeholder satisfaction outcomes. The philosophy is always to plan to give the customer a little more than they expect.

4 A feeling of total involvement of all concerned with ownership of the quest. Senior management commitment is particularly important as a leadership to others.

5 Regular measurement, monitoring, evaluation and adjustment to changing circumstances.

CONCLUSION

The management of retail cannot be divorced from the management of service and quality. The marketing management of retail cannot ignore the primary characteristics which set retail apart from other products. These are the important aspects of being intangible, perishable and inseparable. Retail, as a specialized service, creates a number of important considerations which need to be fully understood if a retail enterprise or organization is to be successful. The customer service approach has to support all other functional strategies with the objective of exceeding customer expectations. At the very minimum it has to be able to provide an effortless retail sales purchase experience.

EXERCISES

The exercises in this section relate to the management of service and quality in retailing. It is suggested that you work through these exercises before moving on to Chapter 5.

1 Provide an analysis of the type of service offered and service levels and standards at Argos, B&Q, and a bank you are familiar with. Assess the service delivery and quality encounter episodes utilizing a checklist of service and quality attributes drawn from this chapter. Comment on the expectations and outcomes experienced.

2 What would be the differences, in service and quality management, if you were the marketing manager of a chain of supermarkets or a well-known shoe shop as opposed to the sales and marketing manager of an e-tailer? What are the service level implications for the retail industry based upon the changes that e-commerce will bring about?

3 Select and visit five similar retail outlets in your local high street. Using the following grid as a guide, assess each store in turn.

External appearance:	Assessment by store:
● paintwork (colours and state of repair) ● cleanliness of windows ● window display ● lighting (list others)	
Internal: ● any welcome by staff? ● was the body language of staff friendly? ● was the layout of the store user-helpful? ● was the standard (of the fitting room, etc.) acceptable? ● did the till transaction look efficient? (list others)	**Assessment by store:**

Compare your findings with what you believe to be the key requirements of quality management for any high street retailer.

4 Look at the literature dealing with service encounters and think about any dissatisfying and satisfying aspects of service encounters you or your friends have experienced. Based upon these experiences, and the literature, describe the policies you would implement if you were responsible for the service quality management of a retail company.

REFERENCES AND FURTHER READING

Blackwell, D. (1998) 'Companies and finance: Granada's rental revamp', *Financial Times*, 9 March.

Buttle, F. (1994) 'Jaeger ladies', in McGoldrick, P. (ed.) *Cases in Retail Management*. London: Pitman Publishing.

Cadotte, E.R. and Turgeon, N. (1988) 'Key factors in guest satisfaction', *Cornell HRA Quarterly*, February.

Cope, N. (1995) 'Jobs cut in Safeway shake-up', *Independent*, 25 May.

The Economist (2000) 'The personal touch', *The Economist*, 11 November.

Ernst, R. and Powell, S.G. (1998) 'Manufacturer incentives to improve retail service levels', *European Journal of Operational Research*, 104 (3), 437–50.

Fant, D. (1998) 'Understanding customers: the key to retail success', *Marketing News*, 32 (4), 7.

Fitzsimmons, J.A. and Fitzsimmons, M.J. (1994) *Service Management for Competitive Advantage*. Singapore: McGraw-Hill.

Gengler, C.E., Leszczyc, P. and Popkowski, T.L. (1997) 'Using customer satisfaction research for relationship marketing: A direct marketing approach', *Journal of Direct Marketing*, 11 (1), 23–9.

Gilbert, D.C., and Joshi, I. (1992) 'Quality management and the tourism and hospitality industry' in Cooper, C. and Lockwood, A. (eds) *Progress in Tourism, Recreation and Hospitality Management*. London: Belhaven Press.

Glyn, W.J. and Barnes, J.G. (1996) *Understanding Services Management*. Chichester: Wiley.

Gronroos, C. (1982) *Strategic management and marketing in the service sector*. Helsinki: Swedish School of Economics and Business Administration.

Gwinner, K.P., Gremler, D.D. and Bitner, M.J. (1998) 'Relational benefits in services industries: The customer's perspective', *Journal of the Academy of Marketing Science*, 26 (2), 101–14.

Hart, C.W.L. (1988) 'The power of unconditional guarantees', *Harvard Business Review*, July–August, 54–62.

Heskett, J.L., Sasser, W. and Hart, C.W. (1990) *Service Breakthroughs – Changing the Rules of the Game*. New York: The Free Press.

Hoffman, K.D. and Bateson, J.E.G. (1997) *Essentials of Services Marketing*. Fort Worth, FL: Dryden Press.

Hurley, R.F. (1998) 'Customer service behavior in retail settings: A study of the effect of service provider personality', *Journal of the Academy of Marketing Science*, 26 (2), 115–27.

Kay, W. (1995) 'Profile: The self-made man from MFI: John Randall', *Independent on Sunday*, 23 April, 20.

Knights, D. and McCabe, D. (1997) ' "How would you measure something like that?": Quality in a retail bank', *Journal of Management Studies*, 34 (3), 371–88.

Kotler, P. (1996) *Marketing Management – Analysis, Planning and Control*. 9th edn. Upper Saddle River, NJ: Prentice Hall.

Mishra, D.P. (2000) 'Interdisciplinary contributions in retail service delivery: review and future directions', *Journal of Retailing and Consumer Services*, 7 (2), 101–18.

Morrison, L.J., Colman, A.M. and Preston, C.C. (1997) 'Mystery customer research: Cognitive processes affecting accuracy', *Journal of the Market Research Society*, 39 (2), 349–61.

O'Reilly, A. (1984) 'Manufacturers versus retailers: the long-term winners', *Retail and Distribution Management*, 12 (3), 40–1.

Palmer, A. (1994) *Principles of Services Marketing*. Maidenhead: McGraw-Hill.

Parasuraman, A., Zeithaml, V.A. and Berry, L.L. (1985) 'A conceptual model of service quality and its implications for future research', *Journal of Marketing*, 49 (4), 41–50.

Rust, R.T. and Zahorik, A.J. (1993) 'Customer satisfaction, customer retention and market share', *Journal of Retailing*, 69 (2), 193–215.

Stern, B.B. (1997) 'Advertising intimacy: Relationship marketing and the services consumer', *Journal of Advertising*, 26 (4), 7–19.

Zeithaml, V.A. and Bitner, M.J. (1996) *Services Marketing*. Singapore: McGraw-Hill.

5 The retail marketing mix and the retail product

This chapter should enable you to understand and explain:

- what constitutes the marketing mix;
- the importance of targeting and the marketing mix;
- a model of the relationships between components of the mix;
- the pressures to increase the four Ps of the mix for services;
- what constitutes a product; and
- the aspects of store layout and atmospherics which affect demand.

When you have finally decided to use a retailer you have probably been influenced by a promotional campaign, have assessed the product offer, considered whether you are willing to pay the price, and finally thought about how easy it would be to buy it. Each of these aspects of purchase is part of the marketing mix, which is carefully planned by marketers in an attempt to convince you to utilize a particular outlet or make a transaction. The four Ps – *product*, *price*, *promotion* and the *place* (channel) of purchase – are the basic ingredients of the marketing mix. However, these ingredients mask a major role of the retailer which is to select and acquire the goods they plan to sell. There is a need for retailers to devise and implement a well-developed merchandise plan in order to be a successful retailer. This will ensure that the proper assortment of goods and services is made available, based upon historical demand patterns and the strategic positioning of the company or store as a brand.

When considering the marketing mix, the part dealing with merchandise becomes part of the product. Because merchandising is so important to the success or otherwise of a retailer it is dealt with in a separate chapter (*see* Chapter 6, Merchandise management) although merchandising falls within the category of the product. Merchandising is a key area as traditional retailing is positioned as the final distribution stage in the channel of sales to the consumer. This is not to deny the importance of the rest of the mix. Each of the areas which make up the marketing mix involves a complex set of management decisions which have to be taken into account for the retailer to prosper. This is both for the individual mix strategy and for the combined effect of the whole mix on the target market sub-groups. In fact the mix has to be combined across its different parts so that each aspect of the mix reinforces and reflects the other parts of the mix. This creates a synergy effect, where the whole becomes greater than the sum of the parts. The combined mix has to be positioned so as to create a clear proposition for the customer. As Ries and Trout (1981) commented: 'Positioning is not what you do to a product; positioning is what you do to the mind of the prospect.' This chapter's information will, therefore, provide you with an overview of the most important considerations for planning the marketing mix.

WHAT IS THE MARKETING MIX?

It is customary to accept the classic marketing mix to be made up from the four Ps of product, price, promotion, and place (channel service).

1 The *product* is the totality of the offer which will normally include the services, store layout, merchandise. It will also include the company, and product brand name.

2 The *price* is what the customer has to be willing to pay in exchange for the benefits of the product and channel service. The price is related to a perception of value based upon the way the whole of the marketing mix creates an image of the transaction experience.

3 The *promotion* is the means by which the retail offer is communicated to the target groups in order to inform and persuade different segments of the benefits of utilizing a specific retailer's outlet or to make a purchase.

4 The *place* is based on the retailer's activities in supplying a channel service. This includes the logistics of inventory management systems.

Kotler *et al.* (1999) indicate that the marketing mix is one of the key concepts in modern marketing theory. The definition of the marketing mix is provided as:

> **the set of controllable tactical marketing tools that the firm blends to produce the response it wants in the target market.**

Figure 5.1 illustrates the approach to the interrelated nature of the marketing mix favoured here. While the four Ps are a traditional way of understanding the key aspects of marketing which are within the control of the company or managers, there are alternative approaches where authors stress the need for an expansion of these four components. This is an interesting development because the four Ps were provided by McCarthy (1978) as an abridged version of a much wider range of what were termed 'marketing ingredients'. McCarthy based his four Ps upon a simplified version of a range of twelve marketing ingredients offered much earlier by Borden (1965).

THE MARKETING MIX FOR SERVICES – ARE THE FOUR PS SUFFICIENT?

The adaptation of the marketing mix by authors such as Booms and Bitner (1981) has been based upon arguments which stress that the four Ps' marketing mix is more appropriate to manufacturing than to service companies, such as are found in retailing. For example, Booms and Bitner add the three extra Ps of people, physical evidence and process (*see* Fig. 5.2). Authors such as Booms and Bitner argue that the marketing mix of four Ps is not comprehensive enough. The major difference is argued to be the intangible element of human behaviour, where quality and its control is of paramount importance. We believe that there is enough scope in Fig. 5.1 to incorporate each of the additional areas of Booms and Bitner.

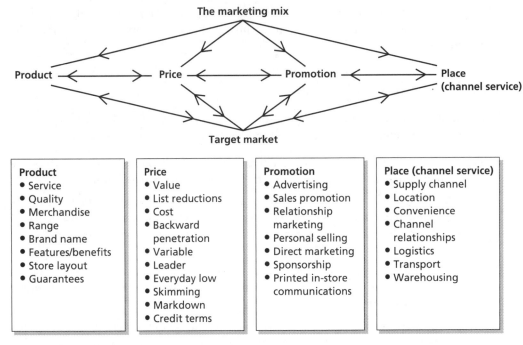

Fig. 5.1 The marketing mix

For the present it is believed the four Ps offer an adequate framework into which the differences can be incorporated. The main task of marketers in retail is to understand many of the complexities of the marketing mix contained in this chapter in order to ensure they will be better prepared to plan, control and manage different types of retail operations. Retail managers have to control the aspects of the marketing mix which have most bearing on the demand creation and satisfaction level of consumers. While it is obvious that there are differences between manufactured and service products, the framework of the four Ps is sufficient for retail planning purposes, based on the content of this chapter and the following chapter on merchandise management. The four mix categories do not presuppose the relegation of service product considerations to secondary importance. On the contrary, the four categories should ensure that within any mix formulation greater emphasis will be placed on the integration of all the different service management considerations.

Whatever approach is taken to the classification of the controllable aspects of marketing there is a need to realize that purchases do not take place unless customers know:

● that an offer exists;

● where it is best to purchase the offer;

● that it offers value and is affordable;

● that the offer is likely to satisfy the need for which it is required.

The essentials of the marketing mix for retail are explained fully in the next chapters of this book. First, however, it is important to understand how the target market plays an essential part in the formulation of any retail mix strategy.

Product	Price	Place	Promotion	People	Physical evidence	Process
Range	Level	Location	Advertising	Personnel:	Environment:	Policies
Quality	Discounts:	Accessibility	Personal selling	• Training	• Furnishings	Procedures
Level	• Allowances	Distribution channels	Sales promotion	• Discretion	• Colour	Mechanization
Brand name	• Commissions	Distribution coverage	Publicity	• Commitment	• Layout	Employee discretion
Service line	Payment terms		Public relations	• Incentives	• Noise level	Customer involvement
Warranty	Customer's			• Appearance	Facilitating goods	Customer direction
After-sales	perceived value			• Interpersonal behaviour	Tangible clues	Flow of activities
service	Quality/price			• Attitudes		
	Differentiation			Other customers:		
				• Behaviour		
				• Degree of involvement		
				• Customer/customer contact		

Fig. 5.2 The marketing mix for services

Source: Reprinted by permission of the American Marketing Association from Booms and Bitner, 1981

TARGET MARKETS

The fundamental starting point for the creation of a successful marketing mix strategy is to ensure that the target market is clearly defined. While the target market is not part of the mix, its role in dictating the different ways the mix is used makes it indistinguishable from the concept, and of paramount importance. In any management decision which is related to the marketing mix, the customer base or target market is always the initial focus of all marketing mix activity. This is because the potential consumer has to remain the focus for all retail decision-making. For example, we need to know what minimum and maximum level of price or what retail offer proposition will be acceptable to target consumers.

The retail market is made up of actual and potential consumers. This total available group of consumers will be analysed and a decision made as to which segments or sub-groups will be targeted. The segments would probably have been identified as part of the marketing planning process and would have been specified at the time of the setting of objectives. A clear specification of the target market allows for a number of benefits, including improved levels of understanding of:

- the characteristics and needs of the group targeted;
- the main competitors;
- the changing/developing needs of targeted consumers.

Benefits of targeting

1 A fuller understanding of the unique characteristics and needs of the group to be satisfied is reached. The target market acts as a reference point for retail marketing decisions, especially as to how the marketing mix should be planned. This should lead to greater effectiveness for the mix, which in turn provides for the success of the programme.

2 A better understanding of the main competitors is gained because it is possible to detect those retail companies who have made a similar selection of target markets. If a company does not clarify the markets it wishes to target, it may treat every other company in its sector as an equal competitor. Once main competitors are identified, their marketing efforts can be more closely followed – or benchmarked if appropriate – so as to improve marketing decision-making.

3 Improvements are possible in the understanding of the changes and development in the needs of the target market. Awareness and knowledge of retail demand is heightened due to the scrutiny focused upon the target group's actions and reactions to slightly different forms of the marketing mix.

Target markets are often based upon socio-economic groups, geographic location, age, gender, income levels, shopper type, benefits sought, purchase behaviour and attitudes. The target market acts as the focus for tailoring the mix so that target customers will judge it to be superior to that of the competition. Segmentation and target marketing is central to marketing because different customer groups should dictate the search for the correct marketing mix strategy. (For further discussion, see Chapter 10, Methods and approaches to retail strategy and marketing planning.)

MINICASE 5.1

Product decisions – the shop as a destination?

Is shopping a leisure activity? Behind that question lies a raging debate over the design and management of shopping centres in which a growing number of real estate professionals are arguing that the two are inextricably linked. 'Shopping is leisure,' says John Milligan, partner in the retail practice at property consultants Jones Lang Wooten. 'If you don't make it a leisure activity, you're dead.' The introduction of a cinema, with its evening operating hours, entices a far wider range of food retailers than may be prepared to occupy a shopping centre and these may be prepared to pay far more for the space. Thus, the addition of a cinema encourages further daytime shopping and the growth of food courts, leading to a virtuous circle resulting in higher revenues for everyone. Mr Ronson (Heron) is developing retailing/

entertainment complexes in Continental Europe. However, he cautions that the retailing element itself must contain a leisure theme. White goods superstores and food supermarkets, he says, will not be a feature. 'We're thinking of music superstores, bookshops, that sort of thing,' he says. 'The shopping centre has to be a destination,' he argues. 'It's a day out.' However, Michael McCarty cautions against a headlong plunge into leisure/retailing development. 'The conventional wisdom is that the entertainment and leisure component can enhance the value of a retail development,' he says. 'But it is not a panacea for a bad centre. It will make a good centre better but it will not make a bad centre survive.'

Source: Norma Cohen, *Financial Times*, 1998

Retailing in shopping centres may need to target the leisure segment of the market in order to encourage that group to use other retail facilities such as food courts and shops. Minicase 5.1 introduces the debate as to what product types should be available in a shopping centre, based upon the link between shopping and leisure.

The marketing mix is put together to ensure the highest expected outcome of demand from the customer. Therefore, when the marketing mix is delivered to the target market it has to produce an outcome of higher value than any competing form of retail offer. What we have to consider is that all retail purchases are related to a cost for the consumer. The marketing mix amalgam has to create greater value than the travel costs if a car or transport is used, the time costs which have to be taken from an individual's total time budget for leisure as well as shopping, etc. Figure 5.3 is a simple illustration of the

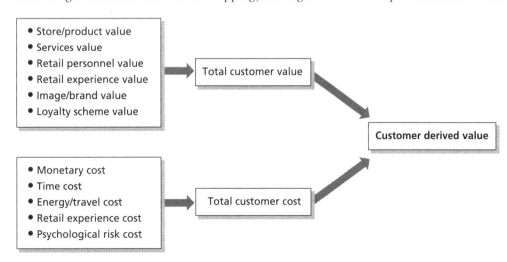

Fig. 5.3 Components of the derived value of purchase for the customer

components of a purchase situation, with the customer-derived value being an outcome of a deduction of value from costs. The figure reflects the need to create perceived or actual positive outcomes from any creation of a retail marketing mix strategy. The object-ive of creating high levels of derived value should be borne in mind when assessing the underlying concepts that follow. Some aspects of value and costs are discussed more fully in Chapter 3 and later in this chapter.

THE RETAIL PRODUCT

The effectiveness of planning the marketing mix depends as much on the ability to select the right target market as on the skill in devising a retail offer which will generate high levels of satisfaction. *A product is anything that can be offered to a market that may sat-isfy a need or a want.* This means a combination of goods and services, which includes the store, the staff and the merchandise. In retailing the complete retail offer of location, price levels, merchandise, store layout or method of selling, brand name and service pro-vided play a pivotal role in a firm's existence and long-term success or survival. The con-ception of the store has to take into consideration the internal and external design fittings and features as well as all the myriad ways the brand, merchandise and pro-motional messages communicate with the customer. The shopper has to believe that the merchandise, or outlet, offers added value in order for it to be successful. Retailing com-prises everything an individual or customer receives – both favourable and unfavourable – as part of the total retail transaction. It should be noted that Chapter 6 is dedicated to a full explanation of the role and functions of merchandise management, which is an important aspect of any discussion of the marketing mix.

A BREAKDOWN OF RETAILING AS A PRODUCT

The formulation of a successful retailing operation involves a combination of:

- service;
- quality;
- merchandise;
- brand name;
- features and benefits;
- atmospherics.

If you envisage the situation where you have taken a holiday and you need to have your hair styled you will call upon many of the above as clues as to whether or not to use one hairdresser rather than another. If you walked around the area the location in terms of other buildings and retail outlets may give you some clues as to the type of service you could expect. You would probably look in the salons to see what the other customers looked like, the age and dress of the staff, the internal fixtures and fitments and decide whether the interior was comfortable enough to wait for a stylist. Perhaps you would see a Vidal Sassoon branded fascia on one salon and this may make the difference in the decision made. All these intangible and tangible product factors will have a bearing on the choice made by consumers. Of course, some of the other aspects of the marketing mix such as price will also have an influence but the product attributes are an important means of communicating the promise of a specific retail experience.

Service

An agreement to service provision is concerned with creating the level of services to be offered. In a store, how much of the service should the client be expected to perform and how much should be provided by staff? For example, in supermarkets the self-service of food and the customer carrying their own purchased items are now thought of as acceptable – and at times desirable – by clients. The use of automatic teller machines (ATMs) at banks extends the availability of the cash retrieval service (and others) beyond typical bank hours, and also allows customers to estimate roughly how long a transaction will take. There are also systems for self-scanning of goods which cut down on the cost of time. A retail operation has to be able to deliver high levels of service. These are judged through the five dimensions that can be used to measure service quality:

- *tangibles* – such as uniforms, toilets, mirrors, fitting rooms;
- *reliability* – based upon the ability to perform the service dependably and accurately;
- *responsiveness* – by reacting in a timely manner with the right level of knowledge and courtesy;
- *empathy* – demonstrated by providing a caring, individualized service performance for customers;
- *assurance* – to provide credibility that the service standard will be upheld.

A full discussion of service and quality management is contained in Chapter 4.

Quality

A decision regarding quality involves deciding on quality standards and implementing a method of assurance on the performance level of staff and facilities. The management of quality is becoming an increasingly important management function. It is important to create a good quality reputation for the product and service offered as this provides a positive image for the company or organization and is a major advantage in countering the perception of risk which, for many retail consumers, is high. Retail service providers are more likely to be successful if they can be depended upon to deliver higher quality service levels than their competitors. Success through quality is often seen as, for certain product categories, the outcome of a relationship between a customer's prior expectations of service delivery and the perception of the actual service experience. Quality is also used strategically: as a way of differentiating merchandise and of positioning the offer or retail outlet in an exclusive way. However, an exclusive position does bring with it the added problems of needing to source more widely to continue to find unique merchandise and having to bear additional overhead costs as a consequence of exclusivity.

Merchandise

Retailers need to decide on the merchandise to offer by engaging in the sorting process of assembling a range of goods and services from a variety of suppliers. The depth and width of this range will depend on the specific strategy of each retailer, who must decide how different products will fit into the overall range of products they offer to the marketplace (Chapter 6 offers a more detailed description of the role of the merchandise manager). A retailer must also decide on whether to include various brands in the range, and whether the offer of traditional or new products should be included. The range of the offer and how each product matches or complements the chosen positioning of the retailer is an important retail consideration; for example, is the company maintaining an upmarket, mid-market or economy position? The decision regarding the range of products is also important as it affects the need for space for display at the point-of-sale as well as stockholding. The width and depth decisions over the range of merchandise to offer have to be linked to both the expectations and the financial considerations of the consumer target group. Decisions over merchandise have to take into account that a consumer may want to choose to purchase from a range of different types of goods. This could encompass the following categories.

National brands

These are the brands which are heavily promoted by companies, such as Sainsbury, Boots and Kwik Fit, to achieve consumer awareness and preference, for example, Kellogg's (*see* Chapter 12 for a discussion of brand management). For the retailer the problem in offering a range which is predominately made up of national brands is that they have no exclusivity and are open to price competition from low-cost retailers discounting national brands.

Advantages of own-brands for retailers

- Good value perceptions which by association enhance store image and may build loyalty.
- Quality improvement of own-brands leads to the belief that they are equal to, or better than manufacturers' brands. As such, the development of own-brands may provide for an enhanced corporate image.
- Own-brands provide a communication function by reinforcing the retailer's name in the consumer's own home environment.
- Retailer promotions can benefit both the retailer and the own-brand products.
- Strategic advantage can be gained if competitors do not have own-brand products.
- More able to create a superior brand through own specification and quality control. The own-brand merchandise then acts as an inducement to visit the store.
- Can be a fast route for new product development and product innovation.
- Supply control as own-brand products cannot be obtained elsewhere.
- Own-brands often have credibility as it is generally assumed by the public that own-brands are sourced from leading manufacturers.
- Financial benefits are the improved control of pricing policy, stock levels and display space. Higher margins (characteristically 5–10 per cent better) and manufacturers' promotional expenses are avoided. Also, allows for a competitive balance and greater bargaining power in relation to leading manufacturers.

Own-brand

Own-brand (sometimes termed own-label) is discussed in detail in Chapter 12. As the larger retailers look for competitive advantage in the marketplace, own-brands have become one of the key weapons in the battle for improved financial returns, channel control and consumer loyalty. In the growing confrontation between manufacturers' and own-brands, retailers can be found to enjoy a number of advantages and increasing market power (see below). Initially positioned as a cheaper value-for-money alternative to national brands, own-brands are now marketed with the advantage of a 'quality' focus. Nowadays a retailer can offer the advantage of exclusivity and have greater control over all aspects of the product. Thus they need not enter into heavy advertising as do national brands, which may give the flexibility of being able to offer lower unit prices.

Licensed merchandise

The importance of TV or film characters has led to the addition of images and symbols on a range of merchandise from everyday items to clothing. Disney characters, Bart Simpson, etc. have appealed to the children's market and led to major opportunities for increasing the desirability of different types of merchandise.

Franchised products via concessions in a store

An advantage may be gained through an exclusive deal with a manufacturer (for example, Clinique, Principles, Alexon, etc.).

MINICASE 5.2

Supermarkets sew up the clothing market

Although the size of Tesco and Asda's ranges are similar, in Compability's survey for *Retail Week*, Tesco has the edge. With 2,244 options, Tesco's clothing offer is 10 per cent bigger than the George range, which has 2,049 options, and more than 50 per cent bigger than the clothing offer at Sainsbury's, which has 1,450 overall options. The survey counted every option for styles and colours for clothing, footwear and accessories.

Tesco's wider range is mainly due to its extensive Essentials offer for women. The Essentials – underwear and hosiery – at Tesco dwarfs the choice in Asda and Sainsbury's. Interestingly however, both the George childrenswear range at Asda and the Adams range at Sainsbury's have more options than the children's range at Tesco. George has the widest choice of footwear.

The George clothing range at Asda relies on one name and one name only, while Jeff & Co articulates the offer via a number of sub-brands. For example, 14oz for denims, CMT for tailoring and Navy Blue for relaxed weekend wear. The bulk of Tesco's range carries the 'Designed for Tesco' label. The newer and more aspirational Florence+Fred branding is not yet available in accessories and footwear, and is at the moment a small element of the range.

In terms of environment, the trading area for Jeff & Co is far better differentiated from the rest of the store than the clothing ranges at Tesco and George. Frosted glass panels, illuminated wardrobe display units and spotlights make for a classy atmosphere. Florence+Fred, on the other hand, does not appear to have been given the same level of support.

Elements of the range incorporate sophist-icated colours and fabrics, which would be better emphasised in a more intimate area, like the one developed for Jeff & Co. George of Asda combines a lot of product on display with wide aisles for ease of navigation, and clearly demarcated sections.

From a product point of view, Tesco is well on the way to developing a lifestyle brand with the launch of Florence+Fred, but it falls short from a presentation perspective. Sainsbury's has made a big impact with the stylish shopfit and wearable appeal of the Jeff & Co clothes. But the range is still in honey-moon mode, and as yet unhindered by the usual problems of broken size ratios and fragmentation. Jeff & Co prices are substan-tially higher than both Tesco and George, and while the Sainsbury's customer is argu-ably better off, it remains to be seen just how much impact a 19-store proposition will have.

Asda has more large-spaced stores than either Tesco or Sainsbury's and with excel-lent prices and ranges will remain the biggest apparel selling supermarket group for the foreseeable future. However, Tesco is aggress-ively expanding space dedicated to clothing and plans to sell its ranges from 140 super-stores and 46 hypermarkets by next year. Ultimately the emergence of stronger cloth-ing ranges within the supermarket sector will inevitably increase the pressure on already struggling middle-market players.

Source: Compability Report, *Retail Week*, 8 June 2001

Brand name

The store exterior and brand name is the initial impression that a customer will have of a store. Branding is also an important portable communication tool which can be utilized on the retailer's bags and packaging of its own-label products. A brand name which is well known and associated with high satisfaction levels imparts an improved image and added value to the product or the store. This can lead to store loyalty or consumers insisting on the product by brand name and being less price sensitive (Chapter 12 dis-cusses branding in great detail). These days a retail brand name may be a national brand or an own-label brand. Brand names can be family brands where each of the company's products adopts the same brand name. Umbrella brands which use a corporate brand symbol are being used to project a consistent image across countries. Nestlé's brand policy, for example, uses umbrella and sub-umbrella branding; corporate branding takes place with Nestlé, Carnation, Maggi, C&B, Chambourcy, Buitoni, Findus, Friskies, Herta and Libby's, while sub-branding is used for Nescafé, Nestea, Nestum, Sveltesse and Lean Cuisine. Additionally, individual product brand names such as Nido, Milo, Crunch and KitKat are used, where each product is branded differently. It is argued that it is difficult to create marketing success across a wide range of products owing to the problem of providing complex brand values to dissimilar products. Marks & Spencer was renowned for having built their success on an umbrella own-brand, St Michael, which was associ-ated with added value but which may now be weaker than in previous times.

Some companies opt for individual brand names such as those associated with the Debenham's organization. The individual brand name approach allows the retailer to search for the most appropriate brand name; its weakness is that the promotional budget for each brand has to be sufficiently large to support that brand. With individual brand-ing, a company is able to position brands and products at the cheaper end of the market without the brand damaging the image of the rest of the company's brands. In addition, if there is bad publicity for one of the company's brands then the other company brands do not necessarily suffer.

With umbrella or family brands there is a spin-off effect for each of the brands from the expenditure on any one brand. Conversely, if one of the family brands attracts poor publicity, because of association there will be damage to the other brands. For family branding, careful attention has to be given to the quality control of the products. One other benefit of family branding is that each product brand performance (PBP) can be measured against the overall family brand performance (FBP). That is to say, when FBP is divided by PBP and the quotient shows an increase over time, without good reason, it may mean that the product brand needs modification, revitalization or a detailed review.

Product levels

The product can be thought of as being an amalgam of four different levels – *the core product*; *the facilitating product*; *the supporting product*; and *the augmented product.*

A product includes everything that the customer receives and this includes the basic level of the core product which is made up of the delivery of benefits and features. We know that consumers buy products for the benefits they deliver to them, as this is the basic outcome value assessment associated with the purchase. Every retail product is a package of problem-solving services that will be successful if the package is valued enough. A holiday consumer in a travel agency is looking for the benefit of relaxing in the sun and having no hassle in the journey or stay. They leave the detail to the travel agent. As Levitt pointed out, the buyers 'do not buy quarter inch drills; they buy quarter inch holes'. Marketing staff have to uncover the subtle benefits that the consumer seeks when utilizing a retail distribution channel or purchasing a retail product. There are also the different features that are the tangible aspects of the product which help to differentiate it from competitors. Adding in the right features increases the probability that a purchase will occur. The features will be the size of the entrance, the aisles and the fixtures and fittings of the store.

The facilitating aspects of the product in a store must be present for the customer to utilize the services of the core product. This will be the service and goods such as checkout and credit card facilities, if clothing then mirrors and fitting room, signage and easy access around the store, acceptable merchandise.

Core products require facilitating products but do not necessarily have to include supporting products. In fact the discounter stores ensure that their cost-leadership strategy is adhered to by having only a minimum of supporting products. Such extras as a play area for children, baby change facilities, higher employee numbers operating fast checkouts, free gift wrap service, free delivery, and so on are all supporting products which may be planned into the product offer.

The augmented product includes aspects of atmosphere and the interaction of the customer with the company. Retailers should take the opportunity to consider factors such as the appropriateness of in-store music at different periods in the week as well as at weekends when the market profile of their customers may change and the need for supporting services will vary e.g. gift wrapping service, loyalty programme benefits, etc. Retail outlets in London are now incorporating advanced thinking as to what can be offered as an augmented product. There are MTV booths for males to relax in while females shop, and there are additions such as juice bars and DJ booths that are able to bring about change in consumer attitudes as to what is expected as a shopping experience.

STORE LAYOUT

The store is a product in its own right. The customer's product decisions can be enhanced, or ruined, by the type of planned store layout. Stores should be designed to facilitate the movement of customers, to create a planned store experience and to allow the optimum presentation of merchandise. The traffic flow of customers has been influenced through the clever design of displays, aisles, signage and overall layout. This also involves the full use of the floor area – to utilizing obscure and unproductive areas. The retailer's goal has to be a store layout which reflects the brand position of the store and ensures the most effective use of the space. It also has to be designed on a proactive rather than a passive basis. This is because the understanding of how customers shop for specific categories of merchandise should be incorporated into the way it is exhibited or displayed within an overall store layout. Donovan and Rossiter (1982) found that the effect of store-induced pleasure is a very dominant determinant of either approach or avoidance behaviour as well as in-store spending patterns. The results of their study indicated that arousal, or the feelings of alertness and excitement created by means of store-induced emotion led to increased time spent in the store by customers and also produced a higher willingness to interact with sales personnel.

Proactive planning should therefore be based upon the manipulation of the in-store experience rather than accepting a passive, totally random experience for customers. Proactive planning accepts and responds to the data showing that store layout can influence the customer's shopping behaviour and perceptions. It is well known that the use of different layouts and aisle design will influence the patterns of traffic flow past the principal merchandising groups. The correct display of merchandise in a highly frequented area can dramatically increase sales; conversely, a poor display will have a negative effect. There is also the time factor related to any shopping trip. Those stores with an appropriate number of checkouts for the square area of the store may influence the shopper to spend longer browsing and purchasing if they believe the checkout time is efficient.

Customers have to feel happy and comfortable in an environment if they are to relax and stay for any length of time. Customers are more likely to want to enter and shop in a store when their senses are satisfied by the way the store environment has been planned. The ambience of the store has to be right for that store's positioning. For example, a discount store with narrow aisles, high density merchandise, bold signs and loud music has consistency with the rest of the marketing mix and this reinforces the perception of low price.

There is a whole variety of layouts available for consideration but the retailer's choice should be determined by the merchandise, the size and type of space available and cost involved. Layouts can contain one or a combination of the following:

- *Grid pattern layout* – is characterised by the regimentation of the layout into long rows of parallel fixtures, with straight aisles. If the aisles are too short, the customer will look to the next aisle – so for maximum effect the aisles have to be long enough so that the customer looks at the merchandise on the shelving as they pass. The layout produces a maze effect as it constrains the customer: they are unable to pass through the rows because there is no opportunity to move at right angles until the end of each row. The merchandise counters are arranged to produce long barriers to cross-aisle

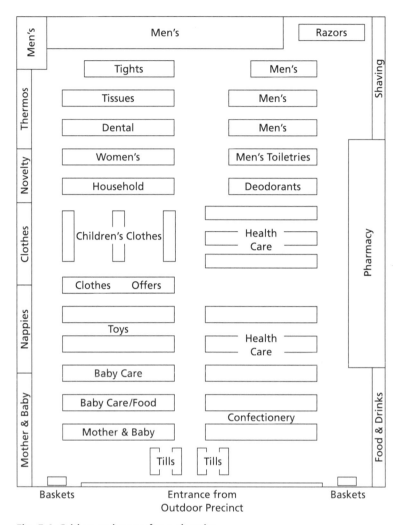

Fig. 5.4 Grid store layout for a chemist

traffic flow. This channels the customer past different store sections. Supermarkets or retailers of fast-moving product lines normally adopt this format.

- *Free-flow layout* – is based upon an irregular pattern with some logic of attempting to create a flow but which allows the customer the choice of whether to move between the fixtures or not. The design allows for more unstructured flows of store traffic. It allows for more relaxed customer shopping and for impulse purchases as customers are drawn to areas they are interested in. This type of layout style is to be found in many clothing stores.

- *Boutique layout* – is a variation of the free-flow layout pattern whereby the departments or sections are arranged in the form of individual speciality areas that can cater for specific customer requirements. This approach is more likely to be adopted by specialist or department stores.

Examples of the layouts described are shown in Figs 5.4–5.6.

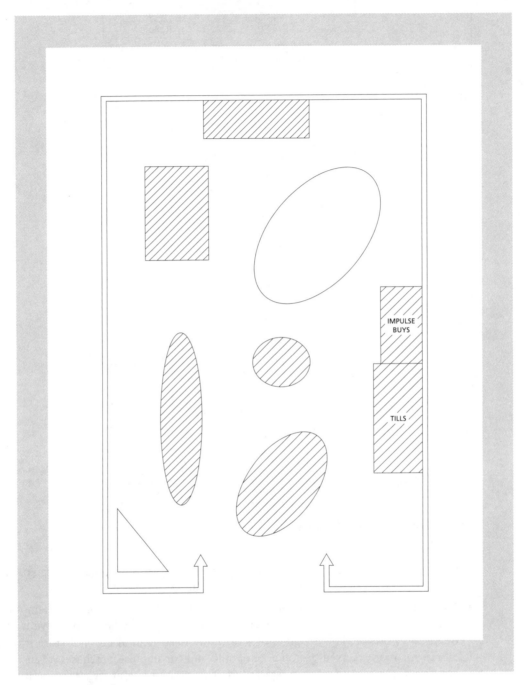

Fig. 5.5 Free-flow layout

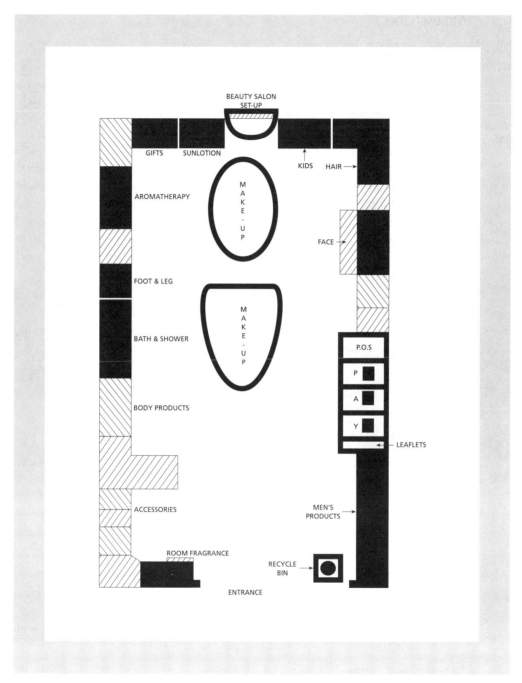

Fig. 5.6 Boutique-style layout

Atmospherics

The act of a retail purchase entails a number of social and psychological states related to the place and time of that purchase occasion. These are based upon:

- *the environmental and physical aspects of place* – which include atmospherics and visible components of the store and the store's location;
- *the social surroundings* – which involves the interaction with other shoppers in terms of judgements of their characteristics and appearance and whether the retail outlet is crowded or not. Crowding can affect behaviour in different ways. Consumers learn to cope with crowded retail outlets by allocating their time by postponing, rescheduling, aborting or focusing their purchase behaviour;
- *the temporal aspects of the occasion* in terms of the time of day, week or year – which may be based upon a seasonal aspect to the shopping experience such as Easter or Christmas. This will lead to different levels of crowding, visual and olfactory changes;
- *the objective of the shopping trip* will affect the emotional state of the individual as a routine shopping task is not the same as one where high expenditure or importance of purchase is present;
- *the predisposition of the individual* will also affect the purchase behaviour. For example, a specific mood state will lead to distinct purchasing behaviour.

The above five factors need to be understood as a composite whole as each will affect the other and provide an overall synergy which will have an impact on the type and timing of the retail purchase.

Atmospherics can enhance the shopping experience through environmental changes which affect the emotional response of customers. Atmosphere is perceived through the different elements in the same store environment which are planned to interact with an individual's senses. This should be understood as a holistic experience where each part of sensory marketing works in combination with the other atmospheric elements. Sensory triggers create a number of changes in the customer's emotions which can influence the type and amount of demand for different types of merchandise in the store. The main sensory mediums are:

- *Visual* – colour, brightness or variation of light, size, shape, texture.
- *Aural* – volume, pitch, beat, harmony – recognized/favoured music. This is based upon the notion that music is composed of at least three primary dimensions: a physical dimension (volume, pitch, tempo, rhythm), an emotional tone, and a preferential dimension (the degree to which a shopper judges they like the music).
- *Olfactory* – scent, freshness – merchandise such as leather, bakery items, food, etc. This comprises ambient scent which should be distinguished from non-ambient scent. Ambient scent is the scent that does not originate from any particular object but is present in the environment while non-ambient scent is given off by objects. Both are controllable by the retailer. Scent includes the affective quality of the scent (i.e. how pleasant it is), its arousing nature (i.e. how likely it is to evoke a physiological response), and its intensity (i.e. how strong it is).
- *Tactile* – softness, smoothness, shape – surface and display area by feel/touch.

Store sensory characteristics	Emotions	Customer behaviour outcome
Spatial aspects, temperature, type of music, lighting either natural or designed, scent, colours, etc. Provides —>	Pleasure, calmness, arousal, non-arousal, anxiety, interest Provides —>	Purchase behaviour changes, time spent in the store is altered, activity patterns are affected

Fig. 5.7 Stages related to sensory marketing

The use of space, colour, walls, pillars, floor coverings, lighting, music, scent and so on can be controlled by the retailer. The combinations of these planned 'physical messages' is known as *atmospherics*. Atmospherics can be defined as:

> **The changes made to the design of buying environments that produce special emotional effects that subsequently enhance the likelihood that a purchase will take place.**

The type of merchandise offered and the method of its display – down to the style and pose of mannequins, reinforce this. Atmospherics are created by the combination of a whole series of cues and stimulants to produce the desired ambience and emotional response from the group of target customers. The emotional state of the shopper will lead to an increase or decrease in the planned level of purchases. It is essential to know what factors stimulate and please consumers as the result will capture individuals for longer periods in a store and make them more susceptible to merchandise offers. Figure 5.7 indicates the links which drive the stages of retail atmospherics. Therefore, the design of stores has to strive to produce an efficient layout with the qualities of ambience that attract members of the target market. The following list of factors is useful but not exhaustive:

1 Space must be used effectively, with territorial areas planned to break up the store into logical sales sections and functional areas such as changing rooms, restaurants and pay points. The store's layout has to be planned for optimum circulation around the store. It should not be forgotten that the entrance to a store, both outside and inside, has to transform the customer's attitude and to create a promise of the experience to come.

2 Layout should be planned to encourage customers to circulate in specific patterns so as to visit as many merchandise areas as possible in order to achieve the optimum productive layout. The retail layout logic has to be easily comprehensible so that the potential customer quickly understands and assimilates the route they can negotiate past the merchandise. This is often achieved by the use of different floor coverings or textures which act as clues to the customer. It may also be accomplished through the use of clear appropriate signage which reflects the positioning of the retail outlet.

3 Stimulants to the senses to improve sales must also be planned. Music can be changed to suit the type of shopper in the store such as playing 'younger' background music just after the school day ends. Faster or slower music will affect the speed at which shopping occurs; national music, such as French or German tunes, played in a supermarket will increase the sales of a particular country's wines. Classical music will lead to sales of more expensive wines. Another option available is to vary the tempo of the music, at different times of day or in different areas, to influence the pace of in-store

traffic movement. For example, when a higher turnover of customers is required in the restaurant around lunchtime, increasing the tempo of the music will achieve this behavioural effect. As evidence of the arousal effect of music, Vanderark and Ely (1993) found that high tempo and high rhythmic content in the music led to an increase in physiological arousal among consumers. While the effect of music can be beneficial, many stores do not have music apart from at the Christmas shopping period. Yalch and Spangenberg (1990) conducted research in a department store setting where they compared the effects of foreground music (top 40 music played), and background music (instrumental easy listening), in relation to a no-music control group. It was found that younger shoppers (under 25) perceived that they had spent more time shopping in the easy listening condition, whereas older shoppers perceived that they had shopped longer when top 40 music was being played. From the results, the authors concluded that encountering atypical environmental factors (e.g. unfamiliar music) might adversely influence consumers' time perceptions. In addition, the fragrances and scents of perfumes, leatherwear, houseplants and so on may influence customers to purchase. The aroma of fresh bread, pastries, cheese, coffee, chocolate, etc. can stimulate sales and some stores or restaurants extract the aroma, pumping it outside their building to attract the passing public. Supermarkets may position a gondola of flowers in the entrance of the store to provide customers with the welcome sight of the blooms and the fragrance of their scent. Spangenberg *et al.* (1996) examined the effect of ambient scents in a simulated retail environment. The conclusion was that the subjects had more positive evaluations and behaviours of the environment in the scented rather than the unscented group. One other interesting finding was that the type of scent did not matter, as even effectively light scents were able to generate enhanced perceptions. Moreover, the intensity of the scent (within an acceptable range) did not alter the overall results.

4 Lighting is an important mood setter and very useful in the production of a desired ambience. Lighting can be soft, bright or produce colour washes. Merchandise can be highlighted by directional lighting or with a combination of low-voltage and energy-efficient systems. Different types of lighting can be used in combinations to create interesting contrasts throughout a display area. The use of sophisticated lighting systems allows the retailer to adapt the ambience at regular intervals. This can alter perceptions of the size of different areas, complement the merchandise by bringing out its colours and direct the attention of the customer's gaze. Glass shelving with lighting in a toiletries area can communicate a bright, clean set of merchandise. One other important aspect of lighting is that in fitting rooms or where there are mirrors to view merchandise the lighting should be flattering.

From a strategic marketing stance, it is important that in highly competitive retail sectors the layout of the store is planned in order to reflect the desired market position (*see* Chapter 10 on retail planning). The position has to be planned in conjunction with clear ideas as to how the atmospherics will differentiate the store as a brand from its competitors. Store layout planners must also take into account who the target segments of the market are and what sort of buying experience they may seek from the store. For example, Boots utilize hard floors to enhance the image of cleanliness, and blue and white colours which are cool and have associations with health and clinical practice. However,

MINICASE 5.3

M&S hopes tills will revive with sound of music

Marks and Spencer is to launch a subliminal attempt to lure back shoppers: playing background music in its stores. The struggling retailer has held out against the high street canned music barrage, allowing its British shoppers to seek out sandwiches and knitwear in dignified silence. But M&S is so confident the initiative will be a success, that it hopes shoppers will be willing to fork out for the soundtrack of their visit. The tunes on offer will come from M&S-branded compact discs, supplied by Universal, the entertainment conglomerate, and are on sale in about 160 stores.

M&S is not the first retailer to offer CDs in an attempt to appeal to customers who are put off by the thumping music and youth culture of a traditional record store. In the US, piped music CDs are becoming big business with Guess, Old Navy and Starbucks, the coffee house group, all getting in on the action. One of the first retailers to make the discovery was Victoria's Secret, a lingerie company with nearly 800 stores across the US. In 1988, it started selling compact disc and tape cassette compilations of the classical music playing in its stores. Of the 11 classical albums to have sold more than 1m copies in the US, five are from the Victoria's Secret collection.

Source: Lisa Clifford, *Financial Times*, 26 July 2001

lighting is utilized to make the products stand out and provide effects that are more dramatic. Boots utilize glass shelving to display their gift items and cosmetics. This in conjunction with the lighting creates a quality association for the displays. The Body Shop have the fragrance of their merchandise but this is complemented by the use of bright, earthy colours such orange and dark greens, as well as mirrors and clever lighting to provide their own unique atmospherics. Boots uses a combination of layouts. Grid patterns are utilized for everyday items such as shampoo and toothpaste whereas free-flow layouts may be adopted for other parts of the store. The Body Shop has adopted the free-flow layout.

Aspects of atmospherics and store layout

These may affect:

- the speed at which consumers move from one point to another in the store
- the degree of well-being felt by the staff working in the store environment
- the total sales revenue, sales patterns and type of product sold
- the image the consumer has of the store and its merchandise

CONCLUSION

You should now be aware that marketing mix decisions have to be linked to achieving the objectives of the company or organization and should be coupled to acceptability throughout the company. While marketing departments often lead in setting the marketing mix strategy they should not ignore input from others, nor should they fail to check with others that the strategy will be workable from an operational standpoint.

The marketing mix offers the range and spread of alternative strategies by which a retail marketer can influence demand. For any retail marketer, while the available range is very similar the choice is not. The process of mix formulation and balancing is quite often unique to each organization because the way the mix is combined allows the company to provide the augmented product with which it will compete with others. In the competitive retail marketplace, a business can be successful only if its complete marketing mix offer matches what the consumer wants. To be truly successful, the offer has to be as good as – but preferably better than – that of the competition. The marketing mix is planned and co-ordinated by marketers, so the onus is on marketing to control the inputs in such a way that the overall effect maximizes the demand and satisfaction of the consumer.

Product planning allows a retail company to understand and pinpoint marketplace opportunities so that the merchandise range can be co-ordinated to ensure that successful products are maintained and undesirable ones deleted. It allows for an understanding of the complexity of the retail product so that aspects of service and quality are considered as part of the overall retail offer. This section on the retail product is brief as the following chapter (Chapter 6) is devoted solely to the important area of merchandise management. It discusses the different approaches to planning and controlling merchandise in terms of the width and depth issues, the assessment of stock levels and issues in buying.

EXERCISES

The exercises in this section relate to the issues discussed in this chapter. It is suggested that you work through them before moving on to Chapter 6.

1 Go to the high street and select two different types of small-sized stores in order to create a floor plan of their layout. Mark the way the entrance is shaped and types of merchandise that are in different areas of the store. Try to create this to scale. Also, provide some analysis as to the height of different in-store displays. Provide a strengths and weaknesses analysis of your findings.

2 Visit at least two large department stores and note the way the overall marketing mix has been formulated. Do you think the product is well integrated with the in-store promotion, window display, pricing policy, etc.? For example, does the total retail product offer and experience match other visible signs of the marketing mix? Produce a report to the manager on what changes are required to improve the current situation.

3 Create a list of the atmospherics you would expect to find in leading supermarkets. Now visit two different supermarkets and find what additions or subtractions need to be made to your list. Based upon your findings you are required to write a report to a charity shop to offer advice on how to improve the atmospherics of the shop.

4 Choose two retail stores in the high street (such as Boots and The Body Shop). Visit the stores and provide a breakdown of the way the fascia, window display, atmospherics, staff uniforms, packaging and layout create an image and positioning for the company using the following grid as a guide. Also, provide advice on any areas in which improvement could be made.

Visit and make notes at:	Make notes on:
● Boots	Fascia
● The Body Shop	Window display
●	Type of materials used in store display
●	Staff uniforms
●	Atmospherics, etc.
Learnt from study the concepts of:	Practical aspects that any other company could utilize to improve their business?

REFERENCES AND FURTHER READING

Bell, J., Gilbert, D.C. and Lockwood, A. (1997) 'Service quality in food retailing operations: a critical incident analysis', *International Review of Retail, Distribution and Consumer Research*, 7 (4), 405–23.

Betts, E. and McGoldrick, P.J. (1995) 'The strategy of the retail sale, typology, review and synthesis', *International Review of Retail, Distribution and Consumer Research*, 5 (3), 303–32.

Booms, B.H. and Bitner, M.J. (1981) 'Marketing strategies and organization structures for service firms', in Donnelly, J. and George, W.R. (eds) *Marketing of Services*. Chicago, IL: American Marketing Association.

Borden, N.H. (1965) 'The concept of the marketing mix', in Schwartz, G. (ed.) *Science in Marketing*. Chichester: J. Wiley and Sons.

Bowden, D. (1995) 'Problems with delivery delay on-line shopping', *Independent on Sunday*, 4 June, 4.

Britt, S.H. (1975) 'How Weber's Law can be applied to marketing', *Business Horizons*, February, 21–9.

Clifford, L. (2001) 'M&S hopes tills will revive with sound of music', *Financial Times*, 26 July.

Cohen, N. (1998) 'Leisure: the shop as a destination', *Financial Times*, 17 March.

Comer, J.M., Mehta, R. and Holmes, T.L. (1998) 'Information technology: retail users versus nonusers', *Journal of Interactive Marketing*, 12 (2), 49–62.

Compability Report (2001) 'Supermarkets sew up the clothing market', *Retail Week*, 8 June, 14–15.

Davies, G. (1993) 'Is retailing what the dictionaries say it is?', *International Journal of Retail and Distribution Management*, 21 (2), 3–7.

Donovan, R.J. and Rossiter, J.R. (1982) 'Store atmosphere: an environmental psychology approach', *Journal of Retailing*, 58 (1), 34–57.

Gilbert, D.C. (1990) 'European product purchase methods and systems', *Service Industries Journal*, 10 (4), 664–79.

Gilligan, C. and Sutton, C. (1987) 'Strategic planning in grocery and DIY retailing', in Johnson, G. (ed.) *Business Strategy and Retailing*. Chichester: John Wiley.

Institute of Grocery Distribution (1997) *Trends in Grocery Retailing – the market review*. Watford: IGD Business Publications.

Institute of Grocery Distribution (1998) *Grocery Market Bulletin*. Watford: IGD Business Publications.

Kiran, W.K. and Kumar, V. (1995) 'The effect of brand characteristics and retailer policies on response to retail price promotions: implications for retailers', *Journal of Retailing*, 71 (3), 249–78.

Kotler, P., Armstrong, G., Saunders, J. and Wong, V. (1999) *Principles of Marketing*. 2nd European edn. Hemel Hempstead: Prentice Hall.

Kumar, V. and Karande, K. (2000) 'The effect of retail store environment on retailer performance', *Journal of Business Research*, 49 (2), 167–81.

Mattila, A.S. and Wirtz, J. (2001) 'Congruency of scent and music as a driver of in-store evaluations and behavior', *Journal of Retailing*, 77 (2), 273–89.

McCarthy, E.J. (1978) *Basic Marketing: a managerial approach*. 6th edn. Homewood, IL: Richard D. Irwin.

Porter, M.E. (1985) *Competitive Advantage*. New York: The Free Press.

Powell, T.C. and Dent-Micallef, A. (1997) 'Information technology as competitive advantage: the role of human, business, and technology resources', *Strategic Management Journal*, 18 (5), 375–405.

Reichheld, F. and Sasser, W.E. Jr. (1990) 'Zero defections: Quality comes to services', *Harvard Business Review*, 68, September/October, 105–10.

Reid, M. (1995) 'Survey of retailing (2): stores of value – computers are no longer enough. To stay ahead, retailers must use them to innovate', *The Economist*, 334, 4 March, 334.

Rhodes, E. and Carter, R. (1998) 'Electronic commerce technologies and changing product distribution', *International Journal of Technology Management*, 15 (1, 2), 31–48.

Ries, A. and Trout, J. (1981) *Positioning: The Battle for Your Mind*. London: McGraw-Hill.

Sirgy, M.J., Grewal, D. and Mangleburg, T. (2000) 'Retail environment, self congruity and retail patronage: An integrative model and research agenda', *Journal of Business Research*, 49 (2), 127–38.

Spangenberg, E.C., Crowley, A.E. and Henderson, P.W. (1996) 'Improving the store environment: Do olfactory cues affect evaluations and behaviors?' *Journal of Marketing*, 60 (2), 67–80.

Turley, L.W. and Milliman, R. (2000) 'Atmospheric effects on shopping behavior: A review of the experimental evidence', *Journal of Business Research*, 49, 193–211.

Vanderark, S.D. and Ely, D. (1993) 'Cortisal, biochemical, and galvanic skin responses to musical stimuli of different preference value by college students in biology and music', *Perceptual Motor Skills*, 77, 227–34.

Yalch, R.F. and Spangenberg, E. (1990) 'Effects of Store Music on Shopping Behavior', *Journal of Consumer Marketing*, 7 (Spring), 55–63.

Yoo, C., Park, J. and MacInnis, D.J. (1998) 'Effects of store characteristics and in-store emotional experiences on store attitude', *Journal of Business Research*, 47 (3), 253–63.

6 Merchandise management

This chapter should enable you to understand and explain:

- the definition and role of the *retail* merchandiser;
- the development of a merchandise plan;
- category management approaches;
- what is involved in space allocation and range planning;
- inventory turnover control.

The development and implementation of a merchandise plan is one of the most important phases in any retail strategy. This is because the primary objective of any retail organization is to ensure the sale of its merchandise. In order to be successful, retailers must make competent decisions over what is to be bought, in what quantities and at what time. The overall choice of merchandise also presents a clear message to consumers about the type of company they are purchasing from. As such, the selection and presentation of merchandise enables a key source of difference to exist which will allow one store to differentiate itself from another. There is an old adage which states 'goods well bought are half sold'. While true, this masks the fact that merchandise has to reflect the different market segment needs and wants and there is a requirement for a sophisticated approach. This is often related to IT application. As Ody (1998) commented, the retailers of today take 'integration as the name of the game' based upon software and IT. This is related to the need to manage merchandise – with a transparent data flow from the buyer's laptop and digital camera to the 'planogram'. Store layouts are capable of being downloaded to branches with the benefit of a seamless supply chain back-up operation. In addition, the product and demand data from raw materials' supplier to end-consumer is all regarded as part of the total 'enterprise'.

WHAT IS MERCHANDISE MANAGEMENT?

Merchandise management focuses on the planning and controlling of the retailer's inventories. The role has to balance the financial requirements of the company with a strategy for merchandise purchasing. We believe the complex role of merchandise management can be defined as:

> the planning and implementation of the acquisition, handling and monitoring of merchandise categories for an identified retail organization.

The definition stresses a number of key points. As merchandise has to be acquired for future purchase opportunities, forward planning is needed in relation to changing consumption tastes and demand. There is a need for acquisition from either wholesalers or manufacturers and for the merchandise to be handled in an appropriate way to ensure it is able to be sold in perfect condition. As the financial aspects of buying merchandise can be treated as an investment decision, there is the final aspect of monitoring all aspects of the process to ensure adequate returns are achieved.

The complexity of modern retail operations often requires the grouping of the buying process into an individual *category*. This is normally structured to ensure that the buyer can understand different market segments such as those defined by age (infants, children's, youth, etc.) or by gender. In general a category is an assortment of items that the customer would broadly perceive as being substitutes for each other while reflecting the extent of possible variants. For example, a customer may substitute a pair of trousers for jeans but not for a swimsuit. This approach enables a customer-led focus on the assortment profile and the issues of the width and depth, quality and cost-to-price implications. Category management, working with key brands, is a feature of modern retailing. Cobb (1997) explains that at the point of purchase, the shop-in-shop concept, traditionally utilized to promote a single manufacturer or brand, has been developed to improve category differentiation in the grocery multiples. A prime example is at Sainsbury's where Cadbury, in partnership with the supermarket, developed a novelty confectionery section in a Treasure Island children's area. Other developments are the retailer's link with Duracell, to create a battery centre area. As brand leader, Duracell commissioned NDI Display to work with the store group to create a specialist merchandising system.

The phases in developing a merchandise plan are listed in Fig. 6.1. In all marketing-led approaches the consumer will ultimately dictate the strategy options. In Fig. 6.1 there is no exception. (*See* Chapter 10 on marketing planning in order to understand the full complexities of a planning approach.) The customer will have expectations of an assortment profile with issues of choice (width and depth), sizes, quality, exclusivity, availability and cost (as indicated in points 1 and 2 in Fig. 6.1). The consequence of understanding the expectations is for these to be translated into a particular structure for

1 Marketing considerations	Store and image, trading format, environment, retail proposition, fashion trends, customer base, potential buyers
2 Merchandise strategy options	Availability based upon assortment profile and issues of choice (width and depth), quality, exclusivity, seasonality of range, estimated cost, promotional agreement
3 Type of customer base	Items purchased, range purchased, length of season, average transaction value for different lines, frequency of visits and purchases
4 Financial considerations	Profitability and sales performance projections, stock investment and stock return, type of contract and payment terms, corporate objectives and pricing
5 Merchandise assortment search	Ensuring merchandise meets criteria of: required range, comparison, cost, price range offer, brand policy, availability, delivery, stockholding needs, financial returns

Fig. 6.1 Merchandise plan considerations

the buying organization (as indicated by point 3 in Fig. 6.1). If exclusivity is required, then there is a consequent requirement for selective sourcing. If quality is important, a great deal of quality control is necessary as part of the buying procedure. Whatever the approach decided upon, buyers will be expected to source only after extensive research and searching out all the alternatives. The next consideration is a financial one (point 4 in Fig. 6.1): having to meet company profit and market requirements before the merchandise stock is acquired (point 5 in Fig. 6.1). Some of the important merchandise decisions related to this plan are discussed below.

Availability is an important concept. Availability is based upon the need to ensure that the level of stock required meets the demand from the consumer. This requires an appreciation that a higher level of cost is linked to increases in the level of stockholding. The importance of wanting to derive the availability measure is based upon knowing what orders will be satisfied over a specified time span. This is typically a percentage – say 90 per cent of orders will be satisfied. The notion of availability introduces a need to manage the reorder/replenishment cycles on an efficient basis. Of course, high levels of stockholding will require working capital to be tied up. On the other hand, improved stockholding may increase sales due to the rapid flow of merchandise. The balance between these two factors needs to be carefully assessed. In current businesses information systems have had a considerable impact on the whole area of availability. (This is discussed in Chapters 5 and 13.)

The availability performance is linked to *inventory turnover*, which can also be described as merchandise stock-turn. The inventory turnover concept allows us to work out how long inventory is on hand prior to it being sold. Goods with a high turnover will need to be planned differently from those with a low turnover. Retailers can call upon different ways to measure this:

$$\frac{\text{Net sales}}{\text{Average inventory at retail store}}$$

$$\frac{\text{Cost of merchandise sold}}{\text{Average inventory at cost}}$$

$$\frac{\text{Units sold}}{\text{Average inventory at retail store}}$$

The inventory turnover concept allows a store to operate at a more optimal level. As an indicator of the differences which can exist, the National Retail Federation of America (1991) found that the annual inventory turnover level of large department stores varied from 1.5 for home furnishings to 1.7 for footwear, leisure and home electronics, 2.3 for cosmetics and drugs, and 2.9 for female apparel, infants' and children's clothing and accessories.

METHODS OF PLANNING AND CALCULATING INVENTORY LEVELS

Basic stock method of planning inventory

The merchandiser may have to plan to have a basic level of stock derived by the basic stock method (BSM) when it is agreed that there should be a particular level of inventory available at all times. The inventory with BSM will meet sales expectations and also allow for a margin of error. This approach is based on ensuring stock levels are not depleted and customers dissatisfied. It is especially important if sales are higher than expected or if there could be any problem with the shipment and delivery of stocks. However, this method is better suited to a low turnover or when sales may be erratic. It has the advantage that stock can be added to over time rather than all of it being purchased in advance, but this method does not take into consideration stockholding costs.

The level of the beginning of month stock (BOM) for a retailer can be calculated by taking the figures for a season (say 6 months in this case) and working out the BOM as the planned monthly sales plus the basic stock. If this were based upon an inventory turnover of 2 and total sales of £600 000 then the calculations would be made as follows:

Note: Calculations are for a season.

Beginning of month stock (BOM) = Planned monthly sales + Basic stock

where

$$\text{(a) Average stock for season} = \frac{\text{Total planned sales for season}}{\text{Estimated inventory turnover}}$$

and

$$\text{(b) Average monthly sales} = \frac{\text{Total planned sales for season}}{\text{Number of months}}$$

and

$$\text{Basic stock} = \text{(a)} - \text{(b)}$$

which is: (a) = £600 000 ÷ 2 or £300 000
(b) = £600 000 ÷ 6 or £100 000

From this we are able to provide the basic stock calculation as:

£300 000 – £100 000 which is £200 000

The final average basic stock requirement for the season is:

£100 000 + £200 000 = £300 000

This means the retailer may require the following inventory:

Beginning of month @ retail	Basic stock + planned monthly sales
March =	£200 000 + £80 000 = £280 000
April =	£200 000 + £110 000 = £310 000
May =	£200 000 + £105 000 = £305 000
June =	£200 000 + £110 000 = £310 000
July =	£200 000 + £100 000 = £300 000
August =	£200 000 + £95 000 = £295 000

Percentage variation method

An alternative method for determining planned stock levels, especially when turnover is higher than 6 or more annually, is the percentage variation method (PVM). The method is recommended when stock is quite stable since it results in planned monthly inventories that are closer to the monthly average than other techniques. If the retailer faces fluctuations in sales but does not want to ensure that a given level of inventory is available at all times then this approach would be acceptable. The technique assumes the monthly percentage fluctuations from average stock should be half as great as the percentage fluctuations in monthly sales from average sales. This would be calculated as follows:

$$\text{Beginning of month planned inventory level} = \text{Planned average monthly stock for season} \times \frac{1}{2}\left[1 + \left(\frac{\text{Estimated monthly sales}}{\text{Estimated average monthly sales}}\right)\right]$$

Since the PVM utilizes the same basic components as the previous example we can utilize the same data:

Beginning of month @ retail	Average stock for season + planned monthly sales ÷ average monthly sales
March =	£300 000 × 1/2[1 + (£80 000/100 000)] = £270 000
April =	£300 000 × 1/2[1 + (£110 000/100 000)] = £315 000
May =	£300 000 × 1/2[1 + (£105 000/100 000)] = £307 500
June =	£300 000 × 1/2[1 + (£110 000/100 000)] = £315 000
July =	£300 000 × 1/2[1 + (£100 000/100 000)] = £300 000
August =	£300 000 × 1/2[1 + (£95 000/100 000)] = £292 500

The PVM is a better choice when the annual turnover rate is greater than 6 as the results will fluctuate less. Below 6 the BSM method of calculation would be preferred.

Weeks' supply method

The weeks' supply method (WSM) for planning inventory involves forecasting average sales on a weekly rather than a monthly basis. The WSM formula assumes the inventory carried is in direct proportion to sales. It is utilized by retailers that need to plan on a weekly basis, such as supermarkets where sales do not fluctuate by significant amounts. The calculation is based upon a predetermined number of weeks' supply that has to be linked to the stock turnover rate desired. In WSM there is a proportional link between the value of the stock and the forecast of sales. Thus, if forecasted sales double then inventory value will triple. In order to understand WSM the following example can be considered:

$$\text{BOM stock} = \text{Average weekly sales} \times \text{Number of weeks to be stocked}$$

where

$$\text{Average weekly sales} = \frac{\text{Estimated total sales for the period}}{\text{Stock turnover rate for the period}}$$

and

$$\text{Number of weeks to be stocked} = \frac{\text{Number of weeks in the period}}{\text{Stock turnover rate for period}}$$

$$\text{Number of weeks to be stocked} = \frac{26}{2} = 13$$

$$\text{Average weekly sales} = \frac{\pounds 600\,000}{26} = \pounds 23\,076.9$$

$$\text{BOM stock} = \pounds 23\,077 \times 13 = \pounds 300\,000$$

With the number of weeks' supply to be stocked at 13 weeks based upon the average weekly sales of £23 076.9, stocks may need to be checked on a regular basis to ensure that there is no danger of stockouts or a build-up of stock which will increase holding costs. It would therefore be clear that this method requires both stable sales and turnover for it to prove beneficial.

Stock-to-sales method

One other method that can be employed is known as the stock-to-sales method. It is beneficial to utilize such an approach if a retailer wants to maintain a specified ratio of goods on hand to sales. The retailer has to use a beginning of the month stock-to-sales ratio. This ratio informs the retailer as to the amount of inventory required in order to sustain that month's estimated sales. A ratio of 2, for example, would require a retailer to have twice that month's expected sales available in inventory at the beginning of the month. The method is not difficult to calculate. Stock-to-sales ratios can be calculated from a retailer's own historical results or from external sources as long as these are reliable.

All the preceding methods of estimating inventory requirements need to be understood in conjunction with a number of other factors. These are the level of shrinkage, markdowns and employee discounts as these will affect both the financial and availability aspects of the business. These reductions will cause the retail value of the inventory to be lower than it was at the beginning and, therefore, the estimates should be included in the merchandise budget. *Shrinkage* is the difference between the amount of merchandise that is reported on the inventory stock system and what is available for sale or on the shelves. The difference in value could be due to any one of a number of actions: shoplifting, employee theft, vendor over-billing, distributor theft, paperwork errors, and breakage and spoilage. The effect of shrinkage is that the total retail value of the merchandise is reduced. The level of shrinkage may alter by merchandise type or by department and therefore adjustments cannot be made without some detailed understanding of the business. *Markdowns* are a lowering of the prices of the merchandise so that the reduction (markdown) acts as a promotion: for special sales periods or for moving sluggish lines, because of damage or soiling of merchandise, due to end of range offers, or because of greater price competition from competitors or manufacturers who may have made adjustments to their prices. *Employee discounts* are part of planned reductions and offer value to the employee in working at the store. However, these sales should be recorded so that all such discounts are accountable.

MERCHANDISER SKILLS AND PROFILE

The role of merchandiser is pivotal between the pursuit of the strategic objectives of the retailer and operational activity. The merchandiser is responsible for planning and controlling stock ranges and replenishment. Successful execution of the role will require close liaison with, and support for, the retail buyer. Also required is a holistic view of the supply chain and regular interaction with central functions such as management accounting and distribution, through to those operating at store level.

The effective merchandiser will therefore need to be an effective communicator with appropriate interpersonal skills. The nature of the job will specifically require advanced numerical capability supported by PC literacy, notably in the use of spreadsheets and databases. Due to the complexity of merchandise management it follows that the post would also require administrative competence. There are a number of key areas to control which relate to the need for attention to detail in order to ensure the plan is always aligned to operational objectives (*see* Fig. 6.1 and boxes summarizing requirements in the text that follows).

Developing the first stage of the merchandise plan

It requires:

- understanding the target market groups
- agreeing regional and branch sales forecasts
- collecting information on competitors and any new branch plans
- taking into consideration branding and corporate policy
- agreeing merchandise budget
- liaison and initial discussion with buyer(s)

While a brief outline of the function of the merchandiser has been given, it should be noted that the parameters of the job vary widely between retailers. The key common element is the support role to the buyer. It follows that an effective working relationship with the buyer will be vital if the trading objectives are to be delivered on the shop floor. Beyond that, the extent to which the merchandiser is expected to be a reactive number-cruncher or a proactive trader, actively seeking and exploiting opportunities, will vary.

The budgeting process is the key driver as to the role of the merchandiser. Budgeting seeks to quantify in financial terms the objectives of the retailer for a defined period of time. Once this financial plan or master budget has been devised, it can then be used to monitor the performance of the business. Retailers need to buy merchandise that can be set at an acceptable market price and also provide a planned gross margin. There are two values as part of this process: the retail value of sales and the cost value based upon the purchase cost of the merchandise. The merchandiser has an important role to play in both planning and controlling retail activity. In the early stages it will be necessary to analyse market research information and sales trends in order to produce agreed forecasts that can be incorporated into the master budget.

M&S' PERFECT SOLUTION?: Can a clothes range with a back to basics approach spark a Marks & Spencer revival?

Marks & Spencer introduced 60 lines of womenswear, menswear and lingerie when it launched its autumn collection two weeks ago in the hope that the range, called Perfect, will help it halt a three-year free fall. The bastion of the British high street has already tried its emergency parachute – a major brand relaunch a year ago – but it failed to open. And unless M&S can win back its core audience of women over 40, it will continue to spiral downward.

Its most recent quarterly results showed the company's descent is quickening. In the 12 weeks to July 7, M&S suffered a 9.1% year-on-year sales slump in its core business of clothing, footwear and gifts, compared with a 6.5% year-on-year fall in the previous quarter. 'Its market share has continued to fall and it must show that sales are bottoming out,' says Richard Hyman at retail analysts Verdict Research. The Perfect collection is an attempt to return to basics. The company describes the clothes as 'wardrobe essentials, timeless pieces'.

A £3m magazine and newspaper campaign for the range, created by Rainey Kelly Campbell Roalfe/ Y&R, shows models – no longer size 16 – wearing products from a rollneck sweater to jeans against a plain background with the word 'Perfect' emblazoned next to them. The theme is repeated in the new M&S magazine, one million in-store leaflets and a mailing to 1.5 million M&S Chargecard-holders. The campaign will also give a strong nod toward textile innovation, for which M&S is justifiably famous, in ads featuring its machine-washable suits and jeans 'that never lose their shape'.

M&S group marketing director Alan McWalter is brutally frank about the aims of this launch. 'The demise of M&S has been closely associated with adult clothing, and particularly womenswear. Getting it right is crucial. We have to get back to what we know best – aspirational quality at accessible prices.' He realises these claims will be met by media and public scepticism. As one M&S

marketing insider says: 'M&S is now like the Dome. Nobody is interested in writing a positive story' – but McWalter believes the huge amount of work put in by the retailer in the past 12 months is close to bearing fruit. Despite better-performing areas such as food – sales grew 5.9% year-on-year in the quarter – M&S continues to prioritise the recovery of its clothing business.

UK clothes sales still represent £3bn worth of business for M&S, well over 50% of its turnover. It has about 11% of the clothes retail market and this autumn will sell nine million pairs of socks alone. But it desperately needs to win back its niche in the middle-market of quality clothing, particularly womenswear. The Perfect collection forms just part of the recovery plan.

In June, M&S handed over its bra manufacture and promotion to Sara Lee Courtaulds, which subsequently hired *Brookside* and *Celebrity Big Brother* star Claire Sweeney to front the bra range. In October, M&S will unveil a range of clothing aimed at 25- to 35-year-old women called Per Una. It has been designed by George Davies, the entrepreneur behind Next and creator of the successful George kids' clothing collection at Asda. The company is also planning a resurgence in the children's clothing market. Last month it announced that it will enter into a £6m joint venture with long-standing clothing supplier Desmond & Sons. The new company, called the Zip Project, will be 75%-owned by M&S, with £1.5m input from Desmond & Sons. Three years ago, M&S had 9% of the clothing market for 0- to 14-year-olds. It now has 7%.

M&S' fightback comes after years of success-bred complacency, which saw it sit back while its market was eaten away by aggressive, agile retailers such as Gap, Next and Benetton. It must also defend its market share against a renewed onslaught from revived department stores Bhs and Debenhams, as well as the heel-snapping price-led retailers such as Matalan and Primark and the foray made by supermarkets such as Asda and Tesco into clothing.

'In a nutshell M&S history is': Christmas 1998 Disastrous trading figures hit share price. March 1999 New chief executive Peter Salsbury announces recovery plan and appoints James Benfield as marketing director. January 2000 M&S hires Alan McWalter as group marketing director. February 2000 Luc Vandevelde joins as chief executive. March 2000 McWalter unveils new look for

brand and hires Rainey Kelly Campbell Roalfe/Y&R. September 2000 First ever corporate brand advertising in £20m campaign. March 2001 Vandevelde unveils business strategy to focus on UK. April 2001 McWalter restructures marketing department for customer focus. July 2001 M&S launches Simply Food convenience stores. August 2001 Major press ad campaign for M&S foods. September 2001 Launch of the Perfect autumn collection and ad campaign.

Source: Daniel Rogers, *Marketing*, 13 September 2001

The merchandise budget becomes a tool for the financial planning and control of the investment the retailer has had to make in the inventory acquired. The master merchandise budget will be required to offer a gross sales projection, stock level requirements, retail reduction estimates and expected profit margins. Following this, a large part of the merchandiser's function is the disaggregation of this figure into merchandise plans that are able to meet the projected sales. The resultant process has three dimensions: the merchandise range itself, the profile of stores in the group, and variations in sales demand over time.

Managing variations in demand

The merchandiser, as part of the above planning approach, needs to contend with the extent to which demand for product lines fluctuates. This was touched upon earlier in this chapter with the discussion of availability and inventory turnover. There are lines which exhibit remarkably constant levels of turnover, all year around. In such cases, the planning is comparatively straightforward. A good match between the retailer's facility to meet demand and actual turnover will meet customer expectations with the minimum of wasted resources. However, many merchandise categories will exhibit a degree of seasonality.

The merchandiser has to have intimate knowledge of customers and the type of demand for the product being sold. The variations on the category lifestyle whereby some products will sustain demand for longer periods is an important aspect in deciding upon the merchandise plan (*see* Fig. 6.2). For example, a *fad product* will generate a high level of sales owing to a large segment of the population requesting the item. However, the demand will only last for a short time and perhaps not even for the whole season. Hula hoops, yo-yos, Rubik's Cubes, Teletubbies and Batman toys are all examples of this phenomenon. Given that a high number of fad items can be sold in a short time they can, or need to, be sold at substantial mark-ups due to their price insensitive nature and suppliers' price increases based on their decisions to 'cash in' while the fad lasts. Fads are difficult to predict and demand often places a great deal of pressure on distribution chains as demand will always outstrip supply. The only way to deal with a fad is to recognize the signs of its importance as early as possible.

The *fashion product* demand cycle will last for several seasons although sales may vary from season to season. The demand depends on the type of customer and the product

	Fad	Fashion	Staple	Seasonal
Sales over several seasons	No	Yes	Yes	Yes
Sales of a specific style over many seasons	No	No	Yes	Yes
Sales difficult to forecast one season to the next	Yes	Yes	No	Sometimes
Demand curve over time	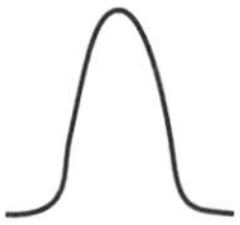			

Fig. 6.2 Merchandise category life-cycle analysis

categories. Men's suits will have a different demand curve to that of teenage clothing. *Staple merchandise* will provide continuous demand over an extended life span. Most food products and household cleaning items are examples of staple products. *Seasonal merchandise* will be characterized by fluctuations in demand according to the time of year. In addition, both the fashion and staple merchandise categories will normally have seasonal variations of demand based upon the season and the weather. The merchandise manager will find the staple category to be the easiest to manage because it offers a reliably repeatable sales history on which to base predictions of planned stock. The inventory system for fads and fashion merchandise requires much more careful appraisal.

CATEGORY MANAGEMENT

It is fairly obvious that selling space is a key resource in retailing given that it will be finite and of specific shape and dimension. For the same reasons that airlines and hoteliers apply yield management techniques to their seats and rooms, retailers seek to optimize the use of selling space, in order to maximize profitability. An important characteristic, as with other services, is that the retail offer is perishable. Unsold merchandise at the end of a trading day represents an opportunity that has been lost for ever. Perhaps other stock lines would have sold? We will never know. An indication of the importance of category management can be found by examination of IGD figures. IGD (2001) have pointed out that 75 per cent of consumer/shopper brand decisions are made in front of the fixture and often within three seconds. Therefore, the category offering has to be managed to maximize sales and profits. This relies on creating ranging and merchandising, pricing, new product introductions and promotions which are based upon the approach to marketing focused upon the consumer, as outlined in this text.

A definition of category management is offered as follows:

> **Category management is related to decisions over groups of products that are selected and placed to satisfy use occasions or consumption patterns. This is based upon strategic retailing principles that attempt to maximize sales and profits and may also include trade partnerships.**

The implication here is that decisions concerning the final assortment, and its display, will have a direct impact on the success of the business. WH Smith is attempting to boost sales of high-tech products. In 2001 the retailer unveiled 'Electronics Zones' in 20 of its UK stores. The zones bring together WH Smith's mobile phone, consumer technology and home entertainment products in one area. Divided into two sections, the zones cover in-the-home and on-the-go product categories. The retailer is attempting to increase sales of mobile phone, consumer technology and its home entertainment products that were previously spread throughout stores.

At the crudest level, profitability is a function of both profit margin and the rate of sale, or rate of stock-turn as retailers would define it, for each individual line stocked. In the case of a single line, there will be a trade-off between the two. The retailer sets a selling price, which in turn sets a profit margin. Customer take-up at that price and margin, as well as the way the customer perceives the category, determines the rate of stock-turn and the gross profit realized. Discount retailers set keen prices with thinner margins in anticipation of relatively high sales volumes. A premium retail offer will command a higher selling price with a healthier gross profit margin, but usually at the subsequent expense of physical sales volume. Either strategy can be effective and can deliver increased profitability.

Reflecting that gross margins are an incomplete measure of operating profitability, retailers have developed techniques to account for the differing cost structures behind product lines. Direct product profitability (DPP) was developed specifically to support space allocation decisions from absorption costing. The argument here is that a more accurate picture of an individual product line's contribution to profitability could be identified by absorbing overheads as part of the calculation. For example, some products are more labour-intensive than others and should therefore bear more of the labour cost. Some lines have higher levels of storage cost by virtue of special temperature requirements or security measures, and should therefore absorb more of these overheads. The resulting DPP for the individual line could then be used to inform merchandising strategy. Such an approach is logical, but compiling such information for an accurate picture carries cost implications of its own and it has limitations. Most significantly, the analysis is concerned with individual lines rather than the product mix in total.

Category management is the current approach to assortment decision-making. It adopts an explicit customer perspective and takes a holistic view of product groups. For a given category of products, the merchandising policy has to meet the range needs of the target customer without unnecessary duplication. Product line proliferation detracts from the operating efficiency of the retail business. Two similar products alongside each other on the shelf are likely to impact on each other's rate of stock-turn. From the retailer's perspective, it may not be worthwhile to be stocking both. In consequence each individual product line has to justify its place in the range in terms of meeting customer needs. However, it should be noted that there is the potential for conflict between retailer and supplier. The primary objective of the supplier will be to ensure that they are successful in getting their own lines onto retail shelves. For the retailer, the issue is whether any lines really add to the offer, or whether a rationalization would make the business more efficient without compromising profitability.

Category management would be relatively straightforward if sales volumes remained constant over time, which of course they do not. For example, retailers need to plan fulfilment for promotions to meet customer expectations efficiently. In the first instance, the promoted line needs to be available. While this is fundamental, it is worth emphasizing. If there is one retail service failure worse than being out of stock, it is to promote an offer heavily and then be out of stock. However, the planning should extend beyond meeting customer expectations of availability to the secondary implications such as the impact on sales of other lines within the category. Effective category management takes a holistic view in planning promotions, with the intention of meeting customer expectations without creating unnecessary inefficiencies in the system. Supported by information systems this practice has become more accurate over time.

Category management is often exercised within a supply chain partnership context. Such partnerships between retailers and key suppliers have emerged in recent years in recognition of the substantial common interests shared by each. After all, they are both serving the same consumer. If we can eliminate cost from the supply chain altogether, then everyone wins. What had been trading relationships characterized by short-term objectives and relatively adversarial dealings have shifted. Partnerships have longer-term perspectives where the trust between retailer and supplier has increased. In such a context, key suppliers are keen to be involved in category management, as it has strengthened their position in what can be seen as a battle over space allocation on the sales floor.

Karonis (1998) indicated that category management is now about creating closer relationships between suppliers and retailers. This is identified to require a multi-disciplinary approach to products that inevitably leads to increasingly complex processes which have to be managed and controlled. Karonis has isolated the challenges facing each component in the traditional retail supply chain as follows:

- *Product development and sourcing*: regional consumer preferences must be identified and products developed or sourced to satisfy these unique needs.
- *Supplier management*: this historically difficult relationship becomes even more complex, as language, cultural, and commercial impediments are introduced.
- *Buying*: negotiating prices based on the true profit contribution is made more difficult by currency fluctuations, extended transportation channels, and commercial practices unique to each culture.
- *Merchandising*: retailers must create the right mix of product to appeal to local needs, and still have rapid response processes in place when the mix must be changed or replenished.
- *Distribution*: this must be more diverse, with typically longer channels to move product from source to consumer. It also needs to accommodate market-specific packaging and environmental needs.
- *Retail operations*: again, there is a need to tailor product presentation and service offerings to each specific market.

RANGE PLANNING

A retailer's stock range can be described in terms of its *width* and *depth*, with the extent of each determined by company policy. This is sometimes termed the *assortment*.

The width will relate to the number of categories that are found in the merchandise line and different generic classes of product or merchandise carried. A wide and narrow stock assortment is normally where there is little choice in brands, styles, etc. within an individual range. Stock-turn could be higher for a broad merchandise assortment, but margins will be slim in order to encourage custom.

The depth relates to the sizes, styles, colours, and prices within a particular generic class of product. There are specialist shops, such as the niche boutiques, which offer a lot of depth but with a narrow product range. We could also compare the typical UK grocery superstore carrying upwards of 20 000 individual lines, with the more restricted 600–1000 lines of the Continental 'hard' discounter. The retail offer of each business is substantially different, with the respective stock ranges of each being an integral part of their strategy. The superstore is seeking to charge a premium price for added value as perceived by the customer. It is important to disguise the premium, and the leading operators are skilled at promoting a limited part of their ranges on a price basis to create this effect. The profitability comes from offering a very extensive range of lines, some with comparatively slow rates of stock-turn, at healthy profit margins. The number of different lines a retailer stocks in store is often referred to as the *variety* of the merchandise mix. Obviously department stores will have many more lines and variety than a store such as Bally or Clarks selling quality footwear. The extent of the range is a key part of the customer's perception of added value. In the case of the hard discounter, the offer is extremely competitively priced – the key concern of the target customer. Profitability stems from achieving a very high rate of stock-turn, and by maintaining management emphasis on keeping costs to a minimum. Product line proliferation would be the undoing of this discount strategy, as it is not what target customers expect and would impact on stock-turn and costs.

In extreme cases, such as toys and lingerie, most of the annual turnover is concentrated in a very few weeks of the year. This represents a significant challenge to the merchandiser in range planning. Treading a course between meeting customer expectations and not wasting resources will not be easy. Stock needs building against an anticipated rise in demand. This will have implications for supply chain management. Distribution networks have limits in terms of capacity. Peak trading will place massive physical demands on the warehousing and transport system and on store staff handling the merchandise.

There are other examples of the central role that range planning plays in retail strategy. Of particular interest is the attempt by some multiple chains to become '*category killers*'; that is, to meet all customer needs within a particular category of merchandise. The 'category killer' is normally a large store that concentrates on one category, thus making it possible for it to carry both a broad assortment and a deep selection of merchandise, coupled with low price and moderate service. A good example of this is the US retail brand, Toys "Я" Us.

Developing the range planning and merchandise allocation plan

It requires:

- understanding the selection process of consumers
- deciding upon core and seasonal merchandise
- agreeing the range – e.g. style, size and colour mix – depth and width
- taking into consideration the sales-to-stock level targets and calculating the optimum level of stock by utilizing one of the stock inventory planning methods
- relating the range plans to individual stores and possible promotional plans
- briefing the buyer(s) on agreed source

The range will need to take into consideration the space constraints imposed upon the merchandise manager. If breadth and depth are important then this requires both stock space as well as display space to separate merchandise. There is also a need to ensure that any move into providing more depth does not affect turnover. To provide more depth the retailer will have to stock more variations of the product for smaller retail segments; this may mean turnover could deteriorate and stock levels would be difficult to control.

Any decision over the range and amount of inventory to stock has to be followed up by the determination of the source. In agreeing the source there should be some consideration of previous sales performance, acceptability of the design or brand name, manufacturing and product quality, reliability of delivery and service, assurance of ability to provide further stock if required, and cost of items. With some high fashion lines, the buyer may want to know who is being supplied and may even specify that the contract will deny their competitors the purchase of a similar range.

In summary, range planning needs to be customer driven. The merchandiser needs to identify which product attributes are most important to the customer and plan accordingly. In under-performing retailers, problems are often most apparent in their ranges as a direct consequence of losing touch with their customer.

The types of depth and width assortment profiles of *narrow and deep*, *square* and *broad and shallow* are more easily understood using a graphic illustration: *see* Fig. 6.3. The main factors that need attention when planning width and depth of assortment are those of estimated sales and profit performance.

Many merchandise lines will be far more successful if given adequate promotional support. Merchandisers will attempt to evaluate the significance of the offer of different types of assistance with the promotion of different items. This can assume many different forms including advertising allowances, co-operative advertising, free display materials, in-store demonstrations or videos, consumer sales inducements – such as special offers, coupon redemptions, free samples, and contests. Also any major advertising carried out by the manufacturer to support the brand, or product, will be an important consideration.

Store grading

Taking a very simplistic approach, store grading can be related to the gross sales forecast. The gross sales projection for the company needs disaggregating across the portfolio of stores. Each store will therefore have its own budgeted gross sales figure. Part of the merchandiser's job will be to see that the merchandise plan for the store will meet the projected target. Rather than produce a unique plan for each store, it is common practice to grade the stores. As shelf or display space is the key yet limited selling medium, this grading is normally conducted on the basis of floor sales area. However, it should be recognized that this must inevitably be a crude device as, depending on the location, there will be smaller stores capable of achieving much higher than average sales densities and larger units with the reverse characteristic. An extreme example of this would be the Marks & Spencer store at Marble Arch or Timberland in Bond Street (both London), where the sales density achieved is uniquely high.

Store grading can be a major source of controversy between store operations management and central merchandise functions. From the perspective of store management,

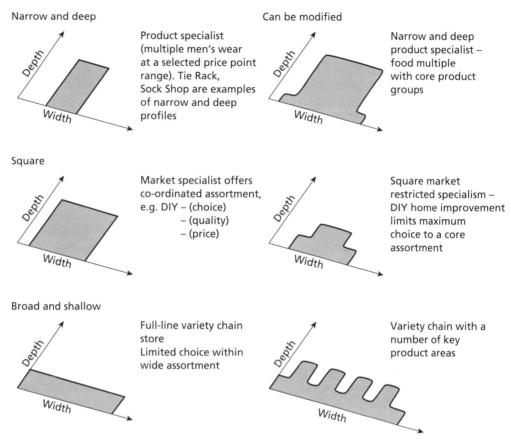

Fig. 6.3 Assortment profiles for differing merchandise strategies

Source: Cook and Walters, 1991

MINICASE 6.2

Tie Rack extends ranges in bid to reposition brand

Niche fashion retailer Tie Rack plans to reinvent itself as a luxury accessories brand, beginning with a review and widening of its product range. The 145-strong chain will expand its womenswear range from mainly silk scarves to include handbags, jewellery and hats. Its tie-focused menswear offer will also be developed to include gloves, plus silk and cashmere goods. A spokeswoman said: 'We define ourselves as being in the fashion accessory business. It was therefore a natural progression to expand the offer to cover the full range.'

The retailer has ruled out branching further into clothing. Instead, Tie Rack aims to become a 'style-conscious accessories house'. The changes are being driven by Tie Rack owner and scarf and tie manu-facturer Frangi, which bought Tie Rack for £22.6 million after the chain saw heavy losses in 1999. Founded in 1981, the chain was hit by competition from mainstream retailers and changes in men's clothing as the dress-down trend took off. The spokeswoman said: 'In re-engineering its core proposition, Tie Rack is evolving with the time. We are moving from a successful 1980s retailer to a style-conscious accessories house catering to the pervasive change in society.'

Price points will remain the same and no store refurbishments are planned for the near future. Despite speculation, Tie Rack's name and branding will be retained.

Source: Rita David, *Retail Week*, 11 May 2001

crude grading may be perceived as yet another example of how head office is out of touch with what is happening at the 'sharp end'. This illustrates the need for effective liaison between stores and the central buying function. This liaison will be an important part of the merchandiser's remit. It will involve making sure that all relevant local characteristics are accommodated in the merchandise planning, while realizing the efficiency benefits that accrue from store grading.

Developing the control mechanisms of the merchandise plan

It requires:

- an understanding of comparative frequency of store visits, based upon the browsing of, or items purchased by, the target market groups
- forecasting sales of range items and profitability
- monitoring stock levels and availability of new stocks and replenishment levels
- assessing value of merchandise through shrinkage, markdowns, employee reductions
- liaising with the buyer(s) to discuss the performance figures
- expanding or reducing merchandise categories, based upon sales performance

---

SPACE ALLOCATION

Beyond the determination of category composition the retailer is faced with decisions concerning space allocation and in-store presentation of the assortment to the customer. The assignment of store space to a category has a twin effect. Firstly it allows for efficient shopping and so attracts customers to the store and, secondly, it will affect the level of sales to these customers once in the store. This is not just for the sought category but also for the alternative categories which offer potential sales. The improved effect on category performance revenue can result from ensuring increased visibility as well as methods aimed at capturing customer attention.

For all retailers such decisions are central to the retail offer. As we note in the section on category management in this chapter, there are yield management approaches that coupled with recent advances in information systems can be used to support space allocation decisions. In essence these seek to establish a relationship between space allocation, sales volumes and, ultimately, profitability. However, there are other constraints which affect the decision, some of a very practical nature, and ultimately the retailer will seek to optimize the layout. There is a need to know:

- Are products easy to locate individually and as part of a basket of goods?
- How long does it take to obtain and purchase a category?
- Is the range broad enough to provide a satisfactory selection?
- Are other retailers offering a superior layout of categories?
- Space allocation and financial performance (margin, profit, activity based costing, loss through waste, damage, shrinkage, etc.).

Multiple retailers have become progressively more sophisticated in their space allocation decision-making and this provides a good example of the trend away from a short-term trading perspective towards longer-term retail brand building. This is perhaps exemplified by the Tesco organization in the UK. The founder of Tesco was a fine example of a very successful trader, an intuitive retailer who had a deep understanding of the grocery business and whose initial philosophy was to 'pile it high, sell it cheap'. From this origin, Tesco has evolved a strong retail brand, supported in part by a consistent in-store presentation.

Beyond the financial emphasis of yield management techniques, space allocation will be driven by competitive strategy and constrained by practical operational and merchandise-related factors. There are clearly differences in the sales generation abilities of store space (positions near the entrance or checkouts, for instance, being more visible and prominent than those in a back corner) but simple rules of thumb are not adequate. To facilitate the stock replenishment process the logic would suggest that proportions of available selling space should reflect market shares, for both inter- and intra-category decisions. This approach will lead to an even 'run-down' of shelf stock, which is easier to manage. However, this overlooks space elasticity. Increasing the space of some categories or product lines will generate a disproportionately high increase in sales. For merchandise with above-average profit margins, this is attractive because the store's gross margin will be pushed upwards. A recent example from the UK grocery sector is the chilled ready meals category. The combination of quality and sheer convenience with this fast food offers tremendous added value to today's time-pressured consumer. Canny retailers have recognized the potential from allocating disproportionate selling space to the chilled ready meals to lever sales and profits. Conversely, some product lines will be relatively unaffected by changes in space allocation. For some commodity items with relatively thin margins there will be the opportunity to reduce selling space without adversely affecting turnover. Such products can be staple lines, which customers expect to find and, significantly in space planning terms, will go looking for.

The use of market shares to determine space allocation is also flawed when it comes to new product launches. One of the objectives that category management seeks to achieve is a smooth new product launch. New products, which by definition have no market share, will always be a potential source of conflict between supplier and retailer. Suppliers know that success is absolutely dependent on retailer support, meaning the allocation of selling space. On the other hand, retailers need to be convinced that taking selling space from established lines to accommodate a newcomer will deliver a net benefit.

Fixture layout

Space planning decisions are supported by dedicated software packages at both fixture and store level. Intuitive expertise still features highly, particularly when the situation demands a radical change or where a high level of novelty is present. According to Davies and Ward (2000) systems to support space allocation and layout decision-making are most advanced at the fixture level. Planograms are maps of the vertical plane of the in-store shelving or units, the view the customer sees. The planogram offers a medium for communicating the display of a range layout to the distributor or acts as a guide to the store. Proprietary software such as ACNielsen's Spaceman is used to devise planograms centrally before dissemination to stores, thus ensuring a consistently merchandised retail offer. These software programs provide a visual representation of the on-shelf merchandise.

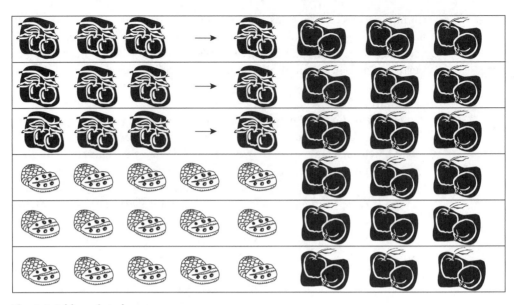

Fig. 6.4 A blueprint planogram

Effective fixture layouts are driven by several considerations. In terms of competitive strategy, the retailer aims to meet the expectations of its target customer. For example, the presentation of simple commodity groups on supermarket shelves is very traditional and perhaps appropriate for a trolley-customer shopping the whole store. However, the time-pressured individual, shopping on the way home from work and looking for a solution to tonight's 'What's-for-dinner?' problem, will not be best served by having to shop the whole store. Shelf layouts will have to accommodate 'logical product adjacencies' or recognize what lines the customer is expecting to find in close proximity. IGD (1998) have indicated that a category strategy document should be provided which contains sections such as Impact of category role on range and space strategies; Consumer specific strategies (e.g. for 'value' or 'healthy' ranges); and Intended range architectures of the stocking holding units based upon differences by store and location. What is required is an analysis of how customers define various category elements and their purchase fit. This requires some mapping research and analysis as to the way shoppers categorize through segmentation and grouping of possible purchases. This can be combined with data analysis of transactions to provide a blueprint planogram that will reflect the optimum allocation of space and position to different merchandise (*see* Fig. 6.4). A blueprint will need to be based upon the dimensions of fixtures and will need to be checked to ensure it meets operational considerations and is able to provide the required financial returns. The blueprint has to consider the physical dimensions of products, packing types, weight(s) of product, and any special requirements. Prior to implementation of the space allocation a planogram can be produced which indicates visually the packaging as a live image of what the final fixture unit will look like.

Temporary shifts in space allocation can be employed as part of promotional strategies. By implication product promotion will stimulate sales and the associated volume increases may place too great a demand on normal shelf capacities. Given the significance of availability in meeting customer expectations of retail service there is a need to co-ordinate space planning with promotional strategies. The use of off-shelf displays will help maintain supply and serve as a promotional element in itself. This will need to be co-ordinated with the inventory management function, as the volume necessary for a promotional display will often exceed standard replenishment levels.

Practical constraints will have a substantial influence over fixture layout. The physical dimensions of the product, the number of items per case and replenishment methods will each have a bearing on efficiency, both operationally and in terms of space utilization.

In-store layout

Space planners have to strike a balance between meeting the expectations of target customers and the pressure to be efficient in their layout of stores. Typically, retailers of fast-moving consumer goods adopt grid-style layouts (see Chapter 5). Grid layouts are extremely efficient in their use of the available selling space, but can convey negative impressions of utility, tediousness and confinement to the customer. Retailers need to plan the space between aisles, around service counters and at entry/exit areas in order to reduce anxiety levels in the customer without unnecessary waste. In retail environments, where purchasing is more discretionary and customers need to be encouraged to be more relaxed and to browse, then a free-flow type of layout will be more appropriate. The in-store layout can be instrumental in creating an ambience that will be conducive to the conversion of browsers into shoppers. For some customers this will be an important added value of the retail offer.

MERCHANDISE ASSORTMENT AND SUPPORT

Having devised the range plan to take account of the nature of the merchandise, the spread of stores in the company portfolio and the variations in demand over time, the role then becomes one of monitoring actual sales performance against the budget. The merchandiser needs to be proactive in seeking out opportunities to maintain and improve the rate of stock-turn. This requires sophisticated analysis of merchandise category performance. If demand exceeds the projected figures, there is the prospect of missed opportunities and disappointed customers. Early warning of this situation may allow some degree of remedial action but, depending on the category, this may be limited. At the very least, the higher than anticipated sales volume will give the buyer greater freedom to increase supply, and, if necessary, from different sources.

The lower than anticipated sales volume of the under-performing category will raise the prospect of markdowns. The merchandiser has a key part to play in the markdown decision-making process. In purely financial terms, retail profitability stems from both the gross margins realized on each product line and from the frequency with which the business is able to turn the product line over, that is the rate of stock-turn. Therefore, in marking down a product line by reducing its selling price, the retailer is accepting a lower gross margin in return for an anticipated increase in the rate of stock-turn. The key point is to recognize that gross margin is only realized when the stock is turned over or sold.

All retailers have to execute markdowns. The merchandiser's skill and expertise is to know when and by how much to mark down in order to achieve the desired effect. Again, this requires careful monitoring of performance and a proactive rather than reactive approach. Given the direct financial implications, strict controls are vital. The markdown policy of the retailer will seek to support positioning strategy. Customer perceptions of reduced merchandise are a key consideration and the public profile of the 'bargain-bin' cannot be allowed to compromise image. So the merchandiser has to strike the balance between stimulating stock-turn with price reductions, and not undermining the perception of added value that the retailer has to preserve in order to command its 'full' price on the remainder of the stock range.

NEGOTIATING THE PURCHASE

When all the different aspects of the merchandise have been assessed and the source has been evaluated and carefully chosen, the retailer has to negotiate the purchase and its terms. This can be carried out through *centralized buying* where co-ordination takes place to achieve scale of purchase discounts based upon full-time buying specialist inputs. However, centralized buying can lack the flexibility of responding to local market needs or ensuring that good communication takes place between the buyers and the store units. *Decentralized buying* may take place at the local level based upon geographic market needs. There has to be some control with this approach as it can lead to inconsistency of the store offer and a loss of economies of scale for purchasing. Some retailers structure the buying function with *specialist buyers* in one or a few merchandise lines and also *generalist buyers* who can buy across a number of lines which need less specialist knowledge. The specialists can become experts in the merchandise areas related to their field and so identify the best suppliers as sources for the company's product offer. The control of quality, cost and delivery are necessary starting points for any discussions.

A new or different type of order will require a *negotiated contract* specifying all aspects of the purchase. Alternatively, where regular orders are already agreed and reorder needs to take place, there will be a *uniform contract* with the standard pre-agreed conditions forming the basis of the agreement. However, the purchase terms should be stipulated whatever the type of contract. These should involve clear documentation of aspects such as delivery date; quantity to be purchased; method of delivery or storage, and who should bear the related charges; price and payment terms, including any discount for level of order or returns allowed by the retailer; advertising or merchandising support from the supplier; the stage in the process as to the title and ownership responsibility; and so on.

CONCLUSION

Merchandise management requires a systematic approach as well as adherence to the concept of marketing. The marketplace is uncompromising when merchandise selection does not reflect consumer tastes and trends. In addition, a company has to ensure that the optimal level of stock is held to improve cash flow and profitability. Merchandise management has to be underpinned by a merchandise plan to ensure the chances of success are maximized. This should be related to: marketing considerations; merchandise strategy options; type of customer base; financial considerations; and merchandise assortment search. The role of merchandiser is central to the pursuit of the strategic objectives of the retailer, and the operational activity surrounding planning and controlling stock ranges and replenishment. Finally, no plan will be able to succeed unless the negotiating and contracting skills of those involved ensure that quality, delivery and cost are acceptable to the consumer.

EXERCISES

The exercises in this section relate to merchandise management. It is advised that you work through them before moving on to Chapter 7.

1 If you had to plan the merchandise stock changes for a food retailer during the Christmas period what would you recommend? What considerations did you make in coming to your conclusions?

2 What checklist of questions would you ask the merchandise manager, to help you make your selections, if you had just been appointed to act as the buyer for children's wear for a leading department store?

3 Discuss the implications of width and depth considerations for a specialist outlet such as a leading women's fashion boutique and compare these to a leading DIY home improvement retailer.

4 You are asked to draw up a list of requirements for the selection of a merchandise manager. With the information in this chapter and from other sources what would you recommend? Use the following grid as a guide.

	Recommended characteristics:
● type of personality ● management skills ● intellectual ability ● experience ● others (list)	

Now identify and discuss a priority list of characteristics you would recommend, including the reasons for inclusion on your list.

5 **Supermarket layout – exercise:**
Supermarket layouts typically follow a grid pattern. This has the advantage of being a very efficient use of space. Customers are 'encouraged' to shop the entire store, travelling the length of every aisle. This behaviour may be true for the weekly family shopping, but many customers will be more selective over their chosen route. As a result the perimeter of the selling area, particularly the first side wall and the back wall, will have the highest volumes of shopper traffic. Identify factors that will help determine the in-store location of the following supermarket product categories and indicate where in a grid layout they should be located:

Wines & spirits; Pet foods; Fresh foods; Paper goods / Tissues & towels; Confectionery; Frozen foods; Fresh milk; Household / cleaning; Clothing

REFERENCES AND FURTHER READING

Boyle, K.B. (1987) *Direct Product Profit – A Primer*. Food Marketing Institute Research Dept., USA.

Branigan, L. (1998) 'The Internet: the emerging premier direct marketing channel', *Direct Marketing*, 61 (1), 46–8.

Cash, R.P., Wingate, J.W. and Friedlander, J.S. (1995) *Management of Retail Buying*. London: John Wiley.

Christopher, M. (1992) *Logistics and Supply Chain Management – Strategies for Reducing Costs and Improving Services*. London: Pitman Publishing.

Cobb, R. (1997) 'Space exploration', *Marketing*, 17 July, 29–32.

Cook, D. and Walters, D. (1991) *Retail Marketing: theory and practice*. Englewood Cliffs, NJ: Prentice Hall.

Corstjens, J. and Corstjens, M. (1995) *Store Wars*. Chichester: J. Wiley.

Cox, R. and Brittain, P. (1993) *Retail Management*. London: Pitman Publishing.

David, R. (2001) 'Tie Rack extends ranges in bid to reposition brand', *Retail Week*, 11 May, 3.

Davies, B.J. and Ward, P. (2000) *Grocery Space Allocation: The Executive Viewpoint*, Contemporary Issues in Retail Marketing Conference, 8 September, Manchester.

Davies, G. (1993) *Trade Marketing Strategy*. London: Paul Chapman.

Harris, D. and Walters, D. (1992) *Retail Operations Management – A Strategic Approach*. Englewood Cliffs, NJ: Prentice Hall.

Hill, T. (1991) *Production Operations Management Text and Cases*. 2nd edn. Englewood Cliffs, NJ: Prentice Hall.

IGD (Institute of Grocery Distribution) (1998) *ECR Range Selection and Merchandising Process*. Letchmore: IGD Business Publications.

Johnson, M. and Pinnington, D. (1998) 'Supporting the category management challenge: how research can contribute', *Journal of the Market Research Society*, 40 (1), 33–54.

Karonis, J. (1998) 'The supply chain: small needs, big solutions', *Financial Times*, 17 March.

Lewison, D. (1994) *Retailing*. 5th edn. New York: MacMillan College Publishing Company.

Lucas, G., Bush, R. and Gresham, L. (1994) *Retailing*. Boston, MA: Houghton Mifflin Co.

MacDonald, M. and Tideman, C. (1993) *Retail Marketing Plans*. Oxford: Butterworth-Heinemann.

Martin, C. and Parfett, M.C. (1992) *What Is EDI? A guide to electronic data interchange*. 2nd edn. Oxford: Butterworth.

Mulhern, F.J. (1997) 'Retail marketing: from distribution to integration', *International Journal of Research in Marketing*, 14 (2), 103–24.

National Retail Federation of America (1991) *Merchandising and Operating Results of Department and Speciality Stores in 1990*. New York: Financial Executives Division, National Retail Federation of America.

Ody, P. (1998) 'A transformation in retailing: information technology is helping to transform retailers', *Financial Times*, 3 June.

Porter, M. (1985) *Competitive Advantage – Creating and Sustaining Superior Performance*. New York, London: The Free Press.

Risch, E.H. (1991) *Retail Merchandising*. New York: Macmillan.

Rogers, D. (1998) 'Barclays offers on-screen links', *Marketing*, 21 May, 2.

Rogers, D. (2001) 'M&S' PERFECT SOLUTION?: Can a clothes range with a back to basics approach spark a Marks & Spencer revival?', *Marketing*, 13 September.

Senn, J.A. (1995) *Information Technology in Business*. Englewood Cliffs, NJ: Prentice Hall.

Shipp, R.D. (1985) *Retail Merchandising*. 2nd edn. Boston, MA: Houghton Mifflin Co.

Smith-Bohlinger, M. (1993) *Merchandise Buying*. Needham Heights, MA: Allyn & Bacon.

7 Retail pricing

This chapter should enable you to understand and explain:

- the concept and meaning of price and price sensitivity in retailing;
- methods used in the pricing of the retail product;
- the price and value comparison;
- approaches to markdown policies.

The pricing policy selected by a retailer will usually be directly related to the resultant level of demand over a period of time and, with the right margins, to the profitability of the enterprise. For the retailer, pricing decisions are critical because without adequate margins the business will not survive for long. As a business, the retailer has to seek cash flow, profitability and growth in order to improve their market position. The importance of selecting the right strategy is growing as battles among retailers to increase market share are fought on the basis of offering quality, selection and availability at competitive prices. To be successful, retailers are having to forge partnerships with manufacturers and introduce technology in order to gain cost advantage without compromising quality. Given this situation it is not surprising that cost, margin and price comprise the most important elements of the marketing mix for most retailers. This is especially the case given the existence of discount store formats, the entrance of Continental discounters and cheap sources of supply. For others, such as convenience stores, price is still important even if it is secondary to the benefits of location and the opening hours for trading. The current situation is that in the competitive retail marketplace, price is a major strategic weapon in the battle with the competition.

UNDERSTANDING PRICE AS A CONCEPT

Price may be usefully described as follows:

> Price is the monetary value assigned by the seller to something purchased, sold or offered for sale, and on transaction by a buyer, as their willingness to pay for the benefits the product and channel service delivers.

This definition clearly separates the way the retailer treats pricing – as a cash flow or income generating function – from the view of the customer, who sees price as more than money. The purchase for the customer includes the complexity of emotional and functional benefits derived from the product and the brand. This means that value for the customer is a complex set of perceptions. This is discussed in more detail later in this chapter.

We believe that of all the elements of the marketing mix, good pricing decisions are the hardest to make. This is because prices for retail products and channel services have to take into account the complexity created by seasonality of demand and the inherent perishability of the product due to factors related to fashion or being past the sell-by date. There has also been a major influence on the grocery sector by the abolition of resale price maintenance (RPM). This in turn has led to the offer of loss leaders and more complex pricing policies, in order to achieve optimal overall profit. In conjunction with this, consumers are now pressurizing retailers to change their pricing policies to offer greater value for money.

A retailer's pricing policy must be consistent with the overall objectives and reputation of the business. This could be in financial terms such as sales, profits, return on investment, etc. or as pricing's role in the growth and expansion of the business. There may also be broader objectives such as the number of sales periods, total number and range of prices to be made available and positioning of the store and merchandise in relation to prices. These pricing goals are important as they provide the consumer with an image of the retail outlet based upon its approach to pricing. In addition, pricing has to be integrated with other aspects of the marketing mix and take account of the target market.

According to research carried out by Datamonitor (1996) the pricing initiatives of the major multiples create distinct differences which pass on specific images of the company brand. ASDA's catalogue and price promotions have reaffirmed the company's position as the most 'value led' multiple and this can lead to long-term loyalty. Tesco's and Safeway's promotions have not only led to loyalty but also created a full-scale customer database. On the other hand, Sainsbury's price promotions are mainly used as an aid to stores facing local competition.

PRICE SENSITIVITY

The understanding of the way different price points affect demand or how demand operates between price points is an important consideration for the setting of retail price policy. Within retailing there are also major differences between market segments, such as youth markets and upper income groups, whose tastes may dramatically change from one period to another. Quite often the relative elasticities of demand for these segments is dissimilar. There is a range of different factors that affect price sensitivity which deserves discussion. First, however, we need to understand the demand curves which illustrate the different market reactions to price change, known as elastic and inelastic demand (*see* Fig. 7.1).

Elasticity is a key element in the understanding of the demand process. It is defined as the ratio of the percentage response in the quantity sold to a percentage change in price or one of the other marketing mix elements, such as the expenditure on advertising. It therefore measures the sensitivity in quantity demanded to a change in the demand determinant. Mathematically, elasticity can be calculated as follows:

$$\text{Elasticity} = \frac{\text{Percentage change in quantity demanded}}{\text{Percentage change in any demand determinant}}$$

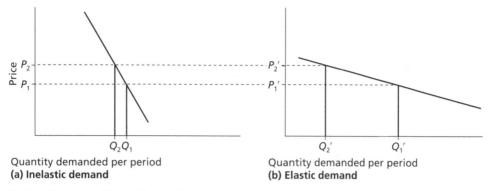

Quantity demanded per period
(a) Inelastic demand

Quantity demanded per period
(b) Elastic demand

Fig. 7.1 Price elasticity of demand

For price elasticity the denominator is simply changed to a percentage change in price. The coefficient of price elasticity is nearly always negative because the price and quantity are inversely related. This means that when the price falls, the quantity demanded tends to rise; and when the price rises, demand tends to fall. Thus the retailer would be interested in the size of the coefficient as a coefficient of more than one indicates that demand is elastic (if price rises, demand falls significantly) and less than one that it is inelastic (if price rises, demand falls but only slightly).

From this it follows that the mark-up on highly competitive merchandise tends to be low because the demand for such items is price elastic. In general, retail mark-ups should vary inversely with price elasticity of demand if profits are to be maximized.

Factors affecting price sensitivity

A number of factors will affect the price sensitivity of products. From a marketing viewpoint a deeper understanding of price sensitivity assists with an understanding of the different retail segments and the development of strategic planning. The main factors when considering retail pricing are listed below.

Perceived substitutes effect

Buyers are more sensitive the higher the product's price is in relation to another product or substitute they could purchase. Therefore, the consumer may choose a substitute or forgo the purchase if they believe the overall value is unacceptable. For example, local residents may avoid an area with higher priced shops frequented by tourists who are unaware of the alternatives.

Unique value effect

Buyers are less sensitive to a product's price the more they value any of its attributes that differentiate it from competing products. For example, many customers are loyal to Heinz or Nestlé products because they perceive them to offer superior benefits.

Importance of purchase effect

If the risk of the purchase increases then the price will not be the most important aspect of the purchase. This occurs when the item is an important present or when there is a need to purchase medicines. The greater the importance of the product, the less price sensitive (more inelastic) the purchase will be.

Difficult comparison effect

Buyers are less sensitive to price when they find it more difficult to compare alternatives. This may lead to a demand for the more established brands, or greater store loyalty, in order to reduce the perception of risk.

Price quality effect

A higher price may signal that the product is of superior quality. The result may be less sensitivity to price. This is not a conclusive effect as it applies to some products, while others may generate different reactions. For example, whisky at a higher price may signal improved quality but very few people would think higher priced petrol offered any quality advantage.

Expenditure effect

Buyers become more price sensitive when the expenditure is larger, either in absolute money amounts or as a percentage of their income. This is most prevalent in low income households in which all expenditure is carefully controlled. This effect is also stronger and more likely to occur in times of recession.

Fairness and transparency effect

If the buyer believes the price falls outside a band of what would be judged reasonable and fair then they become more price sensitive. With some types of products it is relatively easy to judge the offer of alternative brands and products and therefore easy to switch demand to cheaper alternatives. At certain times alternatives are not easy to find. Consumers will perceive retailers, or the brands they stock, to be 'ripping-off' customers if they exploit situations of shortage by being greedy. For example, street vendors are often seen to be selling drinks or ice creams at highly inflated prices when the temperature is extremely high.

> **MINICASE 7.1**
>
> # Reduced prices based upon the 'grey market'
>
> They claim they are waging a war against artificially high prices. But when supermarket chains advertise designer products at reduced prices – against the wishes of the brand's owner – they are sending out subtle messages about their core business. 'The implication is that everything else you buy in the store is sold at competitive prices,' says a supermarket executive, who co-ordinates purchases on the 'grey market', where stores obtain brand-name goods. Food retailers are increasingly waking up to the promotional advantages of using this market. Asda reinforces its low-price image by selling fine fragrances at up to 50 per cent less than department stores and claims to be a leading campaigner for consumer interests as a result. Recently, Tesco said it had gone to 'extreme lengths' to find Ralph Lauren shirts and T-shirts to sell at less than half price. Both stress they cannot

promise a consistent supply of such products, since up-market brand owners refuse to distribute to mass-market food retailers. 'It is difficult for a retailer to get a clear idea of how the grey market works,' says a large chain, 'because traders keep their sources close to their chests.' The market's secrecy makes it difficult for anyone to gauge the size of the grey economy. Tesco estimates last year it sold about £20m of grey market products.

Source: Peggy Hollinger, *Financial Times*, 1998

Update from Chris Tighe, *Financial Times*, 12 April 2001: Asda to use 'grey market'
Asda plans to source more 'grey market' goods, and has this week put on sale its biggest range yet of cut-price designer sunglasses.

The retailer said the sunglasses were ordered before last Thursday's landmark European Court opinion on cheap imported brand-name goods. However, it said the ruling was encouraging, and the timing of its launch of a big designer sunglasses range was not a coincidence. 'We will be looking to source further items within the grey market; it's all about giving the consumer the best value we can,' said the supermarket chain. Last week, in a legal opinion triggered by Tesco's sale of Levi's jeans at cut prices, the European Court said in an initial ruling that primary responsibility for deciding whether makers could block cheap imports lay with domestic courts. However, the complex opinion, which led both Tesco and Levi to claim victory, was not a final ruling.

The choice process of the consumer based upon price is quite a complex matter and each of the effects discussed above may be working in conjunction with each other. While price may be an indicator of quality, the consumer is capable of choosing between several offers. The consumer is able to judge the materials used in the manufacture of the product, the brand name and reputation, and after-sales service guarantees. On the other hand, the consumer may be ignorant of such factors and therefore will rely on a trusted retailer or brand.

Price transparency is a concept which is often used given the growth of e-commerce. Price transparency refers to the ability of a consumer (whether at the wholesale or retail level) to have knowledge of the prices of a given good or service which may apply for a variety of outlets. Until recently the differences in retail prices – based upon such cost factors as distribution and margin applied – have not been transparent. This is because of the lack of information, distance to alternative shopping locations, etc., all of which have hampered the ability of the consumer to engage in widespread comparison shopping. The advent of increasing use of the Internet has given consumers the ability to price-shop by means of the click of a mouse. Therefore, retail pricing policy has to respond to price transparency as the knowledge of the customer is now far better as to where to acquire value for money.

FURTHER FACTORS INFLUENCING PRICING

Price sensitivity is only one of the factors which a retailer has to consider in their approach to pricing. A retail company in formulating price policy decisions has to consider a range of influences, including the following aspects:

1   The perishable nature of some products, such as high fashion items or those with 'sell-by' dates, is influential. Products which cannot be sold on a future occasion lead retailers to engage in various forms of last-minute tactical pricing or seasonal sales.

2 The competitive nature of the industry places emphasis on setting prices at competitive levels or retailers could face losing sales.

3 The market is volatile due to:

- short-run fluctuations in international costs;
- the need to stock saleable items;
- problems of supply;
- shrinkage rates;
- the need for an adequate return for each square metre of floor space or page in a catalogue.

This requires sophisticated forward planning.

4 Cost control is an important part of pricing policy. Many retail enterprises have high fixed costs and yet need to set competitive prices. This can make them vulnerable to financial collapse or takeover if costs are not controlled.

5 Seasonal demand leads to peak and low season periods which require demand management pricing to cope with the need to shift old stock or improve cash flow situations.

6 Price is associated with the psychological aspects of both quality and status. It is therefore always important to gauge the way prices or their change will be perceived by different target segments.

7 Intermediaries may influence prices through changes in costs of supply, bank charges and interest rate changes, increases in wages because of national minimum wage rates, etc.

8 Pricing also has to take into account the legislation that affects the way prices are displayed. For example, from March 2000 the retailer has been required to display the unit price of certain products which are sold by volume (i.e. price per 100ml, 100g, etc.) in addition to the selling price. This affects window displays, price tags and communication via POS as these will require unit pricing calculations of products sold by volume in addition to any other price information.

APPROACHES TO PRICING THE RETAIL PRODUCT

Pricing policy has to consider all the potential influences and factors affecting the market and therefore the scope facing the retailer is remarkably wide. The choice made will probably be one, or a combination, of the following. The major difference is between the *cost-oriented* and *demand-oriented* approach to pricing.

Cost-oriented pricing

Cost-oriented pricing is related to the costs a retailer incurs when purchasing a product or service for sale to their customers. Cost-oriented pricing refers to setting prices on the basis of an understanding of costs to the retailer.

Cost-plus pricing

For the cost-plus method this will be in relation to either marginal costs or total costs including overheads.

The approach could be to:

- select the target market;
- determine the cost of the goods in store – storage costs, selling costs, shrinkage estimates, overheads, etc.;
- determine the ceiling price above which the retailer would be offering expensive prices compared with those of competitors;
- apply the mark-up, given that the possible range has been identified in order to achieve profit objectives. There may be some discretion for pricing individual items within a department or section as it is the overall profit which is important. A percentage mark-up is then normally applied to reach the final selling price. This may be expressed as a percentage of cost or of selling price. It should cover operating expenses and provide the desired level of profit. For example, if we assume a retailer purchases a dress at £60 and prices it at £90 then the mark-up on cost (£30/£60) expressed as a percentage is 50 per cent and the mark-up on selling price (£30/£90) is 33.3 per cent. Some minor adjustments may take place, such as bringing the price to £89.95 – fine-tuning the final price for psychological and other reasons.

Knowing the cost breakdown of the product is extremely important and it is essential to have calculated the operating cost of each retail outlet or page in a catalogue. This allows the marketer to know what the net effect of any tactical price reduction will be.

The weakness of cost-oriented pricing as a method is that it does not give adequate consideration to demand for the product, what prices the marketplace will bear, or the different price levels of the competitors.

Rate-of-return pricing

Another cost-oriented method is that of rate-of-return pricing which provides the company with an agreed rate of return on its investment. Whereas the cost-plus method concentrates on the costs associated with the running of the business, the rate-of-return method concentrates on the profits generated in relation to the capital invested. This approach ignores the need to link the pricing policy to the creation of a sales volume which is large enough to cover overheads or to ensure that demand will remain consistent over time. Cost-plus or rate-of-return methods of pricing are not appropriate for those retail products which have to survive in a highly competitive marketplace.

Demand-oriented pricing

Demand-oriented pricing takes into consideration the factors of demand rather than the level of costs when setting price. In times of shortage of products – from candles at the time of power cuts, to vegetables out of season – prices are usually raised to take advantage of higher demand and scarcity of supply.

Discrimination pricing

Discrimination pricing, which is sometimes called *variable* or *flexible pricing*, is often used when products are sold at two or more different prices. Quite often students, the unwaged and older people are charged lower prices than other consumer segments at attractions or events. A garage will offer different prices for servicing company cars as opposed to private cars. A customer known to a retailer may be given a personal discount as part of a flexible approach to pricing based upon a personal relationship with that individual. Discrimination pricing is often time related, for example cheaper drinks charges in 'happy hour' periods or cheaper meal prices in the early evening prior to the high demand periods. For price discrimination to be successful it is necessary to be able to identify those segments which, without the price differentials, would not purchase the product. To obtain a high flow of business, a DIY retailer will often discount to those customers who offer significant sales demand. This means that small businesses may benefit from volume discount rates and those individual customers building their own extension, for instance, may be offered a special one-off discount rate.

Discrimination may also be based upon increasing the price of products which have higher potential demand. For example, if the product is a fad product (for further explanation *see* Chapter 6) then it is normally in high demand; usually demand is so strong that it outstrips supply. Therefore, such products as Pokémon or Teletubbies dolls could be set at a higher price based upon an increasing level of demand. Another example of this is exhibited on special celebration dates, such as Mother's Day or Valentine's Day, when the price of flowers or plants is raised.

Backward pricing

This is a market-based method of pricing which focuses on what the consumer is willing to pay. The price is worked backwards, as the name suggests. First an acceptable margin is agreed upon. Next the costs are closely monitored so that the price which is deemed to be acceptable is able to be matched. If necessary an adjustment is made to the quality of the product offer or service to meet the cost-led needs of this technique. Retailers selling on a price-led basis often insist that their suppliers meet specified costs, even if this compromises some aspects of the quality.

This approach can be associated with *price lining*. Price lining is a method of simplifying the merchandise comparisons for the customer by establishing a number of lines within price points for each classification. Once the price lines have been determined, the retailers purchase goods which fit into each line. For example, for men's shirts the price lines could be £25, £35 and £45. In order to be a successful trader the monetary difference between the price lines has to be large enough to reflect a value difference for the consumer. Such steps of change in price and value enhance the ability of the salesperson to convince the customer to trade either up or down. The selection of price lines has to be based upon the strength of consumer demand for the bands. The benefit of limiting the number of price lines is that a retailer can achieve broader assortments, which leads to increased sales and fewer markdowns. For example, a retailer which stocks 180 units of an item and has 6 price lines would have an assortment of only 30 units in each line. On the other hand, if the units were divided among only three price lines there would be 60 units in each line. By utilizing such an approach a retailer may specialize more easily in relation to lines and so create a more defined store image for its merchandise. The advantages of price lining are:

- sales volume can be increased by the provision of larger assortments at each price line;
- there is greater clarity of price offer for the customers;

- salespeople can offer stepwise change to the customer to convince them to trade up or down;
- line concentration allows for improved displays and promotional messages;
- with improved effectiveness of pricing there may be fewer markdowns;
- the buying process is improved as buyers have to focus on the retail price point and 'buy backwards';
- control may be easier with greater price co-ordination and fewer pricing variables.

Skimming pricing

Skimming is utilized when there is a shortage of supply of the product or the brand has been associated with added value and, therefore, demand will not be dampened by charging a premium price. Market skimming policies can only occur where there is a healthy potential demand for the product on offer. Top fashion houses dealing in haute couture or cosmetics companies with strong branding utilize this approach.

Leader pricing

Some retail items may be priced very competitively so as to sacrifice profit on specific items in order to generate more overall demand for other items. These are often known as 'loss leaders' if they are sold below cost but in reality retailers seldom make a cash loss on the items even though they are heavily discounted. The leader items are normally sold near to cost rather than at a loss. However, a supermarket may sell turkeys as loss leaders at Christmas in order to achieve extra sales of other Christmas holiday provisions. The purpose behind the use of leader prices is to increase store visits, purchases and the perception of good value.

The items chosen for inclusion as loss leaders should be widely known and bought on a frequent basis. The objective would be to price the item low enough to attract numerous buyers. In addition, if information is made available as to the value of the offer, the promotion will usually be far more successful. The approach is often employed by supermarkets which feature leader items on a regular basis. As with all forms of price promotion, there is an obvious need for retailers to monitor and evaluate their usefulness. In offering leader pricing, the danger is that customers may be selective in what they purchase. If customers are limiting their purchase to the lead item or if that item competes with other items in the store, the price promotion may need to be revised.

Competitive pricing

Competitive pricing is employed to match the market prices of competitive retailers. This is a technique which requires knowledge of actual costs as matching the prices of a more efficient retailer may lead to losses on particular items. It also requires an understanding of the importance of the pricing policies of the competition from a consumer's perspective. Competitive pricing is a reactive rather than proactive form of pricing as a retailer with a strong brand image does not necessarily need to match competitors' offers.

Market penetration pricing

Market penetration pricing is similar to competitive pricing but is adopted when a company or brand wants to establish itself quickly in a market. Prices are set below those of the competition in order to create high initial acceptance for the company's retail offer. A company selling fast-moving consumer goods (FMCGs) may use market penetration pricing in the first couple of years and then, when the product becomes established, will slowly increase the prices. In 1996 there was all-out war between the food retailers and major oil companies over the price of petrol, based upon various supermarkets trying to obtain a major market share. It is estimated that the petrol price war of 1996 cost Tesco £30 million and 2000 independent companies were forced out of business. According to an article in *SuperMarketing* (1996), at the height of the price war the average gross profits were only 0.03p a litre and these rose to 5.5p a litre when the war subsided in July of the same year. The penetration strategy quickly established a 21.5 per cent share of the petrol market in the UK for the combined supermarkets.

Psychological pricing

This is sometimes referred to as *odd pricing*. Retailers will often price products below a round figure, changing a price from say £10 to £9.95 or £9.99 to foster the perception of the price as being below that at which the customer is willing to buy. Just as £9.95 may appear to be significantly less than £10, so a price of £488 may seem more on a £400 level than a £500 level. However, there is no conclusive evidence that such pricing policies make any significant difference to profits.

Everyday low pricing

A number of retailers now adopt the strategy of everyday low pricing (EDLP). This strategy stresses the use of a pricing policy with the continuity of prices at a level between the normal own store price and the price of the deep discount competitors. The term 'low' does not mean 'lowest'; it simply refers to a price position which is competitive and, therefore, can remain stable. A number of retailers who operate EDLP do not believe in markdown policies and sales but attempt to generate all-year-round demand by setting the prices at the right level. One of the most well-known retailers to have adopted this strategy is Toys "Я" Us. EDLP is a strategy which is open to large operators who have significant economies of scale and buying power.

EDLP can offer a number of benefits, as the following list attests:

1 *Perception of fairness*. Many customers have become increasingly sceptical about the mark-up and markdown strategies of retailers. There has been a trend by consumers to wait for sale periods or to attempt to get the best bargains by shopping around for promotions. EDLP allows retailers to withdraw from sale period pricing wars and to concentrate on creating a market position that imparts a perception of fairness of pricing.

2 *Reduced advertising*. The stable price policy of EDLPs eliminates the need for communication of sale or special price offers. Instead, the retailer can use the budget to concentrate on improvement of image or the building of relationship marketing schemes.

3 *Improved customer service management*. If the policy is set to banish sale periods then the demand created is less seasonal and volatile, and sales staff are able to spend adequate time in dealing with customers. This will improve the customer's perception of the level of service they receive. The lack of high demand sale periods also has the benefit of allowing staff levels to remain relatively constant.

4 *Reduced stockouts and improved inventory management.* With more even demand for the products it is easier to control the stock situation. EDLP reduces the large variations in demand and, therefore, periods of stockout when customers may feel dissatisfaction with the retailer's service.

5 *Increased profit margins.* If a retailer can impart to the customer an image of fair pricing then, although the prices may be generally lower, the overall effect can be to increase turnover and consequently profitability.

EDLP has some major benefits to recommend it; however, it would not be appropriate for all retailers. Some retailers would find it difficult to maintain low prices for a continuous period because of a lack of economies of scale in buying or the competitive nature of their business. Also, retailers selling goods which have a strong fashion content are more likely to want to set initial prices at a high level as this is good business practice. Fashion goods are often priced differently because if a subsequent sale is created for this type of merchandise, it often creates a high level of excitement. The motivation to purchase created from the sale enables the retailer to move a large amount of merchandise in a short period. Therefore, adoption of EDLP is not a sensible strategy for all types of retailers.

In order to be clear, the differences are that an EDLP store can be treated as being positioned at one end of the continuum and a store which offers promotional pricing, sometimes known as the HILO store, is at the other. The category management policy of these approaches differs. For example, the EDLP store will often stock a large number of items but based upon a smaller selection of brands and large format. Technically, we can generalize the EDLP stores as having a low fixed utility (less assortment, being less convenient) but offering a high variable utility (lower prices). 'Fixed utility' refers to costs and benefits that are essentially independent of the specific items purchased on a shopping trip, while 'variable utility' refers to factors that change according to which items are purchased. EDLP is more likely to appeal to the cost-conscious customer while the HILO format offers a high fixed utility. The HILO benefit is based upon a convenient format, high quality service and good assortment of products. However, it is more likely to offer a low variable utility because these stores tend to have higher prices. In contrast to the EDLP store, the position of the HILO store is one where competition revolves around better service and assortment for which higher prices are charged.

PRICING AND THE RELATIONSHIP TO VALUE

Whatever pricing policy is adopted, a company has to take into consideration the potential consumer's perceptual assessment. In deciding to buy a product a consumer has to be willing to give up something in order to enjoy the satisfactions of the benefits the product will deliver. This concept is more complex than it seems. The majority of consumers are looking for value when they buy a product and value is derived from the functions of quality and price, as well as the added value of the image or brand. This may be expressed as:

$$\text{Value} = \frac{\text{Quality}}{\text{Price}} + \text{Image}$$

If a consumer believes the image and quality of a product is good they will be willing to make greater sacrifices in order to purchase that product. This explains how first-class travel continues to be successful on different forms of transport such as trains, aircraft and cruise ships, and why leading brands are able to attract higher prices. The interrelationship between price, quality and value plays a significant role in store patronage and the buying behaviour of customers. Value was grouped into four categories by Zeithaml (1988). These are:

- value as low price;
- value as whatever is wanted from a product;
- value as the quality one gets for the price paid;
- value as what one gets for what one gives.

Zeithaml describes value as a 'trade-off between salient benefit components and sacrifice components'. Benefit components according to Zeithaml include intrinsic attributes, extrinsic attributes, perceived quality and other relevant high abstractions. This means value is a judgement about superiority and benefits delivered. Therefore, having the lowest price is not a sufficient strategy as the best route to retail marketplace success.

If prices change, this can affect the consumers' quality perception. A price reduction may be associated with a belief that the company is in financial trouble, that it will have to cut service and quality, or that prices are falling and if one waits, a price will come down even more. The value of the product is thought to have decreased because quality, by association with the changes, is observed to have fallen by a greater ratio than prices. The following shows the perception that the new value is at only half the level of its former position:

$$\text{Value} = \frac{\text{Quality}}{\text{Price}} \text{ then if } V = \frac{Q/2x}{P/x} \text{ then } 1/2 \ V = \frac{Q}{P}$$

The above relationship indicates that the quality of the merchandise or service is perceived to drop by half its former position while price remains the same. With the assumption that this is the same factor of x then value as judged by the consumer drops to half its former value. This indicates the importance of not dealing with price in isolation from other factors.

Alternatively, a price increase may be interpreted as the way the company is going to pay to improve the quality and service of the retail offer. However, some consumers may simply think that the company is being greedy and that quality has not improved. This means the consumer may judge the value to have fallen. The outcome quite often depends on how the retailer explains the increase in price to the consumer.

To ensure the maximum chance of success for the pricing policy adopted there is a need to check each stage of the procedure, as in Fig. 7.2. This figure identifies the important considerations required for the successful evolution of a pricing policy.

Other costs and therefore pricing implications

There are other costs which a retailer needs to bear in mind when attempting to judge how competitive the store product price may be. These can be based upon:

- consumer travel costs such as the need to purchase petrol to travel to a store in a distant or out-of-town location;

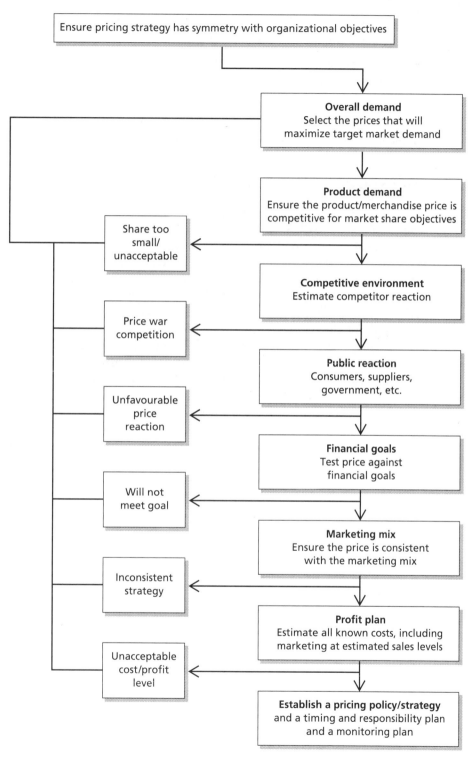

Fig. 7.2 Pricing policy considerations

- any parking charges related to a shopping visit to town;
- the level of traffic congestion in getting to the store;
- whether there is a free transit scheme to a local store or whether a park and ride scheme is available;
- pricing mix changes which affect price in terms of the provision of loyalty rewards or trading stamps. Any change in these is, in effect, a change in price and cost;
- the need for multi-purpose visits to a store or location.

MARKDOWN POLICY CONSIDERATIONS FOR RETAILERS

Price competition is an important feature of the grocery marketplace. Prior to its merger with Somerfield, Kwik Save sparked off a grocery price war in 1995 when it announced a nationwide promotion cutting up to 15 per cent off the price of one in ten of its top brands (Cope, 1995). While rivals such as ASDA dismissed Kwik Save's actions as a 'panic move', others promised to retaliate. Netto, a Danish discount operator, said it would match the prices if any of its lines were directly undercut. Kwik Save had been under pressure in the grocery market where it was caught between the larger superstore operators and the aggressive Continental discounters such as Aldi, Netto and Lidl.

Virtually all retailers will have occasion to utilize price markdowns. It is typical for markdowns to be used as part of a clearance sale in order to provide space for new merchandise. However, while the list below indicates that there are a number of reasons to use markdowns, it should be remembered that other elements of the marketing mix can be used to increase sales, or alternatively merchandise may be carried over into the new season. In the use of price to increase demand, markdown reductions of the original price may be necessary due to a number of reasons:

- competitor activity affecting demand;
- inadequate original pricing policy;
- merchandise did not meet consumer needs or preferences;
- economic or seasonal problems;
- overstocking of merchandise or poor stock keeping;
- quality of merchandise inferior due to manufacture or damage;
- problems of seasonality and poor timing of offer;
- merchandise became shop-soiled or damaged on the shop floor;
- need to release the display space for other merchandise;
- the selling space or display of the merchandise had been inadequate or in the wrong location;
- a policy decision taken to develop improved customer goodwill through markdowns;
- an error by the buyer with regard to style, fashions, research of market, etc.;
- an initial markdown being too small to achieve desired sales results;
- sales staff not being briefed properly or encouraged to sell old as well as new lines.

A retailer has to be clear about how any downward adjustment to original prices (markdowns) should be handled. This is important as markdowns are a consistent feature of retail marketing. For example, merchandise which sold originally for £50 may have to be reduced to £35 prior to the generation of adequate sales. In such a case the markdown is 30 per cent (£15/£50). However, some retailers prefer to express the markdown as a percentage of the new selling price. In the case given above this would be 42.9 per cent (£15/£35). Expressing markdowns as a percentage of the new selling price is often adopted as it can be more easily related to the method of accounting for the markdown for an entire department over a period of time.

$$\text{Markdown percentage on net sales} = \frac{\text{Markdown amount}}{\text{Net sales}}$$

For example, if a department achieved net sales of £10 000 after £2000 worth of markdowns, the markdown percentage of net sales would have been 20 per cent.

Most retailers that rely on a high inventory turnover will endeavour to use an early intervention for markdowns. However, there are a number of considerations which need to be addressed when utilizing markdowns. There is consideration of the frequency and timing; retailers have to be aware of the negative consequences for exclusivity, image and quality of the type and number of sales or other promotional price reduction events. An early markdown policy may move the bulk of the stock more speedily, limit shop-soiling, free up space for the new merchandise and enable the remaining stock to be better presented. A late policy may allow more stock to be sold at a higher profit and could help maintain a more positive image for the retailer. If a markdown is used at a late stage it will necessitate a longer stockholding period, but the price cut should be large enough to ensure that the remaining merchandise is moved quickly. Whatever the policy, markdowns should be of a sufficient size to attract those who would have bought the merchandise but rejected it on the basis of price. The size of the markdown is important. A small markdown may be ineffective and a large one may make the customer question the value of the merchandise – it may be felt that the retailer had previously been greedy. A reduction of 20 per cent is sufficient for the customer to notice the difference. Whatever approach is decided upon, a retailer should not allow unauthorized ad hoc reductions to be made. In some situations it may also be beneficial to remove the old prices, to retain the image of the store and to ensure that customers who bought previously are not dissatisfied. In other situations, however, the need to encourage customer perception that the new markdown prices offer a bargain is important.

In September 1996 Tesco launched their 'Unbeatable Value' campaign, during which they offered discounts on 600 products and challenged shoppers to find the same product on sale for less at a competitor's outlet (Atwal, 1996). This competitive pricing strategy was backed up by an extensive internal and external marketing campaign aimed at communicating the offers to their target market. Other retailers who wished to remain competitive had to react to this initiative in order to have a competitive stance. All companies reacted to varying degrees, with the most notable response coming from Sainsbury. The setting of price cannot be solely concerned with the consumer. Care and attention has to be given to appraising the reactions of both the consumer and the competition. Due to the high risk nature of some sectors of the retail industry, a price

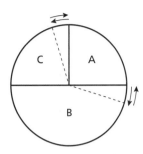

(a) Reactive price cutting, creating medium/long-term stabilization but with less total revenue

(b) Lower prices increasing market size, but not necessarily to total revenue levels before the price cut

Fig. 7.3 Price cutting considerations

advantage which takes share from a competitor may often provoke hostile repricing reaction.

In Fig. 7.3, if company A attempts to increase its market share by price cutting it will need to take share from companies B and C (Fig. 7.3(a)). This is a situation in which C and B react by cutting their own prices. The outcome is that the market shares remain similar and may, as in Fig. 7.3(b), lead the market to grow in volume, but perhaps not in overall revenue. The long-term result is that the market remains extremely unstable due to smaller margins being applied. In this situation a company has to ensure that it has a high volume of business in order to exceed its breakeven point. Price cutting policies have always been a feature of retail businesses in the UK and this has led to the collapse of many smaller companies which could not compete effectively with companies which had advantages of stronger buying power.

CONCLUSION

Price is a very important element in the marketing mix as it has to be set at the right level to ensure retailers have the capability to generate profits. It also represents an essential ingredient for the customer as price is all about the offer of value and benefits as part of the retail exchange process. It will be found that some retailers utilize EDLP but the majority still use price adjustments in order to create the right levels of demand for the ever-changing market conditions of the modern marketplace.

EXERCISES

The exercises in this section relate to the issues discussed in this chapter. It is suggested that you work through them before moving on to Chapter 8.

1 Examine the pricing strategies of different retailers. Make a list of branded and own-brand products which you can compare, using the following grid as a guide.

Visit and make notes at:	How were price and offers displayed?
● Tesco ● Sainsbury ● Boots ● convenience store ● others (list)	
Note prices of similar brands/own-brands, by retailer, of: ● shampoos/toiletries ● over-the-counter medicines ● branded perfumes ● health products	What is your assessment of the different pricing policies by company?

2 Visit a store when it has embarked upon markdowns. Try to assess the level and effectiveness of the different methods and, from discussions with staff, assess the reasons for the markdown policy.

3 Write a report to the marketing director of a large department store about the benefits, or otherwise, of taking an approach where pricing will be based upon a policy of everyday low pricing.

4 Read about price sensitivity and then create a short questionnaire that will measure the importance of some of these points when a person purchases an expensive electrical good of your choice. Now ask a young as well as an older group of people the questions and then write a report as to the importance of the concept and the differences found.

REFERENCES AND FURTHER READING

Alba, J., Lynch, J., Weitz, B. and Janiszewski, C. (1998) 'Interactive home shopping: consumer, retailer, and manufacturer incentives to participate in electronic marketplaces', *Journal of Marketing*, 61 (3), 38–53.

Atwal, K. (1996) 'Sainsbury's cuts prices to counter Tesco scheme', *Marketing Week*, 13 September, 6.

Bell, D.R. and Lattin, J.M. (1998) 'Shopping behavior and consumer preference for store price format: why "large basket" shoppers prefer EDLP', *Marketing Science*, 17 (1), 66–88.

Betts, E. and McGoldrick, P.J. (1995) 'The strategy of the retail sale, typology, review and synthesis', *International Review of Retail, Distribution and Consumer Research*, 5 (3), 303–32.

Blois, K.J. (1994) 'Discounts in business marketing management', *Industrial Marketing Management*, 23, 84.

Carlson, P.G. (1983) 'Fashion retailing: the sensitivity of rate of sale to markdown', *Journal of Retailing*, 59 'Spring', 67–78.

Cope, N. (1995) 'Kwik Save starts price war', *Independent*, 3 May, 34.

Corliss, L.G. (1995) 'Differential responses to retail sales promotion among African-American and Anglo-American consumers', *Journal of Retailing*, 71 (1), 83–92.

Cox, A. and Cox, D. (1990) 'Competing on price: the role of retail price advertisements in shaping store price image', *Journal of Retailing*, 66 (4), 428–45.

Datamonitor (1996) *Loyalty Discount Schemes*. Report. July.

Dickenson, P.R. and Sawyer, A. (1990) 'The price knowledge and search of supermarket shoppers', *Journal of Marketing*, 54 'July', 42–53.

Hollinger, P. (1998) 'When prices are not black and white: food retailers are increasingly waking up to the promotional advantages offered by the "grey market"', *Financial Times*, 16 May.

Kalwani, M.V. and Chi, K.Y. (1992) 'Consumer price and promotion expectations', *Journal of Marketing Research*, 29 (1), 90–100.

Kiran, W.K. and Kumar, V. (1995) 'The effect of brand characteristics and retailer policies on response to retail price promotions: implications for retailers', *Journal of Retailing*, 71 (3), 249–78.

Kotler, P., Armstrong, G., Saunders, J. and Wong, V. (1999) *Principles of Marketing*. 2nd European edn. Hemel Hempstead: Prentice Hall.

Kumar, V. and Pereira, A. (1997) 'Assessing the competitive impact of type, timing, frequency, and magnitude of retail promotions', *Journal of Business Research*, 40 (1), 1–13.

Levy, M. and Howard, D.J. (1988) 'An experimental approach to planning the duration and size of markdowns', *International Journal of Retailing*, 3 (2), 48–58.

Manning, K.C., Bearden, W.O. and Rose, R.L. (1998) 'Development of a theory of retailer response to manufacturers' everyday low cost programs', *Journal of Retailing*, 74 (1), 107–37.

Nagle, T.T. and Holden, R.K. (1995) *The Strategy and Tactics of Pricing*. Englewood Cliffs, NJ: Prentice Hall.

Ortmeyer, G., Quelch, J.A. and Salmon, W. (1991) 'Restoring creditability to retail pricing', *Sloan Management Review*, 33 (2), 55–6.

Schindler, R. (1991) 'Symbolic meanings of a price ending', *Advances in Consumer Research*, 794–801.

SuperMarketing (1996) 'Relief as petrol war cools', *SuperMarketing*, 11 October, 14.

Tighe, C. (2001) 'Asda to use "grey market"', *Financial Times*, 12 April.

Zeithaml, V.A. (1988) 'Consumer perceptions of price, quality, and value: a means–end model and synthesis of evidence', *Journal of Marketing*, 52 'July', 2–22.

8 Retail communication and promotion

This chapter should enable you to understand and explain:

- the importance of setting SMARRTT objectives;
- communication models;
- the concept and application of advertising, PR and sales promotion;
- the growth and use of relationship marketing and loyalty schemes;
- personal selling in the retail context.

Retailers communicate to their customers on a continuous basis through the store atmosphere, the products and services, promotional literature, advertising and other promotional means. *Retail promotion* is the descriptive term for the mix of communication activities which retail companies carry out in order to influence those publics on whom their sales depend. Retailing promotion will have the main objective of influencing consumer perceptions, attitudes and behaviour in order to increase store loyalty, store visits and product purchase. However, the important groups which need to be influenced are not simply the target market group of current and potential customers. There is a need to influence trade contacts such as agents and suppliers as well as opinion formers such as journalists and writers. Even local, national and international politicians and important professional groups may need to be influenced.

SETTING OBJECTIVES

As there is a range of promotional methods which can be employed by the marketer, it is important to define what the promotion has to achieve. The marketing objectives need to be clearly defined so that the most effective types of promotion can be utilized. The mix strategies could specify a need to achieve awareness; to inform; to educate; create purchase action; improve loyalty; change the perception of the customer, etc. Figure 8.1 explains how promotional objectives may be developed.

The promotional objectives should have some precise terms for the purposes of carrying out the promotion and then monitoring the results – so-called SMARRTT objectives. SMARRTT objectives will provide Specific, Measurable, Achievable, Realistic, Relevant, Targeted and Timed results along the following lines:

1 The target audience or market has to be identified (by segment, geographical spread, and for what stores). For example, identifying parents of school-age children living in London.

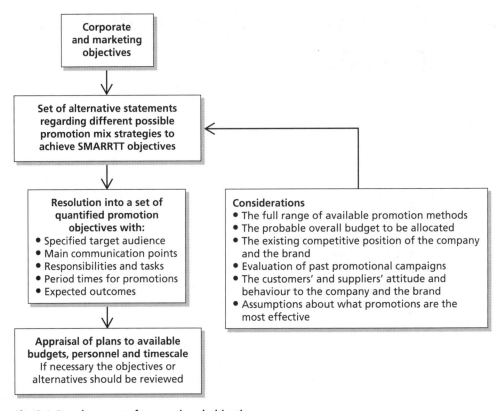

Fig. 8.1 Development of promotional objectives

2 The specific product (goods and service) to be promoted has to be identified. For example, identifying children's school-related products for a 'back-to-school' promotion.

3 Specific goals should be set, perhaps that sales will increase by £x in specific departments or across the store, or that attitudes to the store or brand will become more positive for the 40-plus age group. To continue the back-to-school example: to target an increase in sales of £15 000 for each London store for children's wear and £12 000 for school-related equipment. To fit with the SMARRTT objectives these goals have to be *achievable* in that the company has to deliver to the objectives; also *relevant* to the task required, e.g. changing attitude or educating if this is required.

4 The time horizon of when the expected effect will have occurred should be stated. For example, the objectives have to be achieved by September of a specified year.

Taking up the example used in the list above, a SMARRTT objective would therefore be:

To ensure that the parents of children between the ages of 4 and 16, within 7 miles of each London store, are communicated with and receive information on the back-to-school children's offers. Subsequently, sales for these products will increase by £15 000 for children's wear and £12 000 for school-related equipment by 1 September.

SMARRTT objectives

- *Specific*: Objectives have to be precise and clear enough to offer direction as to the expected outcome.

- *Measurable*: Objectives need a quantifiable outcome measurement statement against which an evaluation can take place.

- *Achievable*: Objectives should be achieved and therefore budgets/resources need to be adequate. Staffing or supply problems may restrict achievements.

- *Realistic*: The expectations of what the promotion can achieve have to be realistic. Promotion can only achieve so much and therefore expected changes in attitude to a brand, or demand for a retail offer, may not be realistic.

- *Relevant*: Objectives have to be appropriate to the task set.

- *Targeted*: All objectives need to be tied in with statements related to achieving results in the target audience(s). Different target audiences may need separate objectives.

- *Timed*: Objectives have to be written with consideration of effect or change within a time frame of achievement.

Promotional budget approaches

The second important step in any promotion campaign is to agree the budget. There are different approaches to agreeing budgets that may be based upon a number of criteria. It is important to realize that there is no one best method to set budgets. This is because promotional campaign measurement is not straightforward given that there is often a time lag between the campaign and any resultant demand patterns. Also other elements in the marketing mix will affect the demand for the retailer.

Various factors determine the overall promotion budget but any decision has to take into account existing or potential sales of the company. The most common approaches are *objective-and-task*, *affordable method*, *percentage of sales method*, and *competitive parity method*:

- *Objective-and-task* – whereby the budget is related to the communication objectives. If the retailer needs to create awareness, change attitudes or build brand then these objectives become the necessary tasks against which the budget is determined.

- *Affordable method* – where the first step is to produce a budgeted period forecast of the expected sales and company costs, excluding the promotional expenditure. The difference between the surplus expected and the desired profit allows for a decision over the communications budget based upon what can be afforded. This approach treats the promotion budget as a cost of business and does not encourage retailers to spend against the likelihood of future problems or as an investment to increase sales.

- *Percentage of sales method* – is an approach where the communications budget is set on the basis of a predetermined percentage of the forecasted sales. The weakness is that the method assumes the historical percentage is still relevant for the current retail marketplace. It also relies on accurate forecasts which provides for the chance of unacceptable error. In addition, if a retailer wants to build preference for a new store or a new format then a system of budgeting based upon the percentage of sales method may not raise the necessary budget to achieve the short-term task of ensuring awareness and acceptability. The other problem is that the method will provide for lower budgets when there is a downturn in the market, or because of a loss of sales based upon increased competitor activity that takes away business. This may lead to further sales decline as less and less money is spent on the company's promotion effort.

- *Competitive parity method* – allows the setting of the budget based upon both the share of market of the retailer and also the estimated expenditure level of its competitors. This method does not allow for specific marketplace opportunities as the parity level of expenditure will be held and consequently a strategic penetration of the market may not be achieved.

COMMUNICATION EFFECTS

There is always the need to plan to achieve the most effective response from the target market. An important part of the promotional effort is the building of *brand and product awareness*. Sometimes it will take a long time for the consumer to learn about the brand and the type of products which will be on offer. A promotional campaign should aim to provide *knowledge* of the product, to ensure that the consumer will feel favourable towards the product and build up a *preference* for it. Any campaign has to sell the benefits that a customer would be seeking in a credible way so that the potential customer feels *conviction* and is more likely than not to make a purchase.

Figure 8.2 shows how a promotional campaign should aim to create increased demand through awareness and information. It also shows that the development of a positive image for a product creates a more price inelastic demand curve (*see* Fig. 7.1 for an illustration of the basics of elasticity), which means that the product is more resilient with regard to price rises and does not have to rely on having low prices. P_1Q_1 is existing demand before a campaign has been developed to create more awareness in the target audience. At P_1Q_2 demand has increased because more people are aware of the company, the product and the benefits it can deliver. At P_1Q_3 the campaign has been planned to improve the image of the company or product so that more status is derived from the transaction process. This changes the shape of the demand curve – it becomes more inelastic.

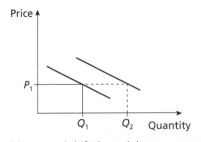

(a) Demand shift through better awareness

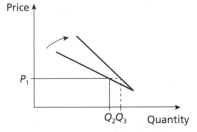

(b) Demand becomes more inelastic due to image improvement

Fig. 8.2 Promotional effect on demand

Advertising and sales promotions are the most widely used forms of promotion. Because of the intrusive characteristic of these forms of promotion most consumers relate ideas of marketing to the use of advertising or sales promotion. The other main forms include public relations and personal selling. Retail promotion can be defined as any communication that informs, influences and prompts the target market about any aspect of the retail sponsor.

ADVERTISING

The term advertising includes any paid form of non-personal communication through the media about a product that has an identified sponsor. The use of payment differentiates advertising from public relations for which no payment is made for the time or space to convey a message. The media may include telephone directories, guides, newspapers, magazines, radio, television, direct mail, Web pages and billboards. Advertising is normally associated with mass communication, where a broad target market is to be contacted.

Advertising is used to achieve a whole range of objectives that may include changing attitudes or building image as well as achieving sales. Advertising is often described as above-the-line promotion with all other forms of promotion being termed below-the-line. The difference between above and below the line is simply academic now as the emphasis is on both areas, for example sales promotion and advertising working together to achieve the greatest impact.

Moreover, in decisions over communication plans, it is the cost-effectiveness that matters most. The use of different combinations of what has traditionally been known as above and below the line has blurred the meaning of the terms and there are many promotional strategies which can be seen to erase the line or, as it is known, pass 'through the line'. With direct mail being used to build awareness and TV being used to sell products direct to the consumer, there is a great deal more flexibility in the use of different promotional mediums.

Communication theorists have proposed several models to explain the way advertising works and each have some similarity. The basic underlying approach is to theorize that the individual will first move to a *knowledge state* or *awareness state* on the basis of information gained through experience and methods of communication. *Attitudes* are then formed and the importance is to move the potential purchaser to a *behavioural action* phase of purchase through desire and *conviction*. One model known as the DAGMAR model (Defining Advertising Goals for Measured Advertising Results) describes the sequence of stages through which the prospective customer has to move:

- unawareness;
- awareness;
- comprehension of the offer;
- conviction;
- action or inaction.

Through advertising, the retailer will make the potential customer aware of the store and its range of offers. As part of the advertising communication process, information has to be clearly transmitted so that it can be decoded and comprehended properly. The process is then to make the offer credible so that the potential customer can be moved to a favourable attitude to the store or product. The act of purchase may then follow.

Advertising has the potential to affect a large number of people simultaneously with a single message. The secondary effect of advertising is personal communications among consumers. This is known as the *two-step flow of communication*. The first step in the process is the communications flow from media to opinion leaders – the individuals whose attitudes, opinions, preferences and actions affect others. The second step is word-of-mouth communications from opinion leaders to others (followers). This communication can occur through personal conversation between friends or with work colleagues based upon communication about the store or its offers. It can also occur through non-verbal communications when someone displays newly bought merchandise in their home or by means of the labels on or in their clothes. One implication of the need to achieve as much benefit as possible from the two-step model is the requirement to reach and influence opinion leaders.

Types of advertising

There are many different forms of advertising. While different, each one produces a highly public exposure of messages and concepts to the general public. The very public nature of this confers a legitimacy and acceptance of the retailer or brand. Consumers are aware that the advertising is an expressive and targeted medium by which individuals can feel they share a set of underlying values which reflect their involvement with the retail offer or store. Some of the different types are as follows:

Product advertising

Product advertising is aimed at enticing people to the store in order to consider specific merchandise. Product advertising will feature the promotion of merchandise that is new, exclusive, and superior in aspects of quality and design as well as creating awareness of complete assortments or special merchandise events. It is aimed at creating awareness of the product, its availability and benefits.

Markdown event advertising

This is used to create some excitement about a special period of lower cost offers for products. It is likely to be more successful if the reduction is believed to be part of a genuine sale of products which in the past had been fairly priced.

Institutional advertising

This type of advertising is used to sell the store or shopping mall as a pleasing place to shop. With the use of institutional advertising, the store attempts to reinforce the image of one or more of the following: a leader in fashion, fair prices, wide merchandise selection, superior service or quality, a leisure experience or somewhere to enjoy visiting. There is now a trend to advertise a shopping centre rather than individual outlets. The communication emphasis is on the available range of shops, ease of parking or other consumer benefits. The frequency of this type of advertising increases at peak demand times such as Christmas.

Co-operative advertising

This is used where manufacturers fund part of a promotion by supplying leaflets or advertising material for use by the store. The store can add its own address to ready-prepared printed material and carry out mail drops or other methods of distribution. Alternatively, a manufacturer may agree to share equally the costs of an advertising campaign. Manufacturers are keen to have their brands stocked and sold; therefore, they often enter into joint advertising schemes with retailers. Co-operative advertising may involve a combination of one or more retailers in an area as well as the manufacturer. In addition, co-operative promotions may well extend to agreements to provide joint branded window display material and point-of-sale material.

Retail promotion in relation to that of manufacturers

There are differences between retailer and manufacturer advertising strategies. Retail advertising is often based upon short-term objectives with the emphasis on value or price of the products on offer. This is unlike manufacturers' approaches; they often attempt to build favourable attitudes or improve the image of the brand or organization over an extended period of time. Whereas a manufacturer will need to create awareness of its brand across major market areas, a retailer may have more geographically concentrated target markets. Therefore, a retailer has to take into account local habits, conditions of the marketplace, availability of local media and have a clear idea of the housing areas where potential customers are living.

The expense of some forms of advertising is excessive – for example, TV advertising is extremely expensive due to production as well as transmission costs, and therefore only the larger companies or franchisers will use this medium. The alternative use of direct marketing is often a more cost-effective form of promotion for smaller, more geographically dispersed retailers.

Window displays

Window areas offer a major opportunity to provide a distinctive image for a store, to promote seasonal activities and merchandise, or to create interest and capture the attention of the public. Think about the Christmas period in any large city centre. It is not simply Christmas street decorations which offer the most fascination. It is often the clever automatons and figures which are used as window displays to bring pleasure to both children and adults alike.

Some store fronts are configured to allow large display areas with either straight, angled or arcade style designs. Some frontage designs dispense with the whole of the built area of the shopfront and window so as to offer a larger sales space and to provide views of the interior display areas. In any type of window the use of good lighting is essential to show the display to best effect and to reduce the effect of glare on the outside of the window. Whatever the shop front design, it should act as a funnel to induce the potential customer to enter the store.

Design of shop windows

- Windows should have simple clear messages as would a poster, and the design should convey the personality of the brand or store. Passing consumers have only a short attention span for the window so it should not be confusiong in any way.

- For upmarket retailers a minimalist, simple approach with a focus on a single communication, emotion or product will provide a powerful image. The approach is used by retailers such as Prada and Versace.

- The utilization of dressing the window space with similar props, mannequins or garments creates impact through repetition. This is often utilized by French Connection and Gap.

- Interest is produced by movement based upon live events, technology based upon changes in lighting, projection of images on screens, etc., or mechanical use of props or products.

- In this integrated communications age the windows must be consistent in their message and positioning with other communications.

- Lighting through colour and graduation or changes in intensity can provide dramatic effect. It also has to be planned to take into account the strength of the daylight.

- The window has to be changed to create interest and relationships with the consumer that provides information as to what is the fashion change or new look they should be informed of.

The window area will need to be thought about in terms of the logic of positioning and grouping of display material and merchandise. There is far more impact gained from the grouping of products in similar categories. Sales can also be enhanced by recognition about how purchases may be primary and secondary. As such the display accessories that may also be purchased along with a main purchase of furniture or an outfit can provide increased sales and a more pleasing display. Like any promotional medium specific areas will attract more attention and so should be utilized for the most important displays – those near eye level, away from corners or pillars, or on moving displays. The window display should be changed on a regular basis and this should always be planned in advance of the event so that the theme is agreed and the assignment of space is controlled.

MINICASE 8.1

Get the most out of window space – Innovative and well-targeted window displays can give stores a competitive edge

Many retailers are turning to a less-trumpeted marketing medium to back their above-the-line activity – their store windows. Fashion brands are at the forefront of the trend, integrating windows into their overall marketing strategy to raise brand awareness as much as show off their latest collections. French Connection, for example, used its store windows to sidestep a ruling by the Advertising Standards Author-ity ordering the removal of posters around London and censoring TV ads for its fcukinky promotion.

Fashion retailers are not alone in making full use of their windows. WH Smith's store window at the Blue-water shopping complex in Kent was created by design agency Fitch in the style of a magazine cover. The window appeals to consumers on two levels – LED screens feature news flashes, while tri-graphics

– billboards with three rotating posters – promote the shop's latest offers. Research by Hauch Research International found that the window draws consumers to it with a welcoming impression that excites them and makes them want to discover more in-store.

But not all behavioural analysis supports the conviction of design agencies and retailers in the power of windows to lift footfall and influence purchase decisions. ID Magasin research suggests that only 7% to 9% of passing traffic will notice a typical window, with even the most entertaining grabbing the attention of only 18% of passers-by. Rather than the window, it suggests the most important element of the store front is the view through the door. So how can retailers ensure they get the most out of their investment?

ID Magasin managing director Siemon Scamell-Katz believes more work integrating behavioural analysis into design will pay off. The bottom third of a window has the greatest impact, he explains, but how many designs take that into account? 'Retailers wouldn't spend money on TV slots without working out what they were doing first, but that's what happening with windows.'

For retailers, deciding which products to showcase is often based on what's hot and what fits with the audience. 'Unlike fashion, which changes on a seasonal basis, music is a fast-moving business and windows change every week to feature new releases,' says Simon Dornan, PR and events manager for Virgin Megastore. 'They are the first place many customers look to see what's new. We are steered by what's new and what is appropriate to Virgin customers. Bob the Builder was popular, but he would never feature in a Virgin window.' But not all retailers have such a clearly defined audience. The window design for book and music retailer Borders requires a careful balancing act, according to marketing manager Matt Taylor. Its windows feature new releases and an extensive backlist. 'While we have many small products to promote, it is essential to keep the window clear and simple. We want it to talk to people passing by as well as those on the other side of the street.' Technology is changing the way many POP agencies approach window design. A recent Borders promotion involved piled-up TVs showing *The Perfect Storm*, while Electronics Boutique re-

cently used lenticular panels – the layering of images to create the impression of movement from different angles – to support the launch of strategy game Black & White. And the Sloane Group is introducing interactive touch-screen technology to allow customers to interact with displays by touching the actual window glass.

Selfridges strives to remain at the forefront of window design and head of creative services David Snaith believes getting people to interact at the street level brings them into the store and reinforces the theatre of the Selfridges shopping experience. It recently used plasma screens and real-time video from Japanese street scenes to support its 'Tokyo Life' spring promotion. In addition, movement sensors inflated larger-than-life Japanese dolls as people passed and one section of its Oxford Street window was turned into a 24-hour Japanese-style convenience store selling a range of authentic products.

Lillywhites teamed up with Adidas to lure consumers in-store earlier this year when it provided Samantha Tomlinson, a 25-year-old runner, with a living space in a converted window in the run-up to the London Marathon. With a bedroom, sitting room and training area, the athlete went about her daily routine in front of thousands of passers-by for two weeks. The exercise, which aimed to drive shoppers to the third-floor official marathon and Adidas store, proved a tremendous draw, both during the display and following the marathon, when the athlete returned to tell shoppers how she had got on.

It's not just stores that benefit from high street windows. Since the 80s, retail banks have used them to push products and reinforce their brands. Sheena Booth, marketing and communications manager at Royal Bank of Scotland, is responsible for the company's retail merchandising and design. She explains that for banks, effective windows are less about attracting footfall than raising brand awareness.

'We try to keep the design as simple as possible, while putting products in the window that really appeal to new customers – highly discounted mortgages or a strong credit card proposition. In a lot of cases, that will be a price-lead proposition. We also want it to be corporate-looking, as new customers want a bank they can trust.'

Source: Belinda Gannaway, *Marketing*, 2 August 2001

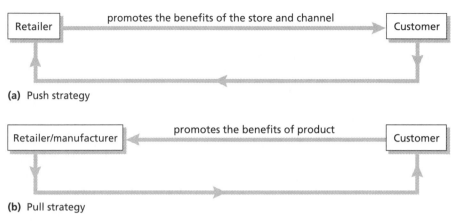

(a) Push strategy

(b) Pull strategy

Fig. 8.3 Push versus pull strategy for a retailer

Push versus pull promotion strategy

The promotional decisions have to consider whether the company chooses a push strategy or a pull strategy or a balance of the two. A push strategy involves 'pushing' the consumer through the channel by directing the marketing activities to promote the store or benefits of the channel (*see* Fig. 8.3(a)). As retailing is a channel service, this approach is unlike that of more traditional forms of product marketing as it is the channel service which is promoted. The pull strategy is where marketing promotion activities are targeted to the consumer to induce them to buy the retailer's merchandise or services (*see* Fig. 8.3(b)). Retailers may enter third party agreements for promotion whereby the cost of the promotion is shared between the retailer and the manufacturer to encourage more sales of the manufacturer's product.

With the growing use of relationship marketing and the compilation of customer databases, retailers have been concentrating more on push rather than pull strategies. Companies are increasing their efforts to select the most appropriate target groups to direct offers at. This allows marketing programmes to be more finely targeted, with literature for sale periods, special events or offers being tailored to suit the individual customer group.

MINICASE 8.2

Persuading viewers to pay for services could be tough

It has been a perplexing year for followers of interactive television (iTV). While there have been signs that the viewing public is finally waking up to the opportunities offered by the technology, operators have appeared as far away as ever from making the services pay. In the UK, world leader in digital television, this year was heralded as the coming of age for iTV when two high-profile interactive events captured the public's imagination.

Nearly 3m people used their remote controls to vote contestants out of the *Big Brother* gameshow and another 2m interacted with the BBC's coverage of the Wimbledon tennis championship, which allowed viewers to choose the match they wanted to watch. Both programmes demonstrated the ability of iTV to enhance the viewing experience and proved there is a mass market for services which are simple and either useful or fun.

What remains to be seen is whether anyone will make very much money out of these services. Forrester Research forecast that iTV would generate worldwide revenues of £9bn by 2005. But this year has seen that potential called into question. Just two months before the success of *Big Brother* and Wimbledon, British Sky Broadcasting, a global leader in iTV, announced a retreat from some services, tacitly admitting its strategy had failed.

Sky had invested heavily in Open, a home shopping portal that allowed viewers to buy goods and services with the click of the remote control. Open was the leading example of the so-called walled garden model of iTV that involved a limited group of retailers and service providers paying Sky large sums for exclusive access to the portal. Viewers were frustrated by the lack of choice and found the technology clunky and inconvenient, having to switch away from television programmes to use the service.

Sky and its retail partners found the economics did not stack up. Open was quietly closed. In future, Sky's interactive services will be integrated with television content rather than separated from it. 'The walled garden approach was totally misguided from the start and is outdated,' says Claes Loeberg, creative director at Rubus, the e-business consultancy.

Some in the industry still believe the future of iTV is on the internet, which has none of the constraints of a walled garden. The web can be delivered to the television by telephone or cable, with viewers operating it by keyboard. ITV Digital, one of Sky's pay television rivals in the UK, is among the broadcasters to have introduced the internet to the small screen, but it has been little more successful than its walled garden competitors. 'Web content is not right for TV,' says Mark Neild, analyst at PA Consulting. 'It looks ghastly and is virtually unusable.'

The failure of both services to attract large numbers of users cast doubt on the ability of television to match the internet as a vehicle for transactions. It had been argued that so-called t-commerce would outstrip e-commerce because television sets are more widespread than PCs and people are more comfortable using them. Many still accept this argument. But others point out that, while the PC is a 'lean forward' medium, which people interact with for services or information, television has people in 'lean back' mode, passively waiting to be entertained. 'Just because you sit in front of the computer and do your banking does not mean you want to sit in your lounge to conduct your finances. It makes as much

sense as building a financial centre in an amusement park,' says Mr Loeberg. The lesson of *Big Brother* and Wimbledon was that for interactivity to be a success, it must be an extension of television's existing role as an entertainment.

'Service providers saw iTV as a chance to sell things. However, for subscribers it has to add value and give them a reason to stop watching *EastEnders* to go to the Tesco site. The interactive experience must be related to what is actually on TV,' says Dennis Jones, of ICL, which helped build services for NTL and the BBC. Viewers have quickly adopted services such as Sky Sports Extra, which allows people to select which footballer they want to watch during a match. *Big Brother* viewers were offered a choice of camera angles and people are able to take part in ITV's *Who Wants to be a Millionaire?* quiz show from their front room.

However, there is still hope that income will emerge from iTV. Broadcasters are relying on it to support them as their audiences are fragmented in the multi-channel world and revenues from traditional advertising declines. Retailers and advertisers also have a stake in t-commerce working as the broadcasting landscape is transformed and iTV becomes the most direct way to market to viewers. 'Advertising will slowly disappear from the slots inserted into programmes as digital TV delivery becomes more non-linear, thanks to TiVo (the personal video recorder) and video-on-demand. Advertisers will choose instead to deliver their message through interactive programmes,' says Patrick Bossert, of KPMG Consulting.

Assuming regulatory approval, retailers could sell food during a cookery programme or DIY equipment during a home improvements show. Viewers might eventually be able to buy a dress worn by a soap star by clicking on the screen. Television operators, content providers and retailers share the spoils. The key to successful t-commerce, most analysts agree, is the ability of viewers to make impulse purchases. 'TV viewers want products and services presented on a plate. All they want to do is select and agree,' says Mr Neild.

When KBHK, a San Francisco broadcaster, screened a rock concert by Melissa Etheridge recently, 22 per cent of the audience ordered a CD through the television during the show. It is isolated hits such as that which makes Sky still confident of reaching its target of generating £50 per subscriber per year from interactivity by 2005. Much of it is expected to come from betting, set to be one of the most successful services by allowing viewers to place bets on the outcome of live sports events.

'Betting, TV-poll voting, and merchandise sales around big live events will drive the future of transactional revenue from TV programming,' says Mr Bossert. There will be no overnight revolution. 'The video recorder took nearly 10 years from launch to household necessity,' he points out. 'Mobile phones and CD players took 7 years each, so why are companies expecting hockey-stick shaped revenue growth curves from interactive television?' But the foundations for iTV's lift-off are taking place. By the end of this year, more than 40 per cent of people in the UK – where digital television subscriptions outstrip internet connections – will have access to interactive services.

Source: Andrew Ward, *Financial Times*, 5 September 2001

SALES PROMOTION

Sales promotion involves any paid non-personal marketing communication activity, other than advertising, which offers an incentive to induce a desired result from potential customers, trade intermediaries, or the salesforce. This is sometimes referred to by the term *sales incentive*. Sales promotion campaigns will add value to the product because the incentives will generally not accompany the product but will typically be offered as mail drops or as coupons to be cut from newspapers, etc. It is usual for a sales promotion campaign to be used as a temporary offer to the customer in order to stimulate an immediate response. For example, free samples or money-off vouchers and offers are frequently used in sales promotion campaigns for brands or companies which need to improve demand at certain periods. Included in these campaigns are displays, contests, sweepstakes, coupons, frequent user (loyalty) programmes, prizes, samples, demonstrations, referral gifts and other limited duration selling efforts not included in the other techniques – *see* the summary of types of sales promotion in Table 8.1. Most incentives are planned to be offered on a short-term basis only.

Sales promotion is often used in combination with other promotional tools in order to supplement the overall effort. However, it has to be remembered that it is sometimes difficult to terminate or change special promotions without causing adverse effects. Loyalty programmes are an example of this (*see* the following section on relationship marketing). A sales promotion (or series of promotions) also has to take account of the likely effect it may have on the image of the brand or outlet due to the negative perception change which may occur because of an association with banal and frivolous promotions.

Example: McDonald's

In 1999, McDonald's celebrated its anniversary with a free BigMac promotion. The special offer of buy one get one free, which was advertised extensively in the national press, resulted in a sales promotion offer that was so popular it caused major problems for the company. The food retailer ran out of supplies of BigMac and had to apologize to the public for the shortage. However, there was the extra publicity surrounding the incident which may, or may not, have been beneficial to the company.

To evaluate a sales promotion the retailer should consider:

● the cost of the promotion in employee time, as well as for the cost of any merchandise, giveaway items or promotional literature;

Table 8.1 Summary of types of sales promotion

Type of sales promotion	Description
Point-of-purchase/ point-of-sale	Retailer or manufacturer displays for the window, floor and counter to enhance impulse purchase
Contests	Reinforcement of brand or outlet through competitions (skill games providing slogans, doing puzzles, etc.) for prizes
Sweepstakes	Similar to contest but winner chosen by chance, by filling in application form, rather than skill
Coupons	Special discounts are advertised with a coupon being cut out and redeemed as part of an at-store purchase. Modern approaches utilize optically read coupon cards at checkout
Frequent shopper	Customers are rewarded by points or stamps for repeat purchase or total amount spent
Prizes	Similar to frequent shopper programmes except retailer offers prizes whereby a piece of a set, such as a glass or part of a tea set, is gained on predetermined threshold purchase levels
Demonstrations	Products or services are shown in use, or what they can achieve and the benefits they give are demonstrated, for example, demonstration of a foot massager to customers
Referral gifts	Presents or gifts are given to existing customers who introduce new custom. Often used by direct sales retailers such as those selling books or tapes and CDs
2 for the price of 1	Extra items of merchandise added to pack free of charge to increase sales
Branded giveaways	Items such as pens, calendars, shopping bags, etc. with the retailer's logo are given to customers
Samples	Free samples of products, tastes, smells given away to customers
Premiums	Merchandise item given free of charge or at substantial reduction for traffic-building or increase in store visits or to encourage sales. Self-liquidating premiums are when the customer pays something towards cost
Special events	Fashion shows, autograph sessions with celebrities, art and craft exhibitions, school holiday activities, topical local interest displays. Retail store openings are often linked to a special event

- the increase in sales and profit, or improvement in awareness, based upon the campaign;
- whether the campaign had secondary effects of switching demand from other retailer products;
- whether there were any additional sales outside of the promotion, due to customers being attracted to the store.

It is not always easy to isolate the above effects from other factors, but it is always important to make some assessment of the benefit of different types of promotion.

RELATIONSHIP MARKETING AND LOYALTY SCHEMES

The retail marketplace is maturing and due to a slowdown in growth is becoming more competitive. Against this backdrop, retailers have sought out different ways of improving sales and profits. In order to address these problems retailers are adopting relationship marketing (RM) schemes which aim to:

- build greater customer loyalty and retention;
- develop methods of creating longer-term relationships;
- lead ultimately to increased sales and profits.

RM has been defined by Gronroos (1990, 1991, 1994a, 1994b), who has consistently argued for the importance of ensuring that relationships with customers should be continuously developed. Gronroos (1994b, p. 9) developed his definition in which he described the objectives of RM as being to:

> **Identify and establish, maintain and enhance and, when necessary, terminate relationships with customers and other stakeholders, at a profit so that the objectives of all parties involved are met; and this is done by a mutual exchange and fulfilment of promises.**

This definition includes many of the aspects of importance in RM but does not necessarily embrace the whole range of concepts utilized in RM. Gronroos argues that all marketing strategies lie on a continuum ranging from transactional to relational marketing, where relationship marketing can be judged in terms of measures of *customer retention* rather than market share. Christopher *et al.* (1996) have developed the idea of a ladder whereby relationships develop as part of growing customer loyalty (*see* Fig. 8.4).

The growth of retail relationship marketing schemes

Early methods of building loyalty were carried out by small shopkeepers who could get to know their customers personally and reward some of them with special services or attention – and even discounts or gifts at times such as Christmas. As companies began to grow, it became increasingly difficult to identify who were the most valuable customers and to collect and retain accurate information.

In the 1950s the Co-op led the way with cash dividend schemes for the 12 million members who regularly shopped at Co-op stores or benefited from the door-to-door services of the Co-op. Then, in 1963, Tesco introduced Green Shield stamps as an incentive scheme. This led to many of the smaller traders having to follow their lead in order to

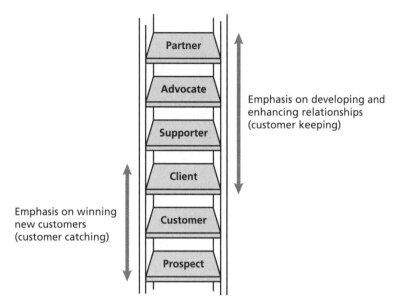

Fig. 8.4 The relationship marketing ladder

Source: Payne *et al.*, 1995. Reproduced with permission

retain business. More recently, petrol retailers introduced point or reward schemes in order to create more regular custom. However, the development of loyalty cards by Tesco is a major departure from any previous marketing promotion scheme operated in the UK. This is because the loyalty card is able to provide instant and accurate feedback information on individual customers and their purchase patterns; this subsequently allows more individualized relationship marketing to take place.

In the UK from 1995 onwards the major grocery retailers embarked upon the development of loyalty cards for their retail operations. The schemes are designed to ensure that a customer is retained and remains faithful to a particular retailer. The Tesco scheme was launched in 1995 and quickly built up a customer base of an estimated 9.5 million. Wanting to go even further, in 1996 Tesco launched Clubcard Plus which allowed customers to pay a set amount of money into the Clubcard scheme each month by standing order and for the cost of a cardholder's shopping to be deducted automatically from their Clubcard account. Any balance on the account earns interest; credit is extended for larger expenditure in any month with low rates of interest charged.

Loyalty card schemes

- Tesco: launched Clubcard in 1995; has 14 million cardholders
- Sainsbury's: launched Reward Card in 1996; has 17 million cardholders
- ASDA: launched ASDA Club Card in 1996; abandoned 1999
- Safeway: launched ABC card in 1995; dropped points collection 2000

This strategy by Tesco aimed at winning new customers was quickly followed by defensive strategies from other grocery retailers who needed to retain their own existing customers. This situation is very similar to what happened in the airline industry with frequent flyer programmes. These programmes brought major competitive advantage in the early stages of introduction but ended up by providing little advantage to the retailers when all airlines created similar schemes (Gilbert, 1996).

Incentivized relationship marketing has become more prominent during the 1990s following the launch of loyalty card schemes. The Tesco scheme collects details of the transaction and club member at the checkout. Money-off vouchers are then mailed out to customers participating in the scheme. The value of the vouchers is proportional to the money having been spent. In addition, other vouchers may be targeted and sent to incentivize the sales of own-brand or other product lines. Alternatively, other retailers reward customers for their loyalty through the collection of points which entitle them to money-off products, free items and other incentives such as Air Miles or charity donations. A loyalty scheme will collect information such as name, address including postcode, sex, date of birth, household size, children's dates of birth, ownership of consumer durables, preferred place(s) to carry out shopping, pet ownership, etc. Once this information is collected, the card customer data on household type and size can be related to the postcode geographic data and then matched to the use of the card – the EPOS sales data. The record of purchase will provide information about time and frequency of visits, expenditure patterns, products and brands purchased as well as the success of any special offers. The combination of this data will allow for data mining and data extraction for further promotions; improved decision-making for new store development; targeted marketing via direct mail to promote sale periods, or to tempt back a 'lapsed' customer by the use of different promotions. Relationship marketing schemes are normally built around communication with members through magazines. With the larger schemes, the membership magazine may be targeted to different groups, such as students, pensioners or other life-cycle groups. This allows a company to target specific segments with information and offers which are attractive to that particular group.

The RM process helps to advance relationships to higher levels until advocate status is achieved. This is where the customer as advocate is not only loyal but also champions the company, the employees and the service to others. RM should not be confused with brand loyalty based upon commitment to the product; RM is a far more complex and wider alliance and association.

The rationale for RM is that it makes business sense to focus on long-term financial benefits which may accrue once a customer has been won for the first time. This is because it has been estimated that it is five to ten times more expensive to recruit a new customer than it is to retain an existing one. This is based upon the estimated cost of prospecting, advertising and selling, commission, product samples, credit checking, administration, and database management. The true value of retaining customers is that it enables the costs of conversion of the prospect to be set against the revenues earned over the longer term. Sales and profits improve in direct proportion to the length of time a relationship lasts.

Lifetime value analysis

Customers will represent a diverse set of purchasing and spending patterns. However, it is important to be able to make marketing decisions which reflect the worth and potential

Points don't always mean prizes in loyalty card lottery

Is the game up for the supermarket loyalty cards? Safeway seem to think so, after announcing two weeks ago that its ABC cardholders will not be able to collect any more points from the end of this month. The scheme will live on, to provide access to Shop and Go and Collect and Go, but without a points element, it is effectively dead. Safeway says it will save £50 million by dropping the bulk of the scheme, and will instead spend £80 million on price cuts – which, it claims, customers prefer. Certainly, Safeway says it has gained 750 000 customers and seen a 6 per cent growth in like-for-like sales since its latest price-cutting offensive in October.

But what about the rest of the big four supermarkets? Tesco was the first to launch a national loyalty card in 1995 with its Clubcard, and Sainsbury's, despite initial scepticism, followed suit the following year with its Reward Card. Meanwhile, Asda last year cancelled its loyalty card trial to concentrate on its Rollback campaign. A spokeswoman for Sainsbury's says that its Reward Card is very much a part of the chain's future strategy. Last week, it underlined its commitment by offering 500 points to Safeway customers who hand in their ABC cards to any Sainsbury's store. But the argument from many in the industry is that such cards do not actually build loyalty, and a shopper with a Tesco Clubcard in their wallet is also likely to have a Sainsbury's Reward Card there as well.

'The point of loyalty cards in the first place was for a store to differentiate itself from its competitors, but when everyone offered one, the cards lost all their value,' says Verdict director Mike Godliman. In fact, a report on customer loyalty by Verdict shows that the two supermarket chains with the most loyal customers are Morrisons and Asda, neither of which offer loyalty cards. Perversely, offering customers cash incentives may actually make them less loyal, in that they will move the moment a higher bribe is offered by a competitor. Aside from rewarding regular customers, the main aim of loyalty cards was to monitor who buys what products. The long-term goal was 'one-to-one' marketing, with data used to target customers with specific promotional information geared to their preferences.

As Marcus Evans, Carlson Marketing Group development director, argues it is this information and how it is used that really builds loyalty. 'The card is only part of the vehicle that allows you to observe a customer's behaviour. But it is the communication behind the programme between the store and customer that generates the real loyalty.' But Godliman believes the supermarkets have not effectively used the vast amounts of data collected. 'Up until now, the information they have collected has not been exploited, but with new technology they should be able to target promotions at the individual,' he says.

Investec Henderson Crosthwaite food analyst David Stoddard believes the growth of e-shopping could spell the end for the loyalty card. He says: 'If e-shopping takes off, and it is my belief that it will, then the supermarkets will have to adapt to retain customer loyalty.' Tesco is already moving in this direction. Following its deal with software company Autonomy, it plans to offer a personalised shopping service to its Internet customers based on data collected from its Clubcard.

Mark Runacus, managing director of Relationship Marketing Group, which operates Sainsbury's Reward Card scheme, thinks that although the physical loyalty card may disappear in the future, the fundamentals of loyalty schemes will not go away. He says, 'New technology may mean we won't have to carry a piece of plastic around, but there will be something to replace it that will enable us to talk to the customer and make the appropriate offer.'

Source: Jose Riera, *Retail Week*, 19 May 2000

of any one customer. In order to take such decisions there is a requirement to assess the worth of each customer over a period of time. The analysis which allows this is known as *lifetime value* (LTV). Lifetime value allows for the measurement of the total worth to the organization of its relationship with a particular identified customer over a period of time with the amounts discounted to provide a net present value. In order to make a calculation of LTV the retailer has to estimate the costs and revenues of each relationship.

The costs will be related to the acquisition, credit clearance, communication and any rewards or incentives given during any one year. The period of time that the relationship is expected to last is discounted for inflation to provide a realistic real value of each customer. This is to compare it to an investment that could have been made in an interest-bearing deposit account. The analysis will reveal the profile of customers who provide high returns as well as those who are costly for the company to service. The LTV information will allow for improved decision-making regarding:

- the assigning of appropriate acquisition allowances as a reflection of the longer-term benefit of certain individuals. The profile of these individuals is utilized to identify and segment the targeting strategy;

- improving media strategies in order to acquire higher LTV individuals. Database analysis will provide information as to the optimal allocation of marketing communications budgets in recruitment campaigns;

- providing selection policies for customer marketing programmes. LTV analysis will allow a division of customers into graded levels of worth to the retailer. This allows for different rewards and privileges to be given to the different levels or categories of customer. It also allows for the cutback in communication for those individuals who represent only breakeven or loss when marketing costs are taken into consideration.

- which individuals to contact and reactivate from the lapsed category. The database can identify the timing and worth of purchases made by individuals. If a previously higher spending individual indicates lapsed behaviour, a 'winback' policy may be triggered. As such a reactivation allowance can be agreed based upon the likely return of the individual and their future revenue potential;

- the asset value of each individual in the relationship scheme. This can provide the rationale for different marketing initiatives based upon the potential behaviour of individuals or groups to these initiatives.

The design and implementation of a relationship marketing scheme

Research by Dibb and Meadows (2001) examines the application of relationship marketing in retail banking. In carrying out the research they utilized a checklist that allows us some insight into the requirements of such schemes. The list included among other items the need to measure:

> Details of the nature of data collection, management and analysis. An explanation of how the data collection process is managed by the bank; primary and secondary data gathering. A discussion of the quality of existing customer records and how they are used. Examination of the way in which available data are used to build customer relationships. For example whether data analysis leads to a better view of segmentation and the customer base; knowledge of customer profitability and lifetime value. Review of whether customers actually want to build relationships with financial services businesses . . . problems that have been encountered and the progress made . . . Examination of the critical success factors and performance measures for relationship marketing.

The paper also examined aspects of the technology applications used by the bank (such as identifying life events based upon house moves and salary increases) as well as the staff's methods of handling relationships (such as contact programmes and customer service reviews). The paper offers a comprehensive overview of the current stage of relationship marketing in the retail banking sector.

RM requires the effective *acquisition* and *retention* of customers for the building of a more efficient operation and, ultimately, a stronger competitive position. Acquisition is based upon the traditional approach to marketing with the identification of customer needs, development of a retail offer to satisfy those needs, and then the targeting of prospects. The movement from acquisition through to retention (based upon Gilbert, 1996) is described in the following seven steps of events:

1 *Acquisition* – different marketing methods are used to acquire customers (sometimes termed prospects), which then require relationship marketing to ensure effective retention. Customer profiling is important and therefore individuals may need to be given an incentive to part with their personal information required for a relationship scheme.

2 *Identify* more about the customer through database analysis of habits and lifetime value.

3 *Improve* and make the retail outlet/offer/service more attractive based upon active feedback processes.

4 *Inform* through communications programmes to build customers' knowledge of the company (this may need to be based upon what the customer wants – permission marketing where they opt to receive certain types of communication).

5 *Tempt* customers through special targeted offers to purchase more regularly, try different products, etc.

6 *Retain* the customer by developing and delivering different forms of loyalty schemes and rewards.

7 *Measure lifetime value*, which should identify a range of customer types. Those providing high LTV will have higher loyalty and will provide *increased* customer value to the company, which should result in *higher* profits and the ability to make increased *investment* in further acquisition of new members to the scheme.

The foregoing process can be viewed as an increasing outward spiral which as a result of the iterative process of increases in profits and subsequent reinvestment places the company in a stronger and stronger position.

Defining loyalty

When attempting to understand loyalty there are two approaches that can be identified (Javalgi and Moberg, 1997).

1 A definition of loyalty provided in *behavioural terms*, usually related to the number of purchases and measured by monitoring the frequency of such purchases.

2 A definition of loyalty in *attitudinal terms*, incorporating consumer preferences and disposition toward brands to determine levels of loyalty.

The first of these is not straightforward in retailing, as the behavioural measures have to be established based upon variables such as the length of time and means by which loyalty should be measured. For example, if two purchases are made for high priced

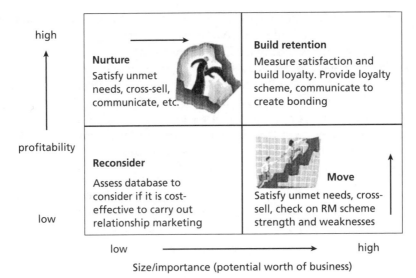

Fig. 8.5 Assessment of customer database

products over a year is this different from a larger number of lower priced purchases? The weakness of the behavioural approach is that patronage can be generated through habit, convenience, income constraint or lack of alternative choices. However, there may be customers we want to retain and develop on a selective basis because we know from profiling them against a database that they will provide longer-term lifetime benefit. In order to provide higher levels of profit, through loyalty, retailers need to ensure that they concentrate on developing a number of key areas that impact upon loyalty. These are: improve perception of perceived value; maximize customer satisfaction in order to create greater commitment and bonding; and ensure that any critical episodes in the interaction with customers have a positive outcome. A retailer has to consider the activity of customers against the profitability and potential of their business over the longer term. When setting up a loyalty scheme the matrix in Fig. 8.5 can help the retailer decide upon what actions to take for the different categories of customer. It should be obvious that the greatest effort needs to be applied to those customers who potentially can deliver the highest returns.

Loyalty should not be confused with satisfaction. However, a high level of satisfaction is a necessary yet not sufficient reason for loyalty as higher levels of satisfaction may reduce the reason for defection or disloyalty. Satisfaction does not always result in retention or loyalty yet on the other hand dissatisfaction does not always result in defection (O'Malley, 1998). Hart *et al.* (1999) offer a number of reasons related to the decisions for setting up loyalty schemes:

- building lasting relationships with customers by rewarding them for their patronage;
- gaining higher profits through extended product usage and cross-selling;
- gathering customer information;
- de-commodifyng brands (i.e. differentiating from the crowd);
- defending market position (against a competitor's loyalty scheme); and
- pre-empting competitive activity.

We should be aware that loyalty schemes are not the same as relationship marketing schemes because many loyalty schemes are run as if they were a sophisticated form of sales promotion. This is in contradiction to the need to create closer bonds and change attitudes based upon the communication and promotional campaigns of RM schemes and marketing campaigns. A good relationship scheme would utilize a loyalty scheme as a reinforcing rather than leading component of the marketing effort. The withdrawal of the main Safeway ABC loyalty scheme has been attacked on the basis that the company failed to embrace the need to maximize the benefits of its scheme in terms of data gathering and profiling. The withdrawal of the Safeway scheme was followed by a clear intent by Tesco and Sainsbury to stay with loyalty schemes as both companies offered 250 and 500 points respectively for any ABC scheme member to switch membership.

It would be useful if we were to define loyalty. Loyalty is

a state of mind which predisposes an individual towards a particular retailer and leads to a higher than normal proportion of expenditure to be devoted to the retailer's offers.

To understand loyalty there are a number of aspects that are important. Those dealing with brand loyalty are covered in Chapter 12 on the management of a retail brand. In essence there is a hierarchy of loyalty and a customer can be placed in different positions for different retailers.

1 *True loyalty* – this is where a single retailer may be used to satisfy a retail need and this retailer will dominate the purchase behaviour unless the first choice does not have the required product in stock.

2 *Latent loyalty* – occurs when the customer feels an element of loyalty yet will not buy from that retailer on every occasion.

3 *Spurious loyalty* – where little difference is perceived between retailers there is often inertia which keeps a customer loyal based upon habit. When there are few reasons to become loyal inertia is the weak bond which retains the customer. Banks are notorious for having spurious loyalty as it is found that only about 10 per cent of customers describe themselves as loyal yet very few customers switch their bank accounts each year.

4 *No loyalty* – is a state whereby customers in a specific retail category will move around from retailer to retailer as there is little benefit and difference perceived between any of the outlets in the marketplace.

Reichheld and Sasser (1990) described the need to look after existing customers as their research of more than one hundred companies in different sectors revealed improving retention can improve profits from 25 per cent to 85 per cent by a reduction in defection by 5 per cent. The analysis of a credit card company indicated that lowering the defection rate from 20 per cent to 10 per cent doubled the longevity of the average customer's relationship from five to ten years and more than doubled the profit stream. Therefore, any increase or decrease in loyalty can produce dramatic impacts on the financial return of an organization. It is for this reason that relationship and loyalty schemes have been adopted to improve the profitability of businesses.

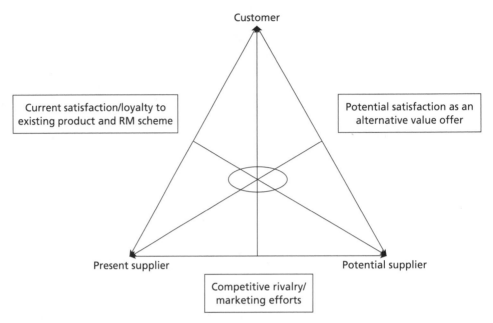

Fig. 8.6 Churn triad

Relationship marketing or loyalty schemes have a number of benefits for the retailer:

● The retailer can accurately track the purchasing habit of large numbers of loyalty scheme members and this enables the acquisition of important data which can be utilized for planning and promotional purposes. This will allow for the acquisition, monitoring and retention of valuable customers.

● A good scheme will lead to repeat purchases through targeted incentives and benefits to visit the retail outlet and make purchases. It can help build business with existing customers.

● The scheme will act as a promotion for acquiring new customers and they, in turn, can tell others about their experience. This relies on good staff morale to deliver the level of service that will help build loyalty.

● The customer may be willing to pay higher prices if the overall scheme enhances the purchase experience.

● Customers will not take as much notice of alternative offers and promotions if they are already linked into a worthwhile loyalty scheme.

A number of companies are affected by the problem of churn, which is the rate at which customers are lost to competitors each year. Churn is reduced by having switching costs such as a number of reward points which cannot then be added to achieve a reward or prize; or a penalty clause such as if an individual changes their mortgage to a competitor they will need to pay a set number of months' interest. Churn is part of the competitive environment where companies forever try to attract new business from their competitors. Figure 8.6 indicates the dynamics of this situation.

Table 8.2 Multiple use of loyalty cards (November 1997)

Cards held by company name	All (%)	Tesco Clubcard (%)	Sainsbury Reward card (%)	Safeway ABC card (%)	Argos Premier Points (%)
Tesco	31	100	35	34	35
Sainsbury	26	30	100	25	29
Safeway*	16	18	15	100	20
Argos	14	16	15	17	100
Boots	12	15	18	17	21
Homebase	10	17	16	15	13
M&S	10	18	19	14	15

Source: Institute of Grocery Distribution, 1998
Note: * Safeway scheme abandoned 2000

Loyalty cards

Loyalty cards normally fall into either the magnetic strip or the smart card category. Relationship schemes are often card-based loyalty programmes using the former type. The cards are inexpensive to produce. Each time a magnetic strip card is used the card identifies the purchaser so that other details of the transaction can be captured within the company database, providing historical information on each card member. Smart cards are more expensive to produce and have a chip on the card on which data is stored. They can be taken from transaction to transaction which means the loyalty scheme can be shared between a number of companies. Boots have introduced a card, containing a microchip, for the 12 million members of its scheme. A card-based loyalty scheme can be expensive to set up; a retail company wanting to collect information on a million of its customers will have to pay from £5 to £10 million on creating the system and then bear the cost of the annual data capture which can be around 75p for each member.

The worry is that a growing number of customers will belong to several card schemes and this will dilute the impact of individual schemes. In 1997 it was estimated that there were 55 million active loyalty programme participants in the UK, indicating a crossover between many of the schemes (IGD, 1998). Table 8.2 indicates that 35 per cent of Tesco cardholders will also belong to the Sainsbury Reward Card scheme and that 30 per cent of Sainsbury cardholders also belong to a Tesco scheme.

With the figures in Table 8.2 in mind, we need to ensure that we realize that there are different types of shopping occasion. It was found by *Which? Magazine* (1996) that customers are more loyal to those stores where they do most of their shopping and are more likely to embark on secondary 'top-up shopping' for daily essentials such as bread or milk. Therefore, the penetration of the market in the use of cards reflects this type of activity. This is because the convenience of the location is a major determinant in the loyalty process, not simply the fact that someone has joined a loyalty scheme.

The use of different cards is expanding and as shown in the information box there are many different varieties of plastic cards in use. These cards are replacing the use of cheques as a means of carrying out transactions.

Plastic cards

According to APACS (2001 website) there are nearly 120 million bank and building society plastic cards in issue in the UK, with over 85 per cent of the adult population holding one or more plastic cards. Plastic cards have numerous uses as listed below:

- *Affinity card*: A credit card that enables the card issuer to provide a donation to an organization (normally a charity) every time the card is used.
- *ATM (Automated Teller Machine) card*: Also known as a cash card, cash dispenser card or cash machine card. A plastic card used in an ATM for cash withdrawals and other bank services.
- *Charge card*: A plastic payment card which requires the cardholder to settle the account at the end of a specified period.
- *Cheque guarantee card*: Also known as a cheque card. These are issued by a bank or building society to guarantee settlement of cheques to third parties or to support the encashment of cheques at a financial institution up to a specified value (£50, £100 or £250). Most debit and some credit cards may also function as cheque guarantee cards (multifunction cards). Around 54.2 million plastic cards carry a Domestic Cheque Guarantee Scheme function.
- *Chip or smart card*: Also known as an integrated circuit or smart card. A chip card holds details on a computer chip instead of a traditional magnetic strip.
- *Credit card*: A plastic payment card that enables the holder to make purchases and to draw cash up to a pre-arranged ceiling. The credit granted can be settled in full by the end of a specified period or in segmented payments, with the balance taken as extended credit. The holder is sometimes charged an annual fee.
- *Debit card*: A plastic payment card which is linked to a bank or building society account and used to pay for goods and services by debiting the holder's account. Debit cards are usually combined with other facilities such as ATM and cheque guarantee functions.
- *Electronic purse*: Also known as a pre-payment card. This card has a stored cash value which can be used to purchase goods and services – it is an alternative to cash. The card can be disposable or re-loadable. Mondex and VisaCash are both electronic purse products.
- *Loyalty card*: Cards issued typically by retailers to promote customer loyalty and allow customers to earn rewards or discounts, e.g. Tesco Clubcard.
- *Payment card*: A generic term for any plastic card (credit, debit, charge, etc.) that is used on its own to pay for goods and services or to withdraw cash.
- *Purchasing card*: A payment card issued to businesses, companies or government departments to make supplier and/or trade payments.
- *Store card*: Also known as a retailer card. A plastic payment card that can be used only with a specified retailer or group of retailers.
- *Travel and entertainment card*: A plastic payment card that operates similarly to a charge card, e.g. American Express and Diners Club cards.

PERSONAL SELLING

Personal selling is an attempt to gain benefit through face-to-face or telephone contact between the seller's representative and those people with whom the seller wants to communicate. This may be based upon sales activity in-store, evening calls to try to sell services or products, or sales calls by paid salespersons either to companies or to private individuals. Whatever situation occurs in the buyer–seller relationship, trust is an important aspect of any interaction. This may be trust in the salesperson, trust in the company, attitude towards product, communication openness, loyalty intention and loyalty behaviour. Trust is a *perceived credibility* of the company and its staff. In the buyer and seller relationship, trust is frequently considered fundamental to the successful outcome of highly priced products. This is because trust affects the credibility in the communication between seller and customer, all of which creates commitment and greater loyalty intention and loyalty behaviour.

The importance of personal selling differs among retail businesses on the basis of the type of merchandise offered. A retailer offering low-risk, low-price goods, which are promoted, need only employ sales staff who can complete the transaction and deal with minor enquiries. The typical information required will be the current policy on reductions or special offers, guarantees or possible methods of payment. While the demeanour of the staff in this situation is important, there is little sales negotiation skill required to conclude the transaction. However, it should be noted that the trend is towards retailers reducing the number of sales personnel by offering greater self-selection of products in order to save on sales staff costs.

In a store where there are highly priced or more complex items for sale the customer has to cope with not only finding a salesperson to relate to but also one who has expert information. Such retail sales employees are often viewed as *order takers* but they should be viewed as *order procurers*. This is because for higher risk purchases customers utilize and seek out expert advice and help. Groom (1998) has argued that the sales assistant is now making a comeback because the need for good advice is more important to the fashion shopper. Situations where it is important to have trained staff are:

- where the item has to be made to fit the customer's specific requirements, for example a wedding dress or made-to-measure clothes;
- where the product is technically complex and the range is wide, for example a computer or a video camera;
- when the product is expensive in relation to the individual's income, such as an overseas holiday;
- when flexible pricing is practised and negotiation over price takes place, for example car sales.

The importance of the service aspects of retail were discussed in Chapter 4, with the one-to-one contact of the salesperson being seen as key to the way the retail company is judged. For this reason sales staff have to be carefully selected and then well trained.

The intention of personal selling is to:

- obtain a sale. Often customers enter the retail outlet after acquiring information and the salesperson needs to persuade them to purchase;

1	Preparing through skills and knowledge	Feedback and learning from prior listening and training
2	Anticipating and identifying a prospective sale	Feedback and learning from prior listening and understanding customers
3	Method of approaching the potential customer and task	Feedback and learning from prior listening plus asking appropriate questions
4	Presenting the features and benefits	Active selling and listening in order to check on acceptability of offer
5	Dealing with customer concerns	Active listening in order to revise the argument to overcome objections
6	Building obligation and commitment	Active listening in order to ensure the offer is acceptable and the sale can be concluded
7	Establishing affinity and relationship	Reinforcement of the relationship through creating a satisfied customer

Fig. 8.7 The retail selling process

- stimulate sales of 'impulse buy' purchases by bringing attention to extra requirements;
- complete a successful transaction with the customer;
- leave the customer satisfied and well informed, no matter whether a transaction has or has not occurred;
- create good customer relations.

The rationale for personal selling, as listed above, means that there should never be a role conflict between whether a salesperson should be straightening and folding stock as opposed to engaging any customer entering the department in a conversation. To reduce any conflict felt by the salesperson, the high service retailer should reinforce the message that the customer is always the priority for attention. The overriding values of the retailer – the commitment to excellence in selling – have to be reinforced through compliments, incentives and rewards, and training. This training should include aspects of merchandise manufacture, buying and control as well as selling techniques. A salesperson can only sell convincingly if he or she understands fully the product and its benefits.

Selling is a process of steps whereby the salesperson builds up a personal obligation for the customer to make a purchase. This selling process is a series of moves and counter-moves to ensure that the offer is acceptable (*see* Fig. 8.7).

The retail selling process is made up of a number of the steps outlined in Fig. 8.7: preparing, anticipating a prospective sale, approaching, presenting, dealing with concerns, gaining commitment and establishing relationships. All these are linked into the feedback process of active listening and response. This is because the approach allows the salesperson to relate to the individual needs which will be specific to that customer. Most salespeople think their job is to talk rather than to listen, but it is only through listening that a good salesperson can provide the right offer and arguments to achieve the sale. The advantage of personal selling is that a salesperson can adapt the communication of benefits to be gained to the specific needs of the customer. The feedback process of listening to the customer's needs allows the salesperson to be flexible in their approach. This is made easier in a selling situation because the personal contact produces heightened awareness and attention by the customer. However, the sales functions of retailers have to be carefully handled because less skilled staff, who lack empathy, will be judged as being 'pushy'.

A salesperson will use questions to focus both on what the customer is looking for and on why, when something is offered, they may have objections to it. An *open-ended question* which requires the customer to explain their response in some detail is often preferable to a *closed question* which will require only a yes or no answer. Open questions such as, 'What are you looking for today?' are far better than, 'May I help you?', which can prompt, 'No thank you.' Asking for the reasons for a purchase, or what the feelings and attitudes are to any merchandise shown will allow the salesperson to select an appropriate type of offer.

PUBLIC RELATIONS

Public relations is non-personal communication which changes opinion or achieves coverage in a mass medium, which is not paid for by the source. The coverage could include space given to a press release or favourable editorial comment. Public relations (PR) is important not only in obtaining editorial coverage, but also in suppressing potentially bad coverage. A company which has good links with the media is more likely to have the opportunity to stop or moderate news that could be damaging to the company. Consumer affairs television programmes quite often berate retailers for poor service or dangerous products. More recently, the use of cheap child labour in the production of merchandise for Western markets has become a newsworthy subject. This all requires sensible public relations reaction in order to retain a positive image for the retail company and industry.

The major benefit of PR is that it can promote and enhance a company's image. This is very important for service-based companies that are reliant on a more tangible positive image in order to be successful. PR is a highly credible form of communication as people like to read 'news stories' and will believe them to be less biased than information provided in advertisements. However, editorial decisions over what is communicated will mean publishers have control over the message, its timing, placement; and therefore coverage is out of a company's hands.

Benefits of obtaining good PR effort and coverage are:

- perceived to be impartial and acts as a neutral endorsement of the retailer;
- credible and believable as it is not identified as a paid form of promotion;
- helps to build image of a brand and develop favourable opinions by the drip effect of the information provided;
- can generate increased sales;
- allows for a cost-effective means to promote seasonal merchandise and new company or sales initiatives; and
- can possibly limit or neutralize negative or hostile opinions.

PR activity can either be planned or unplanned. Planned activity means the retailer attempts to retain control over the activity and news release. With unplanned activity, the retailer simply reacts in the most beneficial way to the chance of some publicity or to suppress a negative news item. Larger retailers will have a public relations agency or in-house department. These will attempt to influence the company's 'publics'. The 'publics' are made up of those important to the retailer – customers, shareholders, employees, suppliers, local community, the media and local and national government. Planned publicity will involve sending press releases and photographs to the media (trade papers, local and national press, radio and television), organizing press conferences for more newsworthy events, sending letters to editors of journals or local newspapers, organizing different creative 'stunts' to acquire the right tone of media coverage, and making speeches (or writing articles) on informed retail issues in order to be perceived as a well-informed company.

Public relations activities

- Media information releases / contact / speeches
- Production of PR materials (video, CDs, Web information, press kits, corporate identity materials, etc.)
- PR events, media conferences and newsworthy 'stunts'
- Advertorials (which require PR copy along with an advertisement)
- In-house and customer magazines
- Facility visits to store etc.
- Sponsorship and donations
- Lobbying

The media are interested in their own circulation, listening and viewing figures and, therefore, to be successful all PR has to be newsworthy and of benefit to media interests. New and unusual information on new products or technology, expansion and development plans, human interest stories about staff and their achievements – all written up and complemented by photographs – may be placed in trade and local press. Finally, the overall PR efforts should be monitored. Measurement may be based upon the actual activity to acquire the coverage – such as whether the conference worked, how many attended and whether they were the right people, was it cost-effective, etc., or the results of the activity such as the amount of coverage produced. Coverage is assessed in terms of the range and number of media, number of column centimetres or mentions or position in the publication. It can also be checked for accuracy of the editorial produced against the initial communication sent and importantly the number of adverse as opposed to favourable mentions. The media coverage can be assessed against important publics targeted or more basically as to whether the readership, listening or viewing public of the coverage matched that of the retailer's target groups.

POINT OF PURCHASE: POP designers add creative ingenuity

Point-of-purchase (POP) material is growing up, becoming more innovative and daring. While POP once accounted for less than 5% of marketing budgets, it now typically takes between 10% and 20%. While the technology behind much POP material is not new, it is cheaper than ever and being used in innovative ways. Whether it's internet access points in banks, fridge sound chips, lenticular ads, fashion or sports on plasma screens in bars and stores or interactive kiosks, the point of sale has never seen so much action – or, indeed, interaction.

With retailers linking POP to customer databases through loyalty cards, the medium is coming into its own. And shoppers' willingness to interact with in-store terminals is great news for marketers. Simply stacking high-tech products on shelves doesn't sell them; demonstrating what they can do, does. Consumers will interact with a device if it offers tangible value. Some may be nervous of computer-powered kiosks, but technophobia will continue to decrease as word-of-mouth spreads news of the benefits of what's on offer, and the PlayStation generation grows up. In the meantime, retailers such as Virgin's V Shops are training staff to offer assistance to interested but wary shoppers. V Shops also uses its interactive terminals to offer a sales route for the huge stock of products that cannot be accommodated in-store. On the back of its £14m investment, Boots now sees 1.5 million customers a month using its kiosks, 50% of whom buy more because of them. Noeleen Kershaw, Boots' Advantage Point controller, says: 'We're looking at using the kiosks as a key way of talking directly to the customer in-store. Shoppers will be able to book services such as opticians' appointments, talk to customer services, access product databases and information, and take part in third-party offers and promotions.' Boots is also looking at installing touch points throughout the store, such as a hair diagnostics point in the hair care section. And Kershaw wants to link the in-store information to Boots' web site to give customers access from home. According to Philip Evason, commercial director at Inter.Act Electronic Marketing, the company behind Boots' and Sainsbury's terminals, targeting is the key to kiosks' success. 'People may have a shopping list, but we give them a reason to do more – go to new categories, try something different and buy more. We don't do that indiscriminately; we know who the

customer is and what they have bought before. The value of that level of targeting is that you can afford to be incredibly generous with your offers because you know who you're speaking to.'

As it seeks to improve customer interaction with its services – particularly PC banking to the PC underclass – NatWest is providing free internet 'clickstart' terminals in branches. John Ryan was behind the design and initial roll-out of ten units and has trained meeter-greeters to overcome consumer nervousness. As well as attracting footfall, NatWest clickstart is gleaning information on existing customers. 'We can find out what people are looking for from the internet once they've been introduced to it,' says branch manager Mark Mackey. 'It helps us work out how NatWest can better help them.'

At the moment, interactive media remains costly, limited in application to areas of high footfall or high-value products. But lenticular devices, that appear to move as you look at them, offer some of the benefits – raising awareness and communicating a message – at a fraction of the cost. As a technology, lenticular is not new, but it has come a long way since smiley-face bike stickers. Posters can now offer 3D images that protrude three inches and appear to move. They can also carry a few seconds of a commercial. A plastic serrated lens magnifies one of a selection of filmstrips and the image moves according to the changing position of the viewer. Rob Kelly, marketing manager of Photobition, the design agency behind Selfridges' blink-and-you've-missed-it lenticular storefront window, says the medium is an extremely powerful communicator because it catches you unaware. 'You think you're looking at something static and then it changes, taking you by surprise – that's a really powerful attention grabber that never wears off.'

On Oxford Street, 70% of passers-by stopped to look at the Selfridges' window or walked back for a second take. Sales rose in the featured women's fashion departments. Other devices, using related technologies, aim to grab attention in a similar way. Nike recently used Media Vehicle's 3D Imager in its flagship London Nike Town store to appear to suspend a spinning sports shoe in mid-air.

For mainstream POP appeal, it is hard to beat the rapidly proliferating plasma screen. V Stores uses them to attract shoppers to its interactive kiosks, while Selfridges has ten of these ultra-stylish flat screens in its London store broadcasting a mix of brand imagery and fashion.

Plasma's potential. Argos is currently trialling Dynamex Technologies' digital signage system in its stores. The agency's managing director, Frank Jones, thinks plasma screens will soon be an everyday part of the shopping experience. 'There are other technologies coming along, but it will be the derivatives of plasma screens and the pricing that will be important,' he says. 'As the price drops, every store that has a message will have one or more screens.' Not all POP developments are taking place off-shelf. In Japan, electronic shelf-talkers show ads next to the product.

Martin Law, chief executive of Fords Design Group, believes that for all the high-tech noise, 'most activity is as it always has been – straightforward merchandising cabinets and displays'. Fords research suggests that 55% of consumers rate shelf displays most highly in terms of POP material which grabs their attention. 'It gives information on the shelf which is where people are looking for it,' says Law.

Indeed, POP works best when it makes the shopping experience easier. Glade made sure its activity covered both bases when it launched Duet earlier this year. It used The Aroma Company's Poparoma device, a unique pump-action mechanism for dispensing fragrances at the fixture. A 3D dispensing tray raises the product up and the dispenser's button is shaped and textured like a child's tricycle hooter. 'We deliberately shaped it like that so people would know what to do with it,' says The Aroma Company managing director Simon Harrop. 'It's successful because the consumer can interact with it, which draws them to the product.'

As POP develops, the various creative elements will begin to merge. It's not lenticular, plasma or interactive that matters, but communicating with an information-hungry, discerning consumer base, which means that effective POP must anticipate and respond to changes in the way consumers react to brands. However innovative the solution, POP material must continue to create a tangible link between the brand and the purchasing decision.

HOW TO INNOVATE – Set a clear brief, including quantities and budget details. POP works best when a client provides sufficient spend to an activity to avoid stretching the budget too thinly; Don't rely on gimmicks; they might affect a response from the consumer the first time, but it won't work the next; Build in flexibility for update and store demands; Talk to the designers, but also the users and producers – they're all in touch with different parts of the market; Merchandising and display, along with packaging, is the only three-dimensional part of marketing. Use every element of that extra dimension for full impact; Interactive POP can be unwelcoming; make sure store staff are trained and able to help customers; Avoid using technology for technology's sake. The best POP is interactive anyway; you don't always need to use computers and microchips to attract consumer attention.

Source: Belinda Gannaway, *Marketing*, 24 May 2001

OTHER IMPORTANT PROMOTIONAL TOOLS

Within the field of promotion, there is the important area of *visual merchandising*. Advertising may encourage consumers to visit the store but the retailer's display may make the difference between making a sale or not. The use of visual merchandising includes visual materials and window displays used in retail outlets to stimulate sales. Visual merchandising is non-personal in-store presentation and exhibition of merchandise, along with printed forms of communication. The approach is to:

● ensure maximum product exposure;

● provide displays which enhance product appearance and create interest;

● provide sales and product information such as display cards and posters;

● allow for storage and security of stock;

● generate additional sales through impulse purchases or by reminding the consumer of what is on offer based upon a message which is directly related to the product.

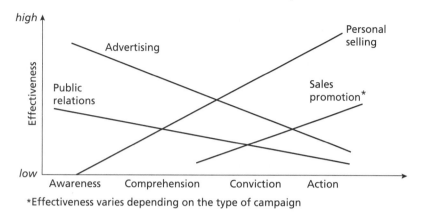

*Effectiveness varies depending on the type of campaign

Fig. 8.8 Effectiveness of the four major methods of promotion

If retailers rely on self-service of items then a selection display such as those found in greetings card or music shops is required. Selection displays are generally open to facilitate easy browsing and inspection. Retailers use selection displays to exhibit their everyday assortments of convenience or shopping goods. Effective use of this approach requires a logical grouping of the merchandise by its usage. Ease of selection through uncomplicated, well-organized arrangements will increase sales. There are also special displays which are placed in well-exposed locations to bring some interest to the store. These can offer a dramatic impact by the use of display equipment and merchandise. Point-of-purchase promotional displays are a particular type of special display which will be on the counter, in the store window or other relevant places. The visual display may include banners, counter cards, end-aisle stands, video-screen displays, floor-stand displays, trolley advertising and shelf extenders. However, they also include in-store broadcasts and interactive kiosks. The point-of-purchase objectives may be to attract *attention*, to *remind* the customer of a need or link to other forms of promotion, *differentiate* the store's image and *attract* more custom. For example Hugo Boss installed a 106-inch television screen in its London outlet to mix fragments of sporting events with its latest fashion collections. As this could be seen from outside the store it achieved an increase in store visitors.

There is a growing use of *sponsorship* and *direct marketing* which do not comfortably fit into the other four promotion categories (*see* Fig. 8.8). Direct marketing is a method of contacting customers and prospects in a direct way with the intention of generating an immediate and measurable response. In the 1990s the use of relationship building and long-term retention became of increasing importance for direct marketing. In order to make direct contact with the customer base there is a requirement to have a database which will allow for: individualizing the communication and collecting data on transactions so that measurement of response can be provided. The use of direct methods can also be based upon not having information regarding the contact address – teletext, direct response advertising. However, most do have a contact address – catalogue company mailing, direct mailing, Internet e-mail, and telemarketing by phone.

Sponsorship is the material or financial support of a specific activity, normally but not exclusively sport or the arts, which does not form part of the sponsor company's normal business. As Meenaghan (1998) has pointed out, throughout its relatively brief history commercial sponsorship has changed in many fundamental ways. Most evident has been its development from a small-scale activity to a major global industry. Sponsorship is treated much more seriously today, with sponsors adopting sophistic-ated planning, selection and evaluation procedures for their sponsorship programmes. Banks have utilized sponsorship extensively to promote and enhance their corporate images.

A range of direct sell companies, by clever utilization of retailers' loyalty-scheme database address lists, is using direct marketing more extensively. The main method is direct mail which is postal communication by an identified sponsor. This is being expanded into database marketing based upon relationship marketing principles and an increasing use of telephone sales campaigns. Direct methods of contacting prospective customers are used to:

- encourage store visits from new customers;
- increase sales when there is a unique or special merchandise offer to be made;
- take full advantage of using the information from one department to cross-sell other aspects of the store or its services;
- build loyalty programmes in order to retain customers and increase revenue;
- improve the image and competitive position of the store in relation to the competitors;
- send out special offers for low season or sales periods in order to increase in-store traffic and sales. There is sometimes resistance to too much direct mail as it is often associated with 'junk mail'. Good direct marketing selects the target carefully and provides the correct offer.

Finally *billboards*, sometimes referred to as *poster sites*, are used as either permanent painted sites or covered in prepared poster advertisements which can be frequently changed. The space is normally available on a rental basis, depending on the site and time of year. The use of this form of promotion can be beneficial if located near to the store, on a transport route which services the store or area or on the vehicles themselves. The costs are relatively low, based upon estimates of numbers of passing observers. However, car drivers, those travelling on public transport and the walking public need to have a short, clear message if the medium is to be successful. It is also important to real-ize that if the site is not illuminated then in the winter there will be less opportunity to see the message than at other times of the year.

CHARACTERISTICS OF PROMOTIONS

Each of the promotional elements discussed above has the capacity to achieve a different promotional objective. While personal selling has high potency for achieving commun-ication objectives only a relatively small number of people can be contacted. Therefore, advertising is a better method of reaching a high number of people at low cost. Public relations is more credible than advertising but there is more control over what is com-municated through advertising messages and these messages can be repeated on a regular basis. When it is difficult to raise advertising budgets, public relations is a lower cost alternative but it is difficult to control the timing and consistency of PR coverage. Sales promotions, such as leaflet drops which offer retail price discounts, may produce an initial trial for a product – for instance, the purchase of a product which is being launched into the market – but this type of promotion is most suitable if used only for a short-term period.

Each part of the promotions mix has its own strength and weakness. While this may include the factors of cost, ability to target different groups, and control, there are other important considerations. Figure 8.8 indicates the relative strengths of each of the four forms of promotion: advertising, personal selling, PR and sales promotion. They are compared with each other based on the level of awareness of the communication and its comprehension, as well as whether it can build conviction and succeed in creating action.

Integrated marketing communications

It should be obvious that many of the activities of retail promotion will occur in different areas of the company and with different activities taking place based upon the predilections of the individuals in control. Therefore, while it is obvious that co-ordination is required it is often not carried out in a systematic way. If it were, all elements of marketing communications could work in unison to create a whole that is greater than the sum of the parts. To ensure such impact is achieved there is a requirement for an integrated marketing communications (IMC) approach throughout the business. However, this will only occur if the various components of the marketing mix and communication effort are co-ordinated. Essentially the use of IMC requires first that the area of marketing and possibly the company are integrated so that a fully integrated effort will follow. To achieve this the retailer has to provide guidelines that direct the efforts in every part of the organization so that all aspects of marketing and communication offer reinforcement to each other. The benefits of IMC are:

- greater efficiency in resource allocations especially as marketing costs escalate;
- provides competitive advantage;
- provides clearer guidelines and direction for all company efforts;
- allows the new types of development – relationship schemes; partnerships, alliances, etc. – to be co-ordinated with existing company practice;
- helps with launch of technological change requirements – Internet, kiosks, etc.;
- realization that consistency and reinforcement of core messages are important;
- awareness that brand reputation and building has to have a co-ordinated approach.

CONCLUSION

Retail promotion involves a complex series of communications to inform the target groups of the retailer's store and its offerings so as to increase demand and profits. There are a number of promotional mix tools available to achieve this. They consist primarily of advertising, sales promotion, personal selling and public relations. Moreover, we should not forget that the store itself will play a part in this process based upon its atmospherics and visual merchandising. Like other elements in the marketing mix, promotion does not work in isolation. Promotion is often used in conjunction with other constituents of the marketing mix, such as pricing markdowns, to stimulate the demand for products and subsequent store visits. Retail promotion is used to convey the store's current offer – whether it is product, place or price, or a combination of these. However, a consistently good set of promotional campaigns will help establish a store's long-term image.

Each component of the promotion mix has unique advantages and disadvantages. The appropriate choice has to be based on which method is most suited to the marketing objectives at any one time. The largest proportion of a retailer's promotion budget will be allocated to advertising and sales promotion. Advertising is used as a means to inform, persuade and remind customers that the retailer's merchandise and service offer is the one best suited to their individual needs. Sales promotion is used as a means to generate short-term increases in sales and, therefore, is an important part of the promotion mix. One other tool is public relations, which does not require large budgets to be successful. Public relations allows the use of other media channels such as journalism, radio and television to act as opinion leaders for the personality and image of the retailer's business and product offering.

EXERCISES

The exercises in this section relate to the issues discussed in this chapter. It is suggested that you work through them before moving on to Chapter 9.

1 Explain what is meant by a sales promotion. Either collect five examples of different retail sales promotions to discuss and/or describe what types of sales promotion would encourage you to buy, and why.

2 You have been asked by the manager of a chain of pet food shops to set up a relationship marketing scheme for the company. Draw up a plan for the recruitment, contact and communication with members and any other factors which you feel are important. Provide a timescale for the events in a flow diagram.

3 If you had to write the communications plan for a department store what are the key aspects of the plan you would need to have agreed by management? Also, what percentages would you allocate from the budget to different aspects of the communication mix?

4 Collect at least three weeks of the local newspaper and other local magazines or publications. Then carry out a content analysis of the publicity that different retailers may have gained. This should be both quantitative and qualitative and the results should be assessed to provide a note of guidance on how retailers can achieve good PR coverage.

Quantitative	Names of retailers receiving coverage
Amount of coverage (measure space)	
Number of times name of company mentioned	
etc.	
Qualitative	
Tone of copy (adjectives used good/bad)	
Image created, etc.	

REFERENCES AND FURTHER READING

Alba, J., Lynch, J., Weitz, B. and Janiszewski, C. (1998) 'Interactive home shopping: consumer, retailer, and manufacturer incentives to participate in electronic marketplaces', *Journal of Marketing*, 61 (3), 38–53.

Allaway, A., Mason, J.B. and Brown, G. (1987) 'An optimal decision support model for department-level promotion mix planning', *Journal of Retailing*, 63, Fall, 215–42.

APACS (2001) Association for Payment Clearing Services, www.apacs.org.uk

Betts, E. and McGoldrick, P.J. (1995) 'The strategy of the retail sale, typology, review and synthesis', *International Review of Retail, Distribution and Consumer Research*, 5 (3), 303–32.

Branigan, L. (1998) 'The Internet: the emerging premier direct marketing channel', *Direct Marketing*, 61 (1), 46–8.

Christopher, M., Payne, A. and Ballantyne, D. (1996) *Relationship Marketing*. Oxford: Butterworth-Heinemann.

Comer, J.M., Mehta, R. and Holmes, T.L. (1998) 'Information technology: retail users versus nonusers', *Journal of Interactive Marketing*, 12 (2), 49–62.

Corliss, L.G. (1995) 'Differential responses to retail sales promotion among African-American and Anglo-American consumers', *Journal of Retailing*, 71 (1), 83–92.

Datamonitor (1996) *Loyalty Discount Schemes*. Report. July.

Dawes, J. (1998) 'Winning new customers in financial services: using relationship marketing and information technology in consumer financial services', *European Management Journal*, 16 (2), 249.

Dibb, S. and Meadows, M. (2001) 'The application of a relationship marketing perspective in retail banking', *Service Industries Journal*, 21 (1), 169–94.

East, R., Harris, P. and Willson, G. (1995) 'Loyalty to supermarkets', *International Review of Retail, Distribution and Consumer Research*, 5 (1), 99–109.

The Economist (2000) 'Handcuffs on the high street: Silly shopping regulations in Europe', *The Economist*, 13 May.

Fiorito, S., May, E. and Straughn, K. (1995) 'Quick response in retailing: components and implementation', *International Journal of Retail and Distribution Management*, 23 (5), 12–21.

Gannaway, B. (2001) 'POINT OF PURCHASE: POP designers add creative ingenuity', *Marketing*, 24 May.

Gannaway, B. (2001) 'Get the most out of window space – Innovative and well-targeted window displays can give stores a competitive edge', *Marketing*, 2 August.

Gengler, C.E., Leszczyc, P. and Popkowski, T. (1997) 'Using customer satisfaction research for relationship marketing: a direct marketing approach', *Journal of Direct Marketing*, 11 (1), 23–9.

Gilbert, D.C. (1996) 'Relationship marketing and airline loyalty schemes', *Tourism Management*, 17 (8), 575–82.

Gronroos, C. (1990) 'Relationship approach to the marketing function in service contexts: the marketing and organization behavior interface', *Journal of Business Research*, 20 (1), 3–12.

Gronroos, C. (1991) 'The marketing strategy continuum: towards a marketing concept for the 1990s', *Management Decisions*, 29 (1), 7–13.

Gronroos, C. (1992) 'Facing the challenge of service competition: the economies of services', in Kunst, P. and Lemmik, J. (eds) *Quality Management in Services*. Maastricht: Van Gorcum.

Gronroos, C. (1994a) 'Toward a relationship marketing paradigm', *Journal of Marketing Management*, 10, 347–60.

Gronroos, C. (1994b) 'From marketing mix to relationship marketing: towards a paradigm shift in marketing', *Management Decisions*, 32 (2), 4–20.

Groom, A. (1998) 'Fashion: the expert shop assistant is making a comeback. Everyone interested in modern style should rejoice', *Financial Times*, 30 May.

Hart, S., Smith, A., Sparks, L. and Tzokas, N. (1999) 'Are loyalty schemes a manifestation of relationship marketing?' *Journal of Marketing Management*, 15, 541–62.

IGD (Institute of Grocery Distribution) (1998) *Grocery Market Bulletin*. Watford: IGD Business Publications.

Javalgi, R. and Moberg, C. (1997) 'Service loyalty: implications for service providers', *Journal of Services Marketing*, 11 (3), 165–79.

Kotler, P., Armstrong, G., Saunders, J. and Wong, V. (1999) *Principles of Marketing*. 2nd European edn. Hemel Hempstead: Prentice Hall.

Kumar, V. and Pereira, A. (1997) 'Assessing the competitive impact of type, timing, frequency, and magnitude of retail promotions', *Journal of Business Research*, 40 (1), 1–13.

Lam, S., Vandenbosch, M. and Pearce, M. (1998) 'Retail sales force scheduling based on store traffic forecasting', *Journal of Retailing*, 74 (1), 61–88.

Meenaghan, T. (1998) 'Current developments and future directions in sponsorship', *International Journal of Advertising*, 17 (1), 3–28.

O'Malley, L. (1998) 'Can loyalty schemes really build loyalty?' *Marketing Intelligence and Planning*, 16 (1), 47–55.

Payne, A., Christopher, M., Clark, M. and Peck, H. (1995) *Relationship Marketing for Competitive Advantage*. Oxford: Butterworth-Heinemann.

Powell, T.C. and Dent-Micallef, A. (1997) 'Information technology as competitive advantage: the role of human, business, and technology resources', *Strategic Management Journal*, 18 (5), 375–405.

Reichheld, F. and Sasser, W.E. Jr (1990) 'Zero defections: quality comes to services', *Harvard Business Review*, 68, September/October 105–10.

Riera, J. (2001) 'Points don't always mean prizes in loyalty card lottery', *Retail Week*, 19 May.

Ries, A. and Trout, J. (1981) *Positioning: The Battle for Your Mind*. London: McGraw-Hill.

Stern, B.B. (1997) 'Advertising intimacy: relationship marketing and the services consumer', *Journal of Advertising*, 26 (4), 7–19.

Ward, A. (2001) 'Persuading viewers to pay for services could be tough', *Financial Times*, 5 September.

Yoo, C., Park, J. and MacInnis, D.J. (1998) 'Effects of store characteristics and in-store emotional experiences on store attitude', *Journal of Business Research*, 42 (3), 253–63.

9 Retail distribution and supply chain management

This chapter should enable you to understand and explain:
- management of the process of logistics and distribution;
- channels and channel flows;
- growth of channel relationships and partnerships;
- distribution logistics and stock control;
- various distribution costs and their source;
- computerized replenishment systems;
- Internet applications and direct systems.

The special characteristics of retail businesses and the emergence of major retailers in the marketplace have led to specific forms of distribution or channel service. Prior to consumption, the retail product has to be both available and accessible. This requires a supply chain distribution system. A distribution system is the channel used to bring items to the place of sale, or the means by which a retail supplier gains access to the potential buyers of the product. More recently the efficiencies of supply chain management linked to IT have made major differences to the effectiveness of retailers and their overall profitability. (Read Chapter 13 in order to understand the way IT has changed the whole field of distribution logistics.) Also, there is a major trend to *disintermediation* which is the bypassing of traditional intermediaries and subsequent selling directly to final buyers. For example, Dell Computer sells directly to final buyers having eliminated retailers from their marketing channel.

With the ever-growing size and dispersal of traditional retail operations, controlling merchandise as part of store operations has been of paramount importance. This goes beyond an administration system; modern supply chain management can achieve competitive advantage through shorter lead times for restocking, reduced inventory size and costs, improved management information and greater overall control.

Retailing cannot be divorced from an understanding of the supply chain as the following retail definition from Davies (1993) indicates:

> **The management of resources to supply the product and service needs of the end-consumer, encompassing the supply chain of any physical products and the exchange processes involved.**

The supply chain includes all the activities and exchanges involved in extracting, processing, manufacturing and distributing goods and services from raw materials through to the end consumer. Supply chain management requires a holistic view of these activities and an innovative approach to their organization, in order to meet customer needs with the greatest efficiency.

CHANNELS AND CHANNEL FLOWS

There are different supply chain structures based upon *extended*, *limited* and *direct channels*. The discussion of supply chain management here will concentrate on the extended channel of retail distribution, as this is the most prevalent. An extended channel (*see* Fig. 9.1) is where the manufacturer, wholesaler and retailer provide a chain of facilitating services in order to sell the right product to the final customer. The limited channel is when a retailer works directly with the producer and, therefore, can eliminate the wholesaler and the extra costs of this part of the chain. The retailers of furniture, white goods, electrical goods, and so on quite often deal directly with the supplier and create limited supply channels. The final alternative is the direct channel. In this case the product is sold direct by either the producer or retailer. By using different direct sales marketing promotions such as direct mailing, Internet services, telephone sales techniques, etc., the channel is kept direct and the extra charges and commissions are thus eliminated. This allows some of the saving to be passed on to the customer who will purchase on the basis of lower price. It is important to realize that whatever part of the chain is eliminated, some of the functions of that link in the chain have to remain. Even if the retailer were to be dispensed with, some of the retail functions have to remain in order to achieve a transaction.

Within any of the different types of channel the flow is not restricted to physical goods alone. Other types of flow of equal importance in ensuring the channel is successful are as follows:

- *physical flow* – the movement of goods and method of transport, from one part of the chain to another;

- *ownership flow* – the transfer of title for ownership/usage from one channel member to another. This is important for legal aspects of delivery, damage and storage by the producer and intermediary as well as for the final customer;

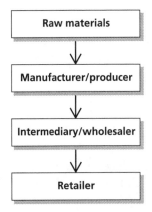

Fig. 9.1 The traditional supply channel for retail products

- *service flow* – if services are rendered as part of the process or the end product is a service or mainly service based, it is necessary to ensure that all the characteristics of the services are fully understood (*see* Chapter 4);

- *information flow* – there is a need for timely and accurate two-way information between all channel members;

- *payment flow* – there is a necessity for agreed payment transfer terms based upon services rendered or goods delivered;

- *promotion flow* – a flow of communication material needs to be used to influence both trade partners and consumers. The objectives of the promotion will be to produce a positive attitude and image for the retailer.

With the extended channel, the distribution of goods ('inventory') by retailers to consumers is achieved through the movement of goods to and from stockholding points (normally warehouses) and then on to points of purchase (stores). In marketing terminology this part of the marketing mix is referred to as 'place' but the stages involved in this chain may be referred to as 'distribution and warehousing' or, more aptly, as 'logistics' and 'supply chain management'. In the modern competitive marketplace, retailers need to achieve high levels of customer satisfaction and service but at acceptable costs. This has led to the development of increasingly sophisticated distribution systems to ensure optimum service for the supply of goods to the customer. According to Davison (1995), large, highly complex and often computerized warehouse facilities may handle several million cases per week (or in excess of £10–15 million worth of stock). Computerized stock management and information systems (for example, Tesco's Dallas, Sainsbury's BRS, Safeway's SM3, etc.) which link retailer communications direct to suppliers have been developed (for example, Tradenet) and transportation is subject to computerized control systems (for example, Paragon). These comprise sophisticated logistics systems that have become not only a means of managing the supply of goods to the customer but are key strategic tools.

Many retailers benefited from the introduction of new logistics systems in the 1980s through increasing market share or increasing profitability. Companies which have benefited from such policies are generally those which no longer consider distribution and warehousing as purely a support function or an operations' headache. Rather than simply a functional supply line, the use of retail logistics is now a valued management area with its own operational and strategic objectives.

THE SUPPLY CHANNEL

The supply channel is the total process by which products reach the end consumer as goods or services. This is a sequence of events that involves strategic decisions over different resources and the maintenance of relationships all focused on delivering optimum value to the end consumer. Figure 9.1 indicates the components of the traditional supply chain channel. Such a chain is an arrangement between paired links, where the emphasis has to be on controlling and managing the relationships in order to move products through the process effectively. This should be based on a strategic marketing and business need for the chain to achieve:

- reduced inventory and storage investment in the chain;
- improved end-user and customer service benefits through productivity and effectiveness (faster order cycle times, improved on-time shipment, lack of damage/defects, etc.);
- development of strong relational links, and hence a strong chain, in order to build competitive advantage; and
- lower procurement, transportation and unit costs which can be used to price more competitively and to increase value-added benefits.

As the whole chain is dependent on the way any two of these parts of the chain interact there is always a question of whether the working relationships will be good and provide the service and economies required. In practice, it is found that the relationships are often ones of rivalry, mistrust and secrecy. With the increasing use of multiple channels of distribution, which are sometimes competitive, this can lead to deterioration in co-ordination and co-operation between channel members. None of these is conducive to a retailer being able to provide increased added value from the supply chain. What is required is a commitment by all parties to invest in continuous improvement in order to create mutual advantage. This is because channel competitiveness is an important focus for successful retailing. Uneconomic channels are characterized by unhealthy support of existing traditional practices; disregard of the importance of information and the need to share it; lack of entrepreneurial ideas regarding innovation, renewal and development; an organizational culture of inflexibility and slow adoption of new ideas; and partial rather than major changes adopted.

New channel forms and processes are emerging which are characterized by the expectation of lower margins and more value for the customer. This means channel success will be based upon the degree to which the supply chain is improved, regardless of the margins and practices involved.

The manufacturer

The manufacturer or supplier processes raw materials into the finished consumable article. For efficiency of the chain manufacturers should not experience overproduction, allow defects, create waiting through shortage or be inefficient in the areas of transport and logistics. Manufacturers need to be aware of the implications to the chain of the elements of time and cost related to their part of the process.

Suppliers may specialize in the type of products that they process (for example, Birds Eye) or diversify into a wide product range (for example, Unilever). Suppliers of leading brands will use a high level of marketing, including sales representatives and advertising campaigns, in order to ensure that their products are given maximum public exposure. They may even reduce the cost of their products to encourage retailers to have their products featured in high flow locations within their stores.

The intermediary function

The intermediary, the wholesaler, is in effect a distributor of goods from the manufacturer or supplier to the retailer. Wholesalers have traditionally been responsible for holding large stocks of products, attempting to anticipate demands and seasonal trends, etc.

Traditionally the wholesaler has also provided a warehousing function for both the supplier and the retailer. This ensures that the supplier does not end up with stockpiles in the factory and is able to continue or switch production; the retailer has similarly benefited from the use of this intermediary in the supply channel by avoiding the need to hold large quantities of stock. This enables the retailer to free up capital, which would otherwise be tied up in stock, for other purposes.

However, modern multiple store groups and supermarket chains have rendered the use of wholesalers unnecessary in the supply chain by assuming the function of the intermediary. This has a cost-saving function. At each stage in the chain of distribution the cost price of a product is added to. This build-up of extra costs may reduce profit margins for the retailer or increase the final selling price to the customer. This is not in harmony with the normal retail objective which is to maximize sales and profitability. Additionally, each extra stage in the supply chain makes it more difficult for the retailer to control the service or the quality of the final product. The more links that are involved in the distribution chain, the less control there may be. This is allied to the risk of conflicts over relationships with each partner attempting to maximize profit.

The larger retailers have, therefore, sought to extend their control over the supply chain and moved away from the use of the intermediary. This has been particularly so in the grocery sector, where currently four grocery chains, Sainsbury, Tesco, Safeway and ASDA, account for a major share of sales in the UK packaged groceries market. The size of market share gives these companies enormous power over suppliers to negotiate discount prices and to absorb the role of the former wholesale intermediary, while ensuring the quality and service of product to the customer. For such companies the traditional supply chain no longer exists. Multiple retailers – with their clearly defined strategic objectives, extensive national coverage, centralized organizational structures and highly accurate information systems – have created logistics networks which supplant the intermediary's role of supply in filling gaps between production and consumption.

GROWTH OF CHANNEL RELATIONSHIPS AND PARTNERSHIPS

A number of interrelated power relationships characterize the UK grocery sector. These range from mutual dependence to alliances based upon secondary suppliers. The relationships are also affected by the concentration of market share in that suppliers are constrained in who they can deal with as the market is dominated by a limited number of multiple-outlet retailers. The negotiating strength of retailers has increased, and this is even more apparent when own-label products are being offered with gross margins higher than manufacturers' brands. The power that individual retailers now exert is also compounded by the centralization of decision-making, with fewer individuals at head office being involved in deciding the fate of numerous different suppliers. This has meant that store managers have little input to supplier choice and are freer to concentrate on personnel and service quality functions. Such developments have had the effect of fundamentally restructuring the supply chain. This does not apply only to food retailers as the new methods of working have affected all aspects of retail.

Driven by competitive pressure to improve efficiency and to deliver added value for customers, major players in the supply chain have been changing the way that they do business with each other. Retailers and suppliers have started to recognize the degree of mutuality between each of their own objectives. Traditionally, supply chain relationships have been adversarial, exhibiting a high degree of conflict; during the 1990s there has been a recognition that there are benefits in closer working relationships. However, there is always a potential problem for the large suppliers, which use logistics contractors, utilizing their power; this may lead to a situation founded on fear rather than mutual interdependence. Any trading relationship will include a measure of conflict and of co-operation. This can be seen as a continuum extending from a single transaction, with a very minimal requirement for trust between the two parties, to a long-term supply chain 'partnership' with a very high degree of trust, at the other extreme. Conflict imposes additional costs on the trading arrangements. Therefore, the aim is to move along the continuum, reducing the level of conflict and increasing the co-operation so that costs are reduced and quality improves.

In pre-checkout scanning days, the retailer had privileged access to current sales data and would use this as a weapon to counteract suppliers' bargaining strength. We can contrast this with recent trends of using EFTPOS and EDI technology to delegate the entire replenishment administration activity to suppliers. Technology has had a major impact on distribution. Inventory management is now driven by the scanning of merchandise at the checkout. This allows sales for all outlets to be collated and communicated straight through to the supplier, who will be responsible – within agreed parameters – for ensuring that fresh supplies arrive at retailer distribution centres to replenish outlets.

It is important to recognize that transformation to a partnership arrangement represents radical change. The previously prevailing adversarial climate, with its relatively low levels of trust, will remain deep-seated. It is not realistic to expect two organizations previously engaged in a form of opposition to each other suddenly to adopt a spirit of openness, and exhibit faith in each other and the co-operative pursuit of mutual goals. Making such changes requires a fundamental shift in the culture of each organization. This is not achieved overnight and can be a slow process, fraught with difficulties.

Leading proponents of supply chain partnerships have been vocal in their support. There has been little public expression questioning the value of these trading arrangements. The existence of a partnership does not change the fact that some large retailers tend to be dominant in their respective sectors and are not afraid to exert their power over the supply chain. In these cases, if the retailer wants a 'partnership', then a smaller supplier is unlikely to object. The very term 'partnership' conveys a message of mutual objectives, trust and co-operation. Whether the benefits of this strategy accrue on an equally mutual basis has yet to be proven.

MINICASE 9.1

Amazon looks for more fulfilment

Amazon.co.uk's effective takeover of the online fulfilment operation for bookseller Waterstone's might be yet another sign of the e-tailer's dominance, but it could pay dividends for both parties. In a market which has more commonly seen the offline incumbents snapping up struggling dotcoms, Amazon has now struck a number of such deals. In April, Amazon.com struck a similar deal with Borders, the second-largest book retailer in the US, while in July, Amazon.co.uk announced that it was to sell mobile phones through a co-branded site with Carphone Warehouse.

The Waterstone's deal means that visitors to waterstones.co.uk will be redirected to a mirror co-branded site within the Amazon.co.uk service using its web-framing format. Waterstone's will provide the content, reviews and articles, but has washed its hands of all fulfilment and customer service. Peter Mitchell, business development director at Waterstone's, explains how the multi-year deal was forged with the company keeping a firm eye on the exorbitant cost of waging an online battle with Amazon.co.uk. 'Amazon has established a clear position of market leadership in online book selling,' he explains. 'So for us to start or continue investment in order to get to an economic scale of operations would be a long and expensive journey.' But he doesn't believe that it means Waterstone's will be left in the technological dust. He says the company will gain the ability to effectively piggy-back on Amazon.co.uk as it develops because 'the deal allows a form of future-proofing for us as Amazon builds online'. However, a telling factor in the deal is that all orders made through the Waterstone's web site will be delivered with Amazon.co.uk packaging. Sally Bain, senior researcher at retail research firm Verdict, cautions that this loss of control over delivery and branding could cost Waterstone's more than money. 'Fulfilment is the key issue in getting consumers to continue to shop online, and to give that away is a risky business,' she says. 'The interface between the retailer and the customer is what retailing is all about. Amazon.co.uk branding means that it will lose presence with its customers.'

Robin Terrell, managing director of Amazon.co.uk, comments that the deal reflects an acknowledgement by some retailers that their core competencies lie offline. 'Deals like this and with Toys "Я" Us and Borders show that the real expertise of these strong offline brands is running physical stores,' he says. 'They want to maintain an online presence, but focus offline.' Waterstone's Mitchell admits that while the company sees the value in online channels, it had to concentrate on its core strength of offline retailing. 'Our investment priorities need to be in maintaining the quality of our stores,' he says. 'This deal enables us to maintain a valuable transactional facility and not just a marketing platform.'

Philip Robinson, founder of music e-tailer CD-WOW, points out that the deal isn't a unique event, with the likes of Superdrug, Woolworths and BOL all scaling back their operations. 'Waterstone's is being very grown-up and what it is doing is best for its shareholders,' he explains. 'However, there won't be many deals like this, because a lot of brands would rather pull out than team up with a competitor.' He can't see the same thing spilling over into the music sector, although there are white-label fulfilment operators around, as everyone has to make a margin at some point and prices would end up too uncompetitive.

Source: Mark Sweney, Revolution, 8 August 2001

DISTRIBUTION LOGISTICS AND STOCK CONTROL

The customer's central expectation of retail service delivery is one of availability. No amount of service enhancement or added incentives will effectively make up for an empty shelf. As a customer, the ultimate measure of a retail service is whether the goods or services are available as required. Modern retailing is underpinned by a complex infrastructure that seeks to meet this central customer expectation. All of this has its cost and, therefore, from a management perspective it will be vital to deliver the retail service in an efficient manner. This is becoming increasingly important as profit growth cannot be easily achieved when sales growth is not high; such extra profit has to be gained from improvements in productivity. The achievement of productivity gains is available from a retail logistics system infrastructure which consists of several elements, as is discussed in the sections that follow.

RETAIL LOGISTICS

The word logistics is derived from the French word '*loger*' which means to quarter and supply troops. Logistics has developed from the systematic planning required when large numbers of troops and their equipment move, to that of the moving of large amounts of goods. Retail logistics is the organized process of managing the flow of merchandise from the source of supply to the customer – from the producer/manufacturer, wholesaler/intermediary through to the warehouse, transport to the retail units until the merchandise is sold and delivered to the customer. The massive increase in product variety in stores has created a need for improved logistics and sophisticated systems. From a marketing point of view the system has to satisfy the customer based upon the old adage of getting the right product to the right customer in the right place at the right time. This requires a starting point at the marketplace and then working backwards to ensure everything is put in place to provide improved delivery, better service, lower prices through efficient logistics and added value. Retail logistics systems incorporate the following functions:

- the physical movement of goods;
- the holding of these goods in stockholding points;
- the holding of goods in quantities required to meet demand from the end consumer;
- the management and administration of the process which, in modern complex distribution systems, is a function in its own right.

All of this is based upon the aspects of:

- order processing;
- transport;
- storage;
- inventory.

Christopher (1992) defined logistics:

> **Logistics is the process of strategically managing the procurement, movement and storage of materials, parts and finished inventory through the organisation and its marketing channels in such a way that current and future profitability are maximised through the cost-effective fulfilment of orders.**

Gattorna and Walters (1996) have added elements of information flow to this understanding but we believe the infrastructure elements supporting availability for a customer can be more easily identified as warehousing, transport, inventory and administration. The cost structure of each will be considered next, but at this stage it is important to recognize the interrelationships that exist between the elements. A holistic perspective is essential if management is to identify the optimal organization and realize the greatest efficiency for the system as a whole. A ruthless pursuit of cost savings within one element is flawed if the result is simply to push a cost burden on to another.

A similarly holistic view is required of the supply chain in a vertical sense. Porter's value chain analysis (1985) recognizes that as well as seeking to improve the internal linkages between the activities of the retailer, it will be important to acknowledge the fit with the wider value adding system. Retailer activity should strive to add value for the customer. This will not be realized if, in seeking to pursue efficiency in the supply chain element under the direct control of the retailer, costs are simply pushed on to suppliers. The cost will remain in the system and will ultimately be borne by the customer. Managing retail logistics requires a vision of the supply chain 'big picture'. How could activities be organized or reorganized to take cost out of the supply chain completely and deliver better value for customers at the same time? Such an approach may see retailers taking on an additional cost burden to facilitate a saving for suppliers and, ultimately, a net saving for the customer. Here, there is a congruence in the objectives of retailers and suppliers. The recent shift towards supply chain partnerships is logical as it is driven in part by the need to exploit the potential for taking cost out of the supply chain completely.

This holistic approach to retail logistics can be illustrated by the trend in the 1980s and 1990s towards centralized distribution. Depending on volumes, retailers have increasingly created central or regional distribution centres: a major investment in property, plant and equipment with associated overheads. Suppliers making individual direct deliveries to retail outlets may then be replaced by suppliers delivering to the retailer distribution centres by the truckload. The centre then breaks the bulk to create store orders, which are then transported on the retailer's own vehicle fleet. Lead times are reduced and so are the levels of stock held at retail outlets. There are major cost savings and improved supply chain efficiency delivers added value for the customer in the shape of the most recent product being available. Centralizing retail distribution represents a very significant redistribution of costs across logistics elements and between supply chain organizations, with substantial net benefit. The store staff are more aware of deliveries, stock is less of a problem and stock space is kept to a minimum.

RETAIL LOGISTICS – THE COST STRUCTURE

Many retailers pursue distribution strategies which explicitly or implicitly acknowledge the importance of the total distribution concept (TDC) which is based on the work of West (1989). In so doing they are taking a holistic approach, strategically and operationally integrating the functions listed below. The TDC encourages everyone in the company to think in terms of all components of distribution – from the moment of manufacture to when, in the case of the retailer, goods are sold through the checkout – as an integrated linear model.

For example, when we think of some of the costs of inventory (*see* section below), we should be aware that all of the total distribution costs (*see* Fig. 9.2) must be considered in relation to each other. This will often involve various trade-offs, for instance between service levels and quality, or between margins and investment in systems. As such, optimizing a logistics system is a difficult and demanding task as each component of the system is affected by the level of investment the company is able to make in it. TDC allows retailers to extend their control over the costs as well as supply of goods to the

---

Total distribution costs (TDC) = TC + FC + CC + IC + HC + PC + MC

where: TC = transport costs
FC = facilities costs
CC = communications costs
IC = inventory costs
HC = handling costs
PC = packaging costs
MC = management costs

Fig. 9.2 Total distribution costs for the supply chain

Source: West, A. 1989, *Managing Distribution and Change*. Copyright John Wiley & Sons Limited. Reproduced with permission

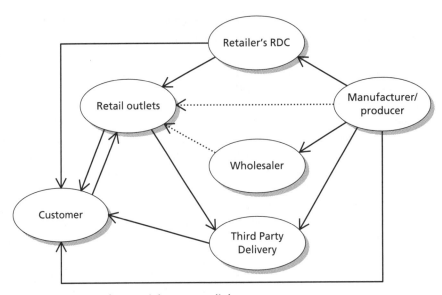

Fig. 9.3 Diagram of potential transport links

Source: adapted from Foresight (2000) @ *your service: future of retail logistics*

Note: The direct link from manufacturer to customer includes electronic delivery mechanisms in some retail sectors

consumer. This requires an understanding of the interaction of all parts of the logistics process. These costs are discussed in the following sections.

Transport

Transport cost structures include substantial fixed-cost elements, but perhaps include greater scope to adapt capacity to match volume. Centralizing retail distribution has had the benefit of dramatically decreasing the number of journeys made with less than full loads, thereby improving efficiency. The use of composite distribution facilities, where the same vehicle handles merchandise categories requiring different storage regimes, has allowed for more frequent full-load deliveries to stores. Computer software now supports route planning, using iterative programmes to identify the optimal schedules for each day's deliveries and thereby achieving lower costs. In addition, retailers make use of back haul, where the trucks make collections from suppliers rather than return empty to the distribution centre.

The marketplace is changing and additional logistic chains need to be considered given the introduction and growth of e-commerce. If the customer is to be included as a direct form of home delivery in the system then this has to be taken into account in transport planning. This may be based upon agreement between retailers to operate common haulage services to reduce the cost per delivery. The schematic diagram for the wider picture of transport needs is shown in Figure 9.3.

Facilities cost – warehousing

As already identified, retail logistics can be reduced to the areas of warehousing, transport, inventory and administration, each with its associated cost structure. Facilities costs are taken as the capital and running costs associated with providing warehousing infrastructure

Table 9.1 UK grocery retailers usage of centralised distribution 1986–2000

Retailer	1986	1996	2000
Safeway (Argyll)	40–80	95	98
ASDA	10	85	95*
Co-op Retail	40–60	95	95
Co-op Wholesale	40–60	93	95
Boots	–	93	99
Iceland	–	100	97
J. Sainsbury	80	95	95
Tesco	40–60	96	97
Waitrose	80	90	99

Source: Institute of Grocery Distribution, 1997 and 2000
Note:* Asda figure of 95 per cent is for 1999

and internal systems to store and pick stock. Warehousing has a high fixed-cost element. The lack of flexibility makes the initial decision to create warehouse capacity crucial. Spare capacity represents wasted resource and short-term measures to cope with insufficient capacity will be expensive. Once created, the ability of the business to match warehousing facilities to fluctuating demand will be strictly limited. This is further accentuated if there is to be capital investment in automated merchandise handling equipment.

A regional distribution centre (RDC) is usually located in a low-cost area. Such a centre can handle a volume in excess of a million cases of product a week as recent advances in information systems have had a huge impact on the efficiency of the operation. It is the application of technologies such as electronic data interchange (EDI) that have facilitated a reduction of stockholding at both store and distribution centre level. The extent of channelling of supplies through RDCs may be gauged by the examination of UK grocery retailers (*see* Table 9.1). Retailers such as ASDA have moved from channelling 10 per cent of their supplies through RDCs in 1986 to over 90 per cent. Similarly, the competitive change in Tesco's position may be gauged from its major increase in usage of centralized distribution.

Within an RDC, communication between the warehouse management system (WMS) and each operative is by radio link, drastically reducing the amount of travel within the centre. The WMS tracks the throughput of merchandise and the activity of each operative. This can allow for individual piece-rates which replace team-based bonuses. The wage bill is a major element within the cost structure of an efficient distribution centre. Hence, with the need to match the labour resource with the volume throughput, 'annualized hours' contracts are now commonplace. This is not always a straightforward task as warehouse staff are often unionized and the union holds power. Developments have to be carefully negotiated and this has led to local agreements, often producing localized differences in working practices and sometimes less efficiency.

The costs and functions of inventory

The first thing to note is that with steadily increasing sophistication in many product categories – and this is particularly the case in retailing – the costs of holding inventory have increased. This, coupled to the increasing concentration in retailing, means that the end consumer currently expects a wider range of products in smaller quantities. Irrespective of the type of inventory system used by the retailer, and regardless of set service levels, attitudes to distribution, etc., there will be costs incurred as a result of the maintenance and replenishment of inventory. The supply chain has to consider the functions of inventory which are to satisfy demand at a level of optimal efficiency. However, this function may be in conflict with supplying to geographic demand with specialist merchandise; the need of the manufacturer to have long not short runs for cost control; poor product forecasts; and the need for safety stock to protect against supply and demand fluctuations.

Maintaining inventory is an investment which ties up large amounts of capital. This has obvious cost implications for (retail) companies, regardless of their size. In accounting terms, the retailer must invest in a certain level of the stock asset in order to service the needs of customers. Greater investment should ensure higher levels of availability and satisfied customers; insufficient investment runs the risk of poor availability and, by implication, customer dissatisfaction.

It is clear that opportunity costs exist in the capital costs of inventory; the capital tied up in inventory could be available for investment elsewhere within the company or outside the company. For these reasons, systems have become based upon demand pull rather than supply push, as demand pull allows for restocking to occur in relation to customer demand. One method of achieving this is through just-in-time (JIT) deliveries. (JIT is discussed in more detail below as part of corporate replenishment systems.)

As previously noted, carrying stock involves a level of risk, which represents additional cost to the business. Some of the costs associated with stock cannot be eliminated by systems such as JIT. There are costs which occur as a result of damage, pilferage, wastage, maladministration, etc. (that is, shrinkage) or markdown action occurring as a result of inappropriate inventory holding. Markdowns, particularly in fashion-related sectors, can account for a sizeable portion of turnover. It is clear that 'risk costs' represent a significant cost of inventory holding.

Administration costs

Communications cost (*see* Fig. 9.2) is largely the administrative cost associated with order processing and electronic data interchange (EDI). Inventory costs include the direct capital costs of buying stock, the opportunity costs of carrying inventory by having capital tied up in stock which could be otherwise invested in the company, insurance charges and, in some countries, a tax on stockholdings. Handling costs (*see* Fig. 9.2) may include the 'risk' costs of damage and spoilage that may be caused by the movement of stock through warehouse and transportation systems. Every time an item is moved or stored, a potential for damage, pilferage or deterioration exists. Packaging costs (*see* Fig. 9.2) will be incurred by the retailer through the use of pallet boards on which deliveries may be shipped and the use of shrink-wrap or cling-wrap film to secure pallets and roll-cages during transit. Management costs (*see* Fig. 9.2) refer to those costs which are incurred as a direct result of control systems and mechanisms which are built into the retailer's logistics systems such as security systems, temperature monitoring computer systems, etc.

Stock management costs, which are essentially the costs of controlling inventory, are not easy to isolate. It may be relatively easy to identify the fixed investment cost of installing an EPOS, or a computerized shelf management (CSM) system of inventory control but it is quite another matter to isolate the stock management costs. It is widely believed that computerized inventory management systems have improved efficiency but it seems equally likely that such systems have increased stock management costs in achieving that goal. When one thinks of the plethora of expert support staff, the costs associated with electronic transmission of data, the greater level of control (and therefore more time required) afforded to management, etc., it is difficult to argue otherwise. Administration costs will occur for every part of the inventory, whether one of the top selling 20 per cent or the remaining 80 per cent of products stocked (the Pareto principle); all inventory has to be tracked and controlled in terms of receipt, location and despatch, for example.

Much of recent innovation in retail logistics has been in pursuit of reducing levels of stockholding in the supply chain. Retailers of highly perishable products have perhaps most to gain from such developments and have led the way. Retail distribution centres have been used for bulk storage of product. This has relieved individual stores of the need to carry stock and, in efficiency terms, has represented an improvement on previous direct delivery arrangements. However, the technology now facilitates the 'stockless' distribution centre. Via EPOS and EDI, suppliers can arrive at the centre with supplies exactly tailored to immediate store requirements. The stock is then 'cross-docked' for shipment to outlets on the same day. Using this just-in-time (JIT) strategy there is no need for bulk storage or double handling at the centre. Figures from IGD (1997) indicate that up to 98 per cent of the UK grocery multiples have committed themselves to EPOS and EDI implementation.

MINICASE 9.2

Battle of the newsagents – distribution change

'What they don't realise,' says Vinod Patel, speaking for Britain's mainly Asian-run independent newsagents, 'is that the Patels can stop London.' The target of Mr Patel's anger is WH Smith, the chain of newsagents that shifts nearly a fifth of the 450m magazines that are sold each year in Britain's $1.8 billion market for magazines. WH Smith is accused of using its might to destabilise a delicately balanced ecosystem.

WH Smith wants to modernise the magazine supply chain. Instead of a system which requires publishers and their distribution companies to 'push' their titles into the wholesale and retail networks, it wants one which lets retailers 'pull' only those products they think their customers want to buy. The present system, says Robin Dickie, the managing director of the firm's retail business, is inefficient. Retailers have to send back one in three of all magazines, which are then wastefully pulped. According to Mr Dickie, this costs wholesalers $24m and retailers $54m. On top of this, he maintains, poorly targeted distribution costs $35m–40m.

To end these inefficiencies, WH Smith has decided to use its own wholesale operation, which already supplies more than 40% of the market, to establish a national distribution system. Some of the big retailers,

including Tesco, which has 7% of the magazine market, and Safeway, support it. Mr Dickie says there are no plans to change the way newspapers are distributed, mainly because there are far fewer titles.

The publishers hate the idea, because it lessens their power to dictate titles and volumes. The other wholesalers hate the idea because it would take business away from them. The reason for the Patels' fury can be found in an analysis of the impact on the newspaper industry produced by Paul Dobson, a retailing professor at Loughborough University, on behalf of the Newspaper Publishers' Association. The 'Dobson Report', as it is reverentially known, argues that WH Smith's plan will duplicate the existing distribution network, thus increasing costs by about $20m. The distributors' customers – the retailers – will end up paying those costs. He suggests that, in consequence, up to 8,000 retailers will no longer find it economic to sell magazines or, as a result, newspapers as well. Were the new distribution system to be extended to newspapers, the number of outlets could be cut by 12,000. He estimates that this could cut magazine sales by $53m and newspaper sales by $97m.

Source: © The Economist, 2 December, 2000

Outsourcing

It is common practice for retailers to contract out some or all of the distribution activity. A strategic argument for this would be to allow management to focus on those parts of the business where the retailer adds value for the customer – that is, their core competence. It is potentially more flexible and spreads risk. From a financial viewpoint, the contractor should find economies of scale that may be enjoyed by both parties and passed on to the consumer. From the retailer's perspective it represents a form of off-balance-sheet financing, with the contractor obliged to invest in assets that are effectively dedicated to the retailer's business. Many such contractors' vans carry the logo of the retailer but remain the contractor's property.

COMPUTERIZED REPLENISHMENT SYSTEMS (CRS)

The benefits of the new distribution systems are numerous and extend well beyond inventory control and replenishment. The systems are becoming increasingly important in the competitive environment of multiple retailing. J. Sainsbury, Tesco and Safeway have almost 100 per cent of stores with EPOS scanning. In the variety chainstores, Bhs has been on full EPOS for several years, their EPOS system being directly linked to their replenishment through central distribution centres at Atherstone and Dundee. Marks & Spencer also have full EPOS and have implemented a computerized inventory system, ASR (automatic stock replenishment), from an initial investment of £78 million in 1988/89.

The perceived benefits of these systems for inventory are shared and are simple: a reduction of stockholding through more accurate ordering and replenishment (which in turn gives better product availability to the customer and thus maximizes sales). There is also the benefit of far more accurate sales data on which improved decision-making can take place. It can be readily seen that EPOS may serve replenishment. By accurate data capture obtained via EPOS, forecasting (for example, on the basis of experimental smoothing) future merchandise requirements and inventory control is facilitated. This enables both more accurate and more economical buying. It also affords greater control of stockholding through greater inventory control, by the removal of the human error associated with other forms of stock control.

CORPORATE REPLENISHMENT POLICIES

Corporate retail planning often involves formalized logistics policies related to distribution networks, warehouse systems, information systems, and replenishment systems. These policies allow the head office of a retail organization to be responsive to operational needs, which include general as well as local patterns of demand, and new market opportunities. Companies that have built into their corporate strategies the logistics of distribution have created dramatic improvements in their return on investment whether that investment be fixed (warehousing, vehicles or other equipment) or current (inventory, accounts due and cash). Corporate replenishment (CR) has thus become an integral part of the corporate strategy and is instrumental in enabling the achievement of financial and strategic objectives.

Corporate replenishment policy is a broad policy based upon the organization's replenishment ethos related to a systems approach. There are two types of stock control systems: the push strategy, where quantities of stock are pushed into stores in anticipation of demand; and the pull strategy, where merchandise is pulled through the supply chain to replenish sales at stores, and a minimum stockholding is planned to be retained in the store. Systems have been developed in the 1990s to encompass quick response or just-in-time (JIT) methods, where the pull strategy becomes the leading method to link inventory to actual customer demand. The channel then becomes a continuous replenishment system triggered by accurate electronic information from the use of EPOS and EDI. As such, JIT systems allow for restocking to occur in relation to customer demand. JIT is a philosophy as much as a technique; it is based on the premise that no products should be made or moved until there is a 'downstream' requirement for them based upon feedback from the supply chain. Within retailing, the fundamentals of JIT are often known as 'quick response' (QR). The logic is that demand is captured as close to the final customer as possible, allowing a logistics response to be made as a direct result. Quick response will thus include the manufacturer in a vertically integrated supply chain so that all means of JIT are triggered based upon changes in consumer demand patterns. Quick response is a series of technologies which comprise the electronic scanning of product codes, the application of EDI, and the identification and tracking of goods in the supply chain. The main users of QR are the grocery multiples but other companies such as Benetton and Arcadia (formerly The Burton Group) developed the systems at an early stage (Dapiran, 1992).

Advantages of corporate replenishment (CR)

There are four different beneficiaries of corporate replenishment systems:

1 the customer;
2 store management;
3 the company;
4 suppliers.

The advantages for each of these groups are discussed below.

The customer

The customer is able to receive an improved level of service as the goods are available at the point of sale, where and when the customer needs them. When items are advertised they are in stock and this adds to customer goodwill as stock is assured through the system. Stores can, and do, order promotional lines in some manual ordering systems. However, across a chain of stores it is unlikely that all relevant managers will order sufficient stock levels – or indeed place orders at all – to meet the promotion, product introduction or range change needs, at the right time. Also, in emergencies, substitute products and so on can be sourced more effectively in advanced CR systems.

Through economies of scale and inventory savings made by being able to carry less 'safety stock' the retailer can pass on savings to the customer. The retailer is able, through feedback from sales systems and the resultant flow of accurate sales information, to forecast bulk buying requirements more accurately. This allows the retailer to obtain greater discounts from suppliers, so making savings which can be passed on to the customer.

Store management

Store management, through corporate replenishment, may be relieved of the time-consuming task of stock checking and ordering if the CR is well designed. Under automatic stock replenishment through EPOS and central distribution, store management may be completely freed from stock and ordering worries. This means that they have more time to manage resources and implement company policies. Under highly computerized goods receipt systems other duties, associated with shrinkage and delivery security, may also change significantly.

It is believed that automated systems will mean that managers will not worry about stock situations. This is possible but it must be realized that a basic function of store managers is to ensure stock counting is accurately recorded, whether they or a head office buyer is responsible for ordering stock. In EPOS replenishment, stockouts occur for a variety of reasons: unpredictable shifts in demand; product unavailability; poor data capture control; loss of information or computer failure, etc. In such a situation it is incumbent upon store managers to ensure that major stockouts are communicated as soon as possible to the head office buyer or allocator so that remedial action may be taken. EPOS merely removes the task of physically ordering stock; it does not remove the manager's responsibility to ensure that maximum customer service, through product availability, is achieved. To achieve this, accurate information input by stores on stockholding is vital. Even with EPOS systems information can be corrupted by poor data capture, by incorrect codes being entered at the checkouts, or by staff coding articles or merchandise incorrectly.

The company

The company benefits from maximizing service and minimizing costs. The central control of inventory replenishment can be managed to keep the amount of stock to an acceptable level. CR avoids dead stock being built up through discontinuity of buying or ordering by store-based management. The main benefit is that reduced stockholding figures prevent capital from being tied up; it may be freed for the expansion and development of the business.

Because of the ability to control stockholding, previously used warehousing and store space is no longer required for that purpose. This enables retailers to maximize store floor selling space. In a self-service environment you cannot sell stock that is in the warehouse. In conjunction with central warehousing, economies of scale can be made through composite transport systems. Whether it is an agency or own-transport network, corporate replenishment enables improved utilization of the transport fleets and improvements in service.

Given the constraints of supplier-fed deliveries, marketing may also benefit from corporate replenishment. It can be assumed that stock will be allocated and received into stores to coincide with advertising, other promotional activities and videos, coupons, competitions, etc. Advertising products which are not available in stores is a major fault – a possibility that can occur in any type of replenishment system. CR ensures that it is not left to department managers, some of whom will – due to other pressures – be unable to meet the requirements of the promotional activity.

Suppliers

It is far easier for a supplier to cope with one order for upwards of 300 stores than for each store independently to place orders. Consequently, the supplier can deliver economically the quantity required in good time. Similarly, it is much more desirable to organize this through central distribution warehousing (CDW). Phoning, faxing or using traditional forms of placing orders is time-consuming and often inaccurate. To deal with one electronic system of ordering is desirable to the supplier as well as to the retailer. However, orders may also be placed by the buyers – professionals who are specialists in their field, knowing the merchandise and seasonal trends. Therefore, from the supplier's point of view, it is preferable not to deal with store-based management who have numerous responsibilities to perform and ordering is only one of a list of urgent priorities.

INTERNET AND DIRECT DISTRIBUTION SYSTEMS

In addition to more traditional methods of channel management, there has been a change of distribution strategy to increase sales through direct channels. Large retailers now offer many of their products online through the Internet. While this is an important trend, retailers' long-term strategies are still hard to discern. In 1995 J. Sainsbury was an early mover by announcing it was offering wine on the Internet. However, the service was not straightforward as consumers had to be linked to the Internet and, after choosing online, had to confirm the order and pay for it by telephone. Any e-commerce system has to provide convenience and will have to be backed by a service that is cost-effective. This affects all of e-commerce from global product offerings to weekly shopping items. The decisions will revolve around many issues:

- When should deliveries be planned for – Monday to Friday or six or seven days a week, and should there be evening delivery services?
- Is there to be a boundary of delivery by miles or time?
- What is the time standard requirement for delivery in hours or days?
- Is there to be a delivery charge and will this be a banded or standard cost?
- What is the minimum order value of product(s) that will be transported direct?
- Should there be a central pick-up point or home delivery?

Ordering is possible via a number of media – the Internet, private online services, interactive television and even special in-home devices. However, the routine business of delivering goods efficiently could prove to be a problem. For example, big retailers are used to shifting pallets of products by lorry but the packing and delivering of single items quickly is much more difficult and expensive. Therefore, any need for home deliveries may lead the retailers to make alliances with parcel companies, the Post Office, or even local dairies. Retailers offering grocery items or regular purchases may need to consider how extra fulfilment costs can be passed on or absorbed. Early adopters may well be prepared to pay a little more for a home delivery service, recognizing the additional value of the saving in time and personal transport. In any assessment of the cost of delivery there is a need to examine the process in detail to ensure efficiencies in the cost of the assembly of each order as well as the geographic density of deliveries. This is because the development of e-retailing capabilities will need to bear the costs of e-fulfilment and still offer value for money. Such costs may involve aspects of communications technology; automated picking technology, unattended goods collection devices; mixed centre RDC and local delivery transport logistics.

CompuServe, the US-owned online information system, announced its UK Shopping Centre in 1995. Subscribers who paid a small monthly charge could buy books from WH Smith, CDs from Virgin and cameras from Dixons. Because CompuServe is considered more secure than the Internet, the retailers ask customers to enter credit card numbers directly into their computers. The results of the early schemes have been commented on as positive. WH Smith, Sainsbury's and Tesco reported the service to have been effective (*see* Chapter 13 on IT and retail for further discussion of the possibilities of the Internet). The question underlying any change in channel level is why anyone would need a superstore if manufacturers started selling their well-known brands online. This would mean that large food retailers may treat online shopping as a threat as well as an opportunity.

Logistical problems will also have to be overcome. These will not be on the high-tech ordering side as the problems of security for customer and retailer have been largely overcome through sophisticated encryption systems; and devices such as an 'intelligent agent' that will search out the best value on the Internet have also been developed.

Distribution based on travel retail

In an increasingly competitive world it has been necessary for most companies to consider different forms of distribution. The ability for companies to sell direct – either from their place of location or through direct marketing methods – currently exists. Some stores combine direct marketing, by use of advertisements, catalogues, telephone sales or electronic media, with their retail outlets. The structure of distribution channels in tourism is illustrated in Fig. 9.4.

In the UK there is the opportunity to have access to a wide network of around 7000 travel agency distribution outlets. The need for travel agents first arose in the 1950s

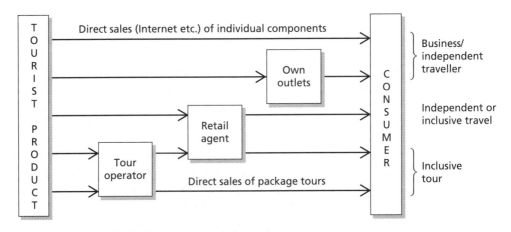

Fig. 9.4 Structure of distribution channels in tourism

because of the rapidly expanding operations of airline/ferry businesses. Transport providers required a means of distribution for their products that was more cost-effective than establishing individual networks of booking offices around the country. Their subsequent development was a direct result of the increasing consumer demand for inclusive tours from holidaymakers who were largely uneducated and unsophisticated, and therefore looked to 'experts' to facilitate the process.

These agents charge commission on the sales they make and they need to hold a stock of the companies' brochures or sales literature. The travel retail agent sells a product that is both intangible and perishable and this is very different from some of the more traditional types of retail. The bookings made for travel abroad, from the UK, are mostly organized through either high street travel agents for holidays or by specialist business travel agents for business travel. The UK has a different pattern of purchase from that of the rest of Europe where most bookings are made direct rather than through agents. In many European countries, twice as many bookings are made direct than in the UK. The Internet has many implications for all areas of business and every sector of society. Its effect can be seen already in the precarious balance of travel distribution. Sales channels for travel were once clear-cut but are now more complex. Disintermediation does not appear to be lessening the travel industry's complicated distribution network, and if anything is adding to it.

To date there has been a lack of conversion of the British holidaymaker to buying direct. There is little doubt that, for many, the convenience of using an agent is an important element in the buying process. This is because a travel agent may offer greater opportunities for one-stop shopping, allowing the parallel purchase of insurance, car hire, rail travel to the airport, traveller's cheques, and so on. The travel agent offers a number of benefits which may have led to the reason more travellers have not booked direct (Gilbert, 1990). The information box summarizes the possible reasons for customers to continue to use travel agents.

However, with Expedia and Travelocity now widely known and accepted, the use of more direct systems of booking is expected to make inroads into traditional forms of distribution.

Possible reasons for the use of retail travel agents and limitation of use of direct channels

Easy accessibility:

- to a range and choice of brochures
- to product components of visas, traveller's cheques, insurance, etc.
- to booking points in every main town and city
- to an alternative agent as well as products and brands

Convenience:

- for obtaining information and advice
- for making the purchase and payment for the holiday
- for making complaints and being represented if things go wrong

▶

Habit:

- people can get into a pattern of behaviour which becomes habit forming. Only a major campaign by direct mail operators could change this habit

Security/risk:

- consumers feel more secure when dealing with a reputable operator or agent. Those who buy from the Association of British Travel Agents (ABTA) feel they obtain ABTA protection and that products which are offered have been vetted

Environment/atmosphere:

- travel agents offer an environment which is part of the holiday experience. The travel agency environment is the perfect setting for personal selling methods which are a powerful means to generate bookings

Economic:

- because travel agents compete on price or added value, and tour operators have the smallest of margins, there is little difference in the price between travel agents and direct sell

CONCLUSION

The movement of goods is a feature of retailing. This movement is becoming of greater importance as a means of creating advantage over competitors. The use of technology, building relationships and driving down costs is important. Each provides an area of focus that a retailer has to consider in relation to their competition. For a company to be successful it has to develop a differential advantage, which will distinguish the company's offer from that of the competition. Only when a company has built an advantage in distribution and other aspects of the marketing mix will it find that store visits increase and profits rise. The advantage may be based upon many aspects of the business but in distribution important considerations are cost reductions in order to create value for money and higher profits, and product availability and quality through overall distribution logistics.

EXERCISES

The exercises in this section relate to the issues discussed in this chapter. It is suggested that you work through them before moving on to Chapter 10.

1 Write a report to the director of a retail chain of travel agencies with your findings regarding whether the trend in the use of the Internet will affect the future business of the company and if so what they should do to counteract any threats.

2 Write a note to the director of a large retail company to explain the way that any new computerized logistics or replenishment systems could affect his managers who have to adopt the new systems.

3 Write a report on the reasons a retailer may outsource distribution activity. If there are benefits to outsourcing what type of retailer would you not expect to outsource and what are the reasons for this?

4 Partnership functions are increasing in importance. Comment on this and provide some arguments, which your manager could use, to convince others that the trend is important and that your company should follow suit.

REFERENCES AND FURTHER READING

Alba, J., Lynch, J., Weitz, B. and Janiszewski, C. (1998) 'Interactive home shopping: consumer, retailer, and manufacturer incentives to participate in electronic marketplaces', *Journal of Marketing*, 61 (3), 38–53.

Betts, E. and McGoldrick, P.J. (1995) 'The strategy of the retail sale, typology, review and synthesis', *International Review of Retail, Distribution and Consumer Research*, 5 (3), 303–32.

Booms, B.H. and Bitner, M.J. (1981) 'Marketing strategies and organization structures for service firms', in Donnelly, J. and George W.R. (eds) *Marketing of Services*. Chicago, IL: American Marketing Association.

Bowden, D. (1995) 'Problems with delivery delay on-line shopping', *Independent on Sunday*, 4 June, 4.

Bowlby, S. and Foord, J. (1995) 'Relational contracting between UK retailers and manufacturers', *International Review of Retail, Distribution and Consumer Research*, 5 (3), 333–60.

Branigan, L. (1998) 'The Internet: the emerging premier direct marketing channel', *Direct Marketing*, 61 (1), 46–8.

Christopher, M. (1992) *Logistics*. London: Chapman and Hall.

Christopher, M. (1997) *Marketing Logistics*. Oxford: Butterworth-Heinemann.

Christopher, M., Payne, A. and Ballantyne, D. (1996) *Relationship Marketing*. Oxford: Butterworth-Heinemann.

Comer, J.M., Mehta, R. and Holmes, T.L. (1998) 'Information technology: retail users versus nonusers', *Journal of Interactive Marketing*, 12 (2), 49–62.

Cooper, J., Browne, M. and Peters, M. (1994) *European Logistics: Markets, management and strategy*. Oxford: Blackwell.

Dapiran, P. (1992) 'Benetton – global logistics in action', *International Journal of Physical Distribution and Logistics Management*, 23 (4), 7–11.

Davies, G. (1993) 'Is retailing what dictionaries say it is?', *International Journal of Retail and Distribution Management*, 21 (2), 3–7.

Davison, J. (1995) *Lecture Notes on Distribution Management*. Guildford: University of Surrey.

Delbridge, R. and Oliver, N. (1991) 'Just in time or just the same', *International Journal of Retail and Distribution Management*, 19 (2), 20.

The Economist (2000) 'The battle of the newsagents', *The Economist*, 2 December.

Fernie, J. (1995) 'International comparisons of supply chain management in grocery retailing', *Service Industries Journal*, 5 (4), 135–47.

Fernie, J. (1997) 'Retail change and retail logistics in the UK, past trends and future prospects', *Service Industries Journal*, 17 (3), 383–96.

Fernie, J. and Sparks, L. (1997) *Logistics and Retail Management*. London: Kogan Page.

Foresight (2000) @ *Your Service, Future Models of Retail Logistics*. London: Retail Logistics Task Force, DTI publication.

Foresight (2001) @ *Your Home, New Markets for Customer Service and Delivery*. London: Retail Logistics Task Force, DTI publication.

Gattorna, J.L. and Walters, D.W. (1996) *Managing the Supply Chain – A Strategic Perspective*. Basingstoke: Macmillan.

Gilbert, D.C. (1990) 'European product purchase methods and systems', *Service Industries Journal*, 10 (4), 664–79.

Institute of Grocery Distribution (1997) *Trends in Grocery Retailing – the market review*. Watford: IGD Business Publications.

Institute of Grocery Distribution (1998) *Grocery Market Bulletin*. Watford: IGD Business Publications.

Institute of Grocery Distribution (2000) *Retail Logistics, 2000*. Watford: IGD Business Publications.

Kotler, P., Armstrong, G., Saunders, J. and Wong, V. (1999) *Principles of Marketing*. 2nd European edn. Hemel Hempstead: Prentice Hall.

Mulhern, F.J. (1997) 'Retail marketing: from distribution to integration', *International Journal of Research in Marketing*, 14 (2), 103–24.

Porter, M.E. (1985) *Competitive Advantage*, New York: Free Press.

Powell, T.C. and Dent-Micallef, A. (1997) 'Information technology as competitive advantage: the role of human, business, and technology resources', *Strategic Management Journal*, 18 (5), 375–405.

Rhodes, E. and Carter, R. (1998) 'Electronic commerce technologies and changing product distribution', *International Journal of Technology Management*, 15 (1, 2), 31–48.

Rogers, D., Daugherty, P.J. and Stank, T.P. (1992) 'Enhancing service responsiveness: the strategic potential of EDI', *International Journal of Physical Distribution and Logistics Management*, 22 (8), 15–20.

Schary, P.B. and Coakley, J. (1991) 'Logistics organization and the information system', *International Journal of Logistics Management*, 2 (2), 22–9.

Sheombar, H.S. (1992) 'EDI-induced redesign of co-ordination in logistics', *International Journal of Physical Distribution and Logistics Management*, 22 (8), 4–14.

Smith, D. and Sparks, L. (1993) 'The transformation of physical distribution in retailing: the example of Tesco plc.', *International Review of Retail, Distribution and Consumer Research*, 3 (1), 35–64.

Sweney, M. (2001) 'Amazon looks for more fulfilment', *Revolution UK*, 8 August.

Walmsley, A. (1998) 'New media choice: The Gap web site', *Marketing*, 19 February, 15.

West, A. (1989) *Managing Distribution and Change*. London: John Wiley and Sons.

10 Methods and approaches to retail strategy and marketing planning

This chapter should enable you to understand and explain:
- the reason why retail companies should adopt planning;
- problems which may occur due to a lack of planning;
- the purpose of a marketing plan;
- the structure of a marketing plan including SWOT, PEST analysis, segmentation and strategic decisions over competitive positioning;
- the need to create ownership of plans through involvement of staff.

The pace of change is unrestrained and nowhere is it more unrestrained than in retail. In the past 30 years we have witnessed a dramatic increase in competition in the marketplace. Within this turbulent arena some retailers manage to stand out from the 'crowd' due to their ability to create successful marketing changes through well-devised plans. All planning options have to be considered within the light of their feasibility and acceptability in the marketplace. This is not to say that planning is not part of our everyday experiences; planning is simply part of daily existence whether it be for social or business purposes. We all have to plan to some extent in order to be successful in life. Very few Olympic medallists could be successful without a planned programme of training and events leading up to their Olympic finals and achievements. Whether it is for examinations, sports events, going on holiday or organizing a party, the use of planning leads to a greater certainty that the event will be a success. Without the right approach, and a sensible plan, alternative courses of action will have seldom been considered and, consequently, there is the likelihood that an individual, company or organization will not function as well as might be expected. Knee and Walters (1985) have referred to the way retail management is alleged to have a propensity for 'the butterfly' spirit and approach to problem-solving rather than adopting a clearly defined approach. If a retail company is to remain competitive, continual improvement in systems of planning and increasingly sophisticated approaches to strategic planning are necessary.

Planning is the most important activity of marketing management. Retailers need to plan for merchandise, inventory control, logistics development, pricing, promotional campaigns, store location and layout, positioning of the business, branding, growth and development of the business – and other functional activities. The plan, which needs to ensure that the previous areas are considered, should provide a common structure and act as a focus for all of the company's management activities. It is, therefore, essential for us to understand marketing planning in its context as a key function of management.

Table 10.1 Comparison of strategic emphasis for different-sized retailers

Areas for consideration	Large retailer	Small independent retailer
Strategic options	Segment and market to large target audience based upon price, assortment, quality, loyalty scheme	Select niche markets, identify gaps in the market, provide specialist sourcing/merchandise, and give excellent service
Property	Managing and developing the property portfolio and making location choice will be a core activity. There is a constant need to acquire and develop prime locations	Need to find cost-effective locations with an emphasis on agreeing the right lease conditions and rent reviews. Early selection of a location in the improving areas of a town/city may be important in reducing the burden of high rent
Physical distribution	Use of third party contracts so have to ensure they offer added value	Combination of self and contracted services with higher ratio of costs involved
Inventory management	EPOS can be afforded and linked to MIS to improve marketing, reduce stock-turn and minimize costs	Less sophisticated IT back-up and need to carry high stock levels to ensure good service levels – which increases costs
Opportunity	Due to higher resources the ability to develop retail initiatives such as Web presence, loyalty schemes, out-of-town or international development	Lack of resources focuses the planning on the short-term building of the business. This may be based upon survival in a time of recession as a high debt burden is common

Planning in retailing is based upon a number of approaches. Retail planning often occurs in cycles due to the seasonality of much of retail activity. Any marketing plan is normally related to company activities which are concerned with a future horizon of one to five years, whereas long-range plans deal with timespans over five years. There are also strategic plans which are concerned more with external environmental influences, and opportunities, and less with the detail of functional company marketing activities. Strategic plans are normally either medium or long term and marketing plans typically cover the short or medium term. The purpose of creating different types of retail plans is to improve the overall business both currently and for the future, and to ensure that customers continue to be satisfied with the retail experience and offer. The size of retailer may place a specific emphasis on the strategic possibilities which are available as detailed in Table 10.1.

The retail industry provides for a combination of different products and services – from the small local convenience store to the larger high street chains, major food retailers, banks or building societies. It can include the fast-food outlet and the petrol forecourt. The concept of change and survival is as important to small businesses as to larger organizations such as Marks & Spencer or Sears. That change will occur, and with increasing speed, is the most predictable aspect of contemporary business life. It would therefore seem sensible to try to become familiar with the underlying trends and forces of change which impinge upon retail business activities. This enables the management of change towards desired objectives rather than the organization being driven blindly before the tide of market forces. We have only to remember retail problems such as the demise of Athena and Rumbelows to realize the importance of clear business planning.

The long-term survival of any company is dependent on how well the business relates to its environment. In spite of its dominant market share, Sears' British Shoe Corporation failed to understand the changes which were taking place in shoe-buying behaviour. The company introduced elementary notions of market segmentation that failed to address the substantial problems it was facing because of increasing competition in that market. All retailers have to devise forward plans of where a company, an outlet or product would be best placed for the future. The plan therefore needs to specify the changes that have to be made, needs to allow for the exploitation of any short-term advantages, and has to demonstrate the application of analysis and reason as part of the planning procedure. The Sears Group in the UK demonstrated a lack of consistent focus in the moves it made. It entered and withdrew from the menswear market, became market leader in sports goods with the Olympus chain, and then divested this business and other parts of the organization when problems arose in the retail marketplace.

PROBLEMS THAT MAY ARISE IF RETAIL PLANNING IS IGNORED

A range of problems may be faced if retail planning is ignored. For example, this could involve a variety of difficulties and/or missed opportunities:

- failure to take advantage of potential retail growth markets and new marketing opportunities – such as the Internet and the expansion of the financial services market;
- lack of maintenance of demand from a spread of markets and erosion of market share due to the actions of competitors – for example, competition for supermarket chains from the deep discounters such as Aldi, Lidl and Netto;
- customers' expectations are not met and service delivery weakens – as almost occurred at Granada Rentals;
- increasing demand problems in low demand periods – such as when the economy is weak and levels of confidence are low when consumers spend less;
- low level of awareness of the competition's strategies whereby there is no strategic response;
- poor image associated with the shop/group name or brand – for example, when the Forte Group was unaware of the intentions of Granada, which eventually took over the hotel group. Companies such as MFI and Ratners suffered this problem;
- lack of support for co-operative marketing initiatives;
- decline in quality levels below acceptable limits;
- difficulty in convincing suppliers of the strengths of the company;
- disillusionment and lack of motivation of employees.

As can be seen from the above, there are many potential problems which face retail organizations when there is a lack of planning. This happened to Arcadia, the former Burton Group, the UK's largest menswear retailer, which had dated outlets and a poor image in the 1970s and 1980s. The problem was that the company misjudged the declining market for men's suits and the emergence of a demand for a wider product range of

235

leisurewear, jeans and other forms of casual clothing. A major change of direction needed to be planned in order to modernize the stores, improve the merchandise, promote the changes and identify with the changing market needs.

While planning cannot guarantee success, it can make the organization less vulnerable to market forces. Day-to-day problems can be more easily avoided if more attention is given to planning activities, especially in relation to cash flow, fixed cost and expansion plans. It has been argued that much of retail management has been reactive, opportunistic and dedicated to crisis firefighting than to long-term analysis and planning. Retail companies need to plan to have world-class service or at least distinctive competence in order to be successful. This means that, through sensible planning, companies will attempt to associate their brands or company name with service excellence in order to establish a reputation for meeting or exceeding customer expectations. The methods of service delivery have to be planned to achieve superior systems and support the nature of the business.

Companies which rely on ad hoc initiatives or fail to manage their future will find that their future has been managed for them. Even though the jewellers Ratners suffered major problems due to bad publicity and over-expansion, no company can ignore the significance of the way this retailer grew through its planned pricing policy. Ratners is a lesson that retailers need to ensure that high margin products should be bought at the appropriate cost and sold at competitive prices. Each company will adopt a different approach to the task of planning, based upon the way senior executives see the purpose of marketing plans. The values of any company may be said to fall somewhere along a continuum which runs from a simple *wait and see*, through a more rigorous *prepare and predict* stance to companies at the opposite end of the continuum who want to *make it happen*. A company will benefit more from a future that is made to happen because the clear direction provides fewer surprises for the workforce and places less pressure on other company resources. At present, great importance is placed on building brand strength and, if appropriate, own-brands. This is because of the realization that retail brand strength can allow a company to be more successful in new ventures such as loyalty schemes or financial services. The German men's clothing company Hugo Boss has managed to develop a strong emotive brand based upon a systematic approach to research, development and promotion. Brands that are strong are said to be elastic and can have a spin-off effect on new products or services. This is important for retailers who wish to expand.

THE PURPOSE OF A MARKETING PLAN

It should now be clear that planning is an important activity for any company. We now need to reinforce the essential points which bring value to a company. Some reasons for planning follow:

● To provide *clear direction* to the overall retailing operation based upon a systematic, written approach to planning and action. The planning system allows direction by virtue of requiring a written mission statement and a set of objectives to be established, which can be transmitted to the workforce. This provides clear leadership principles and allows the workforce to know how their own efforts are essential to the achievement of desired results.

- To *co-ordinate the resources* of the company. This eliminates confusion and misunderstanding so that there is maximum co-operation. Tasks and responsibilities may be set which clarify the direction and objectives of the company. To ensure there is a united effort, recommendations have to be presented in such a way that they can be fully understood at all company levels. The plan then acts as a master guide which will underpin all endeavours and decision-making. The plan should lead to greater employee cohesion and make everyone feel part of a team in which each individual believes they can make a valuable contribution.

- To *set targets* against which progress can be measured. Quantified targets for quantity of merchandise sold or revenue generated provide the focus for individual, departmental or company performance. Some companies will set targets at achievable levels whereas others will set targets at a higher than expected level in order to stretch employees to gain better results.

- To *minimize risk through analysis* of the internal and external environment. The planning procedure allows managers to identify areas of strength and weakness so that the first can be exploited and the second surmounted. In addition, threats and opportunities can be assessed.

- To *assess targeting* by examining the various ways of targeting different retail market segments. This allows for different marketing mix strategies to be appraised prior to their implementation.

- To *provide a record* of the company's marketing policies and plans. This allows managers to check on what has been attempted in the past and to evaluate the effectiveness of previous programmes. It also provides continuity and a source of reference for new managers joining the company.

- To *focus on longer-term action* in relation to business objectives so that the company plans to be in the best current position to achieve its future aims. This allows management to develop continuity of thought and action from one year to the next.

Given that you have understood the previous information in this book, it will be accepted that company objectives should be based upon relevant market-centred opportunities. It is the responsibility of retail marketers to identify these opportunities and to have devised a system of planning which may lead to their exploitation.

REASONS FOR POOR PLANNING EXPERIENCES

The standard approach to planning can be found in most textbooks to follow a series of simple steps. However, the true art of planning is to understand both the human aspects and the procedural necessities of planning. A poor planning experience may be a function of one or a combination of the following issues or problems.

1 One major problem which is difficult to resolve is if there is weak support for the plan from senior people and the chief executive. Any planning requires senior management support if it is to be treated seriously by employees.

2 The system of planning which is adopted may not suit the company. There is often the separation of different planning functions from each other that leads to a lack of integration. Therefore, the system often has to be designed to match the company and to achieve harmony between groups.

3 The planning system is often blamed when the weakness is actually poor planning and management. Sometimes there is confusion over data or planning terms. The requirement is for a plan to be compiled which clarifies times and responsibilities for different actions and meetings.

4 Unexpected environmental changes may create adverse effects on the company's performance. Planning is then often blamed for not having incorporated such a scenario. Plans need to be flexible and updated when necessary.

5 The values of the management team will imply different acceptance levels of the plan and, ultimately, its success or failure. There is often hostility towards plans because of the feeling of a lack of involvement in the planning process. This often occurs when the planning is left solely to a planner or it becomes an annual ritual.

6 Problems occur when there is an over-abundance of information which has to be filtered for its relevance. Too much detail in the early stages can produce what is often referred to as 'paralysis analysis'. There is a need to decide what is important and what is not.

It is distressing that companies which have recognized the need for a more structured approach to planning, and have subsequently adopted formalized procedures found in the literature, seldom enjoy the advantages that are claimed for organizations which embark on planning. In fact it is often planning itself which is brought into disrepute when it fails to bring about the desired changes within a company. The problems faced in marketing planning have led to a growing body of literature which indicates companies should do what they are good at, rather than embark upon higher level planning exercises. This could be a retrograde step because companies should attempt to take the most logical direction and not be hampered by internal failings of the human resource aspects of implementation, lack of planning expertise, or disregard of the involvement of others in the planning process. The argument put forward here is that an understanding of the social aspects of the company is a prerequisite for successful planning.

It is necessary for those involved in planning to recognize the need for involvement of all departments in the company in the formulation of the plan. This will ensure various personnel are more likely to be motivated towards its successful implementation. Such motivation is vital to success, quite apart from the valuable knowledge and expertise which key personnel bring to marketing plan formulation. The reality of this is that most accomplishments, in service industries, are made through people. The control of schedules, budgets, monitoring performance or corrective decisions can only take place with the involvement of people. Each employee who has responsibility requires clear objectives against which to judge whether tactical action needs to be carried out.

It is important to ensure that plans are not prepared within the vacuum of one department or by a marketing team who believe they are an elite. Well-structured management meetings may offer a setting where deliberation, responsibility and authority are shared and taken by all. This precludes dogmatic assertions about the particular methods of preparing and organizing marketing planning.

The marketing planning system offers a structured and market-led approach to organizing and co-ordinating the efforts and activities of those involved in deciding on the future of an organization. However, there is no one 'right' system for any particular company as companies differ in size and diversity of operations, as may the values of senior management, and the expertise of those involved in the planning exercise.

THE BODY SHOP – Has The Body Shop lost its direction for good?

The Body Shop has evolved from a single retail outlet into a global brand on the back of products such as best-sellers Nut Body Butter and Vitamin E Moisture Cream and a brand positioning as a socially respons-ible cosmetics retailer. It now has 1841 outlets across the globe, including 294 in the UK. Yet over the past few years, not everything has proceeded entirely smoothly.

Two years ago, the company restructured dramati-cally and founder Anita Roddick took a back seat as Patrick Gournay of Danone was brought in to turn around the company. Yet a poor Christmas, when sales of Body Shop's gift packages traditionally boost annual figures, forced the company to issue a profits warning. The company revealed annual profits down 55% from £28.8m to £12.8m, as well as a 1% drop in like-for-like sales in the first seven weeks of 2001.

Gournay admits The Body Shop has made mis-takes – most notably poor implementation of its plan to boost revenue from new products. 'We tried to do too much too quickly, not respecting our brand heri-tage,' said Gournay. 'It would have been better to have a small number of big ideas than a big number of small ideas.'

In the UK, The Body Shop finds itself operating in a much more competitive marketplace than at its launch 25 years ago. Its exclusive green proposition has been largely eroded, with most high street retail chains now fielding their own 'natural' cosmetics and toiletries ranges. And a price and promotional battle on toiletries has left its products more expensive than its rivals. The company's attempts at innovation sug-gest it is targeting a younger audience, yet there are no signs this has succeeded. It core customer base is still getting older.

The Body Shop is undeniably one of the world's best-known brands and the only global brand to set out its stall on environmental and social issues. In the past 25 years it has opened up a new agenda for business and allowed people with similar attitudes to express themselves openly without being ridiculed. When you look at what is going on today, The Body Shop's values now seem even more contemporary than they were when it started – consumerism, social justice and environmental issues are now firmly on the agenda across the world. But where the brand has perhaps taken a wrong direction is that the relation-ship between its values and products appears to have been watered down. As a consequence, its relationship with customers has been affected. I think this is at the heart of why the brand is appearing to flounder a bit.

Anita Roddick is one of the world's great mar-keters, but as her involvement has lessened The Body Shop has lost a bit of passion and heart. The Body Shop is a global company, but has a turnover of just £375m with a limited management structure to match the challenges it faces on many different fronts. It operates in 49 markets and has 1841 out-lets globally. This brings inevitable problems – with franchisees, for example – which require manage-ment firefighting. The strong pound has proved a particular challenge, with consequent margin pres-sures making its products seem rather pricey amid growing competition.

In the early- and mid-90s, The Body Shop rested on its laurels while top management allowed itself to be diverted by wider global issues. It is still paying the price, both in the US and in the UK, where Boots, Superdrug, the supermarkets and new entrant Lush have made significant inroads. The company's in-store design is distinctive and idiosyncratic, but also outdated. Attempts have been made at an update, but haven't really worked.

It was right to divest much of its manufacturing in 1999, but it has been followed by product revolu-tion, rather than evolution, which has seen it alienate its core market without bringing in new consumers. [The need is to] make the brand philosophy more obvious in-store; given that Anita has scaled down her involvement, find a team whose hearts beat as passionately as hers to get NPD back on track. The Body Shop marketing expertise was based on the belief that actions speak louder than words – it still holds true, but the company seems to have forgotten it.

Source: Harriet Marsh, *Marketing*, 10 May, 2001

THE STRUCTURE OF THE MARKETING PLAN

The construction of the marketing plan is characterized by a range of headings which have been developed by different theorists. Some authors offer a list of sections with the first headed SWOT issues or situational analysis, the second headed statement of objectives and goals or setting objectives, the third is strategy or marketing programming, and the last is monitoring or control. We prefer to use different stages which are more easily understood by managers and students.

The stages are:

1 What is it we want?
2 Where are we now?
3 Where do we want to go?
4 How do we get there?
5 Where did we get to?

These stages are represented in the model in Fig. 10.1. For an understanding of the model it is important to realize that the system is not always linear, as would appear from the seemingly hierarchical stages. Quite often the process needs to involve an interplay between the various stages, with the flexibility to move backwards as well as forwards in an interactive process. We should also understand that refinements of the plan take place as understanding of the interconnections improves. We should not presume that anything close to perfection will apply until a number of drafts have been completed.

The approach to retail marketing planning is described in the following six main sections:

1 the corporate mission and goals;
2 external and internal audit;
3 business situation analysis;
4 creating the objectives;
5 providing an effective marketing mix strategy;
6 monitoring the plan.

THE CORPORATE MISSION AND GOALS

It is important to understand what is expected of the plan from the long-term goals set at corporate level. A clear mission statement enables the retailer to concentrate on core business objectives and what it wants to accomplish. Mission statements often will have terms such as: 'focus on our customers'; 'our foundation is our people'; 'we strive for quality'; 'renewal and innovation is our mantra'; 'we offer responsible and ethical approaches'.

The mission statement is a confirmation of what business the company is in from a consumer viewpoint and also acts as a guide for employees to know what the purpose of the company is. For example, the statement could stress: 'serving customers better than the competition and supporting the local community and employee needs through excellence in retailing'. The mission statement then represents the overriding goal of the

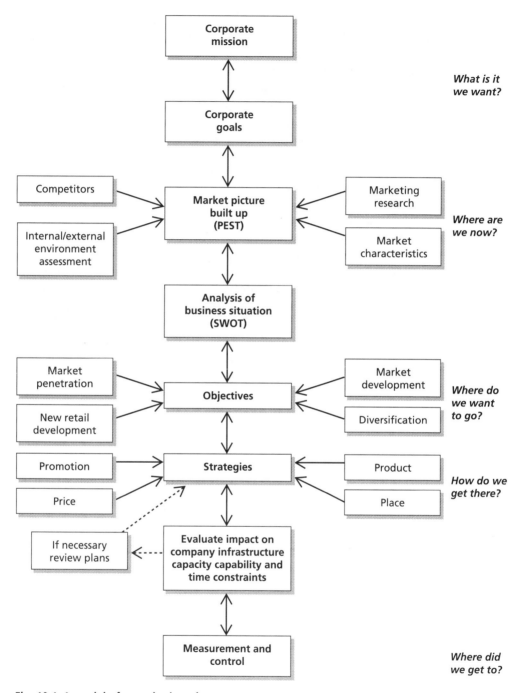

Fig. 10.1 A model of a marketing plan

company or organization. It is a statement of what the company wants to accomplish within chosen markets for the stakeholder groups it will serve. The mission statement is a clear expression of what the company or organization will attempt to achieve from the strategic intent and inputs in the marketing plan. It encapsulates the broad vision of the retailer and facilitates the identification of both the marketing objectives and goals.

The goals of a mission statement may be based upon the values and objectives of the key shareholders, board directors or senior managers. In some situations, goals are set only after the establishment and evaluation of the marketing programmes. This is a parochial, programme-led method of planning where management does not attempt to meet higher level corporate goals within the planning process because managers are more prepared to settle for what they believe will work rather than what should be made to work. A decision to agree easier targets may mean that a company, or organization, will not investigate as broad a range of alternatives, objectives and strategies as their competitors who may be driven to ensure leadership and competitive supremacy. Companies need to invent and reinvent themselves in the modern competitive age and therefore the mission statement should offer some guide as to the direction of this.

The mission statement of Boots is:

> To be the world's leading retailer of products and services that help make our customers look good and feel good.

Whatever approach is taken, the most effective form of planning has to create a balance between setting corporate direction and ensuring employee commitment to that direction by the process of their involvement (*see* Fig. 10.6). If goals are dictated to employees by a 'top-down' approach there is very little sense of ownership of the plan, which can lead to a corresponding lack of motivation. As will be realized from Fig. 10.6 there can be a balanced approach through the combination of bottom-up and top-down processes.

UNDERSTANDING THE FORCES OF INDUSTRY COMPETITION

The plan has to be formulated in relation to those forces which impinge on the likelihood of success. Prime among such forces is competition. The plan cannot exist in isolation of other factors. As Porter has argued (1980), it is easy to view the competition too narrowly and too pessimistically. Porter views intense competition as natural, with the state of competition depending on the relationship between five basic forces (*see* Fig. 10.2). Porter argues that it is the collective strength of these forces that determines the ultimate profit potential of any industry. The model has become widely known as the 'five forces' model of competition.

Any planning approach has to answer key questions about the marketplace. The use of the five-forces model provides an analysis that will help resolve such questions as:

- What are the key factors at work in the competitive environment?
- Are there any underlying forces that need to be uncovered?
- Is it likely that the forces will change and if so at what pace?
- What is the position of particular competitors in relation to these competitive forces?
- What can management (marketing) do to influence the competitive forces affecting their business and sector.

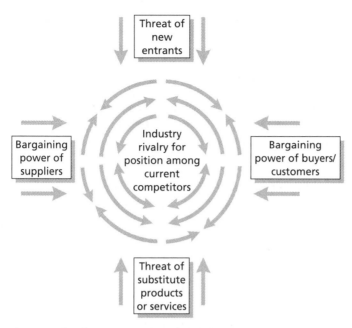

Fig. 10.2 Five forces governing competition in an industry

● Does the analyses provide an understanding of whether some industries or sectors are more attractive than others?

The forces of rivalry among existing competitors are:

1 the outcome of rivalry;
2 the bargaining power of buyers;
3 the bargaining power of suppliers;
4 the threat of new entrants; and
5 the threat of substitute products or services.

Each of these forces, in turn, can be broken down into its constituent elements. The following discussion of these forces helps with our understanding of the retail industry and clarifies the considerations we must take into account.

1 Rivalry among existing competitors

Factors which might affect the nature of competitiveness or 'the jockeying for position' by the use of tactics in the industry include the following:

● the degree of concentration in the industry, and the number and relative size of the competitors;
● fights for market share if industry growth is slow;
● the extent and nature of product differentiation;
● whether fixed costs are high or the product perishable;
● capacity in relation to demand and characteristics of demand;

● high exit barriers keeping companies competing even though they may be earning low or negative returns.

2 Bargaining power of buyers

The bargaining power of the buyers (that is, demand for the products or services whether it is the retail company acting as buyer from suppliers or whether it is the retail customer) is related to the following features:

● the degree of concentration relating to the relative importance of levels of demand on the customer side by comparison with those of the competing suppliers;
● the relative significance of the produce or service to customers in terms of quality, expenditure and service;
● the relative ease and cost of changing to new suppliers (switching costs);
● the amount of information possessed by buyers;
● the ability of buyers to integrate backwards;
● profit levels of buyers;
● the extent to which buyers want differentiated products.

3 Bargaining power of suppliers

Factors relevant to the supply side of the industry will be similar to those mentioned on the customer side of the industry and, thus, include:

● the structure of the supplier side relative to the producer industry;
● the degree of produce differentiation/substitutability;
● the potential for forward integration;
● the relative importance of the industry demand to suppliers;
● the feasibility and cost of producers switching suppliers.

4 Threat of new entrants

The ease, or difficulty, with which new producers may enter the industry affects the degree to which the structure of the industry can change due to the extra competition and the desire to gain market share. The seriousness of the threat is dependent on the type of barriers to entry and on the way existing competitors will react:

● the extent to which there are economies of scale;
● the amount of capital required to capture customer loyalty and create brand identification;
● the capital required for inventories and absorbing start-up costs;
● the learning curve benefits which lower costs experienced by existing companies;
● the level of customer switching costs;
● the existence of government regulation and legal limitations and barriers.

5 Threat of substitutes

- the availability of substitutes and willingness of buyers to purchase substitute products which have the same functional capability;
- the impact on profits of close substitutes;
- the impact of the comparative price and quality of substitutes.

The above approach to industry analysis can allow a retailer to understand the pressures on the industry and the likely effect on the prospects for short- and longer-term success. More specifically, a retailer is able to take into consideration its true competitive position with regard to its opponents and can identify the possible strengths and weaknesses resulting from the current state of rivalry in the industry. It may then proceed to consider what level of importance should be attached to the marketing planning process in order to provide a competitive advantage and a position from which to achieve its financial objectives.

EXTERNAL AND INTERNAL AUDIT

An external and internal audit is carried out as part of the broader process of market analysis to determine the opportunities existing in the retail marketplace. It is necessary to gather enough relevant information about the external and internal company environment to be able to construct a business and market picture of current and future pressure and trends. One important part of marketing planning is knowing what to analyse. Executives have to be careful that they do not have too limited a focus in terms of the environment. Checklists of necessary information are one way to stop companies scanning the environment based upon what they intend to do, rather than in relation to what they could or should do.

The information collected should, at the very least, form the basis of a PEST investigation. *PEST analysis* is an examination of the Political, Economic, Social and Technological changes which may affect the company and the plan. The information gathering utilizing PEST is part of an internal and external audit which could involve the business/economic environment and the market environment – discussed in more detail below.

Business/economic environment

Political: taxation, duty, regulation, policies, local authorities, statutory holidays, Sunday trading, opening times, planning permission for buildings

Economic: inflation, unemployment, fuel costs, exchange rates, average salaries, market environment (*see* market environment list below)

Social: demographics, holiday/leisure time entitlement, values (consumerism), lifestyle, male/female role changes, delay of first child, education, workforce changes

Technology: innovations, new retailing systems, home technology, electronic fund transfer, Internet, distribution systems, stock handling mechanisms and control

Market environment

This is an expansion of the economic category above.

Total market:	size, growth, trends, value, industry structure, barriers to entry, extent of under- or overcapacity of supply, marketing methods
Companies in the market:	level of investment, takeovers, alliances, promotion expenditures, redundancies, profits, expansion plans, trading formats
Product development:	trends, new product types, service enhancements
Price:	levels, range, terms, practices
Distribution:	patterns, trade structure, policies
Promotion:	expenditure, types, communication messages

The information listed above should be gathered on the basis of how it affects the company and service. For example, it will be found that shops in single-site positions are disappearing and that location in areas where the fascia brands will have pulling power is becoming more important. The task is then to analyse and ascertain the way forward. Identification of objectives may be intuitive and based upon a good idea, or systematic through researched evidence, or based upon trial and error from what has been learnt from past events.

BUSINESS SITUATION ANALYSIS

Once sufficient internal and external information has been collected it is necessary to carry out an analysis of the business situation, to identify the major

- Strengths
- Weaknesses
- Opportunities
- Threats

facing the company. This is the so-called *SWOT analysis*. There is also the need to check these against information provided from PEST analysis.

The systematic analysis carried out at this stage provides for the formulation of a number of assumptions about the past performance, future conditions, product opportunities, resources, and service priorities which all lead to the possibility of a range of strategic options for an organization within the retail industry. The analysis may utilize a number of approaches related to life-cycle assessment or portfolio analysis. These are discussed later and describe how to form a clearer understanding of the current position of the retail business which will lead to guidance in the selection of specific objectives and strategies.

The research feedback, from the earlier phase of planning activity, should have highlighted customer satisfaction or dissatisfaction with the current retail offers and services. It will also have highlighted what it is that the competition is doing well, and may indicate the existence of market gaps. For a store, decisions may need to be taken about the merchandise. This may include the width of assortment (number of different product categories carried) and the depth of assortment (the variety of products carried in a specific category). Scanning what is happening in foreign markets will sensitize the planners to what may become new trends or ideas in the home market. The point is that the overall analysis should be far-reaching to ensure that the best possible company options are assessed.

SWOT analysis

A framework of information should be created which is divided into the categories of strengths, weaknesses, opportunities and threats facing the company (SWOT). This will allow further assessment of the information collected and form the basis of a summary of all the main issues which will have been examined. Each of the SWOT points could be fed into the objectives of the plan. For example, if it were found that a weakness existed in the attitude of the target market to the brand or in the lack of knowledge the target market had of the organization, this could become part of the plan as a promotional objective. The example of a SWOT matrix in Fig. 10.3 is for a hypothetical bank which operates traditional branch retailing.

The SWOT analysis may lead to short-term operational imperatives. For example, a SWOT analysis could be a guide for a merchandiser as to how the existing product lines will need to be extended or deleted. It could act as a guide to the buyers to achieve certain price, quality and specification objectives for the retail brand, or even indicate to display people that the different window and in-store promotions need to be more consistent by season across all outlets.

Assessment of the retail operation has to take place in relation to the position of the company in its life-cycle stage (*see* Chapter 1 for a further discussion of this concept). The life-cycle figure (Fig. 10.4) and matrix (Table 10.2) provide our approach to the current retail situation and the strategies which may be appropriate at any one stage of the life cycle based upon a consideration of the competitive position of retail companies. The phases can be characterized as:

Strengths	Weaknesses
• financial position • reputation • branch network • technology • employees well qualified	• poor branch service; 'old-bank' brand image • opening hours restricted • high overheads due to high street locations • no parking
Opportunities	Threats
• expansion of investment and financial services • create a CRM (customer relationship management) system • develop relationship marketing scheme • expand services for retirees and younger investors • Segment and target lost ground taken by 'new' banks	• the development of tele-banking • encroachment by building societies and grocery retailers • international expansion of banking • over-concentration on traditional competencies (mortgages and loans)

Fig. 10.3 Example of a SWOT matrix

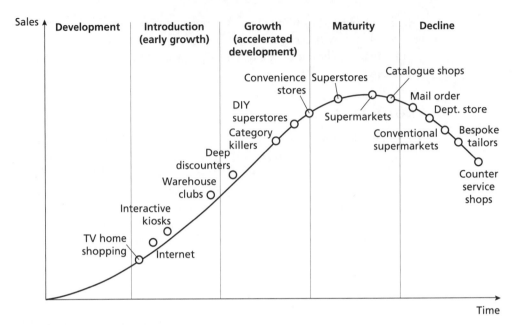

Fig. 10.4 UK retail life cycle

Table 10.2 Management of life-cycle position based upon market strength/weakness

Stages/competitive position	Birth	Growth	Maturity	Decline
Dominant	Fast business growth expected due to competitive strength and focus	Defend position and build in strategy of cost leadership and technological superiority	Aggressively defend position and renew efforts of leadership strategies and taking share	Continue to defend position Find way to relaunch retail concept
Favourable	Need to develop strengths of differentiation, cost control, and focus	Need to improve total business to ensure growth within the industry sector	Ensure focus and marketing is maximizing returns by attacking leaders' weaknesses Control costs	Plan turnaround Retrench Divest
Weak	Improve to ensure growth will occur Find niche	Require a major turnaround or new focus of the business	Start to harvest returns or plan improvements Take quiet route	Harvest Withdraw

- **Introduction** – Slow growth of demand, need to target innovators/early adopters, monopoly or few rivals for first movers, technology important.

- **Growth and shakeout** – Expansion at accelerating pace, need to target early adopters, facing competitive retail services/formats, and diffused technology. If growth declines some of the weakest rivals will drop out.

- **Maturity** – Primary demand does not expand, the market becomes fragmented and a few powerful rivals dominate, technology becomes standardized.

- **Decline** – Zero growth occurs and competitors may leave the market, technology becomes outdated.

As an example, the life cycle for retail can be generalized for different types of business, as illustrated in Fig. 10.4 for the UK.

Retail, like any other industry, can be seen to have stages that reflect different forms of competition. High street retail outlets which are reliant on clothing and footwear, such as Marks & Spencer, Bhs and Littlewoods, have suffered in recent times and a more general shakeout is occurring. The department and variety store retail sector can be characterized by saturation where low levels of demand from the consumer limit the strategic opportunities. Retailers in this sector have to fight to maintain market share and those that are more successful at cost control and brand building will probably win out. Once the position of an individual business (or its category type) is clear, then the strength or weakness of that retailer's position will dictate the most logical objectives and consequently point to the possible strategies which could be chosen. This is made clear in Table 10.2.

Portfolio analysis

A portfolio approach allows for the analysis of an organization's current position in relation to the marketplace, its own companies or products.

Example: Dixons manage their portfolio

Dixons business divisions have prospered within a portfolio management approach. The business has traditionally been made up of high street and out-of-town (Dixons, The Link, Currys, PC World), and Freeserve, Internet and e-commerce (Dixon's Online). The development of Freeserve in 1998 and the subsequent flotation of 20 per cent of Freeserve in 1999 has created the largest UK portal site with over 2 million users. The money raised and the success of investing in growth markets such as PC World has allowed the company to expand internationally (Elkjop, the Norwegian market leader in electrical retail marketing, was purchased in 1999; Ei system, the leading specialist retailer in Spain, was purchased in 2000, and a 15 per cent stake in Kotsovolos, the leading Greek electrical retailer, in 2000). The company understands the opportunities in the marketplace as can be judged by its development of The Link, which in 2001 had 260 outlets specializing in mobile phone sales, and the expansion of tax-free outlets at different airports. Through the years Dixons have divested those businesses which did not fit the portfolio – for example, problems with Silo, the company's US electrical retailer, were deemed so great that a divestment strategy was adopted; and the mail order division of VTG acquired in 1993 was disposed of in order to focus on the retail side of the business. In order to plan more effectively Dixons regrouped its business into the four retailing divisions of high street, out-of-town, PC World and Freeserve.

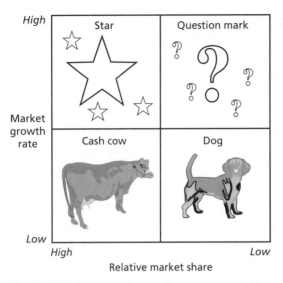

Fig. 10.5 Market growth – market share portfolio analysis matrix

A commonly used technique for consideration of the growth and share of an organization is the Boston Consulting Group Matrix (BCG). Portfolio analysis has been described as a family of techniques with BCG as the most famous (Abell and Hammond, 1979). This is even more true two decades on with the BCG approach being used by a large number of planners in different marketing settings. This approach allows an organization to classify the position of each of its retail strategic business units (SBUs) on one axis in terms of their market share relative to competitors and on the opposite axis to position annual industry growth. By creating a measurement based upon the scales of each of these axes, a spatial plot is derived which by the use of the creation of quadrants places each plot in a specific category. As part of the analysis, a company may identify which SBUs are dominant when compared to competitors, and whether the areas in which the company operates are growing, stable or declining. The two-by-two matrix describes four types of position as: star, question mark, cash cow, and dog (*see* Fig. 10.5).

Stars

These are SBUs or products with a high market share in a fast growing market and, importantly, offering good prospects for growth. As such, the objective would be for an investment in any SBU or product to fall into this quadrant. One objective is to build on the strength of the position and/or to hold on to it in the face of any competition. If the organization has a balanced portfolio, the transferring of money from a cash cow (*see* Fig. 10.5) SBU could be contemplated if this would create higher returns in the long run.

Question marks

These are SBUs or products where there is some question about their position. Spatially there is the potential for high market growth, but there is also low market share. The objectives would be to investigate further the possibility of any future movement, in the market or from the competition, creating a new position of either a star or a dog. If the question mark has the possibility of becoming a star, and if the organization has a cash cow, then money should be transferred to build the question mark position with the objective of creating a star. Alternatively, a poor outcome for the analysis may mean the objective has to be one of becoming a niche retailer – or even divestment. If the unit of consideration were merchandise and certain items fell into this area, there may need to be an expansion of shelf space for the merchandise and the use of in-store promotion.

Cash cows

This categtory is where the SBU or product is enjoying the benefit of a high market share but in a low or zero growth market. The objective would be to exploit the strong, positive cash flow situation but not to devote any investment into the SBU or product apart from that necessary to ensure its maintenance. The objective is normally to hold the position and harvest money that can be used to grow other parts of the business.

Dogs

These are SBUs or products with a low market share and static or no market growth. The inference is that any future earnings are bound to be low and little or no profit will be made. The objective would be either to create a niche area for activity or to withdraw from this area of business by selling out or planning closure. If the unit of consideration were merchandise and certain items fell into this area, there would be a case for reducing or removing the area of shelf space for the merchandise.

Each of these spatial areas allows an identification of what strategies may be most appropriate. This allows objectives to be decided upon which are in the long-term interests of the organization as a whole, so that a balanced approach is taken which considers all aspects of an operation.

The assumption is that the higher the market share of any strategic business unit the better its long-term marketplace position, because of the probability of economies of scale, lower costs and higher profitability. In Fig. 10.5 the vertical axis identifies the annual growth rate percentage of the operating market for the SBUs, companies or products being assessed. It does not normally exceed a growth rate of 12 per cent but it depends on the market being analysed. The logic of its inclusion is related to the notion that any organization in a situation where there is high market growth will have derived benefit from the buoyant development in the marketplace. However, for a retailer, the costs of operation may not decline because of this situation as some merchandise, for stores in a star position, may require prime store sites in order to achieve the optimum level of sales.

Relative market share is the horizontal axis and is used because it provides the unit of measurement as an indicator of the ability to generate cash based upon the relative position to the market leader. The measure of market share is expressed as a comparison to that of the largest competitor. This is important because it reflects market share relative to the leader and shows the degree of power the market leader has over others in the market. For example, if company 'A' had a 25 per cent share of the market and its competitor 'B' also had 25 per cent, there is little advantage. However, the market situation is dramatically different and more favourable to 'A' if it is the market leader with a 25 per cent share and its closest competitor has a 12.5 per cent market share. The horizontal axis provides a relative ratio to the market leader and, therefore, the example given would create a 1:1 ratio in the first example and 2:1 in the second. These ratios are plotted on the horizontal axis against the market leader's share to reflect the individual positions of dominance for different units of measurement. The axis can be divided on any scale which makes sense for the market being considered but should enable the relative positions, across the range of the axis, to be plotted. As there is the use of a market leader share figure, the left-hand end of the scale will be no larger than 1 as no other SBU, product or company can exceed the size of the leader's share.

A certain amount of caution has to be applied to the indiscriminate use of portfolio analysis. At the outset it should be realized that portfolio analysis has more dimensions than simply market share and market growth. In fact, one of the difficulties is to decide upon the scales for the axes. Once these are agreed, it may be difficult to obtain competitive data. With a BCG approach the spatial positioning outcome of any analysis is not necessarily related to profitability, as a high market share could be based upon low profitability if prices are lower than the competition or vice versa. In addition, a higher market share for a retailer or a product may reflect a disproportionate amount of promotional expenditure which in turn could be creating unacceptable cost implications. There are conceptual and practical problems in defining both products and markets when using the matrix. While telephone banking for a bank may be a star, the main business for the bank could be suffering due to the impact of building society and grocery retail activity. Finally, a market which is growing may not be a good environmental fit, or suit the business strengths of the SBU or company. None of these weaknesses indicates there is a major problem with the BCG matrix or its principles, simply that it has to be utilized with some degree of caution.

The human resources considerations for successful planning

The involvement of different departments will help reduce resistance to future changes or tasks. Continuous concern about the human aspects of planning can provide a greater possibility of the plan's success. The planner or planning team should be aware that they are only a technical service to a wider team. However, care must be taken not to make the system too open as to be in danger of creating anarchy. On the other hand, the system should not be too closed, as this leads to bureaucracy and apathy.

Good planning is a combination of qualitative and quantitative factors based upon creative as well as analytical and logical thinking. As Albert Einstein once remarked, 'When I examined myself, and my methods of thought, I came to the conclusion that the gift of fantasy has meant more to me than my talent for absorbing positive knowledge.' Creative thinkers bring specific benefits to the planning process. They enable:

- challenges to norms and assumptions and the ability to question what others automatically accept as true;
- the focus on chance and the unexpected rather than safe answers;
- a group to develop new ways of altering familiar ideas into unconventional approaches and so provide new ideas and means of thinking of situations;
- individuals to make associations and so combine seemingly unrelated events, topics and ideas;
- retail product, service and promotion ideas to be updated and revised;

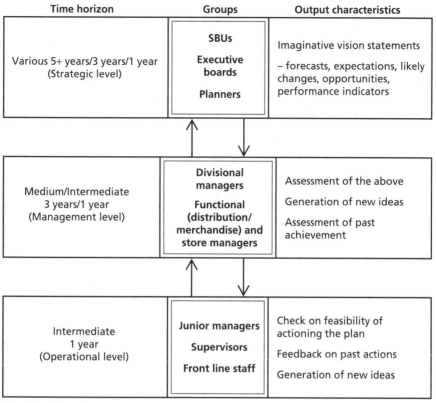

Time horizon	Groups	Output characteristics
Various 5+ years/3 years/1 year (Strategic level)	**SBUs** **Executive boards** **Planners**	Imaginative vision statements – forecasts, expectations, likely changes, opportunities, performance indicators
Medium/Intermediate 3 years/1 year (Management level)	**Divisional managers** **Functional (distribution/ merchandise) and store managers**	Assessment of the above Generation of new ideas Assessment of past achievement
Intermediate 1 year (Operational level)	**Junior managers** **Supervisors** **Front line staff**	Check on feasibility of actioning the plan Feedback on past actions Generation of new ideas

Note: SBU = Strategic Business Unit

Fig. 10.6 Involvement levels for marketing planning

- planners to keep the planning function from being too boring by bringing humanistic values to the whole process.

One vital behavioural consideration of any plan, which affects all aspects of the company, is that it should not clash with the company culture. Such a clash may be overcome by ensuring that staff values are incorporated into various stages of the planning cycle and the planning method. The involvement of the full range of staff leads to a situation where the company culture values of staff are reflected in the 'bottom-up' comments. This helps to ensure that the plan is created as part of a process which makes it compatible with the company culture.

As you are now aware, we stress that companies have to plan for the involvement level of staff as well as for the market. Figure 10.6 provides one approach to dealing with marketing planning involvement levels.

One other important aspect of influence when including a cross-section of people in planning is their capability to hinder or help the plan. Within any company or organization, a manager's competence to plan will reflect the level of activity, the degree of preoccupation with other business, career goals, and their experience and ability to think conceptually and analytically. These attributes are linked to other managers' values and the cultural climate within the company, which may be more or less responsive to change and adaptation, and the willingness to adhere to and use the planning system.

A plan when completed should be read and understood by as many people as possible throughout the company. This is often not possible due to lack of time among busy executives and the complexity of the plan. To overcome the problem, all plans require the addition of a good executive summary – written in clear, concise language – which will ensure that the most salient points and important themes are communicated. The summary should be cogent and logical and should concentrate on objectives, main target markets, opportunities and threats, key strategies and timings.

MINICASE 10.2

7-Eleven wants to cut it the UK way: The US store chain FT hopes to copy British success with portable food

Jim Keyes, chief executive of 7-Eleven, has just returned from an unusual fact-finding tour in the UK. His mission: to discover the secret of the high-quality packaged sandwich. Portable fast food is hard to find in the US, he contends: 'You can't throw a McDonald's in your briefcase and eat it three hours later.'

Mr Keyes spent a week touring British supermarkets and the Prêt-à-Manger sandwich chain for inspiration, and is confident that the model can be emulated in the US. The expansion into fresh food is part of the group's strategy to offset a long-term decline in tobacco sales but could also help counter the impact of the US economic downturn.

The group has begun to take a more aggressive approach towards merchandising. Mr Keyes argues that the chain's technology can provide manufacturers with information about what shoppers want. Recently, for example, the group spotted that customers who bought Kraft's Crystal Light powdered soft drinks were buying bottled water to mix it with. It suggested that Kraft make a bottled drink, and secured an exclusive deal to sell the 20oz bottles. Mr Keyes says this inverts the relationship between retailers and suppliers to create a 'demand chain management system' that allows it to introduce 50 new items a week to its 5,700 US stores. The retail

industry has not been very proactive with manufacturers, he says, but 7-Eleven's experience showed that 'we have a lot more strength with manufacturers than we gave ourselves credit for'.

In search of replacement revenues, he has settled on fresh food. This accounts for just 6–10 per cent of US sales, but Mr Keyes is encouraged by 7-Eleven's Swedish stores, which have expanded fresh produce sales from 4 per cent to 25 per cent in five years. Such improvements may allow 7-Eleven to ask for a higher royalty from franchisees. About 3,300 of its US stores are operated by franchisees, who pay 7-Eleven between 0.25 per cent and 1 per cent of sales.

Mr Keyes says 7-Eleven's history has taught him to be selective. After a period of over-expansion in the 1980s, the group was privatised through a leveraged buyout in October 1987. Caught out by its $4.5bn debt burden and double-digit interest rates, it was rescued by its Japanese licensee, and has retreated from areas where it has little critical mass. Mr Keyes is comfortable opening 150–200 stores a year, but says 'this company has some credibility building to do' before bolder moves can be on the agenda.

Source: Andrew Edgecliffe-Johnson, *Financial Times*, 25 July, 2001

CREATING THE OBJECTIVES

This stage involves communicating the company's objectives, which are a combination of what is expected of the company by its shareholders or directors, and an evaluation of the options emerging out of the first three steps. For a small company, the objectives are often less ambitious than for larger concerns, but in terms of achieving market success, no less important.

If at the earlier stage of analysis it was found that waiting times in the shop were affecting frequency of visits in a negative way, then the retailer has to have the following objectives:

- improve the retail operation's service levels;
- enhance the waiting time experience;
- inform customers as to the likely time they will have to wait;
- apologize and give a reason for the delay;
- ensure the customers can judge the progress of their turn in being served.

These objectives will be translated into tactics or operational changes but, as a starting point, it is necessary to know what the main objectives are. At a later stage, changes could be made similar to those at Disney where those queuing for rides can watch TV, listen to music, are organized so that they can see people moving and are given approximate waiting times. In busy booking offices or shops, customers can take a numbered ticket that will guarantee their place in the queue without anyone else pushing in.

The objectives should emerge as the most logical course of action the company ought to embark upon, given the analysis which has occurred in the preceding stages of the plan. We have to ensure that the objectives include not only sales volume and financial objectives, but also broader marketing objectives. Objectives should also include the expected market share achievements because the performance of the company may only reach realistic levels if certain budgets are made available.

At this stage of planning it is possible to circulate the assumptions and forecasts to different stores, functional units and company divisions. These should be offered as a range of alternatives. For example, if you have assumed the market will grow at X per cent and this will create £Y with a specific strategy, then it is also wise to create alternative scenarios. You should estimate sales at lower and higher rates than expected, so that the potential impact on profits can be assessed. For example, a rate of growth of X + 2 per cent (where X is the expected demand) may create a profit of $1.3 \times £Y$, or alternatively X − 2 per cent may give $0.5 \times £Y$. Managers may need to involve their team in discussions about the relevance of the material created from the previous environmental scanning stage to ensure agreement to expected demand level.

One danger in planning is that large companies often set only financial objectives – for example, in terms of growth rate in earnings per share, return on equity or investment and so on – and ignore or forget to set marketing objectives such as the selection of specific segments as target markets and the improvement of merchandise selection, brand image or consumer awareness. Retailers have to establish and maintain a distinctive image in their chosen markets. This image is created only if objectives are set which recognize the need for appropriate physical and attitudinal attributes. These goals need to be related to retail design, ambience, the location decisions based upon surrounding area, and the impact of the retail window area and front of building. The use of promotional techniques and customer service strategies all enhance the position and image of a retail company.

Objectives are often complex. For example, an objective may be to *increase sales revenue*, which could be achieved in a number of ways, such as:

- increasing average transaction values;
- converting browsing visits to purchase behaviour;
- increasing the frequency of customer visits;
- improving merchandise selection or placing merchandise in proximity to corresponding mix and match items;
- increasing hours of trading, such as Sunday opening.

Another example could be an objective to *create improved productivity*. This could be achieved in various ways:

- increasing sales and contribution per retail employee;
- introducing technology to provide efficiencies;
- increasing throughput of distribution facilities;
- redesigning the store layout to improve customer flow;
- improving stock control.

Retail companies involve many labour-intensive operations and will often set objectives of reducing costs through greater use of technology or systems design. MFI, the furniture retailer, attempted to increase operating efficiencies and sales productivity. There was an investment in systems in order to reduce staff numbers, to improve stock control and merchandise and warehouse space. In addition, store layouts were improved and visual merchandising introduced. The initial changes allowed the company to improve substantially on its previously weak sales and profit results.

In the current marketplace, retailing technology is advancing swiftly with inventory control, automated checkout facilities, vending machines, etc. Any change due to technology innovation has to be carried out with due concern for the marketing implications of that improvement. Any reduction in personal service may be interpreted as a decline in the standards of service. Therefore, objectives need to be a balance between the aspirational and the realistic, so that the company attempts to improve its market position within acceptable risk limits.

Growth objectives

The alternative objective inputs, as shown on the marketing plan schema in Fig. 10.2, are based upon the possibility of the selection of growth strategies, borrowed from the work of Ansoff (1988), whereby a company is attempting to expand by adopting a specific strategy from those of *penetration, market development, product development* and *diversification*.

Companies may want to attack the market share of others by *penetrating* the market to increase their own share of that market. This takes place within the company's current markets and normally involves a more aggressive use of the marketing mix. The company may attempt to increase existing customer usage rates or attract competitors' customers. For example, VISA used promotion in an attempt to get their cardholders to use their card while on holiday and in preference to those of competitors. Some of the

current large DIY outlets started as home improvement specialists with initial links to paint and wallpaper stores. These companies realized the growth potential of the whole DIY marketplace and wanted to take market share from their competitors. To back up the setting of the objective of market penetration, there should be some evidence from the analysis that there is buoyancy and growth in the marketplace. Sales can be increased by reaching non-users of the outlet or service, attracting competitors' customers and raising the frequency of store visit of existing customers.

Larger organizations or companies will try to increase sales through *market development* by attempting to sell current products in new markets. As an objective, this is often linked to those retailers which are located on a local or regional basis and want to widen their market by geographical expansion. Companies may develop their markets by expanding internationally, as did the IKEA group, for instance. Market development may also involve the addition of new locations, such as McDonald's outlet openings to compete at airports, at tourist attractions, and even within office buildings. Market development is related to the objective of a retailer wanting to widen its market, attract new market segments or convince the customer that the business has been repositioned and offers new benefits.

Rapid market development may be achieved through franchising. Franchising is the method by which a company (the franchisee who owns the right to a brand name) will sell, for a fee or a royalty, access to the company's supply of merchandise and the right to trade under the company's name to a franchisor. There will also be a transfer of know-how to those individuals who are deemed suitable to run a franchised operation. The most famous franchises in the UK are Benetton, The Body Shop and Tie Rack. There are advantages to the franchisees as promotion is carried out on a national basis, the niche market is already established through clear marketing strategies, and supply chains are highly developed.

Example: Diversification development at Tesco

Tesco Personal Finance (TPF) was launched in July 1997 and is a joint venture with Royal Bank of Scotland. Products include Clubcard Plus, a grocery budgeting account. A Tesco Visa card was launched in July 1997, Tesco Instant Access Savings Account in September 1997, home insurance in April 1998, loans in May 1998, pensions in June 1998, travel insurance in July 1998, ISAs in April 1999, pet insurance in October 1999 and mortgages in June 2000. The joint venture has over 1 million customers, 1.6m accounts and is already profitable. In addition, Tesco is Britain's largest independent petrol retailer, with 325 petrol stations, including Express sites, and has 12.5 per cent of the market for petrol sold in the UK.

Source: Tesco company accounts, 2001

Company objectives may also include *product development* or *diversification*. Product development is a sensible objective for retailers which have strong brands and a good market presence. One of the reasons own-brands have been successful is related to the market presence of those companies which have introduced the concept. Companies often develop new ideas for retailing which need to be planned as new product development. An example of new product retail development is the advent of factory outlet shopping centres. This type of outlet started as an American concept and was developed during the 1990s in the UK. Factory outlets should not be confused with discount centres. They are groups of shops, normally away from town centres, specializing in the selling of seconds or end-of-line goods, usually under a named manufacturer rather than the retailer.

Diversification is an objective linked to a desire not to become dependent on one type of retail business. Diversification has occurred where retailers have created mail order operations and vice versa. We have also seen the diversification of retailers such as Virgin into the airline business or Marks & Spencer into food; the diversification into food set a positioning for the M&S business which differentiated it from all other supermarkets rather than M&S appearing to move into line with them. The company planned and implemented a high quality and value added range of premium priced food products targeted at affluent consumers.

Integrative growth

Growth, as an objective, can also be achieved through *integrative growth*, which is based upon the three areas of backward, forward and horizontal integration within the supply chain. An objective to increase sales by incorporating one or more levels of the supply chain into the business would be based upon integrative growth. If this were based upon *backward integration*, company changes would need to involve taking ownership or control of the supply aspects of the supply chain (for example, a retailer acquiring a wholesaler or manufacturer). In the case of *horizontal integration*, the retailer would seek ownership or control of competitors at the same level within the marketing channel; mergers, acquisitions and takeovers are the logical outcome of this objective. *Forward integration* is often the objective of manufacturers who want to gain greater control of their distribution through the development or acquisition of retail businesses. For example, British Airways, American Express and the tour operator Thomson with the Lunn Poly brand, have opened a number of travel shops to ensure they can have some presence – and control of sales – in the high street.

Competitive advantage

When retail companies decide upon strategies which may lead them towards market success they need to consider generic routes to competitive advantage. Porter (1980) describes the three generic strategies of *cost leadership* (a company that seeks, finds and exploits all sources of cost advantage – providing for a standard, no frills package); *differentiation* (a company seeks something distinctive to set it apart from others that can bring in good profit returns – typically having attributes that are different from the competition); and a *focus* strategy (a company selects a segment of the market and targets that to the extent of excluding other segments).

Cost leadership

Using Porter's terminology, the discounters – such as Aldi and Lidl from Germany, and Netto from Denmark – entered the UK market in the late 1980s and early 1990s with a cost leadership strategy. The only way for them to prosper was through the achievement of competitive advantage by sustaining lower prices than the competition. This placed a great deal of emphasis on their being able to reduce and control the costs of their operations. Cost leadership can be adopted by low cost retail operations which are aiming to penetrate the market and exploit experience curve effects. The low cost super-markets and discount warehouses have taken this approach. Low priced retailers need to:

- choose to locate outlets on smaller sites that are less expensive than their competitors;
- provide an outlet design which has no lavish facilities and where stock can be moved straight into the sales area, on pallets, with boxes that can be opened when they are needed;
- streamline all systems and employ a minimum number of staff. However, the staff may be paid more to ensure that multi-skilling and productivity gains are achieved;
- keep stockholding to a minimum;
- develop many outlets to achieve improved economies of scale.

Cost leadership normally requires economies of scale and the ability to control costs better than the competitors. Cost leadership would not be a viable strategy for a small retail operation such as a hairdresser because local competitors could probably offer a similar range of prices. Smaller companies can grow on the basis of cost leadership if they identify segments which offer lower costs. For example, in insurance and banking there are low cost clients who seldom complain, take up less time for any transaction, and are willing to communicate by letter or phone. Such an approach will eliminate many of the costs associated with the running of a traditional retail business. An example is the Abbey National attempting to attract savers to its postal service savings account by offering competitive interest rates. By creating this service, Abbey National can gain the advantage of lowering costs and freeing up its branches to deal with other types of transaction.

Differentiation

Differentiation, as a generic strategy, involves a company developing a product or service that is unique or superior in some way. Retailers that achieve differentiation through quality are often able to charge higher than average prices. As indicated earlier, one major success story is that of Marks & Spencer. In the early 1990s Marks & Spencer were achieving a 40 per cent share of total sales for their range of quality food products. This diversification occurred with a service design back-up to ensure that their food arrived in the freshest of conditions and was then stored at optimal temperatures. This reinforced the commitment to differentiate on quality which is the hallmark of the positioning of their overall retail offer.

A bank could differentiate itself on the basis of its service by offering to pay for the installation of modems and terminals in the homes of its most important customers to enable them to have instant access to their accounts and investments.

Focus

There is often a need to ensure that a business has a clear focus because that is precisely the way a customer needs to have the offer positioned in their mind. Focus, in relation to the retailer, allows the retail offer to be more precisely defined in terms of price, quality and range. This will enable a retailer to be single-minded in creating a highly focused retail mix offer. The success of Mothercare in the early stages was that they built a reputation on the positioning slogan, 'Everything for the mother-to-be and children under 5' and then put together a product range and marketing policy which reflected this. When Mothercare attempted to extend the range to teenagers, it transpired that the baby shop image had been such a strong focus that these younger consumers resisted the change.

As indicated, with a focus approach companies concentrate their efforts on specific segments of the market. This may be because they have insufficient resources to concentrate on a broader market base. Tie Rack, Knickerbox, Accessorize and Sock Shop are examples of such a strategy. However, this does not preclude Tie Rack having a small part of its stock as socks. This can also be a dangerous position. Sock Shop made the mistake of underestimating both the strength of the competition from companies such as Marks & Spencer and the limited size of the market for socks. Although the niche approach has its attractions in terms of being able to concentrate on a focused offer, there is always danger inherent in such a singular and exposed position. If success occurs there is a risk of being attacked by stronger companies and of not being able to find alternative competencies in order to survive a strong marketing assault.

Each of the above ways of gaining advantage can be successful, but companies have to be clear about their strategy or they will become 'stuck in the middle' and fail to achieve any advantage. Customers will not have a good reason to utilize a particular retailer who is either unfocused, offers no cost advantage or has an undifferentiated store or service image.

There are a number of operational areas where retailers should plan to create sustainable competitive advantage. An adaptation of the article by Knee and Walters (1989) provides the following ways that advantage can be gained:

- strong customer loyalty;
- good location;
- supplier partner relationships;
- technological superiority;
- low cost efficiencies.

In addition, we should also add a further point – higher quality staff, as they are an asset that can provide advantage. The retail business is based around the performance of staff as part of interpersonal relationships. Over 90 per cent of Waterstone's staff are graduates; given the nature of the business, this is an ideal fit both for giving informed advice and for the ability to delegate management functions and buying decisions. (The importance of a service culture within retailing was dealt with extensively in Chapter 4.) Companies are attempting to meet the challenges to improve operations and some, such as Marks & Spencer, have built competitive advantage over many years through the relationships they build with their suppliers. Another area mentioned above is the use of information technology. In the retail industry, IT is in widespread use as its application to merchandise control allows for the more efficient use of retail space, improved inventory control and the collection of detailed customer information. The advantages are to be gained by those companies who have developed their systems to create greater efficiencies and customer satisfaction than their competitors.

Location advantage is very important for both large and small companies. The Savile Row tailors gain a great deal of advantage from their location; it provides a focus for their exclusive services, provides synergy of image, and signals the quality and price positioning of the outlets.

Retail market segmentation

One important part of the analysis stage of marketing planning is the selection of the most desirable target markets. Arising from the SWOT analysis will be the objective to target specific sub-markets – also known as segments. The target market will consist of a group of customers sharing some similar characteristics towards which the retailer will direct its products and services. For example, Harrods will have a different target market from that of Littlewoods and the positioning of the stores will be planned to appeal to the main segments who will shop at each type of outlet.

Market segmentation is based upon the breaking down of a large heterogeneous market into smaller subdivisions in which there is some similarity of character. In practice, there is always the problem of identifying a large enough group of customers with clearly differentiated needs so that a retailer can position its outlets and offer to that group. The consequence is that the retailer has to think clearly about the image, layout and service levels of the store in order to achieve the most advantageous position against its competitors. Retailing, by its nature, includes a whole range and type of different customers. Even some of the niche retailers, such as new entrants, The Perfume Shop and Games Workshop, or more traditional companies seeking a revival such as Sock Shop, appeal to a cross-section of the public who have very little in common. The determination of the retailer's choice of segments to target relies on the company resources, the nature of rivalry and competition, and the volatility or stability of the marketplace.

We believe that market segmentation, in the context of retailing, can be defined as:

the process of dividing the total retail market into subsets, whereby the potential segments have characteristics in common which lead to similar demand needs for a type of store format, product and service.

It would follow that retailers should be concerned with the examination of the marketplace to identify those groups which can be differentiated on the basis of shopping habits, desired shopping experience, and demand patterns and needs. The general trends in society have led to a number of changes which create viable opportunities for retailers. Changes in disposable income for the younger groups in society led to the emergence of the opportunity for positioning of brands such as Miss Selfridge, River Island, Top Shop and Top Man. In addition, the accent on healthy living has given rise to specialist shops such as Holland & Barrett. The retailer has to decide upon the coverage of the target market. This can be any one of a selection from a broad *mass market*, a selective *market segment* strategy, or aiming at two or more *multiple segments*.

Example: Arcadia's portfolio approach to segmentation

Arcadia Group's portfolio has been planned for the mass market and covers menswear, womenswear and childrenswear. Each brand is carefully positioned to provide coverage of specific market targets. With the exception of Wade Smith (now sold) which stocked designer labels, all of the group's chains offered own-brand offers. Outfit, the out-of-town chain, retails own-label products from the other brands within the group.

Arcadia Group: Product offer and own-brands, 2000

Chain	Product offer	Target market	Brands
Dorothy Perkins	Womenswear	20–45 year olds	Dorothy Perkins; Secrets; DP Petites; DP Maternity; DP Denim; Liza Bruce; Whistles Express; DPL (DP Leather)
Evans	Womenswear	Size 16+ women	SeVen; East Coast; Essence; Petites; Sixteen47; Active VIII; Design; Images
Top Shop	Womenswear	15–25 year olds	Topshop; Moto; TS Design
Principles for Women	Womenswear	25–40 year olds	Principles; Principles Petites; The Collection at Principles; The Collection at Principles Petites
Wallis	Womenswear	30–40 year olds	Wallis; W.woman
Richards	Womenswear	30–40 year olds	
Miss Selfridge	Womenswear	15–25 year olds	Miss Selfridge
Warehouse	Womenswear	15–40 year olds	Warehouse
Top Man	Menswear	15–25 year olds	Moto; Willson; Jibe; Bloc & Tackle; Nico
Burton Menswear	Menswear	25–40 year olds	Burton Menswear; Atlantic; Centaur Atlantic Sport; Jonathan Adams;
Principles for Men	Menswear	25–40 year olds	Principles For Men; PFM Sport; The Collection
Hawkshead	Womenswear/ Menswear/ Childrenswear	Outdoor and casualwear	Hawkshead
Racing Green	Menswear/ Womenswear	25–40 year olds	Racing Green
Outfit	Womenswear/ Menswear/ Childrenswear	15–40 year olds	Burton Menswear; Dorothy Perkins; Evans; Topshop; Topman; Miss Selfridge; Wallis; Warehouse; Racing Green; Hawkshead; Principles
Wade Smith	Menswear/ Womenswear	25–35 year olds	Designer brands
SU214	Menswear/ Womenswear	15–30 year olds	SU214; Moto; Designer brands

Source: Retail Intelligence, 2001
Note: Entries in italics have either closed or are being closed. Wade Smith has now been sold

Retail outlets selling general products, such as supermarkets and chemists, will target the broader mass market. This is because their trading success lies in offering a wide range of popular items at value-for-money prices. By contrast, a specialist retailer can attempt to identify a new segment, or adopt an upmarket or downmarket position. Anita Roddick is the classic example of someone who identified a gap in the market – one which she successfully exploited with The Body Shop range of natural products merchandise. In the 1980s George Davis successfully used lifestyle and age segmentation for the Next group of outlets. The product was then chosen to reflect the individual's status, lifestyle, gender and age, with a higher quality standard to the clothes which was reinforced by above average prices. Following the success of positioning stores to target specific groups, a number of retailers decided to adopt segmentation strategies based upon different aspects of lifestyle. There were several successful approaches at this time, including those of Habitat, Harrods, Laura Ashley and, more recently, IKEA. A current lifestyle change is towards being healthier. The medical profession and a number of magazines and newspapers have helped to change attitudes to both leisure pursuits and eating habits. These trends will, in turn, have repercussions on fashion and merchandise selection as well as provide an opportunity for new product development: for example, Boots having specialist boutiques for health care.

Department stores are likely to judge multiple segments to be a viable business alternative. This is because they supply distinct groups of customers for whom they choose to provide specific goods and services. Department stores are often subdivided within the store, thus creating different shopping experiences for different segments. However, they will design a restaurant to cater for the needs of all the targeted groups.

Psychographic segmentation

Within retailing the need to understand psychographics is increasingly important. This is because individuals from the same socio-economic group can have vastly different preferences and purchasing behaviour. Lifestyle is a term for the way individuals or groups lead their lives based upon differences determined by their attitudes, opinions and interests. The modern consumer's behaviour can be found to reflect the lifestyle they have, or aspire to. As society becomes more affluent there is the possibility for individual consumption patterns to be personalized. This allows an individual to seek out a set of brands and embark upon shopping habits that provide symbolic meaning to others about their lifestyle. For example, a person with concerns over the environment may be more likely to shop at The Body Shop. Different lifestyles also set the cultural norms by which individuals define their aspirations towards certain consumption behaviour. Massive queuing to patronize the premises of McDonald's followed the first retail premises opening in Moscow. This is because McDonald's is an ultimate icon of what it means to have an American or Western lifestyle. Psychographic segmentation can be understood in different ways:

- At a stable level, as the individual's system of evaluation based upon personality and attitudes.
- At an intermediate level, as the values of the individual based upon their opinions, activities and interests.
- At a weak level, as the individual's lifestyle reflected in the purchasing habits they demonstrate and the resulting use or consumption patterns of these.

The use of psychographic analysis has to be constantly updated as social forces will affect the way individuals act and react in their shopping habits and purchasing behaviour. There is therefore a need to track emerging trends within society. Hasson (1995) identified a number of social forces that will affect lifestyle habits:

- *self-development* – affirming oneself as an individual;
- *hedonism* – giving priority to pleasure;
- *plasticity* – adapting to circumstances;
- *vitality* – exploiting one's energy;
- *connectivity* – relating to others: clicking in and out; mixing cultures;
- *ethics* – searching for authenticity and meaning in life;
- *belongings* – defining social links and cultural identities;
- *inertia* – actively, or more often passively, resisting change.

Each of the above is thought to influence and shape our society and in particular European society.

Approaches to retail segmentation

The identification and selection of segments will require judgement based on the analysis of different data. The main method of segmentation is to select a segment (target market) with the best potential from a range of criteria. Then the objective is to create product benefits, features and promotional messages which will appeal to the needs of the selected segment(s). A number of characteristics are examined when deciding upon target groups. For example, K Mart in the USA describes its target market as middle-class (ABC1), value-conscious consumers. It is geographically located in mid-range shopping centres and offers both national and K Mart brands for sale. On a geographical basis, retailers in America will plan significant variations in the product mix due to geographical segment differences, e.g. between West Coast and East Coast consumers. The size, type and tastes of the population within any geographic area may be different from other areas and, therefore, require a different marketing mix (*see* Chapter 3 on consumer behaviour in retail for further discussion of some of the segmentation characteristics profiled in Table 10.3 and the following text).

The approach illustrated in Fig. 10.7 utilizes the list of segmentation characteristics given in Table 10.3 and disaggregates the detail in steps 1 and 2 so that all possibilities can be considered. In step 3 the information is analysed, then aggregated and assessed. The retailer will then make a decision in step 4 based upon the consideration of a combination of factors, including the segment's potential sales volume and profits, the retail competition of those companies currently selling to the segments, as well as the company's abilities and objectives. Therefore, the retailer attempts to assess the needs of different sub-groups to see if it can offer now, or in the future, a form of distribution service that will prove successful.

In order for segmentation to be successful, intellectual rigour must be applied to the segmentation procedure. When a target group is identified it is prudent to use a checklist, such as the retail segmentation checklist shown in the box, to ensure that the segment offers a viable opportunity for the company. The check is based upon whether

Table 10.3 Some general characteristics of segmentation variables

Characteristic	Typical classification
Geographic	By differences in the distances individuals live and have to travel in relation to the location of the store. Type of shopper – Country, area of country: north, Midlands, south, coastal; County, TV areas: urban, suburban, rural areas, city, town, postcode or type of house
Demographic	By age group, gender, education, family life cycle, ethnic group, socio-economic classification of household based upon A, B, C1, C2, D, E classifications
Psychographic	Lifestyle Personality type – introvert, extrovert, high/low ego drive, green consumer, health consumer, independent, group worker
Usership	Non-user, current user, past user, potential user, heavy user, medium user, light user, merchandise preferences
Type of shopping occasion	Store type, regular, special occasion Convenience, speciality, comparison shopping, place of shopping
Attitudes	Towards product area, toward brand Towards usership and use situations
Benefits sought	Utility, convenience, luxury, economy, etc.

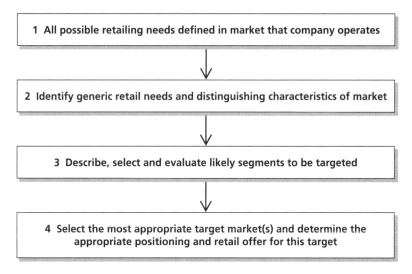

Fig. 10.7 Steps in selection of target market

the segment is identifiable, measurable, accessible, substantial, sustainable, actionable and defendable.

Retail segmentation checklist

- *Is the segment identifiable and measurable?* There is the need to identify different types of retail consumers and how different types of marketing mix activity will affect sub-groups. If any changes occur, such as an expansion into loyalty schemes, will the potential market segments (there are several being targeted – *see* Chapter 8) be measurable in the locality of a store?

- *Is the segment accessible?* The segment requires that individual buyers may easily visit the store or be contacted through promotional messages. Also, with new forms of retailing utilizing electronic means of transaction, accessibility of segments is a key consideration.

- *Is the segment substantial?* The segment must be large enough to provide a viable level of business and profit. The Body Shop started in the area of Brighton and its success in targeting a particular lifestyle group was substantial enough to support expansion throughout the country.

- *Is the segment sustainable?* The choice of segment has to take into account whether the demand will last. Fashion and 'lifestyle' market segments are prone to change and demise.

- *Is the segment actionable?* Are there any impediments in putting together a local or national marketing mix so that the target market can be reached with a specific retail offer, positioning and message which fits with the plans of the company? A retail group may want to target a segment in order to offer a specific range with acceptable width and depth at acceptable cost, but the reaction of the segment – especially on a local store basis – should dictate the final offer.

- *Is the segment defendable?* Can the target market be defended against competitor activity if the competitors also target the same group? In a small catchment area will increased retail rivalry cause any viability problems for the retailer?

The approach to segmentation selection is as wide as marketers make it. There is no single way which will prove successful. For example, the general list of segmentation variables shown does not include retailers segmenting by size (Evans, High and Mighty, Long Tall Sally). Even when a segment has been identified, customers' needs and attitudes are multifaceted and, as such, they move from one segment to another as part of their shopping behaviour.

In the postmodern fragmented market composed of an array of different retail experience choices and images there is a weakening pattern of predictable behaviour. For example, a consumer may buy groceries in a low cost outlet yet go to an Armani store for their clothing. Such behaviour is an expression of a multiplicity of selves and a less static consumer which makes it more difficult to carry out successful segmentation. These consumer changes need to be understood in relation to the symbolic meaning of positioning which is described in the following section.

Positioning the retail offer

As part of the segmentation analysis, sub-groups will emerge as the ideal customers to market to. Because of the potential of these segments they will form the target groups for the business. The target groups will need to be satisfied with the retail offer. Thus there has to be a clear understanding by consumers of where the company wants its business to be positioned. Positioning is a marketing term which is used to describe the process of establishing and maintaining a distinctive place for a business in its marketplace. There is no easy approach to positioning as different consumers will look for something mean-ingful to them. The retailer has some basic alternative choices but other positions, such as lifestyle-led choices, are an option. Positioning can be on the basis of:

- the type of service given, or the merchandise sold, by the retailer;
- the delivery of benefits and problem solutions for retail consumers;
- the different usage occasions of the service or merchandise;
- the specific retail category of the service or merchandise;
- in an opposite position, or gap, to that of another retailer.

There has to be compatibility between the product offer and the segment being targeted. Marks & Spencer achieved this with the successful launch of food as well as home fur-nishings. However, if M&S had launched a cheaper range of furniture – similar to that of the MFI position – they would have confused their customers and compromised their existing position as a service and quality-oriented retailer. The successful strategy of MFI in selling cheap furniture is not a strategy M&S would want to adopt because it would not fit with the existing spatial positioning of its current retail offer.

Achieving strength of positioning

To achieve success at positioning there is a need to ensure the position has *clarity*, is *credible*, has *consistency* over time and will remain *competitive*. This is explained as follows:

- **Clarity.** It is important to realize that positioning is about communicating a message to the consumer so as to spatially place the retail service offered in their mind. This has to be a clear message with no confusion. If the message is not clear the consumer will not understand what the brand or offer is about. A positioning strategy requires a clear message that most people will understand.

- **Credibility.** A positioning message has to be believable. If we claim that our retail company offers better service than it delivers in reality, consumers may well utilize it a first time but never again. They may well feel cynical about the company claims if they find the delivery does not match the promise. This is particularly vital in the case of services where it is not possible for customers to sample an offering very easily. Also, customers have a preconceived set of relative positions already in their mind and therefore they have learnt what is possible in terms of any claim to a specific position.

- **Consistency.** It has been pointed out that positioning is all about creating an image in the mind of the consumer. Clearly for this to be achieved the message has to be consist-ent. If a company changes its communications policy there will be no clear messages and the public will not be able to visualize the positioning the retailer is attempting to occupy. Of course, it is possible to change positioning but this takes time to achieve. A good example from the motor trade is that of Volvo. Volvo was always positioned as being a very safe car. This was a good position first because there were customers who wanted that and secondly because the product actually delivered it through safety design. In addition, Volvo was consistently at the top of crash test safety results. However, Volvo was also perceived as a company that produced very boring cars. In order to reposition the brand the company then embarked upon the production of both high performance and more stylish cars. Volvo knew the strength of its position and attempted to retain its safety image. The communication is, 'We still make safe cars, but they are fun as well.' This is part of a gradual repositioning of the brand and while change is occurring the message remains consistent from the customer's point of view.

● **Competitiveness.** In any decision over position there needs to be a strategic decision which positions the company relative to that of the competition (we are friendlier, larger, offer more value, have better service, are more modern, safer or whatever) and this has to be accepted by the customer. Positioning the brand with a set of attributes that the customer does not care about is never going to be effective.

The selection in terms of position is based upon how the retailer wants to be perceived by its target group of customers in terms of any one of the factors which it decides is of importance. Any positioning has to take into consideration the three generic strategies of Porter (1980) which are to decide upon only one approach, be it *cost leadership*, *differentiation* or *focus*. A company has to be clear about where it needs and wants to be positioned in the marketplace. One way of ensuring this is to create a perceptual map that reflects the current marketplace. This is one of the customary ways a planner would plot the company's retail business in relation to the competitors. The plots would be based upon customers' and employees' perceptions of where a particular store or retail service would be located on the perceptual map. This approach could be used to identify gaps in the market based upon customer desires or lack of competition in certain market positions. The identification of gaps in the marketplace may offer opportunities for new retail formats or product development. There is a wide range of polar opposites which could be utilized for the ends of the continuums such as high to low value for money; traditional to modern; wide to narrow range of merchandise, etc. The most simple positioning can be achieved through spatially plotting price and service levels, as illustrated in Fig. 10.8.

High value – low price and high service position

If a retail business is to provide a high service and low price there is a need to examine the business very closely. This is because the cost of delivering a high service has to be recouped and relatively low prices do not usually allow sufficient margins to achieve this. More recently, changes in retail have opened up opportunities for retailers to fill this position. The new retail format of the 'category killer' has allowed this position to be filled because of the ability of retailers to buy in bulk, therefore ensuring merchandise costs are low. Such a format also allows the category specialist to sell in high quantity, thereby achieving high enough revenue to make the operation viable. The use of electronic systems for sales is another area where costs can be controlled more easily and after-sales service levels may therefore be planned to be high.

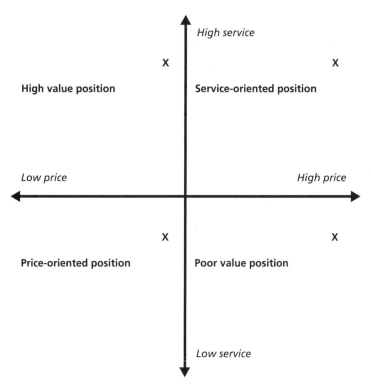

Fig. 10.8 Retail price and service positioning map

Service-oriented – high price and high service position

This position is based on providing a very high level of service and charging the customer higher than average prices. In order to be successful within this spatial position, there has to be a segment of the market willing to pay higher prices for the benefit of receiving superior levels of quality and service. The concern of managing this position is whether the higher prices offer perceived value or not. Many companies will attempt to ensure that prices are competitive and this may mean a slide of position towards a more central area, nearer to where the axes cross. This more central position provides little differentiation and can cause problems, as it is open to attack from the other quadrants. Positioning as a strategy has to be clear to both the consumer and the retailer's employees.

Price-oriented – low price and low service position

The low price and low service position is based upon a no-frills retail operation which leads on price as the means to generate sales. Such a position fits with the theory regarding the wheel of retailing, which was covered in Chapter 1 of this book. The example given was that new forms of retailing enter the market as low cost, no frills, low margin operations. However, unlike the development process associated with the theory whereby retailers attempt to move upmarket, the modern low price retailer understands the strength in occupying this position. The deep discounters develop their strategies to ensure that they will remain securely situated in the low price and low service position over the long term. This is a highly competitive position to occupy as competitive buying, cost control, management systems and lean organization structure all need to be constantly monitored to ensure a sound basis for long-term survival. Such efficiency is not necessarily based upon minimal investment. A high initial investment in technology is required to ensure that just-in-time inventory and management systems are available and utilized. A price-led position can only be achieved if the retailer is relentless in driving down costs, with the clear goal of increasing margins while retaining low price levels and market share.

Poor value – high price and low service position

The least viable position to occupy is one where a high price is charged for a low level of service. This position will only be filled when a retailer can survive due to a lack of competition for a particular good or service. For example, some rural grocery shops are run by older people who give poor service because they have lost interest in the business. However, they have higher costs because of small orders to their suppliers which are passed on as higher prices to customers. The shop is caught in a spiral of decline, with the more mobile people shopping elsewhere while the old and less mobile groups will continue to have to pay the higher prices.

Positioning in the mind of the consumer

To be successful in positioning a retailer has to understand how to modify the perception of the consumer by improving, reinforcing or defending a company or store's position in the marketplace. Ries and Trout (1986) argue that positioning has to be correctly addressed, as it is the only way to counteract the confusion created by the communication jungle. According to Ries and Trout, 'the best approach in our over-communicated society is the over-simplified message'. This has to happen at the right time and as such the secret of positioning becomes the organized system for finding the window in the mind. Ries and Trout contend that:

> Positioning starts with a product. A piece of merchandise, a service, a company, an institution or even a person . . . But positioning is not what you do to a product. Positioning is what you do to the mind of the prospect. That is, you position the product in the mind of the prospect.

Thus communications strategies are important and any attempt to achieve success with the retail mix has to ensure some consideration of the importance of producing a favourable image in the mind of the target consumer. Positioning should be coupled with the exercise of segmentation as this allows for a more rigorous approach which considers differentiated targeted segments rather than a total market coverage. Matalan is successful in its chosen position as it offers a clear retail proposition to its customer base. The typical questions to be asked for positioning are:

1 What are the distinctive features and benefits, real or perceived, that will be considered in utilizing a channel or retail outlet?

2 What are the perceived positions of the main channel or retail competitors?

3 Given the changes in the retail marketplace, and the strengths and weaknesses of our position, what is the ideal positioning strategy to adopt?

4 What is the most appropriate marketing programme to maximize the chance of achieving our chosen position?

Kotler (2000) identified that there are four possible positioning errors a company has to ensure it does not make. These are adapted to be applied to the case of positioning in retailing:

- *Underpositioning*: The retail brand is not well known and is just another entry into a crowded marketplace. Several e-commerce brands have suffered from lack of knowledge as to the product proposition and positioning of the channel.

- *Overpositioning*: Potential customers may have too narrow an image of the retail brand. For example, Tiffany's diamond rings may be thought of as outside the budget of the average consumer when in fact they have a range of rings to suit each level of purchase.

- *Confused positioning*: Buyers might have a confused image due to a retailer making too many strategic changes in positioning and changing its communications campaigns. Marks & Spencer are currently attempting this but many consumers are confused as not all stores are repositioned and the communications campaign does not provide a clear message.

- *Doubtful positioning*: Customers may not find the positioning credible due to a mismatch of the communications claims in relation to the features, prices and company.

In summary, the use of market positioning is to ensure that the target customers have a clear reason to use a company's shops rather than those of the competitors. The positioning creates a retail offer which is relevant and of value to the different segments, but it is one that needs to be communicated to those segments through promotional campaigns and store design so that the position is both reinforced and clearly recognized. Finally, a strong position in the minds of the customers creates marketing advantage because it clarifies the reason why someone frequents the company's stores – and it may be one that competitors will find difficult to copy.

PROVIDING AN EFFECTIVE MARKETING MIX STRATEGY

The success of the marketing plan relies on creating the right marketing mix strategies for achieving the objectives (*see* Chapter 5 for a clear explanation of the different aspects of the marketing mix). The use of the marketing mix of price, product, promotion and place – with its special emphasis for retail – involves balancing the marketing mix to achieve the highest expected probability of meeting the plan's objectives. However, mix strategies have to be checked to ensure that they are acceptable. This is because they also involve uncontrollable factors such as the reaction of competitors, or changes that may occur in a market due to shifts in fashion, or effects due to changes in the economy.

If it is found that there are no problems with the objectives and the plan is to be adopted, there has to be some assessment of whether the objectives can be achieved within specific time constraints. Competitors may be able to react more quickly or the company may find it too difficult to change in a short period of time. The ability to change is often related to the availability of resources. It is necessary to question whether the resources available are sufficient to achieve the objectives (in terms of budgets, personnel, technology, existing outlets, service improvements, brand building). If, after evaluation, it is decided the strategy is unacceptable there is a need to review and revise the plan's objectives.

Agreeing the marketing mix strategy has to be linked to laying down task-related programmes which will allocate budgets and create responsibilities and timings for the plan's implementation. There is an important need to link planning with budgeting and monitoring, which will allow for the adoption and execution of an effective marketing mix strategy to achieve the objectives of the plan. The control and managing of budgets and planned performance are dealt with in the next section.

MONITORING THE PLAN

A business needs a mechanism to monitor the achievements of the marketing plan so that actions can be taken either to get the plan back on course or to take advantage of new opportunities. As such, there is a need for the provision of assessment, as well as measurement methods which will monitor progress towards the achievement of the overall objectives of the plan. Retail businesses are characterized by their diversity and wide range of goods with differing qualities and attributes. However, all managers are required to make appropriate decisions on the basis of sales and performance and deviations from the initial objectives and targets. Managers need to decide if these fluctuations are either acceptable or unacceptable, based upon the effect of over- or under-performance on overall company performance. Effective monitoring of performance will allow for the review and amendment of the plan on a continuous basis, to facilitate decisions, such as the introduction of tactical action if sales are behind target. Effective control hinges on the quantity, quality and timeliness of the information made available. The information has to flow on a regular basis to decision-makers in a form that enables ease of understanding and the carrying out of effective response.

The retail industry has invested in integrated systems, such as EPOS and EDI, which provide for a continuous flow of financial and stock/sales pattern data. This has allowed for the modelling of different performance indicators. These may include forecasts of likely demand factors or purchase levels, as well as assessment of the effectiveness of regional or national sales promotion, price changes and store campaigns. Sales measurements are the basic measure of evaluation based upon sales transactions. With this information a company can analyse sales in terms of cash volume by period or market share, or by location or allocated space. Retail companies regularly use cash volume sales as the figures allow a common denominator of sales, costs and profits. However, changes in retail prices, either up or down, will affect sales figures and may not reflect the actual sales position. Total sales figures are more useful if broken down by size and place of geographic unit, salesperson, product code, price including any discount, customer type and time of the transaction. It is also beneficial to have details of the timing and type of any promotion which may have affected demand. Figure 10.9 indicates the measures that are often utilized to assess previous retail decisions.

It is also necessary to monitor 'softer' aspects of the business, such as brand awareness and customer satisfaction. If these weaken, attention should be paid to them; they are usually early signals of future problems related to the financial performance. An example of how the monitoring of retail products may lead to important change is to be found in the video games market. The video games market was flooded with too many games titles by Nintendo, Atari and Sega. Consumers became confused and disappointed by the

Output measures	Input measures	Productivity (output/input)

Net sales
Net profits
Performance in sales and profits
Cost of labour
	Square metres of retail space
	Number of employees
	Promotional expenditures
	Number of customer
	    transactions
	Linear shelf space area
		Sales per square metre
		Sales per employee
		Return on asset
		Asset turnover
		Wage cost per outomer
		Average profit per
		    customer
		Sales per linear shelf
		    space area

Mechandise net sales
Merchandise gross margin
Performance in merchandise sales
	Inventory levels over time
	Markdowns
	Cost of merchandise
	Advertising costs
		Gross margin return on
		    investment (GMR)
		Inventory turnover
		Advertising and markdown
		    as a percentage of sales

Fig. 10.9 Retail performance measurement indicators

numerous lookalike products having similar names. By monitoring customer reaction, companies such as Nintendo were able to withdraw from the market a high percentage of their games to allow space for new product introductions. This allowed the games market to recover after the fad period of the 1980s.

CONCLUSION

The marketing plan is a structured guide to action. It acts as a systematic discipline for data collection, objective setting and logical analysis of the most appropriate direction for the organization, retail unit or its merchandise to develop. If a marketing plan is to be accepted by all concerned, then the compilation of the plan has to involve all levels of personnel. This is because marketing plans require company-wide commitment if they are to be successful. The plan has to reflect the dynamic nature of the marketplace and, as such, the plan needs to be thought of as a loose-leaf binder rather than as a tablet of stone. This means the plan acts as a working document which should be updated to take into account opportunities or problem situations. Finally, any worthwhile plan will contain the expected results for the business based upon different periods of operation. Planning functions have to include the means by which the business will measure its performance in a quantifiable manner that is timely, relevant and accurate. This will allow the plan to achieve its objectives and enable management to function more effectively in its decision-making activities.

EXERCISES

The exercises in this section relate to the contents of this chapter. It is advised that you work through them before moving on to Chapter 11.

1 Read the newspapers over a four-week period (*Financial Times*, trade papers, *The Economist*, etc.). Write down the changes that large retail companies are making and also what may be happening, by application of a marketplace PEST analysis. Try to relate your findings to what is

contained in the approaches to the compilation of a marketing plan as outlined in this chapter. You should also try to identify the link there may be between the theory and the practice of the changes taking place.

2 Think about your own experience in doing things you initially did not want to do. Why did you subsequently agree to do them? How do you think the plans in a retail company could be adopted more effectively throughout the company utilizing the ideas in this chapter, further reading and from your own experiences?

3 Identify the different market segments and their reasons for the use of a post office, building society and a bank. Is there anything you may have learnt from this exercise which may assist the bank to change to attract new segments? What would be the outcomes of any repositioning the bank may adopt?

4 List some of the retail changes that have taken place in recent years. How can a medium-sized retailer develop an improved competitive position through the use of a planning approach? Use the following grid as a guide.

List competitive changes, for example:	What would you need to know about your competitors and the marketplace in order to develop an improvement in competitive position?
• greater use of loyalty schemes • more direct channel operations • differentiation through improved service • more women working • development of the Internet • others (list)	

REFERENCES AND FURTHER READING

Abell, D.F. (1982) 'Metamorphosis in Market Planning' in Cox, K.K. and McGinnis, V.J. (eds) *Strategic Market Decisions*. Englewood Cliffs, NJ: Prentice Hall.

Abell, D.F. and Hammond, J.S. (1979) *Strategic Market Planning Problems and Analytical Approaches*. Englewood Cliffs, NJ: Prentice Hall.

Ansoff, H.I. (1988) *The New Corporate Strategy*. New York: John Wiley and Sons.

Baker, L. (2000) 'Youth obsessed retailers must look to an older group of big spenders', *Independent*, 25 April, 15.

Collins, A. (1992) *Competitive Retail Marketing*. Maidenhead: McGraw-Hill.

David, R. (2001) 'Tie Rack extends ranges in bid to reposition brand', *Retail Week*, 11 May, 3.

Davies, G.J. and Brooks, J.M. (1989) *Positioning Strategy in Retailing*. London: Paul Chapman.

Edgecliffe-Johnson, A. (2001) '7-Eleven wants to cut it the UK way: The US store chain hopes to copy British success with portable food', *Financial Times*, 25 July.

González-Benito, O., Greatorex, M. and Muñoz-Gallego, P.A. (2000) 'Assessment of potential retail segmentation variables: An approach based on a subjective MCI resource allocation model', *Journal of Retailing and Consumer Services*, 7 (3), 171–79.

Hasson, L. (1995) 'Monitoring Social Change', *Journal of the Market Research Society*, 37, 69–80.

Hooley, G.J., Saunders, J.A. and Piercy, N.F. (1998) *Marketing Strategy and Competitive Positioning*. Hemel Hempstead: Prentice Hall.

Jaworski, B.J., Stathakopoulis, V. and Shanker Krishnan, H. (1993) 'Control combinations in marketing: conceptual framework and empirical evidence', *Journal of Marketing*, 57 (1), 57–69.

Knee, D. and Walters, D. (1985) *Strategy in Retailing: Theory and application*. Oxford: Philip Allan.

Knee, D. and Walters, D. (1989) 'Competitive strategies in retailing', *Journal of Long Range Planning*, 22, December, 27–34.

Kotler, P. (2000) *Marketing Management: the millennium edition*. 10th edn. Englewood Cliffs, NJ: Prentice Hall.

Kotler, P., Armstrong, G., Saunders, J. and Wong, V. (1999) *Principles of Marketing*. 2nd European edn. Englewood Cliffs, NJ: Prentice Hall.

Marsh, H. (2001) 'THE BODY SHOP – Has The Body Shop lost its direction for good?' *Marketing*, 10 May.

McDonald, M. and Tideman, C. (1996) *Retail Marketing Plans: How to prepare them: How to use them*. Oxford: Butterworth-Heinemann.

McGoldrick, P.J. (1998) 'Spatial and temporal shifts in the development of international retail images', *Journal of Business Research*, 42 (2), 189–96.

Palmer, A. (1994) *Principles of Services Marketing*. Maidenhead: McGraw-Hill.

Porter, M.E. (1980) *Competitive Strategy: Techniques for analyzing industries and competitors*. New York: Free Press.

Quinn, J.B., Mintzberg, H. and James, R.M. (1988) *The Strategy Process – Concepts, Contexts and Cases*. Englewood Cliffs, NJ: Prentice Hall.

Retail Intelligence (2001) 'UK retail report', no. 119, April, 113.

Ries, A. and Trout, J. (1986) *Positioning: The battle for your mind*, New York: McGraw-Hill.

Walters, D. (1994) *Retailing Management: Analysis planning and control*. London: Macmillan.

11 Retail location strategies and decisions

The chapter should enable you to understand and explain:

- the importance of retail location decision-making;
- the different types of retail trading areas;
- theories which explain the historical patterns of retail location;
- a range of analytical techniques for assessing the suitability of a retail location;
- different approaches to property development.

It is often said that within the retailing industry only three things matter: location, location and location. The logic of this is that if the right site is acquired, success should be a simple matter of opening for business. It is not that straightforward; selection of merchandise, sound pricing policy, layout and presentation, as well as other retail marketing factors are also required as prerequisites for success. For example, the customer service policies may be the reason a customer will return again and again. A problem could be a weak strategic approach if the fit between location and the format planned will not meet customer expectations. This should highlight the point that while this chapter deals with location strategies and decisions there is the need to consider a whole range of marketing issues. Having identified the importance of marketing factors, the actual selection of the location site has to be carried out utilizing a systematic approach whereby there is logical acceptance or rejection. This is because of several issues:

1 *consumer choice*: the location is often the most important consumer behaviour consideration in a customer's decision of where to shop;

2 *the need for competitive advantage*: the decision over where to develop a retail outlet will be of strategic importance because retailers can gain long-term competitive advantage if they develop in the best location;

3 *consideration of trends*: any decision on location has to consider the recent social and structural changes – greater use of the motor car, the importance of out-of-town shopping centres, regional shopping areas, the growth of multiple retailers, the power of retailer brands, and so on;

4 *high investment*: development of a retail site is accompanied by high investment and rental costs and long lead times, which require decisions regarding long-term financial implications;

5 *property asset*: it is important to select carefully as the final property assets of a company can be valued as high as their annual turnover;

6 *declining number of sites*: there are a restricted number of new sites for development and, within government policy guidelines, less opportunity to obtain planning permission easily.

The dimensions of location decision-making are extensive. Locational decisions engage the different disciplines of strategic marketing, the geography of retailing, town planning, operations research, consumer behaviour, and economics. If a company has a weak approach to location analysis it may not just be a financial dilemma but could threaten the long-term progress of the retailer. As pressures mount on the availability of sites and the propensity of local authorities to allow development, retail companies have to become better at both the politics and the technical aspects of planning. The obtaining of planning permission is being severely restricted in the UK. The planning policy guidelines issued by the government (Department of the Environment, 1996) has the objectives of:

1 sustaining and enhancing the vitality and viability of town centres;
2 focusing retail development in locations where the proximity of business facilitates competition from which all consumers are able to benefit and maximizing the opportunity to use means of transport other than a car;
3 maintaining an efficient, competitive and innovative retail sector; and
4 ensuring the availability of a wide range of shops, employment, services and facilities to which people have easy access by a choice of means of transport.

The above guidelines are to be utilized on a regional planning basis, with local considerations taken into account. However, developers and local authorities have to prove that they have thoroughly investigated all central sites prior to the contemplation of a greenfield site.

In the light of the increased market or political pressure and the resultant government guidelines, Tesco embarked upon the development of smaller stores (*see* Table 11.1). This strategy of different-sized stores, developed in different locations, also has the advantage that each format is serving a different consumer demand. While the out-of-town, or edge-of-town superstores offer one-stop shopping services for weekly outings,

Table 11.1 Tesco Group, UK store development programme (total stores built)

Store format and size	1991	1993	1995	1996	Total developed 2001
Superstore (26 500+ sq. ft)	17	20	12	8	274
Compact superstore (<25 500 sq. ft)	3	4	15	14	96
Metro store (c. 10 000 sq. ft)	–	1	6	2	38
Express store (c. 1500 sq. ft petrol station site)	–	–	2	10	45

Source: Tesco Group annual reports

the smaller in-town stores offer top-up shopping facilities. In this way, they are complementary formats within Tesco's portfolio. Even if allowed by the authorities, the development of a new superstore often has a negative impact on other stores owned by the company that are operating in the wider area due to cannibalization of demand.

Long-term strategies have to take into consideration the dynamics of change. Transformation is ever present, as Schiller (1994) has shown in his exploration of retail changes. Schiller identified three different phases of a move away from the town centre. The first wave he identifies as the 1970s, when supermarkets enjoying high demand had to find extra space for supply and at lower rents. This led to out-of-town development as it offered good growth potential. The second wave was in the 1980s, when the retail parks aided the movement of DIY, furniture, carpets and electrical goods from the town centres following the pattern set by the supermarkets. The third wave was identified as the mid-1980s, when retailers such as Marks & Spencer and other comparison retailers moved out of town. Fernie (1995) added to this understanding when he identified the new wave of factory outlets and warehouse clubs that also had an impact on retail format and concentration. These waves are quite interesting as the retailers were proactive in these strategic location selection procedures and were not influenced by government legislation. It is important to realize that locations are only successful when the consumer decides that there are benefits in utilizing them. This means government pressure may attempt to stop development in specific areas but at the end of the day viability rests on satisfying the needs of the customer.

Any retail location decision requires sophisticated analysis. Once the strategic direction is clear, retailers can increase the size of existing premises, refurbish, reformat premises, build new stores in or out of town, internationalize or acquire other companies, etc. Figure 11.1 gives a strategic overview of a supermarket's format choices available and how smaller units are expanding the fastest.

GEOGRAPHIC LOCATION DECISIONS

How then can a retailer find an optimum location? In the past many location decisions would have been made on the basis of intuition or, more likely, the availability of a particular property or 'going concern'. Planning today requires some idea of population shifts, consumer mobility and increases in discretionary income as each will affect shopping habits. With the application of technology a number of developments have taken place. Technology can aid in location decision-making: analytical techniques such as SLAM (store location assessment model) allow the assessment, profiling and comparison of market opportunities; the screening of potential sites; the definition of catchment areas; and modelling of the possible impact of competitor strategies (Simkin, 1989, 1990). Clark (1993) has attempted to outline the future usage of geographical information systems with the prediction that they will be integrated more with financial and strategic planning.

A starting point for the understanding of location decisions is based upon the *location area*. There are zones or locations which attract higher levels of custom than others. The location decision may take into consideration the broader considerations of the *region*, which would involve a large section of the country or county; or the *market area*, which would be a geographic sector containing zones, of which one would be the *primary trading zone* (*see* Fig. 11.2) which provides the major customer base for a retail outlet.

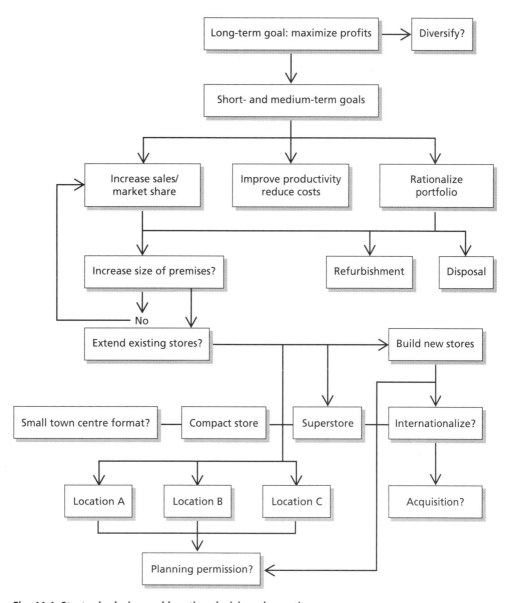

Fig. 11.1 Strategic choice and location decision alternatives

Regions may contain many specific types of consumers due to average incomes, density of population, climate, geography, and type of economic development – for example, rural or industrial. From a strategic planning perspective, some retailers concentrate on dominating or being successful in regional markets prior to any expansion. Decisions regarding regional markets are based upon the strategic posture of a company; whether it wants to achieve dominance and leadership in the region or whether it wants to be a follower or market niche retailer. The typical assessment of regional markets is based upon the use of secondary information sources because other, more sophisticated, approaches are very expensive.

Market area is a geographic area that will contain the potential customers of a specific retailer or shopping area. This is based upon three zones which take the retail outlet or shopping centre as the epicentre from which bands emanate, based upon access, distance and travelling time. While these may be treated as concentric rings (*see* Fig. 11.2), due to the effect of different road routes and local geography the pattern is somewhat less regular. The zone pattern will also be affected by the location of the competition as well as ease of final accessibility and parking in the primary zone. The market area is made up of the following three zones:

1 *Primary trading zone* where the majority of customers will be based (60–65 per cent or higher if it is a local retail outlet such as a video rental or convenience store).

2 *Secondary zone* which can be any distance from two to seven miles, or under 20 minutes drive time, from the outlet.

3 *Fringe* or *tertiary zone* which will include those who occasionally shop there as an alternative to local shopping. This zone depends on the type and size of outlet, and the alternative size and experience to be enjoyed in other market areas. Typically, this zone can extend as far as 50 miles when there is a lack of acceptable alternatives.

Figure 11.2 describes the market area breakdown for a store. The store could be located in any one of a number of sites across a wide area. If we look at this more carefully, and examine the use of land in a city, there will be different pressures which will lead more of the major retailers to locate in the central district area than on its outskirts. Figure 11.3 indicates how the city could be divided. As will be discussed later, retail development in different areas will occur due to the benefit of mutual physical location, specialization of district, rent effects, and problems of loading and unloading. The physical, social and business elements of the city will determine and support a specific type of retailing development. This will lead to specialized land use patterns emerging as retailers, developers and other land users compete for sites which will be the most favourable for them. The result of competitive bidding is a land use pattern which will form the spatial patterns most capable of supporting an urban environment. A group of spatial models is provided in Fig. 11.3 which offers a basic way to describe the distribution of land for different business and social uses.

Concentric zone approaches stress that a city will develop by forming different concentric urban zones focused around a central business district. Growth occurs as each zone expands out into the next zone. This approach recognizes that as the residential areas move further out from the centre some of the existing shopping facilities,

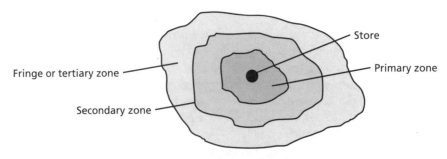

Fig. 11.2 Market area zones

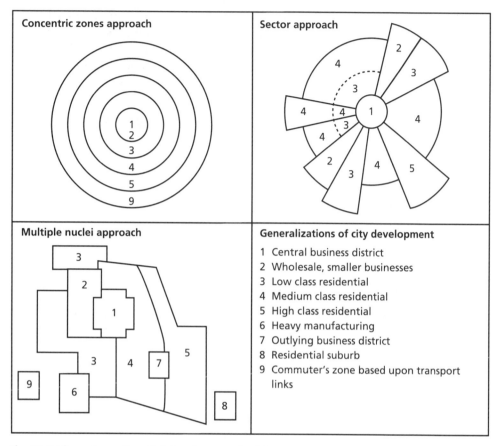

Fig. 11.3 **The nature of spatial development in cities**

near the business centre, are liable to be replaced by new retail facilities in the outlying areas.

Sector approaches place the stress on understanding residential areas but take into consideration the importance of commercial areas in relation to residential development. The approach utilizes a wedge pattern of development which occurs in relation to major transportation routes and through the creation of sector rent patterns. The model is dynamic. High rent residential areas are believed to move away from the city and to pull the city in the direction of such movement. In this movement, the stronger and more sophisticated retailers are most likely to follow the high rent areas and move from the business area of the city.

Multiple nuclei is an approach that accepts that different types of activity will tend to group together: shopping centres, business districts, residential areas, and so on. The nuclei effect is created by:

● the mutual need for close proximity of different activities;

● the need for accessibility of shopping;

● the different abilities to afford higher rents;

● any significant physical aspects of the land – such as steep hills or rivers affecting spatial development.

No urban area will conform exactly to any of the above approaches, but in total they help us to understand the development of different districts – some of which will be developed for retailing activities. The underlying ideas derived from the above approaches can be developed in greater detail by reference to the spatial distribution theories discussed in the next section.

EXPLANATIONS FOR THE SPATIAL DISTRIBUTION OF RETAIL ACTIVITIES

The spatial distributions of different retail activities have been evaluated as to their locational pattern, size and function of shopping centres and districts, the agglomeration of similar retail outlets and retail intra-spatial arrangements.

Emerging from this approach, it is clear that there are three main spatial patterns which describe most cases of retail location. These are:

- central place theory;
- bid rent theory;
- the principle of minimum differentiation.

Each of these theories may be found to have specific limitations but, in combination, they help to explain the existence of specific variations of hierarchical patterns to retail location.

Central place theory

Central place theory attempts to explain the existence of city and town shopping districts or regional shopping centres, based upon a description of their size, retail function and relative positions to one another. The central place theory proposes a hierarchy of retail centres. A large retail centre that offers a variety of different retail functions is surrounded further out by smaller centres with less choice and specialist retailers, which in turn are surrounded by smaller centres comprising basic goods retailers. The central place theory is based upon the premise that as distance to a retail centre increases, demand for a product will decrease due to the increased cost of transport. Eventually the demand will drop to zero as this is the cut-off point past which consumers will not travel further to obtain the product. This distance is often termed the *market area* or *range* of a good. Concurrent with this, a retailer will not trade if the level of demand is too low. This level is known as the *threshold* and its level will differ according to the product offered. *High threshold* products are relatively expensive and infrequently purchased – for example, jewellery and furniture. *Low threshold* products are relatively inexpensive and purchased on a regular basis – for example, groceries.

If the market range of a good exceeds the threshold then it can be made available by retailers at a profit. This is because enough potential consumers exist who are willing to travel to acquire the product or product range. Thus, it is predicted that there will be many retailers of *low order* goods which are based upon low threshold and low range criteria. This means that there is a local demand for frequently purchased, inexpensive goods because consumers are not willing to travel very far to obtain them. At the same time there will be only a small number of retailers offering *high order* goods which are based upon high threshold and high range criteria. The demand for high order goods is

Table 11.2 Consumer changes which may affect the basic assumptions behind central place theory

Central place assumptions of consumer	Modern retail consumer
● Trips are regular to purchase small amounts, especially those with product perishability	● The use of large refrigerators and freezers allows less frequent purchases from superstores or retail centres
● Purchase response is based upon price and product range	● Non-price factors are increasingly a more important determinant of the purchase decision
● Trips are home location based and often single-purpose trips to the nearest shopping district where goods are available	● Improved road systems, increased numbers of cars and drivers per family allows multi-purpose trips and greater distances to be covered
● The shopping visit decision is based upon the necessity of the trip	● There has been an increase in leisure shopping
● The consumer treats each shopping area as a similar experience, i.e. all retailers are assumed to adopt a uniform retail strategy	● Retail innovation has taken place, with themed and purpose-built facilities creating retail experiences which appeal to different types of consumers

based upon infrequently purchased and expensive items, for which the consumer will travel longer distances in order to assess and make a purchase.

As a way of generalizing the reasons for the spatial pattern of existing retail sites, the central place theory helps our understanding of the different shopping districts to be found in developed countries. However, the basis of the theory requires a similar pattern of retail outlets equidistant from their counterparts. However, this approach does not account for the agglomeration of retail outlets where centres exist based upon a high number of similar retailers. For example, within two district centres there may be an agglomeration of footwear and fashion retailers in each of the high streets. Additionally, one centre may have developed an agglomeration of electrical retailers while the other has developed a specialization in antique retailers. The overall functional composition of the two areas may be considered to differ and, therefore, this contradicts the underlying premise of central place theory. The theory is a useful tool to apply in order to generalize about the existence of shopping areas and the hierarchical distribution of retail outlets but, in order to explain some spatial patterns, more detailed analysis is often required. For example, consumer changes may be affecting the patterns, as shown in Table 11.2.

Bid rent theory

Bid rent theory attempts to explain the internal spatial organization of planned and unplanned shopping districts. The theory assumes that retailers would always prefer to locate in the city or town centre, but this in turn increases the rents and costs of these locations. Because of the increased costs, only some types of retailers are able to afford such prime sites and so different types of retailers will be found further out from central locations (*see* Fig. 11.4). Central place theory, as discussed above, describes the hierarchy

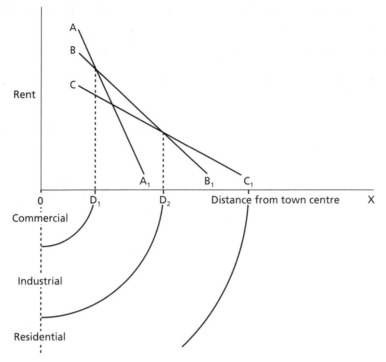

Fig. 11.4 An illustration of bid rent principles

Source: Brown, 1992, p. 54

of retail centres but bid rent theory assumes that the spatial composition of retail outlets is based upon the economics of land value theory. In reality, the use of land is based upon a whole range of different factors, including land-use planning regulations, individual choice and decision-making, and perhaps even chance. Bid rent theory is based upon the premise that all economic activities aim to be located in the city centre as it is the most accessible location.

The theory assumes that different types of land use are segregated by the amount of rent that a prospective tenant can pay and that competition ensures that, in the long run, all sites are occupied by a retail activity capable of paying the highest possible rent; as such, it is argued, the land is employed to its maximum utility. The important premise is that land use is based upon access, because consumers will seek out the most accessible location. As with other neoclassical economic approaches to location, it is grounded on the assumption that an inelastic supply of land exists and therefore land does not become readily available as the demand for it increases, or vice versa. It also assumes the existence of uniformly priced travel which will be as easy to make in any direction, and that land can be acquired through an open and fair competitive bidding process where the highest bidder will acquire a site. Under these circumstances the price a bidder is likely to pay will depend on the use which will be made of the site. For example, a commercial user will earn more from the land and therefore pay a higher price than an industrial user, and an industrial user will in turn pay more than a residential user. This assumes that a plot of land can be equally used for each of the above purposes. In essence that is seldom the case.

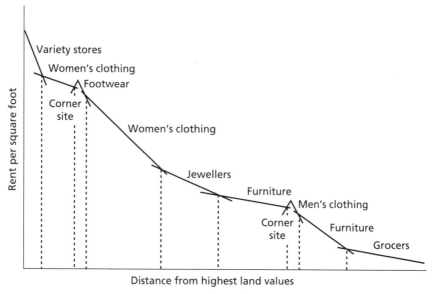

Fig. 11.5 Intra-centre adaptation of bid rent theory
Source: Scott, 1970

In a city centre location there is normally a better transport service and network than in the outlying areas. The highest market potential and optimum access is related to a city location – for both consumers and the labour market – even though city centre congestion may cause secondary problems. This is why the more central the location the more desirable the plot, and consequently the higher will be the price as different users will compete to purchase the land. As the economic activity that can gain most utility from that site will be able and willing to pay the highest price, it follows that the land will naturally attract that form of activity. The result is that bands of activity will occur in concentric patterns emanating from the city centre (*see* Fig. 11.2) as the different forms of economic activity 'naturally' segregate themselves from each other.

Retailers require access to consumers more than any other land use function and this will lead to retailers being prepared to pay very high rents for city centre locations. The bid rent demand from retailers falls away quite sharply as the distance from the city centre increases. This is because the potential in outer city areas is non-existent or too low for major retailers. In contrast, the demand curves for commercial and residential use are more elastic since there is a willingness to accept poorer access in return for lower cost which produces a shallower demand curve. The two-dimensional Fig. 11.2 can be associated with the three bands illustrated in Fig. 11.4: 0–D_1, commercial use, D_1–D_2 industrial use, and D_2 and beyond for residential use, where each activity will produce a concentric pattern at varying distances from the city centre.

Figure 11.5 indicates how the retail sector will be further segmented into different demand schedules, with some types of retail activity being more willing to bid higher rents in order to obtain a central location. Department and speciality stores selling women's clothing, for example, are likely to attach far greater importance to having a central location than would a convenience store or grocery retailer.

Figure 11.5 indicates how the gradient for some retailers is steeper than for others; for example, variety stores as opposed to furniture retailers. This reflects the relative importance attached to a central location by specific types of retailer. The difference in rents paid per square foot is because retailers understand their own marketplace needs and are unwilling to pay prices beyond the attractiveness of the site to their potential customers. Empirical evidence supports the general assumptions associated with bid rent theory, but land may also be affected by planning restrictions on types of use and the type of buildings constructed. On the whole the principles of the theory are a useful way to understand the historical spatial location of different types of business emanating from a city centre.

The principle of minimum differentiation

The principle of minimum differentiation describes the intra-centre agglomeration of similar retail outlets. It is found that many retailers choose to locate near similar types of retail activity in order jointly to attract a higher flow of customers. In addition, some retailers will aim to locate near complementary rather than similar retail functions, in order to maximize the demand from potential customers. Bid rent theory is based upon the assumption that all economic activities aim to be located in the city centre because the centre is the most accessible location. This assumption does not explain why some retailers seek sites that are near to their competitors, or stores providing a similar product offer, rather than choosing to be sited in the city centre. This means proximity to complementary activities is sometimes more important than the benefits of general access. As Richardson (1978) pointed out, the 'agglomeration of retailers may be more attributable to "*economics of concentration*" rather than "*economics of centralisation*"'.

The principle of minimum differentiation has been developed from the work of Hotelling (1929). The assumption behind the theory is that only two firms will be considered although in reality there will normally be more than two. These two firms are located on a linear market line and both are considered to have the ultimate aim of seeking to maximize profits. It is also assumed that transport costs are constant, based upon the distance travelled, and that demand is stable. Potential consumers are assumed to be evenly distributed over the linear market. Therefore, stability exists as no marketing or other influences are brought to bear on the situation. The consumers are considered to be rational and utility maximizing, which means they are going to choose the nearest retailer in order to save on transport costs.

The principle of minimum differentiation suggests that a retailer would be able to maximize profits by locating or relocating closer to a competitor in order to gain a larger market area. However, after the relocation the competitor losing out on market share may then move or leapfrog in order to gain a larger market area share; *see* Fig. 11.6 which illustrates the dynamics of the repositioning. Figure 11.6 indicates the movement of the stalls of two ice cream vendors on a beach. Starting initially at opposite ends of the beach, vendor A realizes that an advantage can be gained by moving nearer to vendor B as the bulk of the market will be captured by those walking to areas of the beach from X. However, vendor B can retaliate by leapfrogging vendor A to gain the main part of the market and leave A the smaller market share up to Y. Finally A responds by leapfrogging B and assuming a position where a stalemate equilibrium occurs such that both vendors are competing in locations adjacent to each other and with equal shares of the business from the beach.

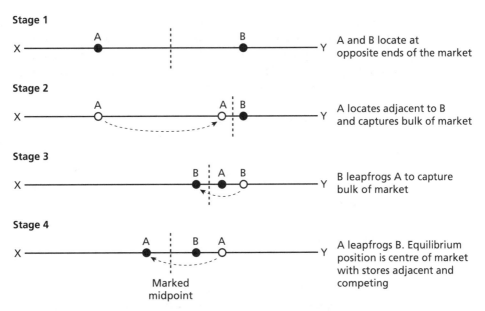

Stage 1

X ——————————•A————————¦————————•B———————— Y

A and B locate at opposite ends of the market

Stage 2

X ——————————○A————————————○A¦•B———————— Y

A locates adjacent to B and captures bulk of market

Stage 3

X ————————————————•B¦•A ○B———————— Y

B leapfrogs A to capture bulk of market

Stage 4

X ——————————•A¦ •B ○A———————————— Y

Marked midpoint

A leapfrogs B. Equilibrium position is centre of market with stores adjacent and competing

Fig. 11.6 The dynamics of the principle of minimum differentiation

Source: Hotelling (1929), in Brown (1992), p. 68

The long-term outcome of the dynamics of the principle of minimum differentiation is that there is a tendency for some retailers selling similar categories of merchandise – for example, motor car dealers – to cluster together in a pattern of agglomeration. The same phenomenon has been identified for compatible but contrasting retailers such as restaurants and cinemas or grocers and florists.

The evidence of agglomeration patterns suggests that there is a relationship to the type of retailing function. For example, it is much more likely that high order retailers (*see* the discussion on central place theory above) will cluster rather than low order retailers; while boutiques, jewellery or antique shops are often found together in an area or street, lower order outlets such as supermarkets or superstores attempt to be as far from each other as possible. Additionally, there are complementary activity clusters where theatres or cinemas will be positioned near to restaurants, or an accessories outlet near to a fashion retailer.

LOCATION SITE AND TYPES OF RETAIL DEVELOPMENT

The types of location are associated with different types of site selection. A number of different permutations exist but a retailer may decide to locate in one of three types of site:

- a solitary site;
- an unplanned shopping area site;
- a planned shopping district/centre.

Each of these site selections is associated with specific strengths and weaknesses. The following is only indicative of what a site may provide; there is a range of complex and different factors which will need to be assessed.

The solitary site may be a single free-standing retail outlet isolated from other retailers and positioned on a road or street. Its strengths are the lack of competition, low rental costs, lower operating costs which can be passed on to the customer, higher impact of presence given traffic visibility is not a problem, and probable ease of parking. For some larger companies a free-standing site offers the benefit of lower cost, provision of a larger display area and a store layout to suit their own specification. It should be noted that free-standing stores, as part of their strategy of differentiation, emphasize location. This is because consumers tend to go to the nearest grocery store; this is in direct contrast to complementary retailers, such as fashion retailers, who agglomerate together to achieve a critical mass to create an attraction to consumers. The site's weaknesses will be the difficulty in attracting initial/new customers, as a single outlet may not have a great deal of gravitational pull. Promotional costs may therefore be higher and there is no shared benefit of security, grounds maintenance or environment improvement. The solitary site is often operated by convenience stores, garages, fast-food restaurants or discount warehouses as other types of business find it hard to attract and retain a large enough customer base.

The unplanned shopping area site may be a retail location with two or more outlets in close proximity to each other. Unplanned retailing, as the term implies, has evolved in a gradual or piecemeal pattern. Buildings may have been converted to retail use and the ownership of unplanned retail centres is frequently fragmented among a number of companies or owners. The majority of central shopping areas in cities or towns and small shopping areas are unplanned. Increasingly, though, they will include planned areas, especially in edge-of-town or out-of-town developments. Normally a number of retailers will coexist, with perhaps an oversupply of some business types and a shortage of others. No quotas will exist as to number and types of retail businesses. The strengths will be the variety of retail choice in a single area, the ability to compare price, higher levels of pedestrian traffic, probable access to public transport, and convenience of saving time by utilizing different stores. The weaknesses will be the problems of traffic congestion and parking, organizing deliveries, high rents and taxes, poor condition of some of the properties in older city centres and, if travel is expensive to the centre and parking difficult, problems of recruiting and retaining staff.

The planned shopping area site may be a retail location which has been architecturally planned to provide a unified theme for a number of outlets. The planned retail area is a deliberately developed site with complementary retail outlets. Planned shopping sites are developed as an amalgam of different retailers to reflect the market catchment area. The plan is often based upon having some large, key brand stores and a number of smaller retailers adding diversity and interest. Normally a centre will be developed and operated as a single unit, with adequate parking facilities and a balance between the types of stores represented in the centre. The retailers will be allowed to rent space on the basis of being able to complement other centre retail businesses and on the grounds of the quality and type of goods, or services, offered. The strengths will be the balance and comprehensiveness of the retail offers, the freedom for individuals to shop in comfort and satisfy all their needs in the single centre, the creation of a single unified image and sense of place, an ability to funnel consumers into a zoned location, the ability to increase security and reduce theft – this all fits in with the growing popularity of malls and shopping centres which have no vehicular traffic and are all-weather or temperature-controlled environments. Generally, planned centres tend to be marketed and managed holistically. The weaknesses will be the inflexibility stipulated in the rental agreement such as opening hours; rents may be higher than in other locations; there are often restrictions as to the type of goods which may be sold by the different stores; the smaller stores may not be as successful as the more established ones; and some centres are ageing and are in need of upgrading.

Types of planned shopping areas

The retail park and shopping mall as planned shopping areas are discussed below in more detail.

The retail park

A retail park is normally developed on the outskirts or at an out-of-town site and consists of a purpose-built cluster of free-standing stores with parking facilities. These are usually a minimum of three warehouse-type stores based in a retail park of at least 50 000 square feet and built and let as a retail entity. Retail parks were initially developed in the early 1980s and later were developed alongside leisure facilities such as bowling alleys or cinemas. The retail park is different from the shopping mall in that the mall is a single building and marketed as an individual place. The mall often contains small retail outlets but a retail park has retail units that are of at least 10 000 square feet.

The importance of the right anchor store for the development of a shopping mall

No matter which innovative sales angle developers dangle in front of shoppers, a centre cannot attract a critical mass of shoppers without a significant purveyor of a critical mass of goods. And that means finding the right 'anchor' – the mass retailer with the single largest floorspace in the centre – to draw in the right mix of shoppers. So who, then, is the ideal anchor?

In the UK, there is growing consensus that food retailing and shopping malls – at least larger ones – do not mix. Capital Shopping Centres, owner of some of the UK's leading centres, recently announced plans to move Asda, the food retailer that is one of the anchors of its landmark MetroCentre in Gateshead in the north-east of England, to a new site and replace it with Debenhams, a department store. 'At the MetroCentre, we found that the footfall into the Red Quadrant (where Asda is located) from that entrance was not as high as from other

entrances,' says Douglas Leslie, chief executive of Capital Shopping Centres. 'People were entering through Asda but they were going right back out again. It is highly debatable whether food shopping ever had any synergy with comparison shopping.' David Robinoff, managing director at Eastdil Realty Co. in New York, says: 'People who have stocked up on perishable goods do not want to lock them in their cars for a few hours while they take in the other sights at the mall.' Moreover, food and clothing shopping trips are really about different things. According to research by Healey & Baker, it is typical to find supermarkets as anchors in many European countries, including Belgium, Denmark, Germany and Portugal. France shows a preference for a so-called hypermarket anchor. Yvonne Court, retailing specialist at Healey & Baker, says restricted shopping hours in some European states may be part of the explanation. Also, the degree to which supermarkets are desirable anchors may depend on the degree of retailing sophistication of the population generally, says Jonathan Tinker, of Chelverton Properties which specialises in European retail and leisure parks. 'The richer economies anywhere will have less focus on basic goods relative to overall consumption,' he notes. In Poland, where the average annual per capita income is $3,000, a higher percentage of expenditure goes on food than on anything else. But in Germany, with income of $22,000, shopping patterns differ. Thus, understanding the nature of shopping depends on the socio-economic context in which it occurs. In developing economies, it is a necessary chore and in wealthier ones, a leisure activity. And in the most well-off, it is an art form.

Source: Norma Cohen, *Financial Times*, 9 January 1998

The shopping mall

A shopping mall contains a high number of retail outlets in a large building of at least 100 000 square feet in size. The mall normally forms a covered building with open pedestrian walkways which are lined with shops linking the main retailers' sites. If the mall is more than one floor high then the major 'anchor' stores may extend to each of the floors. The mall development may be free-standing or within an existing shopping area. This is because some malls have been built as an infill, as part of an unplanned town centre, whereas others are located on greenfield sites. The property developer's aim is to create a modern themed entity with a balance of types of store. A shopping mall normally contains one or more major branded stores plus several smaller enterprises. They are different from retail parks as the range of store offers is much wider and often includes luxury and leisure items as well as clothing, footwear and other typical central location merchandise. There are a number of examples of shopping malls, ranging from small district size centres to regional malls such as the MetroCentre near Gateshead or Meadowhall in Sheffield in the UK. Regional malls are at least 300 000 square feet in size and often include leisure functions such as cinemas, food courts, ice rinks and restaurants.

A shopping mall is strongly marketed as a unified shopping destination with one name and logo. The success of a mall, however, is quite often dependent on the range and quality of the shops it can attract. The mall is more likely to want to attract non-discount retailers. Table 11.3 explains the differences which often exist between a discount operation and that of a department store.

Two types of retailing in location decisions

Based upon the preceding theories, there are two basic types of retailing which need to be explained: proximity and destination retailing. The nature of any regional development will affect the nature of the sites available for retailers. Each area can be generalized to identify the type of retailing which may be successful. Therefore, two broad types of retailing development may be considered in the location decision: proximity retailing and destination retailing.

Proximity retailing is development-led by locating where the consumer is to ensure high levels of convenience – in the workplace, related to the patterns of movement, near the home or at home. Specific examples include petrol stations, chemists, small convenience stores, newsagents, video outlets, fast-food outlets, mail order and teleshopping. A

Table 11.3 Retail strategy differences between a discount store and a traditional department store

Discount clothing store strategy	*Department store strategy*
1 Low cost rental location – which may reflect in a lower level of passing potential consumer traffic or a less prosperous area	1 More expensive rental location in an established shopping centre which has a high level of pull on potential consumer traffic
2 Simple fixtures and fittings, cheap floor covering, few displays, single fitting room	2 Elegant fixtures and fittings, carpeted flooring, individual fitting rooms, an abundance of window and interior displays
3 Promotional strategy is based upon price leadership	3 Promotional strategy is based upon developing brand image, offering quality brands, achieving a positive image and providing superior service
4 Little flexibility in service (few, if any, of alterations, phone orders, gift wrapping, credit, etc.)	4 Flexibility in service (will alter, arrange home delivery, have relationship marketing or loyalty schemes)
5 Reliance on self-service, basic displays, most merchandise being visible and in crowded conditions	5 Thorough sales assistance, depth and breadth of stock, attractive display of merchandise
6 May stock limited lines and cheap discounted brands	6 Full selection of branded products and reluctance to have discounted items
7 Continual use of low price offers	7 Sales limited to specific end-of-season clearances or special occasions
8 No changing rooms	8 Changing rooms

retail outlet wishing to be successful in this category has to identify sites with maximum passing traffic and visibility, and ensure that the retail offer matches the needs and characteristics of people working or living in the immediate vicinity. Proximity retailing is often associated with convenience or staple goods which are purchased on a frequent or routine basis.

Destination retailing is based on drawing consumers to travel to a store: brand leaders, the major multiple grocers, large outlets for DIY, toys, clothing, as well as the large 'discount' retailers are included in the category of retailers using this type of location. Relatively mobile, car-owning consumers are more likely to be attracted by this type of retailing. Destination retailing is often associated with speciality goods which are characterized by unique attributes that will attract specific segments. For these goods, purchase behaviour is often associated with higher involvement as part of the buying process and more pre-purchase planning than for other types of goods. A recent trend has been the movement of electrical, carpet and furniture stores away from existing centres to fringe and out-of-town locations, usually grouped together in retail parks. The marketing strategy for this trend is often based upon the proposition of providing products which offer good value for money.

Fig. 11.7 Retail location and consumer behaviour consideration

Other factors also come into play. From a consumer behaviour point of view it is important to understand the type of shopping occasion (*see* Fig. 11.7). A suitable location strategy needs to be underpinned by the type of merchandise and how time dependent the purchase may be. Convenience goods by their very nature should be in close proximity to the customer's home. However, there are also comparison goods that are associated with more time taken to decide on the ideal purchase. These may be in a central high street location. If a retailer is offering bulky goods, such as furniture or white goods, then quite often the ease of parking and a large selection offered by a retail park is an ideal location to plan for. Finally, a retailer distributing more portable purchases can locate in the high street where consumers can choose between competing outlets.

LOCATIONAL TECHNIQUES

The use of different forms of analysis is essential to the selection of an appropriate retail location. The appropriateness is based upon the characteristics of the retailer's business and this means different types of analysis will need to be undertaken according to the type and range of products being sold, where the business would ideally be based, and the ideal catchment population.

Factors in the location decision

In order to determine possible catchment areas, to forecast sales and to calculate likely demand and profitability, a substantial number of factors may need to be investigated. Chu and Lu (1998) have argued that within any discussion on spatial economics and location decisions it is assumed that the firm in question can choose only one store site. This may be restrictive, as spatial decisions may be far more complicated based upon geographic distribution of competitors and competitive prices. The list in Table 11.4 is not exhaustive but serves as an example. All sites need to be examined on a preliminary basis prior to the more detailed location analysis. Road and traffic systems, parking

Table 11.4 Sample of location factors

Customers – potential/actual	Accessibility	Competition	Costs
• Numbers by demographics	• Site visibility	• Amount and level	• Building costs
• Income/employment by occupation, industry, trends	• Pedestrian flows	• Type and numbers	• Rent costs
• Spending patterns	• Barriers such as railway tracks, rivers	• Saturation index	• Rates payable
• Population growth, density and trends	• Type of location zone	• Proximity of key competitors, traders, brand leaders – for example, Marks & Spencer	• Delivery costs
• Lifestyles	• Road conditions and network		• Insurance costs
• Car ownership	• Parking		• Labour rates
	• Public transport		

facilities, competitors and pedestrian flows may be easily assessed; some of the other items listed in Table 11.4 need more detailed analysis.

Location assessment techniques

Techniques for assessing a location for a retail outlet range from the simple to the sophisticated. An obvious method, which is the simplest way of assessing a site's viability, is to count the flow of people during five-minute periods at the busiest times of the week. Based upon a crude 'rule of thumb', if it were a site where on average 100 people passed within five minutes then that could be equated to expenditure per person based upon a money weighting, of say £150 each, which would represent a potential of £15 000 a week. Two hundred people would represent £30 000. Obviously there are certain variables which also need to be assessed to ensure the viability, such as being in a central place location among shops with a high customer utilization. Eppli (1998), in a study of consumer shopping behaviour, revealed that the effects of location, comparison shopping, and department store image are a composite when estimating both shopping centre patronage and retail sales.

The most logical step would be to use a checklist of factors similar to those in Table 11.4. Factors relevant to a potential site could be identified and then allocated a score on a scale of 1 to 10 (1 = poor, 10 = excellent). The final score would act as a management decision input when considering whether or not to proceed in one area as opposed to another. While a small retailer without large resources may adopt such an approach, the location of a superstore would need a more sophisticated approach. This is because of the size of the investment involved, the complexity of the operation and the profit required to secure a return on any investment. Destination retailing, as previously described, requires a much more detailed assessment as part of the location determination process.

Table 11.5 Framework for catchment area analysis

(1) Travel time (minutes)	(2) Population	(3) Weekly potential sales	(4) Competition (total square footage)	(5) Square footage per head	(6) Forecast sales
0 to under 10 10 to under 20 20 to under 30 30 to under 40 40 to 60					

CATCHMENT AREA ANALYSIS

Catchment area analysis together with the analogue method (a comparison of similar stores in the group) serves as a useful basis for forecasting sales of a proposed superstore. A superstore wanting to locate to a new site may turn to catchment area analysis. The basic framework is shown in Table 11.5.

The columns of Table 11.5 require some explanation.

- Column 1, although expressed in time bands, could equally be stated in terms of distance. However, distance does not take local road conditions into consideration.

- Column 2 could be broken down into socio-economic groups, age bands, car ownership, etc. It could also be based upon percentage of working population.

- Column 3 would initially be calculated by multiplying per capita expenditure on merchandise lines/goods by the population figure. More detailed analysis would determine per capita expenditure in different consumer categories multiplied by the number of such consumers in the various time bands. The superstore, for example, may be looking to attract the higher socio-economic groups or may be surrounded by specific household types.

- Columns 4 and 5 enable an assessment to be carried out into the potential market for a new store on the basis of existing provision.

- Column 6 – by utilizing the data from a number of similar stores in the group (analogue method) a realistic forecast can be made. The forecast will indicate the levels of penetration in each of the travel bands, adjusted to take the effect of competition into account.

Ultimately, the decision as to whether or not development proceeds will depend on the sales and profit requirements of both retailers and property developers.

Computerized databases as an aid to store location catchment area decisions

In order to evaluate the trade area for a store with some accuracy, a range of different computerized mapping techniques is available. Trade area mapping may be provided by software such as SYMAP, GIS (geographic information systems) or Pinpoint analysis. These systems can assess the geographical and demographic attractiveness of a site with much more accuracy than other methods. Retailers have often been slow to use spatial decision software in order to improve decisions regarding the retail location and operation. The larger multiples, especially food multiples, use GIS because it can give competitive advantage as part of marketing planning over smaller retailers.

Gravitational model

The use of models is another way to assess the feasibility of a location decision. With the gravitational model, the selection of a primary trading location is based upon the idea that consumers are attracted towards one location as opposed to another by its draw or pull effect. One of the original exponents of the 'pulling effect' of a location was W.J. Reilly, who published his law of retail gravitation in 1929. The law set out to allow a point of indifference to be established between two cities or communities so that the catchment area could be determined. The point of indifference is the geographic breaking point between two communities, that is, the point where consumers would be indifferent to shopping at either location. This aids one of the crucial tasks in retail location, which is the necessity to delineate the catchment area or geographical area from which a retailer draws custom. According to Reilly, more consumers will be attracted to the larger city or community to shop due to the greater amount of store facilities and choice which would make any extra travelling time worthwhile. Reilly's law may be expressed as:

$$D_{AB} = \frac{d}{1 + \sqrt{\dfrac{P_B}{P_A}}}$$

where D_{AB} is the limit of city A's catchment area measured in miles along the road to city B, d is the distance in miles along a major roadway between A and B, P_A is the population of city A and P_B is the population of city B.

Based on this formula, a city with a population of 450 000 (A) would draw people from three times the distance that a city with a population of 50 000 (B) could manage. If the cities are 20 miles apart, the catchment area for city A extends to 15 miles and for city B, 5 miles (*see* Fig. 11.8).

However, Reilly's law rests on three major assumptions:

- the two competing areas are equally accessible from a major road;
- retailers in either of the two areas offer no additional competitive advantage and are equally effective;
- the areas are similar and that no bias will occur due to differences in ethnic, civic and general architecture, facilities or parking restrictions.

Consequently, the law has its limitations. Not only is the focus on distance rather than travel times, but also actual distance may not correspond with the consumer's *perception* of distance – for example, a store that offers limited merchandise, few services and parking problems may be at a greater perceived distance from one with an attractive, pleasant environment. Alternatively, consumers may be willing to travel further due to ease of parking or to visit a particular store, etc.

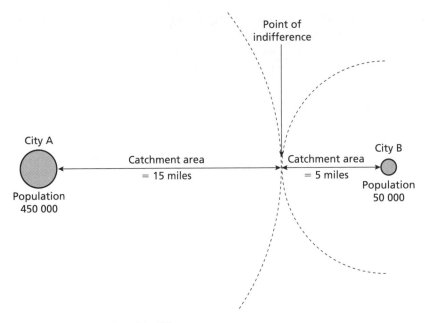

Fig. 11.8 Reilly's point of indifference

However, despite the above weaknesses, Reilly's law still represents an important contribution to our assessment of retail location as it formalizes the interrelationships between competing retail trading areas. In particular, it includes some of the basics of location:

- *spatial convenience* – the increase in travel time and distance to any destination to utilize a store or market centre will restrict and limit the potential size of the market;
- *range* – this is the maximum distance that customers are willing to travel to a shopping destination;
- *threshold* – this refers to the smallest market size needed to support a certain type of store or shopping centre.

REGRESSION ANALYSIS

The large stores may also utilize regression analysis in order to forecast sales. As seen previously, existing stores similar to the proposed new store are used to estimate an equation relating variations in sales to a set of variables, for example population, competition store size, and so on. A hypothetical example will illustrate the procedure:

$$Y = a + b_1x_1 - b_2x_2$$

where Y = retail sales
               x_1 = population (within 20 minutes' drive time)
               x_2 = competition (floor space of all stores over 20 000 ft^2 within 20 minutes' drive time)
       b_1, b_2 = regression coefficients
          a = intercept value

Twenty-five observations from analogous stores give us the following regression equation:

$$Y = 200\ 000 + 0.74x_1 - 1.35x_2$$

The overall explanatory power of the regression equation above is known as the coefficient of determination, R^2, which for this equation is 0.83. (The figure of 0.83 is, in turn, the squared value of the correlation coefficient, r, which in this example would be 0.91. Therefore $0.91^2 = 0.83$.)

What does $R^2 = 0.83$ mean? An R^2 of 0.83 means that 83 per cent of the differences in sales among the 25 analogous stores can be explained by variations in population and competition. Only 17 per cent is left unexplained (owing to some other factors, for example income levels, promotional expenditure, product range).

For the regression coefficients: b_1 is equal to 0.74, which means that for a 1 per cent increase in the population, sales will increase by 0.74. On the other hand, a b_2 of -1.35 means that with a 1 per cent increase in competitor's floorspace, sales will decrease by 1.35 per cent. Using the area's population and competition figures, a proposed new superstore can use the above equation to estimate sales.

Whereas superstores consider travel times and distance proximity, retailers study geodemographic profiles for an understanding of catchment areas. More specifically, proximity retailers wish to know the types of people in the immediate vicinity of the proposed site, as it is from here that the vast proportion of its business will come. Geo-demographic systems like ACORN or MOSAIC (*see* Chapter 3 for further explanation), along with Target Group Index (TGI) information on consumption, can provide detailed information on the catchment area: for example, type of housing, consumer character-istics, consumption patterns, suggestions on product ranges, etc. Statistical data and databases can show the influence and distribution of, say, ACORN types within a city, town or village. Further analysis enables an estimate of market size and sales potential.

Index of retail saturation

The level of competition between stores will affect the retail opportunity in an area. Therefore, the competitive structure of a catchment area needs to be studied in order to assess a location accurately. Put simply, a catchment area can be under-stored, over-stored, or saturated. An under-stored area has too few stores selling specific goods or services to satisfy the needs of its population. An over-stored area has a superfluous number of stores and some retailers may not be able to earn an adequate profit. A satur-ated area has just enough retail facilities to satisfy the needs of its population.

To assess the above, a general ratio model has been developed to measure store satura-tion in a specific area based upon an index of retail saturation (IRS). The calculation can be made as follows:

$$IRS_i = \frac{C_i \times RE_i}{RF_i}$$

where IRS_i = index of retail saturation for area i (where i = local market area)
C_i = number of customers in area i for the product/service category
RE_i = retail expenditures per customer in area i for the product/service category
RF_i = total retail square footage in area i allocated to the product/service category

Table 11.6 An example of the use of the index of retail saturation

	Catchment area		
	1	*2*	*3*
Number of customers buying annually	60 000	30 000	10 000
Average annual purchases per customer	£60	£75	£100
Total square footage (including the proposed store)	20 000	15 000	75 000
Index of retail saturation (including the proposed store)	180	150	133
Index of retail saturation (excluding the proposed store)	240	225	400

Consider the following example of food store saturation in a catchment area. There are 15 000 consumers in the area and they spend, on average, £20 per week in food stores. (Figures for different per capita expenditure on retail products are available from the Family Expenditure Survey.) There are three stores serving the market with a total of 30 000 square feet. Hence:

$$\text{IRS} = \frac{15\,000 \times £20}{300\,000} = £10$$

The revenue of £10 per square foot of selling area measured against the revenue per square foot necessary to break even provides the measure of saturation.

The use of the IRS can also be illustrated by an analysis of three catchment areas under consideration by a shoe retailer. The company has predetermined that its sales must be at least £160 per square foot of store space to be profitable. The catchment area chosen will be the one that yields the best index of retail store saturation. In this case, the retailer selects catchment area 1 which has an index of saturation of £180 (*see* Table 11.6).

When calculating the index, the retailer has to remember to include the proposed store. If the store is not included, the relative value of each calculation may be distorted. If the proposed store is excluded in Table 11.6, for instance, area 3 has the best level of sales per square foot (£400). However, this area is not desirable after the prospective store is added to the computation. It should be noted that sales per square foot decline most when new outlets are added to a small area. The retailer should also examine the impact of its business and whether a new store will expand the total market or not. The information in Table 11.6 assumes that sales will remain the same. In the food retailing industry it has been claimed that there should be approximately one square foot of retail space for each head of population living in a catchment area. So 80 000 people should be matched by 80 000 square feet of retail space. However, the complexity of any retail sales situation quite often means that such rules of thumb are too crude an approach. It should be noted that a market may be saturated in some sectors, for example grocery and superstores, and yet be very much underdeveloped in others such as footwear retailing. Each retail organization must analyse the situation as it affects its business. In addition, the company has to have the resources to afford the developments. According to Edgecliffe-Johnson (2001) the problems of Gap led the company to change its plans from its 30 per cent expansion of square footage to only 10 per cent.

RETAIL PROPERTY DEVELOPMENT

Retail property development can be considered as the change of use of a piece of land in order to develop it for retail use. This may be based upon the refurbishment of existing buildings from what used to be a warehouse or factory into retail units. The general definition relating to transforming a plot of land from one state to another is based upon the premise that if there is a higher demand for retail sites in an area and a decrease in the need for industrial sites then it will be inevitable that suitable sites for retailing will be developed. The other type of development is the planned development of new centres in out-of-town locations or the development of retail parks. The latter type of retail property development has been a more recent phenomenon but the overriding motivation for all development is the financial return on any project and the commercial value of the new property.

Retail property development is also reliant on:

- local factors of supply and demand;
- appropriateness of the available site(s) for different types of retailer;
- the experience and preferences of the developer and local planning officers;
- the minimum amount of land required to provide different scales of development and change;
- the costs of the development;
- the time factors in the completion of the development;
- the level of financial risk in undertaking the development.

Retail Location Problems: Market forces

Like many small market towns in Britain, Romsey has seen better days. New towns, garden suburbs, cars, ring roads, innovations in retailing, refrigeration, e-commerce and even women working outside the home have all been blamed for the declining fortunes of Britain's 1,000 or so small towns, with a population of under 20,000. The closure of banks and railway stations has added to their isolation.

But most local planners agree that one thing above all has damaged traditional small towns – the growth of out-of-town superstores. In the past 40 years, the market share of large multiples, national brands and franchises that have homogenised Britain's high streets and shopping malls has almost doubled to 65% of retail turnover, according to a small-business review by Barclays Bank. This has hurt independent shops, particularly small grocers, whose numbers have declined from 275,000 in 1950 to fewer than 80,000 today. The latest threat to Romsey is West

Quay, one of Britain's largest shopping centres, which is just opening in nearby Southampton. But after years of gentle decline, a movement is under way to try to save Britain's small towns, which are still the homes of much of the country's most attractive architecture, as well as its sense of the past. Record numbers of delegates went to Ripon last month to attend the fourth annual conference on market towns, advertised as 'the battle for survival'. Pleas to 'Save our Countryside' and 'Save our Cities' are now competing with a new chorus of 'Save our Market Towns'.

Despite the growth of the superstores, small retailers own nearly 250,000 shops across Britain and employ more than 750,000 workers, a good proportion of them in small towns. A quarter of the country's population continues to live in or very near small towns. Nicholas Falk of the Urban and Economic Development Group, a consultancy, argues that the most important things small towns can do are to improve their shops and to emphasise their distinctiveness. The superstores may offer convenience, keen prices and a range of products that small-town shops cannot match. But they are homogeneous, and market towns can take advantage of the search for something a bit more picturesque and individual than the average out-of-town Tesco.

Some market towns are going back to their roots, by rediscovering the pulling power of the farmers' markets which have done so much to keep small towns going in France. Wellington in Shropshire took on the superstores in nearby Telford by expanding its outdoor market under colourful awnings. Other towns are putting on 'medieval' craft fairs and seasonal festivals in an attempt to attract visitors.

Other towns are being urged to adopt an American formula, capitalising on bars, books and bread. Romsey is trying bits of several of these strategies, with some effect. Its population of 17,000 is growing slightly after years of stagnation. Not so long ago, 20% of the town's 85 shops were vacant. The remaining merchants banded together, sought help from the borough council and chamber of commerce, and aggressively promoted the town. A co-ordinator helped organise civic and commercial improvements, emphasising attractive window dressings and courtesy to customers. This simple strategy appears to be paying off. Just two shops remain vacant, and shop-owners claim that trade has picked up.

Source: © *The Economist*, 7 October, 2000

THE LEASING OF A RETAIL OUTLET

Once a specific site has been agreed upon a retailer needs to assess the contract or lease offered. There are different types of leases and a variety of terms which may be applied. On the whole it is more usual for a retailer to lease a store site than enter into a loan or mortgage in order to purchase the property. This provides for a more flexible response by the retailer and the ability to free the capital for alternative projects. In addition, it will be found that shopping malls and similar purpose-developed locations are only available as part of a leasing agreement. There are straight leases, percentage leases or net leases.

With a *straight lease* a retailer will pay an agreed fixed amount per month or quarter over the life of the lease. With a straight lease, both the landlord and the retailer know in advance what payments are expected over the life of the lease. One modification of the straight lease is the *graduated lease* where the amount due increases by a fixed amount after specified periods of time. This may be based upon inflationary clauses using government figures as to how much the lease may increase each year or there may be some pre-agreed increase.

The *percentage lease* is based upon an agreement made on the principle of the rent being linked to a percentage of sales. Given that leases can run from 5 to 20 years, there is some protection for the retailer if the rent can fluctuate on the basis of inflation and sales results. In America, this is a very popular form of leasing, accepted as a fair way to set rent as the local and national economy would force rents down if there were a general decline in sales demand – or vice versa. This approach is often combined with an accepted minimum or maximum increase so as to incentivize the retailer and also protect the landlord. The scheme may also be based upon a sliding scale of change in rent whereby a retailer may pay 4 per cent on the first £250 000 of sales and 3 per cent on the next £150 000, etc. This will offer a further reward to those retailers who can improve the achievement of their operation.

The above leases may be based upon *maintenance recoupment*, where a landlord will have the right to increase the rent if it can be shown that the property insurance, taxes or utility bills have increased beyond a specified agreed level. The above may also be allied to a *net lease*. With a net lease the retailer is responsible for all maintenance and utility charges; the property owner, therefore, can base the rent on a more stable set of circumstances.

A lease is a formal contract and therefore agreement has to take place regarding the conditions and terms by the lessor (property owner) and lessee (the party signing the lease). A lease may be negotiated to achieve the best conditions for each participant; the outcome, however, is often based upon the relative power of each party and their knowledge of what can be added to the agreement as specific clauses. These clauses may include the following.

A *prohibited use clause* is used in order to limit the landlord from leasing to tenants who may affect the image of the business or building(s) or restrict the demand for the retailer's goods, due to alternative business which may affect the use of parking space and not increase the retailer's sales. For example, certain types of leisure facilities such as a fitness club or day centre may reduce the number of shoppers. There may also be a wish for the list of prohibited businesses to include sex shops, bars, pool halls or other establishments which may affect the overall image of the area.

An *exclusive use clause* will prohibit the landlord from leasing to retailers who will then become direct competitors. For example, if the retail outlet is a video hire business the clause may limit the landlord from renting to another similar business unit; it may also restrict other outlets – such as a convenience store – from hiring out videos from their store. Alternatively, a retailer may wish to protect their business on the basis of the continued trading of strongly branded retailers within the area. The exclusive use clause may therefore ensure that the agreement is reliant on key, named retailers remaining in the area.

The lease may also need to include clauses to restrict a landlord from placing any objects or kiosks in a position which may affect the sight line to the store or its visibility to passing potential customers. With the development of stand-alone automatic teller machines, public Internet machines and advances in technology there is the possible threat of land being rented for the establishment of an obstacle which may affect the original lessee's business.

CONCLUSION

The decision regarding where to locate a store is critical to the future performance of that outlet and the retailer's prosperity. This is compounded by the fact that all location plans are important on the basis of the resources required to develop a new store, and the time this takes. Any decision over a retail site requires an appraisal of the potential site area based upon a number of analytical techniques. The retailer's task is to identify the size and profile of the potential market of consumers, assess the different potential sites of an area and then utilize methods of screening the alternatives so that the chosen site offers the best likelihood of maximizing the store's retail profitability. This process has to be one of matching the site to the type of business represented by that retailer. It also has to be carried out in a timely manner to ensure there is the maximization of profits for the retailer.

EXERCISES

The exercises in this section relate to retail location strategies and decisions. It is advised that you work through them before moving on to Chapter 12.

1   What are the major consumer and business influences which have produced the current location patterns of retail outlets in developed economies?

2   Given the recent trends in retail shopping and customer behaviour, what changes may occur in the location of retail outlets in large city centres?

3   Do you believe that some aspects of location analysis techniques are better than others? If so, what are the techniques you would employ and which key aspects would you want to assess prior to location decisions being made? What were the reasons for your choice?

4   In your opinion, what are the most important aspects of location decision-making? Use the following grid as a guide.

Location analysis factors	Comment on the importance of these from a marketing viewpoint:
● proximity of competitors ● type of housing and lifestyle of households ● development costs ● in-town, edge-of-town, out-of-town location ● others (list)	

Now comment on how you think location analysis will change over the next 20 years to encourage increased purchases.

REFERENCES AND FURTHER READING

Bennison, D., Clarke, I. and Pal, J.J. (1995) 'Location decision making in retailing: an exploratory framework for analysis', *International Review of Retail, Distribution and Consumer Research*, 5 (1), 1–20.

Brown, S. (1992) *Retail Location: A micro-scale perspective*. Aldershot: Avebury.

Brown, S. (1993) 'Retail location theory: evolution and evaluation', *International Review of Retail, Distribution and Consumer Research*, 3 (2), 185–229.

Chu, C.Y.C. and Lu, H. (1998) 'The multi-store location and pricing decisions of a spatial monopoly', *Regional Science and Urban Economics*, 28 (3), 255–81.

Clark, M. (1993) 'Mapping out retail direction', *International Journal of Retail and Distribution Management*, 21 (2), 36–8.

Clarke, I. and Bennison, D. (1997) 'Towards a contemporary perspective of retail location', *International Journal of Retail and Distribution Management*, 25 (2/3), 59–69.

Clarkson, R.M., Clarke-Hill, C.M. and Robinson, T. (1996) 'UK supermarket location assessment', *International Journal of Retail and Distribution Management*, 24 (6), 22–3.

Coates, D., Doherty, N., French, A. and Kirkup, M. (1995) 'Neural networks for store performance forecasting: an empirical comparison with regression techniques', *International Review of Retail, Distribution and Consumer Research*, 5 (4), 415–32.

Cohen, N. (1998) 'Property market: an anchor in the centre', *Financial Times*, 9 January.

Department of the Environment (1996) *Town Centres and Retail Developments, Planning Policy Guidance* (Note 6). London: HMSO.

Drezner, Z., Wesolowsky, G.O. and Drezner, T. (1998) 'On the logit approach to competitive facility location', *Journal of Regional Science*, 38 (2), 313–27.

The Economist (2000) 'Market Forces', *The Economist*, 7 October.

Edgecliffe-Johnson, A. (2001) 'Gap reins in plans to expand number of stores', FT.com site, 22 June.

Eppli, M.J. (1998) 'Value allocation in regional shopping centers', *Appraisal Journal*, 66 (2), 198–206.

Fernie, J. (1995) 'The coming of the Fourth wave: New forms of out of town retail development'. *International Journal of Retail and Distribution Management*, 23 (1), 4–11.

Guy, C.M. (1984) The Urban Pattern of Retailing within the UK, in Davies, R.L. and Rogers, D.S. (eds) *Store Location and Store Assessment Research*. Chichester: John Wiley.

Guy, C.M. (1994) *The Retail Development Process: Location, property and planning*. London: Routledge.

Hallsworth, A.G., Jones, K.G. and Muncaster, R. (1995) 'The planning implications of new retail format introductions in Canada and Britain', *Services Industries Journal*, 15 (4), 148–63.

Hotelling, H. (1929) 'Stability in competition', *Economic Journal*, 39, March, 41–57.

Jones, K. and Simmons, J. (1990) *The Retail Environment*. London: Routledge.

McGoldrick, P.J. (1994) *Cases in Retail Management*. London: Pitman.

Reilly, W.J. (1929) 'Method for the study of retail relationships', *Research Monograph No. 4*, Austin, TX: University of Texas Bulletin No. 2944.

Richardson, H.W. (1978) *Urban Economics*. Hinsdale: Dryden Press.

Schiller, R. (1994) 'Vitality and viability: Challenge to the town centre', *International Journal of Retail and Distribution Management*, 22 (6), 46–50.

Scott, P. (1970) *Geography and Retailing*. London: Hutchinson.

Simkin, L.P. (1989) 'SLAM: Store Location Assessment Model – theory and practice', *International Journal of Management Science*, 17 (1), 53–8.

Simkin, L.P. (1990) 'Evaluating a store location', *International Journal of Retail and Distribution Management*, 18 (4), 33–8.

Smith, C.A. and Webb, J.R. (1997) 'Using GIS to improve estimates of future retail space demand', *Appraisal Journal*, 65 (4), 337–41.

12 The management of a retail brand

This chapter should enable you to understand and explain:

- what a brand is;
- the positioning and differentiation of a brand;
- the role and purpose of branding;
- the development and importance of own-brands;
- corporate branding;
- strategies of brand extension.

In the modern competitive retail marketplace, growth markets are increasingly scarce and consumers are sovereign in dictating what shape the market will be. The consumer is faced with an increasing array of essential, as well as non-essential retail products over which to exercise the power of choice and dictate trends. If a retailer is to be successful, improvements and investment in stores or retailing operations are not enough. Returns can be made only if the customer decides to purchase, and purchase again, as part of a relationship with the store and the brand. Simply put, retailers and suppliers of products or services need to understand that consumption has symbolic meaning which transcends mere utilitarian purchase in that people seek out a lifestyle when deciding upon a retail offer. One current marketing method of achieving positive symbolic meaning is to embark upon a strategy of *brand building*. This can be adopted by a chain of retail outlets, financial service providers or by a producer of branded merchandise. A successful brand strategy will both aid and convince consumers in the decision-making process to select out certain companies and merchandise. To build retail brand requires more than trading ability; it requires that the company institutionalize marketing as the means to manage the long-term development of brand values.

The benefit of developing a strong brand is that consumers are often prepared to pay a price premium for perceived added values related to buying well-marketed brands. The price premium, also known as *brand equity*, is the price customers are prepared to pay above the commodity value of a product or service. This being the case, well-respected stores or brands – if well positioned and managed – can give a better return on floor space or investment. Brands with a strong personality are attractive to companies who own them and predator companies wishing to buy into their potency. A successful brand is a flag bearer as it provides visible signals of positional strength in the marketplace. In this way successful brands provide their parent companies with a competitive advantage.

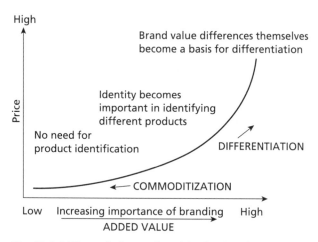

Fig. 12.1 Differentiation and positioning in relation to added value

Figure 12.1 illustrates the benefit of creating a strong brand which is able to add value to the retail offer. A differentiated position from that of the competition with a clear identity allows the brand to achieve higher prices and achieve higher levels of demand in periods of recession.

In the UK, Boots the Chemist, the Early Learning Centre and Dixons are examples of strong brands which communicate a clear position for both merchandise and service. A secondary consideration is that strong domestic retail brands provide a good base on which to build an international or global presence. Therefore, brand management may become more important for those companies that want to escape the competitive domestic market and attempt international growth. There are few truly global retail brands. The retail financial services market has American Express, VISA, MasterCard and Diners Club. There are some large banks that have followed their domestic business, and private customers overseas, to business centres, tourist destinations or expatriate communities. However, the growth of non-branch banking could lead to far faster global competition due to the low cost operations of direct services and the economies of scale to be found in international expansion. In addition, the activity of financial services utilizing the benefits of the Internet is an emerging trend whereby the brand has to be considered in both an offline and online experience and how this affects perceptions of the consumer.

Companies produce strategies based upon long-term commitment to brand building as a way out of the heavy reliance on offering low prices as the primary reason for consumer choice. More recently, branding in the retail sector has taken on increased significance due to the importance of the own-brands (sometimes termed own-label), which make up a significant percentage of retail sales. However, the long-term success of a particular brand, be it own-brand or not, is based not on the number of customers who purchase it once, but on the number who become repeat purchasers. They become *brand loyal* or *store loyal*. The concept of selling a product to as many people as possible at least once may have been relevant in a growth market, but when a market matures companies need to realize that it is of paramount importance to maintain loyal customers as well as search for new customers. For consumers, the familiar associations and standard guarantees embodied in brand offers reduce the perceived purchase risks often associated with high involvement, intangible retail products.

Branding has become even more important nowadays due to the relentless evolution of the marketplace from an environment where satisfaction of basic needs has given way to the need to have brands that engender positive associations. We live in a world where symbolic meaning linked to brand use provides status and social significance for the consumer of that brand. Historically fashion brands have held great significance in retailing. These include such brands as Yves Saint Laurent, Chanel, Christian Dior and Jean Paul Gautier from France; Giorgio Armani, Gianni Versace and Emanuel Ungaro from Italy; Issey Miyake and Kenzo from the Far East; and Ralph Lauren, Calvin Klein and Donna Karan from the USA. These fashion brands are all names that have a strong international reputation. Branding is a powerful phenomenon in that it is one of the most successful ways of satisfying customer recognition needs. To understand the phenomenon we need to know specifically the intrinsic properties that constitute a brand.

DEFINITION OF A BRAND

Kotler (1997) defines a brand as:

> a name, term, sign, symbol or design or a combination of them, intended to identify the goods or services of one seller or group of sellers and to differentiate them from those of competitors.

This describes a brand as a purely functional means of distinguishing a retail offer and would have been apt in the early days of branding, but by the 1990s other aspects had been introduced and extensively discussed.

In total abandonment of the focus on aspects of product, Kapferer (1992) produces the more esoteric statement:

> A brand is not a product. It is the product's essence, its meaning and its direction, and it defines its identity in time and space.

An individual's awareness of the world is made up of experiences, learning, emotions and perceptions – or, more accurately, the cognitive evaluation of such experiences, learning, emotions and perceptions. Such awareness may be described as knowledge producing a specific image of the world. This image will obviously affect an individual's preference and motivation towards products, as it will provide a 'pull' effect resulting in different demand schedules. The success of a brand is, therefore, not just what the company puts into the brand but is based upon what the customer associates with the brand – the added value it provides for them. To examine branding from the viewpoint of consumer behaviour, the starting point is to comprehend the way a customer perceives and classifies brands – for example, Benetton and Body Shop are each both a brand and a retail product – prior to specifying how companies can build positive images to reinforce that perception.

The process of brand management has to distinguish a brand from a commodity. The latter is typically characterized by the lack of a perceived differentiation by customers between competing offerings. This being the case, the purchase decision for a commodity is usually taken on the basis of price or availability and not on the brand. Store loyal and brand loyal customers choose on the basis that the shopping experience is 'more than the sum of its component parts'. In other words, the successful brand has *added value* over its commodity content.

Aaker and Biel (1993) give the following definition:

> A brand is basically a name that refers to the product of a particular manufacturer in a particular product category. A brand includes tangible or intrinsic qualities, such as appearance, performance data, package, and the guarantees or warranties that are attached to it. Perhaps more importantly, a brand involves aspects that the consumer attributes to it, beyond its tangible features. These aspects may include attitudes towards the company that produces the product or towards the brand itself, beliefs about the brand in relationship to self and others, and so on.

They further stress that their definition applies not only to consumer products, but to people (for example, politicians, pop stars, and so on), places, ships, companies and services. This at first seems to be comprehensive. However, brands have to be clearly positioned so as to give distinct signals and demarcations from their rivals. This requires a clear distinction encompassing the need to provide focus and personality for the brand. The need to understand this argument introduces two further aspects – *positioning* and *personality* – which will be discussed below.

THE ROLE OF THE BRAND

Before discussing what brand management involves, we will examine why it is considered a pertinent marketing tool for retail companies in the current developed and highly competitive markets. As the marketplace becomes mature, there is a need to rise above the mass and confusion of competing offers. The brand, if managed properly, confers individuality – something different among the crowd. In a mature market, companies experience slow growth and declining returns. Each company will, therefore, attempt to defend its market share, encourage consumers' purchase loyalty and profitably differentiate their outlets and offer. We believe a brand provides an icon or symbol which helps to identify the promise of a particular retail offer or service and helps to distinguish it from competing offers.

Successful retail outlet brand building enables organizations to:

1 build stable, long-term demand based upon increasing store brand name strength;
2 build and hold better margins than stores that have weak or unsuccessful brand names (e.g. even though Marks & Spencer have had problems their food products sell at premium prices);
3 differentiate themselves through creating associations that can endure over long periods of time and which may allow brand stretch (e.g. Starbucks from coffee to ice cream and CDs);
4 add values that entice customers to visit and buy, especially in relation to own-brands;
5 act as a signal to the customer implying trust in the fulfilment of service expectations;
6 promote customer loyalty and launch relationship marketing schemes for their retail offers/services;
7 protect themselves against the growing competition of alternative intermediaries and to gain leverage in the distribution channel;

8 protect themselves against aggressive competitors by strengthening barriers to entry;

9 transform themselves into companies that are attractive to work for and to deal with;

10 negotiate with suppliers from a position of improved strength.

The latter are the potential results of successful retail outlet brand building, but all involve substantial initial, and ongoing, investments to ensure there are long-term returns. Furthermore, brand building needs to be a comprehensive exercise which covers every aspect of the company and every point of contact with the consumer. This puts brand building under severe pressure in modern markets where short-term profits are more commonly the measure of success.

A company may introduce a brand and keep it exclusively for itself, or it can either franchise a brand or manufacture a brand of another company under licence. Franchising is being used extensively by companies in order to expand the brand as quickly as possible in a domestic or global marketplace. With franchising, the company owning the brand will allow others to utilize the brand but with certain preconditions attached. These may be related to an obligation to purchase goods exclusively from the franchiser or to pay a certain percentage of the turnover as part of a royalty payment. The consumer is offered the benefit of the consistency and recognized standards of quality which have been built up in conjunction with the brand. This has led to a number of successful retail operations such as Pizza Hut, Caffé Uno, McDonald's, KFC and Hilton International.

BRAND LOYALTY

Some consumers use the same retail outlet or purchase the same brand of product on most occasions or on a regular basis. This buyer characteristic is known as *store* or *brand loyalty*. In particular, store or brand loyalty will mean that a person will:

- feel positively disposed to the brand, based upon *brand attitude*;
- utilize the store more than other stores or buy the brand more frequently. This will be based upon *store* or *brand preference*;
- continue to utilize the store or brand over time. This is the *brand allegiance*.

The above description of store or brand loyalty can be based upon a number of consumer behaviour variables which were mentioned in Chapter 3. There is the case of *monopoly loyalty* where there is often no alternative choice such as in rural areas; *inertia loyalty* where no alternatives are sought due to existing high levels of satisfaction; *convenience loyalty* due to the location of the retail outlet; *price loyalty* where other alternatives are considered not to offer value for money; *incentivized loyalty* where a loyalty scheme ties in the customer to shop on a regular basis; and *emotional loyalty* which is built up through the intangibles associated with the brand.

Therefore, there is no simple behaviour which indicates the reason for a specific form of loyalty and it may be the case that loyalty is expressed for one or more brands. If we assume that there are five brands, or five properties of brands, that the consumer can choose from – A, B, C, D and E – then we can further segment the demand, based upon brand loyalty, as follows.

1 *Hard core loyals*. These consumers buy one brand all the time and demonstrate strong allegiance. They would therefore on five occasions buy AAAAA, because they have undivided loyalty to the brand.

2 *Soft core loyals*. These consumers will be loyal to two or three brands. Thus a buying pattern of ABABA represents a consumer whose loyalties are divided between two competing brands.

3 *Shifting loyals*. This type of consumer shifts their loyalty from one brand to another. The buying pattern AACCC suggests a consumer whose loyalty has shifted from one brand 'A' to brand 'C'.

4 *Switchers*. These consumers show no loyalty to any one brand. The pattern ABCDE suggests a switcher who is prone to buy when there is a deal being given (price offers, sales, extra benefits). They may equally be a variety shopper who wants something different each time they purchase.

Brand loyalty can be explained in a number of ways: habit; maximization of value over price; a cost may be involved in switching brand; the availability of substitutes; perceived risk of alternatives is high; past satisfaction with the brand; the frequency of usage; influence of the media; the awareness of the alternatives; and so on. For obvious reasons, the loyal customer is of key importance to the retail industry, especially those loyal customers who are high spenders or provide long-term patronage. Loyalty schemes are being introduced in an attempt to retain customers over longer periods of time (*see* Chapter 8 for a full discussion of this). Such schemes are often based upon database programs that provide benefits for those with loyalty shopping cards whose expenditure and frequency of purchase can be assessed. The database can identify individuals' birthdays, when a person is 21 for example, or it can identify lapsed customers to whom a special offer can be made. In addition, the information can be used to understand the patterns of preference and demand at different periods so as to convert soft core loyals and other customers into hard core loyals.

POSITIONING OF A BRAND

The positioning of a brand places it in its competitive context. It may be determined on the basis of product usage: for instance, Müller yogurt may be positioned as a substitute for dairy cream or as a child's pudding alongside ice cream. Alternatively, a brand's position may be determined on the basis of price: for instance, top designer branded clothes have a high upper market position which will attract customers who want exclusivity and a positioning which is associated with other luxury items. Benetton's bold and distinctive colours, Laura Ashley's English country patterns and The Gap's understated American casualwear all provide for brand differentiation.

Registering a clear brand positioning is becoming increasingly difficult because competitors proliferate, media costs escalate, and shelf space becomes more difficult to negotiate as retailers exert more influence over manufacturers' brand strategies. Theorists maintain that focusing on brand positioning is essential for a brand to survive. They express their lack of faith in the intellectual ability of brand managers to assess fully the competition and in the intellectual ability of the consumers similarly to assess the range of brands available to them. The brand managers, who regularly take a sounding of consumer opinion, are the most likely to maintain a brand's positioning successfully. Once the target has been clearly identified, attention needs to be lavished on planning the brand. Furthermore, a brand which is not differentiated from others in its sub-group of brands risks having no distinguishing characteristics and a weak brand position:

Brand differentiation × Brand segmentation = Brand position

Branding places a premium on achieving appropriate positioning. A brand may be made distinctive by its positioning relative to the competition, the main objective being to develop sustainable competitive advantage. As such, a key task for the strategist is to identify those bases which offer the most potential for defensible positioning. In marketing, choosing segments and positioning strategies are inseparable. While segmentation identifies homogeneous groups of potential customers, positioning needs to take into account how customers perceive the competing retail store brands, merchandise offers or services. Both segmentation and positioning research are, therefore, ways of focusing on how customers in a market can be identified and grouped, and then how those customers (segments) perceive the variety of retailers or brands in the marketplace. The furniture maker MFI adopted the strategy of repositioning its retail offer in the late 1980s by the acquisition and use of the Schreiber brand name so that it could sell its higher priced kitchen and bedroom furniture more easily. This complemented its other brands, such as its self-assembly Hygena brand, Pronto its low price point products, and Greaves and Thomas and Ashton Dean for upholstery products. The brand segmentation benefits of Schreiber allowed MFI to attract older ABC1 customers and to produce differentiation based upon style and quality. A new brand position can be created by deliberate strategic repositioning. Interbrand helped reposition Austin Reed stores to provide a more modern image so as to attract a younger market.

The use of positioning in marketing shifts the emphasis away from the tangible changes a retailer makes towards the mental perception of the prospective customer. It emphasizes the share of mind and judgement of mind based upon brand identity. This is what Ries and Trout (1981) referred to as the 'battle for your mind'. Positioning is the clearest way to establish a distinct place in the minds of the consumer and counteract the proclamations and calls for attention by the competitors.

The market is the ultimate judge of any organization's work and, although customer perception can be irrational and ill-informed, the way a consumer perceives the brand and the image of the brand is a powerful influence on the way the retail marketplace reacts to different initiatives and changes. In the fluidity of retail market conditions, the more powerful brands will be successful. The challenge, therefore, for any organization is to position its offer in a way which will be most appealing to the target audience. Market position can also be affected by pricing, distribution and, of course, the product itself. This is why the 'grey' market of selling goods not sourced directly from the manufacturer, and at lower prices than parallel suppliers, has resulted in legal arguments. Tommy Hilfiger, the trendy US fashion label, brought what is believed to be the first legal action of its kind in the UK (Hollinger, 1998). The US group issued a writ claiming damages and demanding that Tesco reveal its sources for the £3.5m worth of Hilfiger caps, T-shirts, jackets and other products it began selling at cut prices in 1998. Hilfiger said it had examined the items and believed certain products were not genuine.

A firm can position a product to compete head-on with another brand. Like-for-like positioning is relevant if the product's characteristics are at least equal to competitive brands and if the product is priced lower; it may be appropriate, even when the price is higher, if the product's performance characteristics are superior. Conversely, a product may be positioned to avoid competition. This may be the best approach when the product's performance characteristics are not significantly different from those of competing brands, or when that brand has unique characteristics that are important to some buyers. For example, Aldi sells many items which are sold at Tesco but at deeply discounted prices.

Brand strategy is essentially about two variables: the exact composition of the offer made to the market and the part(s) of the market to which the offer is made (that is, brand differentiation and brand segmentation), either of which may provide a competitive advantage. Within this approach brand positioning provides the vehicle to integrate the marketing mix and create overall consumer perception. The Argyll Group decided in the early 1990s to build their business around the positioning of three store brands: Safeway, Presto and Lo-Cost. Safeway was the leading brand, bringing in about 85 per cent of Argyll's profits, and therefore this brand was retained as the major flagship. This use of different brands was in direct opposition to the brand strategies of most of their competitors. The larger stores with the Presto brand were progressively refurbished and rebranded as Safeway stores and this allowed the Presto brand to be related to medium-sized units of around 5000 sq. ft. The Lo-Cost brand was positioned as a discount brand and was made up of the smallest units – around 3000 sq. ft. The positioning of the brands allowed the Safeway brand to compete head-to-head with Sainsbury and, due to the brand rationalization, it provided a clear positioning statement for its customers.

It can be seen that the positioning process is to make the offer into a clearly defined brand. Ideally the strategist should consider whether the position is:

- apparent to consumers and offers real added value to them;
- built upon real brand strengths which reflect performance potential;
- clearly differentiated from competitor brand positions but not too narrow;
- capable of being understood and communicated to all stakeholder groups;
- able to be achieved, and then defended if attacked by competitors (British Home Stores were unable to position their brand as the first choice for dressing the modern woman and family due to the strength of the Marks & Spencer brand).

The risks of poor positioning

A poorly positioned brand with a fuzzy position, or not offering a clear proposition, is likely to be eclipsed or weakened by a stronger competitor. Weak positioning can occur if a retailer consistently cuts a brand's price. The Ratner stratagem of bringing in foreign stock which was cheaper but not hallmarked was at first successful. However, the overstretching of the business in takeovers to expand the brand and then a widely reported statement by Ratner himself that his products were 'crap' led to the demise of the group. Ratner had to leave the company and the brand name was subsequently changed to Signet. In effect, Ratner management had repositioned the brand without thinking beyond the 'price' effect to the 'brand' effect. This led to the alienation of the company's target market.

There are other undesirable consequences of not having the right positioning strategy for a product or service in the marketplace. Among the most common in the retail trade are:

- the retail organization (or its own-label products) may find itself in a position where it cannot escape from direct competition from stronger competitors;
- the retailer may find itself in a position which is weak as demand may be falling and others have left that position knowing there is little customer demand there;
- the retailer's position, or that of its own-label products, is so confusing that nobody knows what its distinctive competence or personality really is;
- the retailer has no apparent position in the marketplace because there is little awareness of the brand or its personality.

PERSONALITY OF A BRAND

As markets have become more competitive and products have only marginal differences in their physical formulation, it becomes more important to create distinction by adding relevant psychological values through advertising, packaging and other aspects of the marketing mix. It is interesting to examine the trend in advertising expenditure for retailers (*see* Table 12.1). This shows a willingness by major retailers to release large promotional budgets to support their brands. Some of this can be seen to have commenced only in the late 1990s, or to have doubled in the case of Boots the Chemist since 1992 to over £37 million, representing a major share of all expenditure shown.

Hankinson and Cowking (1993) define the brand personality as being a unique mix of functional attributes and symbolic values. Functional values are extrinsic, tangible product properties such as 'hardwearing' or 'easy to use'; whereas symbolic values describe intrinsic, intangible properties such as 'friendliness' or 'fun'.

Ultimately, each company needs to find ways of encouraging consumers to build a relationship with a brand for it to have any strength or staying power. This is why *brand personality* is important and has consequently developed as a term. Well-positioned brands are more effective problem-solvers, due to marketing techniques which mould their image into a 'brand personality' that can be understood and accepted.

A strong brand personality is an effective added value at the augmented stage and is reflected in the way consumers describe a brand. The extent to which people perceive and identify brands in different ways is illustrated in the Saatchi and Saatchi Compton Worldwide 1984 Annual Report. This report stated that, 'When probed deeply, consumers described the products they call brands in terms that we would normally expect to be used to describe people. They talk about a brand's persona, its image and its reputation, and it is this "aura" or "ethos" that characterises a brand.' The personality then stands for the *essence* of the corporate or product brand. This essence or personality is the succinct cue that a consumer will use to judge the brand. Some brands have a spokesperson or figurehead to represent them and this produces an instant personality around which the brand can be developed. Famous fashion designers or individuals such as Richard Branson, Mary Quant and Anita Roddick have all created a human persona association for their company brand.

Table 12.1 Advertising expenditure of selected retailers, 1992–98 (£000s)

	1992	1993	1994	1995	1996	1997	1998
Booksellers							
Books Etc.	–	–	–	–	158	169	189
Dillons	577	591	1 900	617	220	173	176
Waterstone's	506	–	–	848	1 150	1 431	2 249
Chemists							
Boots the Chemist	18 816	23 040	26 596	34 850	40 083	38 684	37 660
Superdrug	5 216	6 330	8 141	7 209	6 532	3 117	4 746
Unichem	–	260	1 015	613	514	293	236
Opticians							
20/20 Vision	–	–	530	879	1 155	1 020	1 056
Boots Opticians	1 547	2 937	4 354	2 320	4 885	5 560	6 071
Dollond & Aitchison	2 467	2 310	2 979	4 508	5 658	5 409	4 784
Optical Express	–	–	–	–	676	1 359	2 065
Specsavers	2 198	2 200	5 276	8 588	11 873	15 589	18 286
Vision Express	3 172	4 173	5 250	6 445	6 559	7 881	7 784
Sports shops							
Allsports	–	486	522	930	1 327	1 347	1 068
American Golf Discount	–	206	369	426	453	495	546
Blacks Leisure (First Sport)	–	170	227	193	–	592	735
JD Sport	–	–	–	–	368	263	444
JJB Sports	–	236	534	1 078	1 087	1 380	2 008
Sports Division	710	–	464	1 138	954	3 648	4 050
Toy shops							
Early Learning Centre	–	487	180	751	666	1 085	1 068
Toymaster	360	245	445	766	824	622	619
Toys "Я" Us	2 939	3 257	3 988	4 592	5 158	5 450	5 571
Jewellery							
Asprey	1 406	996	579	633	2 798	1 387	1 991
Goldsmiths Group	–	–	1 183	1 241	1 509	1 492	1 428
Signet	384	1 302	952	3 160	3 096	1 837	1 856
Photographic stores							
Jessops	685	766	670	450	298	633	605
Tecno	259	–	180	256	313	512	595
Total of above	41 242	49 992	66 334	82 491	98 314	101 428	107 886

Source: ACNielsen-MEAL (1998), ACNielsen House, Oxford

The right to Grey Goods?

Levi's court battle with Tesco, which has been selling jeans imported on the so-called 'grey market' at a discount, is raging on. The case, which seeks to clarify whether EU retailers can legally sell grey, or 'parallel', imports originally destined for a non-EU country, has given rise to passionate arguments on both sides.

Retailers argue that consumers demand lower prices and that brands are keeping EU prices artificially high. But brand owners say their own investment in innovation and brand image, as well as quality control, will be undermined should they lose control of distribution. As well as damaging their own business, they argue that this is not in the long-term interest of consumers. Although it is Levi's, Calvin Klein and Davidoff that have taken this battle to the courts, the question is not restricted to luxury goods and designer names. Every brand – 'from soap and razor blades to film' – could potentially be affected by EU rulings on parallel imports, according to John Noble, director of the British Brands Group, which represents branded goods owners.

Since grey-market goods first started to appear in the early 90s, the legal pendulum has swung one way and then the other, in favour of brand owners or retailers. In 1998, a ruling on Silhouette sunglasses said retailers could not import goods from outside Europe without the manufacturer's consent. But in 1999, UK courts ruled that fragrance brand Davidoff had given 'implied' consent to its perfumes being imported from the Far East by not 'explicitly' forbidding their resale in Europe. Since then, both parties have sought clarification. At the Levi's interim ruling in April, the EU indicated that it would refer the matter back to the national courts, and that parallel traders' rights should be recognised by the law. Good news for retailers. But it also indicated that the national courts cannot apply a 'general presumption' that the manufacturer has waived its rights to control imports – in other words, a reversal of the 1999 case. Good news for brand manufacturers.

The main reason Tesco was quick to shout victory in April is that UK courts are likely to look favourably on parallel importers. The government certainly does: Stephen Byers, former trade and industry secretary, aggressively backed a campaign led by Sweden to overturn the EU's current block on parallel imports for trademark goods. Byers has also repeatedly called for lower prices on branded goods in Britain, and early indications are that his successor at the DTI, Patricia Hewitt, will do likewise. But in yet another twist, the European Commission itself is against a change in the regime. It has said that parallel imports inhibit investment in new brands and may make trademark-holders withdraw products from the market. Only one thing is certain: the issue is not going to go away.

Retailers such as Tesco and Asda are confident about their justification for selling branded goods sourced on the grey market. 'We do it because it's what our customers ask for. It's about the price the customer pays, not the price the retailer pays,' says David Miles, head of specialist businesses at Asda, which sells a range of grey-market brands, from Ray-Ban sunglasses to Armani fragrances.

'Brands argue that they have created an attitude and an ambience for their products – but we don't believe this is consistent with the location of purchase,' he adds. 'How can perfume brands say that environment devalues the brand when consumers can buy these products off a trolley in the gangway of an aircraft?' The retailers' argument is endorsed by a growing anger among consumers about 'rip-off Britain'. Consumers see that prices are higher in the UK than the US or the rest of Europe and believe greedy brands are to blame. But British Brands Group's Noble argues that 'rip-off Britain' has nothing to do with brand manufacturers. He agrees that the UK is expensive, but says there are many reasons, such as lack of available retail space and fuel costs. This means brands such as Gap are more expensive, but actually less profitable, in the UK. Alan Christie, vice-president of public affairs at Levi's, echoes this claim. He says retailers such as Tesco are well aware there are price differences due to different economic regimes around the world but are 'happy to perpetuate the myth that the retail price in the UK is set by the manufacturer'.

The brand manufacturers' case has been furthered by research revealing that the outcome for consumers of allowing parallel imports is on the whole negligible. Products are, in the end, only about 2% cheaper. 'You have to look at whether retailers are selling these brands as promotional items to get people into stores or selling them at a consistent price,' says Noble. But the same study showed that should parallel imports become fair game, there will be a major shift in profit from manufacturers to retailers. A study commissioned by the EU into the consequences of this change shows that the effect on reducing prices is small – between 0% and 2% – whereas the transfer of profits from manufacturers to traders is high – up to 35%. This is because retailers purchase the goods at low prices and can sell them at a reasonable mark-up, while still making the products cheaper than an approved outlet. Despite the slight discount, consumers are still far more willing to buy discounted goods. Indeed, when questioned, by Taylor Nelson Sofres, an overwhelming majority – 88% – of UK adults said they would rather buy discounted Levi's from a supermarket than full-price at a Levi's store. Only 8% said they were prepared to pay the extra.

Companies such as Levi's, Calvin Klein and Microsoft have invested millions in their advertising and marketing to create their brand image. They argue that not only are brands devalued by becoming just another supermarket item, but the retailers are profiting without making any investment themselves.

Christie points out that while Asda and Sainsbury's created their own 'designer' clothing ranges, Tesco took the cheaper option in selling someone else's. 'Tesco knows exactly what it is doing; it is trying to grow its non-food business.' Brand owners also believe supermarkets do not give the consumer the same quality of service and advice they would get in an approved outlet. 'A brand is a combination of things, including the quality of product and the retail experience,' says Christie. 'If you attack any of these things, you change the consumer's perception of that brand.' However, the brand owners maintain that there is still an issue of quality control. Noble says that even more worrying than the Levi's court case is the ongoing Davidoff saga, which hinges on whether removal of batch codes on products amounts to them being 'damaged'. If it doesn't, parallel importers can go ahead and sell them. Noble says that this has many implications. In the event of a health scare, for example, manufacturers might have to withdraw products globally as they would not be able to trace the faulty batch. It also means customer guarantees on quality and safety, which are arguably part of the brand promise, effectively disappear.

So what can brands do to protect themselves? By fighting public battles, they do their reputation no favours. Levi's Christie admits that Tesco has scored a PR coup by positioning itself as the consumer champion in the court battle, but adds that Levi's had no choice but to try to control its brands' distribution.

One way of protecting a reputation is to invest in brand security technology. Companies such as DeLaRue offer solutions that allow brand owners, retailers and even consumers to track and trace products, so that the origin can always be guaranteed. Chris Clark, business development director of DeLaRue, says: 'At the moment there is too much fire-fighting going on, such as raids of warehouses when a problem occurs. It's all very well investing in above-the-line advertising, but brand owners also need to ensure their product is going where it should be.'

Another solution is for companies to tighten up on their brands' distribution. It might see a short-term sales fall, but the strategy provides long-term benefits. In June, Gucci announced a rescue plan for its struggling Yves Saint Laurent brand, which involves cutting licensed manufacturers from nearly 200 to just 12. Yves Saint Laurent had expanded so widely in the 80s that it now appears on a range of products from socks and baseball caps to plastic shoes – arguably losing its exclusivity in the process. Burberry has carried out a similar exercise and has successfully repositioned itself as an exclusive, must-have label. This strategy doesn't only apply to luxury goods. Gillette has announced a new plan to control its supply chain more strictly and match production to consumption in an effort to protect its brand. And Christie says Levi's is taking a hard look at its distribution.

Philip Evans, principal policy adviser, Consumers' Association, believes consumers are much more cynical about prices than they used to be, and brand owners are out of touch with the way shoppers and retail are changing. 'It's what is known as the "Florida and Calais" effect. People used to go on holiday to Spain and Greece and they would understand that prices were cheaper because the standard of living seemed lower than ours. But now they go to Florida and Calais and they can't believe that it's so much cheaper – people coming back from holiday abroad are much more questioning.'

'Brand owners think they control their brands' image, but it's simply not true, particularly when you can buy stuff they've over-ordered or last year's goods – with their blessing – in designer outlets or discount stores such as Matalan or TK Maxx. Do they think people don't go to these places? The average punter doesn't know or care that it's last year's stock, unless they are a real brand obsessive. John Noble, director, British Brands Group, believes consumers' interests are not served by allowing grey market imports. They would lose out in the long-run, he says, because of a lack of quality control and the fact that brands' very existence would be threatened.

Source: Alexandra Jardine, *Marketing*, 9 July 2001

CONSUMERS' CONCEPT OF 'SELF-IMAGE'

When consumers choose between brands they rationally consider practical issues about a brand's functional capabilities. At the same time they evaluate different brands' personalities, forming a view which fits the image with which they wish to be associated. In fact, image can be seen to be the sum of impressions about the brand – as that which it is perceived to be and, at the same time, what it is perceived to signify about the purchaser/user. When two competing brands are perceived as being equal in terms of their physical capabilities, the brand that comes closest to enhancing the consumer's self-concept will be chosen. Consumers look to brands not only for what they can do, but also to help say something about themselves to their peer groups. Rolex watches are not worn simply for their functional excellence, but also to say something about who the owner is. According to de Chernatony and McDonald (1998), the symbolic nature of brands increases the attraction for consumers as they:

- help set social scenes and enable people to mix with each other more easily;
- enable consumers to convey messages about themselves;
- provide a basis for a better understanding of the way people act;
- help consumers to say something to themselves.

In effect, consumers are transmitting subtle messages to others by purchasing and displaying the use of particular brands in the hope that their reference groups decode the messages in a positive and acceptable way. This can be related to the sportswear market in the UK where shoppers identify with the leisure associations of different brands. According to Neely (1997), brand loyalty for sportswear is high in the UK, especially for the upmarket brands which confer a certain cachet. Consumers hold a view of themselves – what is called their 'self-image' – and buy brands which conform to that image. Consumers may be said to admit brands and their 'personalities' into their social circle, in much the same way as consumers enjoy having like-minded people around them. When friends or colleagues admire someone's newly bought brand, that person feels pleased that the brand reinforces his or her self-image and will continue to use the brand. The situation in which consumers find themselves will dictate, to some extent, the type of image that they wish to project. Through anticipating and subsequently evaluating the people that they will meet at a particular event, consumers then seek brands to reflect the situational self-image that they wish to display.

BRAND PROPOSITION

The term 'proposition' is used for a set of statements which summarizes the combination of positioning and personality. The proposition allows the brand to emerge from the fuzziness of the competition. However, the secret of success is to have a simple proposition which consumers understand; brand propositions which are complicated or inconsistent will simply confuse consumers.

As part of this concept, two non-functional aspects of brands have been highlighted and are discussed below: *brand image* and *brand identity*.

Brand image

Image is the outcome of the consumer's interpretation of the brand. In a postmodern world this is all about the constructed meanings which offer symbolic identity as to what individuals 'want to be' and are convinced they can be through marketing communication and personal experience processes. Brands are complex and their identity is often regarded by consumers as incorporating human-like characteristics. Such characteristics are projected on them by consumers who experience the brands not only as functional products or services, but also as bundles of associations. Consumers 'see', 'hear', 'smell', 'taste' and 'get gut feelings' about different brands. This profile or 'essence' is called 'brand image'. It represents the consumer counterpart perception of brand personality which, as has been discussed, has to be endowed by the brand marketer. It is important to understand that when a brand image is developed, through communication and experience, consumers do not judge the image in relation only to other stores – they also adopt best-in-class processes. This means that if other service providers outside of retail – such as British Airways or Marriott Hotels – provide world class standards these can be benchmarked as the best-in-class expectation for the way retailers should deal with their customers.

Brand identity

Brand identity is the central concept in promoting a brand. Identity comprises durability, coherence and realism, embodying the personality of the brand. It sends out signals which the consumer decodes and interprets in terms of image. Identity is the solid enduring concept of the brand and is not subject to the idealism, fickleness or opportunism of brand image. A graphic description used is that of the *brand fingerprint*, the unique

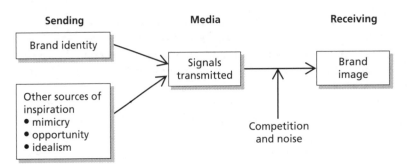

Fig. 12.2 Identity and image
Source: Kapferer, 1992

identity of the company's offering. The power and recognition of brands has become so powerful for some brands that in certain circumstances the brand logo – even without the name – will suffice to provide a clear brand identity. Nike, for example, can rely on its 'swoosh' logo to promote its products. In the UK at least 80 per cent of consumers associate the swoosh symbol with Nike – which is higher than for the recognition of the 'golden arches' as standing for McDonald's (Snowden, 1997).

Figure 12.2 shows the relationship between identity and image.

BRAND NAME

A brand name is that component of the brand which consists of words or letters to provide a means by which the company can be recognized and distinguished from other companies in the marketplace. It is the part of the brand which can be vocalized, unlike the trade mark which is a symbol or design. A name cannot make or break a retailer or company. What matters is how well a retailer's stores, merchandise or services meet its customers' needs. However, a brand name is imbued with associations which conjure up an overall brand image. The choice of a name is only one part of the overall company strategy that has to be backed up by a sophisticated and cohesive branding programme. Consumers normally seek to process only a few rich pieces of information as quickly as possible. Labelling presents shorthand pieces of this information which can highlight key points and facilitate brand choice. A good brand name can communicate a brand's promise and potential. Brand names thus facilitate the consumer purchase decision by acting as a useful and convenient shorthand device. There are instances where there are a number of sub-brands, which also act in this shorthand way to confer association with the brand. For example, BigMac is a coded way of linking a sub-brand to the McDonald's master brand name or Miss Selfridge to that of Selfridges.

Consumers have restrictive cognitive capacities which are protected from information overload by perceptual selectivity. This channels consumers' attention on those attributes considered to be important. To process the minimum of information, consumers develop ways of coping with the extensive – even excessive – information available. It is widely accepted that consumers have a preference for using a brand name above all other informational cues in order to make a decision. There is a school of thought which views the consumer as an efficient information searcher and processor, relying on a brand name as an informational memory device. Through the use of the brand name, the consumer is able to recall numerous attributes, for example quality, availability, guarantee, advertising support, and so on. This emphasizes how vital it is for marketing managers to communicate associations for the brand and affect the emotional memory in the consumer's mind in order to form the brand entity successfully. The retailer's name alone, no matter how apt, is not going to ensure a company's success unless there is a well-co-ordinated marketing and communications programme in order to build the brand around the name.

BRAND AWARENESS

People will often buy a familiar brand because they are comfortable with things familiar. There may be an assumption that the brand that is familiar is probably reliable, in business to stay, and of reasonable quality. A recognised brand will thus often be selected in preference to an unknown brand. The awareness factor is particularly important in contexts in which the brand must first enter the evoked set – it must be one of the brands that are evaluated. An unknown brand usually has little chance (Aaker, 1991).

Creating awareness of a brand is one of the biggest challenges for marketers; to put their product in a customer's 'evoked set' of brand options. In Fig. 12.3 a customer's evoked set is shown by 'top of the mind' recall; this is the optimal awareness of a brand. This pyramid is only representative as there are no established scales or measurements connected with it, but it does serve as a conceptual framework.

Marketing strategy should take the 'evoked set' into consideration because the actual choices of individual consumers depend crucially upon which brands are considered and evaluated by consumers and which are not. According to research it is found that consumers generally carry only a limited number of brands in their 'evoked set' – often no more than three to five brands.

Consumers do not necessarily select brands only from their 'evoked set' nor is their selection process logical, but if buyers recall a company's brand first the likelihood of them purchasing it increases. This concept accounts for the enormous amounts of money companies spend in buying out a well-branded competitor, to erase the visibility and reinforcement of alternative brands in the marketplace.

Advertising is often aimed at facilitating the growth of brand awareness. Furthermore, it can develop an image and manipulate consumers' perception, which is

Fig. 12.3 The awareness pyramid
Source: Aaker, 1991, p. 62. Adapted with the permission of the Free Press, a Division of Simon & Schuster, Inc. from *Managing Brand Equity: Capitalizing on the Value of a Brand Name* by David A. Aaker, Copyright © 1991 by David A. Aaker

fundamental to building values over and above the price–value relationship. Brand advertising communicates the consumer-oriented benefits of owning, displaying or consuming a brand, which increases confidence in the selection process. The process is enhanced by the shopper being provided with bags which communicate the store logo. However, the problem facing the marketer is that consumers are selective in their search for brand information and may distort some of the information to ensure it matches their existing beliefs. All brand promotional activity must, therefore, be regularly scrutinized, to gauge the extent to which consumers 'correctly' interpret the desired message.

Good brand advertising ensures that the perceived brand image is not product-based but overrides it in its influence on the target market's mental processes. Brand advertising can also aid repeat purchase and brand loyalty. Advertising's major role is to reinforce and protect brands which, in turn, reinforces and holds market share. The promotion branding role is very much about reinforcing core values and keeping the brand uppermost in the choice process.

MANAGING BRANDS OVER THEIR LIFE CYCLES

Life-cycle theorists believe that a brand is launched, wins market share, enjoys a period of maturity and then declines. These theorists are wrong insofar as they predict an inevitable decline of a brand. The product life cycle refers to the product not the brand. There is no reason why a brand cannot adapt to new technologies and move from mature into relaunch or new growth markets. Therefore, a brand that has been managed properly can extend the timeframe associated with the product life cycle. We may find that well-managed brands are evidence that some brands have longevity. The leading brands are constantly fine-tuned to keep them updated, making it possible for them to survive more than one generation.

Compared with the literature on how to manage a product or service over its life cycle, there is relatively little written about how to manage a brand's image over time. Brands which successfully stand the test of time build up a considerable amount of goodwill with their consumers, so much so that when sales start to fall it should not be automatically assumed that they are in a terminal state and investment must be cut. It is less expensive to revitalize an established brand than it is to develop and launch a new brand consumers are less familiar with. Some brand owners become complacent about their brands, almost preferring to ignore the threat of competitors until it becomes too late. Having lost contact with their consumers, they respond to competitive threats in a less effective manner, for example through pricing.

If a brand is to survive, within the notion of product life cycle, it must first be recognized as symbolizing lasting values. An example is Gillette. Its core value in its 90 years of existence had been performance in shaving – it had become a symbol of manhood. In the 1980s disposable razors entered the market, offering convenience and cheapness. Gillette responded according to classical product marketing and introduced its own disposable razor. As a result, the Gillette brand name became subsidiary to the product name and the traditional values attached to the brand were being lost. In order to restore its position, Gillette stopped advertising disposables and emphasized systems. Its successful slogan 'The best a man can get' was an expression of what the Gillette brand had always stood for. To manage a brand properly there is a need to ensure the marketing effort does not endanger the brand's development.

Sales promotion tactics that may endanger brand building

1 While brand-building activities such as advertisements are very much individual creations, sales promotions are easily replicated by competing firms.

2 Strategic activities can be thought of as building up brand loyalty. Sales promotions may be viewed as the reverse: helping to break down competitors' brand loyalty.

3 Sales promotions often cause a catch-22 situation, in which competitors must retaliate or suffer losses. When a promotions/price-cutting cycle begins it is most difficult to stop; both the customer and the trade become used to it and begin planning their purchases around the promotion cycle – they perceive it as part of the standard product, price or terms of trade. Kotler suggests that 'probably there is risk in putting a well-known brand on promotion more than 30% of the time' (Kotler, 1997). That is why Marks & Spencer almost never have a sale and Harrods only has one a year. They are protecting the brand name and its position.

4 An emphasis on price as a retail strategy can put pressure on organizations to reduce the quality, features and services offered. In extreme situations, a retailer or the merchandise may revert to the status of a commodity as brand added values decline in importance. One danger is that sales promotions can seem even more attractive for their short-term impact, though consumers can quickly become bored with one particular promotion.

5 Sustained sales promotions also cause serious erosion of profitability, which highlights the need to limit them. They can also engender a degree of boredom and acceptability which undermines the impact of the sales promotion effort.

6 Poorly presented sales promotion campaigns may create negative images for the brand. Though sales promotions are not the only brand debilitating device, they remain one of the most visible and often used.

Decisions over branding are strategic issues. The most astute tactical decisions will only build real brand strength if a strategic view underlies all activity. A brand needs to evolve slowly and yet there is the responsibility to consider every response to unco-ordinated short-term stimuli. A tactical brand strategy has to be associated with the outcome and impact on the brand. Companies which employ 'brand managers' to cover an individual product line very often have a high turnover in personnel. This may be dangerous as too many changes in advertising strategy or programmes, or in decisions on brand extension, promotion or discounts, confuses distributors as well as consumers. It is significant that brands which have maintained a continuous, consistent message are those belonging to businesses with clear strategies and sustained consistency of brand management. Decisions by these brand managers should have led to successful brands.

SUCCESSFUL BRANDS

De Chernatony and McDonald (1998) describe the necessary attributes of a successful brand:

> A successful brand is an identifiable product, service, person or place augmented in such a way that the buyer, or user, perceives relevant, unique added values which match their needs most closely. Its success results from being able to sustain these added values against competitors.

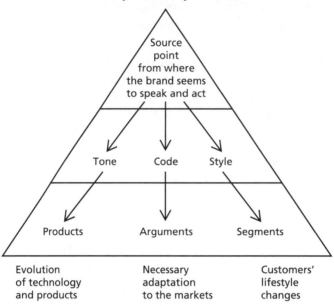

Permanence

Core values, sources of inspiration or
continuity and identity of the brand

Fig. 12.4 The pyramidal model of a brand
Source: Kapferer, 1992

Successful brands therefore are required to have unique added values. Examples of added value are:

- rituals (Moët et Chandon champagne at celebrations);
- symbols (Perrier as a statement about a sophisticated consumer);
- heritage of good (Kellogg's as a reflection of time-honoured family values);
- aloofness (Carlsberg's time spent brewing and storing);
- belonging (Carling Black Label as one of the crowd);
- legend (Sandeman, Johny Walker black label);
- quality and trust (M&S food);
- exclusivity (Gucci, Harrods).

To succeed, brand marketers have to ensure that their current added values are appropriate to the preferences of their intended consumers.

Kapferer (1992) introduces the pyramidal model of a brand as a means of successfully managing a brand through time (*see* Fig. 12.4). At the top of the pyramid is the brand's 'core value', its 'essence' or 'kernel'; in the middle are the styles and codes – a brand's specific means of conveying a message in words and images; the lower level represents the brand's communication themes – its current advertising position.

The art of managing a brand over time depends on brand managers being totally aware of what their brand's kernel is and realizing that this must not be changed. At the same time, they must beware of two extremes: an 'excess of democracy' – relying too much on the consumer to dictate how the brand should evolve; and an 'excess of code' – fear of changing the brand. Kentucky Fried Chicken faced increased competition during the 1990s from newly launched, chicken fast-food outlets as well as from McDonald's and Burger King who introduced chicken products following the BSE scare. It also had to contend with the growing problem of fried food being perceived as less healthy. Evolving the brand to KFC, in order to be able to stand out from the new competition, and introducing grilled, baked and rotisserie-cooked chicken solved the dilemma.

BRAND UPDATING

Kapferer (1992) maintains that a brand is updated not, as many think, by communication but through its products and meaningful actions. For instance, technical progress alerts the public to a brand's revival and intentions.

Branded products with long histories, for example Kellogg's various cereals, have been forced subtly to adjust their offerings to keep them relevant to the changing market conditions. For some companies this has been little more than adjusting packaging to update the product; for others it has meant putting the brand's core values in a different context. For example, Lucozade used to promote their drink as providing energy for the sick. When social trends indicated a shift towards a more active population in the early 1980s, Lucozade adapted successfully by presenting the brand as a source of energy for highly active people.

However, updating can have its dangers. It must be undertaken in line with customer expectations. Coca-Cola's move into the caffeine-free Coca-Cola Light was one which achieved consumers' acceptance because the product was essentially unchanged, but the creation of New Coca-Cola, an attempt to introduce a totally new taste, was at odds with the original brand's identity and it had to be dropped.

Some of the largest brand owners have been complacent about their brands in the past, appearing to ignore the changing surrounding environment and the threat of their competitors until it was almost too late. The notion of brand revival was then introduced. Babycham, for example, suffered from its lack of acknowledgement of different social situations and changing consumers. In 1993 the brand was forced to 'grow up' as it entered the decline stage in the product life cycle. Gaymers launched the Babycham revival. The name has remained the same but the product has been reformulated; the packaging has been changed and the well-known fawn logo revised. Brand line extensions have also been introduced to suit different consumer tastes – Xtra Dry Babycham, for example.

Ideally a product should not be allowed to get so close to terminal decline and it must be recognized that initial market research for a brand, however thorough, has limitations in that it only investigates attitudes, beliefs and social norms at that one specific point in time. However successful a brand is, its managers have to be constantly vigilant about potential rivals and their tactics, and need to adapt strategy accordingly.

Pricing and brands

In 1993 Philip Morris cut the price of the company's flagship brand of cigarettes, Marlboro, by as much as 25 per cent to stem the loss of sales and market share to lower priced rivals. City analysts criticized the move as 'killing the brand'. Although the brand

Monsoon – How should Monsoon go about expansion?

Monsoon has carved a distinctive niche on the high street with an ethnic, Liberty-meets-Goa-hippie style, described by the company as 'deluxe boho chic'. This positioning has been conveyed through much in-store panache. The little above-the-line activity it has carried out has mainly been created in-house.

Chairman Peter Simon started importing brightly coloured ethnic clothes from the Far East and India in 1972, naming his store Monsoon because he was born in Sri Lanka during such a storm. The company soon branched into houseware and accessories, and opened the first Accessorize store in 1984. But while Monsoon, which floated in 1998, has been largely successful, and its latest results, announced on Monday, show like-for-like sales up by 15% for the year to May 26, it faces strong competition in the high street from Jigsaw, Karen Millen and a reju-venated Laura Ashley. With all its product sourced in the Far East, it is also suffering from the strong pound. It is thought that Monsoon needs to widen the appeal of its brand and communicate its strengths to a younger generation of women in order to expand. So how can it create a storm? We asked Juliet Warkentin, former Arcadia marketing chief and editor of *Marie Claire* – Brands such as Monsoon that are not owned by big retail groups sometimes fall off the marketing and advertising world's radar. Retailers with store portfolios of 100 to 150 stores usually focus on getting their core skills right. Service, card marketing, positioning are all critical in converting a browser into a sale.

With all that retail floor space and all those win-dows, clothing retailers are often lazy marketers. If the sun is shining and the collection is good, who needs marketing? But with an aggressive growth strategy planned both in the UK and overseas, Monsoon now stretches beyond its signature floaty, high street/ethnic dresses into homeware and kids clothing and an extremely successful sister brand in Accessorize. It has to start thinking carefully about the clarity of its brand position. The company's deci-sion to focus on marketing is absolutely right – it signals a move from thinking just about the product to thinking about the customer as well.

Lindsey Roberts [said] his guess is that Monsoon is currently doing better than most retailers. The keys to its success include being genuinely differentiated on the high street, remaining true to its core values and being content to dominate a niche. In fact, it dominates not just one niche, but two – creating a new market with Accessorize was a masterstroke.

Go blindfolded into most fashion retailers and you'd struggle to know where you are when you take it off. Not so with Monsoon. This is a real brand that has perennially succeeded in connecting its brand name with its product, by taking the best of the ethnic influence in fabrics and transforming it into wearable, glamorous and contemporary fashion. Right now, the stores are teeming with jewel colours and spangling brocades – just going in gives you a lift.

Source: Alexandra Jardine, *Marketing*, 2 August 2001

dropped in value by £2.4 billion, the real issue in this case was not what it cost, but what it would have cost the company if they had done nothing. Higher price is associated with higher quality and some brands are positioned to be expensive. During the 1980s, price was considered a purely tactical marketing tool. Since 1981, premium lager brand Stella Artois has used the promotional line 'reassuringly expensive' in its advertising. The phrase explains to the consumer that the reason for the brand's high price is the quality of the ingredients.

A more common approach to using price to defend the brand is illustrated in the battle that has been raging between different UK newspapers. Both *The Times* and the *Daily Telegraph* have used price as a short-term weapon to defend market share. However, once a company has decided to embark on the road of using price as a tactical weapon, the process of increasing price is made all the more difficult. In most cases, tak-ing the price war option signifies that the company has failed to build a sustainable com-petitive edge and price disparities only serve to devalue the brand.

Deciding whether or not to choose price as a marketing tool will depend on the role of the brand within the company's portfolio. For example, it would not be an option for Coca-Cola to introduce price as a weapon against rival colas. The one big advantage they have is that of image, and their pricing points reflect part of that perception. To destroy that position could lead to commercial and strategic suicide. Richard Branson's Virgin Group attacked the giant cola manufacturers in 1994. The Virgin Cola Brand was launched in November 1994 mainly through Tesco, Iceland and the Thresher chain, with an estimated market share of about 10 per cent (Fagan, 1995). This indicates the strength of the existing Virgin brand in the launch of a new product.

COUNTERFEIT OR COPYCAT BRANDS

Counterfeit trade marks are especially dangerous to brands which rely upon a high price to give them a superior image to the consumer. Cheap imitations lead to proliferation and hence dilute the brand image. Manufacturers are quick to use legislative action wherever possible so as to kill off such imitations. A more generalized threat has been 'copycat' brands which, until recently, have been difficult to fight on legal grounds. These are brands which so closely copy the packaging of an established brand that the consumer is seduced into choosing them, either because they think they are the original brand or because the copy's price is lower and it is assumed represents better value than the original.

However, the Trade Marks Act 1994 gives some protection to the initial brand. Any sign can be registered as a trade mark if it can be represented graphically, and an important new facility is the registration of the shape of goods or their packaging, for example the distinctive prismatic shape of Toblerone or the classic Coca-Cola bottle. The recent Act greatly strengthens a trade mark owner's rights. Previously, if a very similar trade mark were used it had to be proved that the public would be confused between the two marks. This is no longer the case. Secondly, a trade mark can be infringed verbally, not just in printed or other physical form. Thirdly, where a trade mark is registered for particular goods or services, and has acquired a strong reputation, the owner of the trade mark can, in some circumstances, prevent it from being used with other goods or services. Finally, action can be taken against a person who applies a trade mark to labelling, packaging or business documents when they ought to know that the use of the trade mark is unauthorized. However, trade mark owners must proceed cautiously before making an allegation since any person who is threatened by court proceedings for registered trade mark infringement without justification is able to seek compensation from the trade mark owner.

OWN-BRANDS

On an international basis own-brand retail power is most developed in the UK where Boots, M&S and the supermarkets have led the way. Own-brands are the names given to consumer products produced by, or on behalf of, distributors and sold under the distributor's own name or trade mark through the distributor's own outlet. The development of own-brands has reinforced the position of large-scale concentrated retailers due to the extra control they gain over the value chain. Own-brands, sometimes referred to as own-label brands (but this has restricted meaning related simply to groceries), evolved initially as a cheap and inferior alternative to manufacturers' brands. There are four main types of own-brands and their characteristics that we can recognize:

- *Generic* – simple low-cost plain packaging with no branding but may have the retailer's name. Typically unadvertised and offered as a lower grade alternative purchase. Will be more popular in poorer areas and in times of recession.

- *Price-led retailer brand* – the name of the retailer is shown and the packaging is designed overtly to communicate the impression of value and of lower price. The strategy is based upon providing better value than the manufacturer brands and to reduce their power by setting a lower price. Tend to be based upon products which offer large volume product purchases.

- *Quality-led own-brand* – the packaging is designed to reflect product quality and to compete directly with established manufacturer brands. The strategy is to attack any product positioned as a close competitor, build brand image of retailer, expand product assortment and increase margins.

- *Exclusive own-brand* – this is manufacturer based and produced to be sold through one agreed retailer. This is a selected niche strategy often based upon differentiation in order to achieve higher margins.

The Co-operative movement in the 1870s initiated the first own-brand products. As time passed own-brands grew to replace generic brands, which were commodity foods or household lines which were sold in basic packaging. In the 1970s generic brands were perceived to be similar to own-brands and this aided their initial launch. By the late 1980s, own-brands had replaced the generic brands which had taken up shelf space and brought in lower margins. With the expansion in the number of supermarkets, own-brands became more prolific. This occurred at a time when there was little differentiation in the marketplace and there were a number of similar products. In addition, the economic conditions in the late 1980s made consumers more price conscious, while at the same time own-brands were improved in relation to their quality and packaging to such an extent that they became brands in their own right. By the 1990s, own-brands in Tesco and Sainsbury accounted for over 50 per cent of all sales. The own-brand concept is thus a broader concept than that of manufacturer brands as it embraces both the store proposition and that of individual product lines. It should be remembered that Marks & Spencer's St Michael's clothing, as a brand, had for decades been 100 per cent of all sales. If a retailer such as Marks & Spencer can inspire confidence in a brand as an own-label brand then the company has a distinct advantage in also being able to raise prices. The company is considered to be Britain's largest own-brand retailer but has no manufacturing capacity within its direct span of control. This type of own-label strategy is not easy to achieve and has required Marks & Spencer to have complete domination over its suppliers. The St Michael label was backed by stringent buying and manufacturing specifications. More recently Northern Foods became the supplier for St Michael foods, operating what is termed a mixed brand policy in producing own labels and a number of well-known brands.

The development of own-brands may have certain advantages, some of which are listed below.

1 The exclusivity of a good quality own-brand, at the right price, can boost store patronage. There is, therefore, the benefit of improved store loyalty due to consumers

seeking out a popular own-brand. Also, when the retailer brand is on the packaging this acts as a constant reminder when the product is in the cupboard or in the home and this can reinforce brand loyalty.

2 Goods carrying an own label cannot be directly compared on price or attributes in other retail outlets. The result is that own-label offers greater price flexibility and does not need to be repriced as often as some other lines.

3 If the own-brand is well received, the store image is enhanced. In fact, the two reinforce each other as there is a circular reinforcement effect of one on the other.

4 A range of own-brand products which offers advantages over the competition will attract higher levels of custom and lead to purchase from a wider range of the store's products. This will consequently lead to higher profits through increased sales and the ability to achieve high margins.

5 Own-label products are free from the restrictions which relate to methods of display, promotion or pricing which often apply to manufacturers' brands.

6 Supermarket own-brands can become powerful enough for the company to place pressure on some of the major branded manufacturers to make concessions to avoid their brands being delisted.

7 Own-brands can be used as a co-ordinated range or positioned to fill gaps left by the competition. There is also the opportunity to create an own-brand which is positioned to appeal to the specific tastes of a store's customers.

8 Launch and distribution costs for new products are far lower than those of conventional manufacturers. The shorter, cheaper route allows for less risk and opens up the market to innovation.

One way that retailers have tried to achieve the advantage of the image of well-known brands is by use of copycat packaging, but the recent Trade Marks Act (as discussed above) will seriously inhibit this and we may see a decline in proliferation of own-brands which are hardly distinguishable in packaging and design from their national brand counterparts. Products which are largely image based, such as Coca-Cola, are protected from the threat of price-cutting rivals by the consumers' desire to support the status brand. The retailer danger is that consumers will buy rivals' products unknowingly, if they are lookalikes, and that the 'in' brand will shift from being theirs to that of a newer younger rival, for example Virgin.

On the other hand, manufacturers such as Mars are being forced into own-label ventures due to the problems which may face their business if they decide not to co-operate with the larger retailers. However, the own-label phenomenon is probably a serious threat – not only to the survival of a particular brand, but also to the very concept of branding. Manufacturers invest heavily in research and development before launching a brand, and the price has to reflect this. If own-labels can step in and capitalize on this investment, it is impossible for the initial brand to survive unless the manufacturer can convince the consumer that the price premium is worth paying. This is becoming increasingly difficult as the public acquire a more sophisticated approach to purchasing. The more functional the product, the more threatened it is. For example, BP tried to counteract the price cutting of the new entrant rivals – the multiples – by claiming that BP's petrol contained engine cleaning detergents, but consumers did not acknowledge this product differentiation as important. Within a product category all brands may be perceived as similar and, in this case, all petrol is apparently regarded as essentially the same.

MINICASE 12.3

Back to cheap and cheerful – Own-Label

Private-label products – also known as own-label or store-brand products – are rapidly stealing market share from established brands. In part, this is because own-brand products are usually priced well below their branded equivalents. But private label is no longer competing on price alone. Exclusive deals with big retailers and heavy investment in product innovation have made private-label brands more attractive for the cost-conscious shopper.

Private-label goods are not new. It is more than 20 years since Sam Walton, the founder of Wal-Mart, introduced a pet food called Ol' Roy, named after his favourite hunting dog. The product now outsells the big national brands. But the US slowdown has encouraged US retailers to devote fresh attention to a part of their business that offers higher-than-average profit margins and a chance to differentiate themselves from their rivals. A recent JP Morgan analysis of the grocery industry found this month that store brands are gaining market share in 55 of the 61 categories it monitored.

The businesses suffering most from the incursion of private label are often those where the market leader has stumbled and failed to keep an old product up to date, such as Campbell's Soup. In part, this is because private label has shed its cheap and cheerful image and large stores such as Wal-Mart have invested heavily to ensure that their own-branded produce keeps up with innovations in their categories. On rare occasions, private-label suppliers have even beaten their branded rivals to the punch. Co-operative Group, the UK retailer, rushed out liquid detergent capsules before Procter & Gamble and Unilever, the two giants of the laundry industry, could bring their own new products to market.

Dan Barry of Merrill Lynch says retailers are focusing on investing in such innovations more than ever: 'The quality of private-label [goods] is dramatically better than it was 10 years ago.' But private-label goods serve another purpose for retailers: 'They are using it at the opening price level, where the branded guys don't have what they need.' In short, as companies such as Procter & Gamble and Unilever have sought to increase returns by focusing on high-margin, top-of-the-range goods, they have neglected the cheaper end of the market.

A.G. Lafley, chief executive of P&G, says he sees private label as a relatively small problem in most of the group's categories, which range from nappies to toothpaste. 'We don't want to be in the commodity end of the market. We want to be in the differentiated end of the market,' he says. He admits, however, that competition from private label has been a factor in considering which businesses it no longer wants to be in. 'People ask why we're getting out of Crisco [cooking oil],' he says. 'In cooking oils you have a couple of brands and a lot of private label, because it is essentially a commodity.' Mr Lafley says that P&G decided it no longer wanted to compete in such a business as more consumers switch to olive oil.

Consumer-branded companies are also responding by seeking private-label status for some of their own products. Retailers such as Target and manufacturers such as P&G have signed agreements ensuring that certain products will appear only in certain stores. While store brands are gaining significant ground in the US, they have never been as large a force in North America as they have in much of Europe. Ahold says private label contributes one-third of its revenues in the Netherlands and Scandinavia, compared with just one-fifth in the US. In the UK, own-label goods often account for more than half of a supermarket's sales.

Edited source: Andrew Edgecliffe-Johnson, *Financial Times*, 19 June 2001

CORPORATE BRANDING

There is a school of thought that believes that brand building will increasingly mean developing the whole company as the brand. The service industries, which include retail, are ideally placed to produce this change because it is difficult for them to sustain a differentiated, competitive product advantage over their competitors. Thus, it will become increasingly important to position organizations as 'brands' in the minds of actual and potential consumers.

According to King (1991), increasingly the company brand will become the main discriminator. That is, consumers' choice of what they buy will depend rather less on an evaluation of the functional benefits to them of a product or service and rather more on their assessment of the people in the company behind it, their skills, attitudes, behaviour, design, style, language, greenism, altruism, modes of communication, speed of response, and so on – the whole company culture could be said to reflect this.

The communication of a company brand is necessarily targeted at a wider variety of 'audiences' rather than simply consumers. Relevant audiences include shareholders, suppliers, government agencies, banks, employees and potential employees, as well as immediate customers. In short, all the company's stockholders. For Hankinson and Cowking (1993) these audiences should understand:

- what the company is;
- what the company does;
- how the company does it.

From a company's point of view, de Chernatony and McDonald (1998) state:

> a characteristic of successful brands is the way that their position has been precisely defined and communicated internally. Everyone working on a particular brand is regularly reminded of the brand's positioning and an integrated, committed approach is adopted, ensuring that the correct balance of resources is consistently applied.

In essence, brand building involves designing and controlling all aspects of a company which may require new initiatives and activities outside of the traditional skills of the marketing department and the agencies that it engages. This is an all-pervasive approach requiring constant and convincing communication with several audiences offering positive images of product or company values, styles and behaviour. This is becoming more, rather than less complex. As it is becomes increasingly necessary for companies to grow, through extension, brand acquisition or brand alliance, we increasingly live in an age whereby large corporations need to use corporate brand management to build brand portfolios. According to Fisher (2001) Unilever, the Anglo-Dutch consumer products group – with brands including Birds Eye foods, Ben & Jerry's ice cream and Lipton tea – is restructuring with a brand strategy that involves greater focus on its top 400 brands, taking into account the supply chain and innovation areas. It has already reduced its brands to around 900 from 1600.

Corporate brand building also needs to be highly controlled, especially where there are retail franchises involved. Closely managed franchises, such as McDonald's, are an example of where the corporate brand is not owned by the retailer. In order to control the standards and service delivery there is very strong control of all aspects of the retail experience and service delivery to protect the brand equity. This will be legally binding and enforceable through a franchise agreement. It will be found that protection of the brand can also apply in a non-franchise environment, such as a Bang & Olufsen outlet where an exclusive retailer not owned by the manufacturer utilizes the manufacturer's brand.

If a company wants to support a corporate brand it can decide upon one of three options:

- a central hub system;
- an endorsed brand system;
- a hybrid approach.

A central hub system will place the brand at the heart of the business and all products, services and communications are managed with the same brand name, corporate family identity and corporate brand values. For example, Richard Branson has utilized the Virgin brand name across the whole of his business empire. The benefits are obvious in that there is the benefit of goodwill, economies of scale in brand building and instant credibility when the company launches its new products. Therefore, the benefits accrue to the centre and are transmitted out along the spokes. The difficulty with the central structure is that each business has to adapt easily to the whole breadth of the business to ensure fit with the core brand values. More importantly, if there is any negative communication from one part of the spoke system it may lead to a dilution of corporate brand equity for the whole group.

An endorsed brand system is where the corporate brand's values (trust, security, competence, etc.) are used to endorse product brands within the portfolio. For example, 3M with Post-it and Scotch Tape which is endorsed by having the 3M corporate association.

A hybrid approach by its very nature is a mixture of different approaches whereby competitive advantage of the corporate name is subsumed within other leading brands. For example, Nestlé, the largest food group in the world, have grouped their portfolio into ten global banner brands such as Perrier, Carnation, etc.

TYPES OF BRAND EXTENSION

A brand can be stretched in the process of product development, by introducing minor product variations (line extension), as in the extension of the Coca-Cola line to include Diet Coke. This approach has been used by Gap, which was founded in America in 1969 and in 1986 stretched its brand to launch GapKids, having identified the growing importance of the children's market. More recently in 1990 they expanded to BabyGap and diversified into aftershave, perfumes and deodorants. A report of leading consumer product companies in 1993 found that 75 per cent of new product introductions were line extensions. Another example of the way extension is used is exhibited by the introduction of flanker brands to monopolize shelf space in retail outlets, for example Cherry Coke, Cadbury's Twirl and Procter & Gamble's different washing powder brands. Completely new products can be introduced. A brand may also be stretched in the process of market development, when the original brand (and product) is launched into segments of the existing market and then into new markets (brand leverage) – as in the extension of Yamaha from motorbikes to musical instruments. The Tesco supermarket

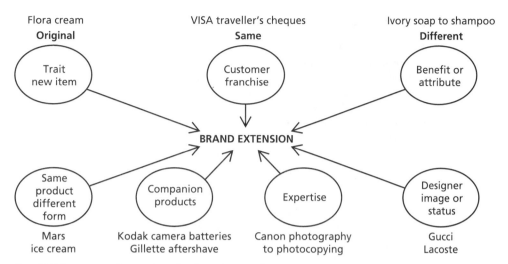

Fig. 12.5 Leverage alternatives for brand extensions
Source: Tauber, 1988

chain extended its brand to petrol retailing and gained very good publicity for the brand due to low pricing policies and a campaign supporting unleaded petrol.

In many cases, the stretching is a combination of both factors – for example, Dunhill, where the original brand product (cigarettes) was simultaneously extended into a new segment (pipes), a related product category (lighters), and over time into totally new product sectors (clothing, accessories and cosmetics).

After studying a sample of 276 brand extensions over a long period, Tauber (1988) concluded that there are seven types of leverage, which he illustrated graphically (*see* Fig. 12.5).

Advantages of brand extension

- When market entry barriers are high or rising, brand extension is a means by which a company can achieve growth by capitalizing on its existing brand assets.

- It gives ready-made and lower-cost access to an existing distribution and retail operation. For example, traditional menswear brands such as Diesel, Paul Smith and Ted Baker have all incorporated womenswear into their ranges.

- There may be economies in promotion and advertising, since there is no need to build public awareness of the name.

- The use of an existing brand name gives own products or new businesses an instant position and reputation. The customer has an immediate awareness of the brand, and thus has existing confidence transferred to the new product on offer.

- The perceived quality of the existing retail offer is transferred by the customer to the new product.

- A recognizable brand name reassures a prospective purchaser that the retail offer is well supported and hence encourages initial purchases, for example, General Motors or Ford car dealers.

Disadvantages of brand extension

- Brand extension may discourage innovation and may lead to companies producing too many 'lookalike' products.
- The brand extension may weaken the core brand by diluting its appeal, for example, Pierre Cardin's extension into too many other product areas.
- The company may waste resources producing products which are very similar to the original, and which may gain their sales at the expense of the original (cannibalization).
- There is a temptation for the company to rely on the power of the core brand name and hence not give sufficient financial support to the extension.
- Any bad publicity for the original product will affect any other products with the same brand name (spillover). For example, the failure of the Sinclair C5 electric vehicle added to the demise of the company's Spectrum computer range.
- An inappropriate extension in the eyes of the consumer can lead to negative associations, for example, Levi's extension into suits, or if a cigarette company extended into health products.
- Research shows that extensions which are successfully launched are seldom as successful as the original brand.

Risks of brand extension

Risk associated with brand extension has two dimensions:

1 the ability of the brand to travel across products;
2 the capability of management to market a new product while not neglecting the core business and overestimating the new brand.

Some markets seem logical and therefore harbour little risk. For example, Paxo's move from supplying dried stuffing mix to other dehydrated food products or Mars's move into ice cream. However, as markets become more competitive there is pressure for companies to create diverse product portfolios. We have witnessed amazing leaps, such as Swatch extending from manufacturing watches to designing cars, and Virgin diversifying into controversial markets such as airline and train transport systems where failure or distrust could have a knock-on effect on other services or products under the Virgin brand name. Levi Strauss in the 1980s extended its brand from jeans into other clothing and shoes. However, the consumer did not accept this and Levi had to return to its core business and reclaim its former position through a relaunch focusing on the 501 jeans product.

Extending successfully

Four brand extension options were identified by Peter Doyle (1989) and are illustrated in the brand positioning grid (*see* Fig. 12.6).

The following is an explanation of the four quadrants of Fig. 12.6:

1 If the brands appeal to the same target segment and have the same differential advantage, then they can safely share the same company name or range. Here, there is consistency in the positioning strategies.

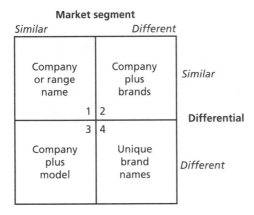

Market segment

	Similar	Different	
Similar	Company or range name	Company plus brands	Differential: Similar
	1	2	
	3	4	
Different	Company plus model	Unique brand names	Differential: Different

Fig. 12.6 Brand positioning grid
Source: Doyle, 1989

2 If the differential advantage is the same but the target market differs, then the company name can be extended because the benefit is similar. However, it is important to identify the group.

3 If a company has differential advantages, then it should use separate brand names.

4 If both the target customers and the differential advantages are different, then using unique brand names is the most appropriate strategy.

Studies have shown that groups of related products reinforce the brand, particularly where technical expertise is important and perceived to be so. Consumers categorize goods or services in their purchase decision and transfer attitudes associated with a core brand to its extensions. An extension into a separate category has less risk of a resulting negative feedback on the core brand than when the extension is very similar to the core brand. Keller and Aaker (1992) report that high quality brands stretch further than those of average quality. The stronger the brand, the easier it is to extend it into diverse product areas. The question to ponder is how tolerant the customer is if the product differs from the core brand. Toyota did not believe that new product positioning can be achieved by stressing the attributes of the extension; in trying to capture the more luxurious sector of the car market, Toyota believed that a brand extension into a quality position would not be successful. The company, therefore, launched the Lexus brand in order to enter the quality marketplace.

Recent research has shown that a brand name which has a strong association with functional benefits can be extended more readily into product areas which are themselves bought for functional benefits. Similarly, if the original brand is more linked to prestige then it may be extended into a product field also bought for its prestige. For example, a Timex watch which has functional associations would extend readily into stop watches, whereas a Rolex brand might be extended to luxury clocks.

Problems may appear when attempting to move a brand down the income scale rather than up it. However, attempting to move a brand to a higher income group is possibly the most risky form of brand stretching because it involves stretching consumers' perceptions. In such cases the management strategies have to be carefully planned for such a move.

CONCLUSION

In order to maintain a brand successfully, it is essential that its managers thoroughly understand its intrinsic properties – its core values, added value, its positioning, proposition, personality, image, and identity – and constantly update themselves on consumer concepts of their brand in relation to others. Any modification of the store brand or offer must be in line with customer expectations of the original positioning.

Branding is a necessary feature of the marketplace because without brand management there would be no strategies to understand the essence and position of the retail operation. The ultimate aim of management must be that of brand strength and immortality. Such an aim requires adaptation of the brand to the new and evolving demands of customers, competitive moves and the changing marketplace.

New legislation has strengthened the hand of manufacturers in defending their brands against counterfeits and copycat products. However, own-label entrants are one of the most exciting changes taking place. If an own-label brand is very similar in packaging to an existing brand, it does seem unfair to benefit from the reputation of the original brand without having had the expense of development and launching. Another key trend is brand extension. This enables companies to introduce new products and product modifications to new and existing customers. However, their success cannot be guaranteed, and it is important that there is a perceived quality and 'fit' with the core brand. The range of products currently offered may also influence the success of the extension – very similar extensions succeed in narrow ranges, whereas wide ranges can sustain more variety in the extensions. Even the strongest brands have boundaries and the art of brand extension is fully to exploit a brand's possibilities without overstepping the boundary limits.

EXERCISES

The exercises in this section relate to the management of a retail brand. It is advised that you work through them before moving on to Chapter 13.

1 Write down a list of brands or stores you believe you will always patronize. Now refer to the theory you have read to compile a list of reasons for the strength of the brands you have listed.

2 Do you believe that own-brand products will be even more successful in the future, and if so why? What reactions do you think manufacturers will have to these changes in terms of defensive strategies?

3 Read Minicase 12.1 and then write a briefing document to your marketing director (of a leading high fashion jeans manufacturer) as to the damage to different aspects of the brand which may occur if a discount retailer sources your product and sells it at discount prices. You need to cover the different aspects of branding as described in this chapter and in any other reading you may carry out.

4 What brands have launched (extension strategy) new products or retail concepts which do not fit easily with the core brand? Were they successful? If not, why not?

5 How does Chanel perfume keep its brand strength? Can marketing ensure there is more to a brand than simply a name? Use the following grid as a guide.

Consideration of Chanel attributes:	Identify the marketing approach:
<ul><li>distribution</li><li>promotion</li><li>pricing</li><li>range and position of products</li><li>others (list)</li></ul>	

Now discuss what you have learnt about the success, or otherwise, of Chanel which could be applied to a high street fashion retailer.

REFERENCES AND FURTHER READING

Aaker, D.A. (1991) *Managing Brand Equity: Capitalising on the value of a brand name*. New York: The Free Press.

Aaker, D.A. and Biel, A.L. (1993) *Brand Equity and Advertising*. Lawrence Erlbaum Associates.

Davies, G. (1992) 'The two ways in which retailers can be brands', *International Journal of Retail and Distribution Management*, 20 (2), 24–34.

Davies, G. (1998) 'Retail brands and the theft of identity', *International Journal of Retail and Distribution Management*, 26 (4), 140–46.

Debling, F. (2000) 'On brand banking: An examination of the factors contributing to effective branding and brand development through direct marketing in the consumer financial services sector', *Journal of Financial Services Marketing*, 5 (2), 150–73.

Doyle, P. (1989) 'Building successful brands: the strategic options', *Journal of Marketing Management*, 5 (1), 77–95.

de Chernatony, L. (2001) 'Succeeding with brands on the Internet', *Journal of Brand Management*, 8 (3), 186–95.

de Chernatony, L. and Daniels, K. (1994) 'Developing a more effective brand positioning', *Journal of Brand Management*, 1 (6), 373–9.

de Chernatony, L. and McDonald, M.H.B. (1998) *Creating Powerful Brands*. 2nd edn. Oxford: Butterworth-Heinemann.

de Chernatony, L. and McWilliam, G. (1989) 'The varying nature of brands as assets', *International Journal of Advertising*, 8 (4), 339–49.

Edgecliffe-Johnson, A. (2001) 'Back to cheap and cheerful – Own-Label', *Financial Times*, 19 June.

Fagan, M. (1995) 'Virgin steps up cola campaign', *Independent*, 3 January, 26.

Fisher, A. (2001) 'Unilever sharpens its focus on its top 400 brands', *Financial Times*, 8 August.

Hankinson, G. and Cowking, P. (1993) *Branding in Action: Cases and strategies for profitable brand management*. London: McGraw-Hill.

Hildebrandt, L. and Klapper, D. (2001) 'The analysis of price competition between corporate brands', *International Journal of Research in Marketing*, 18 (1–2), 139–59.

Hollinger, P. (1998) 'Hilfiger sues Tesco over "counterfeit" goods claim', *Financial Times*, 29 May.

Institute of Grocery Distribution (1996) *Brands: Their future on the supermarket shelf. A survey of retailers' and manufacturers' attitudes to brands*. Watford: IGD Business Publications.

Interbrand. Web site: www.Interbrand.com

Jardine, A. (2001) 'The right to Grey Goods?' *Marketing*, 19 July.

Jardine, A. (2001) 'Monsoon – How should Monsoon go about expansion?' *Marketing*, 2 August.

Jary, M. and Wileman, A. (1997) 'Retail brands. Is this the real thing?' *Retail Week*, 11 July, 12–13.

Kapferer, J.N. (1992) *Strategic Brand Management: New approaches to creating and evaluating brand equity*. London: Kogan Page.

Keller, K.L. and Aaker, D.A. (1992) 'The effects of sequential introduction of brand extensions', *Journal of Marketing Research*, 29 (1), 35–50.

Key Note (1993) *Own-brands: A market sector overview*. 5th edn. Hampton: Key Note Publications.

King, S. (1991) 'Brand building in the 1990s', *Journal of Marketing Management*, 7 (1), 3–13.

Kotler, P. (1997) *Marketing Management: Analysis, planning, implementation and control*. 9th edn. London: Prentice-Hall.

Meyers, H.M. (1994) 'The role of packaging in brand line extensions', *Journal of Brand Management*, 1 (6), 348–56.

Monk, H. (1997) 'Gentlemen prefer brands', *Retail Week*, 17 January, 5.

Neely, J. (1997) *UK Fashion Report*. London: EMAP Fashion.

Reid, M. (1995) 'Survey of retailing (4): Make it your own – Own label is good for profits, good for the image and good for consumers. No wonder it is spreading', *The Economist*, 4 March.

Ries, A. and Trout, J. (1981) *Positioning: The battle for your mind*. London: McGraw-Hill.

Rubenstein, H. (1996) 'Brand first management', *Journal of Marketing Management*, 12, 269–80.

Snowdon, R. (1997) 'No name – just images', *The Times*, 30 September, 29.

Tauber, E.M. (1988) 'Brand leverage: strategy for growth in a cost-controlled world', *Journal of Advertising Research*, September, 26–30.

Vishwanath, V. and Mark, J. (1997) 'Your brands best strategy', *Harvard Business Review*, May/June, 123–9.

Webster, F.E. (2000) 'Understanding the relationships among brands and resellers', *Journal of the Academy of Marketing Science*, 28 (1), 17–23.

13 The applications of IT to retail marketing

This chapter should enable you to understand and explain:

- how retailers add value to their business through the use of IT;
- the use of IT to improve marketing and merchandising performance;
- the role of customer databases in developing effective retail marketing;
- the contribution of business e-commerce to improved retail performance;
- the development and significance of consumer e-commerce, the Internet, multimedia and future IT trends likely to have an impact on retail businesses.

THE GROWING ROLE OF INFORMATION TECHNOLOGY IN RETAILING

A visit to any large store will show that information technology (IT) has become a vital part of retailing. The laser-scanners used in most of the large stores to read product bar codes, check the details on their product file, and provide the correct price *in fractions of a second* are among the most distinctive examples of modern computer technology. In addition, the development of the Internet has enabled consumers to order books, CDs, clothing or groceries at any time of day or night and have them delivered to their homes. These are merely the *visible* components of the investment of substantial resources by retailers throughout the world in extensive computer and high speed communications networks which collect and exchange data between stores, distribution centres, suppliers, head offices and consumers. Such systems are not the sole preserve of large companies. The relative costs of IT systems have fallen considerably in recent years, enabling retailers of any size to purchase IT. As Management Horizons (1995) predicted, technology is becoming a virtual prerequisite to successful competition. Retail-supplier partnerships utilize technology where information is a key to reduce costs while improving productivity.

The current success of many retail companies is related to the way they have improved the operation of their businesses through investment in technology. The significant contributions to efficiency can be directly related to the application of scanning and stock control systems, data interchange and management support systems. For all large retailers and for many smaller ones, ever-growing investment in IT is not simply one option among many, but a necessary condition of remaining a serious competitor in the marketplace. Modern technology is transforming the retail environment and has helped many retailers to expand their operations. In this chapter we shall examine the role of IT systems in enabling retailers to increase efficiency, productivity and marketing needs as well as the role of electronic commerce (e-commerce) in providing new ways in which retailers can serve the public and compete with one another.

INFORMATION TECHNOLOGY – SOME EXPLANATIONS AND DEFINITIONS

IT or information technology refers to the technology of the production, storage and communication of information using computers and micro-electronics. IT includes both the *equipment* used to produce, store and communicate information and the business uses or *applications* to which IT is put. It requires '*hardware*' (the term used for the equipment which handles data, using computer equipment), '*software*' (the instructions that control the way hardware accepts data input, and then processes, stores, and communicates that data), and '*communications*'. Communications deals with the equipment (including any cabling) and software used to transmit data between computers within a store or across a wide distance.

Companies use a range of different computers including mainframes, minicomputers and PCs. *Mainframes* are the largest computers used to run major systems with specialized software often produced by the mainframe supplier or by closely associated companies. *Minicomputers*, as the name suggests, are smaller computers with much of the power of mainframes but which can use commercially available packages, representing considerable savings in cost and development time. *PCs* or *personal computers* vary in computing power from those which are simply advanced word processing devices to those which are small minicomputers capable of running an electronic point of sale (EPOS) system or store administration system. Each system will normally have *terminal equipment* (often known simply as *terminals*), which is the equipment at each end of a computer system, used to input data (via a keyboard or from reading a bar code) or to display data output on a screen, store it or print it out as text or graphs (known as *hard copy*).

Although the phrase 'information technology' may seem to focus mostly on computer hardware, in this book we follow current usage to cover both computer equipment and the business applications of IT. The context of IT is primarily about how it can be used to help solve retail business problems. A simple case illustrates the advantages of IT to a retailer of modest size. The bigger the retailer, the more necessary the application of IT.

Example: Grantham Fashions Ltd, Reading

Grantham Fashions Ltd is a chain of only five clothing shops. Each store is equipped with a PC which holds information about the stock in the store by item and by range, size and colour. A hand-held device reads when an item is sold to a customer and the bar code on the label deducts the item from the shop's stock. Overnight, the sales information on each store's computer is downloaded automatically over a BT telephone line to the company PC in the main store.

Every morning the owner of Grantham Fashions is able to review the previous day's sales performance of every one of her stores. When deciding how much to order, she has available the weekly and monthly sales figures for each type of article last year and this year. She is able to spot product lines that are selling very well in the first few days and quickly place 'top-up' orders with her suppliers. She can also reallocate stock between different branches to ensure that every store has a range of sizes or colours of each range.

The computer is also used to maintain the company accounts, calculate the salaries and bonuses of every employee, and hold customer information used to keep in touch with the best customers. When the owner had only two stores she was able to act as manager for both of them as well as doing all the buying and her own marketing. With five stores she has found that the only way she can keep tight control on all her stores as well as buying is through her computer system, although she still visits every store at least twice every week. She uses the Internet to access her bank account, pay her suppliers, and check the progress of orders and often e-mails her regular customers to tell them about new merchandise that may interest them.

IT FOR COMPETITIVE ADVANTAGE

Grantham Fashions Ltd, like major retailers Tesco, Delhaize Le Lion and Carrefour, uses IT to carry out basic functions including selling items, capturing the sales data by item, stock control, buying, management reports, customer information, and managing the finances of the business. The main uses of IT in retailing are shown in Fig. 13.1. However, the most advanced retailers attempt to use IT to give them competitive advantages over their rivals. For IT to provide competitive advantage it needs to cut costs, differentiate the retailer's service offer, or provide innovation in ways that are prized by the customer.

Taylor (1998) argued that in the increasingly competitive retailing sector, advances in IT systems such as data mining, multimedia kiosks and Web-based commerce are helping businesses differentiate their services and are enabling them to develop closer relationships with their customers. Lowe and Wrigley (1996) suggest that since the 1970s there have been three main ways in which retailers have used IT, 'positioning themselves

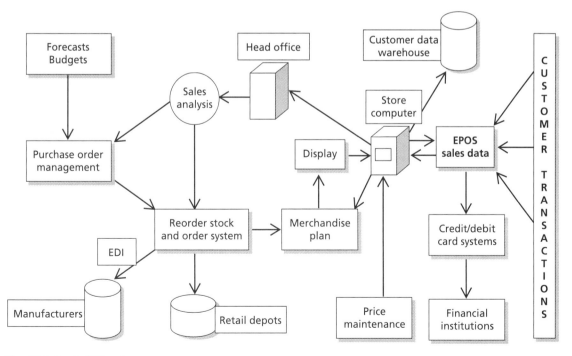

Fig .13.1 A retail IT system

at the cutting edge of technological development', compared with manufacturers. These are:

1 investment in IT along with organizational changes, improved retail logistics, reducing delivery lead times, resulting in a progressive reduction in retailer inventory holdings;

2 better information about consumer demand supported retail policies in own-brand, product development, and the refocusing and redefinition of many of the most successful firms.

3 cutting labour costs by effective staff scheduling and by using more part-time and casual staff. Retailers were able to use IT to measure staff performance, enabling costs to be further reduced with the help of better information about transactions and performance levels.

IT is having a major impact on the modern retail business. Article bar-coding, combined with the advent of business-to-business electronic commerce, creates phenomenal efficiencies for the retailer, as listed below.

Cost and productivity benefits

- efficiency of time/transaction speed increases;
- reduced queuing times;
- operating cost reductions, e.g. less ticketing;
- increased accuracy of all aspects of the sales transaction;
- improved administration/invoices;
- no new keying required;
- shorter lead times;
- reduction in stockouts and stockholding;
- pricing can be changed easily and accurately.

Marketing benefits

- improved data – effectiveness of promotions, forecasts of sales, stock records, etc.;
- faster distribution cycle system;
- improved trading partner relationship;
- ability to incorporate faster responses to changing market conditions;
- consumer benefits from operational efficiencies, e.g. shorter queues;
- can lead to the building of loyalty schemes and databases;
- additional selling space owing to reduced stockholding.

Automating processes

Automating a process may cut costs, increase accuracy, reduce processing times, enable decisions to be made more quickly, and speed up customer service. For example, the application of electronic point of sale, or EPOS, which uses scanning systems to ensure the charge is based upon accurate prices, enables checkout staff to work faster, and, in a food environment, to eliminate the need to apply price labels to goods. All these factors cut labour costs. In addition, accurate 'shopping basket' data can be collected and stored for analysis.

Collecting data about the customer

Data about what individual shoppers buy is collected and analysed. The purchasing patterns of different types of shopper can be analysed, assisting decisions about ranging, product extension, or promotions. (*Note*: Data protection legislation in every EU country controls what personal information can be held on an individual and bans the export of personal data to other countries which do not have equivalent data protection.)

MINICASE 13.1

Opinion: Online shopping – the next five years

We expect shopping online in the UK to be worth GBP12.53bn ($17.9bn) by 2005, or 5 per cent of total retail sales. Shopping on the Internet is accelerating and women are fast catching up with men as a spending force. Our latest research shows that the number of UK Internet shoppers has reached 3.2m people, while the number of women shoppers has doubled to 1.1m. Some GBP581m was spent online in 1999. About a third of this was in the fourth quarter of the year. This may sound high but in fact it is only 0.3 per cent of all retail sales. However, our work shows that spending levels have continued to increase as the year has unfolded. Our forecast for 2005 is partly explained by developments in the grocery market, which will drive sales forward over the next few years. Online food business will grow to GBP4.9bn, or 4.9 per cent of sector sales. More players have entered the market and the leaders such as Tesco, Sainsbury, Asda and Iceland are all pushing ahead faster.

We also predict that the development of Internet shopping via the TV will be particularly beneficial to the clothing sector where sales will rise to GBP1.8bn, or 4.0 per cent of sector sales, by 2005. Clothing sales will be driven by technological innovations such as body scanning, enabling measurements to be stored electronically. As well as interactive digital TV services, growth drivers will include mobile phones. However, this growth will not be in addition to existing retail sales. By far the largest part will be cannibalised from

existing sales through stores and mail order catalogues.

We forecast that about 6 per cent of Internet sales will be new growth and that 94 per cent will be transferred from existing channels. Despite recent blips there is no escape from the inevitability that retail must become multi-channel to cater for consumer needs. Just as physical retailers are moving online, it will not be too long before pure players open a physical presence, making their brands better known and reaching more customers.

There will be consolidation. Many businesses will fail as there is a 'flight to quality'. Mergers and acquisitions will be rife including between dotcoms and established retailers. Despite the rapid growth of online shopping via PC over the past two years, it is still a very small part of consumers' lives.

There are two main barriers to stronger Internet retail growth – security and delivery. Some 41 per cent of Internet users – 48 per cent six months ago – are still worried about giving their financial details over the Internet. The increase of trust in secure servers, new ways to pay, including online currency, and the rise of the 'walled gardens' of digital TV where providers limit Internet access to the bundle of services they are offering will all help. As for delivery, 25 per cent of shoppers have a problem with the fact that many companies cannot deliver when it is convenient.

Retailers are on a steep learning curve in understanding what motivates the Internet shopper. Behaviour patterns and expectations are very different online than they are physically. There is a significant time lag between going online and buying a product. Shoppers are also much more demanding about seeing and experiencing constant newness, and 'getting the best deal'. While price discounting has typified retail Internet activity, we believe that upping added-value elements of the offer and leveraging brand values will be essential for retailers, as it will lead to greater profitability. Creating 'communities' around the brand and targeting people by lifestyle, interests and aspirations, rather than by age and class is key, with new levels of communication required.

Retail brands which can diversify as Amazon has done will be the strongest, as consumers trust the core brand whether it sells clothes, toys or pensions. The retailing landscape will change significantly over the next five years, but online shopping and physical shopping will co-exist. Online and offline retailers can learn much from each other.

Customers still favour going into shops rather than going online for many important products. They trust those retailers more, feel they get better help and advice and prefer the ease of transaction. Shoppers view Internet shopping as more convenient, better for sourcing unusual products and more cost-effective.

Source: Richard Hyman, Chairman, Verdict Research Limited, FT.com site, 26 October 2000

A loyalty card database will hold the customer demographic information and the addresses of card holders. These entries can be linked to transactions data provided by EPOS to show what individual customers buy and this data can be used to profile the customer base. This then allows specific offers to be made to certain types of customer. Boots the Chemist launched its first mail order catalogue, *Mother and Baby*, by sending copies to all loyalty card holders who had bought baby products from Boots in the previous year. In addition, many Internet e-commerce sites attempt to use previous transaction information to *personalize* their sites for each shopper by offering them items that have been related to their last few transactions and by automatically greeting them by name when they enter the site.

Feedback on marketing decisions

EPOS data can be analysed to show quickly the effects of promotions, prices, new products, and packaging changes. The impact of changing the layout or merchandising of stores can be rapidly assessed in terms of category sales, competitor brands, gross profit and sales elsewhere in the store. New ideas and concepts can be carefully tested against marketplace realities. For example, the DIY company B&Q has a rigorous policy of using its EPOS data to evaluate its promotions, enabling it to calculate customer price responsiveness for core and seasonal products at different times of the year. This enables the company to plan its promotions more scientifically and predict the outcomes with greater accuracy.

Communications

Stores can communicate with suppliers to send documents such as purchase orders, stock and sales information over third-party communications networks. This is known as e-commerce (electronic commerce). This is cheaper and faster than paper-based

Table 13.1 Remote grocery shopping operation options

Ordering method	Picking and packing	Delivery charge	Payment method	Availability
Internet, intranet, phone, fax. Sometimes incentives are offered to join scheme	Minimum worth of order required or free at any level. Sometimes restricted range only	Minimum worth of order required, free to home or work or collection (can be drive though) from store only	Debit / credit card, cheque on delivery. E-cash payment is undergoing trials	Mainly large city, or within 5 miles of named store

systems, so that many stores only need to place their orders 24–48 hours in advance compared with seven days earlier with traditional ordering methods. Store computers also transmit daily EPOS data and other information to head office so that senior managers are more in touch with the performance of every store and product group, and can respond appropriately. For example, in the Tesco Stores Group stock replenishment occurs automatically, made possible by a computer system which receives daily EPOS data from each store and generates the next day's stock requirement using a computer model of predicted sales. The system automatically sends the requirement electronically overnight to the distribution centre for picking and delivery the next day. This creates efficiency as the *lead time* (time between sending an order and receiving the merchandise) has been slashed. This system has allowed Tesco over a period of five years to halve the amount of stock it carries and to improve the freshness of its product on offer to the consumer.

A number of options are possible as to the way a remote shopping operation is set up to service customers. Table 13.1 indicates the current methods employed for grocery shopping services from the larger companies.

Tools to plan the business

Sophisticated computer software packages may help retailers to plan, budget and forecast, to choose the most successful locations, and to control their business. Expert systems can model decision-making, statistical packages can forecast sales, data-mining tools can extract and analyse information in a database, and neural networks can 'see' changing patterns in complex data. Retailers use geographic information systems (GIS), which draw on socio-demographic data by postcode, along with company transaction data, and intelligent analytical tools to forecast the likely turnover of stores in different locations.

Adding value to the retail transaction

IT-assisted transactions can be preferred by at least some customers to 'traditional' retailing in shops, because they provide transactional speed, accuracy, and convenience. The use by bank customers of automated teller machines ('hole-in-the wall' cash machines) at any time of day or night demonstrates that customers welcome lower levels of involvement if they receive clear additional benefits which they value.

Example: Self-scanning

Safeway in the UK and Albert Heijn in The Netherlands are the European pioneers of self-scanning for customers. On entering the store, the customer collects a small hand scanner, which is used to read the item bar code before putting the goods into the trolley. Customers can go at their own pace, they can check the accuracy of the prices they are being charged, they can change their minds and replace merchandise back on the shelves, and there are virtually no queues. When they reach the end of the store a quick check on the items purchased may be made, the customer pays the member of staff and leaves the store. It took Safeway five years to develop the system, which is now being taken up by other food retailers such as Sainsbury's and Waitrose.

Technologically enabled shopping

Selling goods over the Internet is likely to become increasingly important, although its progress has been much slower than was predicted in the 1990s. The trend is fully discussed in the last two sections of this chapter. Electronic means of selling include the following:

- **Products**: range of grocery, clothing and footwear, music, books, videos, DIY, electronic goods such as washing machines and hi-fi, garden products, motor vehicles and motor bikes, sports goods, cameras and photographic goods, computer hardware and software, pharmacy goods, etc.
- **Services**: home betting, retail banking, personal insurance, financial service, estate agents, stocks and shares, travel and holidays, flower delivery, entertainment tickets, virtual education, information services.

Example: Amazon.com

Amazon.com, founded in 1995, had by 2000 taken 7 per cent share of all book sales in the US as an Internet retail bookseller selling millions of different titles. As a *virtual* bookseller it does not invest in stores but has concentrated on building brand and dominating the World Wide Web. More recently it has expanded into selling other products and also carrying out fulfilment services for other companies. It has therefore merged the role of the wholesaler/distributor and the retailer. The business strength is that cost is taken out of the operation as all they need is a massive warehouse and no shops as all their business is Web based. The marketing benefit is the low price and convenience they can pass on to the customer because of their shorter and more cost-effective supply chain. They have succeeded, based upon Porter (1980), due to a generic strategy of industry-wide differentiation and having smaller overheads than their rivals. The company have questioned existing accepted ways of doing business and are specializing in a commodity item market. However, the costs of operating at the leading edge of retailing are huge and Amazon.com has not yet earned a profit in any year of its operation.

Further reinforcement of the powerful role of IT in business has been developed by Porter and Millar (1985). They felt that new technology was transforming the nature of products, processes, companies, industries and even competition itself. Companies could not stand aside from the massive changes that were going on and survive indefinitely. Porter and Millar's *transformational* view of IT is widely accepted today.

Limits to using IT for competitive advantage

IT was originally used by retailers to automate central services such as finance, payroll, and management accounts. The first EPOS systems appeared in the 1970s, usually in department stores that were large enough to be able to justify a computer installation. The use of EPOS across most retail markets did not occur until the mid-1980s, and even the largest and most IT-committed retailers did not complete the installation of EPOS in all their stores until the early 1990s. Retailing is a highly dispersed business and the cost for retailers of providing elaborate IT equipment in all their stores has been high. Complex systems are required to handle the large number of product lines and the wide range of purposes the systems are to serve. Only the very largest retailers can afford to employ computer specialists so systems have to be designed which require little maintenance and can be used in stores where staff may have limited knowledge about computers. Thus the costs, both of routine investment in automating processes (such as EPOS) and the *transformational* IT investment, may simply be too high for many retailers. Moreover, the more adventurous and radical the IT investment, the longer it may take to garner the rewards. Many IT projects fail and the risk of a novel application failing may simply be too great for many companies.

Professor John Dawson (1994) felt that there was little evidence that European retailers made sufficient use of IT to transform their businesses. He argued that large European retailers devoted proportionately smaller amounts of their budgets to IT than manufacturers, many retailers were untouched by significant involvement in IT, they concentrated on operational improvements rather than transformational ones, and that the expected pay-offs from IT had not been fully realized. Porter's (2001: 66) analysis looked at the Internet and found that 'the Internet per se will rarely be a competitive advantage' on its own, that 'Internet technology provides better opportunities for companies to establish distinctive strategy positionings' and 'gaining such a competitive advantage will not require a radically new approach to business'. Following this argument, it is suggested that companies should utilize Internet technologies alongside their traditional competitive strategies to maximize their profitability and competitive advantage.

Effective use of IT

IT is not a single event or product and this will also limit the ability of many retailers to gain the maximum competitive advantage from IT. 'Computerization' is usually dependent upon many other changes in related IT and processes. Getting the full benefits of IT may take a long time while the retailer attempts to *learn* how best to exploit the new systems. Although many UK grocers invested in EPOS in the 1980s, they were able to make little effective use of information about patterns of individual customer shopping behaviour (called 'shopping basket data' in grocery) until the late-1990s when cost-effective ways of creating and analysing masses of data became available. It has taken Tesco seven years of heavy investment and learning from experience to create one of the most advanced IT-based stock replenishment systems, using EPOS sales data, expert forecasting systems, and electronic data communications (Seth and Randall, 1999). Dawson (2001) describes the way changes in markets and increased technologically enabled productivity were helping to create a new low-cost commerce (the *new commerce*) in Europe. Powell and Dent-Micallef (1997) investigated the linkages between

345

IT and the performance of firms. The research examined the IT literature and included a retail study; they found that IT alone had not produced sustainable performance advantage in the retail industry, but that some firms have gained advantages such as flexible culture, strategic planning-IT integration, and improved supplier relationships. This underlines the point that the real advantage lies in people and systems rather than systems alone.

Obtaining the full competitive advantages from IT requires long-term investment for an IT strategy which supports the retailer's strategic direction. It is likely to involve not simply heavy investment in one or two applications but continuous investment and improvement in most functional areas where IT can add value.

CAPTURING AND TRANSMITTING DATA AT THE POINT OF SALE

To be able to plan effectively there is a need to collect and transmit timely data on retail transactions, which may be fulfilled in a number of ways.

Retail data capture (or data collection) of every sales transaction at the point of sale is one of the most important elements of retail IT, whether data capture occurs through an EPOS (electronic point-of-sale) device or is directly entered into a computer using a keyboard. It provides accurate information about customer purchases, the sales of individual merchandise lines and other data the retailer wishes to capture, covering, for example, how the customer has paid for the item, a loyalty card reference, the time and date of transaction, the sales assistant and amount spent.

This means that, for marketing purposes, the likely performance of new product lines can be assessed quickly by using a number of well-located trial stores. The impact of new lines upon the sales of other products can also be measured by comparing how sales of different lines have changed in the trial stores and in control stores. Many retailers offer an EPOS-based service to manufacturers, which allows them to market test the impact of new products in their stores. The effect of new promotion can be analysed in the same way. There are many retailers with pronounced *seasonal* sales for whom rapid feedback about new product lines is not merely important, it is vital. To know exactly how well or badly the new season's colours or designs are selling in the first week enables merchandisers and buyers to turn provisional orders into firm orders and to make purchases in the Far East, for example, with confidence. Mistakes can still be made, but EPOS data can provide buyers with accurate and timely information.

Extensive, timely and accurate sales data generated by EPOS systems has become a critical source of marketing information for retailers and supplier marketing departments.

Data capture involves three elements on a practical level:

- a coding system;
- a code symbology;
- the means used to capture the data in a form that can be fed to the computer.

Coding systems

The retailer must decide how merchandise will be coded. In practice, this usually involves the retailer deciding whether to use the dominant European Article Numbering

(EAN) system using 13 digits (EAN13), which has become the international standard, or to develop a different one. The code structure adopted must uniquely identify every product line to prevent confusion (and pricing errors). To provide continued improvement, in 2005 a new 14-digit system known as GTIN will replace current systems.

Code symbology

How will this code be represented in a machine-readable form? Retailers who use EAN will naturally expect manufacturers to deliver merchandise to them already bar-coded. The EAN13 code is omni-directional which means that it can be presented to the scanner in any direction and be successfully read in any orientation. Where retailers have adopted their own coding system, they usually adopt a version of EAN13. There are also new symbologies that are just starting to be introduced which can represent considerably more data within a comparatively small space. Such new systems include *snowball*, a two-dimensional symbology that is read vertically as well as horizontally. For most retailers, however, the use of the international standard, EAN, will provide considerable benefits.

Data capture

There are several options available to the retailer in capturing sales data. Although the price of laser scanners has fallen, it is still a considerable investment for retailers to adopt a policy of high-speed automatic data entry. Flat-bed scanning systems provide the best pay-off in supermarkets or mass merchandising environments, which require fast transaction speeds for high densities of relatively low-cost products. Data can also be captured *automatically* by using a *hand scanner* or some other portable scanning device. Alternatively, the item code can be captured manually by keying in the product identification numbers to the cash till or computer keyboard. On each occasion a sale is registered, the retailer will have captured on a transactions database the brand name, size, colour and price – and perhaps details of the individual if a loyalty card is used or where expensive items are involved. This information can be combined with other forms of market research to help the retailer improve both marketing and retail planning decisions.

At the point of transaction, credit or debit cards need to be read. Computerization of credit card transactions has created a more efficient and secure way for retailers to accept payment. In addition, retailers realize the advantage of increased sales due to accepting credit cards as the higher the cost of the merchandise the more likely it is that a credit card will be used. Credit and debit card information (and most loyalty card information) is coded on the reverse of the card using *magnetic strip* technology, which can only be read (or decoded) by specialist devices called *card-swipes*. Tamper-proof *smart cards* incorporating electronic chips have been introduced throughout Europe to combat fraud. Smart cards are able to hold much more data than a magnetic strip and could themselves hold personal information, payment limits, and act as loyalty cards for several retailers.

Most standard bar codes do not include prices, they simply identify the merchandise. If the merchandise price is kept on file within the EPOS terminal or the central store computer, then the correct price is automatically entered every time the bar code is read.

This system of *price look up* (PLU) saves the need to price-mark goods and is much faster than entering prices automatically. PLU systems make it easier for the retailer to amend prices as only the shelf edge label needs to be changed. Some non-food retailers have taken advantage of this facility to create extra excitement in-store by reducing prices for 30 minutes or an hour. Newer EPOS systems allow multiple purchase promotions to operate automatically, with the EPOS system recalculating the correct price for a multi-save, or buy-one-get-one-free, or linked transactions thus enabling the retail marketer to be more adventurous with pricing mechanisms.

Communicating store data

Stores and depots transmit EPOS sales data files, financial transactions data, the amount banked, along with a range of other data such as staff hours worked, despatch information, and stock levels, electronically to head office computers for processing and analysis. This is called *retail data transaction file exchange*. Much of this information is transmitted automatically. The store may be *polled* at night by one of a number of central computers and the required data downloaded to head office. In larger stores the store computers automatically exchange data with a central computer several times every day, enabling the merchandise director to view the progress of that day's trading in every store by 11 a.m. The same systems are used by retailers to update the price files held by stores. The new prices are downloaded from head office to the store computer, often on a Thursday night to take effect the following Monday morning. Depending on exactly how the system is configured, the new price files may finally be passed to every EPOS terminal by the store computer.

DATABASE MARKETING, DATA MINING AND BUSINESS INTELLIGENCE

A database is a computer system used to store and analyse large volumes of data. Data relating to item sales, customer information, and the range of goods bought by customers can be held on a database and used for marketing purposes. A department store can develop a specialized catalogue aimed at affluent customers with teenage daughters. Postcodes uniquely identify a small location and the demographic information available commercially for each postcode area (for example from CACI) will allow the department store to target affluent areas with a degree of precision. Customers of bookshops who mainly buy management books can receive mailings of the retailer's management offerings along with something more frivolous such as a selection of thrillers or humour to purchase. In practice, retailers have found it difficult and expensive to target customers with precision. Wal-Mart, USA, found, from analysis of its shopping basket EPOS data, that sales of beer and nappies were linked and that joint sales were highest on Friday evenings. The company's reasoning was that males were buying nappies on their way home and were stocking up on beer at the same time. When beer and nappies were merchandised next to each other the sales of both increased.

This use of a database to trigger off a large number of mailshots or telephone sales is probably the most typical use at present. However, most large retailers are investing in *data warehouses* (*see* Fig. 13.2). These are large systems collecting *internal* information from inside the company (such as electronic point of sale, loyalty cards, and customer services) and *external* information from other organizations (such as third party

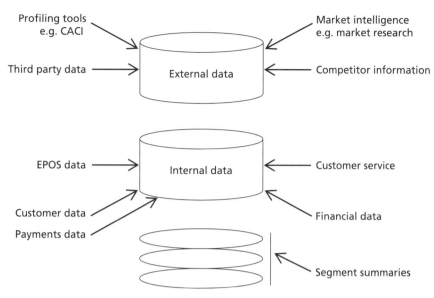

Fig. 13.2 Data warehouse

suppliers, customer profiling tools, competitor information and market research). These data are usually stored in a separate computer system so that the data warehouse does not interfere with normal day-to-day operations. The data then need to be analysed by easy-to-use tools, often in conjunction with other external data. If the analytical tools can mimic normal patterns of thought they will be much easier to use. The retailer hopes that trawling through masses of data can derive key marketing patterns or relationships about types of customer that can be exploited to increase sales or profitability. *Data mining* involves extracting and analysing different types of data to detect patterns that are not immediately obvious and might never be discovered using normal reporting systems.

Data mining and analysis will permit data to be organized to assist customer segmentation. Virtually all retailers need to be able to answer these questions:

- Who are our best customers and what do they buy?
- Where are they price sensitive and where are there possibilities for price advances?
- What products do they tend to buy or order at the same time, during a single visit to a store? How much do they spend per visit?
- What can we do to hold on to these customers and to attract others like them?

However, many data warehouses have been poorly designed making it difficult to access and analyse the data except by specialists. The problem is that there has often been a tendency to store 'everything', which is not a cost-effective approach. Several North American retailers, such as JC Penney, have suffered expensive failures with data warehouses, which were badly delayed and failed to provide the business with new insights. However, expectations of the new systems may have been too high. A more focused approach involves creating what is known as a *data mart*, a smaller data warehouse used for one functional area such as marketing consisting of sales, stores promotions and consumer profile data. These data can be quickly analysed with a set of specialized analytical tools that can spot trends (and problems) and support merchandising much more easily than by attempting to extract data from an unwieldy data warehouse.

The growing interest in data marts and data warehouses is all part of a trend towards developing methods of assessing the massive volumes of data which retailers typically collect every day. Data warehousing is one, large-scale approach towards doing this, but there are many other systems called variously: executive information systems (EIS), business intelligence, or decision support systems (DSS). Enterprise-wide business data, often stored in different places and databases, is modified and simplified and stored in what is known as an 'online analytical processing engine' (OLAP). This *moulded* or transformed data can be looked at by end users in several different ways, for example at sales by store, by product and product group, and by supplier. The manager utilizing a desktop computer can interrogate some versions of business intelligence, although these have difficulty in handling large quantities of data. Once data is in the right form, decision-makers can look at several aspects of the business simultaneously.

Many retailers have only a few years' experience of data warehousing, data mining and business intelligence systems and are learning how to configure them to the best advantage. While there will continue to be failures, these systems are likely to be a fundamental method of enabling managers to understand and make decisions about their own company within the retail market. For example, Allders International, the UK department store group, uses data mining to analyse the performance of its 82 stores to identify poorly performing lines and to establish the reasons for problem stores. They have used the system to take out lower margin lines, even though they were selling well, substituting them or adjusting their location within stores.

BUSINESS E-COMMERCE AND DATA COMMUNICATIONS

Rapid data communications have been an essential element in the application of new IT systems to retailing. Computer files with the data arranged in a specified way are switched between individual retail stores, depots, head offices and suppliers using a range of networks including ordinary public telephone lines, dedicated networks and secure public data lines or by satellite link.

Business electronic commerce with other businesses (increasingly described as 'business-to-business e-commerce' or B2B) has grown rapidly since the early 1990s. This automates such critical business functions as placing orders for merchandise, checking delivery, and exchanging order or payment documentation. *Business* electronic commerce needs to be carefully distinguished from *customer* electronic commerce (otherwise known as 'business-to-customer' or B2C) by which retailers sell goods to the final consumer. Creating even further jargon, the whole area of data communication for trading purposes, both as 'business-to-business' and as 'business-to-customer' (B2B and B2C), is also known as e-commerce or e-business.

What types of data are exchanged in business e-commerce or B2B? The most significant involve computerized ordering and messages providing sales or promotional information, which help suppliers to know how and where to keep retailers effectively stocked with merchandise. Stockholding (or *inventory*) is one of the retail sector's largest costs. Tight control over inventory – exactly what is in stock, what is on order, what new items are out of stock, what potential problems exist – is a necessary requirement for modern retailers. From a marketing approach it is necessary to improve service and product availability, and simultaneously reduce the stock levels in order to improve profitability. To be able to cut inventory to the minimum at the same time as ensuring that product is never out of stock represents a trading ideal. *Computerized ordering* speeds up the stock ordering process, thereby cutting costs – including the costs of safety stock – and providing more information. The use of electronic data interchange (EDI) provides an electronic administrative management system of replenishment through controlling product despatch and returns. The technology allows the retailer to:

- be more efficient due to enhanced merchandise availability;
- have higher stockturn rates;
- incur lower spoilage and shrinkage costs;
- achieve improved merchandise tracking;
- have less need for discount lines;
- lower administration costs;
- provide fresher products for customers and timely offers in store, particularly valuable for food retailers.

There are four main types of systems for business communications and exchanging data:

- e-commerce and EDI;
- trading exchanges and e-tendering;
- extranet;
- intranet.

E-commerce and EDI

Sending orders to suppliers and to depots electronically saves time and avoids the need to re-key order information. In principle, an e-commerce order can be received by a manufacturer, accepted, and immediately passed into the distribution system for order picking in the warehouse and delivery. After processing the order, the supplier or depot can then electronically transmit despatch information to the store (i.e. what goods are going to be received) and send an invoice.

EDI (electronic data interchange) is a highly structured variant of e-commerce used mainly for order messages between large retailers and their suppliers. EDI messages between companies conform to a common standard, the worldwide standard being UN/EDIFACT. This defines

- the core information being exchanged; and
- where and how that information must appear.

There are many different EDI messaging systems which retailers, manufacturers and shippers use. In the UK the dominant system is one called 'Tradcoms', developed by the 'e-centre UK', which resulted from an initiative led by UK grocers. One of the oldest EDI systems is Bookshop Teleordering, which supplies books from 20 000 different sources of book supply in the UK to bookshops of all sizes. Other examples include Interflora (independent florists transmit customer orders to the most convenient member store) and Odette (car distributors search for the right model and colour of motor car for their client).

Trading exchanges and e-tendering

While EDI provides a highly structured means for a retailer to send orders or instructions to a supplier, less formal approaches, including trading exchanges and extranets, are gaining ground. An electronic trading exchange provides a relatively simple method for retailers to put contracts out to suppliers without the costs and delays of preparing documents, advertising and waiting for the tenders to arrive. More than 30 per cent of retailers in the UK and the USA are already members of one or more trading exchanges. A tender can be circulated to the supplier members of a trading exchange with the tenders returned within hours or a few days, enabling the retailer to make a decision about suppliers quickly. Sainsbury's has used trading exchanges to place three-month contracts for goods as diverse as cheese, frozen lamb, jeans, and VCRs. Trading exchanges can also be used by suppliers to auction off existing stocks quickly, thus providing continuity in sales. A number of trading exchanges are provided by third parties, such as BarclaysB2B, a partnership between Barclays and Accenture. Large retailers have established two separate international public trading exchanges, GlobalNetXchange and World Wide Retail Exchange. GlobalNetXchange includes Carrefour (France), Sears (US), Kroger (US), Sainsbury's (UK), and Metro AG (Germany). World Wide Retail Exchange has Albertsons (US), Boots Group (UK), Tesco (UK), Coop Italia (Italy), Dairy Farm (Singapore/Australasia). Very high numbers of retailers are concerned that confidential information sent to their suppliers via public trading exchanges may leak to other users of the scheme and this has assisted the development of private exchanges (also known as extranets) which bring together a small number of participants.

Extranet

Also termed *Web EDI* this is likely to be the way that many businesses will use Internet technology for B2B (business-to-business) communication. Normal EDI transactions can be very costly to manage and many companies have said that EDI is not cost-effective for data exchange with all but the top 100 or 200 suppliers. Smaller suppliers are increasingly using dedicated (i.e. closed and secure) Internet services to receive orders from retailers, which also have the advantage of being intuitive and very easy to use. Woolworths (UK) uses an extranet to control new product introduction by sending EPOS sales data to suppliers. Both DHL, the international parcels courier, and Dell Computers, the Internet computer company, permit customers to track the progress of their orders by accessing the information over a dedicated extranet. Sainsbury's, the UK food retailer, has set up an extranet with its suppliers to help with promotions and other events. One-third of its suppliers are part of the scheme. The EQOS extranet facilities have improved joint planning with suppliers, thus smoothing out 'spikes' in supply. Information about regional publicity is shared with suppliers and any differences in perception about start dates and deadlines are resolved. Further developments include the exchange of current EPOS sales data with selected suppliers to ensure that their stock replenishment plans are always accurate.

Example: The Retail Extranet Optimizer

So much retail EPOS information is now sent to suppliers that 17 of the UK's main consumer goods suppliers have established an e-business portal, which collects daily sales and other data automatically from retailers and passes these back to the supplier. Heinz, Elida Fabergé and Cussons among other suppliers need to track hundreds of different products across multiple store sites on a daily basis for many different retailers. This portal system does it automatically. A *portal* is a Web presence which passes information between users.

Intranet

An intranet is a formal system to permit the electronic exchange of business data *within* an organization, mostly between managers and senior staff. Managers may have access to a range of software to create or amend text, spreadsheets and graphs. They should be able to send the documents electronically to colleagues. Staff in the 'field' (i.e. visiting stores) can download required information about the store's performance and other documents over a telephone line or even down their mobile phone. This means that staff are able to have access to current data, whether marketing or logistics, in order to make decisions or provide advice.

Data communications and merchandise reordering systems

Two *transformational* reordering systems are:

● automatic stock replenishment systems;
● efficient consumer response (ECR).

Automatic stock replenishment systems use daily or weekly EPOS sales data to generate a fresh order for rapid delivery overnight or within the next 48 hours. Sales data are sent electronically to the depot or to the manufacturer by EDI. The order from the store can be automatically converted into a picking list, a despatch note and an invoice without the need to key in the data. The amount sold one day is the amount replenished the following day.

Efficient consumer response (ECR) makes EPOS sales data available to suppliers so that they can programme their production and distribution systems to ensure that the retailer never runs out of stock. The retailer creates a supplier partnership with key suppliers using a confidential EDI link to the retailer's weekly or daily sales of relevant merchandise so that suppliers can be responsible for maintaining the target inventory levels of the retail business. ECR is increasingly common in clothing and fast-moving food and non-food merchandise.

We can expect the use of e-commerce and other electronic ordering and remerchandising systems to grow rapidly. The only question mark involves the extent to which the formal EDI systems might be sidelined by informal and intuitive systems such as trading exchanges and extranets. Although the Tradcoms standard has come to dominate many retail applications, only 8 per cent of Western hemisphere trade is carried out using EDI. However, both formal and informal e-commerce systems will have to find their role in serving the business community. Some retailers are already complaining that the lack of data format standards in extranets and trading exchanges is creating difficulties in dealing with different companies, so it is possible that further development of trading exchanges and extranets will be dependent upon greater discipline than has been seen so far.

ELECTRONIC RETAILING

Electronic retailing to consumers (or B2C) was first developed on a large scale in the 1980s. The area is advancing at a rapid rate with retail organizations realizing the growing importance of the sale of products through these new distribution channels. Electronic delivery systems do not necessarily require direct human interaction and, as such, they offer specific advantages. In principle, quality can be assured, the costs are lower, there is consumer convenience of access, and distribution can be wider than normal retail channels. The key underlying reasons behind electronic retailing are: consumer time poverty, consumers wanting to have more control over time and place of transaction, the technology convergence allowing change to take place and growing experience of the benefits of the medium. The different categories of this major growth area fall into two distinct systems: passive or interactive:

1 *Passive systems.* These are non-interactive one-way media, where the retailer can decide upon the content and timing of messages. They include all forms of one-way communication media such as shopping pages, or clubs on television, or one-way cable systems. The success of the Quality Value Convenience Network (QVC), using such an approach, is discussed below. This form of selling includes video catalogues or electronic media which demonstrate the product in use or provide further information.

2 *Interactive systems.* This type of electronic retailing allows for two-way interaction and includes the Internet or promotional touch-screen booths and kiosks for items such as airline or holiday bookings. Some systems can demonstrate the product in use and, in the case of touch-screens, give printouts or allow further enquiries from the database. A feature of both systems is that a credit card can be used in order to secure the sale.

The retailers that undertake electronic commerce can be classified in three main ways.

1 *Virtual retailers*: these have no shops or stores or physical presence in the high street, malls or out-of-town locations. They trade exclusively on the Internet or on television and have to find new ways of attracting custom and serving consumer needs. Examples of these are Amazon.com and lastminute.com.

2 *Two-channel retailers*: these are established retailers with stores that have developed an electronic retailing capability as a major or minor aspect of their business. Tesco can be regarded as a two-channel retailer.

3 *Multi-channel retailers*: these are established retailers which service customer needs in a number of ways, including shops, telephone ordering, the Internet, catalogues, and TV. Examples would include Littlewoods and Boots UK and Ireland. As well as 1400 UK stores, Boots has mother-and-baby catalogues, the *Wellbeing* digital TV channel – although its introduction has been postponed – and transactional and information websites, handbag.com as well as wellbeing.com.

Although many observers originally felt that electronic retailing would be dominated by new *virtual* retailers, it now seems likely that the e-commerce market will be made up of all three categories of retailer.

Passive systems and home shopping

Home shopping through direct mail, agency catalogues, and direct response advertising already accounts for a significant proportion of spending by European consumers. New technology will add greater variety to the routes that already exist. However, many innovative IT home shopping systems have failed because they were not based on what customers needed but on what the technology could provide. This is surprising as most surveys of customers show that although they dislike routine shopping for commodities this does not mean they welcome technologically enabled retailing. In practice, service levels are poor, with considerable amounts of time spent staring at unchanging computer screens; lead times are much longer than popping into a shop on the way home; and there are abiding concerns about security. One clear trend that is successful is the growth of the home shopping networks, especially in the USA. These are based upon the use of studio demonstrations of products while a telephone salesforce stands by to receive orders. As the number of calls diminishes, the network operator is able to demonstrate a new product. The system is therefore characterized by instant feedback on what items are popular and should remain on screen for longer periods or those that should be replaced. In addition, the overheads are low as there is only the need for warehouse storage, a telephone salesforce and the rent of studio time.

In the USA, a number of retailers offer televised home shopping. They include JC Penney Shopping Network, Home Shopping Network, QVC Network, Cable Value Network and Sky Merchant. The USA television retailing marketplace is segmented by product, brand and price. The cable and home shopping networks are targeting the lower end of the market whereas QVC offers well-known national brands. The different networks are able to offer easy payment plans because they own company credit facilities and use promotional techniques such as direct mail coupons. The means of response is by telephone.

TV-based retailing (for example, home shopping programmes such as QVC in Britain and Germany, and the extended TV advertising called *infomercials*) has proved extremely successful compared to the comparatively slow growth of retail sales on the Internet. The British retailers Boots (pharmacy) and Sainsbury's (food) have set up home shopping channels on pay-TV designed to provide information about health/wellbeing and good food respectively, although the Sainsbury's channel was closed down in 2001. Many commentators believe that the introduction of digital TV in several European countries will enable shoppers to use their TV to buy goods on the Internet rather than by using a PC. The telephone/cable company NTL has 900 000 customers in Britain able to log on to any Internet website while watching digital/interactive TV. However, in 2001 only 15.9 per cent of digital TV viewers used their television sets to go online, while those that did so were rather more interested in entertainment, leisure, computer games and electronic gambling than in shopping online, although this may change. Retailing via digital television may be slow to build a critical mass, but it is eventually likely to become a formidable sector in its own right.

How the fittest survived the dotcom meltdown: Online Retailing

In the back room of a Tesco store outside London, a woman looks over bags of items for an online order to be delivered later that afternoon. 'We need a box of peaches,' she tells a young man she is training. He fetches some from the shop floor. The operation is conspicuously low-key: it has no fancy conveyor belts, no big warehouses, no cutting-edge computer systems. Yet Tesco's Internet delivery service has achieved what so many others have not: it is profitable. Other online grocers have shut down, including Homeruns, Streamline and the fabulously well-funded Webvan. Given the sector's dismal record, Tesco surprised many with its announcement last month that it was expanding its online service to the US by a joint venture with Safeway.

In spite of the demise of thousands of dotcoms, Internet retailing is not dead. In May, US consumers alone spent $3.9bn (£2.7bn) online, according to Forrester Research. That compares with $3.4bn in the same month last year. Even more remarkable, several online operations are now turning a profit. Their success proves that businesses can thrive online. And the key to profitability is something so mundane that it was dismissed as overly limiting two years ago: cost control. Profitable Internet operations tend to have modest ambitions. At the peak of the dotcom hype, the creation of the Internet was often compared with the industrial revolution. As it turns out, the web may have more in common with the invention of mail-order catalogues. 'The Internet is another channel that companies can tap,' says Mr Kurtzman. 'It's that simple – but that doesn't mean the web is not important.' The most successful sites concentrate on ease of use. To make the channel accessible and fast, companies have abandoned plans for complicated video streaming and links. 'You don't need to be a software engineer to use our site,' says Brad Newcomb, director of marketing automation at Southwest Airlines. Conventional wisdom had it that bricks-and-mortar chains would fade away as the pure plays took over the world. But bricks-and-mortar groups have emerged as leaders in online sales. 'Two years ago, pure plays looked like the sure winners,' said Tom Stemberg, chief executive of Staples. 'And if the dotcoms could have spent with no regard to cost for 10 more years, they might

have been. As head of a bricks-and-mortar company, of course, I'm glad it turned out this way. In retrospect, I wouldn't have set up a separate tracking stock for Staples.com – but that's the only thing I would have done differently.'

Traditional retailers, it turns out, had something pure dotcoms didn't: existing infrastructure. That infrastructure has proved to be important in allowing companies to create new sales opportunities at the lowest possible extra cost. Victoria's Secret, for example, uses the same photographs online as in its catalogues.

'You have to sweat your existing assets,' says David Reid, deputy chairman of Tesco. 'That's the key to profit on the Internet, or in any area.' Webvan, the defunct dotcom grocer, planned to set up warehouses all over the US within a few years. Tesco, the UK food chain, perceived that it could use its existing stores. Tesco invested only $56m to build its online business. Webvan had spent $1.2bn by the time it folded. The dotcoms' desire to do everything quickly added to their expenses. Pets.com (USA) tried to build a consumer brand almost overnight and wasted a small fortune on expensive television commercials during last year's Superbowl. Traditional companies, by contrast, have been able to rely on existing brands.

There were frivolous moments. Victoria's Secret's online fashion show for St Valentine's Day in 1999 attracted a stampede of viewers that caused the company's website to crash. But for the most part these companies limited their marketing efforts to low-cost outlets – direct mail to existing customers, or simply printing their net address on retail bags.

Pure plays were willing to pay almost any price to win customers because they were judged on how many people visited their site. Successful Internet companies study numbers carefully. Delivery costs are of particular concern and managers struggle to come to terms with what can be provided and at what price. Staples, for instance, has calculated the average online order is about $150. With an average gross margin of $45, the company decided it could afford to provide next-day delivery free. 'If our average order were $75 and we had $25 to work with, it would be a different story,' says Mr Stemberg. Tesco operates with lower average order sizes and thinner margins. To make a profit on its online service, the group charges £5 an order. Many of the failed US grocery sites, by contrast, offered the service free. The key, say managers, is to be realistic. 'The customer comes first but not to the point of putting people out of business,' says Sharen Jester Turney, chief executive of Victoria's Secret Direct. 'Our customers won't get same-day or next-day delivery; that's just the way it is.' Victoria's Secret tapped a new demographic group by its Internet operation, albeit inadvertently. A big surprise of the company's dotcom experience has been the many orders it receives from men. At Christmas, one-third of online purchases are by male customers. 'Some men are too embarrassed to go to the stores,' says Jester Turney. 'And they weren't on our mailing lists, so they didn't do catalogue orders.' Internet retail is in its infancy but the earliest evidence of successful online strategy is just becoming clear: keep it simple, with stringent cost control.

Source: © Victoria Griffith, *Financial Times*, 27 August 2001

Interactive systems – the Internet

The Internet is an open worldwide computer network, linking together by fast data communication countless thousands of computers owned by government, education, commercial and other organizations. No one actually owns it. The Internet is a set of protocols governing how data is presented by individuals and organizations wishing to provide information to others. Within the Internet, the World Wide Web (WWW) is a collection of linked documents or pages that span the Internet. They are accessed from the user's own PC or computer terminal by what are called Web browsers, which are software products enabling the user to load and view a document relatively quickly or switch to other related documents.

Most large retailers of any size and many small retailers now have their own website, including Tesco, Iceland, Virgin, the Boots Group, Comet, Arcadia, HMV, and Gratton. Once established, the website allows a retailer to conduct a targeted business 24 hours a day, 365 days in the year, with a potential worldwide audience. The Web is available and open to anyone with an Internet connection, irrespective of geography, time zone, or computer system. This makes the offer of retail products more accessible to the new global marketplace. A small retailer with a new business idea can, in principle, use the Internet to access millions of customers in the same way as an international retailer. The technology also allows sophisticated digital images, video and sound. 'Electronic brochures' could include 'three-dimensional' aspects of the product that the potential customer could explore continuously.

Example: Small retailers

Some smaller retailers are able to use the Internet to give themselves a national or international market. **Mike Maloney**, butcher and sausage maker in the small town of Mansfield, Nottinghamshire, now derives 35 per cent of his turnover from national sales over the Internet of his award-winning sausages. **Ron Higgins** in Slapton, Devon, has set up the successful Slapton Village website to promote tourism and book accommodation, thereby encouraging additional turnover for his convenience store (the only shop remaining in the village).

Mike Maloney   www.emnet.co.uk/Mike-Maloney
Ron Higgins   www.slapton.org

Initially, most retailers' websites were passive and static: they provided simple information and photographs about a limited range of goods. To buy anything customers needed to telephone or to visit a store. Setting up this form of website is relatively cheap, but an interactive site for a large retailer, which allows customers to interrogate the site to find product details and to purchase items online, can cost more than £15 million per year. When the grocery retailer Somerfield closed down its grocery Internet shopping site it had to write off more than £30 million in debt. However, by 2001, large retailers across the world had tended to replace their previous static websites by making them transactional and many of the better websites were also fully interactive.

From a marketing perspective, the major benefit of the Internet is the much greater degree of interactivity than other communications media. The most valuable Web applications are those that allow companies to transcend communication barriers and establish dialogue directly with customers. For example, websites can contain electronic forms for customer completion and retailers can reply directly via electronic mail (e-mail). This kind of connection will improve customer relations and contribute towards the building of customer loyalty. The Web can give access to a greater store of information than other traditional communications media, and provide visitors with the means to select and retrieve only that which appeals to them. A number of sites such as www.diy.co.uk, www.wellbeing.com and www.WineWarehouse.com differentiate themselves from retailer 'catalogue' websites by providing in-depth objective advice, but provide links to appropriate products. Information for customer-specified travel guides are available from booktailer.com, customized CDs, newspapers, and videos will follow. Customized promotional material could be produced at the touch of a key. For the modern retailer, it provides a useful tool in the adoption of micro-marketing in this 'age of the individual' and relationship marketing. However, it must be remembered that the true determinant is the willingness of customers to use the Web to make purchases.

The progress of an Internet e-retail business can be monitored by measuring the following:

- number and types of visits to the site;
- length of time on the site;
- number of orders placed, broken down by timing of order;
- average basket or transaction value for each order;
- number and profile of different customers;
- number of repeat customers;
- value of transaction by individual customer;
- average time and clicks prior to making an online order;
- delivery accuracy and timing;
- customer satisfaction levels.

Example: Tesco.com

Tesco, Britain's largest grocery retailer, is now the largest online grocery retailer in the world, fulfilling 70 000 orders per week with Internet 2001 sales of more than £300 million. It started delivering groceries to the home in 1996. Because of poor Internet response times, Tesco provided its users with a CD-ROM containing its product file. Customers could telephone or fax orders for home delivery or order on the Internet. Unlike many other retailers, it assembles the orders in stores and will achieve coverage of 80 per cent of UK shoppers in 2002: in 1998 it operated this service from only 10 stores. This approach avoided the need to establish separate (and costly) preparation and distribution depots for home shopping before customer demand was sufficient to justify this. Tesco.com is now regarded as a brand in its own right. A joint venture with Safeway Inc., USA, intends to make the Tesco approach to grocery home shopping available to US customers. Note that the Tesco.com operation lost £9 million in 2000, but was expected to break even in 2001.

Table 13.2 provides some basic statistics about Internet use in 2001 in some major countries, with the USA still dwarfing all other users of the Internet for e-commerce combined. In the UK, 39 per cent of adults had access to the Internet, compared to 52 per cent in the USA and 21 per cent in Spain. The patterns vary between countries, but in these developed countries one-fifth or more of the population have access to the Internet and there is a relatively high use of Internet shopping sites. However, B2C Internet sales to consumers over the Internet was relatively low as was consumer m-commerce revenue using mobile phones.

What sorts of customer wish to use the Internet to buy goods? An attitudinal survey of Internet users carried out by the market research agency BMRB segmented likely Internet users as shown in Table 13.3.

It will be seen that the attitudes of consumers are mixed, with only a small proportion of shoppers showing unalloyed enthusiasm. This is likely to change somewhat as customers start to use the Internet simply as one of the many shopping options that are open to them and retailers become more expert at understanding and meeting customer needs over the Internet.

There are a growing number of ways in which people can access retail sites via the Internet. Thirty-nine per cent of UK adults have access to the Internet through a PC at home or work (and, increasingly, both); there is digital TV; and, increasingly, customers will be able to shop through their mobile phones or small hand-held computer devices such as Palm Pilots (Minicase 13.3). Although, according to IMRG, retail sales over the Internet in both the UK and the USA accounted for only 1 per cent of total retail sales in 2001, it seems likely that Internet retail transactions will continue to grow rapidly.

Table 13.2 Use of e-commerce in selected countries

	Percentage of population with Internet access	E-commerce revenue for year to June 2001 ($ bn)	B2C revenue for year to June 2001 ($ bn)	Consumer m-commerce revenue for year to June 2001 ($ bn)	Visitors to shopping sites in month of June 2001 (m)	Percentage of Internet users who visit shopping sites
France	21	2.74	0.34	0.19	38.1	25.3
Germany	32	5.26	0.65	0.34	44.7	41.6
Spain	21	0.69	0.69	1.47	15.1	8.5
Sweden	58	0.86	0.11	0.04	24.6	17.4
UK	39	4.02	0.5	0.34	38.8	33.1
USA	52	91.55	11.35	2.39	41.2	42.1

Source: Derived from Net Figures (www.netprofiteurope.com), figures correct to end June 2001

Table 13.3 Attitudinal survey of Web users

Name of segment	Percentage of users	Description
Realistic enthusiasts	16	Prize the Internet's convenience more than low prices, but often want to view before they buy. Will buy goods/services costing more than £500 at a time.
Confident brand shoppers	14	Confident in using Internet, tendency to buy well-known brands and believe that Internet prices are lower than standard stores. They are prepared to spend more than £500 over the Internet on goods/services.
Carefree spenders	16	Confident Internet users, they do not restrict themselves to well-known brands and do not need to see before they buy.
Cautious shoppers	20	Refuse to buy goods through Internet auctions, are concerned about the quality of goods they buy on the Internet and need to try before they buy.
Bargain hunters	16	These are driven by low prices not by convenience, will buy from any website however little known, but will not spend more than £50 over the Internet.
Unfulfilled	18	These users find purchasing items on the Internet to be extremely difficult, they are suspicious of little-known websites, concerned about low quality and believe that it takes too long before items are delivered.

Source: Derived from BMRB (August 2001), *The Internet Monitor,* London

MINICASE 13.3

Mobile phone and m-commerce futures?

The increased popularity and extensive use of mobile (cellular) telephones and the introduction of the WAP (Wireless Application Protocol) was heralded as the start of wider access of the Internet in order to purchase goods and services from any location (sometimes called m-commerce). There has been an exceptional increase in text messaging but no corresponding developments in relation to mobile phone use in purchasing from the Internet. However, it is reported that business use of m-commerce has been significant. A problem that needs to be overcome is that GSM (Global System for Mobile Communications) runs at one-sixth of the speed of a PC's modem and the screen size of a mobile phone is restricted to comparatively few characters. This may not last as in the next few years new developments such as General Packet Radio System (GPRS), and Universal Mobile Telephone Systems (UMTS, alternatively known as G3) are to provide many times the capacity of the existing phone network and should be lower cost. In addition, new wireless technologies such as Bluetooth permit data to be exchanged at high speed whereby information about special offers or last minute discounts in nearby stores can be picked up on a shopper's mobile phone, Palm Pilot or electronic diary. The forthcoming technology is more suited to sending short messages and therefore this is the way it will be harnessed and the potential is enormous.

Source: various reports

Online auctions

A popular way of buying goods on the Internet is through online (electronic) auctions – 1.5 million auction transactions take place every day on the Internet. Such sites as ebay.com and QXL.com bring together individuals and companies to buy and sell items both new and second-hand, ranging from works of art to CDs and computer software. However, the anonymity of the Internet has allowed fraudsters to operate pretty freely: 64 per cent of the complaints made to the US Internet Fraud Complaint Center concerned online auctions. In many countries Internet auctions are so recent that they are not covered by relevant laws to protect buyers. Auction technology can also be used by retailers to sell batches of merchandise quickly at a higher average price than if they were advertised at a fixed price. For example, the electrical goods retailer Comet is selling its surplus stock for higher prices in Internet auctions than it would achieve in its clearance outlets. US retailers such as Wal-Mart and JC Penney use the same tactics, but also target consumers whose bids have been rejected with offers of other stock at a fixed price. The use of dynamic pricing (fluctuating prices reflecting customer demand) and the creation of an electronic 'market stall' atmosphere for these leading websites manages to convert 25 per cent of failed bidders into purchasers.

The dotcom revolution

At one stage, many commentators (for example, Cope, 1996 and Gonyea, 1996) believed that electronic retailing would grow at a very rapid pace and would account for more than 20 per cent of the retail markets of advanced economies by 2005–8. They thought that most of the new B2C e-commerce sector would be dominated by new virtual retailers at the expense of traditional retailers with shops. It was this widely held belief that led to the 'dotcom revolution' in the period 1998–2000 that brought into existence thousands of untested business formats for new virtual retailers, many of which were heavily funded by private shareholders, merchant banks and venture capital. Eighty per cent of these ultimately collapsed, and by June 2001 US Internet stocks had fallen 83 per cent from their peak and UK Internet stocks had fallen 98 per cent (Lloyds TSB Economic Bulletin, 2001). The reasons for their failure were primarily: the e-commerce market was not big enough at that time, the set-up costs were huge and unlikely to be recovered unless rapid growth was achieved, they experienced heavy operating losses as they advertised heavily in order to attract custom, and they were frequently badly managed by inexperienced young persons. All these businesses had predicted a massive growth in sales in order to garner the economies of scale which would make them profitable. When this did not happen, they vanished. Frequently, also, Internet technology was insufficient to provide customers with a rapid interactive service, leading to disappointment among many users. The World Wide Web became popularly known as the 'world wide wait', exciting special effects would not load, or the customer order would not get through. According to Forrester Research, 65 per cent of Internet shopping baskets were abandoned by customers and did not lead to an actual sale (Taylor, 2001).

Example: Boo.com

Boo.com was a sports and leisurewear virtual retailer which planned for sales of $1 billion by 2003 in 20 countries. The centrepiece of the site was Miss Boo, an animated shopping adviser who would be able to show the effects of different colour schemes and options. Lifelike rotating models would demonstrate clothing for the customer. The founders had previously set up an online book retailer in Sweden. Boo.com received $120 million from investors. However, the launch in November 1999 was 7 months late, the stock was dated, the technology never worked properly, sales were low, there were heavy operating costs and high advertising spending to win customers. When the business collapsed in 2000, 300 jobs were lost, there were debts of $50 million and all investors' money had been spent.

E-commerce futures

Internet retailing has gone through several stages of development. Initially it was felt that users would prefer to access WWW retailers through virtual shopping malls, with a range of different retail businesses, similar to actual retail shopping centres. In fact, these electronic malls have been generally unsuccessful and some important ones, like IBM's World Avenue, have disappeared from the Internet. The most successful Internet retail marketplaces have been those in which the quality is known and customers are searching for low prices, availability, or convenient delivery. Jupiter (2000) estimated that the largest single sector traded in B2C commerce was electronics (30 per cent of all online purchases), followed by computer hardware and software (27 per cent), books and music (18 per cent), and then 'other' retail sectors. NOP Research (2001) found a 42 per cent increase in the number of Internet e-commerce users compared to the previous year and found that although computers, music and books were the largest retail e-commerce sectors, much of the new growth had come from toys, electrical goods and clothing. While new Internet users came from across the spectrum, the majority of new users were female and the largest single age group was that over 50 years, the so-called 'grey' market. Netvalue (2001) estimated that the percentage of Internet users aged over 50 was 24.4 per cent in the USA, 19.3 per cent in the UK, 17.2 per cent in Germany, and 15.7 per cent in France.

Retailers, whether virtual or real, found e-commerce a tough marketplace to be in. By 2001, many major retailers had dropped their Internet operations including Somerfield, Superdrug, Kingfisher, Boots' Bootsphoto.com, and Disney's Go.com, while virtual retailers including boo.com, Letsbuyit.com, and the health and beauty site Clickmango.com closed. Figure 13.3 indicates the way Porter has analysed the current influences of the Internet on industry structure.

The Consumers' Association report covering the Internet (*Which?*, 2001) found that 36 per cent of people surf the net but less than one-half had ever bought anything there. Only 15 per cent said that they visited shopping sites frequently; and a mere 10 per cent found that Web-based retailers provided a better service than stores. A Mintel report found that only 8 per cent of its respondents had ever bought groceries online, while 61 per cent had never visited a grocery retail site. Both reports commented on the problems many shoppers experienced in using the websites, found that the main reasons for using Internet shopping were convenience and time savings rather than low prices, and expected the growth of Internet shopping to continue.

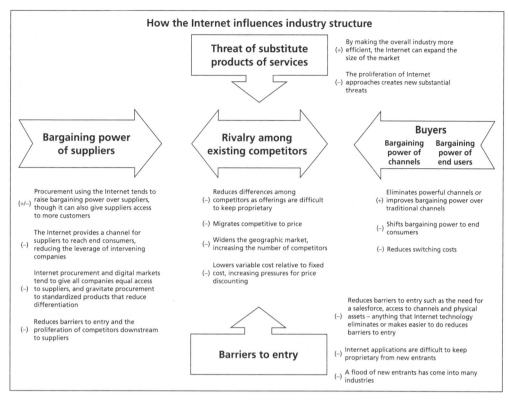

Fig. 13.3 An application of Porter's 5 forces model indicating the influences on industry structure (Porter, 2001).

One of the major issues facing Internet retailers is what is now called 'fulfilment', or the ability of the business to deliver the customer orders accurately and quickly. According to Accenture, two-thirds of deliveries by Internet companies contain at least one error and 12 per cent of goods ordered for Christmas 2000 were delivered late (Revolution, 2001). Rather than commit resources to a dedicated fulfilment operation, most Internet companies outsource fulfilment to parcel couriers or Royal Mail and it is felt that companies that send out small easily deliverable packages like DVDs, software or books have a fulfilment advantage. Among other options being considered include delivery direct to a customer's home by a milk roundsman, customer collection from a local extended-trading-hours convenience store, or delivery to a service box fixed to the house or garage. The need to deliver a bulky assortment of goods within a specific timeslot to a house when the customer is not present is a major constraint for grocery Internet sales. Companies in the US and the UK are experimenting with storage boxes that can be rented from a third-party supplier such as M-boxes, Homeport, Home Delivery Access, or PoD Systems. At their crudest these may simply be lockable boxes securely fastened to a building, but they may additionally provide proof of delivery and incorporate a refrigerator for chilled and frozen grocery items. Once these external storage boxes have been installed, then obviously any Internet delivery company can use them, thus facilitating growth in the use of Internet ordering.

Most surveys show that a major barrier to the use of the Internet for transactions is security. There are now several systems for making payment and credit card details secure, usually involving data encryption. Authorities around the world are currently working on a complex payments security project called *secure electronic transaction* (SET), which will allow cardholder and merchant to authenticate each other during an Internet transaction.

The ideas expressed by writers such as Cope (1996) that a large percentage of conventional shopping would be transferred to the Internet by 2006, forcing the closure of many shops and superstores, now look outdated. Existing retailers with shops are themselves playing a major part in the Internet revolution, while the competitive threat from the virtual retailers failed to materialize. However, even though e-commerce sales are comparatively small, the Internet is having an effect already on high street retailing, but it seems likely that a two- or multi-channel approach will be the most favoured, while existing retailers learn how to make the most effective use of electronic commerce. The research company Zygon found in 2001 that three-quarters of the 100 largest UK retailers expected to adopt a multi-channel strategy (Retail Week, 2001). The e-commerce options for existing retailers are discussed in publications from the UK Government Foresight Programme such as *Clicks and Mortar: The New Store Fronts* (Retail *e-commerce* Task Force, 2000) and *The (R)etail (R)evolution: From a Nation of Shopkeepers to a World of Opportunities* (Retail and Consumer Services Panel, 2000) (both are found at www.foresight.gov.uk).

Limitations of the Web

There are potential problems and limitations that the retail industry must address. The Butler Group suggests that effective Web applications are those that demonstrate an understanding of network limitations, demographics, and culture (URL: www.butlergroup.com, June 1996).

Network limitations

The visual impact of the website is important, but raises conflicts. Graphics and multimedia attributes require that the customer (client) end has access to a high specification PC. Also, the experience of slow data transfer can result in customer frustration and even the premature termination of the access.

Demographics

Successful Web applications should demonstrate clear relevance to the customer base. Websites can be structured so that pages are targeted to specific online customer groups. These pages must be dynamic enough to keep pace with the ever-changing interests of such groups. The challenge here is to monitor the interests and to be flexible in responding to them.

Culture

It is important that customers are comfortable with electronic shopping if they are going to purchase via the Internet. Consumers have been reluctant to supply credit card details over the Internet as they judge it to be risky and have a fear of breach of security. Both popular Web browsers, Netscape and Microsoft Explorer, have now incorporated secure payment encryption algorithms. Electronic cash (e-cash) projects, which secure payment without having to transmit card details over the Internet, have generally been unsuccessful (note the failure of Digicash), although it seems likely that they will finally be successful when they receive the wholehearted backing of the banking system. It would appear that users, as potential customers, are not aware that it is often easier for hackers to obtain credit card details passed over a cordless or mobile telephone, or by criminal activity to take a copy of a credit card as payment in a restaurant or alternative retail outlet. E-wallet or e-purse projects will enable small amounts to be debited automatically from a user's e-purse credits making it easier for WebPages providers to charge for access to parts of their sites.

The commercial success of Internet technology depends not only upon connectivity but also on the fundamental question of social acceptance. Electronic commerce will flourish if users of technology are motivated to become customers and to change their patterns of buying. Shopping by catalogue, TV and phone marketing, and phone banking are increasingly accepted as part of the way society works. While the home PC market is growing at speed, the home Internet market is also set on an upward trend. This means that society is becoming more familiar with information technology and in particular with PCs and the Internet. Therefore, the retail industry has an opportunity to deploy the Web as an effective marketing tool, providing it is able to respond to the demands of Internet commerce by being responsive, agile and innovative.

Many commentators on the WWW believe that, in addition to the competition conventional stores face from Internet retailers, manufacturers of heavily branded goods may also start to use their websites to bypass retailers and supply WWW customers direct. CDs, jeans, videos, cosmetics, perfumes, cameras and so on could all be sold over the WWW by manufacturers who have invested heavily in their brands, such as EMI, Levi, Warner Bros, Estee Lauder, J-P. Gaultier and Kodak. The success of Napster, a website which made available software to exchange music over the Internet (thus avoiding both the retail mark-up and record company licence fees), indicated that there seemed to be a large market for Internet music downloads, although the low cost of the operation reflected the fact that it was illegal. The US record industry is now to make popular music available for downloading via MusicNet and Press Play, reducing production, distribution and retail costs, and this will operate in parallel to CD sales of music in conventional shops and over the Internet.

FUTURE TRENDS

IT has already had a tremendous effect on the retail sector. A number of new IT innovations lie in store for shops. There are many different possibilities. The main difficulty is to assess how quickly these new IT products will be used in stores. The Internet has generated a tremendous level of excitement and sensational predictions have been made with regard to the future of electronic commerce. However, it is argued by Burke (1997) that the Internet is only one of many tools available to manufacturers and retailers for advertising, selling, and distributing their products to customers. He indicates that marketers are most likely to use the Internet in cases where its unique characteristics make it a viable and attractive substitute for the functions of traditional channel intermediaries.

He suggests that, because of its ability to transform information quickly and inexpensively, the Internet will have the greatest impact on marketing communications, a moderate effect on sales transactions, and a minimal impact on logistics. The Foresight Programme published *Retailing 2010*, presenting a number of case studies for discussion based upon possible futuristic scenarios for retailing at the end of the decade (Retail and Consumer Services Panel 2001). However, it is possible to argue that these scenarios may be more typical of 2025 than 2010.

Some of the trends predicted for the future of IT innovations in retailing are discussed below.

Smart cards

Smart cards equipped with a silicon chip will have replaced magnetic strip credit and debit cards (and possibly loyalty cards) by 2003 in the UK and Europe. However, they will also carry a magnetic strip to allow them to be used abroad. Smart cards are more secure than conventional cards and can carry additional information. Smart loyalty cards could include the customer's name and address, preferences, points awarded and be capable of being used across a number of retail companies and services.

By the mid-2000s, it is thought that smaller versions of smart cards will be applied to many articles in the form of 'smart tags', to provide full information about their manufacture (essential for food or pharmaceutical products), monitor their progress down the supply chain, provide stock control in the stores, and may be a partial replacement for EAN codes at the checkout. These smart tags will provide proof of ownership and may help to combat theft instore as well as helping householders to protect their goods. Retailers may be able to charge a premium for goods that are protected by smart tags. A tagged domestic TV or video playback equipment can be protected from unauthorized use in the home (for example, by children when the parents are away). Similarly, without knowledge of the code or the activation device, such products would be unappealing to burglars because

- the goods could be used only by the legal owners;
- the legal owners of goods can be identified;
- stolen goods can thus be returned to their owners.

The price of silicon chips, which are the key ingredient of smart cards and smart tags, is falling rapidly, suggesting that the next few years will see a considerable growth in the use of these products.

E-cash

E-cash or electronic purses consist of smart card systems which can be used in the same way as cash or debit cards with retailers whose stores are equipped with special card readers. Users of the scheme 'deposit' funds into the cards, which are then debited every time they are used until further deposits are made. The pilots carried out in Britain and other European countries show that the technology works but that there is not yet a widespread consumer acceptance of the scheme. Development is, therefore, likely to be slow. Some form of e-cash is proposed to enable young people to buy goods over the

Internet as they do not usually have credit cards or bank accounts. A sum would be credited to an account which would be available for Internet transactions either via an online account (one early model was called Beenz) or a form of Internet debit card with a low credit limit such as £20. An alternative approach would involve an account linked to a mobile phone, which could be debited in order to buy goods, or where a telephone payment card can be topped up with a credit which can then be used to buy goods over the Internet: liability would therefore be strictly limited. Progress is likely to be slow, but it would permit people who do not own credit/debit cards to buy goods over the Internet and also help to overcome customer security fears.

Multimedia kiosks

Multimedia kiosks placed in stores, shopping malls, libraries and railway stations are likely to become increasingly important over the next few years. For the retailer, they will add value in a number of ways. The kiosk can be used by loyalty cardholders when entering the store to receive details of special offers, check the number of points they have, receive updates about new products, and spend their points as shown by Boots UK and Ireland. In DIY or gardening, heavy or cumbersome items could be ordered electronically and be assembled ready for collection in 15 minutes. The retailer could use multimedia to cross-sell related products, for example, a session with a beautician may be booked in a healthcare store; customers booking holidays could arrange insurance, purchase tickets for the cinema, or check and book concessionary train fares.

Example: Service Merchandise Inc.

Service Merchandise Inc. is the USA's largest catalogue retailer with over 400 showrooms across the southern states. It has a customer database of 27 million people and segments them by lifestyle. Over the last five years it has spent millions of dollars in developing customer-friendly kiosks which people would use to buy their goods without the need to involve staff. Current versions use touch-screen technology, show pictures and video clips of the product, and allow customers to compare different items through a comparison screen. Customers can place their orders and pay by credit card for home delivery. These have been so successful that Service Merchandise is now starting to locate single kiosks in shopping malls and airports.

Customer-specific offers

Customer-specific offers are another possibility in the grocery store of the future. The customer's loyalty card (loaded with customer preference information) inserted into a card reader on a shopping trolley would trigger individualized offers at different parts of the store. Some offers would attempt to induce the customer to buy different ranges of product; others might reward a highly loyal customer; yet others might attempt to retain the custom of a consumer who has become less loyal than before.

Electronic body scanners

Electronic body scanners are devices that can provide an exact set of measurements for the perfectly fitting pair of jeans, underwear or suit. This allows customers to be scanned 'in the round' when they place their order. The goods can then be ready for them about 30 minutes later. Marks & Spencer customer advisers are currently able to use a small electronic device to check bra size and fit.

Other ideas being discussed or developed include the virtual reality store (to mimic shopping, but used by home delivery companies) which may also be used to help with space planning and the positioning of checkouts and new gondola designs in retail outlets; 100 per cent customer self-scanning stores with no staff; and the integration of smart tags into products to provide information about product integrity, prices, and to act as an anti-theft device. Also available are electronic shelf edge labels (ESELs) which are liquid crystal modules that replace paper labels on the shelf front. These ESELs may be automatically linked to the head office EPOS system and so enable the changing of all prices on outlet shelves to coincide with scanned prices at the checkout.

CONCLUSION

We have seen how IT has transformed the operation of retail marketing by providing accurate sales data and a mass of high quality information about customers. Fast data communications have enabled retailers to make their merchandise reordering systems more responsive to customers at the same time as cutting the costs of inventory. Data communications are also at the heart of the development of the Internet, which will have a considerable effect on retailers of all kinds – even if the hopes of its greatest supporters prove over-optimistic. A major task facing retailers is to discover new opportunities in the customer and product data now being held in databases and data warehouses. Retailers are attempting to be more customer-focused and hope to use customer information and loyalty systems to increase the average amount spent, and to understand consumer sensitivities about pricing and ranges. The costs of investing in the new IT systems and getting the most from them, and the penalties of *not* investing, will continue to make retailing a high risk area.

EXERCISES

The exercises in this section are related to the applications of IT to retail marketing. It is advised that you work through them before moving on to Chapter 14.

1 Taking the short-, medium- and long-term trends, how is electronic retailing going to displace the current patterns of retail purchasing? Relate this to different segments such as business-to-business as well as consumer sub-groups. In addition, comment on the implication for electronic advances in retailing and the changes which may occur in the social aspects of shopping.

2 What is the supportive role of IT systems for retail (such as EDI) and how can any of the systems you have identified be used by retailers to improve further the management and cost-effectiveness of their operations?

3 Look up the websites listed in the grid below and record your impressions of them.

Company website:	Note your impressions of the Web pages:
Boots www.wellbeing.com Co-op Group www.co-op.co.uk Iceland www.iceland.co.uk www.ebay.co.uk Sainsbury www.sainsbury.co.uk Tesco www.tesco.co.uk Top Shop www.topshop.co.uk	
Note others you looked up:	Note your impressions of the Web pages: (interest, ease of purchase, further links, etc.)

Then explore the Internet for the retail methods of selling different types of merchandise such as cars, travel and CDs, or visit foreign sites such as www.carrefour.fr Report which websites you visited and again note your impressions, particularly recording any differences you find.

4 Discuss, with reasons, what you believe to be the most important future applications of IT to retail marketing and retail operations in the next 20 years.

REFERENCES AND FURTHER READING

Alba, J., Lynch, J., Weitz, B. and Janiszewski, C. (1998) 'Interactive home shopping: consumer, retailer, and manufacturer incentives to participate in electronic marketplaces', *Journal of Marketing*, 61 (3), 38–53.

Barnatt, C. (1994) *The Computers in Business Blueprint*. London: Blackwell Business.

BMRB (2001) *Internet Monitor*, August.

Branigan, L. (1998) 'The Internet: the emerging premier direct marketing channel', *Direct Marketing*, 61 (1), 46–8.

Burke, R.R. (1997) 'Do you see what I see? The future of virtual shopping', *Journal of the Academy of Marketing Science*, 25 (4), 352–60.

Comer, J.M., Mehta, R. and Holmes, T.L. (1998) 'Information technology: retail users versus nonusers', *Journal of Interactive Marketing*, 12 (2), 49–62.

Cope, N. (1996) *Retail in the Digital Age*. London: Bowerdean Publishing.

Curtis, G. (1995) *Business Information Systems: Analysis, design and practice*. 2nd edn. Wokingham: Addison-Wesley.

Davies, G. (1995) 'Bringing stores to shoppers – not shoppers to stores', *International Journal of Retail and Distribution Management*, 23 (1), 18–23.

Dawson, J. (1994) 'Applications of European management in European retailing', *International Review of Retail, Distribution and Consumer Research*, 4 (2), 219–38.

Dawson, J. (2001) 'Is there a new commerce in Europe?', *International Review of Retail, Distribution and Consumer Research*, 11 (3), 287–99.

European Consumer Research (2001) *Maintaining the Web's best customers: Profiting from segmentation*, London: Jupiter Research.

Fidler, C. and Rogerson, S. (1996) *Strategic Management Support Systems*. London: Pitman.

Gonyea, J.C. (1996) *Selling on the Internet: How to open an electronic storefront and have millions of customers*. Maidenhead: McGraw-Hill.

Griffith, V. (2001) 'How the fittest survived the dotcom meltdown: Online Retailing', *Financial Times*, 27 August.

Haeckel, S.H. (1998) 'About the nature and future of interactive marketing', *Journal of Interactive Marketing*, 12 (1), 63–71.

Haigh, M. (2001) *The E-Marketing Handbook: An indispensable guide to marketing your products and services on the Internet*. London: Kogan Page.

Hogarth-Scott, S. and Parkinson, S. (1994) 'Barriers and stimuli to the use of Information Technology in retailing', *International Review of Retail, Distribution and Consumer Research*, 4 (3), 257–75.

Hyman, R. (2000) 'Opinion: Online shopping – the next five years', FT.com site, 26 October.

Institute of Grocery Distribution (1998) *Grocery Market Bulletin*. Watford: IGD Business Publications.

KPMG (1997) *Home Shopping Across Europe: Experience and opportunities*. KPMG Publication 5670.

Lindstrom, M. (2001) *Clicks, Bricks and Brands: the marriage of Retailer and E-tailer*, London: Kogan Page.

Lloyds TSB Economic Bulletin (2001) 'The tech market crash: the end of the new economy?' (39), June, London: Lloyds TSB Bank.

Lowe, M. and Wrigley, N. (1996) *Retailing, Consumption and Capital: Towards the new retail geography*. Harlow: Longman.

Mahadevan, B. (2000) 'Business models for Internet based e-commerce: an anatomy', *California Management Review*, 42 (4), 55–69.

Malmster, E. (2001) *Boohoo.com*, London: Random House.

Management Horizons (1995) *Retailing 2005*. New York: Management Horizons.

Margolis, B. (1996) 'Digital commerce: the future of retailing', *Direct Marketing*, January, 41–6.

Mulhern, F.J. (1997) 'Retail marketing: from distribution to integration', *International Journal of Research in Marketing*, 14 (2), 103–24.

NOP Research (2001) *Internet User Profile Survey, June 2001*. London: National Opinion Polls.

Packaged Facts Inc. (1994) *The Electronic Retailing Market*. New York: Wiley.

Porter, M.E. (1980) *Competitive Strategy: Techniques for analyzing industry competitiveness*. New York: The Free Press.

Porter, M. (2001) 'Strategy and the Internet', *Harvard Business Review*, March, 63–78.

Porter, M.E. and Millar, V.E. (1985) 'How information gives you competitive advantage', *Harvard Business Review*, 63 (4), 149–60.

Powell, T.C. and Dent-Micallef, A. (1997) 'Information technology as competitive advantage: the role of human, business, and technology resources', *Strategic Management Journal*, 18 (5), 375–405.

Retail and Consumer Services Panel (2000) *The (R) etail (R)evoution: From a Nation of Shopkeepers to a World of Opportunities*. London: The Foresight Programme, Department of Trade and Industry.

Retail and Consumer Services Panel (2001) *Retailing 2010*. London: The Foresight Programme, Department of Trade and Industry.

Retail *e-commerce* Task Force (2000) *Clicks and Mortar: The New Store Fronts*. London: Department of Trade and Industry.

Retail Week (2001) 'Retailers explore the potential of multi-channel', *Retail Week*, 5 October.

Revolution (2001) 'Revolution Guide to E-commerce', *Revolution*, 1, March.

Reynolds, J. (2000) 'E-commerce: a critical review', *International Journal of Retail and Distribution Management*, 28 (10), 413–44.

Rhodes, E. and Carter, R. (1998) 'Electronic commerce technologies and changing product distribution', *International Journal of Technology Management*, 15 (1, 2), 31–48.

Rogers, D. (1998) 'Barclays offers on-screen links', *Marketing*, 21 May, 2.

Rowley, J. (1996) 'Retailing and shopping on the Internet', *International Journal of Retail and Distribution Management*, 24 (3), 26–37.

Seth, A. and Randall, G. (1999) *The Grocers: The Rise and Rise of the Supermarket Chains*. London: Kogan Page.

Taylor, P. (1998) 'The electronic revolution: making close links with shoppers', *Financial Times*, 17 March.

Taylor, R. (2001) 'Brand and Deliver', *Retail Week*, 28 September, 19.

Further information

The e-centre (Article Number Association (UK) Ltd), 11 Kingsway, London WC2B 6AR.

The Foresight Programme (UK Department of Trade and Industry): www.foresight.gov.uk. *Clicks and Mortar* and other e-commerce reports can be downloaded from the Retail e-commerce Task Force sector of the Foresight site.

World Wide Retail Exchange: www.wwre.org

E-commerce Times is a valuable central source of press articles about IT and e-commerce.

www.nua.ie/surveys

IMRG is an international research and consultancy body dealing mainly with the development of e-commerce: www.imrg.com

Jupiter: www.jup.com/home. jsp

www.Netvalue.com is a French research company specializing in the Internet.

www.netprofiteurope.com/nf

14 Consumerism and ethics in retailing

This chapter should enable you to understand and explain:
- the different pressures for companies to become more socially responsible;
- what would be deemed a constraint of trade or unfair methods of competition;
- the criticisms levelled at different aspects of marketing;
- the societal marketing approach.

It is not uncommon for reports to reach us of unacceptable service, poor quality, shoddy goods, marketing malpractice and the belief that a company has no interest apart from the profit motive. In the 1990s Sears, as part of its portfolio, managed the largest independent auto-repair concern in the USA. It lost the trust of its customers after the company had to provide a refund of $50 each to around one million customers for auto-work that had been unnecessary. The case damaged the image of Sears and its long-held reputation for reliability. Such situations are now less likely as retailers manage image far better. This is because there is the growing awareness that long-term customer satisfaction and the building of a positive image is a prerequisite for success. In light of this understanding companies are discovering the need to identify and react to the new wave of consumerism and its associated values.

As indicated, the problem of negative attitudes to the modern business world is associated with faceless, large companies attempting to increase their profits. We should, however, be aware that companies are made up of people similar to us and the problems may not be divorced from what we all do. Some studies have highlighted that up to one-third of middle managers have submitted deceptive reports to their supervisors and that even more would bend the rules to gain personal advancement. We know of companies that can be viewed as 'bad barrels' because they have 'bad apples' working for them. To be successful, retail companies need to discover approaches to the marketplace that will build a socially responsible and ethical company culture. There is a need to understand the following three basic issues:

- *Consumerism.* This is organized group pressure, by all consumers, to protect and benefit consumer groups and the environment. This means it is not solely those consumers buying from a company, it is a broad movement to bring about improved exchange relationships.

- *Corporate social responsibility.* This is the decision of a firm to conduct its business in the interest of society as a whole as well as its own interests.

- *Ethics.* This involves personal decisions on the moral principles of what would be the right or wrong activity for individual employees. These decisions will be linked to the values and culture of the organization. Ethical values are the core beliefs and standards such as honesty and fairness that will dictate the stance a company takes in relation to retail marketing.

THE DIFFERENT PRESSURES FOR A COMPANY TO BE SOCIALLY RESPONSIBLE

The concept on which to base the ensuring of long-term satisfaction is not a straightforward one. Consumer satisfaction is linked to aspirations and these may change in relation to political systems, and the products and services other consumers enjoy. For example, the basis of satisfaction of consumers in Eastern European countries prior to and since 1989 will be totally different. Similarly, the USA will not have the same cultural values as less industrialized countries. Satisfaction is based upon personal concepts of acceptability of the type of products available, the potential to purchase them, and how companies act in the transaction process of creating and supplying products or services. This points to the premise that we often use relative standards when judging the circumstances of a specific action. But we need to understand this in more detail as the study and description of ethics is quite complex.

There is a need to understand the subtle differences between the meaning of corporate social responsibility and business ethics. Corporate social responsibility relates to the social aspects of the responsibility a company may adopt for its own business operation within the society it serves. To be corporately responsible, a company would develop and operate economic, stakeholder, or philanthropic policies which were beyond its required legal duties. On the other hand, business ethics is the code by which an organization should behave based upon carefully developed rules of moral philosophy. The two are different as a service company could act in a socially responsible manner of providing local sponsorship money to a worthy activity while telling consumers they required service on their appliances that was not actually needed. Even this is not a straightforward description as the judgement of ethical standards can be culturally determined by a relative approach based upon:

- *utilitarianism* – which judges not the actions but the consequences of those actions. If the result is that there is a net increase in the happiness or welfare of society then the action can be believed to be morally right;
- *intuitionism* – the premise that a decision is right if the individual's intuition or conscience informs him or her that it is right. If a person believes his or her motives are good and honest and no other person is harmed by a decision then that decision can be made.

However, there are arguments that stress that there are *absolute standards* that can be applied:

- *Absolute standards* – are based upon rigid rules which provide clear guidance as to the judgement of whether any action is right or wrong. As such there is no ambiguity as to what constitutes ethical behaviour and no account is taken of the circumstances which may surround the situation. These standards are based upon religious teachings such as 'thou shall not lie' or 'thou shall not steal'.

One major change in the acceptability of the behaviour of companies can be traced to the widespread realization that the world needs to have its environment protected. Green issues are creating more awareness of the environment in Western societies. Pollution due to acid rain, the motor car and leaded petrol, nuclear waste, chemicals in farming and untreated sewage is of topical concern. This has led to the emergence of the 'green' consumer who will seek out and buy environmentally friendly products. The same consumer will expect a retail company to adopt responsible attitudes in terms of the way it carries out its business. This could be related to the organization of waste recycling, energy conservation and some control of the products it stocks or sells. There is the further concern that financial services institutions should work with acceptable political regimes and provide loans only for ethical business ventures. In the late 1990s, various retailers were accused of exploiting workers in developing countries. The recognition of the power of the consumer, based upon emerging values which deem unethical processes unacceptable, has led companies to adopt more socially responsible policies. The recognition by different companies of the need to be more aware of the personal values of those in society is primarily due to consumerism.

Consumerism

This is organized group pressure which has become a set of values held not only by the consumers of a company's products but also within the wider society. Hence consumerism has the objective of protecting all consumers from organizations with which there may be an exchange relationship. As a movement, it attempts to influence the policies and behaviour of organizations and groups to minimize the likelihood of detriments being inflicted on individuals, society or the environment. The values of the movement are based upon scepticism of the motives of businesses. There is a belief that businesses are more likely to maximize their profits than think about issues of public interest. This leads to a large number of individuals believing that retailers combine with producers to ensure that they, the consumers, are 'ripped off'.

In recent years the consumer has not been passive. Consumers have realized their economic power and have used this to bring about change. Consumerism has been used for political ends with purchasing power being applied to influence the policies of different governments. The boycott of goods from South Africa prior to the change of government is one example of this. Similarly, there has been concern over the sale of fur products, genetically modified foods, or the use of cheap child labour in developing countries. In 1996 a boycott took place related to retailers sourcing in Burma, a country where the military regime abused human rights. A campaign was targeted on the fashion retailer, Bhs. In this instance Bhs promised to sever their connections with the country by the following year. However, other companies such as Levi withdrew more quickly.

Ralph Nader is an influential individual in the history of the modern consumer movement. His book on the US automobile industry, *Unsafe at any Speed*, focused consumers' minds on the need for large companies to be more responsible to the users and to society in general for the products they make. Whereas each individual is relatively powerless against large companies, the consumer movement champions the needs of individuals through a collective voice. President Kennedy, following the tradition of Thomas Jefferson with his 'inalienable rights' in the Declaration of Independence, signalled the need for organizations to recognize the rights of the consumer when he incorporated the following four areas into his 'Consumer Bill of Rights':

1 *the right to safety* – that there are no hidden dangers;
2 *the right to be informed* – that there should be honest communications;
3 *the right to choose* – that there should be real competition among sellers;
4 *the right to be heard* – that there should be channels or bodies for complaints.

The protection of the consumer and supplier is often represented by pressure groups. Consumerism as a movement is often based upon the activities of a number of pressure groups who influence government, the media and affect the values within society – groups such as ASH (Action on Smoking and Health) who have organized and promoted national non-smoking days and sensitized the public to the problems of smoking; CAMRA (Campaign for Real Ale) who have forced significant changes on the brewers of beer; and RoSPA (Royal Society for the Prevention of Accidents) which has improved safety regulations in various industries. The self-financing Consumers' Association has been in operation since 1957 and has done much to improve standards through its publication of *Which? Magazine*, which provides comparative information on different products.

The idea of a free marketplace seems, at face value, to be good for the consumer. However, complete freedom in the marketplace is not in the interests of consumers or suppliers. Complete freedom can lead to monopoly situations, may restrict competition and allow price fixing. Consumers are most concerned when a monopoly situation exists. Where effective competition cannot be provided – as was the case with the privatization of many of the UK public utilities in the 1980s – other means of control are needed. The result has been the creation of a number of regulatory bodies that can determine the level and structure of charges made by these utilities. Oftel, Ofwat and Ofgas control the utilities of telecommunications, water and gas respectively. In the case of British Gas, Ofgas regulations allow the company to raise gas supply prices in line with energy prices but the price for ancillary services, such as standing charges and repairs, can only rise in relation to the rate of inflation. However, some groups argue that the regulatory bodies are not as powerful as they should be as they cannot insist, by statutory requirement, that the utility companies should meet their recommendations.

The Monopolies and Mergers Commission, the Office of Fair Trading, trading standards officers and different government departments are consistently ensuring that the consumer has some protection from unfair methods of competition and selling. There is also an EU minister responsible for competition. In recent years that minister has ruled on anti-competitive practices ranging from financial services to airlines, and forced companies to alter trading practices. The Monopolies and Mergers Commission in the UK is an independent body whose members are drawn from a variety of backgrounds including lawyers, economists, industrialists and trade unionists. This commission has the power to take action to remedy or prevent harm to the marketplace. Their power can be applied if the marketplace changes where at least a quarter of the supply is controlled from a single source and leads to a distortion of competition. Historically, much of the regulation of retailing has been designed to encourage and maintain competition and to limit or end deceptive or unfair business practices. What is required is control of restraint of trade and unfair methods of competition.

Restraint of trade

The following indicates measures which can be introduced to provide an improvement in business practice.

1 Retailers should not be able to place pressure on manufacturers to prevent them from selling products to their competitors.
2 Retailers should not acquire their competitors with the intention of substantially lessening competition or creating a monopoly.
3 Retailers should not conspire to fix prices at levels that are unfair.
4 Retailers should not price their products lower in some areas with the objective of driving some retailers out of business so that they can then raise average prices.
5 Retailers should be allowed to sell foreign imported products if they compete fairly with domestic supplies.

Unfair methods of competition

1 Retailers should not use deceptive labelling, advertising, pricing or sales techniques. Consumers believe that the most misleading forms of selling are those by telephone, followed closely by direct mail techniques.
2 Prices of certain products such as drinks, ice creams, etc. should be displayed so that customers can check on what they have been charged. Prices have been removed from the items in many food retailers, with the prices being marked on the aisles and shelves only, because of the use of computerized checkouts which scan pre-marked bar codes. Some groups believe this process to be deceptive as it makes it harder for consumers to judge if the final total is correct or not.
3 Advertised special offers should be available so that the initial customer request is fulfilled.
4 Credit practices should be fair and unambiguous.
5 Warranties should be clearly written with an affirmation of a guarantee to the performance of the product and freedom from defects.
6 If a customer enters into a contract it should have clear wording about cancellation and liabilities. The contract should be written in easily understood terms.
7 When a product is ordered there should be no long-term delay in its delivery.
8 Deregulation of services should occur if it is in the interest of the consumer to have wider choice. For example, building societies moving into banking is a change with positive repercussions for the consumer due to increased competition.

Rights

When considering the above points, it should be realized that both the retailer and consumer have certain rights.

Sellers have the right to:

- sell any product determined by the retailer as long as it is not injurious to health and safety and has a description or label as to the correct use and contents;

- price products at any level provided that there is no discrimination among similar classes of buyers;

- claim any points about the product in their promotions as long as they are not dishonest and misleading;

- utilize whatever level of promotional expenditure they wish, based upon incentive schemes or other means of increasing sales, as long as these schemes are classed as fair competition.

Buyers can also be considered to have demonstrable rights:

- the right not to frequent a store or purchase the products offered them. The silent vote of consumers demonstrates consumer sovereignty by staying away from stores which create consumer problems. This is a very powerful sanction;

- the right to expect that a supplier will have ensured that the product is safe. With the increasing amounts of artificial additives in foods and the alarmist coverage of the press, this is a major concern. The whole food chain is under suspicion from worries of carcinogenic effects of food substitutes or additives to the worry over diseases which can be transmitted through fresh meat and other products. To ensure their fast food did not suffer from health hazard scares, McDonald's reformulated the cooking process of its french fries in order to make them more healthy and Dunkin' Donuts spent two years in an attempt to remove egg yolks and reduce levels of cholesterol in its doughnuts. The question is whether these are only minimal health improvements. These issues are discussed further in the section on product misuse and safety issues;

- the right to expect that the product will be essentially the same as the seller has represented it. This means that a fully informed buyer should be able to make a rational decision.

Criticism of the exploitation of workers

Western retailers are accused of attempting to make maximum profits through the exploitation and manipulation of suppliers in Third World countries. Whether it be a fruit farm worker in South Africa, a toy worker in China or a factory worker in Bangladesh, Sri Lanka or Pakistan, many are on subsistence wages; some are forced to work unpaid overtime, may be fired or even beaten if they cannot keep up with the production schedules. An Oxfam leaflet (1996) shows how a banana from the Caribbean costing 10p provides 4p to the retailer, 2p to the importer/wholesaler, 3p for shipping and handling charges and only 1p for the picking and growing.

The criticism is not confined solely to overseas labour; the National Group on Home Workers estimates there are currently a million home workers in the UK on extremely low wages. Whatever any retailer believes about the current situation, a number of pressure groups are now quite vociferous regarding the terms and conditions of different workers who are considered to be exploited and lacking in bargaining power. It is not just the small companies who are held up as examples of bad practice; Marks & Spencer were at the centre of a *World in Action* TV programme in January 1996 regarding the ethics of retailers and Toys "Я" Us have similarly featured in the *Wall Street Journal*.

CRITICISM OF MARKETING ACTIVITY

As we move further into the twenty-first century there is a growing concern for ethical practice which leads to business policies that aim to sustain the earth's resources. The new values emerging are placing pressure on the underlying concepts of marketing. This is creating a great deal of debate around the ethical standpoint of marketing. In examining criticisms of marketing it is important to distinguish between micro (the individual firm) and macro (how the whole system works) levels of marketing. Some complaints are only directed to one level, say the advertisements of Benetton. Other types of criticism, however, may be levelled at the industry as a whole – for example, that society is over-materialistic owing to the actions of the advertising industry in its prolific use of promotional techniques. Some of the most significant criticisms are discussed in the following subsections.

The disregard of the effects of promotion

The marketing concept can lead to a tunnel-vision focus on potential retail consumers without consideration being taken of the wider society. Promotion targeted on a specific segment may be criticized by other groups who may find it annoying, insulting, misleading or socially unacceptable. Promotional campaigns are often judged adversely to affect others due to the insensitive nature of marketing policies. Many women are offended by the use of the female body to sell products. It is argued that this indirectly creates symbols and meanings which bear no relationship to the place of women in modern society. While advertising is recognized as a powerful medium, it is criticized because it is not used in a socially responsible way. The critics often feel that individuals are manipulated by promotion to buy products that they do not need – and often products that should not exist. It is difficult to know whether the critics or consumers should lead on this. For example, some critics would ban many recreational products such as private boats and planes as well as motorcycles and some pets. On the other hand it is argued that marketing can only inform people and stimulate interest, it cannot manipulate people.

In addition, pollution and damage as a by-product of retail activities is treated as an environmental and social cost carried by the whole of society and not simply the company's consumers. Marketing pollution is the over-abundance of promotion which makes an area less attractive. There are roadside poster sites, advertisements on taxicabs and buses, messages painted on buildings, and leaflets given away which are then discarded – all of which create invasive pollution. There is also a trend to produce advertisements which aim to shock, such as those of Benetton, and there are others which offend, such as the amount of promotion for sex-talk telephone numbers. The overall effect of these trends is to lead the general public to mistrust marketing generally and to suspect the motives of advertisers.

In 1990 Benetton accepted the earlier emphasis of Oliviero Toscani to create a unified corporate trade-mark approach of reflecting the different nationalities of its customers throughout the world. This culminated in the launch of the 'United Colours of Benetton' campaign, where the company's communications were replaced by a series of advertisements related to social concern. Critics condemned the programme because of its ultimate goal to sell more products rather than to deal properly with the issues it raised. The management of Benetton responded by pointing out that other retailers simply provided a 'perfect world' style of advertising which was based upon an association that buying products leads to happiness. Toscani took the stance that if consumers were concerned about the world situation, they would be better to shop at Benetton. The use of large billboards to publicize the company and to bring about change was not fully accepted by major sections of the public – but this did nothing to stop the Benetton communication campaign. Such images as a priest and nun kissing on the lips; a bloody newborn baby with uncut umbilical cord; David Kirby dying of AIDS surrounded by his family; human body parts, marked like a side of beef with an 'HIV Positive' stamp; these are just a few examples of images taken from the campaign. This type of controversial advertising is not new. Calvin Klein has been accused of projecting images of child pornography based upon images of young people in seductive and vulnerable poses.

MINICASE 14.1

Changing values related to retail consumer issues

The UK government has produced a code of practice to crack down on misleading 'green' claims on consumer products. The new rules, which will ban terms such as 'environment-friendly', set standards for retailers and manufacturers. Claims will have to be accurate, capable of being substantiated by hard evidence, relevant to the product in question and used in an appropriate context. So boasting that a deodorant does not contain CFCs would not be allowed because CFCs are already banned by law. Nor could greeting cards be advertised as 'biodegradable', because all paper is over the longer term. Such claims have helped generate cynicism among consumers. But the government has ignored calls from consumer groups to make the code legally binding. The National Consumer Council, which demands statutory rules, will monitor products to see whether the code has any impact. The environment, regions and transport department, which is publishing the code after a year of consultation, hopes retailers will take it up voluntarily. 'The code's effectiveness will depend on how enthusiastically it is taken up by retailers,' the NCC said. B&Q, the DIY chain, said the company is to make the code mandatory for its suppliers. It has also changed the labelling of some of its products to make them comply with the rules. As a result, labels on insulation materials had already been changed to read: 'This product helps conserve energy.'

Source: Leyla Boulton, Financial Times, 17 February 1998

An overemphasis on profitable products

The marketing concept dictates that products should only be offered to the marketplace when they are profitable. This has culminated in the axing of bus and train transport routes and the disregard of low-spending individuals. The loss of the supporting services of transport may affect poorer individuals disproportionately and, in turn, will have an impact on their choice and selection of retail outlet. Where a want exists and the marketing opportunity cannot deliver the required profit return, then a retail offer is seldom developed. The market-based system is guided by self-interest and profit motivation; therefore consumer preferences are only accounted for if an ability to pay is demonstrated. These values are represented by a lack of concern for those who cannot afford to purchase certain items, travel to cheaper priced stores or obtain credit. In addition, it is widely questioned whether retailers want to cater for those who are disadvantaged or disabled. Facilities for blind and disabled people are of low priority in most business planning.

Marketing is sometimes blamed for the drive to the development of monopolistic competition. It is often felt that marketing is the catalyst in the constant attempts to create monopolistic competition. Retail price control by manufacturers has led to the domination of markets and is taken to be a key marketing strategy in order to create premium prices, obtain greater control and make higher profits. The question remains, however, as to the choice or alternatives different consumers have. Accordingly, it can be asked whether some are disadvantaged by the way business is organized. *The Economist* in 1997 highlighted that the Monopolies and Mergers Commission had concluded that the appliance manufacturers had used recommended retail prices to fix many of the prices at which electrical goods were sold. More recently the report by the EU Commission discussed in Minicase 14.2 highlights the ongoing problem of whether retail prices are fair or not.

There is greater profitability to be gained by developing in new site areas. Therefore, there is growing concern over the demise of the high street with the relocation of large retailers to out-of-town sites. The large retail companies have continued to develop new out-of-town areas, forcing out smaller alternative retailers, and creating change without due regard to the cost of environmental or social impacts on the area and local population. The concern over the pollution and waste of resources due to the increased use of the motor car may heighten the pressure on the development of future out-of-town sites or may lead to the introduction of parking fees which could subsidize other forms of transport.

MINICASE 14.2

Brussels drops compact disc price-fixing probe

The European Commission has dropped an investigation into possible price-fixing for compact discs by the world's biggest music companies. The inquiry was launched after a similar investigation in the US, where CD prices are generally much lower than in Europe.

Some officials thought that they had uncovered signs of collusion of prices while scrutinising a planned joint venture between EMI and Time Warner, which was eventually abandoned. But on Friday the Commission said that it had closed the five separate investigations into Bertelsmann Music Group, EMI, Sony Music, Universal Music and Warner Music. 'As the possible infringements were confined to the territory of single member states the Commission is informing the relevant national competition authorities of the results,' it said. It would 'continue to keep the industry under close scrutiny' and might re-open the inquiry if additional information came to hand. Companies found guilty of price-fixing in the EU can face big fines.

The big record companies agreed last year to drop a policy of requiring retailers to display a minimum price for CDs in their advertisements. In May, the five companies settled with the US Federal Trade Commission after it accused them of over-charging for CDs in the US for five years. The FTC said the companies' practice of setting minimum prices with retailers had cost consumers \$480m since 1997. They argue that CDs are not overpriced. The retail price should not be directly compared with the cost of manufacturing the CD, which is low, but also include the cost of finding or acquiring talent and developing successful acts, they say.

Separately, music companies are being investigated by UK competition authorities over allegations of collusion to block cheaper imports from continental Europe. Sony, EMI, Warner, Virgin, Universal, BMG and Pinnacle are being questioned under the inquiry launched in February. If found guilty of contravening competition laws, they could each be fined up to 10 per cent of their UK turnover for every year of the infringement, up to a maximum of three years. The European Commission is also continuing an investigation into whether the market for DVDs is being artificially fragmented in the EU.

Source: Ashling O'Connor and Daniel Dombey, FT.com site, 18 August 2001

The invasion of privacy

The power of modern computers allows companies to capture a complete range of personal information for use in targeting direct mail campaigns. As retail companies such as Tesco begin to spend more on loyalty programmes there is a growing database of information that can be utilized by retailers for different purposes. Also, there is a greater use of telephone and high street interviews to collect information. If this is for a reputable survey, there are no problems, but a number of companies use the disguise of research to collect information on individuals who are then targeted with specific insurance or financial offers or for fund-raising activities. There is also a distrust of Internet sites with over 50 per cent of online consumers citing privacy and security as a major concern. The fear is that private information will be shared between site providers and that the likelihood of fraud, poor service and abuse of credit card details is higher through Web transactions. This places the emphasis on companies to ensure that they have a trustworthy image by a demonstration of social responsibility in all business dealings.

A personal computer is not that personal when e-mails can be sent which are unsolicited. It is estimated that about 30 million e-mails are sent each day. Of these around 30 per cent are unsolicited and form what is known as 'spam'. Spam e-mails are those which are not welcome and therefore should not have been sent. As a result, companies should be considering permission marketing as a means to decide whether a recipient is happy to receive information and messages. Good permission marketing is where the individual opts in to receive the messages rather than has to tick an 'opt out' box in order not to get the mailings. The concern to companies and individuals is that spam is a cost to the company. This is based upon: the cost of time taken up in deleting or dealing with the mailings; the waste of resources due to the cost of the e-mail being carried through third party systems; and the annoyance factor of having to check unwanted mail and finding it irrelevant.

Another area of concern for intrusion is that of CCTV cameras in retail outlets. The benefits of CCTV are well recognized as a crime deterrent for customers as well as staff in retail environments. However, as a general surveillance tool they can be used for anything from monitoring the flow of store traffic, to maintaining safety of environment as well as monitoring staff. The modern CCTV is a covert miniature video camera hidden inside an everyday appliance such as a clock, a smoke alarm or a PIR (passive infra red) detector. As such, a covert installation is virtually impossible to detect and is not used in the same way as overt cameras to act as a deterrent to move a prospective thief on to another location.

Being able to detect crime is a key benefit to retailers using covert cameras. According to Home Office figures, total UK retail losses through theft are estimated at £1500 million per year. Interestingly, staff steal more than 40 per cent of this figure and over 50 per cent of staff apprehended are management. It is also estimated that £300 million per year is lost to fraudulent void and refund entries. In the case of till fraud a covert camera can be used as evidence to compare the video footage to the till data to establish a possible theft. The question is whether these unseen cameras are an intrusion or not. If it is known that covert cameras are in use perhaps this will deter possible thieves but it may place a greater level of stress on the retail staff as they may feel a 'big brother' is watching them.

The waste of resources on retail marketing

Marketing is seen as a waste of money because of the large amounts spent on promoting products. The money given over to retail promotion is often associated with convincing consumers to buy merchandise which they do not want. It is believed that the most disadvantaged of consumers are the ones most likely to be influenced by high expenditure on retail marketing promotional campaigns. Promotion is often criticized as a wasteful cost. In addition, competitive advertising is argued to be responsible for higher costs and subsequently higher prices. It is therefore argued that if advertising were reduced, or did not exist, there would be more competition based upon price and service. The consumerist standpoint is that it would be better to spend the money on informative advertising rather than competitive advertising. It is interesting to note, in this context, that when the US government banned cigarette advertising the sales did not fall significantly and the relative market share of the cigarette manufacturers remained very similar.

The levels of marketing expenditure are often blamed for changing consumer attitudes and bringing about a materialistic society where status is derived from the number and type of products we own or consume, the number of shopping trips we undertake, or what areas we shop in, rather than how good we are as a caring member of society. There is little doubt that marketing panders to materialistic values. However, the question is, does marketing create these values or simply appeal to the values already within society? It is found that the most simplistic of societies have members who want to accumulate possessions. In many tribal societies status comes from the number of animals or possessions an individual owns. On the other hand, marketing may well enhance or reinforce the appeal of materialism.

Need for more protection of children

Children are often believed to require protection from different products (Aacker and Day, 1974). While there is an age ban on certain products which are thought to be harmful to the young – alcohol, tobacco and gambling – it is often believed that retailers' profit motives lead to sales to those who are under age. Also, it is thought that the way scratch cards and the lottery product is offered alongside sweets and other pleasure purchases will lead to the young having a weakened set of values related to gambling.

Some retailers are careful to ensure that products such as toys or games are not sold to inappropriate age groups. The retailers take the responsible action of insisting on age labelling to ensure the safety of younger children. They also help individuals to purchase presents which will provide higher satisfaction for the recipient.

The targeting of children with advertisements can be seen to be unfair rather than misleading. This is because children often find it difficult to understand the advertising messages. The important questions in respect of children that need to be asked are:

- Can children tell the difference between commercials and the programmes they are watching?
- Do children understand that advertisements are attempting to influence them to buy?
- Can commercials make children want products that are of no benefit to them?

Misspent youth

The launch of Schools Plus, a scheme which aims to pour millions of pounds into the rapidly emptying coffers of schools across the UK (*MW* last week), has brought the subject of marketing to pupils back into the spotlight and once more questions the ethics of marketing to children.

Since Tesco launched its Computers for Schools scheme in 1990, Walkers Crisps tied up with News International to market its Free Books for Schools on-pack promotion in 1998 and the *Mirror* and United Biscuits launched a free maths equipment deal two years ago, major education marketing exercises have been thin on the ground. Now Schools Plus aims to become the mother of all corporate funding schemes in primary and secondary schools across the country. The company is on the verge of signing up global giants such as Coca-Cola and Burger King to an initiative which, it claims, could raise millions of pounds for impoverished schools.

Brands which join the scheme will be included in a book containing vouchers worth up to £250, which can be refunded against participating sponsors' products. The books will be sold to parents for £10, of which £7 will go into school funds, with the remaining £3 going to Schools Plus to cover costs. This raises the question of whether the parents are being encouraged to pay for their children's education themselves, in exchange for discounts on brands. There is also the added worry for parents that if they don't buy the vouchers their children will not receive a proper education. The company says the initiative differs from other school incentive schemes, such as Walkers' and Tesco's offers, because it allows more than one brand to participate 'in an unobtrusive way' and includes brands children buy as a matter of course.

Schools Plus was set up at the beginning of last year by a group of senior marketing figures who have all been involved in education, either as school governors or through the running and creation of school promotions.

Two teaching unions, the National Association of Head Teachers and the Secondary Headteachers' Association, are backing the scheme and must be rubbing their hands with glee at the prospect of securing funding from these global giants. But despite Schools Plus's ostensibly altruistic approach, opponents of the scheme are worried that brands are fostering relationships which will give them more control over children – their own future consumers.

Rumours in educational circles that McDonald's is planning to install outlets in school canteens in the UK, similar to those it already operates in colleges in countries such as Australia, have so far proved unfounded.

But Naomi Klein's polemical anti-corporate book *No Logo* outlines two startling examples of corporate classroom interference. One US school, sponsored by Coca-Cola, held a 'Coca-Cola day' and suspended a rebellious pupil for wearing a Pepsi T-shirt. Klein also highlights another school, which was sponsored by US TV station Channel One on the understanding that pupils watch ten minutes of the broadcaster's programming every day in the classroom, including three minutes of ads. Some observers find this approach outrageous and are intent on having all types of marketing and advertising to children outlawed.

The UK's National Consumer Council (NCC) drew up a list of guidelines in 1989 and relaunched in 1996, which it hoped brands would adhere to when approaching schools with sponsorship or branding possibilities. The NCC guidelines covered branded information packs and other educational resources, but did not deal specifically with marketing. But the organisation has been criticised for failing to widely publicise the code or produce any follow-up research on marketing to schools. Many parents still believe regulations exist to prevent advertising from invading classrooms.

The NCC has now passed on responsibility for the regulations to the Consumers' Association (CA), which is set to release a code of practice this summer, in conjunction with the Incorporated Society of British Advertisers (ISBA) and the Department for Education and Employment (DfEE). The previous code did not have DfEE backing and the new guidelines have no legal status as yet, and are not expected to gain it. The new code embraces emergent forms of marketing, including voucher schemes like Schools Plus. The CA is taking a controversial stance on the issue. A spokesman says: 'The CA has no objection in principle to advertising to children. They (the children) need to become informed consumers and if the CA opposed that it would undermine the empowerment process. A good proportion of commercial activity is of high quality, can add value to the curriculum and can provide additional resources that would otherwise be unavailable.' However, the CA's admission is that children are 'a particularly vulnerable group of consumers'.

Source: Marketing Week, 31 May 2001

PRODUCT MISUSE AND SAFETY ISSUES

The most dangerous aspect of any purchase concerns the way the customer uses the product. In fact, the most dangerous aspect of any purchase often relates to the type of consumer utilizing it. Most of us realize that electrical appliances in the bathroom can be extremely dangerous or that electrical garden tools have to be used with care; such dangers have prompted public policy makers to urge or insist on safe designs and testing. However, there is a limit to the precautionary notes which can be presented on a label and a manual or leaflet may often be discarded without due notice to safety hints. Consumerism would like greater safety but individuals may easily misuse products simply because of the type of user they are.

1 *Enthusiastic users* may focus more on using the product as early as possible than on studying the directions for use. There is also a problem in the self-assembly of products whereby care in construction and checks are not carried out in the rush to use the product.

2 *Desensitized users* are often unaware of the consequences of their action, or they may carry out the activity routinely and thus become less vigilant and alert. In addition, when the consumer takes risks which do not lead to problems – they 'get away with it' – they may be more prone to risky behaviour.

3 *Hedonistic users* focus on the fantasy and fun of using products and are less likely to assess the risks of their actions. The use of alcohol, or even glue, may also lead to misuse and abuse.

Critics of the safety of products believe that thousands of accidents could be avoided if companies made better use of improved design and safety standards. The Consumer Product Safety Commission (CPSC) is the federal US agency with major responsibility for product safety in about 15 000 product categories. The CPSC can exercise its powers to:

● require products to be marked with clear warnings and instructions;

● issue mandatory standards that may force firms to redesign products;

● require manufacturers and resellers to notify if they find a product has a defect that would create a substantial risk of injury;

- require manufacturers to conduct reasonable testing programmes to make sure the products conform to established safety standards.

When the CPSC finds a product that may be a potential danger, it can issue an order for the firm to bring the product into conformity with the applicable safety rule, repair the defect or exchange it for one that meets existing safety standards. They can also insist that the original price is refunded. Firms found breaking the safety rules can be fined, and executives are held personally liable and can be fined or jailed for up to a year. The CPSC may also instigate product recall – so that the product can be modified or discontinued.

Consumers in the US have the right to sue the maker or seller of an injurious product, in addition to the powers held by the CPSC. These are so-called class-action suits and there are over 100 000 in the USA each year.

GREEN ISSUES

As society develops there is an emphasis on the need for a more holistic approach to the relationship existing between the economy, society and the environment. The emphasis of this is on the marketing activities of companies and whether they are affecting local and global sustainability of different resources. This presents itself in a green consumerism movement which expresses a preference for less environmentally harmful goods and services. Of course, environmentally friendly is a non-specific term and, in reality, no mass-produced good can be entirely environmentally friendly. Such misleading terminology has allowed considerable freedom for retailers to declare their operation or processes as being green. At the same time, there has been a rise in the awareness and concern of green issues due to pressure group activity, increased media coverage of the issues, and the adoption of new legislation. The trend is strong throughout Europe, with Germany leading the way with organizations adopting a formal environmental policy. The Germans are also keen to introduce schemes whereby scientific testing takes place to assess the claims of various products that they are environmentally friendly. The German consumer is seen as being more environmentally conscious than other European consumers. Sriram and Forman (1993) found that 82 per cent of German supermarket consumers make decisions on environmental considerations. This can be compared to 67 per cent in the Netherlands, 55 per cent in the UK and 50 per cent in France.

However, the key question is whether the consumer will be willing to pay higher prices for green products. There is a segment of about one-quarter of the population which is willing to pay higher prices but this is affected by times of recession, competitive pricing and the media. The retail industry may also be affected by the use of more friendly chemicals in products. If the new ingredients are perceived to be inferior in terms of achieving the results required by the consumer, the implication is that the consumer would sooner buy the more harmful product if it is thought to be superior. There is another segment that believes that the retailer will claim the products are green on the basis of wanting to charge higher prices. The cynical view held by many is that greenness is a way to exploit the consumer through:

- making only marginal or cost-free shifts in the responsibility of the company towards the environment;

- saving on costs by using cheaper packing or other measures;

- using so-called greenness simply as a public relations exercise;

- disguising the prime objective of achieving higher profits behind a mask of social responsibility.

Retailers need to identify and quantify the processes and activities of their operations in relation to the use of materials and energy. There is a need to consider any waste or emission produced and opportunities for environmental improvement. Some retailers have carried out this process and adopted change. B&Q has taken a holistic approach to green retailing practices with its logistics planning such as: the control and reduction of vehicle emissions, improved distribution logistics to reduce vehicle movements, working with suppliers to reduce the use of packing such as corrugated board, recycling policies and systems at store level, and the promotion of awareness in its staff. Some companies, such as The Body Shop, who follow EU Eco-Management guidelines, and Boots the Chemist, are being proactive in the area of environmental responsibility. Others merely jump on the bandwagon and offer recycled or disposable packaging without examination of their own environmental practices and policies within the organization or giving any consideration to wider ethical concerns. Sainsbury have taken bold initiatives in the writing of an environmental policy and undertaking a constant review of policies. Their initiatives included the early removal of CFCs from own-label products and refrigeration equipment, a plastics and waste recycling facility for the company and customers, new energy management systems – plus a wide range of environmental and organic products.

Finding merchandise which is environmentally acceptable

The chemical compounds chlorofluorocarbons (CFCs) are/were used in the production of aerosols, packaging materials, refrigeration and air-conditioning plants. It is widely recognized that there are long-term dangers to the ozone layer from CFCs, which could culminate in a greater number of skin cancers and other wide-ranging problems. Many companies have taken a responsible attitude and voluntarily found alternative chemicals to CFCs. This has led to far greater pressure on those companies who did not change quickly to new compounds. Most aerosols have now adopted more benign chemicals which – given the diversity of range of spray applications, from hair sprays to furniture polishes – has provided strong evidence of the speed at which companies can adopt the above guidelines.

One of society's main problems is based upon the lack of space to dispose of refuse. This makes the disposal of non-biodegradable materials such as plastics and styrofoam packaging a major problem. It also makes the sale of products such as disposable nappies a long-term environmental problem. In the USA, a number of states have banned the use of all plastic packaging in stores and restaurants. This trend has caused problems for McDonald's and other fast-food restaurants which have had to find alternative forms of packaging. McDonald's has changed to wax-paper packing rather than attempting to dispose of polystyrene from the estimated 22 million customers it serves each day. Some firms are recycling plastic to make the most of the relatively recent concerns about environmental issues. Procter & Gamble market cleaning products in recycled plastic bottles. The important question to be posed by retailers, however, remains whether the customer will be willing to pay higher prices for products that are less harmful to the environment. There is also a supplementary question: will the consumer be satisfied with lower quality recycled packaging? There is no clear answer to this as some consumers will accept these changes but others will not. The young and the affluent are more likely to accept pro-environment changes irrespective of whether they lead to higher costs and changes.

THE ACCEPTABILITY OF A SOCIETAL MARKETING APPROACH

It has been argued that the pressures affecting the image of marketing need to be taken into account. This has culminated in the movement towards a societal concept of marketing which stresses the enhancement of the needs of society as well as those of the consumer. The importance of any changes a company makes to improve society has to be balanced with how much else could be achieved. Some companies, such as brewers and distillers, are creating campaigns to warn people of the excesses of drinking but it is questionable whether they are as worried about the customer as they are about the legislation which could affect their operations. While some companies may pay lip service to a societal concept for PR purposes, in a competitive situation many of the problems related to retail, and its marketing, will continue. It is also important to recognize that consumers are now better educated and informed, and are competent enough to select products which are not creating undue problems for society. If companies or their products do create problems, there are articulate pressure groups and government legislation available for consumer and environmental protection. A truly societal marketing approach is problematic because of the need to resolve multifaceted decisions over profit, pollution, and environmental concerns such as energy and land use. However, some companies perform their marketing activities better than others and are judged in positive terms by the public. The disposition of the public to buying and promoting the brands of retailers is an important aspect of contemporary marketing. The image of retailers, based upon the expectations of the public and the behaviour of the company, may lead to different patterns of negative or positive demand. It is therefore important for companies to adopt a more societal stance by showing that they are ethical and considerate in their marketing and planning. This is important for both retailers and marketers who should accept responsibility for any consequences of their activities and actions. Good business managers are being urged to put themselves in the consumer's position with regard to how they or their family feel they should be treated by others. The following points are relevant in this context:

1 Good business managers should be socially responsible to all stakeholders (customers, employees, suppliers, shareholders, society, etc.) related to the company or retail offer so as to minimize social costs. They should also have regard for laws or regulations, and be ethical in management decisions. For example, not selling certain products such as alcohol and tobacco to children or placing sweets at the checkout counter.

2 Managers should be honest in claims and promotions, not be deceptive or agree to misleading advertising. They should show fairness to third parties. In addition, there should not be any hidden costs – identify extra costs which may be applicable.

3 The retail products offered should not cause harm when in use or on disposal and managers should communicate any risks which are known to be associated with any product.

4 Marketers should undertake not to adopt sales techniques or fund-raising under the guise of research. Also, it is unfair and unethical to use promotions as research when adequate stock is unavailable because the research is being used as a method of deciding on the stock requirements.

Some retail companies such as The Body Shop have attempted to become benefactors of the local environment in which the stores are located, so as to bring about improvements to inner-city neighbourhoods and communities. This is a proactive approach to social responsibility. Community relations programmes may include:

- ensuring that no retail outlets limit or hinder access for disabled people (millions of consumers find it difficult to carry out shopping as they may have arthritis, visual or hearing impairments and difficulties in walking, reading signs, reaching or stretching or manoeuvring in confined spaces – this means any steps or obstacles, heavy doors and product positioning may make it difficult for them to shop in comfort);

- demonstrating an ecological approach by clearing up packaging and the local environment as well as recycling waste (a slogan of The Body Shop is refill, reuse and recycle);

- supporting local charities, and young and old people's centres;

- setting up links with local colleges and schools;

- training and employing local residents;

- giving special promotional offers to senior citizens or disadvantaged groups.

Cause-related marketing

The use of sales promotion techniques is not always well accepted when such techniques are used under the guise of helping the community. There is a proliferation of schemes aimed at schoolchildren – encouraging their families to patronize certain retail chain outlets so that the children's school will receive some benefit. Tesco have used computers for schools, WH Smith have offered books for schools and Boots, sports equipment. Teachers have shown some concern that the underlying purpose of the retailers' ventures is to benefit themselves in the long run in terms of improved profits and improved image. However, there is also some public concern as to the true purpose of such schemes.

The strength of 'good cause' related marketing is that the majority of parents as well as children are more interested in buying a company's products if they are associated with a charity. Mintel found in 2000 that the majority of those questioned about cause-related marketing would be likely to purchase a product which supported a good cause. The public, especially females, were even willing to pay higher prices for products which were linked to charitable causes. Camelot, Virgin and The Body Shop were the companies most frequently associated with charitable causes. Apart from these, there were few other companies mentioned. Therefore, the use of cause-related marketing can play an important role in the marketing of a retail company to enhance its corporate image and increase sales.

Iceland – socially responsible or utilising marketing promotion?

Iceland, the frozen food retailer, challenged the food industry yesterday to follow its lead in refusing to accept genetically modified ingredients in own label products. The group pledged that all own label products would be manufactured without soya, or any of its derivatives, which have been genetically modified to resist weedkiller. It also revealed it was exploring the possibility of eliminating all processes involving genetically modified products in the manufacture of its own label ranges and will seek to use meat from animals fed only on non-modified products. Malcolm Walker, chairman, said the introduction of genetically modified soya into the food chain represented unquantifiable risks to consumers. It was 'even potentially more devastating . . . to health and the environment than BSE'. 'Genetic engineering is an issue which should concern us now. We urge all other food retailers, manufacturers and farmers to campaign for crop segregation and tighter safety legislation,' he said.

However, the big food retailers said it would be impossible for them to follow Iceland's example. 'You cannot equate a niche frozen food retailer with a supermarket as the quantities required are so different,' said Safeway. Four supermarket groups – Asda, J. Sainsbury, Tesco, and Safeway – have volunteered to label products containing genetically modified ingredients. Although EU and US authorities have declared modified soya safe, some scientists are concerned that the long-term effects are unknown.

Source: Peggy Hollinger, *Financial Times*, 19 March 1998

Update: It was reported in the *Financial Times* on 4 July 2001 that Iceland had very poor results in 2001 and admitted they were suffering from a disastrous switch to organic produce and therefore the company's trading remained weak.

CORPORATE SOCIAL RESPONSIBILITY

The issues of corporate social responsibility cover a company's approach not only to its markets but to its employees, the local community, its suppliers and the way it treats the environment. This places a duty on the organization to seek social approval for its policies because of the potentially detrimental effect on the quality of life of others. Many companies are attempting to provide a green, caring image for their organizations and project the message that they have a social conscience. Sponsorship for the arts, the environment or worthy causes is taking a growing share of marketing budgets. B&Q ensures that almost the whole range of its wooden products has been independently certified as coming from well-managed forests. The Body Shop is entering into a long-term plan to have partnership agreements with staff and managers in nearly half its 40 stores; Thomas Cook is funding local hospital construction; Butlins is offering day visits for underprivileged children; and ICI is transforming redundant sites into nature reserves. Kentucky Fried Chicken is co-operating with the Tidy Britain Group to remove litter and educate people on how to improve the environment. The cynics of all this argue that it is impossible for companies to provide for society without an accompanying high environmental cost such as global warming, damage to the ozone layer or a waste of scarce and non-renewable resources.

Some companies are offering to give donations to good causes in order to improve their image. The Leeds VISA card has made it into the *Guinness Book of Records* twice for its charitable money-raising efforts. By March 1995, it had donated £6.1 million to three charities – the British Heart Foundation, Mencap and Imperial Cancer Research. Some 20p is donated for every £100 spent using the card. In addition, those spending more than £1500 a year on their card have their £12 annual fee refunded or £7 refunded and £5 given to charity.

Many retail companies are leading the field in environmental concern by their participation in recycling initiatives. Boots, ASDA and Tesco have all set up recycling units. Reusing newspapers, aluminium cans, bottles and packaging is a saving on resources and does not add to the ever-increasing need for landfill sites. Collection banks for different types of refuse and return policies on carrier bags for reuse are to be seen in most advanced countries.

The different company initiatives explained above are part of a wider need for companies to have a posture which gives them comparative marketing advantage over their competitors. Companies now need to be doing things better than their competitors if they are going to survive and prosper. To be socially responsible, it is not enough to have a hidden agenda of saving on costs – although improved quality management will often reduce wastage and management time. Today's consumers are able to judge the actions of retailers. There is often a need to undertake a strategy which may have cost implications but which should lead to longer-term increases in profitability. The actions of companies have to link their performance into medium- and long-term benefits. The best strategies being adopted are often proactive and honest and are not knee-jerk reactions to pressure groups. They include:

- integrated management policies aimed at protection of the consumer and environment;
- a policy for the continuous process of improvement in relations with all stakeholders as shown in Fig. 14.1;
- a continuous education programme for all staff in order to train and motivate them into conducting all company activities in an ethically agreed way;
- a system to check that all retail products and services are safe, fairly priced and promoted with full information, and where possible to assess the possibility of the products and packaging being recycled, reused or having directions related to safe disposal;
- advising and, where relevant, ensuring that there is provision of information to customers, suppliers and the public in the safe use, transit, storage and disposal of retail products. The retailer as a condition to the supplier may stipulate this;
- running the operation in an energy efficient way and to minimize the problems of waste disposal and impacts on the environment;
- supporting and conducting research which identifies the ways and means of improving the retail product and services in relation to preventing adverse impacts and improving quality;
- promoting partnership relationships with suppliers so that they also adopt a consistent approach to socially responsible policies;
- having contingency plans and emergency preparedness in case a hazard or health risk is associated with any of the company's products.

Figure 14.1 illustrates the relationship factors with retail stakeholders (employees, banks, government, local community, landlords, service providers, shareholders, pressure

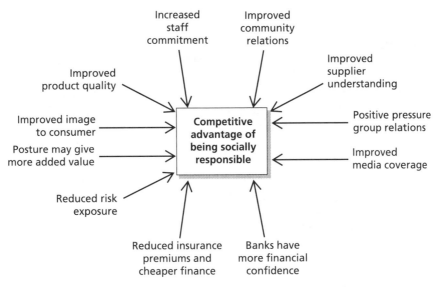

Fig. 14.1 The relationship factors of stakeholder social responsibility

groups, media) which need to be considered when contemplating the benefits of adopting a socially responsible approach to the marketplace. It is increasingly important for retailers to realize that they cannot simply follow the sole pursuit of profit without due consideration to the diversity of stakeholder interest. Corporate social responsibility has to be treated as a strategic process which delivers a more effective means of achieving core mission objectives. The way some retailers approach strategic planning to achieve the advantages of social responsibility are discussed in the following sections.

Strategies for corporate social responsibility

There are different components of corporate strategy which are critical to the success or otherwise of delivering a truly socially responsible service or product.

1 The first is to ensure that the mission and objectives of the company reflect the posture and stance of the organization towards social issues and are central to its functioning. There has to be a close fit between the company's mission and its social responsibility programme.

2 The second is to ensure that whatever responsible policy is carried out there is some competitive advantage gained that is specific and measurable as a benefit to the company. This may be visibility of actions or change of attitude by the different stakeholders.

3 The third is based upon ethical leadership or degrees of compliance to adoption of corporate social responsibility. Voluntarism is far more beneficial than externally imposed compliance requirements.

The different approaches to the adoption process are discussed in the next section.

Self-regulation

The setting up of voluntary codes of practice is valuable for the consumer and creates benefit for those companies who join such an initiative. Once a code has been agreed companies are more likely to abide by the code because they will be in danger of being judged to be a deviant if they contravene the procedures agreed by every other company. Voluntary codes do not protect the consumer from companies that are determined to stay outside of such schemes. The Office of Fair Trading is a useful arbitrator in consumer or trade disputes as one duty of the Office is to approve, monitor and revise codes. The advertising industry set up the British Code of Advertising Practice in 1962. Any complaint is brought before the British Advertising Standards Authority whose job it is to ensure advertisements are 'legal, decent, honest and truthful' and that any advertisement is produced with 'a sense of responsibility to the consumer'. The US Direct Marketing Association has a code of ethics. The main directives are:

- all offers should be clear, honest and complete;
- offers suitable for adults only should not be made to children;
- sweepstake prizes should be advertised in a clear, honest and complete way so that the consumer may know the exact nature of the offer;
- merchandise should not be shipped without first having received the customer's permission;
- telemarketers should remove the name of any customer from their telephone lists when requested by the individual.

Self-regulatory programmes have certain advantages over government laws and regulatory agencies. They are usually less expensive to establish and implement, and the guidelines that make up the code are normally more realistic and easier to apply. In addition, self-regulatory programmes reduce the need to expand government bureaucracy and costs. However, with some trade associations, the worst offenders are not members and therefore are not required to abide by the code. When an association attempts to revise its members' actions it may find it has little authority to enforce guidelines. Therefore, self-regulation is often less strict and has less sanctions than would be the case if the regulation were applied by a government office.

The Body Shop was one of the first retailers to adopt a company policy against the testing of products on animals. The company has raised public awareness on the issue of animal testing over many years, having worked closely with the British Union for the Abolition of Vivisection. While such policies are now commonplace, almost 3 million experiments on live animals took place in Britain in 1994 and as such this will remain a contentious issue. A leaflet from The Body Shop states:

> The Body Shop never has, and never will, test ingredients or final products on animals or authorise such tests on its behalf. We adhere to the BUAV's five year rule – every six months, our suppliers and manufacturers must sign a declaration stating that they are not testing our ingredients on animals and have not done so within the last five years. This dynamic policy is proving successful in changing the practices of suppliers and manufacturers who used to test on animals.

The strategic options for any company policy are as follows:

Non-compliance

Companies with poor long-term strategic planning and 'tunnel vision' may choose non-compliance with the new trends and regulations sweeping the world. Alternatively, other companies will decide that because of cost constraints they are not able to change their policies or products.

Compliance

Companies that pick up pressures from their operating environment are going to be more reactive to the demand by legislators and consumers for changes in the methods and organization of business practices. Compliance as a posture will not achieve competitive advantage, as the company is more likely to be a follower than a leader in social and environmental concerns.

Proactive compliance

Companies that are well aware of their operating environment, due to the systems they apply to understanding the environment, will be ahead of the need for legislation or change and will be more proactive. These companies will be the first to introduce policies and change, and this may enhance their image and reputation.

Social and ethical leadership

These companies will strive for best practice in all their standards of business. They will be the leaders in their sectors, with environmental management and social responsibility being a pivotal basis for their business. The Co-operative movement and The Body Shop are examples of this type of organization.

CONCLUSION

Consumerism is a growing, powerful force which has to be treated seriously. Clearly the retailer's reaction to consumerism must reflect the changing attitudes of the customer. The benefit of living in a pluralist society is that pressures are brought to bear on organizations to encourage them to be more socially responsible. Retailers need to be increasingly sensitive to the needs of society and to practise improved community relations. The demands made by the consumer are often realistic and should be an indicator of what needs to change. The dilemma from the retailer's perspective is how to bring about change while still being able to compete with other stores. It has been argued here that there are advantages in being responsive to consumer pressures. In fact, retailers should actively encourage and seek feedback on consumer issues to ensure that they are abreast of the trends.

The change in different individual and pressure group values towards the acceptability of business actions creates the preconditions for a change in strategic planning within retail companies. This change needs to address the ethical concerns of different stakeholder groups and provide for assessment of policies related to society and the environment. We cannot expect any dramatic voluntary short-term change by companies; we can, however, expect a gradual and continuous adjustment to the need to satisfy not only existing consumers but members of the wider society.

EXERCISES

The exercises in this section relate to consumerism and ethics in retailing. It is advised that you work through them before moving on to Chapter 15.

1 Having read this chapter, what ethical guidelines, if any, would you now recommend to a chain of children's clothes shops?

2 With regard to ethics, think about the future issues for retailing and write down what you believe are the most important aspects of concern for an improvement in the way UK retailing or business will operate in the next 20 years. Use the grid below as a guide.

Business operations/interfaces:	Issues to be faced in next 20 years:
• retail marketing • purchasing from stores and electronically sourcing and buying • local community • EU and government legislation • pressure groups • others (list)	
Issues identified as of most concern:	**How you believe these will be resolved:**

3 Explain all the different pressures there are for a retailer to become more ethical. Can you explain why a retailer or the retail industry is so resistant to pressures for change from consumer groups?

4 It can be said that consumerism provides the ideal business opportunity for retailers. What is meant by this statement and do you believe it is valid?

5 What can be done to improve the safety of retail products? What are the cost and other implications of your argument?

REFERENCES AND FURTHER READING

Aaker, D. and Day, G. (1974) *Consumerism: search for the consumer interest.* New York: Free Press.

Bansal, P. and Kilbourne, W.E. (2001) 'The ecologically sustainable retailer', *Journal of Retailing and Consumer Services*, 8 (3), 139–46.

Body Shop (1996) *Measuring Up: A summary of The Body Shop values report 1995.* The Body Shop Consumer Literature.

Boulton, L. (1998) 'Ministers to publish guidelines for "green" labelling', *Financial Times*, 17 February.

Chryssides, G. and Kaler, J. (1993) *An Introduction to Business Ethics.* New York: Chapman & Hall.

DeGeorge, R. (1986) *Business Ethics.* New York: Macmillan.

Eadie, A. (1995) 'Money: if you want a new Vauxhall, get a GM card', *Independent*, 24 June.

The Economist (1997) 'Upheaval on the high street: The Monopolies and Mergers Commission is about to demand an end to the use of recommended retail prices by electrical-appliance makers. A wave of discounting could follow', *The Economist*, 31 May.

Hollinger, P. (1998) 'Iceland challenges rivals on genetic soya', *Financial Times*, 19 March.

Hollinger, P. (1998) 'Probe into profitability set to fire a warning shot at the big four food retailers: inquiry by Office of Fair Trading may signal that any further concentration of power among supermarket groups will only be acceptable if customers see benefits', *Financial Times*, 31 July.

Marketing Week (2001) 'Misspent Youth', *Marketing Week*, 31 May, 26–9.

Mintel (2000) Cause Related Marketing Report, July, Mintel International Group, London.

Nader, R. (1966) *Unsafe at any Speed*. New York: Pocket Books.

O'Connor, A. and Dombey, D. (2001) 'Brussels drops compact disc price-fixing probe', FT.com site, 17 August.

Packard, V. (1960) *The Wastemakers*. Harmondsworth: Penguin.

Simms, C. (1992) 'Green issues and strategic management in the grocery retail sector', *International Journal of Retail and Distribution Management*, 20 (1), 32–42.

Sriram, V. and Forman, A.M. (1993) 'The relative importance of products' environmental attributes: a cross cultural comparison', *International Marketing Review*, 10 (3), 51–70.

Suchard, H.T. and Suchard, J.C. (1994) 'Corporate environmental marketing: an environmental action model', *Business Strategy and the Environment*, 1 (1), 25–34.

Whysall, P. (2000) 'Addressing ethical issues in retailing: a stakeholder perspective', *International Journal of Retail Distribution and Consumer Research*, 10 (3), 305–18.

15 International retailing

This chapter should enable you to understand and explain:

- international retailing;
- differences between national retail structures;
- motives underlying retail internationalization;
- the direction of expansion;
- different market entry methods;
- typologies of international retailing.

THE MOVE TO INTERNATIONAL RETAILING

Retailers have long operated on an international basis, yet it is only since the last decade or so of the twentieth century that they have done so on any significant scale. In the past, companies trading outside their home market were rare by comparison with the number of retailers operating solely within the domestic market. Also, international operations usually accounted for a much smaller part of the business than domestic trade. However, the larger retail companies that have successfully developed their marketing strategy and human resource base in the domestic market are well suited to extend development into international markets. Other smaller players that have a powerful brand and a strong retail concept also have the ability to internationalize successfully through using a lower cost and risk strategy such as that of a franchise.

Luxury goods retailers are among some of the earliest internationalists, seeking to serve a similar consumer niche in a number of cosmopolitan cities around the world. This is exemplified by Harrods, which operated a store in Argentina in the early twentieth century in order to meet the needs of colonial expatriates. However, international expansion was not just limited to luxury goods retailers. Around the same time, in 1909, Woolworths (then FW Woolworth) expanded its variety store operation from the US to Europe. International retailers are often perceived as companies serving consumer niches, such as The Body Shop or Benetton; however, mass merchandise retailers are also moving across national borders, as exemplified by Tesco's move into Eastern Europe and WH Smith's and Sainsbury's entrance into the US market.

This is not to say that we have witnessed significant international expansion by many retailers. Even today, it is noteworthy that many retailers remain essentially domestic operations. In addition, many of those retailers we might perceive to be developed internationalists, or indeed global operators, receive only a minority of their turnover and

Table 15.1 Overseas turnover: examples of European retailers

Retailer	Origin	European ranking (1999)	Percentage of turnover from non-domestic operation(s)
Carrefour	France	1	48
Tesco	UK	3	12
Ahold	Netherlands	20	20
H&M Hennes & Mauritz	Sweden	54	85
IKEA	Sweden	137	92

Source: Retail Intelligence, 2001b

profit from their operations outside the home market (Table 15.1). Thus, it might be suggested that while the process of retail internationalization has increased at a substantial rate, particularly since the late 1980s, international retailing is still at a relatively early stage in its development.

Why do retailers choose to enter new geographical markets? The motivations underlying the strategy to internationalize include *saturation*, namely that retailers in developed markets such as the UK are forced to move into new markets because of limited opportunities for growth at home. While this is certainly a factor, it is only part of the reason. Increasingly the forces driving the process of internationalization are seen as a complex interplay of push and pull factors. The growing importance of retail internationalization is illustrated by the fact that not only are more retailers operating internationally but, increasingly, they are moving into markets that are distant – both geographically and culturally. As part of this change retailers must also assess which market entry method is most appropriate. Their selection will be the outcome of the interplay of a number of different factors such as the nature of the host market, the sector of retail activity, and the nature of the organization.

THE DEVELOPMENT OF INTERNATIONAL RETAILING

This chapter examines the concept of retail internationalization by uncovering some of the variations within Western European retailing. The motives underlying retail internationalization are then explored. While in the past much prominence has been placed on a *reactive* interpretation of internationalization, namely that retailers only move outside the domestic market when opportunities for growth at home are severely limited, more recently a more *proactive* stance has been taken. Prominence has been placed upon the notion that retailers actively seek opportunities outside the home market, regardless of the potential for growth within it. Both the direction of expansion (choice of host market) and the method of entering a market are considered (the pros and cons of acquisition, joint venture, franchise and so on). Emphasis is placed upon the different requirements of retailers operating in different sectors and with various retail offers.

Prior to examining the nature of the contemporary international retail arena, we will discuss the factors that constrained retailers from operating on an international basis in the past, and how those influences have changed to promote the modern international retail environment. Manufacturers and retailers are at opposite ends of the distribution channel (*see* discussion in Chapter 1). They may also be viewed as dichotomous in other ways. Until recently, manufacturers have dominated retailers within the channel of distribution. For example, Coca-Cola, as a supplier, has had the advantage of utilizing the expertise of overseas distributors familiar with local consumer attitudes and preferences. However, retailers faired less well. US players such as Sears had major problems in Belgium and Spain, and JC Penney were not successful in Italy and Belgium. Many of the problems of these US companies have been related to their lack of awareness of the European consumer. In fact, the problems have been multifaceted. There was a lack of awareness of the consumer market and the retail infrastructure.

Conditions constraining the international development of retailers

1 Retailers have traditionally been perceived as operating in a localized manner and holding limited market power, whereas many manufacturers have long since had an international presence.

2 While manufacturers have been characterized as large companies with sophisticated organizational structures, retailers have been perceived as small scale and unsophisticated in comparison.

3 Manufacturers have established brands, while it is only recently that retailers have created strong brand images capable of international transfer.

4 There has been a lack of understanding of the consumers in foreign markets.

Before discussing the motivations leading to internationalization, it is important to have an understanding of the structural changes that have occurred in the retail industry in the last few decades. Although these trends have not in themselves caused internationalization, they may be considered as prerequisites to significant levels of retail internationalization.

As was discussed more fully in Chapter 1, there have been major changes in the retail environment since the Second World War. While to some extent these structural shifts have occurred throughout Western Europe, they are most apparent in the advanced retail markets of the UK and Germany, and particularly within the food sector.

Structural changes in post-war retailing

1 Retailers have grown in strength relative to manufacturers and in some cases are now characterized as dominating the distribution channel.

2 Traditional independent retailers and co-operative societies have lost market share to multiple retail organizations.

3 Larger but fewer stores and retail companies.

4 Increasing consolidation of the retail sector measured by increasing rates of market concentration and claims of saturation.

5 Higher profitability of major EU and US retailers and subsequent ability to embark on expansionist strategies into foreign markets in order to achieve growth.

Each of these structural shifts have allowed, or indeed promoted, the process of retail internationalization. The fact that retailers have grown in size and strength has given them the capability to operate on an international basis. Intrinsically linked to this is the dominance of the multiple organizations. Their sheer size has given them the necessary financial resources and backing required to move internationally and as they have grown in size so they have developed in terms of organizational structure. The multiples, therefore, have the management expertise and sophistication, as well as being more likely to have access to sufficient capital, to operate internationally while smaller, more traditional, firms have not.

The first three structural changes listed in the box are prerequisites for international retailing on a mass scale, but the fourth provides the prompt. If retailers are to continue to grow in a concentrated market then they must look to diversify from their core activities. While some may follow a strategy of diversifying their activities within the home market – for example, one of the largest retailers in Germany, Rewe, operates a number of types of food store, from hypermarkets to convenience stores, as well as DIY stores, Klee garden centres, Idea and Sconti drugstores, Frick carpet outlets and Kressner clothing stores – others look to transfer their offer to a new market – for example, US clothing retailer The Gap's entry into Canada, Japan, France, Germany and the UK.

The type of decisions made, whether to internationalize or not, will be based upon the following strategic concerns, discussed in further detail later in the chapter:

The strength of the 'push' factors

- saturation of the home market or strong competition;
- national economic recession or limited growth in consumer spending;
- a declining or ageing population which will affect the market size;
- strict planning policies on store development which will constrain growth;
- operating costs which are considered too high (labour, rents, taxation);
- shareholder pressure to maintain profit growth and so be seen 'to be doing something';
- inability to find any further competitive advantages in the home market.

The strength of the 'pull' factors

- international opportunity due to the underdevelopment of some markets or weak competition within them;
- strong economic growth or rising standards of living;
- population growth in relation to the target market of the retailer;
- a relaxed regulatory framework of employment and retail site development;
- favourable operating costs (labour, rents, taxation, etc.);
- a geographical spread of trading risks;
- the opportunity to innovate, in new market conditions.

INTERNATIONAL RETAILING: A DEFINITION

Before discussing retail internationalization, we need to define the actual process. Within the body of the academic literature, no single comprehensive definition is used. There are numerous attempts to describe the process and, although they have obvious similarities, distinct differences between them exist which can make discussion of the topic confusing.

The term 'retail internationalization' may seem clear enough, yet a number of complexities underlie it. For example, does internationalization encompass only the operation of stores outside the domestic market or does international sourcing count as international activity? Should a company with one store in a neighbouring market be differentiated from retailers with a global strategy operating in many diverse markets? Is a company with a portfolio of different brands/fascias going through the same process as a retailer which operates a single brand around the world?

Alexander (1997) has highlighted the varying conditions that international players operate in, suggesting that retail internationalization is:

> the management of retail operations in markets which are different from each other in their regulation, economic development, social conditions, cultural environment, and retail structures.

Perhaps the most obvious definition of retail internationalization is the transfer of retail operations outside the home market; indeed, much of the research into retail internationalization is concentrated precisely on this. However, it is more sensible to consider it as a wider and more complex process than merely the transfer of stores. It may involve the international transfer of retail concepts, management skills, technology and even the buying function. Based on this we would suggest a usable definition for retail internationalization is:

> the process of a retailer transferring its retail operations, concept, management expertise, technology, and/or buying function across national borders.

These factors are discussed in the following subsections.

Operations

A literal interpretation of retail internationalization is the expansion of a retailer's operation into a foreign market. The type of store may or may not be similar to that in the home market. Even if it is an all but identical operation, it may well trade under a different brand/fascia than that operated in the domestic market. This decision is dependent upon (among other things) the sector of activity and the method of market entry. If a foreign retail operation is acquired, very often the new owner may chose to retain the original fascia, particularly if it is an accepted and respected brand. For example, when in July 1999 US giant Wal-Mart bought UK grocery chain ASDA it retained the valuable ASDA brand. It was not until a year later that it established its first ASDA/Wal-Mart Supercentre fascia, and even now plans are to roll out this joint fascia to only a few of the very largest stores in order to differentiate them from the standard ASDA hypermarkets.

If a retailer chooses to enter a new market by organic growth, or perhaps by franchise, it may transfer an established domestic fascia. For example, the Arcadia Group operates numerous clothing brands in the UK including Top Shop, Miss Selfridge and Dorothy Perkins and has transferred these, and other, fascias into numerous countries around the world. In 2001 Arcadia operated 284 non-UK outlets across many of its different store brands. In contrast, although US clothing retailer The Gap operates two other chains at home (Old Navy and Banana Republic), it is only its core fascia that has been expanded internationally. A new fascia is particularly attractive and gets attention in sectors such as clothing where a new foreign brand is perceived as more glamorous or fashionable than its competitors, exemplified by the success of Swedish brand H&M Hennes & Mauritz and Spanish fashion players Zara and Mango on entering the UK.

Concepts

Retail concepts include innovations in the industry, such as the self-service concept which first emerged in California in 1912, with the later establishment of the first supermarket in New York in 1930. This concept was transferred to a number of international markets within the next two decades; for example, to Sweden and Germany in 1938, and France in 1947. Similarly, the convenience store format, which originated in the USA in the late 1920s, was subsequently the focus of internationalization with its transfer to Europe in the 1970s (Sternquist and Kacker, 1994).

The process of internationalization may introduce new retail formats into markets. For example, the hypermarket was initially developed by Carrefour in France in 1963. Carrefour subsequently transferred it into foreign markets – sometimes extremely successfully, as in the case of Spain and Brazil, and other times with less success such as the UK and USA (Dupuis and Prime, 1996). Retail concepts also encompass particular retail offers focused on niche consumer segments. The internationalization of The Body Shop brought with it the idea of environmentally sensitive products and a socially responsible organization. The success of such concepts has meant that they have been adopted by competitors in the markets The Body Shop has entered, both in terms of the development and growth in natural toiletries and cosmetics, and the spawning of similar retail offers, such as Nectar based in Northern Ireland and O. Boticario, a Brazilian company now also operating in Europe.

The retailer who originally developed the concept may carry out the transfer of retail concepts into a new market or they may be copied. One scenario is when a retailer sees a successful concept in a foreign market – for example, a style of retailing, a particular format or a niche retail approach – and then transfers the concept into its own home market. Although it may not have experience of operating that particular concept, it would have knowledge of the domestic market and the prevailing conditions. An example of this includes Sainsbury's (among others) importation of the supermarket format from the USA to the UK in the late 1940s.

Conversely, a retailer who is operating a particular retail concept and perceives that a similar format would be successful in a foreign market may carry out concept internationalization. Examples of such actions include Swedish based furniture retailer IKEA, which felt its concept was strong enough to transfer into other markets. IKEA perceived its offer was not reliant on particular market conditions, and hence could be successful in a variety of non-domestic markets. IKEA seek to target a specific part of the market, mainly those setting up home for the first time, an audience that is found around the world, and aims to be the destination store for this consumer group.

Example: Aldi develops new outlets across Europe

The majority of UK grocery retailers have relentlessly moved into middle to upmarket positionings with their retail offers. They have concentrated on developing own-brand offers, improving quality and service levels, and designing large outlets with car parking and other facilities. The budget sector position has been left to a few limited line, no frills service providers which concentrate on manufacturer brands. However, Aldi, the German heavy discounter which is one of the largest grocery retailers in Europe, has entered the UK market. Aldi is a no frills retailer with little spent on store fittings and atmospherics.

The way Aldi and other international players gain advantage from being international is:

- *system transfers* – planning, budgeting and distribution systems which have been tested in different markets can be implemented easily;
- *people transfers* – skilled people can be assigned across national borders, thus drawing upon an international experienced workforce;
- *economies of centralization* – rather than duplicating the main company systems functions across different countries, they can be centralized, thereby developing greater competence and reducing costs;
- *global perspectives* – international retailers are well positioned to understand the different opportunities and retail changes which may benefit the whole of the business given the right strategies.

Management expertise

The transfer of concepts is related to the internationalization of management expertise. This includes the internationalization of skills and techniques used in the management and running of the company; also included is the transfer of characteristics of the company culture. An important means of transferring management functions is through the formation of alliances. Retail alliances were once seen primarily as a means of achieving economies of scale in buying; modern international alliances go much further than this. Retailers' motives for joining alliances include: operational synergies, buying economies of scale, increased retailer power over manufacturers, the development of retailer own-labels, and joint defence building against the market entry of foreign competitors. International retail alliances are an outcome of the growing trend of globalization. Successful alliance management requires close co-operation, communication, synergistic performance measures and an agreement to common objectives.

The focus of alliances has altered somewhat in the last couple of decades. The 1980s saw the development of strong alliances, particularly in the food sector, in order to gain a scale advantage in relationships with manufacturers. For example, Associated Marketing Services (AMS) was set up in 1988 – members include Ahold of the Netherlands, Casino of France and Safeway of the UK. With the boom in retail internationalization in the 1990s, alliances geared themselves towards providing scale for retailers to compete with the retail giants, such as Wal-Mart which has a massive turnover of €207 billion and Carrefour which operates in 27 countries.

Advances in technology have spawned a new type of alliance in the form of business-to-business (B2B) online exchanges, for example, the WorldWide Retail Exchange and the GlobalNetExchange whose members include Carrefour, J. Sainsbury, Metro of

Germany and US grocer Kroger. The aim here is to increase efficiencies throughout the supply chain rather than solely trying to give retailers a better bargaining position.

Technology

The scale and sophistication of retailers, especially those operating internationally, means that they require the use of technological advances to remain competitive. The introduction of IT has also allowed the development of new techniques and systems used in the central management of retail operations to improve decision-making in functional areas such as finance, personnel and logistics. These areas are increasingly complex functions for international players. Technology is also implemented at the operational level, for example EPOS systems in stores.

Internationalization may not always involve the introduction of state-of-the-art technology, but generally will involve employing technology that is relatively advanced. Retailers may justifiably feel that it is preferable to move into a market where they have a technological advantage. In such a situation the technological advantage would confer a competitive advantage over indigenous retailers. So, although technology may be employed for the purposes of efficiency and cost savings, it may also be used as a form of competitive advantage in itself.

The implementation of technology in many aspects of the retail industry internationally has numerous implications. Notably, a changed working environment is imposed upon the recipient country. The process of internationalization can result in changes in the retail environment of the host country. This is particularly the case when a retailer originating from a developed market moves into a country with a less-developed retail structure. It is not just the introduction of specific formats or new technological tools that impacts on the host; the use of sophisticated management structures may also have a significant effect on the host country. For example, a study of non-indigenous retailers in the Greek market suggested that the major impact is not the introduction of new forms of retailing, but 'the diffusion of modern management thought and practices' (Boutsouki *et al.*, 1995).

Buying

Finally, as in retail operations management expertise and technological know-how are being increasingly transferred across national borders, so is the function of buying – indeed it is sourcing that has had the greatest impact in terms of internationalization. In the post-war era many manufacturers have grown in size and have become transnational corporations. In many cases this has resulted in retailers, even those whose retail operation is based solely in the domestic market, dealing with manufacturers and wholesalers in foreign markets.

One of the major motives for retailers to join an alliance is still the efficiencies and leverage they can attain in sourcing. When dealing with transnational manufacturers, the benefits of joining together to increase size are evident: to use their collective influence with suppliers to reduce prices and improve quality. For example, the European alliance EMD explicitly stated its aim of exerting the combined purchasing power of its members: 'In unity there is strength. In international unity even more strength' (Retail Intelligence, 1991, p. 18).

It is suggested that internationalization of one function of a retail company often follows the internationalization of another aspect. For example, if a retail company internationalizes its product sourcing, this may lead to the international transfer of certain technologies and management functions. This in turn develops the experience and confidence of the retailer in operating in the international environment, which may act as a catalyst to them following a growth strategy of internationalizing their operations. It is therefore possible to consider the process of retail internationalization as following a learning curve.

INTERNATIONAL RETAIL STRUCTURES

As indicated by Davies and Finny (1998), until the mid-1970s the level of international retailing was limited and characterized by many failures. The early companies were mostly American: Woolworths in 1909 – although now not American owned; British Home Stores (now Bhs) was incorporated in 1928 by two Americans, and Safeway in 1963 prior to being acquired by Argyll (now Safeway plc). European retailers were far less ambitious, with the exception of early moves by C&A, Boots and Marks & Spencer.

While we may talk of a global retail environment there remain fundamental differences between national retail markets. Despite the existence of truly global retail brands, which are found throughout the world, retail structures remain traditional in many parts of the world. Informal retailing, such as open trading markets, characterize developing regions. Even though modern forms of retailing are emerging in such markets, traditional retail styles remain an inherent part of the market structure and are inescapably bound to the local culture and lifestyle. For example, even in Singapore with its sophisticated shopping malls and whole array of international retailers, shopping for produce at markets remains a daily way of life for many people.

Measuring retail structures

So what do we actually mean by the term retail structure, and how do we measure it in order to compare markets? The structure of the retail environment generally refers to the nature and characteristics of the market: for example, the type of retail operations, the variety of retail offers, store location and nature of ownership.

In terms of measuring the retail environment, levels of market concentration are often used. Higher levels of concentration are associated with more developed markets. For example, the top three retailers of each country account for 58 per cent of all sales through food retailers in Germany and 47 per cent in the UK and in France, indicating that these are highly developed retail environments. Compare this with concentration levels of just 22 per cent for Italy and 8 per cent for Poland, illustrating their less developed retail industries (Retail Intelligence, 2001b). This is explained by the fact that, as retail industries develop, so multiple organizations begin to take market share from traditional independent and co-operative retailers; thus, a smaller number of larger organizations are taking a greater proportion of the market.

The level of retail structure development can be measured not just by the number of retail organizations, but also by the number of stores (Davies and Whitehead, 1995). As illustrated in Fig. 15.1, as a demand-led retail market begins to develop, so the number of stores, and also the number of retail companies, increases. As the market becomes

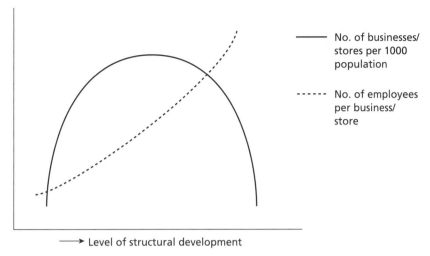

No. of businesses/ stores per 1000 population

------ No. of employees per business/ store

———➤ Level of structural development

Fig. 15.1 Measures of retail development
Source: Adapted from Davies and Whitehead, 1995

more structured, the number of retail organizations begins to drop off due to the dominance of fewer but larger multiple organizations. The number of stores begins to decrease because the size of individual shops has increased in order to gain scale economies and efficiencies, and so one store can serve a larger group of the population. In the developed retail market of the UK there are some 185 inhabitants per retail outlet, this compares to just 66 people in Greece, implying that stores in Greece are much smaller (Retail Intelligence, 2000a).

The number of employees per retail business or per store also increases since traditional retail businesses are characterized as small scale, and employ few people per outlet and per company. As the retailer develops, the size of the store tends to increase, as does the number of outlets per business. Hence, more developed retail industries have more employees per business and more employees per store.

A more general measure of prosperity and development in a market is the proportion of consumer expenditure that goes on retail. As the population becomes more wealthy a greater proportion of income is spent on non-essentials, thus a smaller percentage of total spend goes on food and clothing (although the actual amount may increase) and a higher share of spending power is directed towards non-essentials such as holidays and leisure activities. This is exemplified by the fact that in Germany some 28 per cent of consumer expenditure went through retailers, while in Portugal a much higher proportion, some 60 per cent, was accounted for by retail (Retail Intelligence, 2000b).

Tordjman (1995) has divided the markets of Western Europe into a four-stage matrix of structural development. The *advanced* markets of the UK and Germany are characterized by having the highest levels of concentration and a clearly segmented market. Next are the *structured* markets of France and the Netherlands, followed by the *intermediary* markets of Spain and Italy and, finally, the *traditional* retail structures of Portugal and Greece. Rather than regarding these as unchanging distinct phases, it is perhaps more useful to consider these markets as being at different points along a continuum of retail development (*see* Fig. 15.2).

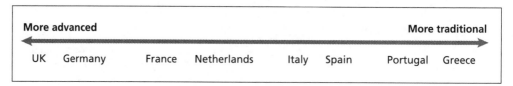

Fig. 15.2 A continuum of European retail structures
Source: Adapted from Tordjman, 1995, p. 25

The retail environments of former centrally planned economies (CPEs) may appear similar to other developing markets whereas there are fundamental differences. For example, the Russian retail industry is based on a legacy of a supply-led, not a demand-led economy. Retailing has traditionally been perceived as an unproductive link in the channel of distribution. The outcome of this is that concepts such as marketing, product advertising or the role of the salesperson were previously unknown – or at least absent. While many foreign operations are moving into former CPE markets as a result of consumer demand and limited indigenous competition, the former state-owned operations are finding it difficult to transform themselves.

It is important to note that the above description does not fully explain the structure of CPEs and former CPEs. With a retail industry based on supply rather than demand, the pattern of growth in terms of size and number of retail businesses does not follow the same rules. The nature of the economy dictates that increased consumer demand is not met by more stores or the development of multiple organizations, thus former CPEs need to be analysed separately.

The following section refers to markets by their national borders, which suggests that there are various differences between national retail markets. While fully supporting this assertion, it is also necessary to point out that there may be similarities between markets – retail characteristics do not necessarily change abruptly at national borders. For example, it may be difficult to distinguish differences between retailing in western Germany and conditions across the Dutch border. It is also true to say that conditions may vary considerably within national markets; indeed, this was a point made by Hollander (1970) in a seminal study of international retailing. He suggested that differences between retailing on the East Coast of the USA and on the West Coast far outweighed variations between the retail environments of north-east USA and Canada, despite the national border separating them. This concept, that variations may be greater within a market than between them, has also been supported in a European context (Dawson, 1994; Myers, 1996).

MOTIVES AND REASONS FOR INTERNATIONALIZATION

A question fundamental to the discussion of retail internationalization asks why retailers follow such a strategy. Invariably operating in a new market is a high cost and high risk method of growth. Indeed, it has been suggested, 'Global retailing demands huge investment and gives no guarantee of return' (quoted in Lamey, 1997).

While there are certainly successful international retailers, there are many examples of failure. Failure is, undoubtedly, the result of a series of complex and interrelated factors. For example, although a successful domestic retailer, Boots the Chemist has had a number of international ventures that it has subsequently pulled out of. It has retreated from Canada, New Zealand, France and the Netherlands and most recently its Japanese operation. It still has stores in Taiwan and concessions in Thailand.

Just because a retailer successfully internationalizes into one market does not mean it can necessarily repeat this success elsewhere. For example, Tesco entered Ireland in 1978 only to pull out in 1986 after incurring substantial losses. Tesco re-entered the Irish market in the late 1990s and also operates stores in Eastern Europe and Asia.

Growth strategies

If it is assumed that retailers want to grow their company, then they have three options (Pelegrini, 1994; Treadgold, 1991):

1 From operating their core offer in the home market they may choose to follow a strategy of *sectoral expansion*, whereby they move into new formats, retail sectors or even outside the retail industry.

2 The second growth strategy open to retailers is to remain with the core offer and to transfer this into *new markets*. The advantage of this is that they are experienced in the operation; however, they may need to learn about and adapt to new market conditions.

3 The third method of growth is to use a *combined strategy*, whereby a company may move away from its core offer and also internationalize. Although this may balance the risks somewhat it may mean the board lose focus. If this strategy is taken to its extreme, the company then becomes an international portfolio or holding company.

Examples: Growth strategies

Sectoral expansion

The John Lewis Partnership runs a chain of some 25 department stores. In addition it also operates 120+ Waitrose supermarkets. There may seem little connection between the two but both are pitched at the mid to upper market and so have a similar target market and complementary retail offers. The company also has its own manufacturing operations and own-brand is important for both chains. The advantage of being a multi-sector retailer concentrating on the home market is that it is familiar with the domestic consumer market and its brand image is strong enough to transfer from one sector to another.

International expansion

An example of such a retailer is the German 'hard discounter' Aldi. The company was founded in the immediate post-war years with an orientation on heavily discounted limited lines of generic products. Since the 1960s Aldi has moved into numerous European markets and also the US, using a method of organic growth. Although a number of alternative fascias are used, all stores are practically identical. This generates vast economies and efficiencies of scale. Despite moving into a variety of markets, Aldi has made the very minimum of adaptations to its retail offer.

Combined sectoral and international expansion

Kingfisher operates in a number of chains in sectors including DIY (e.g. B&Q, Castorama) and electrical (e.g. Comet, Darty) but is divesting in general merchandise (e.g. Woolworths). It has stores in numerous European countries as well as the Far East, Canada and Brazil. The company has also ventured into e-commerce. The advantage of this strategy is the array of opportunities it offers; however, it also increases the problems associated with working in unfamiliar markets and in unfamiliar sectors. A danger is that the company may lose direction. It is a strategy perhaps more appropriate for experienced international companies.

Reasons for internationalization

The motivations underlying the decision to internationalize have been addressed in a number of ways. One of the first studies, by Hollander in 1970, proposed five reasons for retail internationalization:

1 inadvertent internationalization;
2 non-commercial motives;
3 commercial objectives;
4 government regulation;
5 capitalizing on existing or potential sales opportunities.

By *inadvertent* internationalization Hollander was referring to political instability. Changes in the demarcation of national borders may mean a retail company is operating in a different market although its stores have not physically moved. This is exemplified by changes in Eastern Europe. The US retailer K Mart entered Czechoslovakia and within a year found itself operating in two distinct markets, the Czech and Slovak republics (Alexander, 1995; Loker *et al.*, 1994).

Milton Friedman (1970) controversially suggested that the only responsibility that businesses have is to increase their profits. However, Hollander (1970) perceived that some retailers may move into new markets not to make money but for *non-commercial* reasons of political, personal, ethical or social responsibility. For example, retailers may move into markets for reasons of social and environmental responsibility, notably The Body Shop's 'Trade not Aid' sourcing policy, or to help develop infrastructures in order to stabilize economies, such as in Eastern Europe.

Commercial objectives include entering a market in order to establish a presence before a competitor, to gain important market knowledge before moving in on a larger scale, or to learn about innovations to transfer elsewhere.

The impact of *government regulations* is perhaps more likely to influence the choice of market rather than be a prerequisite to internationalization. Retailers are obviously more likely to enter markets with fewer restrictions on their growth. If regulations at home are severely restricting growth plans it may be the catalyst that pushes them into the international arena. A prime example of such a situation is the Loi Royer in France, which severely restricted the development of large out-of-town stores. The outcome was that French hypermarkets turned to less restrictive markets, such as those in Spain, to continue their expansion.

Hollander's fifth suggestion is probably the most obvious. Retailers are businesses seeking the best *growth potential* possible, therefore if they perceive significant opportunities in overseas markets they are likely to capitalize on them despite the risks involved.

The proactive–reactive debate

The strategic focus of retailers is shaped by a set of underlying forces. If a retailer expands by moving into foreign markets, it is due to the influence of a set of specific conditions in both the external environment and the internal factors within the company. Traditionally, internationalization has been viewed as the outcome of forces pushing the retailer from the domestic market. It is proposed that if market conditions make it

Fig. 15.3 The proactive–reactive continuum

increasingly difficult for retailers to continue to expand, then they will be forced to seek opportunities for further growth in a new market. This has been termed the *reactive* school of thought.

The other perspective suggests that retailers internationalize not because of limitations at home but rather because they seek opportunities in other markets. This has been defined as the *proactive* response. The debate about these two ideas continues and it is now suggested that there is a need to use an integrated approach when studying retail internationalization (Alexander and Myers, 2000). In many cases, it is true to say that retailers internationalize as a result of a combination of both push and pull factors. If this is indeed the case, it is perhaps more appropriate to view motivations for internationalization not as dichotomous forces, but rather as two ends of a continuum (*see* Fig. 15.3).

Forces acting to push retailers from continuing to expand within the home market include:

- *structural* conditions that inhibit the development of further growth – for example, competitive pressure from increasing rates of market competition, retail format maturity, retail sector concentration and the proximity of saturation levels;
- *legislative* factors, for example, the impact of planning restrictions controlling the development of large-scale out-of-town food stores or regional shopping malls such as Bluewater;
- *political* issues, such as the unstable environment of Eastern Europe;
- *social* and *demographic* factors, such as the effect on consumer demand of an ageing and declining population;
- *economic* issues, an example being the impact of a recession on consumer spending power.

Pull factors are the opposite. In some respects they may be considered to be the reverse side of the coin. For example, a market that has comparatively unrestrictive legislative measures concerning such issues as store opening hours may serve to highlight the potential for growth. A retailer faced with a restrictive environment in its home market may therefore seek to move into one with less regulation. A market with a growing population may appear attractive to retailers from countries with ageing demographic structures. Similarly, a market with a high amount of consumer expenditure is likely to be more attractive than one where consumers have limited spending power (*see* Table 15.2).

The traditional interpretation of internationalization is the reactive school of thought. Primarily based on observing the actions of retailers in the 1960s, 1970s and early 1980s, it suggested that the underlying motives for increasing numbers of retailers moving into foreign markets were push factors, namely the lack of opportunities at home (Kacker, 1985; Salmon and Tordjman, 1989; Treadgold, 1988). It was considered that retailers would not undertake a high risk and high investment strategy of

Table 15.2 Push and pull factors

Factors	Push examples	Pull examples
Structural	Maturity of superstore in UK	Competitive advantage of importing hypermarkets to Indonesia
Legislative	Planning restrictions for large out-of-town stores in France	Laissez-faire regulations in Greece
Political	Instability in Eastern Europe	Stable political environment in Germany
Social/demographic	Declining population in developed Western markets	Increasing and unfulfilled consumer demand in developing parts of Europe
Economic	Economic recession in Japan	Increasing consumer expenditure in Latin America

internationalization unless prospects for continued growth within the domestic market were severely curtailed and they had few options or opportunities for domestic growth.

In contrast, it has been suggested that pull factors motivate retailers actively to seek and identify opportunities in foreign markets. Proactive internationalization occurs when perceived opportunities in foreign markets outweigh the associated risks and high investment necessary for internationalization, regardless of the opportunity for continued growth in the domestic market. It is a more aggressive strategy, and potentially more successful as it may be implemented more slowly and with less initial investment. There is also less risk, as there is still growth within the home market. Even within the reactive school of thought, the influence of pull factors is not ignored. Instead, it is suggested that rather than being a reason for retailers seeking to internationalize, pull factors are an important influence in the choice of one market over another.

In contrast to research based on observing retailers' actions suggesting a reactive view, empirical work conducted in the early and mid-1990s proposed a proactive interpretation (Alexander, 1990a, 1990b; Williams, 1992a, 1992b; Myers and Alexander 1996, Myers, 1996). Alexander (1995) suggests that the degree to which a retailer is willing to exploit opportunities in the international arena – the extent to which they are proactive internationalists – is partly dependent on the operation's format and merchandise as well as saturation levels within the domestic market. While the reactive school of thought proposes that retailers internationalize when there is a high level of market saturation, despite the fact that they operate formats with low levels of global relevance, the reactive interpretation suggests that retailers internationalize when operating a format with a high degree of global relevance, despite there being low levels of saturation within the home market.

The importance of the proactive debate in the latter research does not necessarily contradict the reactive school of thought, but simply provides an analysis of the perceived motives for internationalization in the 1990s. It may be viewed as a continuum along which the motives underlying international expansion can be placed. It would appear that at different times and to different extents for individual retailers, factors of both a reactive and a proactive nature work in conjunction as underlying motives in the decision to internationalize.

Driving forces

In addition to analysing environmental influences such as economic growth and legislative conditions, *internal factors*, for example the opinion of senior directors and management philosophy, are also considered part of the complex array of factors underlying the motives for retail internationalization. McGoldrick and Davies (1995) have constructed a model of the driving forces of internationalization. This is a development of the dichotomous push–pull theory. In addition to analysing the effects of environmental factors, consideration is also given to the impact of various influences within the organizational sphere. Defining and understanding the factors of influence within the organizational sphere is particularly useful as they are more easily controlled, unlike the environmental factors which are often beyond the control of retailers.

MINICASE 15.1

Creating a warm, fuzzy feeling: Factory outlet centres are set to do well in Europe only if they are able to master the art of US-style customer service

Anyone who has ever savoured the smug feeling that comes from buying upmarket goods at downmarket prices will understand factory outlet centres. They offer the opportunity to get the feeling in well-designed, comfortable surroundings with access to food, leisure and ample, free parking. Factory outlets are little more than shopping centres where the distributors are the manufacturers rather than retailers. They are a necessary adjunct to any producer of consumer goods that has to clear unsold inventory to make way for the latest line.

Typically, the products sold at factory outlet centres are not damaged seconds but prime merchandise in last year's styles and colours that are unlikely to sell at full price. For consumers who may not care whether the Versace suit they buy is the latest look, factory outlet centres are a boon. Given their inherent attractiveness, the question is why factory outlet centres, a long-time staple of the US shopping scene, have taken so long to come to Europe. Do Europeans not want the warm, fuzzy feeling that comes from buying that Prada handbag at a 50 per cent discount? Research says that of course they do.

According to the European Factory Outlet Center Report by the Institut für Gewerbezentren, based in Starnberg, Germany, the number of factory outlets in Europe has soared over the past two years. From 40 in 1998, the number will have grown to 77 by the end of this year and is expected to reach 93 by the end of 2002. Total retail area for this format is expected to exceed 1m sq metres by the end of next year in an industry that was represented by just three European centres in 1992.

What is interesting, the report notes, is that while the number of factory outlets in Europe is surging, the data suggest that in the US – where the concept first took off – the sector is showing signs of decline. The number of centres opened in the US has been declining steadily each year since 1993, according to data from Value Retail News, the Florida-based newsletter of the International Council of Shopping Centers. Currently, there are 278 centres in the US, down from 329 in 1996.

Momme Falk, project director for the European Factory Outlet Center Report, says the decline in the number of centres does not mean they have already passed their zenith. On the contrary, he says, older, smaller centres are closing while much larger centres are opening. Indeed, the VRN data show that the average size of a factory outlet centre has nearly doubled to 207,469 square feet from 122,000 in 1988. But the big challenge for factory outlet centres in the US, according to Linda Humphers, editor-in-chief of VRN, is saturation. 'The problem for Europe will be that, eventually, you cannot build any more of them,' she says. Outlet centres, she says, sprung up originally in areas that were desperate for some retail offering well away from urban centres. 'Manufacturers aren't going to go into their own distributors' back yards,' she says.

While the dominant location in the US is one equidistant between two conurbations, more than half all European factory outlets are located in edge-of-town locations. The second most popular location is 'in the middle of nowhere', where 24 per cent of the centres are to be found. Mr Falk says that the challenge of saturation that has affected US factory outlet centres is far more likely to arise in Europe because planning is so much more restrictive. In countries such as Germany, he says, there is also fierce opposition from local retailers and manufacturers, making approval of new sites very difficult. German consumers, he says, are very price-conscious and would probably like more discount shopping outlets.

'But are people going to take to the streets to protest against this?' he asks. 'I don't think so.'

Still, a look at the evolution of the US market suggests some challenges for factory outlet centres in Europe. For one thing, even the casual observer of the US retail scene cannot help but notice the strong gains in market share by cut-price retailers such as Wal-Mart and Target at the expense of full-price department stores and fashion retailers. But with discount goods available on every street corner, who needs factory outlet centres? Ms Humphers says that shoppers in outlet centres are typically seeking more than just low prices.

'Who shops at outlet centres isn't just the bargain hunter,' she says. 'It's the brand shopper, the aspirant shopper.' Similarly, Mr Falk makes the same distinction in looking at the customer base for outlet centres in Europe, separating 'bargain hunters' from 'value hunters'. Value hunters, he says, are as motivated by the opportunity to buy quality as to buy cheap goods. They want to shop in comfort and to take advantage of a high standard of customer service. The centres in Europe most likely to thrive, even in a saturated environment, are those catering to the most sophisticated shopper, he says. Ironically, it is probably in the area of customer service – an absolute essential to US upmarket consumers – that European factory outlet centres fare worst, Ms Humphers says. 'I believe that in Europe, the outlet industry is run by the developers. In the US, it's a retail-run business,' she says. Even at a 50 per cent discount, a Prada handbag needs to be sold with tender loving care in order to induce that warm, fuzzy feeling that is the essence of factory outlet shopping.

Source: Norma Cohen, *Financial Times*, 31 August 2001

Environmental factors include those that:

- *promote* international activity, such as the availability of suitable targets for acquisition and lower political and economic barriers;
- *push* retailers from their home market, elements such as domestic trading restrictions and market saturation.

In addition to environmental influences, the framework gives prominence to influences within the organizational sphere that:

- *inhibit* the implementation of a strategy of international expansion, such as start-up costs and fear of shareholder reaction;
- *facilitate*, for example, the effect of international alliances and the bandwagon effect.

As illustrated in Fig. 15.4, findings from an empirical study of the international activity of the largest European food retailers supported McGoldrick's model in Chapter 1 of McGoldrick and Davies (Myers, 1996). While structural factors in the home market – such as the maturity of domestic food retail formats – push retailers to internationalize, demographic conditions in potential host markets may pull retailers into the market. Environmental factors such as the establishment of the Single European Market promoted the opportunities available in other markets, while obstacles such as language and

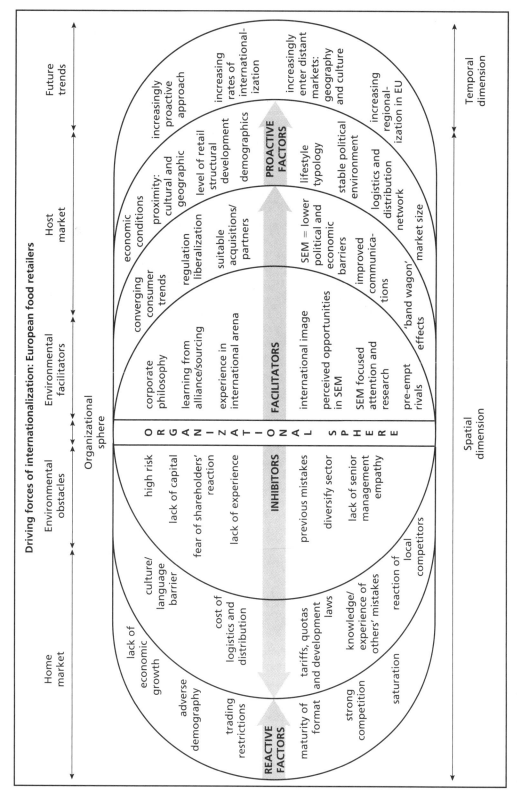

Fig. 15.4 Driving forces: European food retailing

Source: Myers, 1996; adapted from McGoldrick and Davies, 1995

culture barriers had a negative effect. In terms of internal factors, though lack of experience may have held retailers back from making an international move, the image of wanting to be perceived as international was an important factor promoting international activity.

Kingfisher's chief executive wants a run of good fortune

Sir Geoffrey Mulcahy will next week travel to China for the opening of the biggest B&Q store in the world on what should be an auspicious day. The Kingfisher chief executive will be in Shanghai on Wednesday, the eighth day of the eighth month of the year – with the number eight signifying luck in moneymaking in China. The flotation of Woolworths (by Kingfisher) follows the sale of the Superdrug health and beauty chain and marks the end of Kingfisher's involvement in general merchandise retailing. Sir Geoff will lead a group focused on the more highly rated DIY and electrical sectors and with a strong exposure to a series of international markets.

Internationalisation may be a buzz word in the retail sector more often discussed than achieved, but Kingfisher now operates in 16 countries. 'A lot of people talk about their international operations and their international businesses – but there aren't many who make a whole lot of money out of them,' says Sir Geoff.

He says the main priority is making sure that the group is getting the most out of all its businesses – particularly given their geographic spread around the world. Next he wants to fix any underperforming businesses – most notably the ProMarkt electrical chain in Germany, which has never found the right formula.

Only after that will he turn his attention to acquisitions. 'If, after we have tackled those main priorities, there are other opportunities that come up we will then actually be in a position to tackle them,' he says. His caution is well founded. The internationalisation of Kingfisher has not all been plain sailing. The expansion in Europe has been achieved mainly via France, where the group bought the Darty electricals chain in 1993 and engineered a merger with Castorama, the DIY business, in 1998. He has still to buy out the minority interests in Castorama, a deal which under current circumstances would be highly dilutive as the French business is more highly rated than Kingfisher.

Taking heart from the US market, where electricals and DIY are each dominated by two big companies, he says Europe will move the same way. In particular, he says changes to the German capital gains tax regime due to come into force at the start of next year should make some of the big retail groups there, many of which are family-owned, reconsider their positions. 'Europe is going to rapidly consolidate now,' he says. 'It is quite clear to me that the train is out of the station and moving down the line. But it is difficult to predict exactly what will happen.'

Source: Susanna Voyle, *Financial Times*, 2 August 2001

DIRECTION OF EXPANSION

The direction of international expansion taken by retailers has received a good deal of attention in recent years. Much of the recent research on internationalization describes either the development of new markets or the invasion of home markets by foreign competitors. Burt (1993) suggested that the initial direction of international retail expansion is primarily determined by three factors:

1 *cultural* proximity;

2 *geographical* proximity;

3 the *stage of development* of the retail market.

Retailers, at least in early stages of international activity, tend to choose markets that are *spatially* close. Border hopping has obvious advantages in terms of logistics and distribution. A retailer may be able to service international stores from a domestic distribution warehouse, which is a more efficient and less costly and risky option than setting up an entirely new distribution chain. This type of activity provides retailers with the option of moving into a market on an incremental scale, perhaps building their stores at a slow pace as they learn about the market.

When first operating internationally, retailers will often try to move into markets they consider *culturally* similar. Knowledge of both the consumer and business culture is important to success. Indeed it has been suggested that the degree of psychic distance is a key determinant of success (Evans, Treadgold and Mavando, 2000). Defining cultural similarity may not be as easy as assessing levels of geographical and structural development, not least because culture is not necessarily dependent on national boundaries. However, culture might well be one of the most salient factors; this being the case, the difficulties of defining and analysing its impact should not result in culture simply being ignored. The information box indicates the significant cultural considerations in internationalization.

It has also been assessed that retailers usually prefer to enter a market that is less *structurally* developed than their home market in order to have competitive advantage over indigenous players. While there are many examples of such strategies, such as Carrefour moving into Brazil or Makro moving into South East Asia, it is not always so straightforward. For example, the UK is characterized as one of the most competitive food sectors in the world, yet US giant Wal-Mart entered the UK despite knowing that they were moving into a market equally competitive to their home market. However, it is assessed that this was outweighed by the expected positive attitude of the UK consumer to the Wal-Mart concept (Arnold and Fernie, 2000).

The social and cultural environment

- Buying processes vary between different cultures. For example, the role of women may differ on an international basis.

- Different family structures may place more emphasis on the family producing some of the retail goods that would otherwise be purchased in developed societies.

- Services that are taken for granted in one country may be rejected in another; for example, interest charges levied on a store credit card scheme will not be acceptable in some Muslim cultures.

- Attitudes between cultures differ when promotions are utilized. Symbols, colours and product claims can be perceived in different ways. In most of the Arab world a woman's cleavage should never be utilized in promotions and bare arms are not acceptable in Thailand and Malaysia. In addition, merchandise that is bright in colour may not be acceptable in a number of countries, including Japan.

- The knowledge of the importance of 'face' and the need for the development of social connections in business transactions in oriental countries is a key to success.

Example: Entry into the UK food retail sector

The UK is one of the most concentrated markets, the top three food retailers taking about half of sector sales. The primary format in the food sector is edge-of-town superstores. They are characterized as providing ease of access and car parks, high levels of service, a large proportion of quality own-brand lines, a strong retail image, an increasingly wide range of goods and services and the ability to command high profit margins.

Failure

The French company Carrefour transferred its hypermarket format to the UK only to subsequently withdraw. The venture failed for a number of reasons, not least its unacceptability to British consumers. For example, shoppers were not used to buying high priced non-food items from food stores and thus profit levels were hit. Superstores were already beginning to offer the advantages of a hypermarket, namely ease of access and parking and longer opening hours, and shoppers preferred higher levels of service and the familiarity of the trusted UK retail brands.

Success

Continental 'hard discount' operation Aldi entered the UK in 1989. Again, the format was heavily price oriented and with a limited service. Typically it offered generic brands at prices one-third cheaper, made possible by limited lines – typically 550 – and high sales volumes. The company now operates over 225 stores in the UK. Its success is based on its strategy of not competing head-on with the big superstore chains, but rather offering a non-directly competing and indeed complementary format.

Retailers can be successful not only by entering markets that are less developed than their home market, but also by filling a gap in the market. In terms of the wheel of retailing (McNair, 1958; Brown, 1987), the UK food sector had traded up from its price orientation to service and quality. Consequently a gap had been left at the bottom of the market which was filled by the hard discounters.

While the factors of geography, culture and market structure are fundamental to an understanding of the direction of expansion and are observable within the commercial environment, it is dangerous to assume that attitudes towards the direction of expansion remain static. Consequently a fourth factor, which alters perceptions of international opportunities, should be considered; it is *time*. This fourth factor has been recognized by Treadgold (1991) who suggests that retailers, while initially *reluctant* to follow the high risk and cost strategy of internationalization, over time become less *cautious*, more *ambitious*, and are inclined to seek expansion outside the confines of the markets implied by those factors.

> **Stages of international retail development**
>
> 1 Reluctant
> 2 Cautious
> 3 Ambitious

The underlying logic of Treadgold's (1991) model (*see* Fig. 15.5) is that retailers are initially reluctant to internationalize due to the high investment and high risk involved.

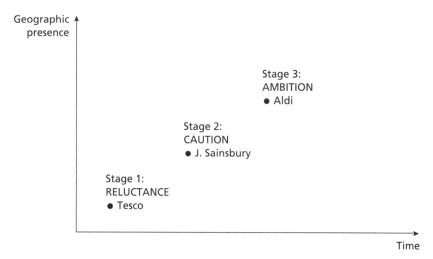

Fig. 15.5 Stages of international development

Source: Adapted from Treadgold, 1991, pp. 20–1

At the time Treadgold assessed Tesco to be in the category of *reluctant* internationalist. The argument suggests that once they moved into the international arena, most likely as a result of push factors from the domestic market, their experience in operating on an international basis grew and they became *cautious* internationalists. J. Sainsbury was cited as an example of a retailer in the second stage of internationalization. Over time, they are likely to move into markets of increasing geographical distance from home. The third stage in Treadgold's model is when retailers have significant experience in the international arena and have a wide geographical presence. Carrefour and Aldi are quoted as *ambitious* internationalists.

Retailers do not necessarily develop along this line of expansion and, once they have reached a certain stage, it is possible for them to retreat rather than progress. A decade after Treadgold's work was carried out it is interesting to evaluate whether the positions of these companies have changed. Tesco is now certainly an accomplished international company with operations in Ireland, France, Eastern Europe, Thailand and South Korea. Currently Tesco might be assessed as being in the ambitious stage. And what of Sainsbury? They still operate only in the US. Perhaps we could now categorize them as cautious going towards reluctant internationalists. Carrefour has operations throughout southern Europe and Latin America and is concentrating its efforts on South East Asia. The company is ambitious and its substantial operations in more than 25 countries make it one of the most global retailers in the world. Aldi continue to roll out their stores in the more developed markets of Europe and the US, perhaps with a more cautious yet single-minded strategy.

MARKET-ENTRY METHODS

Retailers may enter new markets in a number of ways. Although various terms are used, the basic choices are between *acquisition, joint venture, organic growth, shareholding* and *franchise*.

Common market-entry strategies

- *acquisition* – taking over a retail company already established in the market;
- *joint venture* – establishing a company with a partner, most usually one which is indigenous to the market or has experience of operating there. 7-Eleven entered Japan utilizing this method as it needed a partner that understood the complexity of the Japanese distribution systems;
- *organic growth* – opening new outlets using existing brand/fascia or creating a new brand;
- *shareholding* – acquiring shares of a retailer already operating in the chosen market;
- *franchise* – allowing entrepreneurs to open outlets under a single brand/fascia which are operated under certain controlled conditions. US fast-food giants such as KFC, Burger King and McDonald's are key exponents of this approach. In the non-food sector, Benetton is a good example.

Each one of these methods of market entry offers particular advantages and is subject to specific disadvantages (*see* Table 15.3). The choice of market-entry method is dependent upon a number of issues. The *sector* of retail activity will influence the way in which a retailer enters a new market. For example, food retailers are somewhat restricted in their choice of entry strategy because they generally need to enter on a

Table 15.3 Market-entry methods

Market-entry method	Example of advantages	Example of disadvantages	Retail example
Acquisition	Fast substantial market presence	High cost and risk	Wal-Mart's acquisition of ASDA in the UK
Joint venture	Each brings own skills, e.g. market knowledge and format experience	Need suitable partner, can be clash of company cultures	Carrefour JV with PT in Indonesia
Organic growth	Incremental process, can learn and adapt as you go	Slow growth, delay before returns against investment	Aldi's growth in the UK since 1989
Shareholding	Reduces risk, can learn about company from the inside and decide whether to invest further	Culture clash between teams of management	JS shareholding of Shaws in USA in 1984 leading to full acquisition in 1987
Franchise	Very fast and low cost way to roll out stores	Limited control, need suitable franchises	Toys "Я" Us in Indonesia

substantial scale because of distribution requirements. In contrast, niche retailers with a strong brand image have the option of franchising or using licensing agreements. So, they may achieve a widespread presence fairly quickly but at a lower cost and risk than many other strategies.

Conditions within a new *market* will shape the decision on how to internationalize. In markets that are economically and politically stable, retailers may feel it is safe to develop quickly by utilizing a high cost strategy such as acquisition. Entries through acquisition can have a higher post-entry failure rate than entries through setting up new ventures. This is typically attributed to difficulties of integrating the acquired businesses into the existing system, and lower levels of managerial commitment to acquired outlets. In more risky environments retailers may favour a less costly strategy such as franchise and proceed at a more controlled pace. The geographical and cultural distance of the host market will also influence the decision. In markets perceived as distant, a slower more incremental entry strategy may be used in order that the company learns about market conditions and adapts accordingly. Acquiring a company outright in a culturally distant market is a very risky option, and one that may be extremely costly if the retailer subsequently withdraws.

The *size* of the company is also a determinant of market-entry method. Large, powerful companies have the financial backing to follow high investment strategies such as merger or full acquisition. They can also achieve large-scale entry which may provide volume-driven cost advantages. The greater the scale of an initial set-up then the less growth is needed before the minimum-efficient scale of business is obtained. Smaller companies are obviously not in a position to follow the same path. Private companies also have the freedom of perhaps taking a longer-term view of expansion, as they are not restrained by the opinion of shareholders.

Linked to this, the *management* culture often influences strategy. While some retailers have a clear mission to be global or international players and will take risks to achieve this central aim, others are not willing to consider such strategies. The opinion of senior management often determines whether a retail company becomes international or not. Research suggests that it often takes a main board member to champion the idea of going international for it to occur (Myers, 1996). As a result, financial analysts place great importance on the opinions of senior executives.

The degree of *control* required is also a major factor shaping the way in which a retailer will internationalize. Some retailers require very high levels of control and are willing to use more costly and often risky strategies to ensure they maintain it; for other retailers it is more important to establish a diverse international presence. A rapid and lower cost method such as franchise might be used; despite the fact they have only limited control over international operations. Indeed franchising is becoming one of the most important means of internationalizing a retail brand (Quinn and Doherty, 2000). The length of *time* over which the process is to take place is also a constraint on some entry methods. If a retailer wishes to establish international operations very quickly, it may choose to acquire an existing company, or to internationalize the retail brand it may develop concessions or use licensing agreements. However, if a retailer prefers to take a slower pace of internationalization it may open stores on an incremental basis, providing the advantage of learning about the market and adapting the offer as a presence is built in the new market.

MINICASE 15.3

UK plc: overspent, overstretched, over there

There are few places on the globe where the sun has not recently set on the expansionary ambitions of British business. Marks and Spencer, the retailer, has pulled out of continental Europe and is selling its US clothing and supermarket chains. British Telecommunications has disposed of shareholdings in a clutch of Japanese companies, while Belgo, the restaurants group, has pulled out of a loss making venture in New York.

Even Boots, the inveterate optimist, has been forced to withdraw from the Netherlands and scale down its ambitions in Asia. This was the third foreign sally by the healthcare company, following moves into France in the 1970s and Canada in the 1980s – both of which were subsequently reversed. Does this catalogue of failures demonstrate that the British cannot make a success of overseas expansion?

They seem just as inept in parts of their former Empire, where institutions often mirror those back home, as in continental Europe, where languages, legal systems and cultural differences lurk to trap the unwary. Management often set themselves up for embarrassment with brash forecasts of success abroad. In the late 1990s M&S executives boasted of virtually unlimited opportunities overseas, predicting that because clothing styles were becoming increasingly international a quarter of M&S's sales would soon come from outside the UK. But M&S was forced to announce that it was withdrawing from

the Continent after more than 25 years and selling Brooks Brothers, its US clothing chain.

Boots trumpeted in its 2000 annual report that: 'We've proved that our brands can travel, and you'll now find more Boots stores in Bangkok than in Birmingham.' A few months later it was forced to admit to a poor performance in Thailand and Japan, while it blamed the failure of Europe to liberalise pharmaceuticals retailing for a decision to sell its stores in the Netherlands.

But these companies, and many of their compatriots, may have committed some elementary errors when moving abroad. Experts in international business management warn against acquiring a company the locals have rejected because their knowledge tells them it cannot be made to work. They should also avoid attempting to export, say, a retailing format that works on home ground but is less attractive overseas. Market testing can also be deceptive. When M&S opened its first French store on the Boulevard Haussmann in 1975, sales were strong for the first two weeks. But once local expats had stocked up on home comforts and underwear, sales fell back while the retailer slowly built up a French customer base. The finances of overseas operations may also not stack up. In the UK, M&S had the benefit of prime sites it either owned outright or on which it paid very low rents. But, abroad, it had to rent expensive locations.

Source: News Analysis, ft.com/retail, *Financial Times*, 19 June 2001

Factors determining market-entry strategy

- retail sector
- market conditions/level of competition
- company size/capital
- management culture/philosophy/calibre of staff
- degree of control
- time scale
- capital available

Perhaps the best way to consider market-entry strategies is to work from a realization that there is no 'best way', rather some methods are more appropriate for some retailers than others. For example, food retailers tend to use strategies of acquisition or shareholding. This is a high cost option; however, logistical requirements of food retailers mean they need to operate on a substantial scale to be competitive. There are exceptions, however, such as the hard discounter, Aldi, which is growing organically. Aldi prefer this option because they are a very large private company and can take a very long-term perspective that other retailers would be unlikely to use due to shareholder reaction or lack of access to capital.

Some entry method decisions may be made on opportunistic grounds. For example, a company may enter a particular market not because of specific conditions within it but because of finding an appropriate company for a joint venture or an acquisition. Thus, the direction of expansion and choice of market-entry method is very much interlinked in the decision-making process. There is no perfect strategy of retail internationalization. Each method has specific advantages over others and each has particular disadvantages. Retailers use a strategy that is most appropriate given the nature of their operation, the organization and the host market.

TYPOLOGIES OF INTERNATIONAL EXPANSION

Terms such as global, international, multinational and transnational are often used interchangeably and without much regard for the differences in implication. While on one level they all suggest the movement of retailers into new markets, they also imply differences in terms of the nature of international activity. Classifications of retailers have been determined partially by their direction of expansion and market-entry method. For example, Salmon and Tordjman (1989) categorize three types of international strategy:

- investment;
- global;
- multinational.

Companies with diverse portfolios that are seeking new growth opportunities and want to spread their risk often use *investment*. Attaining shares in a foreign company or acquiring the entire company allows swift expansion and may allow the transfer of know-how from the indigenous retailer. Unlike the other two classifications, it is a strategy implemented by both retailers and non-retailers. It implies no real international marketing strategies as the companies are treated autonomously within the portfolio.

Global retailers replicate a concept in a new market. Typically they have a strong brand such as IKEA and Benetton. The replication of the retail offer implies a standard global marketing strategy which allows savings from economies and efficiencies of scale because of the replication of factors such as assortment, store designs and advertising. There is opportunity for vertical integration in terms of design, production and distribution. However, the lack of autonomy as a result of a centralized management structure requires, and leads to, the development of excellent information and communication systems. Global retailers are then likely to achieve the greatest rates of international expansion due primarily to efficiencies of operation.

With the third category, *multinational* retailers, the basic concept is unchanged in the international transfer, but the offer is adapted to suit local conditions, as exemplified by the initial activity of C&A (now withdrawn from the UK). Although the concept is replicated, the marketing mix is adapted to suit local demand. The store decor, service and pricing are similar throughout the world, while the assortment and advertising are subject to local determinants. The management structure is decentralized, providing operations within different markets with a significant degree of autonomy. This is an important source of the transfer of knowledge from one market to another, but the philosophy of adapting to local conditions means that there are few savings from economies of scale on a global level. Although multinational retailers are set to expand within the global arena, it is thought unlikely that such expansion will be to the same extent as the global retailers.

Treadgold (1991) divides retailers into categories of:

- multinational;
- transnational;
- global.

There is a great deal of similarity with Salmon and Tordjman's (1989) model in that the position of a retailer within the typology is dependent upon the level of local responsiveness and the degree of benefits from integration. An example of a multinational retailer is Vendex of the Netherlands. It employs a high degree of adaptation to the local environment and subsequently has few benefits from integration because it has a variety of diverse retail formats. Global retailers are at the other extreme. They provide the same offer in every market with limited, if any, change made to suit different environments. This does, however, provide them with savings from economies of scale; an example of this is The Body Shop. The other category, transnational retailers such as Carrefour, are in the middle ground and show a degree of responsiveness to local conditions and achieve limited benefits of integration.

CONCLUSION

This chapter has set out to define the term retail internationalization, suggesting it includes not only the transfer of retail operations across national borders, but also the international transfer of retail concepts, management expertise, technology and sourcing. Retailers operating on an international scale are still in a minority and for most companies the domestic market remains a far larger proportion of their business than international operations. The internationalization of retailing is still a relatively recent phenomenon and it is suggested that it is a process likely to continue to increase.

Retailers who internationalize may be characterized as doing so for predominantly reactive reasons – because they are being pushed out of the home market due to lack of growth opportunities – or for proactive reasons, that is they are actively seeking international opportunities irrespective of growth potential in the home market. The extent to which a retailer is reactive or proactive depends upon conditions in its sector of the home market, relevant international opportunities, and/or the culture of the organization. It is important to realize the position on the proactive–reactive continuum may change over time.

Retailers tend to move into markets that are geographically and culturally close, and into those that are less developed than their own. As they develop into experienced internationalists, they are more likely to move into more diverse markets. Their choice of market-entry strategy is dependent upon the type of operations, the organizational structure and culture, and the nature of the host markets.

More and more retailers are developing their experience of internationalization and increasingly we are witnessing retailers from all sectors moving into more distant and diverse markets. While for many retailers the developed market conditions at home are becoming increasingly competitive, other opportunities are opening up. For example, developments within Eastern Europe are offering opportunities for expansion that were previously impossible. The advent of the Single Market of the European Union is also facilitating intra-European expansion. Retail internationalization is a growing phenomenon and one that is set to characterize retailing in the new millennium.

EXERCISES

The exercises in this section relate to international retailing. It is advised that you work through them before moving on to Chapter 16.

1 Think of four non-European markets that might be characterized as advanced, structured, intermediary and traditional. What are the factors that can be used to classify them?

2 Select a retail company with an international presence. Consider what might have motivated this company to internationalize. In order of importance, list five factors that you think motivated the retailer to internationalize. For each factor decide whether it is an internal or external force and to what extent it was a push or a pull factor. Overall, to what extent do you consider your chosen retailer to be a reactive or proactive internationalist? Use the form/grid below as a guide.

Company name:

Home market:

Host market(s):

Motive	Internal–1–2–3–External	Push–1–2–3–Pull
1		
2		
3		
4		
5		

3 Select two companies, each active in a different retail sector. For a destination of your choice, decide which would be the most likely market-entry method for each. Justify your answer with reference to the nature of the retail sector, the company and market conditions.

4 It has been suggested that retailers are initially reluctant to internationalize, but over time become cautious and finally ambitious. Using examples of retailers from more than one sector, discuss the extent to which you agree with this theory.

REFERENCES AND FURTHER READING

ACNielsen (2001) *The Retail Pocket Book 2001*. London: NTC Publications.
Akehurst, G. and Alexander, N. (1996) (eds) *The Internationalisation of Retailing*. London: Frank Cass.

Alexander, N. (1990a) 'Retailers and international markets: motives for expansion', *International Marketing Review*, 7 (4), 75–85.

Alexander, N. (1990b) 'Retailing post-1992', *Service Industries Journal*, 10 (2), 172–87.

Alexander, N. (1995) 'Internationalisation: interpreting the motives' in McGoldrick, P.J. and Davies, G. (eds) *International Retailing: Trends and Strategies*. London: Pitman.

Alexander, N. (1997) *International Retailing*. Oxford: Blackwells.

Alexander, N. and Myers, H. (2000) 'The retail internationalisation process', *International Marketing Review*, 17 (4/5), 334–54.

Arnold, S.J. and Fernie, J. (2000) 'Wal-Mart in Europe: prospects for the UK', *International Marketing Review*, 17 (4/5), 416–32.

Boutsouki, C., Bennison, D. and Bourlakis, C. (1995) 'The impact of retail internationalisation on the host country: a case study of Greece', *CESCOM 8th International Conference on Research in the Distributive Trades*, Universita Bocconi, Milan, 1–2 September, A7.11–A7.18.

Brown, S. (1987) 'Institutional change in retailing: a review and synthesis', *European Journal of Marketing*, 21 (6), 5–36.

Burt, S. (1991) 'Trends in the internationalisation of grocery retailing: the European experience', *International Review of Retail, Distribution and Consumer Research*, 1 (4), 487–515.

Burt, S. (1993) 'Temporal trends in the internationalisation of British retailing', *International Review of Retail, Distribution and Consumer Research*, 3 (4), 391–410.

Cohen, N. (2001) 'Creating a warm, fuzzy feeling: Factory outlet centres are set to do well in Europe only if they are able to master the art of US-style customer service', *Financial Times*, 3 August.

Davies, R. and Finney, M. (1998) 'Retailers rush to capture new markets', *Financial Times*, 13 March.

Davies, G. and Whitehead, M. (1995) 'The legislative environment as a measure of attractiveness for internationalisation', in McGoldrick, P. and Davies, G. (eds) *International Retailing: Trends and Strategies*. London: Pitman.

Dawson, J.A. (1993) 'The internationalisation of retailing' in Bromley, R.D.F. and Thomas, C.J. (eds) *Retail Change: Contemporary issues*. London: UCL Press.

Dawson, J. (1994) 'Internationalization of retail operations', *Journal of Marketing Management*, 10, 267–82.

Dawson, J. and Burt, S. (1989) 'The Evolution of European retailing', *Report for ICL*. Vol. 4. Institute of Retail Studies, Stirling: University of Stirling.

Dupuis, M. and Prime, N. (1996) 'Business distance and global retailing: a model for analysis of key success/failure factors', *International Journal of Retail and Distribution Management*, 24 (11), 30–8.

Eurostat (1993) *Retailing in the Single European Market 1993*. Brussels: Commission of the European Communities.

Evans, J., Treadgold, A. and Mavando, F. (2000) 'Psychic distance and the performance of international retailers: a suggested theoretical framework', *International Marketing Review*, 17 (4/5), 373–91.

Friedman, M. (1970) 'The social responsibility of businesses is to increase profits', *New York Times Magazine*, 13 September.

Hellferich, E. Hinfelaar and Kasper, H. (1997) 'Towards a clear terminology on international retailing', *International Review of Retail, Distribution and Consumer Research*, 7 (3), 287–307.

Herman, G. (1995) *The Impact of Information Technology in Retail: Globalisation and customer focus*. *Financial Times* Management Report. London: James Capel and Company.

Hollander, S. (1970) *Multinational Retailing*. East Lancing, MI: Michigan State University.

Institute of Grocery Distribution (1997) *Grocery Retailing*. Letchmore Heath: Institute of Grocery Distribution.

Kacker, M. (1985) *Transatlantic Trends in Retailing*, Westport, CT: Greenwood.

Lamey, J. (1997) *Retailing in East Asia. Financial Times* Management Report. London: Financial Times.

Loker, S., Good, L. and Huddlestone, P. (1994) 'Entering eastern European markets: lessons from Kmart', *Recent Advances in Retailing and Services Science Conference*. Banff, Alberta, Canada: 7–10 May.

Marks & Spencer plc (1998) *Annual Report and Financial Statements 1998*. London: Marks & Spencer.

McGoldrick, P.J. and Davies, G. (1995) (eds) *International Retailing: Trends and Strategies*. London: Pitman.

McNair, M.P. (1958) 'Significant trends and developments in the post-war period' in Smith, A.B. (ed.) *Competitive Distribution in a Free High-Level Economy and its Implications*. Pittsburgh, PA: University of Pittsburgh.

Myers, H. (1996) 'Internationalisation: the impact of the European Union. A study of the food retail sector', Unpublished PhD Thesis, University of Surrey.

Myers, H. and Alexander, N. (1996) 'European food retailer's evaluation of global markets', *International Journal of Retail and Distribution Management*, 24 (6), 34–43.

Myers, H.A. and Alexander, N. (1997) 'Food retailing opportunities in Eastern Europe', *European Business Review*, 97 (3), 124–33.

Pelegrini, L. (1994) 'Alternatives for growth and internationalization in retailing', *International Review of Retail, Distribution and Consumer Research*, 4 (2), 121–48.

Quinn, B. and Doherty, A. (2000) 'Power and control in international retail franchising: evidence from theory and practice', *International Marketing Review*, 17 (4/5), 354–72.

Retail Intelligence (1991) *European Retailing in the 1990s*. London: Retail Intelligence Research Publications.

Retail Intelligence (2000a) *The European Retail Handbook 2000/01*. London: Retail Intelligence Research Publications.

Retail Intelligence (2000b) *Retailing in Europe – A Strategic Overview*. London: Retail Intelligence Research Publications.

Retail Intelligence (2001a) *Grocery Retailing in Europe*. London: Retail Intelligence Research Publications.

Retail Intelligence (2001b) *The European Retail Rankings*. London: Retail Intelligence Research Publications.

Robinson, T. and Clarke-Hill, C. (1993) 'European retail alliances: the ERA experience' in Baker, M. (ed.) *Perspectives in Marketing Management*. Vol. 3. Chichester: J. Wiley.

Robinson, T.M. and Clarke-Hill, C. (1995a) 'International alliances in European retailing', *International Review of Retail, Distribution and Consumer Research*, 5 (2), 167–84.

Robinson, T.M. and Clarke-Hill, C. (1995b) 'International alliances in European retailing' in McGoldrick, P.J. and Davies, G. (eds) *International Retailing: Trends and Strategies*. London: Pitman.

Salmon, W. and Tordjman, A. (1989) 'The internationalisation of retailing', *International Journal of Retailing*, 4 (2), 3–16.

Sternquist, B. and Kacker, M. (1994) *European Retailing's Vanishing Borders*. Westport, CT: Quorum Books.

Tordjman, A. (1995) 'European retailing: convergences, differences and perspectives' in McGoldrick, P. and Davies, G. (eds) *International Retailing; Trends and Strategies*. London: Pitman.

Treadgold, A.D. (1988) 'Retailing without frontiers', *Retail and Distribution Management*, 16 (6), 8–12.

Treadgold, A.D. (1991) 'The emerging internationalisation of retailing: present status and future challenges', *Irish Marketing Review*, 5 (2), 11–27.

Whitford, F. and Hope, A. (1994) 'The grocer's tale', *Sainsbury Magazine, Sainsbury's 125 Years: Celebration Supplement*. London: New Crane Publishing Ltd.

Williams, D. (1992a) 'Motives for retailer internationalization: their impact, structure, and implications', *Journal of Marketing Management*, 8 (2), 269–85.

Williams, D. (1992b) 'Retailer internationalization: an empirical inquiry', *European Journal of Marketing*, 26 (8/9), 8–24.

Voyle, S. (2001) 'Kingfisher's chief executive wants a run of good fortune', *Financial Times*, 2 August.

16 The future of retailing

This chapter should enable you to understand and explain:

- the future retail environment due to consumer change;
- prospective retail development;
- learning curves and their benefits;
- the advantages of retail as opposed to manufacturer brands;
- some of the key variables affecting the future of retailing.

Shopping has existed since the advent of civilization. Communities grew and prospered due to local markets based at suitable places on certain fixed days. Markets have always attracted different groups of purchasers who had either money or the means to barter. While the need for disposable income is an important prerequisite for successful retailing there is little correspondence between the early beginnings of retailing and the modern marketplace. The changes taking place are dramatic; and the pace of change in the modern business world is intense – change takes place at rates that would be incomprehensible to the retailers of the 1950s and 1960s. The last 30 years of change have witnessed dramatic increases in the power and scale of major retailing organizations, with the relentless trend of power changing from the locus of the manufacturer, moving first to the retailer and then through to the consumer. By the latter half of the 1980s, the consumer was dictating a whole series of improvements in the retail service offer as well as expressing the need for price and value for money to be carefully managed. In response to the growing power of the consumer, retailers expanded product lines, became concerned with the strategic issues of discounting, but then needed to move on to everyday low pricing and then value retailing.

The background to this is that the social structural changes in society have fuelled the increased rivalry and competition of the retail marketplace. There is slow population growth combined with less available time for conventional shopping and this is producing changing patterns of demand. Consumers are better informed and, given that much of the information gathering process has been completed, the 'shopping experience' is becoming more a 'buying experience'. This change will be even more pertinent for those consumers who have experienced a real or perceived reduction in their discretionary income. The overwhelming amount of store choice and the tendency of retailers to cross traditional lines of business in their assortment decisions has meant excessive supply. All this is leading to a downward pressure on prices relative to costs whereby the majority of retailers need to survive on lower margins. As such we are witnessing higher numbers of takeovers, bankruptcies and closings within the retail industry. In the clothing retail sector M&S has been forced to find a new way of retailing, C&A has closed down and Bhs was sold at a low price to a new management team.

During the 1990s, recessionary times meant that retailers had to ensure that they were more effective in the management of their retail offers. At the same time there was the need for greater productivity to ensure that costs were controlled and efficiencies could be passed on to the consumer. This heralded the adoption of a systems approach to retailing where computer applications and EPOS were pivotal in the development of all strategic improvements. At the same time as these changes were taking place, the retailer had to contend with the emerging values of concern for the environment and the need for more user-friendly products. The changes are continuous throughout society. There are new economic constraints, rapidly changing attitudes and new business relationships. The future is never clear but we can say, with some certainty, that the retail structure will continue to respond and evolve. Change will take place in relation to the pressures and trends in the internal and external environments of retail organizations. Retailers will need to ensure they have strategies which will relate to changes in consumer demand, social trends, government legislation, improvements in technology and competitor actions. The future will require innovative ways of structuring and carrying out business. This may involve improving the productivity of existing businesses, increasing or improving direct selling methods, and development of partnership and loyalty schemes. All this is going to happen within the constraints of greater government and EU involvement in retail planning and employment issues.

IMPROVED UNDERSTANDING OF THE KEY CHANGES

The main emphasis of this book is that the consumer has to be at the centre of any decision-making carried out by retailers. Modern consumers are very different from those of the 1970s and 1980s. In the UK the youth market has declined dramatically while, at the same time, the student population in higher education has almost doubled to 1.2 million. This has produced a ready part-time workforce for retailers and a growth in the consumption of education and leisure-related products. Consumers as a potential market are easy to predict even as far as the year 2025 as they are already born. Given the rise in the number of older people in society and the values of individualism, there will be a growth in smaller households which will be higher than the population growth rate. However, the population of the UK is set to decline by just over 100 000 by 2036 and by just over 150 000 by 2046. This is due to a general trend in lower birth rates throughout developed countries where the population will ultimately decline. Long before this happens there will be a high number of older consumers with specific needs in relation to retail consumption. The growth rate of ethnic minority groups in the UK offers opportunities for retailers. In the UK the consumption potential of the various ethnic minority groups will become more important as these groups numbered over 2 million in 1995 and represent a substantial market for retailers, especially in inner city areas. Changes in the demographic profile and shopping habits of UK consumers is providing for a much more fragmented and specialist retailer marketplace. A further background to the consumer marketplace is the emerging economic situation in world markets, as discussed below:

1 The establishment of a common currency among most EU member countries – European Monetary Union – and further relaxation of trade restrictions. This should further stimulate retail trade. In addition, national debts are better controlled in European countries due to the needs of monetary union.

2 There are growing concerns over the ability of some geographical areas to solve their financial problems in the short term – South East Asia, former Soviet Union countries and South America. Banking practices in many countries have had to be re-engineered in order to provide more confidence and to solve bad debt problems. As a trend there is global improvement as geographical problem areas are now much more aware of the political and economic need to bring more order and stability to their economies.

The proportion of women working is increasing with a resultant increase in household income. This financial boost, however, will be accompanied by a decrease in available time to shop and make decisions over household choices. There are changes already occurring, with food retailers considering opening smaller stores, or specialized retail environments, in working districts where convenience is important. There will also be an increase in the choice at which time to shop, correspondingly longer opening hours and the employment of part-time staff. The impact of more women working is going to result in many women making a trade-off between convenience and making economies. The trend will also extend opportunities for more fashion-oriented outlets aimed at dressing the working woman and providing for leisure wear. We have yet to find out if technology will provide the impetus for more direct sales or ordering of food and other retail related items.

The Internet

There was a time when location was a key term but now channel, channel, channel could be a far more apt description of the importance of knowing where consumers are most likely to purchase. The retailers who adopt the Internet as a channel of distribution will have to develop competencies and expertise to carry out successful e-tailing. The route is not easy, as Internet retailers Boo.com and Webvan have failed and Somerfield has abandoned its 24–7 service. According to Tesco plc (2002), Tesco.com, its own subsidiary, is the world's leading online grocery retailer and has coverage of 95 per cent of the UK with over 1 million registered users. The site service in the UK receives over 70 000 orders per week. According to statistics from NetValue Tesco received over 1.6 million unique visitors during November 2001. Tesco.com in 2002 operated as an Internet grocery home shopping service in the UK, Republic of Ireland and South Korea. However, the technology is in demand. The site architecture of Tesco.com has been utilized in joint ventures with Safeway in the United States based upon the system developed in the UK (http://www.tesco.com/corporateinfo). As in the case of Somerfield, if grocery retailers have to carry out the fulfilment of e-tailing in terms of picking, packing and delivery this takes out all the benefits they have acquired to date in terms of having developed low cost operations. According to Mintel (2000) the grocery market will be worth around £120 billion by 2005 – with up to 10 per cent of this business going online. This in itself should motivate grocery retailers but the Internet also attracts a high incidence of the sought-after ABC1 shoppers. In addition, the Internet allows for growth of sales of non-food items, which is not hampered by store size. Therefore we can expect much more investment in this area from the food retailers. We do know that Tesco has invested most heavily to date and is well ahead of its competitors. The future is debatable but perhaps the trend will be to regularize routine purchases by the use of technology, while leisure shopping and recreation will be combined as a more pervasive form of retail. We can only indicate that this seems to be the trend but the evidence is too sparse, at the moment, to forecast more precisely what the shape of future retailing will be. However, there is an increase in personal disposable income that could support the payment for home delivery services; there are a growing number of retirees who find shopping a major chore; people are working longer hours and are time-poor; and there are more women working – all of which will lead to e-commerce development.

M-commerce

Mobile commerce or m-commerce should not be confused with the use of the Internet as a sales channel. The existing strengths of the Internet, with graphically intensive page displays and well-developed e-tailers, cannot be easily mirrored by m-commerce. This is especially the case given the drive to make mobile telephone handsets smaller and lighter which does not allow for the optimum display of images or text. However, mobile phone operators are establishing their own portals and while the area is newly emerging the close contact between phone operator and customer may be utilized for a number of key retailing developments. The key technologies are WAP, Bluetooth, Epoc and IP, each of which is based upon open standards of operation which have industry support. The strengths of m-commerce applications are: the system is *portable* and stays with the user; it is *personal* as it is chosen and kept by the user; the user is *known* to the telephone company; the handset may be switched on continually with the benefit of messaging e-alert offers and other information. It can therefore be a transaction device; an information storage device; an entertainment/games device and a payment device with the storage of digital signatures.

Virtual banking as an indicator of future change

Virtual banking is a recent development that may herald changes in other retail areas. In 1989 the Midland Bank (later to become HSBC in 1992) set out to understand the consumer and increase its market share among more prosperous customers. Research was conducted by MORI, which indicated that customers were making less use of their branch network. One in five people said they had not visited their branch in the previous month and over half (51 per cent) said they visited as rarely as possible – which was reinforced when 27 per cent of the sample indicated they would prefer a telephone banking service. The team working on the project concluded that there was a need for a direct banking service, which included some form of human presence. More significant was a recognition that telephone services, such as request of balance, were already provided successfully by the bank and therefore a non-branch service could be offered as long as transactions were added. Therefore, for those who were happier to utilize the telephone a dedicated bank providing only services over the telephone was advocated. The cost savings were another business reason for such a departure. First Direct was launched as a 24-hour banking service and by 1996 had 560 000 customers. The Woolwich (now part of Barclays) developed an Open Plan Service which is an umbrella set of financial services which includes e-banking as well as other financial services. The use of the Internet for e-banking is being promoted by high interest benefits subsidized by the lower costs created by the customer moving money or creating the transaction. These developments are an indicator of how the future may progress for other service sectors.

Retail banks have identified the benefit of e-banking and therefore consumer access to online services will be developed based upon new direct channels. Reuters Business Insight (2000) identifies three main drivers for investment in e-banking solutions:

- distribution channel focus allowing cost reduction and efficiency improvement;
- improved customer service with an emphasis on information collection and management;
- wider e-commerce strategy as a means to link to WAP, interactive TV and other emerging technologies.

There is a move to multi-channel integration which allows banks to obtain a complete picture of their customers' financial activities in real time. This enables the banks to offer an all-encompassing service when managing customers' finances. The key difficulty faced by banks at present is a lack of integrated systems to share data from perhaps that of an ATM transaction to one of e-banking. The complete information allows for improved customer relationship management (CRM) benefits. This data will offer a reliable profile of a customer to aid in assessing the 'value' of each customer to the bank, whereby profitable and unprofitable customers are identified. This will provide the bank with the information to manage high yield customers and to migrate unprofitable customers to cheaper channels of the business.

The problem with such a strategy is that the poorer consumer is unlikely to have access to the Internet.

On a more general level banks are in a unique position to be able to offer services to provide for the entire e-commerce marketplace. They have trusted brands which allow for portal development, credit checking, e-transactions, offline payment processing and authentication as well as wider services in the B2C e-commerce marketplace.

Consumer issues

As the consumer learns to be more sophisticated in their purchasing habits, they will also acquire the values from the media and pressure groups about environmental and consumer issues. This consumerist movement is often treated as a concern and many firms react defensively, as if consumerism were a major threat to the retailer rather than an opportunity. In fact, because of the overt nature of the movement, the retailer can often be over-defensive. Taking a marketing approach, then, the type of concerns expressed by the general public are an indicator of the wishes of the customer and these should trigger changes in the business policy of retail operations. We have discussed the ways in which companies have approached social responsibility in an earlier chapter. We discussed the need for companies to adopt policies for continuous improvement in respect of recycling, directions on product use, storage, energy usage, partnerships with third parties, responsible decision-making, and employee education in the adoption of more socially responsible procedures. The issues that will be more important in the future relate to expectations regarding the quality of the product and retail service, the after-sales service

MINICASE 16.1

The microchip moves into the supermarket

It is Saturday morning and Mary Duffy is getting ready to do the weekly grocery shop. She goes to the kitchen cupboard and has a quick look. The kids have been at the biscuits again and three packets stand half empty. She picks up a pen and runs the point over the bar code on the biscuit packets. The brands are automatically added to an electronic shopping list via the scanner built into the pen. The list will also include products which, once used, have been thrown into a bin specially adapted to read radio signals emitted by intelligent labels. She splashed out on the Trashscan just two months ago, but was annoyed to discover there are still some bugs: such as when the baby repeatedly lifts rubbish out of the bin and puts it back in again. Frustrating, but it is simply a matter of adapting the shopping list, which has been downloaded on to the interactive television or the family's personal computer. Both now use a Microsoft-designed Windows navigation system. Although Mrs Duffy usually has the groceries delivered, this Saturday she decides to shop herself. So after adapting the list on the PC, she sends it to the store. Everything but the fresh fruit and meat will be waiting for her when she gets there. She, like most customers, prefers to choose these items herself. On the way she remembers at least three things she forgot to put on the list. No problem. The voice-activated personal computer fitted into the dashboard of her car will send an updated list. Mrs Duffy's shopping trip sounds far-fetched, but all the items she used can be purchased today. The penscanner is available from Symbol Technologies of the UK, interactive television will launch in the UK this year, and leading car manufacturers such as Mercedes and BMW are planning to launch models with voice-activated computer screens. The only fantasy item might be Trashscan, developed by ICL, the computer services company, two years ago. Technology is the new battleground of retailing.

As she wanders round the store to get ideas for the dinner party tomorrow night, she notices a special offer on compact discs. Pressing the trigger on the keyring given to her by the supermarket chain after she built up 100,000 points, the CD's electronic price tag flashes up a further 10 per cent off just for her. The price looks good, but just to double check, Mrs Duffy runs the scanner in her mobile phone across the album's bar code. It dials up the bargain hunting search engine on the Internet and lists the 10 retailers who sell the CD at the lowest prices. Only one is cheaper than the supermarket's offer, so she decides to buy it.

Source: Peggy Hollinger, *Financial Times*, 3 April 1998

component as part of added value, acceptable containers and packaging, as well as fairness in business practices.

Changing values towards debt

It is clear that social values are changing. We are witnessing the widening acceptance of debt, especially by the young, who are now taking loans to fund their education or to purchase more freely. An indicator of this is the expansion of the use of credit card facilities (*see* Table 16.1). However, the real picture is even bigger given the recent development of over 5000 convenience ATMs in places such as garages, licensed premises or retail outlets.

According to APACS, the use of plastic money in 2000 meant that cheque cash withdrawals were 5.4 per cent less than in 1999. This indicates the importance of the use of plastic money as can be seen in Table 16.1 where the number of cheque transactions reduced by over 1200m in the ten years from 1990 to 2000. The use of credit cards is clearly at a very high penetration level as can be seen in Table 16.2.

Table 16.1 Increasing numbers of transactions by plastic card

	1990	1995	1996	1997	1998	1999	2000
Total transactions in the UK (millions)							
All plastic card purchases	930	2 023	2 413	2 759	3 094	3 537	3 909
Debit card	192	1 004	1 270	1 503	1 736	2 062	2 332
Credit and charge card	690	908	1 025	1 128	1 224	1 344	1 452
Plastic card withdrawals at ATMs and counters	1 045	1 512	1 656	1 809	1 917	2 025	2 102
Direct debits, standing orders, direct credits and CHAPS	1 741	2 402	2 613	2 826	3 056	3 255	3 470
Cheques	3 975	3 283	3 203	3 083	2 986	2 854	2 700
For payment	3 537	2 938	2 901	2 838	2 757	2 641	2 515
For cash acquisition	438	345	302	245	229	213	185
The UK ATM network (banks and building societies)							
Number of ATMs	17 300	20 900	22 100	23 200	24 600	28 300	30 400
ATM withdrawals (millions)	1 012	1 471	1 599	1 745	1 850	1 968	2 027
ATM cards (millions)	45	55	57	60	65	69	71

Source: APACS 2001

Table 16.2 Percentage of cards in use in the UK population

	Percentage of UK adults		
	1989	1995	2000
Credit/charge card	37	39	53
Debit card	30	57	82
Retailer card	–	23	34
Cheque guarantee card	–	62	70
ATM debit card	43	71	86
Any plastic card	67	82	89

Source: APACS 2001

Future developments will encourage smart card usage because of the benefits of the card and the lowering of production costs. This is because the card allows the limiting of the value of the card in order to control expenditure, and spending is instant and can be tracked through the use of a simple device.

Service will always be important

In most developed countries the retail industry is becoming more and more concentrated and better at carrying out its business. The advantages gained by location decisions and the application of technology are important technical aspects of the business. However, the ultimate winners in the marketplace will be those companies that can harness their workforce's energy and motivation to deliver a world class service – which is why we

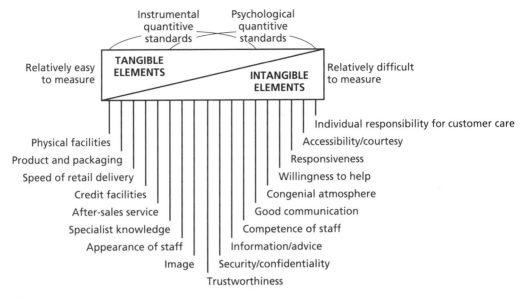

Fig. 16.1 Dimensions of retail customer care

Source: Based on Carson and Gilmore, 1989

provided a great deal of theory and discussion on managing service in earlier chapters. Service excellence is important in the retail product amalgam and the ability of retailers to differentiate on service will be of greater significance in the future. Non-price aspects of the marketing mix will grow in importance and, as such, more research and emphasis will need to be placed on understanding the attitudes and beliefs of the retailers' target market. Figure 16.1, which has been compiled from the marketing of services literature, indicates the full range of skills and functions required by retail operations. This emphasizes the ideas and concepts discussed in Chapter 4 on service and quality in retailing.

MORE EMPHASIS PLACED UPON BRAND, IMAGE AND POSITIONING

In order to take full advantage of the efforts retailers will place on both functional and service improvements, there is a need to distil the retail offer into a clear proposition based on the retail product, brand image and positioning. Each brand will need to be reassessed in light of the changing nature of the retail marketplace. We have discussed in great detail the important trends and concepts behind branding, especially those of own-brand developments. As the retail market continues to mature, it will be interesting to monitor the use of advertising by the different retail organizations to identify those which are attempting to alter the perceptions of consumers to their offers. It may be a while before we witness an expansion of the majority of the 'big players' into advertising campaigns based upon the type of marketing carried out by McDonald's. Whatever happens, all this will take place against a backcloth of manufacturers' attempts to hold on to the strength of their own brands and products, while at the same time the power of the retailers will continue to grow. There are going to be a number of challenges in the future retail marketplace. Manufacturers will attempt to reorganize the shape of the market to ensure that they continue to have some influence over the marketplace. This

Retailers	Manufacturers
Ownership of the stores which provides or means: • ability to communicate directly with customer • full control of retail marketing mix • timely and accurate feedback and information • ability to be efficient with new product introductions and to reinforce the store image • staple food products can be own-branded without worry of prestige or need for communication, e.g. spaghetti • advantage of habitual, low interest purchases occurring and therefore brand acceptability is not difficult • high margin sales will attract competition • sales are more likely to occur when the retailer is of a mass appeal level	*Critical mass and specialization which provides or means:* • specialist manufacturing technology • use of media communications and advertising to influence customer • use of market research in order to understand the consumer • advantage of image especially for quality • advantage of ubiquity of the brand and potential placement in all outlets • can develop a whole range with great deal of variety which provides for a sense of choice • outside of the retailer versus retailer battle and would benefit from overcapacity • able to be sold through a variety of different channels

Fig. 16.2 Comparison of branding advantages between retailers and manufacturers

may mean a trend to the use of categories, as brands become less important. Whatever happens, the manufacturer will not be able to counteract the power of the retailer and this may lead to the need for manufacturers to assess their portfolio of brands in order to rebrand or dispose of those brands which may not survive a prolonged battle. The ultimate threat of powerful retailers to delist a manufacturer's products is a very serious threat that all suppliers will need to take more and more into account as specific retailers continue to grow in size and power.

Corstjens and Corstjens (1995) have offered the concept that there is a battle for mindspace of the retail consumer. They have uncovered a number of arguments regarding advantages to the retailer and the manufacturer of their specific branding exercises. A number of these are summarized in Fig. 16.2.

The retail organization of the future will have to be poised to take a much more proactive stance to the retailing and shopping behaviour of its customers. To have a greater understanding of the dynamics of consumer behaviour will provide an advantage for retail managers. A great deal more research should be carried out into understanding satisfaction or dissatisfaction with the whole service delivery process. The use of techniques such as critical incident technique (CIT) will enable companies to uncover the hidden factors which may lead to disenchantment with the existing retail business operation and its products. Research by Bell *et al.* (1997) at a Tesco store indicated how CIT can be utilized to improve the management of retail operation. There is a need to know more about store choice, shopping habits, and in-store behaviour and decision-making. Consumer behaviour studies are set to be a more important aspect of retail management. We have attempted to cover the fundamentals of consumer behaviour in this book (*see* Chapter 3) because it is a key area of retail management. Minicase 16.2 indicates the importance of ensuring that both consumer behaviour and managing the brand is fully understood.

KFC – How can KFC catch the UK's fast-food leaders?

KFC is in third place behind its burger-based competitors – it has 536 UK outlets to Burger King's 660 and the 1000-plus of McDonald's – it is in the enviable position of achieving better organic growth than either of its rivals. Burger-based chains have watched their profits wane as consumers steer clear of beef products as a result of the BSE and foot and mouth crises, and chicken merchants reaped the rewards. Mintel figures show that the fast-food chicken market grew by 33% between 1996 and 2000 to £633m. The success of KFC, which has seen sales rise by 61% in the past three years, has been attributed to its high-profile advertising, the product's family appeal and its comparatively healthy image.

With a target of 1000 outlets by 2008, KFC is the only national fast-food chicken chain. Under Prior, its ads, created by Ogilvy & Mather since 1994, abandoned the use of celebrities and reverted to a more overt US product-focused style fronted by an animated version of the brand's white-moustached founder, Colonel Sanders. Product choice has changed little – apart from a vegetarian cheeseburger, the menu has remained true to its chicken and fries menu – although it has extended its core offering with products such as Twister, Popcorn Chicken and Crispy Strips.

Julian Borra said the success was – 'I am told by fans, that KFC still makes great chicken. I am told that families still love a good rummage around the family 'bucket'. I am told that its new products are highly successful. And I know that KFC is a uniquely recognisable brand with a uniquely recognisable spokesman. Sadly though, protecting your brand icons while trying to contemporise them can be a risky business. There is a danger of them becoming faintly ridiculous and anodyne. Making a historic brand spokesman 'trendy' to reconnect your brand and your business is also, I believe, only a short-term fix, and has the potential to weaken the brand. Icons can quickly lose their potency and their relevance. As a brand, I believe KFC has the punter's permission to rediscover itself properly. I wish it would. In the meantime, I wish someone would take the Colonel outside and give him a strategic kicking. Or with KFC's desperate bid to be trendy, it could be Lock, Stock and Two Smokin' Buckets next.'

Source: Tania Mason, *Marketing*, 16 August 2001

This is because:

- improving customer satisfaction is a key to gaining store or brand loyalty;
- knowing what to provide, so as to deliver value for money, will become more important. As such, premium price policies can exist on the basis of the willingness of a customer to pay higher prices because of the image and value delivered;
- there is a need to deal with customer dissatisfaction, but first it has to be uncovered and understood;
- with a hyper-segmented store clientele, there is a need to understand the range of customer needs;
- customer satisfaction surveys will not easily uncover the complexities and subtleties of customer reactions to the existing and future business.

EMERGING TRENDS IN I.T.

Retail and information technology are inextricably linked. Some changes will be directly related to the new technologies entering the industry or based upon the way retailers utilize existing technology within their retail operations. IT may also serve to stabilize the future retail industry structure because current applications – and the need to specify and invest in new systems – make for barriers to entry and exit.

The trends emerging in relation to IT are:

- an increased level of intelligence being incorporated into computer systems;
- the increased availability of multimedia technology. As television, telecommunications and audio systems converge, there will be interactive multimedia systems developed to provide exciting new opportunities for retail developments;
- an increased usage of IT to improve levels of retailer productivity;
- miniaturization of electronic systems will continue. It is already possible to fit the processing power of an early mainframe computer into a space smaller than the average briefcase. The electronic wallet will be available soon. It will allow electronic payments and carry a wealth of information, including shopping lists;
- the back office workforce will be able to work at home via special modem and computer links. This will place more pressure on rural rather than city properties as the need to commute will become less necessary. This trend will be reinforced through the policies of local authorities, who are keen to cut down on traffic congestion in city centres;
- stand-alone sales kiosks which can provide voice recognition communication and real comprehension of queries and transaction processes. Ultimately holographic projection will be possible to enhance the sales experience.

Recent IT applications allow for extremely high levels of sophistication and intelligence. The diverse situations to which they can be applied range from operational analysis to decision support systems. This development has been paralleled by an array of software tools known as artificial intelligence (AI). AI includes many different branches of computer technology which are designed to mirror the human thinking, reasoning and decision-making processes. These can be *expert systems*, which contain a knowledge base and decision-making protocols so as to provide the type of answers an expert may suggest if given a similar situation. Expert systems contain an inference engine which has been programmed to tolerate uncertainty. They do this by incorporating probabilities into their logic which is often referred to as 'fuzzy logic'. On the basis of this, the system can take into account a number of uncertainties such as the weather, consumer tastes and environments. Expert systems can be developed into neural networks which, through the identification of patterns, will allow the system to learn as it operates. This can have applications to the calculation of complex pricing policies, diagnosis of operational problems within the organization, or decision-making support for managers to plan the staffing requirements during any time period. The systems will be able to learn from financial reports and returns and from demand patterns how to change and allocate space to different items and brands.

Robotic technology is another branch of IT. *Robotic systems* can help with the manipulation of objects by picking them up and moving them to where they need to go. Robots are different from automatons in that they can be programmed to perform a variety of tasks. The system allows for motion to let the robot move around, sensory processing by use of infrared, ultraviolet or sonar scanning to recognize shelf or stockroom areas, and it also allows actuation to lift and move items whether by electric hydraulics for light movement or pneumatics for heavy objects. Robotics could be used in the future to replenish shelves, clean shop floor areas, collect trolleys, or replace the non-skilled work carried out by retail employees.

In the future, consumers will be able to use robots that will use a card or could learn to pick their regular shopping items for them while the consumer carried out some other task. The checkout will be automated and an electronic fund system will be available to allow for the debiting of the merchandise. Additional functionality will be gained from checkouts in the future, as they will move from point-of-sale to become equipped with point-of-service technology so that customers and staff will utilize touch technology for a whole range of information and services. There is a question of whether self-checkout will be adopted. The answer is that staff will probably still work on checkouts as they are much more efficient than a self-checkout system utilizing the customer. It is estimated that self-checkout is 15 per cent slower than conventional methods. However, there could be combined systems of service with self-checkout for loyalty members at busy periods and full service systems when the store is less busy.

In the home, the packaging of different food items will have information able to be scanned or read so as to communicate directly with the microwave or cooker to ensure perfect cooking. Finally, *multimedia systems* will increase the marketing facility to transmit information and communicate with potential and actual customers, employees and suppliers. Use of the Internet and other systems has been discussed in Chapter 13, along with the realization that there is global connectivity for retail businesses.

Call centre improvements

Call centres are becoming more sophisticated. Anton (2000) talks of information-hungry consumers and the improvements being made to serve this need. For example there will be:

- *Voice of Internet protocol* (VOIP) whereby a customer calling a customer service centre can use the Web (via the Internet) to input the key data which would normally be asked for at the start of a call. This will save money and time as part of the call discussion. New technology would also allow the customer to see the representative and to move the cursor for other information.

- *Interactive voice recognition* (IVR) – interactive recordings will allow consumers to make selections and route them to the specific service representative who can provide specific information and service.

- *Value-based consumer routing* is a system for recognizing and segmenting consumers based upon their value rating profiles related to the company database. This system will provide queue priority for some customers over others. This can be driven by computer telephony integration (CTI) whereby the identified number from ANI (automatic number identification) and DNIS (dialled number identification service) will automatically retrieve information from the company's database to enhance the transaction as it can provide essential background information.

THE PHYSICAL ASPECTS OF RETAILING

Some predictions indicate that stores as we know them will disappear, to be replaced by interactive modules or kiosks which can display the product, provide for a series of questions, take an order by capturing information from the customer, make the transaction by way of a credit card and then create a confirmation printout. All this has been available for some time but has not been fully developed. The store of tomorrow may well look different from that of today, but all indications for the short term suggest that technology will be harnessed to make retailers more productive rather than radically to alter the way consumers shop. The kiosk systems can also be harnessed to the EPOS terminals in a store. The kiosks can be linked to loyalty card swipe technology in order to dispense vouchers or sales promotion offers or allow a card member to look at personal rewards. As automation can be expensive, its increased use favours the larger organizations that will be able to utilize it to create a competitive advantage. There will be the use of technology at head office to automate the business and reduce the number of personnel, and to provide improvement in information so that less profitable lines can be discontinued, inventory control improved, more room be given to selling space rather than for stock items, workforce planning improved, etc. IT has become a vital part of modern retailing. These changes are described in Chapter 13 on IT applications to retail. Relationship marketing, by the capture and use of database information, will become increasingly important along with the development of Internet retail possibilities.

SMART CARDS: Finally going for an all-round smart solution

It has taken time, but smart payment cards – around 20 million of them – are now nestled in shoppers' wallets. Within two years, the banks' estate of payment terminals will be capable of handling smart cards and PIN authorisation at point-of-sale. There is Home Office backing for the move, which is seen as supportive of government strategies for fighting credit card fraud, and necessary changes to the Banking Code will no doubt be mooted before much longer.

Retailers are gearing themselves up for change and the British Retail Consortium is deep in discussion with APACS (Association for Payment Clearing Services). Both parties claim to have identified 'cost benefits' for retailers in moving to smart card systems, although they are surprisingly reluctant to enumerate just what these benefits might be. According to APACS head of public affairs Richard Tyson, while the banks are already well advanced in converting their 300,000–400,000 payment terminals for smart card, most major retailers have yet to bite the bullet.

'The cost of bringing PIN to point-of-sale is likely to be in excess of £1 billion, and although we're cooperating with the British Retail Consortium, the major retailers have not yet committed to chip card,' he says.

Given the positive support from the Home Office, however, Tyson believes that it will not be long before this changes. APACS is optimistic that by 2005, both retail and bank payment terminals will all be smart.

That £1 billion figure covers not only the cost of new smart card readers and PINpads, which are both comparatively inexpensive, but the rather more daunting task of converting sophisticated in-store systems to cope with the complexities of the EMV standard used for card security. Industry speculation suggests that some of the bank savings from credit card fraud might just be channelled into retail coffers to help cover the conversion costs.

PIN authorisation at point-of-sale will require checkouts to be equipped not just with a smart card reader, but with a separate PINpad. These are usually hard-wired to the EPoS or payment terminal, but new technologies could render this technology redundant. At Smart Card 2001, Ingenico Fortronic was demonstrating a Blue-tooth-enabled payment terminal and printer that allows staff to use a portable card reading device with the receipt printed at a remote checkout. The demonstration was equally applicable to the hospitality sector for order-taking with remote printing or could be used with PINpads to give greater flexibility to operations.

Loyalty schemes are no longer guaranteed winners and other sorts of multi-application could be needed: smart transport tickets are one option although these often use contactless technology rather than the contact cards favoured by the banks. Dual chip cards offering both contact and contactless functions are available, but are expensive. Others suggest that government support for smart cards

could raise the ID issue again with a smart identity token that could be linked to bank credit or debit functions, which could be promoted as part of an official crackdown on benefits frauds, for example.

Whatever the 'incentive' smart cards and PINs at point-of-sale are firmly on the agenda – add the conversion of retail systems to handle Euros into the equation and retail IT departments could have a hectic couple of years ahead.

Source: Retail Week, 30 March 2001

COMPANY LEARNING CURVES

The concept of companies experiencing the benefits of learning curves is widely accepted. It is believed that as companies gain more experience of increasing the size of the business they will develop specific efficiencies which can be exploited in the market. Therefore, as retailers expand their business they are able to deliver better value and be more profitable because of the experience gained. The form of the learning or experience may differ, as some companies emphasize improving technology and the development of technological know-how whereas others may focus more resources on research and understanding the customer. Companies make strategic decisions in order to move them down the cost curve to provide added value. In the footwear market, Adidas and Puma invested in setting up large-scale European manufacturing capacity. On the other hand, Nike and Reebok used the learning curve to gain cost advantage from Far East manufacturing locations which had the ability to switch designs quickly – enabling these companies to introduce a flexible fashion element to their marketing. Large retail companies are able to use the learning curve to improve productivity as this is one of the easiest ways for them to prosper. The larger companies are well positioned to harness the benefits of the learning curve. This places a barrier on the entry of new competitors in different retail sectors.

As retailers prepare for the future they have to form a vision and scenario of what the future may hold. This has to take into consideration competitive benchmarking of the business against the best examples in the wider business world. This will push them into improvement and repositioning to become best in class. The exciting aspect of marketing is that there are always a number of alternatives available. The choice has to be made on the basis of the existing company resources, the expected changes in the environment, consumer trends and the most logical direction. The following section lists just some of the possibilities.

Possible areas of change

The areas of possible change which retailers need to decide on are:

- increased access and variety through vending machines and kiosks as well as the development of m-commerce, Internet sites and virtual stores;

439

- more precision marketing through telesales and specialist catalogues. The use of portable stores based in mobile truck or van units could be taken into specific neighbourhoods. The less mobile and rural communities are a key area for the expansion of specific ranges of merchandise;

- greater customization of stores to suit niche markets;

- increased market coverage through cable and TV shopping networks or extending opening hours;

- improved turnover through the development of new areas of retailing such as financial services, specialist merchandise within department stores, or franchising;

- reduction in staff, and therefore costs, through the application of technology, with computerized sales information, inventory and display control, increased security and anti-shoplifting devices, improved scanning systems;

- reappraising the size and location of stores with a more balanced approach to small-scale development in key locations due to future legislation and working trends;

- creating longer-term retention of customers through relationship marketing and loyalty programmes;

- improving information database through introduction of smart card technology, EPOS developments, etc.;

- international expansion strategies in order to realize the opportunities in countries such as India with 850 million people and a growing middle class or China with a population of 1.2 billion – 300 million of whom are adults living in just 95 cities. Forecasts of growth in these countries indicate that a huge market will exist in the near future. That is why Wal-Mart and Carrefour have built stores in China, on the basis of learning how to harness the predicted improvement in the Chinese economy and political situation.

As a background to the changes taking place, there are development trends involving the renovation of older retail areas or the redevelopment of large areas to create major new shopping areas in urban locations. At the same time it is becoming more difficult for retail developers to dictate what their requirements are. Government legislation introduced in 1996, as described in Chapter 11, creates problems for retailers who may want to expand into new greenfield site developments. Retailers may need to examine other ways to expand but there are few true innovations as the risk is quite high.

If there are to be major changes in store design then we should expect the development to favour the niche markets. If a more specialist form of targeting takes place, there is a need to offer a more customized approach. This means that the stores will need to have a format that will target clearly defined segments – for example, more age-specific or lifestyle and cultural-specific design innovations. The new age for retailing is witnessing stores which have an ecological influence in their format, with products aimed at helping wildlife and reminding us of the environment. The atmosphere of the store is enhanced by countryside sounds, such as bird calls, and the range of merchandise is carefully selected to complement the store's market positioning. This is indicative of the efforts made by some retailers to bring the ambience of the store closer to their target customers. Other forms of this approach can be found in the way merchandise displays can be planned to become a retail attraction in their own right. The Disney stores, with their use of costumed characters, movies and videos, create an entertainment leisure environment that relaxes and pleases the customer, which in turn leads to themed purchases.

CONCLUSION

This book has been structured so that the reader will have been exposed to the underlying logic of a marketing approach to retailing. The concepts that you should have mastered from reading the chapters create a useful framework of approach. However, any company adopting these ideas has to be both flexible and adaptable in order to take the course of action with the highest expected value outcome. Retailers will need to react consistently to the environment by ensuring that their offer meets current and future needs. This may mean giving up the established positioning of the brand in order to change contemporary perceptions. Kentucky Fried Chicken became KFC so that it could offer more than simply chicken meals and British Home Stores become Bhs to appeal to younger consumers. There is no short-cut route to deciding on the future. It requires a great deal of analysis of emerging trends and the signals of change. Retailers that can create a company culture which seeks to understand and manage change are the ones who are best suited to survive and prosper.

EXERCISES

The exercises in this section are related to the future of retailing and the issues discussed throughout the book.

1 As we move inexorably toward Internet e-tailing, is branding becoming less important than in the past? Provide a report on this and the future impact of the Internet on retail marketing.

2 What is going to happen in the battle between retail and manufacturer brands? Are alternative distribution channels or other changes going to affect the power struggle?

3 What will be the key skills and knowledge requirements of retail marketing managers in the next decade? What are the reasons for and implications of your ideas?

REFERENCES AND FURTHER READING

Anton, J. (2000) 'The past, present and future of customer access centers', *International Journal of Service Industry Management*, 11 (2), 120–30.

APACS (2001) 'Association for Payment Clearing Services', www.apacs.org.uk

Bell, J., Gilbert, D. and Lockwood, A. (1997) 'Service quality in food retailing operations: a critical incident analysis', *International Review of Retail, Distribution and Consumer Research*, 7 (4), 405–23.

Brown-Humes, C. (1998) 'Barclays to launch "screenphone" service', *Financial Times*, 20 May.

Burke, R.R. (1997) 'Do you see what I see? The future of virtual shopping', *Journal of the Academy of Marketing Science*, 25 (4), 352–60.

Carson, D. and Gilmore, A. (1989) 'Customer care: the neglected domain', *Irish Marketing Review*, 4 (3), 49–61.

Corstjens, J. and Corstjens, M. (1995) *Store Wars: The battle for mindspace and shelfspace*. Chichester: Wiley.

Ernst and Young (1991) 'Survey of retail information technology expenses and trends', *Chain Store Age Executive*, September, Section 2.

Griffith, V. (2001) 'How the fittest survived the dotcom meltdown: Online Retailing', *Financial Times*, 27 August.

Hasty, R. and Reardon, J. (1997) *Retail Management*. London: McGraw-Hill.

Hollinger, P. (1998) 'The microchip moves into the supermarket. Imagine a dustbin that knows what you've thrown away and what should go on the shopping list', *Financial Times*, 3 April.

Keh, H.T. and Park, S.Y. (1997) 'To market, to market: The changing face of grocery retailing', *Long Range Planning*, 30 (6), 836–46.

Long, S. (2000) 'A Survey of Online Finance: The virtual threat: The Internet has already forced wrenching change on the financial-services industry – and the revolution has barely begun', *The Economist*, 20 May.

Mason, T. (2001) 'KFC – How can KFC catch the UK's fast-food leaders?', *Marketing*, 16 August.

Mintel (2000) '*Grocery e-tailing*', Mintel International Group Report.

Retail Week (2001) 'SMART CARDS: Finally going for an all-round smart solution', *Retail Week*, 30 March, 24.

Reuters (2000) '*The Future of European Retail Banking*', Business Insight Report.

Index